Growth, Imbalance and Indian Economy

Growth, Imbalance and Indian Economy

Editor

K R Venugopal

I.K. International Publishing House Pvt. Ltd.

NEW DELHI • BANGALORE

Published by

I.K. International Publishing House Pvt. Ltd.
S-25, Green Park Extension, Uphaar Cinema Market
New Delhi–110 016 (India)
E-mail: info@ikinternational.com
Website: www.ikbooks.com

ISBN 978-81-89866-22-8

10 9 8 7 6 5 4 3 2

Reprint 2011

Published by Krishan Makhijani for I.K. International Publishing House Pvt. Ltd., S-25, Green Park Extension, Uphaar Cinema Market, New Delhi–110 016 and Printed by Rekha Printers Pvt. Ltd., Okhla Industrial Area, Phase II, New Delhi–110 020.

Dedicated to

Prof. K Venkatagiri Gowda

Smt. Savithri Venkatagiri Gowda

Preface

Dr. K Venkatagiri Gowda obtained his Bachelor's and Master's Economics from the University of Mysore and Ph.D in Economics from the London School of Economics. He began his career as a Lecturer with the University of Mysore, where he went to become Reader. From 1967 to 1983, he worked as Professor and Chariman of the Department of Economics in Bangalore University. He had specialisation in Monetary Economics and International Finance.

His works have been internationally acclaimed as definitive and path breaking in the area of Monetary Economics, International Finance and Planning. He published the following books: Fiscal Policy and Inflation (1959), Appreciation of the Indian Rupee (1960), Keynes-Triffin Plans for International Liquidity (1961), European Common Market and India (1962), Commonwealth Common Market (1963), International Currency Plans and Expansion of World Trade (1964), Euro-Dollar Flows and International Monetary Stability (1979), A Plan for Eradication of Black Money and Black Wealth (1983), Perestroika and Glasnost for India (1988), Democracy in Deficits (1995), New Dimensions for Indian Planning (1995), Economic Performance of the Government (1997).

Professor Gowda was an incisive man par excellence. His economic analysis on the budget was greatly valued by the economists and administrators in the country. He was invited by the Government of U.S.A. to deliver lectures on "Oil Crisis" in U.S. Universities.

He represented the Bangalore South Constituency (from BJP) in the Lok Sabha during 1991-96. As a Member of Parliament, his contribution to the economic policy was substantial. I was closely associated with Prof. Gowda for nearly three decades. I had the opportunity to be his Doctoral Pupil from 1986-89. I used to have long and frequent discussions with him. He possessed an uncanny analytical ability and a perfect command over English. Prof. Gowda received Lord Leverhulme Special

Research Award, London School of Economics. In 1983, he received the Karnataka Rajyotsava Award.

He was a great scholar and perfectional, known for his sincerity and honesty. His scholarship, frank opinions and expertise in economics was always appreciated by the prime ministers of our country. His five decades of crusade to bring about economic reforms in our country will never go unnoticed in the annals of our history.

The present book is a collection of memoranda of Professor Gowda mostly addressed to the Late Hon'ble Prime Minister Sri P V Narasimha Rao and the present Hon'ble Prime Minister Sri Manmohan Singh, during 1991-96.

The articles in the book are on topics like Fiscal Structure, Industry Policy, Bank Restructuring, Exchange Rate of Rupee, Gold policy, Inflation Management, Deficit Financing, Liquidity Crisis, Oil Fueled inflation, Oil Exploration, Oil Crisis, Privatisation of Insurance, Foreign Capital Inflows, Foreign Investment, IMF and its Conditionalities, Foreign Exchange Reserves, Public Expenditure, Budget, Disinvestments, Buyoncy of Indian Rupee, Inflation Trap, Subsidies for food and fertilizers, MNCs, Trade deficits, Public Borrowing, External debt, Short and Long Term Capital Flows, Banking Policy, Deregulation of Interest Rates, Convertibility, Liberalization, Industrial Sickness, Export-Import Strategies, NRI Investments, Subsidies, Industry and Agriculture Growth, Debt Crisis, Wage Freeze, etc.

The observations made by him are very critical and useful. They are of special interest to postgraduate and research students, academic planners and policy makers and statesmen.

The book comprises 83 articles, which provide solutions to myriad economic problems in our country. This great personality left us on 5th July 2004 at the age of eighty-one. This book is brought out in the memory of my beloved Professor K Venkatagiri Gowda.

Venugopal K R

Acknowledgements

I wish to place on record my deep debt of gratitude to Sri M.C. Jayadeva, who has been a constant source of inspiration. His gentle encouragement and taste for perfection have been the key to my growth and success in my career. Moreover his timely suggestions and counseling have been of immense help to me.

I am also grateful to Prof. S. Lakshmana Reddy, Prof. N.R. Shetty, Prof. P. Sreenivasa Kumar, Justice N. Rama Jois, Sri. N. Krishnappa, Prof. K. Mallikarjun Chetty, Prof. H.N. Shiva Shankar, Prof. N. Srinivasan, Prof. L.M. Patnaik and Prof. M. Venkatachalappa for encouraging me to bring out this book in the present form. I sincerely thank Sri K.P. Jayarama Reddy, Sri T.G. Girikumar, Sri P. Palani, Sri M.G. Muniyappa, for their support in preparing this book.

I express my gratitude to Sri K. Narahari, Sri Y.K. Raghavendra Rao, Sri P.R. Ananda Rao, Justice T. Venkataswamy, Prof. Y.V. Somayajulu, Sri Sreedhar Sagar, Sri N. Nagabhusan, Sri Prabhakar Bhat, Prof. K.V. Acharya, Sri Khajampadi Subramanya Bhat, Sri V. Nagaraj, Sri Dinesh Kamath, Sri D.M. Ravindra, Sri Jagadesh Karanath, Sri N. Thippeswamy, Sri H. K. Mohan Kumar, Sri Sudhir, Sri V. Manjunath, Sri N Dinesh Hegde, Sri Nagendra Prasad, Sri Sripad, Sri K. Thyagaraj, Smt. Savithri Venkatagiri Gowda, Smt. Karthyayini V. and Smt. Rukmini T, my well wishers for inspiring me to write this book. I thank Dr. P. Deepa Shenoy, Sri K.B. Raja, Sri K. Suresh Babu, Smt D.N. Sujatha, Sri K.G. Srinivasa, Smt. S.H. Manjula, Smt Suraiyya Taranaum, Smt. Vibha L. for their assistance.

I am indebted to Tejaswi Venugopal, T. Shiva Prakash, T. Krishna Prasad and Lakshmi Priya K. for their help. I thank L. Nalini and G. Hemalatha for neat composing the book.

Venugopal K R

Contents

Preface vii

Acknowledgements ix

1. Reform of the Fiscal Structure 1
2. Proposed Amendment to the New Industrial Policy 42
3. Reduction of Import Duties 44
4. The Entry of Foreign Banks to the Indian Financial System is Desirable 49
5. Independence for the Reserve Bank of India 52
6. Are Subsidies the Cause of Fiscal Deficit and Inflation? 57
7. The Problem of the Rupee 62
8. Is India getting into the Debt Trap? 68
9. Structural Adjustment: Human or Brutal 76
10. Holding down the Fiscal Deficits of the Centre and the States 81
11. Prohibit the Import of Gold and Silver 88
12. The Basu Committee on the Norms for Regional Rural Banks 91
13. Precautions against a Rise in the Rate of Inflation 97
14. A Mechanism of Curbing States' Deficits 100
15. Exchange Rate Bank, Import Liberalisation and Full Convertibility of the Rupee on Current Account 106
16. The Problem of Inflation Management 119
17. Conditions Favouring a Reduction of the Rate of Inflation 126
18. Easing the Liquidity Crunch 130

19. Oil Prices and Inflation 135
20. Privatisation of Insurance Business 141
21. Forecasts about the Indian Economy 146
22. The Liquidity Crunch in the Indian Economy 160
23. Focus should Shift from Social Banking to Commercial Banking 167
24. The Prime Minister on Foreign Investment 173
25. Relaxing the Rigid Stance about Monetary Growth 177
26. Need to Re-constitute the Audit Committees of Public Sector Banks 181
27. A Case for Additional Food Subsidy 184
28. Exit Policy is an Immediate Necessity 187
29. A New Dimension to the Mexican Crisis 193
30. The Spring Meeting of the IMF and the World Bank 201
31. The Impatient G-13 with Economic Reforms 208
32. How to Structure the Union Budget for 1995-96 215
33. Problems of Food Storage 258
34. India's Foreign Exchange Reserves 265
35. Integrated Approach to Poverty Alleviation 269
36. A Case for Deferring Payment of Additional Salary and Dearness Allowances 273
37. Economy in Public Expenditure 278
38. Whither the National Renewal Fund? 283
39. The Wheat Import Scandal 289
40. Supply-side Economics: Its Relevance to India 291
41. Union Budget, 1985-86 304
42. Dash to High-tech Production: Problems and Prospects 316
43. Wheat Imports to Restrain Inflation 331
44. Disinvestment in Public Sector Equity 336
45. Enhanced Support Prices for Food Grains 342

46. Modifications of the Loan Waiver Scheme 345
47. Partial Privatisation of Banks is Dangerous 350
48. Ceiling on Borrowing to Reduce the Fiscal Deficit 354
49. Fiscal Consolidation, Inflation, Balance of Payments and the Exchange Rate 358
50. Stabilisation of Coffee Prices 370
51. Can a Strong Rupee Deliver Goods 373
52. Fears about a "Dollar Trap" Unfounded: Adequate Dollars can be Mobilised to Overcome Dollar Shortage 378
53. The Planning Commission on Devaluation of the Indian Rupee: The Case Rebutted 393
54. Banning the Movement of Essential Goods to the Neighbouring States 408
55. Alternative Guarantee Proposals in the Power Sector 411
56. Capping of Coffee Exports is Necessary 414
57. Economics of the Power Sector 417
58. Monetary Financing and Debt Financing of the Fiscal Deficit 424
59. Need for an External Economic Strategy 430
60. Is the Decision to Appreciate the Rupee Desirable 435
61. Will the Rate of Inflation Decline? 438
62. No Devaluation, Please 442
63. Reducing the Interest Cost of Public Debt 445
64. A Note on Railway Finances 450
65. The SSI Sector and Economic Reforms 454
66. Managing India's Food Economy 458
67. The Proposed Madras School of Economics 463
68. Mexican Crisis: A Figment of the Pessimists Imagination 470
69. A Revised Gold Bond Scheme is Necessary 477

70. Foreign Companies in the Power Sector 481
71. How to Rescue the Economy from the Inflation Trap 486
72. Final Act of Full Convertibility of the Rupee on Current Account 495
73. Economic Growth Holds the Key to the Reduction of Fiscal Deficit 503
74. The Reserve Bank of India and a Stable Rupee 506
75. India's Export Performance Emulating the Korean Model is Needed 512
76. Freezing Dearness Allowance is Imperative 520
77. Case for Retaining Food and Fertiliser Subsidies 525
78. Hiking Procurement Prices: Lack of an Integrated Perception 530
79. Liberalizing Farm Exports 535
80. Revenue without Tears 541
81. Export Growth and External Solvency 545
82. Multinational Corporations (MNCs) to be made Growth-promoting 557
83. How to Bridge the Trade Gap 561

Prof. K Venkatagiri Gowda

Dr. Venugopal K R, Prof. K Venkatagiri Gowda,
Smt. Savithri Venkatagiri Gowda

Prof. K Venkatagiri Gowda, His Excellency S M Krishna, Prime Minister Dr. Manmohan Singh, Hon'ble Minister Mallikarjuna Kharge

Hon'ble Prime Minister Dr. Manmohan Singh, and Prof. K Venkatagiri Gowda

Hon'ble Prime Minister Dr. Manmohan Singh,
Dr. Venugopal K R, Prof. K Venkatagiri Gowda

Indian Economist Forum 1991-92

Prof. K Venkatagiri Gowda, family and friends

1

Reform of the Fiscal Structure

It is the budget deficits and the mode of their financing that are the root cause of inflation in the Indian economy. The actual budget deficits are invariably larger than the estimated deficits. These deficits are financed partly by money creation and partly by public borrowing both being inflationary each in its own way. The budget deficits can be closed by increasing revenue and reducing expenditure. Increase in revenue can be realized by changing the tax structure in such a way as to promote built-in flexibility. The objectives of taxation are the provision of incentives to saving, investment and capital accumulation and realize quality in income distribution. Reduction in Government expenditure can be realized by reducing unproductive and inessential expenditure. In all these cases an integrated system of fiscal reform is necessary.

Fiscal reform is the need of the hour in India. The Long Term Fiscal Policy formulated as early as December 1985 was not fiscal policy in the strict sense of the term. It was in fact tax policy which did not take account of public expenditure, public debt, monetary and balance of payments aspects of fiscal policy. Even within the tax segment the reforms it suggested were at variance with the policy actually adopted. With the passage of time the ingredients of the Long Term Fiscal Policy were totally forgotten.

The Union Minister of Finance is confronted with the arduous task of enforcing austerity measures during 1991-92 the austerity being enforced by the rising rate of inflation, yawning balance of payments gap, relentless monetary growth, an overambitious VIII five year plan, the external shocks administered by the frequent oil price hikes and the need to implement and conditionality clauses imposed by the IMF which has extended and is to extent further loans of large dimensions to enable India to tide over the foreign exchange crisis. These compulsive forces have necessitated adherence with marginal modification to the supply-side economic philosophy as the basis of economic policy in general and fiscal policy in particular. It is in this context that the present Memorandum is presented to the Finance Ministry of the Government of India. The components of fiscal policy have to be viewed as an integrated whole as change in any one component has its effects on the other components and their segments. It is necessary to set the different components of fiscal policy in a general equilibrium framework of mutual interdependence.

Objectives of Fiscal Policy

1. Promotion of built-in flexibility of the tax system.
2. Equity in income distribution.
3. Stimulus to savings and investment.
4. Promoting non- inflationary growth.
5. Promoting balanced regional development.
6. Holding down the rate of monetary growth.
7. Reducing the balance of payments deficits and at the same time arresting the depreciation of the rupee.
8. Alleviating poverty and unemployment.

These objectives are a coordinated and mutually consistent set and they are to be pursued in unison.

Fiscal Deficits

In the pursuit of growth through capital accumulation there seems to be alternative to running fiscal deficits in order to finance development expenditures. The reasons advanced are (1) tax bases are inadequate to allow a high tax burden (2) even when adequate tax bases are available, the country's tax administration is too inefficient to take advantage of them; (3) the political realities are such that high tax burdens are not possible. In the absence of a developed capital market the fiscal deficits are financed wholly or in part by domestic borrowing, external borrowing and money creation by the Reserve Bank of India. Monetary financing of the fiscal deficit causes a rise in the price level and this reduces the real value of the monetary unit, this reduction being seen as a tax on those who are holding money.

India has thus been living with fiscal deficits. They have been the development tools of the Government to the extent that they powered growth. The recent escalation of the fiscal deficits has more to do with runaway Government consumption. The lesson for the future is that even while reflecting the investment expenditure of the Government fiscal deficits have been caused by a vision of economic growth that sees the Government playing a central role. This view is no longer shared by the rest of the world. The idea of Government as a guardian is fundamentally flawed—the interest of the politician is power and his concern with economic efficiency is only secondary.

Budget deficits have been the bane of Indian economy. They are evidence of the Government's profligacy which increased sharply from 1982. The revenue account deficit till then was nominal. For the first time it crossed Rs. 1,500 crore in 1982-83 and the country has never looked back since then.

The revenue account deficit increased sharply in 1984-85 when it reached almost Rs. 5,000 crore and continued without respite with each year creating new records. The revenue deficit in 1989-90 crossed Rs. 13,000 crore. Warning signals were given from 1985 but they were brushed aside with assurances that the economy was in excellent shape under the able management of the ruling party. When matters became too difficult to conceal, it was concealed that there were temporary problems but no danger of a debt trap.

The Finance Minister, in his budget for 1990-91 budgeted for a deficit of Rs. 7,206 crore and assured the nation that the actual deficit would not exceed this figure. In September 1990 he stated that the deficit had grown to Rs. 9,000 crore. In January 1991 the Finance Minister stated that by the end of November 1990 the deficit had grown to Rs. 13,500 crore. At this rate of growth, the budget deficit till the end of the fiscal year was expected to be Rs. 20,000 crore. However, he announced on the floor of the Lok Sabha in January 1991 that the deficit would be within the Rs. 10,500-11,000 crore limit. The two figures are not in agreement with one another. He also stated that the deficit would be restricted to 8.1 percent of GDP. In 1990-91 the estimated GDP would be of the order of Rs. 50,00,00 crore. The fiscal deficit of 8.1 percent would work out to Rs. 40,000 crore. If the estimated capital receipts of Rs. 29,391 crore is taken out of the deficit for 1990-91 it would work out to Rs. 10,700 crore. This of course, was dependent on crude oil prices remaining at $21-25 per barrel. The GDP for 1991-92 was projected to Rs. 5,40,000 and the fiscal deficit at 6.5% of GDP would work out to Rs. 35,000 crore or Rs. 5,000 crore less than that in 1990-91. The overall deficit is unlikely to be below Rs. 11,000 crore. The situation would become much worse in the event of a prolonged Gulf War which is not only likely to result in a hike in international prices of petroleum products and consequent building up of inflationary pressures but also in a worldwide recession the symptoms of which were already too glaring to escape attention. While there would be a larger inflow of petroleum products at higher prices, India's exports would be squeezed as a result of the recession which would curb demand the world over.

Pending consideration of the possible hike in the prices of petroleum products, the estimated deficit of Rs. 11,000 crore for 1991-92 was patently inflationary calling for efforts to reduce the fiscal deficit to not more than Rs. 3,000 crore. A fiscal adjustment effort must be based on policy actions designed either to raise revenues to whatever level is necessary to finance Government expenditure or to contain Government expenditure within bounds that are consistent with available revenues. In either or both these ways the aggregate demand-supply maladjustments to which the deficits are contributing can be corrected. At this general level the key issue at stake is the extent to which the Government's resource demands are commensurate with its ability to raise revenues. This dimension of fiscal policy is called the fiscal aspect of macro-economic management. The divergence between the flow of fiscal outlays and receipts has to be met by borrowing-domestic and external and money creation. If the deficit is brought down to

Rs. 3,000 crore the resort to these expedients will be minimal with salutary effects on the macro economy.

In 1991-92 the revenue deficit is on the order of over Rs. 7,700 crore. But it is difficult to contain it at this figure. The restoration of subsidy and the abolition of the dual pricing policy for fertilizers will impose on additional burden of Rs. 800 crore. The pension scheme for defence personnel will cost an extra Rs. 1,200 crore, thus pushing the figure to Rs. 9,700. The frequent award of dearness allowance in keeping with the rising price index will add another Rs. 1000 crore before the 1992-93 budget thus taking the deficit figure to 10,700 crore. It is not known what other forces will emerge to increase Government expenditure and to widen the budget deficit. Even at a conservative estimate the budget deficit before the 1992-93 budget will be not less than Rs. 12,000 crore exacerbating inflation in the economy and generating inflationary expectations. Any corrective measures adopted at this stage will yield results, if at all, only after a time lag. Immediate relief cannot be expected.

There is a logical connection between budget deficits and deficits in the balance of payments. The effects of budget deficits on the balance of payments deficits will be compounded by the new industrial policy which lays emphasis on liberalization of imports and the slashing of import duties with the declared objective of reducing prices. Imports are bound to drain the foreign exchange reserves of the country thus necessitating recourse to external borrowing. Between 1947 and 1984 India's external liabilities rose by about Rs. 800 crore a year to a total of Rs. 30,00 crore in 1984. But during the five years of liberalization policy the external debt increased by Rs. 18,000 crore every year. At present it is in the neighborhood of Rs. 2 lakh crore.

The Finance Minister first assured that there was no danger of a debt trap and no need for an IMF loan. A little more than a year later the nation was told that no IMF loan would be taken at the cost of the nation's honour. Within months came the now very familiar statement from the Finance Minister presal that there was now "no option to the IMF Loan." Before the people could recover from their shock, came devaluation of the rupee by 18%. The

Finance Minster stated that after the steep devaluation ("adjustment" according to him) "the rupee could only rise." The rupee can only rise if the internal depreciation is arrested and the trade balance improves. Internal depreciation cannot be arrested and the trade balance will not improve unless domestic inflation is held in check; it will not be held in check unless the budget deficits are reduced. This calls for the imposition of a ceiling on the budget deficits by means of a constitutional amendment.

State Budget Deficits

It is not sufficient if the budget deficit of the Union Government is brought down; it is equally necessary to bring down the deficits of the State and local governments. The Union Government finances its deficit by money creation by the Reserve Bank of India while the State Governments finance their deficits by overdraft facilities provided by the Reserve Bank. The state Governments thus constitute an overdraft economy. In a tri-fiscal system the deficits in the State Budgets are as inflationary as the deficits of the Union Budget. At present the deficits of the two layers of Government are misaligned and the inflationary effects of the budget deficits of the two layers of Government are additive. There is thus need for coordination of fiscal policies of these two layers of Government. Coordination can have several meanings which may range from a vague understanding that each state will do its best to keep or put its own budget in good shape, to a commitment by each state to adopt specific policy actions agreed to jointly in coordination with the other states. For example, in a period of inflation a group of states may agree to pursue contractive fiscal policies. Alternatively, under circumstances in which the fiscal policies of the states are misaligned some states may commit themselves to pursuing a policy aimed at reducing their budget deficits on condition of the other states agreed to pursue similar polices. In all these cases the institution of the newly constituted Inter-state council can be used to coordinate the fiscal policies of the states and to align them with the fiscal policy of the Union Government.

The need for activating the Inter-State council arises for three reasons: economic and specifically fiscal polices of states have been widely misaligned; the economies of the states are much more interdependent at present than they were in the past; there are important externalities in policy-making implying that when states act independently and in their own self interest policy changes may not be carried to the degree necessary to maximize the collective welfare of all the States.

The need for reduction of budget deficits being admitted, how does this policy affect economic growth? The policy of fiscal expansion undertaken to finance economic growth, however defensible it may be from a purely political point of view, is a misguided economic exercise based on the untenable assumption that fiscal expansion leads to faster growth. The connection between expansion any fiscal policies and faster growth rates is tenuous at best. There is no convincing empirical evidence that the countries that have pursued restrictive, anti-inflationary, policies have grown any less fast than those that have pursued expansionary fiscal polices; there is also no convincing empirical evidence that countries that have pursued overly expansive fiscal policies have grown faster than those that have pursued restrictive fiscal policies. The realization of the goal of non-inflationary growth demands that the budget deficits of both the Union Government and the state Government should be reduced.

This policy required placement of a constitutional ceiling on the Union budget deficits, placement of a constitutional ceiling on the volume of borrowing by the Union Government both domestic and external and the placement of a constitutional limit on the overdraft facilities allowed to the State Governments by the Reserve Bank of India. It is, of course, different to convince the parliament of the need to legislate on these limits but given strong political leadership this should not be an impossible task. The sooner this step is taken the better it is for the country.

Reducing budget deficits tends to reduce the price level. The deficit can be reduced by raising revenue or by reducing Government expenditure or by doing both in a agreed proportion. When non-inflationary growth is the goal, restrictive fiscal measures must be chosen with special care. In a situation where inflationary pressures are exacerbated by insurance systems like tying wages to the cost of living index deficit reduction through raising indirect taxes, reducing subsides or raising public sector fees or tariffs may impart an upward thrust to the price level which more than offsets the disinflationary effects of budget contraction. When the attempt is made to cut the budget deficit through revenue measures, it is necessary to remove the insurance systems. Hence the simultaneous implementation of tax changes and the removal of insurance systems is crucial to the success fo budget contraction as an anti-inflationary exercise. Hence the need for a freeze of wages, salaries and other items of expenditure which are tied to very directly with the price level. If the insurance system cannot be removed real Government expenditure will have to be reduced on goods and services and other items of non-developmental expenditure. Cuts in transfer payments affect inflation after a lag if the recipients of the transfer consider the cuts to be transitory. Their demand will not fall immediately by the full amount of the cut in their current income.

The IMF was assured by the Government that the fiscal deficit would be brought down to 6.5% of GDP in 1991-92 and further down to 5% in 1992-93. However, the IMF does not seem to be happy with the way the Finance Minister sought to reduce the fiscal deficit from 8.5% of GDP to 6.5% in 1991-92. The IMF wants its to cut serious anomalies in the budget projections. For instance, the IMF feels that the Finance Minister's estimate of the revenue receipts was on the higher side and expenditure on the lower side. The IMF feels that the Finance Minister's claim of having reduced the fiscal deficit to 6.5% of GDP, the possibility of bringing it down to 5% of GDP in 1992-93 is remote. This assessment of the IMF is perfectly justified. If anything, the deficit would rise above 6.5% and not fall to 5%. If this is so, there will be no respite to inflation. On the basis of the present budgetary trends it can safely be assumed that the rate of inflation would rise to over 20% before the presentation of the 1992-93 budget. This calls for a merciless slashing of inessential and unproductive expenditure which is in a large magnitude and also sealing down of the proposed outlay of Rs. 7,92,000 crore on the Eight Plan.

Cuts in Government Expenditure

Budget deficit cut can be undertaken from two directions: reduction of Government expenditure and raising of tax revenue. Reduction of expenditure differs from raising tax revenue in respect of impact and in respect of certainty and speed with which it yields results. Measures of reducing expenditure carry more certainty in their impact on the budget deficit than measures to raise tax revenue. Care must be taken to ensure that cutbacks in expenditure are focused on less productive activities. Obvious political sensitivities may limit the degree to which these expenditures can be cut and, as a consequence, the expenditure policies many not be supportive of the growth objective. There is the danger that cuts in expenditure may be borne by the more productive projects. Cutbacks may affect productive projects financed from domestic and external sources. There may be higher implementation rates for lower priority projects.

We should not be merely concerned with reducing the quantum of expenditure. The transition from the quantitative to the qualitative approach requires an analysis of the impact of expenditure structures on long-term growth and inflation and calls for some kind of conditionality on the composition of expenditure. Such an approach implied the development of micro-economic analysis as a basis for achieving macro-economic balance in the development process.

If the macro-economic effect of fiscal restructuring turns out to be higher inflation, a run down of foreign exchange reserves or a crowding out of private investment, the chances of success of fiscal restructuring will be weakened. The manner in which the fiscal gap is closed is very important.

Experience shows that at the margin structurally valuable elements of the budget (eg. operations and maintenance expenditures or high quality capital projects) are often the most susceptible to cuts required to realize the required budgetary target. Meanwhile, less productive elements remain protected because of the perceived political and social implications. Similarly, at the margin revenue measures may adversely affect production and investment patterns. In the final analysis, the private sector will have to bear the burden of fiscal choices made and the important task is to determine the choices consciously that are least detrimental to macro-economic stability, external adjustment and growth.

In the matter of expenditure cuts the Government should not fall prey to the frequently used assumption that any expansion of expenditure represents a sub-optimal use of resources. After all, the Government provides, among other things, social goods that are the preconditions for any development process. Furthermore, the authorities should scrutinize more closely the costs and benefits stemming from groups of expenditure items as a measure of strengthening the economic system.

While expenditure cuts are necessary the authorities have to decide which item of expenditure should be cut. Cuts in productive expenditure are ruled out in the interests of growth and price stability. The three items of expenditure which suggest themselves for pruning are:

1. Defence expenditure
2. Subsidies, and
3. Interest payments on public debt.

Some have suggested a drastic cut in defence expenditure on the ground that defence outlay is excessive and is beyond the capacity of the country to bear. But this view is myopic.

In the 1980s defense expenditure increased dramatically. In rupee terms it more than trebled in an eight-year period from Rs. 3820 crore in 1980 to Rs. 12980 crore in 1988. However, calculated in terms of major western currencies at the Indian exchange rates in the year of spending, defense expenditure doubled in that period. From the equivalent of $ 5.7 billion in 1980 to peak of $ 9.9 billion in 1988. This calculation reflects true increase in real defense expenditure in that eight-year period. After the record expenditure of 1988 India's defense spending has not increased in real terms because of the depreciation of the rupee against major western currencies and high domestic inflation. The Union Budget for 1991-92 unveiled after a 20% rupee devaluation represents a sharp fall in the real value of the Indian defence outlay. Against the $ 8.8 billion spent on defence in 1990 the Government this year (1991-92) has budgeted $ 6.3 billion—a cut of 28 percent.

India's security environment is causing acute concern. India is encircled by hostile neighbours warranting an enhancement of defence outlay. The argument that India should cultivate good neighbourly relations with her neighbors and in this way India can cut down defence expenditure is too facile to be acceptable. It would be risky to trust our neighbours in view of past experience. India must seriously ponder over the Churchillian doctrine of "defence through deterrence". If this is accepted, defence preparedness should be the watchword of India's foreign policy. This necessarily calls for a rise in defence expenditure. This means that defence outlay does not admit of any reduction.

Another item of expenditure which some argue for reduction is the item relating to subsides on food, fertilizers and exports. In a regime governed by supply side economic philosophy subsidies have no place. India is not yet a fulfledged market economy though it is on the road to it. For this reason, India cannot afford to do away with subsidies immediately through over the medium term they can be dispensed with. Food subsidies hold down food prices and are a stabilizing factor. In India it is the food prices that govern the general price index and therefore the rate of inflation. Seen in this perspective food subsidies are necessary to hold down food prices and thus the rate of inflation. Fertilizer subsidies are also necessary to increase agricultural productivity and production especially food production. The removal of fertilizer subsidy will increase the market price of fertilizers. If the demand of fertilizes is price elastic, the demand for them falls, and the input of fertilizers falls causing a fall in agricultural productivity and production, especially food production. A fall in food production assures a rise in food prices and the rate of inflation. If the demand for fertilizers is price inelastic, the input of fertilizers will not fall, farm productivity and production will not fall. But the rise in input prices causes a rise in the cost of production and therefore a rise in food prices.

Thus the abolition of fertilizer subsidy whether the demand for fertilizer is inelastic or elastic causes a rise in food prices. For this reason subsidies on fertilizers must be retained for some more time. Export subsidies make the rupee prices of India's exports fall and this helps export promotion measures. Abolition of export subsidies holds down India's exports and hinders export growth. For this reason export subsidies are necessary.

This is not to argue for institutionalizing subsidies in the Indian economy. Far from it. As the economy has been adjusted to subsidies, sudden removal of subsidies will causes maladjustments which hinder macro-economic stabilization efforts of the Government. Therefore, subsidies have to be retained for the time being and their removal must be arranged in a phased programme. But for the present we cannot expect any relief from the side of subsidies.

Interest payments on the public debt are growing year by year. The Government has been financing the budget deficits by money creation and by borrowing. As observed already borrowing involves interest payments which widen the budget deficit and help to accelerate inflation in the economy. A firm resolve to reduce the budget deficits and to finance whatever deficit is inevitable more by money creation than by domestic borrowing will reduce interest payments. For the time being this is the only way in which expenditure can be cut. Constitutional amendments imposing ceilings on the size of budget deficits and on the size of public borrowing will help reduce interest payments.

For the time being it is necessary to keep subsidies and to maintain/enhance expenditure on defence. Subsidies are necessary for some more time as their abolition or even reduction are bound to exacerbate inflation besides generating popular resentment. Furthermore, while China and Pakistan are increasing their defence expenditure it is incumbent on India to increase its defence expenditure. The IMB has included into in subsidies and defence in its conditionality proscriptions. In view of the special circumstances in which India is placed the IMF should be requested to exclude:

1. Subsidies
2. Defence expenditure and
3. Devaluation of the rupee

From the conditionality prescriptions. On the other hand the industrialized nations should themselves reduce their defence expenditure and free resources for aiding the developing countries.

The Government of India on Friday 13, September 1991 adopted a decision to impose a 5% cut on the expenditure provisions in the sanctioned budget estimates for 1991-92 for all ministries and departments. This decision followed criticism by the IMF that the Government had underestimated the expenditure in the budget to show fiscal deficit at 6.5% of the GDP.

This cut will not be applicable to statutory grant to State Governments recommended by the Finance Commission, black loans and grants to States for State Plan Schemes and pension payments including defence pensions. The cut will also not be applicable to interest payments. In respect of commercial departments and public sector undertakings the cut would be applied on the expenditure provisions in the budget. These steps are in fulfilment of the assurance given to the IMF that steps would be taken to prune expenditure.

This is not the first time that decision has been taken to reduce expenditure by 5%. In 1988-89 budget and in the 1989-90 budget a similar decision was taken but no follow up action was taken. It will not be a surprise if the same fate falls the present decision also. Furthermore, it would be simply juvenile to reduce by 5% the grants estimated for all departments. Whether they are productive or not. What is necessary is to reduce inessential expenditure in all the departments and not to reduce by a uniform percentage the grants estimated for all the departments.

Tax Structure

The need for fiscal restructuring was at no time in the history of Independent India more urgent than at the present moment when the economic crisis of unprecedented magnitude is threatening our survival as a nation. Fiscal restructuring, therefore, calls for immediate attention. In 1985 the Government of India formulated the Long Term Fiscal Policy (LTFP) meant to give a new thrust to the economy in its march towards "growth with stability". This policy was based on the supply side economic philosophy of classical liberalism whose offshoot was the Laffer Curve Analysis. The main idea was to use fiscal policy tax policy in particular to stimulate savings, investment, work effort stand economic growth. Tax rates were to be reduced to achieve those objectives and to induce greater tax compliance so that even at lower rates of tax yields might increase. There was also to be a shift from indirect to direct taxes so as to reduce the regressivity of the tax structure and to provide relief to the common man. The budget deficits were to be reduced in order to contain inflation. However, the debt, monetary and balance of payments implications of the new fiscal philosophy were either not understood or, if understood, were not considered to be of much significance. The new fiscal philosophy represented a revolution in thinking and not revolution in practice. Tax rates were reduced, of course, and though the tax yields increased the entire increase cannot be attributed to tax rate reduction; it was due, in part, to rising incomes which engendered "bracket creep" to operate bringing into the tax bracket many tax payers who were formerly outside it. Despite the aim of shifting to direct taxes there has, infact, been and shift to indirect taxes. The rates of saving and investment have raised marginally, if at all. In the absence of expenditure cuts expenditure has been rising at a greater rate than tax revenue widening the fiscal gap and causing monetary expansion which has a proportionate impact on the price level. The tax policy based as it is on the Laffer Curve Analysis is good in the sense that lower tax rates result in larger tax yields. This is corroborated by the experience of post-war German, Japan, Singapore, Sri Lanka and Hong Kong where tax rate cuts resulted in larger revenue yield, stimulated savings and investment and accelerated economic growth. But the mode of implementation of the Long Term Fiscal Policy in India leaves a lot to be desired. The unsuccess of this policy in India can be attributed to the excessive rise in Government expenditure and excessive resort to public borrowing and monetary expansion to finance it and the exacerbation of inflation which generated expectation of further inflation and caused an inter-temporal substitution of present goods for future goods making expected inflation come true. This did not allow the savings ratio to rise as much as it would have done in the absence of inflation stability of tax rates is the exception rather than the rule. Tax rates are announced in the budget and are approved by the Parliament but subsequently they are changed. Fiscal stimulus to industrial investment is too weak to enable the corporate sector to realize the targets of investment and production. Public debt has increased and has been increasing making the country perch precariously on the brim of an internal debt trap. Excessive budgetary deficits and the associated monetary expansion have generated balance of payments deficits and the rationale of the connection between budget deficits and balance of payments deficits is provided by the analysis of the Cambridge Economic Policy Group. As the foreign exchange reserves are not adequate to meet the deficits the country has to resort to external borrowing which has put it on the brink of the external debt trap also.

Direct Taxation, Income Tax, etc.

It is in the area of direct taxation that decisive changes are necessary. The Long Term Fiscal Policy of December 1985 proposed a reduction in the rates of direct taxes on personal incomes and raised the exemption limit to Rs. 18,000 in the hope that they would induce greater tax compliance and yield larger tax revenues. This measure was founded on the Laffer Curve Analysis which states that the tax yields and tax rates vary inversely. It is true that the tax yields rose in the following years but this cannot be attributed to lower tax rates so much as to the rise in personal incomes. Though the Long Term Fiscal Policy aimed at shifting from indirect taxes to direct taxes the direct tax yields as a preparation of total tax receipts fell while indirect tax yields rose thus indicating that the taxes shifted in favour of indirect taxes.

In the 1990-91 budget the Finance Minister, raised the exemption limit from Rs. 18,000 to Rs. 22,000 ostensibly to provide relief to lower income groups. But this enhancement of the exemption limit was only notional and did not provide any relief to the salaried employees in the lower and middle income groups. In a period of inflation when the real income is falling raising of the exemption limit is only fair, just and equitable.

At the same time, there is an imperative need to raise the tax rates on each successive slab so that those on the higher slabs may contribute to revenues. This, besides yielding more revenue, will achieve equity in income distribution. The incomes of husband and wife should be jointly assessed as a single income.

In a period of inflation, given the tax rates, the tax yields rise and the rise in tax yields is greater. But the lags in tax collection work in the opposite direction each month or each quarter though at the end of the fiscal year the yields will be found to have risen. As the taxes are paid quarterly, half yearly of annually, the tax-GDP ratio in each quarter or half-year falls though at the end of the year it shows a rise. But the Government has to finance its expenditure every month. If, due to collection lags, the taxes are not paid every month but are paid annually, the Government, in order to meet its expenditure, has to borrow from the Reserve Bank of India which is inflationary. Thus, while the progressivity of the tax structure causes a rise in the Tax-GDP ratio at the end of the year, the collection lags cause a fall in each month. Thus, along with increasing the progressivity of the tax structure there is need to shorten the collection lags by requiring the payment of direct taxes every month. This helps to maintain the tax-GDP ratio each month results in a larger revenue yield in absolute terms and makes money financing of the deficit unnecessary. This helps to reduce the size of the budget deficit.

The rate of economic growth depends on net new investment which depends on savings. This means that savings are to rise to finance the targeted rate of investment. The eighth five year plan envisages a rise in the savings rate from the present 21.2% to 23%.

Therefore, there is need to provide tax incentives to savings. At present savings are taxed whether it is consumed or saved and again when savings generate interest income. If this scheme is ended total saving should increase. There is need for exempting interest income or certain types of dividend income from taxation.

The Government may also require the employees to put 10% of their salaries into untaxed bank accounts in their names. The company reserves designed to purchase capital equipment should not be taxed. Abolition of inheritance tax may also favour savings. Empirical evidence shows that savings vary directly with real interest rates. This requires that money interest rates should be raised in a greater proportion than the rate of inflation so that the rise in the real interest rate may stimulate savings. Tax incentives to savings involve a loss in revenue to the Government and this may widen the budget deficit but this loss should be made good by increasing other items of revenue or by a commensurate cut in Government expenditure.

The Government can also plan for a budget surplus which could then be made available on a competitive basis to the private sector and to viable public undertakings. This could be seen as an integral part of fiscal policy meant to direct funds to productive channels. This scheme, besides stimulating productive investment, legitimizes the tax collection that generated the surplus. A progressive tax system associated with prudent macro-economic management may make higher tax rates more acceptable than they would be in a tax system with many exemptions perceived to be unsustainable in the long run.

The savings ratio reacts to the inflation rate in two ways: Savings ratio falls if people expect the inflation rate to rise as in that case they shift to consumption in order to avoid the loss of purchasing power; inflation may also be associated with a rise in the savings ratio as people react to the erosion of the real value of their nominal assets by reducing consumption. In the Indian case the fall in the savings ratio can be explained in terms of the expectation effect which causes a rise in consumption at the expense of savings: a rise in the inflation rate, causes a fall in the real interest rate and this reduces the savings ratio. Savings ratio can also be increased by issuing new savings instruments at attractive terms including interest rates/maturity value.

Gift taxes are to be increased as the gifts are made normally by the wealthy individuals. Wealth tax rates should be increased in the interest of equity. But in order to encourage the inflow of foreign funds wealth tax on all NRI remittances should be withdrawn and conditions for NRI investments should be liberalized. The agricultural sector has performed well. Higher farm incomes have enhanced purchasing power in the rural areas and this will have to be neutralized by taxing the rural rich and also owners of plantations. This will, to some extent, neutralize the adverse consequences of the large internal and external deficits which are the bane of Indian economy.

Direct Taxation—Corporation Tax

Drastic restructuring of the corporate income taxation is absolutely necessary. At present, the corporate sector has voiced many legitimate grievances and a few exaggerated complaints. The manufacturing sector has been growing and its contribution to GNP is also growing. But the rate of growth of this sector is slow and sluggish. The banking sector has generated severe constraints on the availability of credit and this accounts in part for the sluggish rise in investment. If borrowing is a major constraint on investment expansion, we should expect to observe an increase in corporate savings rate and hence a decline in the ratio of borrowed funds to total investment. However, this did not happen. The sluggish investment is due to a decline in the retained earnings rate for a few industries which have recorded a secular decline in the profitability rates. This analysis suggests that interest rate management will be of limited effectiveness in increasing investment. The profitability is falling because of the increase in the product-wage rate. This increase is a consequence of the expansion of public sector employment at rising real wages. In the presence of full equity markets an increase in the wage bill can generate a positive income effect on investment. The transition to perfect capital markets can be achieved with reforms in equity markets.

The earlier budgets had allowed for investment allowances in order to help the industries to undertake modernization and technological upgradation exercises. However, in the 1980-90 budget the investment allowances were withdrawn. This adversely affected the corporate surpluses thus inhibiting investment activity and efficient performance.

The proprietary small scale units are the worst hit by the withdrawal of investment allowances under section 321 and investment deposit under Section 328 AB of the Income Tax Act, 1961. This caused a sharp increase of 10.8% of tax liability in the case of proprietary firms. These units can be provided relief by continuing Section 328AB for non-corporate assessees.

The objective of planning is rapid growth. This has been affected by the withdrawal of benefits under section 80 HHA for newly established firms in backward areas. This is at variance with the policy of industrialization of backward regions. The regional development schemes can be helped by atleast 45% tax deduction for corporate units and 40% tax deduction for non-corporate new small scale industrial units established in backward areas under Section 80-1 of the Income Tax Act. At the same time, liberal depreciation allowances based on replacement cast are necessary to promote the growth of the corporate sector.

The corporate sector has been stridently demanding the reduction of the marginal rte of personal income tax to 40% and applied to income above Rs. 2 lakh and the abolition of the tax on dividends. The revenue implications of this demand are adverse as they cause a fall in revenue. The social implications are adverse to equity in income distribution. In a country with a per capita income of less than Rs. 4,000 per annum at current prices and half the population is eking out a meagre living, this demand is unacceptable. The total number of income tax assesses in India is just about 6 million in a population of 850 million. Their number will come down if income tax is applied only to incomes above Rs. 2 lakh. While the restoration of investment allowances is in order the demand to limit the marginal income tax rate to 40%$ and the application of income tax to incomes above Rs. 2 lakh goes against the ideal of reducing the budget deficit.

Tax on dividends involves double taxation and for this reason dividends should enjoy total exemption or should be given liberal exemption. Inter-corporate dividends should also be exempted. While long-term capital gains should be taxed, short-term capital gains should be tax-exempt on reinvestment in certain activities. The businesses should be allowed to set off business loses against capital gains and capital losses against pre-tax business profits. Wealth tax on closely held companies appears to be unfair. There should be a minimum non-taxable limit of wealth of such enterprises. The imported cares should be wealth taxed while domestically produced cars should be tax-exempt. Double taxation of firms and persons should be dropped as it goes against the norms of equity.

The corporate sector demands the reduction of indirect taxes from the present 17% indirect tax GDP ratio as it is alleged to be crippling the industry. This is unreasonable, in addition, the case of duty exemption on imported capital goods and other inputs on the plea that this duty is a tax on investment and modernization is not strong. Though there is an element of justification for this demand it can be argued that this duty is hardly inimical to investment and modernization. It has been calculated that the incidence of duty of capital goods imports in relation to the price of the commodity produced works out to only 2% in respect to customs and 1% in respect of central excise. The customs and excise duties as a factor enhancing the cost of production cannot be regarded as crippling the industry. However, investment in energy-efficient techniques can be considered for tax exemption.

The objective of all these proposals is to stimulate investment in industry and in its modernization. This objective gains significance from the fact that at present investment activity in the manufacturing sector is sluggish. Investment proposals fall sharply in 1990-91 by 5% in number and 21% in terms of value. Allowing for a 10% inflation and a 15% depreciation in nominal terms, the real fall in investment proposals is of the order of a third in April-November 1990 compared to the previous year. There has also been a parallel fall in approvals for the import of capital goods of 34.7% between April and November 1990. The disbursement of long-term loans by the financial institutions was 5.5% higher than in April-September 1989. But this was the effect of investment proposals made a year ago. Even so, it compares poorly with the annual 20% growth of earlier years.

Generating Employment

There is considerable unemployment in India. According to an estimate unemployment is of the order of 5 crore. Several employment schemes in the past have failed to make a dent into this colossal problem. According to the Deputy Chairman of the Planning Commission the plans have so far failed to generate employment of the required magnitude. Every year million of people are entering the job market generating excess supply of labour unemployment.

This problem has to be tackled from the demand for labour side and the supply of labour side. The demand for labour must be made to increase. For this purpose there is need to levy an employment generation tax on all the employed workers. The proceeds from this tax should be pooled and it should be used to generate employment. This is the contribution of the employed workers to the alleviation of the problem of unemployment of their hapless brethren. The rate of tax should be uniform subject to a minimum.

As the supply of labour to the job market is more than the demand for labour generating unemployment there is need to reduce the supply of labour. This requires the imposition of a tax on every child born over and above two children. This serves as a disincentive to getting more children. At the same time the family planning programmes should be applied to all sections of society irrespective of their caste or religion. Thus fiscal disincentives are necessary to reduce the supply of labour. In this manner unemployment can be alleviated to some extent.

Rising the Income Tax Exemption Limit

Tax reform will not be complete unless the income tax exemption limit is raised to a round figure of Rs. 50,000. In a regime of continuously rising prices the real income of the tax payer goes on falling. The real income falls when, money income being constant, prices rise or when money income rises at a slower rate than prices. Tax exemption is given to tax payers in order to provide partial relief from the rigours of taxation. With a constant exemption limit, a rise in prices causes a fall in the real exemption limit and proves burdensome to the tax payer over and above the general burden of inflation tax. This cuts into his living standards and/or savings margin. It is this reason that justice and equity demand that with a rise in the inflation rate the exemption limit should also be raised.

In the 1989-90 budgets, the exemption limit was set at Rs. 18,000. In the 1990-91 budget the Finance Minister raised it marginally to Rs. 22,000. This limit was maintained in the 1991-92 budget. With a rise in the rate of inflation and the erosion of the real value of money income, the relief provided to the taxpayers was only notional. Despite the rise in prices, the Finance Minister in his budget for 1991-92 maintained the exemption limit at Rs. 22,000. The taxpayers are groaning under the burden of taxation. It is for this reason that there is a strong case for raising the exemption limit to Rs. 50,000.

It is true that raising the exemption limit narrows down the tax base, leaves many taxpayers out of the tax net and results in lower tax yield. This may be so. But at a time when even a family earning Rs. 4,000 a month is not able to make both ends meet because of the rise in the prices of food, clothing and shelter, quite apart from other expenses of an essential nature it appears unjust to make him pay the tax. Therefore, such families can be left outside the tax net. Any loss in the tax revenue can be more than made good by raising the rates of wealth tax and gift tax which have become a fruitful source of income at the present time when gifts are made out of black money accumulations and wealth, for the large part, is black wealth. This step will reduce the accumulation of black money and black wealth but it will also reduce the incentive to accumulate them.

Tax on Interest Income

The Union Budget for 1991-92 envisages taxing at source of income from interest accruing on deposits and those who get an income of over Rs. 2,500 have to pay this tax. The majority of the depositors are salaried employees and retired personnel who have deposited their gratuity amount and their savings in banks at the prescribed interest rates and the interest income supplements their pension payments. Even so, they are unable to make both ends meet on account of the steady depreciation of the rupee. If the tax is collected at the source of their income it will cut into their income and make it difficult for them to live even with the minimum degree of comfort. Furthermore, at a time when the banks are advised to intensify their deposit mobilization efforts, this tax acts as a disincentive to the depositors. After the period of the maturity is over, they may not renew their deposits in the banks but may shift to other avenues where the interest income is not taxed. These avenues are many and valid in India. This is bound to adversely affect the banking system. At a time when many banks are sick this tax is bound to increase their sickness and to increase the number of sick units. Therefore, it behoves the Government to withdraw this tax considering its inequity and unfairness and to refund the tax collected before the damage is done to the banking system.

Indirect Taxation

Both direct and indirect tax revenues have been increasing but in recent years they have become less buoyant. Indirect taxes contribute 82 percent of total tax revenues. Though the long Term Fiscal Policy envisaged a shift in favour of direct taxes, there has, in fact, been a shift in favour of indirect taxes. Raising the indirect tax rates raises the prices of goods. This reduces demand which results in a recession in economic activity besides creating a high cost economy. As the impact of the indirect taxes is uniform, their burden is borne primarily by the poorer section of society. A planning commission study estimates that for every rupee of indirect taxes 55 paise is borne by the poor; the burden of inflation is also borne more by the poor than by the rich.

Considerations of equity and revenue yield demand that the indirect taxes on goods of mass consumption should be lower than at present; the revenue loss emerging from this can be more than made good by the raising of indirect taxes on luxury goods of both domestic and external origin. With rising incomes and rising accumulation of black money there has emerged in the country a kind of "kit-culture" which makes the rich purchase luxury goods domestic and imported more out of ostentation than out of necessity. However, high their prices may be, the demand for them will not fall. Conspicuous consumption is not price elastic but it is income elastic. Goods coming in this category can be taxed at very high rates and the indirect tax yield can be increased considerably. The impact of these levies on the general price level can be mitigated by keeping the stock of money constant under a policy of monetary targetry.

At present indirect taxes contribute about 80% of tax revenue representing a gradual shift towards indirect taxes. This is one of the causes of inflation. This should be gradually reversed and the yield from direct taxes should be increased.

There is a controversy regarding the inflationary effects of indirect taxes. One view is that the enhancement of indirect taxes is anti-inflationary. According to this view a rise in indirect taxes on certain goods or goods in general takes away purchasing power from the consumers and leaves less in their hands. This causes a fall in demand and a fall in prices. Another view is that indirect taxes are inflationary. It is held that indirect taxes which are shifted forwarded to the consumers cause a rise in prices and are inflationary. These view are valid as far as they go but they do not go far. For they do not take account of the monetary conditions.

In a situation approaching full employment a rise in indirect taxes on all goods causes, through forwards shifting, a rise in prices and is therefore inflationary. But, if the supply of money is held constant the rise in prices create conditions which make them fall for the following reasons:

1. A rise in prices represents a rise in money national income. Assuming that the demand for active money (Keynesian L1 Balances) is a linear function of national income, the demand for active balances rises. As the supply of money is held constant,

the transactions who need cash have to sell their bonds in the market. This causes an excess supply of bonds which in turn causes a fall in bond prices and a rise in interest rates. The rise in interest rates checks investment activity. Furthermore the fall in bond prices, through the bond effect checks consumption also.

2. When the prices rise the money illusion effect will be in operation. The consuming units spend the same amount of their income on consumption. As the prices have risen the same amount of spending purchases less and less goods. This results in a fall in real consumption. In this manner both investment and consumption fall representing a fall in aggregate demand and a fall in the price level. Thus, inflation brought about by the imposition or enhancement of a general tax on goods brings about its own remedy. Prices will be rolled back to the pre-tax level.

However if the supply of money is expanding these effects will not be operative. Rising money supply finances the demand for active balances and does not cause a sale of bonds, a fall in bond prices and a rise in the interest rates. Furthermore, rising money supply does not allow the money illusion effect to operate also as it finances rising expenditure in money terms. In view of this the restrictive effects on aggregate demand become inoperative and the higher prices caused by indirect taxes are sustained by monetary expansion. The conclusion is that if the higher indirect taxes are to be price neutral the supply of money should be held constant. In the Indian case, the supply of money is expanding at the rate of 15-18 percent per year on account of budget deficits and therefore indirect taxes are not price neutral. If indirect taxes are not to be inflationary the supply of money should be held constant or better still should be reduced.

Privatisation of Public Sector Units

One of the causes of the fiscal deficits is the budgetary support being extended to the public sector units. These units which were once considered to be temples of India and represented the advance of socialism are, by and large, in the red due to overstaffing and inefficient management. The prices of the goods and services supplied by these enterprises have to be raised in order to render them viable units. As a result, the prices of these goods and services rise and add to inflation; the budgetary support extended to them widen the fiscal gap and they in their own right generate and exacerbate inflation. It is held by everybody including the IMF that these public sector units constitute a major drain on the fiscal resources of the Government.

Budgetary support to the loss-making public sector units has already been reduced considerably. It will have to be further reduced in order to prevent the drain on the fiscal resources of the Government including the drain in borrowed funds. In mid October 1991 the total external borrowing stood at $ 9 billion, this included $ 6 billion under current account deficit and $ 3 billion for repayment. (In the aggregate it was, at the current exchange rate, Rs. 22,600 crore).

The Government of India has undertaken major reforms for the public sector enterprises. In future the units which are unviable will have to be closed down. The Government will have to start the process of transferring 20 percent of the equity of viable public sector units to mutual funds which, in turn, would list them in the stock exchange. This would release a total of Rs.2,500 crore. This process would be in two stages—one in 1991 and the other in 1992.

It must be emphasized that the public sector units are not, as expected, temples of India, nor do they represent and advance of socialism. They have, in fact, proved to be an avoidable burden on the scarce fiscal resources and a source of inflationary pressure which is at variance with philosophy of socialism as it results in unequal distribution of income and wealth. The IMF does not have to advice the Government of India to privatize the public sector units or to close down those which are non-viable. The decision has to be taken by the Government itself in the interests of prudent management of the nation's resources.

Fiscal Planning

The efficiency and effectiveness of public spending need improvement. This requires fiscal planning, budgeting, implementation and monitoring. Fiscal planning ideally involves the formulation of a phased investment programme, projections of current spending needs, an assessment of revenue availability and borrowing requirements over 3-5 years; all set in the context of a consistent macroeconomic framework. The annual budget would then be a one year slice of the medium term fiscal plan. For plans and budgets to promote effective decision-making by individual public agents, the trade-offs among the agencies, programmes and projects must be explicit and the budget constraints for each agency, once set, must be rigid, that is, the agency must not be permitted to exceed the budget on its own initiative.

The planning authorities can develop procedure to ensure that careful attention is paid to the recurrent cost implications of investment spending; they can also employ cost-benefit analysis to screen potential investments before official green signal is given; the Government payrolls must be trimmed through hiring freezes, civil service censuses and voluntary retirement schemes; attempts must be made to rationalize civil service wage structure i.e., by eliminating inter-state salary dearness allowance and pension differentials. Through these measures efficiency and effectiveness of public spending programmes can be secured.

Actual developments in the economy as reflected in the financial reporting process are to be compared with the expected developments. Since the fiscal policy decisions are reflected in the annual budget, the budget becomes a natural basis for this comparison. However, if the budget data are to serve this purpose two requirements must be met:

1. The budget estimates must be realistic and kept that way as the year progresses. This can be done by relating them to a macroeconomic framework and by undertaking periodic reviews of the key budgetary and macroeconomic assumptions on which the budget is based;

2. The components of the budget must be phased over each month of the year (or quarter as the case may be) as accurately and realistically as possible indicating the likely path of each component and the overall fiscal position. There is need to improve the level of sophistication of forecasts.

Such forecasts can be prepared on the basis of the past seasonal patterns of the main revenue and expenditure components adjusted in the light of coming policy changes or events likely to upset past patterns. Individual large-scale development projects would have to be treated separately.

There are two methods of financing the budget deficits:

Money financing and debt financing. The Government of India has been using both these methods of financing the budget deficits and both of them have inflationary consequences. Money financing causes a rise in the price level in consonance with the mechanism underlying the Quantity Theory of Money as modified by Don Patinkin. A rise in money supply, demand for money being constant, causes an excess supply of money which generates a real balance effect which in turn generates excess demand which causes a rise in the price level. This causes a rise in the demand for money to the level of supply and reestablishes monetary equilibrium at a higher level of prices. When, in the following year, the supply of money is expanded to finance the budget deficits the operation of the mechanism is repeated and monetary equilibrium is reestablished at a higher level of prices. This process goes on continuously until the monetary financing of the budget deficit is stopped. This mechanism is in operation in India.

Debt financing of the deficit is also inflationary. Debt financing involves the payment of interest on debt. Interest payments are an item of public expenditure. The larger the debt larger the interest payments and larger the interest payments the bigger the budget deficit. Seen in this perspective, public debt is a source of inflation.

In India public debt is growing at a rapid pace. It was about 44 percent of GDP in the early 1980s. This increased to about

60 percent of GDP at the close of the Seventh Five Year Plan. With the growing volume of deficit financing the quantum of public debt will also increase causing a rise in interest payments and further increasing the size of the budget deficit with all its inflationary consequences. For this reason there is need to impose a ceiling on the size of the public debt by means of a constitutional amendment.

Whatever debt remains outstanding should be diverted of its inflationary potential. It is an essential ingredient of Radcliffe Monetary Theory that expenditure depends on liquidity and that greater the liquidity, greater the volume of expenditure. Short-term debt is more liquid than long-term debt and for this reason it is more inflationary than long term debt. In an inflationary situation it is necessary to reduce the liquidity of the economy. This calls for reducing the volume of short term debt and increasing the volume of long term debt. Therefore, it is necessary to issue long term debt and/ or to convert short term debt into long term debt. It is true that long term debt carries a higher interest rate than short-term debt and therefore long term debt imposes a greater interest burden than short term debt. But the gain to the economy in terms of reduced rate of inflation more than offsets the burden of higher interest payments.

An associated innovation is the freeing of interest rates. At present interest rates are determined by the authorities and not by the market. Interest rates are thus held low in order to hold down the burden of debt. It is necessary to free interest rates from official controls and to allow the market forces to determine them. Furthermore, investors should be free to shift their funds from the debt of one maturity to debts of other maturities. This will prevent market segmentation and allow free mobility of funds between segments.

At present market support policy is the cause of monetary expansion and of inflation. When the debt holders want cash they sell their bond holdings in the market. The authorities, under the market support policy, stand ready to buy the bonds in order to stabilize bond prices and to stabilize interest rates. The bond holders secure in the though that the sale of bonds does not impose a capital loss on them sell the bonds for cash and use it for spending. If it is the banks they sell them for cash and use cash as a basis of multiple credit expansion with all its inflationary consequences. If, on the other hand, the authorities give up the market support policy any sale of bonds causes a fall in bond prices and the accompanying capital loss deters the bond holders from selling bonds for cash. This causes a reduction in expenditure/reduction in money supply and holds down the rate of inflation. Freeing of bond prices and interest rates is necessary to strengthen the forces of macro-economic stability.

Stagflation

In September 1990 industrial production fell sharply by 7.4 percent after having registered a growth of 12.4 percent from April to August 1990. In the months following there was another steep fall because of the shortage of foreign exchange to import raw materials and other inputs. The imports of capital goods allowed fell to Rs. 360 million in November 1990 against an average of Rs. 910 million a month in the previous six months. In theory, this should increase the premium on import licences against exports which can be sold in the open market, encourage exporters to export more in order to get more licences and ease the foreign exchange shortage by increasing exports. In practice, more is needed to export effort than simply a greater profit margin or a lower price. India does not produce goods of the type and quality demanded in foreign markets. Thus, while the premium on import licences has gone up there are few signs of a pick up in exports. In this manner domestic production is bound to suffer.

In the context of the Gulf war one witnessed the signs of a recession in the economy. This was bound to slow down both the growth of production and the growth of employment. A drop in investment in industry of the order of Rs. 1,000 crore will generate unemployment of the order of 50,000. The effect of a recession on investment will be long lasting for, while it reduces investment, it also reduces profitability and revenues and this reduces future investment. It is, therefore, necessary to prevent the economy from sliding into a recession now. While it is necessary to reduce the budget and balance of payments deficits, it is equally necessary to step up investment activity in sectors with the highest growth potential in order to achieve non-inflationary growth.

A policy of trade liberalization is necessary to expose Indian industry to the bracing winds of foreign competition. There is a limit to which imports can be squeezed considering the fact that exports are import-intensive. The exports are to be pushed more vigorously. Exports are only 6 percent of GNP and therefore they cannot provide the entire stimulus to growth. At present, exports are rising at 19.3 percent per annum imports are rising at 22.3 percent. With further liberalization of imports exports have to grow by 10 percent more if the balance of payments gap is to be bridged and if the country is to grow free from the balance of payments constraint.

It must be noted that Indian industrial environment is not suited to international competition. The Journal, "World Competitiveness Report, 1990" published by the Geneva-based World Economic Forum dumps India at the bottom of the heap among emerging developing world competitors much below countries like Thailand, Indonesia and even Mexico. This is because of the persistence of high-cost syndrome. This is mainly because of the 'think small' slogan of the Government which encourages small units so that the industries are not able to reap the economies of scale. The arbitrary hikes in administered prices of coal and steel raise the cost of production. Entry into industry, until the formulation of the New Industrial Policy in July 1991, was on the basis of permits and licences and big industries required more permits and licences. A FICCI study stated that delays in clearance led to cost overruns of Rs. 17,160 crore in the Seventh plan period. As a result, the technology gap between India and the other countries at 15-20 years. Technological upgradation which results in unemployment requires labour law reform without which it is impossible to retrench workers thrown out of jobs.

The macro signals are towards greater export competitiveness. The export profits are rising because of the depreciation of the rupee. The rupee depreciated by 30 percent vis-à-vis the US dollars over 1986-90. The incentives have only helped the corporate sector to export more of the old products. India has, therefore, miles to go before it can achieve a breakthrough on the export front. The reform of the corporate tax structure adumbrated above will be of great help to the corporate sector to improve the quality of products produced, to improve international competitiveness and to reduce the prices in the domestic market. For, under the reformed corporate tax structure, the corporate sector will be left with adequate internal resources to undertake modernization and technological upgradation and to achieve price and quality competitiveness in the external and domestic markets and to make an increasing contribution to accelerating economic growth with price stability. A rising income of the corporate sector will yield greater revenues which help to hold down the budget deficits.

Eradication of Black Money

The colossal sum of black money whose estimates range from Rs. 40,000 crore to Rs. 1,00,000 crore is playing havoc with the Indian economy. This money spent in several unascertainable ways is adding to aggregate demand and aggravating inflation. It has also rendered contractive fiscal-monetary policies ineffective. The Government has not done anything other than its intention to control its menace. How to control it, is a problem.

The Finance Minister in his budget speech while presenting the budget for 1990-91 stated that this black money could be diverted to house building activity, the investors being assured that they would not be asked to disclose how they acquired this money and that they would not be subjected to penal action. The Finance Minister in his budget for 1991-92 presented on 30.7.1991 proposed that the black money could be induced into the housing industry and that the investors would not be asked to divulge the sources of black money. Quite apart from the assurances that could be given to the black money barons, this kind of investment of black money in the current period will be in excess of current domestic savings and will generate inflation in the same way as money-financed budget deficits. Neither budget contraction nor monetary contraction will be able to control this inflation. Therefore, the right remedy for black money is a change in the monetary unit requiring those in possession of black money and white money also to surrender it to the banks in exchange for the new monetary unit by offering satisfactory explanation of how they came to acquire it and why they kept huge stocks of money in secret vaults. They will then surrender only a small part of it to the banks and destroy the other larger part in order to avoid penal action and social obloquy.

Gold Bank Plan

The Reserve Bank of India has proposed a plan to establish a Gold Bank, as recommended by the Rangarajan Committee in 1988, in order to garner at least 100 tonnes of gold of the estimated gold stock of 7000-8000 tonnes of virgin gold and gold jewellery in the country. The plan envisages the issue of gold bonds for six-year or nine-year terms based on international market price of gold prevailing at the time of deposit. The bonds carry an interest rate at 6 percent per annum. At the end of the term, the depositor can reclaim his gold deposit or renew the deposit for a further period. The scheme is to net in at least 100 tonnes of gold which, at the current market price, would be worth Rs. 3,000 crore. The interest payment would be Rs. 180 crore per year or Rs. 1080 crore over the six-year period. The depositor would thus earn an interest income on his unproductive gold and the Government can pledge this gold to meet the foreign exchange crisis.

As is obvious a large part of black money is invested in gold and gold jewellery. Lower and middle class families keep jewellery, however unproductive it may be, as a mark of social prestige and they rarely keep virgin gold. They cannot be induced to part with it by the offer of 6 percent interest. It is the affluent sections of society that are in possession of large stocks of virgin gold and gold jewellery. A large part of it is hidden wealth. If they deposit more than a modest quantity of virgin gold or gold jewellery they would be exposing of themselves as black money barons and would be subjected to social obloquy. There is no guarantee that the depositors of jewellery would, after the six year term, get back the same jewellery; there is also no guarantee that the Government which pledged the jewellery would be able to retrieve it at the end of the six year period to honour its commitment to the depositors. If the foreign exchange crisis continues, the Government may extend the period of the pledge and the depositors of jewellery may not be able to reclaim it after six years. Furthermore, the interest income of Rs.180 crore per year will add to private consumption expenditure and aggravate inflation besides, to that extent, widening the fiscal gap and adding to inflation on Government account.

The Gold Bank Plan is good in theory but unworkable in practice. The quantum of gold that the Gold Bank can mobilize in this manner will not be more than a modest amount. It is part of the gimmickry which the Reserve Bank proposes at frequent intervals. When the country is facing a grave economic crisis gimmickry will not pay. What are necessary are hard decisions however unpalatable they may be.

Cutting the Size of the Eighth Plan

The Eighth Five Year Plan (1992-97) with a gross investment outlay of Rs. 7,92,000 crore including a public sector outlay of Rs. 3,42,000 crore and a targeted growth rate of 5.6 percent is patently over ambitious. In doing so the planning commission has assumed an incremental capital-output ratio (ICOR) of 4.1, an average rate of 21.6 percent for domestic savings, a current account deficit of Rs. 49,000 crore (1.4 percent of GDP) and a 13.6 percent growth in exports per annum.

The aggregate investment outlay for the plan by the Government was Rs. 6,10,000 crore and the growth target was 5.6 percent. The present outlay is 1,62,000 crore more than the earlier outlay. This outlay is in nominal terms. If, as is bound to happen the price level rises, the nominal outlay has to rise in the same proportion if it is intended to maintain the real outlay. This means that the proposed

Eighth Five Year Plan as a built-in hyper inflationary bias and the objective of achieving non-inflationary growth will not be realized. Furthermore it accentuates the balance of payments crisis of grave dimensions rendering recourse to the IMF for a fresh loan of a bigger magnitude and committing the nation to the observance of stiff conditionally clauses. We can trust that the Government and the Planning Commission will not be so misguided as to hamper us too severely in our difficult task of growing at the right pace to the right size. The nation ought to try to form an idea of what size it wants to be on a realistic assessment of its capability, more precisely, at what rate it desires to see its national income growing and what proportion of its current income it should save and invest in order to achieve the desired result.

Growth prospects for 1991-92 are bleak indeed. Massive budgetary deficits, grave foreign exchange crisis, poor performance of infrastructure industries and deceleration of the rate of growth of exports are pointers towards slow down of the rate of growth of Indian economy in 1991-92. The Reserve Bank of India avers that in this situation of macroeconomic imbalances it would be a "very satisfactory performance" if the economy records a gross domestic product (GDP) of even 3 percent against the 1990-91 figure of 5 percent.

From the very beginning the economy has been passing through resource crises. At present 98 percent of the plan outlay is financed from domestic sources but the resource mobilization capacity of the country seems to have reached a plateau. For further augmentation of resource mobilization capacity what is required is a high rate of growth. But high rate of growth would call for a very large plan outlay which is not possible to obtain from domestic sources.

The incidence of indirect taxes which account for over 80 percent of tax revenue is already very high and there should not be any further dependence on indirect taxes for the purpose of additional resource mobilization though the Government has been doing it.

Under these circumstances the dependence on deficit financing has increased very significantly and it is continuing and will continue to increase leading to uninterrupted increase in the growth of money supply and building up of huge inflationary pressure. There is, in consequence, a cause and effect relationship between inflation and budget deficit. Budget deficits lead to inflation and inflation leads to budget deficits. There is thus a two-way causation. If non-inflationary growth is the goal resort to budgetary deficits should be minimal.

The genesis of the resource crisis in India lies not so much in shortage of resources perse as in demand for resources due to escalating plan and non-plan expenditure. Steep increase in expenditure is primarily responsible for the serious resource crisis. Apart from Government extravagance inflation itself is contributing to growing expenditure and budgetary deficits are initially contributing to inflation. In fact, massive budgetary deficits have proved to be the real villain of the Indian economy. Reserve receipts lag behind while aggregate disbursements outstrip the original estimates. While the non-developmental expenditures of the Centre and the states is going up the graph, the developmental expenditure is declining fast. It has already reached a state where non-developmental expenditure is far higher than the developmental expenditure.

The continuing inflationary pressures in the Indian economy accompanied by a declaration of investment have posed a big uncertainty about the possibility of non-inflationary growth.

International credit rating agencies have observed that the Indian economy is faced with the grim possibility of a high level of inflation in 1991-92 and, taking into account the combination of political forces at the Centre this may cause serious political conversions affecting the pace of the sweeping economic reforms announced by the Government. They even talk of an inflation rate of 18 percent in the current fiscal year if the Government fails to take special measures to check the rise in prices. The Planning Commission has been urging the Finance Ministry to take emergency measures to bring down the rate of price rise.

There is the onset of stagflation in the Indian economy and this is sure to affect the rate of growth. The index of industrial production for April 1991 shows a growth of 0.9 percent as against that of 11.1 percent for April 1990. Overall approvals granted by the Capital Goods Committee for import of Capital goods during April-June 1991 shows a decline of 41 percent compared with the value of approvals in the corresponding period of 1990.

What is worrying the Planning Commission is the emergence of signs of real stagflation in the economy and since 1991-92 is the first year of the three year adjustment programme to bring the economy back on rails any dislocation in the first year will adversely affect the prospects in 1992-93, the first year of the Eighth Plan Period.

The continuation of a stagflation scenario will adversely affect the flow of NRI deposits, as they will be nursing hopes that the Government will be compelled to opt for another bout of devaluation in order to restore exchange rate parity.

The Planning Commission has urged the Government to adopt emergency measures to reduce the rate of inflation ordinarily from November onwards prices decline but if this process does not take place this year, that will be giving a dangerous signal to the economy. Even the foreign investors, otherwise interested in investing in India will hold back for some more time till they are sure that the stagflation has been averted and the country is opting for a single digit inflation. This necessarily calls for cutting the size of the Eighth Five Year Plan.

The question of the rate of growth with which the country is faced was posed long ago with exquisite simplicity. The catterpillar was the first to speak: "What size do you want to be"? it asked. Alice's reply was: "Oh, I am not particular as to size; only one does not like changing so often, you know: Ultimately, the country has to grow to the right size and so, like Alice, finding ourselves "at last in the beautiful garden, among the bright flower beds and the cool fountains". We must learn from Alice that trying to grow at a fast pace and to a bloated size in a short span of time is fraught with grave problems unless there are means to do it. The means available to India are means to do it. The means available to India are inadequate to achieve a non-inflationary growth rate of 5.6 percent. This makes it necessary to reduce the investment outlay of the Eighth Plan to Rs. 5,00,000 crore and to set the growth target at a reasonable level of 5 percent-not at 5.6 percent. The objective of policy being non-inflationary growth the quantum of deficit financing has to be kept low and the balance of payments gap has to be set at a reasonable level which does not make recourse to the IMF for a loan inevitable and which does not necessitate devaluation of the rupee whatever be the experience of the other countries in this regard. The promise that devaluation remedies the payments gap is a poor consolation to the poverty stricken, harassed Indian consumers befogged in the inflation jungle.

Domesticism and Globalism

In the pursuit of growth policy there appears to be a clash between domesticism and globalism. The difference between the two approaches is relative and not absolute. Both rely on national and international policy. Domesticism refers to act at the national level but it seeks international consensus on key aspects of national performance which ultimately limits national choice. Globalism refers to action at the international level in order to secure more, not less, autonomy and effectiveness for national policymaking.

The culprit which has caused the problems for the Indian economy is India's domestic economic policy, specifically the growing fiscal deficits and accelerating monetary growth that began at the start of the 1980's. The collapse of price stability facilitated and reflected the loss of commitment to market forces and flexibility. Through the 1980s the role of Government increased inexorably, as citizens demanded more and more from the Government. The ratio of total public expenditure to GDP increased considerably. State owned enterprises, often required to pursue non-market as well as market objectives, mushroomed. These developments weakened market forces and market pricing and further reduced national economic efficiency and competitiveness. India could have negotiated on international trade for a fair trade and investment. But India squandered its diplomatic bargaining power by pursuing inflationary domestic economic policies that weakened its power in the marketplace. At present there is need to revert this approach to economic policy and to engage in assertive use of economic power in the market place based on non-inflationary policies. If the Indian economy could be revitalized and steered back to price stability market incentives could be easily employed to allocate resources efficiently. The budget issue remains control to India's hopes to restore price stability, market incentives and liberalized trade practices. Budget deficits cannot be less frightening than their earlier counterparts. From a purely economic perspective cutting spending will do more to ensure price stability than tax increases since the level of Government expenditure, not the fiscal deficit perse is the ultimate drain on private resources.

Credibility of Policy

Policy makers should recognize the importance of consistency in the design and implementation of the reform programmes and of generating the credibility required for the effectiveness of economic policies. Economic agents must be able to perceive that the Government's targets and instruments are mutually compatible and that they will not be subjected to unpredictable swings. Appropriate incentives and signals must be in place to guide decision making towards the realization of the desired objectives.

Two factors will contribute to the creation of a credible policy environment. The Government must eschew fiscal expansion in order to alleviate the inflation crisis and the balance of payment crisis; it must take a decision to implement rapidly a medium-term programme encompassing both demand management and correction of structural deficiencies coupled with fairly rapid action on both fronts. A policy commitment to liberalize the economy will also contribute to the credibility of the reform process. While such commitments may, at times, constrain the authorities' policy options they will reduce the possibility of policy reversals and infuse confidence in the Government's commitment and enable sure-footed sections to be taken.

The Government must recognize that the long-term interests require an acceptance of international economic interdependence.

It is agreed that a reduction of tariff protection and the liberalization of foreign direct investment will have beneficial effects. Although reduction of tariff may initially increase imports, it will facilitate the renovation of capital equipment and lead to increased investment in export-oriented industries. However, the process of tariff reduction should be gradual giving local industry sufficient time to adjust and pre-empting protectionist pressures. The short-term effects of reforms on output and employment are likely to be offset by the favourable supply side-effects in the context of a credible policy environment.

Policy makers must first announce the policy measures and then express their commitment to the pursuit of these policy measures unless circumstances warrant a change of policy. It is only then that the policy measures enjoy credibility. Otherwise uncertainty shrouds the policy package and frustrate the economic agents in their efforts to make their plans to spend, to save and to invest. This uncertainty is not conducive to the smooth functioning of the economy.

The success of the fiscal programme rests on the Government's fiscal package and its ability to implement this package. The creation of institutional support for its implementation will enhance its ability. Otherwise, fiscal reform may fall short of the targets and adversely affect the reform process. Improvements in tax administration machinery is a vital component of any such effort. Revenue will not be collected and planned without strong tax administration, simple tax codes, effective penalty systems, the use of modern information technologies and the adoption of administrative shortcuts such as the presumptive taxation of small tax payers, traders and professionals. The mere announcement of the passage of a tax law will have little or even a negative fiscal effect if the appropriate and honest administrative machinery to implement the policy is not in place.

In the same manner, a strong budgetary and expenditure control system is to be introduced and this can be achieved by making its objectives clear and by improving fiscal reporting mechanism. Timely fiscal data are necessary for effective fiscal management and to monitor the performance of the Government and public enterprises. In this regard, the restructuring of the public enterprise sector cannot only improve the efficiency of Government expenditure but can also provide a signal to investors and creditors—domestic and foreign—about the economic policies and growth potential of the economy.

The need for close co-operation and consultations between the several agencies cannot be overstressed. When the departments realize that these forecasts are to be used as an integral part of central financial management, their interest and involvement in the exercise are likely to be enhanced. Such involvement will help to make the forecasts more accurate and realistic as well as prompting their timely submission to the Central Government. These forecasts can also be used to facilitate the conduct of monetary policy.

Conclusion

The integrated fiscal structure envisaged in this memorandum represents a mutually reinforcing and harmonious package of measures. It constitutes a viable and coordinated fiscal strategy designed to achieve the objectives laid down already and it represents an interdependent and integrated whole. A change in one inevitably causes changes in the others. There may be minor clashes between the objectives of a couple of measures but in an integrated strategy these clashes are not of much import; there are other measures in the package to offset the untoward consequences of any deviations of others. The incorporation of this package of measures in the Union Budgets will go a long way in reducing the budget deficit, controlling monetary growth, holding down the rate of inflation, reducing the balance of payments deficits and promoting the non-inflationary growth objective. This fiscal strategy is designed to achieve these objectives simultaneously for the good of 850 million people of this ancient land. Imposition of "financial emergency", nebulous and undefined, as proposed by some economists is impracticable in a vast country like India and it provokes hostile and violent reactions all round as it curtails human freedom and damages human dignity. It is unnecessary also if the package of fiscal measures elucidated above is adopted in the Union Budget in the coming years.

2

Proposed Amendment to the New Industrial Policy

The New Industrial Policy (NIP) announced by the Government of India desired that the industrial system be unshackled from bureaucratic controls and licensing procedures. The foreign investment in Indian industry was allowed with 51 percent equity participation, under the NIP the dividend payments royalty etc., had to be made in foreign exchange at the going rate.

But this provision had to be amended in consonance with the new exchange rate policy announced on 29.2.1992 by the Union Finance Minister in his budget speech. Under this amendment all payments flowing from approval of foreign technology agreements accorded by the Government and the Reserve Bank of India will have to be met through the foreign exchange purchased at the market rates. This amendment to the NIP has been made in keeping with the new exchange rate policy-partial convertibility of the rupee will apply to three types of foreign collaboration approvals specified in the NIP. They are: automatic approvals for foreign technology agreements in high priority industries upto a lump sum payment of Rs 1 crore; five percent royalty for domestic sales and eight per cent for exports, automatic approvals for units other than high priority industries on the same lines if no foreign exchange is required for any payment and specific approval for all other proposals.

Under the new dispensation, the conditions relating to free foreign exchange and EXIM scrips for financing such payments approved will no longer be applicable. The Budget for 1992-93 has discontinued EXIM scripts and has stipulated that the foreign exchange required for paying dividends, royalties and other remittance will have to be obtained by the payer at the market rates. In respect of technology agreements approvals issued in the past all original conditions about the payments have become inoperative and all payments will now have to be met through foreign exchange purchased through market rates. The companies will not be required to seek an amendment to the approval letters. But the condition relating to export obligation remains intact. The NIP states that the new projects with majority equity of 51 percent and those companies which intend to raise the foreign stake to 51 percent would have to service their dividend payments through export earnings for seven years. This amounts to an indirect export obligation.

Under the partial convertibility dispensation the exporters have to sell 40 percent of the export earnings to the Reserve Bank of India at the official rate and the balance of 60 percent of the export earnings to the intending buyers at the going market rate of exchange. It goes without saying that the market rate is higher than the official rate. If, those who have to pay royalties and dividends, have to buy foreign exchange at the market rate, the amount of rupee, they have to surrender in the foreign exchange market to the sellers of foreign exchange at the market rate will have to be considerably larger than they would at the official exchange rate. This requirement would impose a loss on the Indian industries without conferring any gain on the foreign investors.

The Government of India and the Reserve Bank of India can both consider the alternative of enabling the industries to purchase foreign exchange at the official rate (not at the market rate in the open market) from the Reserve Bank in order to make remittance for royalty and dividends. The Government has adopted the 40-60 percent formula by which the exporters have to sell 40 percent of the export earnings to the Reserve Bank at the official exchange rate and are free to sell the balance of 60 percent in the open market at the market rate. If the industries are allowed to purchase foreign exchange at the official rate it will be a boon to industries without being a burden on the foreign investors. This will increase the internal resources for the industries and enable their modernization and technological upgradation. This suggestion could be favourably considered in the interests of Indian industries.

3

Reduction of Import Duties

In the attempt to integrate the Indian economy with the global system, the Government of India adopted liberalization of the various sectors of the economy. In this connection the Government appointed the Raja Chellaiah Committee to make a report on tax reform. The Committee initially made an interim report and subsequently submitted its final report. In the Union Budget for 1992-92 the Finance Minister incorporated certain recommendations and the remaining recommendations are likely to be incorporated in the Union Budget for 1993-94. In what follows the committee recommendation regarding the import tariff is examined.

The Chellaiah Committee has recommended that over the next five years the average rate of import-weighted customs tariff should be reduced to 25 percent. The committee wants a six-tier advalorem (i.e. based on the value of goods) rate of duties ranging from 5 to 30 percent and in the case of in essential goods it has recommended a tariff of 50 percent. The acceptance of this recommendation involves the slashing down of import duties which, in the case of several products at present, vary from 60 to 110 percent by at least 50 percent. It is feared that Indian industry which all these years has been flourishing behind the tariff wall will become vulnerable to foreign competition.

Indian industry should become internationally competitive and this requires that it be exposed to the bracing winds of foreign competition. Seen in this light the case for reducing import tariff is strong indeed. But the industrial sector feels that the reduction should take place on a selective basis. While reducing import duties certain allowances should be given to Indian manufacturers. In the first place, the Indian industries have to encounter a number of infrastructural bottlenecks. For instance, because of power shortage, some industries have to build captive power plants of their own costing several crore of rupees and this capital cost the industries have to recover. This bottleneck does not exist in the foreign countries. In the second place, the interest rates in the developed countries are around 6 percent per annum while in India they are as high as around 16-18 percent. In addition, the industries have to pay high local taxes, incur a lot of expenditure on transport etc. All these variable costs push up the total cost of production. In the light of these factors, import tariffs should be reduced after taking due note of the disadvantages under which the Indian industries are labouring. If the tariffs are reduced in phased manner industries can plan their cost reduction exercise. Furthermore, a sharp reduction in import tariff will reduce Government revenue. But the Chellaiah Committee has not taken into account the impact of the recommendations on Government revenue, industrial production and economic growth. That there will be no adverse impact on Government revenue assumes that the demand for the imported goods is highly price elastic so that a reduction in the market price of the imposed goods causes a rise in the demand for them and that the demand for them has an elasticity greater than unity. This may not be the case always. If the demand for imported goods is price-inelastic the demand for them will not rise which means that the tax revenue will not rise after the import tariff is reduced.

A few months ago, the Government reduced the import duty on metal scrap, a substitute for sponge iron in the manufacture of steel from 35 percent to 10 percent. This was undertaken in pursuance of the Government's resolve to reduce the burden of import duty on certain products. As a result this reduction of import duty the sponge iron manufacturing units were rendered unviable as the cost of imported scrap turned out to be lower than the price of sponge iron manufactured in India. This reduce the profit margin of the industrial units considerably and adversely affected the growth of the industry. What happened to the sponge iron units could happen to other industrial units if there is a sudden and sharp reduction in the import tariff.

The Chellaiah Committee assumes that the foreign exchange reserves of the country will be so healthy that it will be possible for the Government to allow import of goods at lower duties. The foreign exchange reserve position looks healthy at present because of the loans obtained from the Fund-Bank Combine. If these reserves do not increase rapidly, the entire scheme of liberalization which includes the reduction of import tariffs will be in trouble. However one thing must be said in favour of the Chellaiah Committee recommendations. The proposed reduction of duties over a five-year period can be commended as during this period, the Indian industries will view with each other to be better prepared to take on competition from foreign manufacturers.

The effects of trade liberalization on the macro-economy have to be analyzed. The advocates of reduced tariffs must confront the question: When jobs are lost in the previously protected industries which are now exposed to foreign competition. Where will the new jobs come from? Partial equilibrium analysis suggests that when the tariffs are reduced employment will fall not just in that industry but in the economy as a whole and would generate a current account deficit, if the demand for the imported goods is highly price elastic. This unemployment can be alleviated by sufficient expansion of aggregate demand and the deficit could be eliminated by a sufficient reduction of aggregate demand. Thus large scale macro-economic imbalance would result from trade liberalization. The exchange rate must depreciate in real terms through nominal depreciation. This will partially restore profitability of the previously protected industries and increase profits and employment in export industries and in import-competing industries that were previously not protected. The new jobs will be found in these industries. We have to take into consideration the general equilibrium considerations also. The export industries may be relatively capital-intensive and initially may not be able to create as many new jobs as the decline in the import-competing industries has closed down. There will be shift to profits. This will increase the Government's corporate tax revenue and if this is spent the demand for non-tradeable goods and for tradeables and employment will go up. This will have the effect of depreciating the exchange rate further and this will raise employment. If the effect of trade liberalization is to raise the efficiency of resource use and hence real national income, the demand for non-tradeables must rise. In consequence, some new jobs will be created in this sector. If the export industries are highly capital-intensive and are foreign owned; greater dividend remittances will help to depreciate the exchange rate further and re-protect the import-competing industries; higher tax payments will enable larger Government spending which will generate employment; larger corporate savings will increase corporate investment. In this manner jobs may be created at different points but in this process the exchange rate depreciation is crucial.

The foregoing analysis implies that trade liberalization should cause exchange rate depreciation. Further, the argument against reducing import duties, namely, that this would increase unemployment is based on the partial equilibrium analysis and this ignores the general equilibrium consequences which would follow if the exchange rate depreciates and appropriate macroeconomic policies are followed. If the import duties are cut suddenly there will be transitional effects especially in the context of low overall growth of the economy. Employment lost in one segment will not be suddenly made good by employment gained in another segment. Thus, there can be short-term localized unemployment, but this is the effect of any kind of change in the economy. In this manner, the reduction of import duties generates unemployment which is only temporary and this can be remedied by expanding Government demand. The reduction of import duties has to be phased so that the industries have the time necessary for adjustment. In the light of this, the Chellaiah Committee recommendation that over the next five years the average nominal rate of import-weighted customs tariff should be reduced to 25 percent has to be welcomed. Sudden and dramatic reduction of the import duties has harmful consequences on the economy and therefore the reduction of import duties has to be gradual.

Several industries in the recent past were set up after paying import duty of 110 to 180 percent. They cannot be expected to be competitive overnight. In some industries saddled with high cost plants the phasing of tariffs should take seven to ten years. The

Indian industry, therefore, should be given a clear direction about the rate and timing of duty reduction. At the same time, there is need for reducing banks' lending rates. Even the interest rate should be brought down in a phased manner so as to prevent a sudden spurt in the inflation rate. There is a wide spread between the lending and deposit rates from 7 to 11 percent. But there should not be more than 2-3 percent. At present though the interest constitutes only 5.5 percent of cost of production, a study published by the Reserve Bank of India revealed that interest as a percentage of gross profits was 71 percent in 1987-88 and 62 percent in 1988-89. If the interest burdens of only profit burden would come to 42 percent in 1988-89. The burden must be higher now in view of the hike in interest rates during the past 15 months. A reduction in interest rates would stimulate investment activity and help to ward off the recession.

The conclusions are:

1. The reduction of import duties should be gradual.
2. The reduction of import duty should take account of the infrastructural deficiencies of the industries;
3. The interest rate should be brought down gradually.

4

The Entry of Foreign Banks to the Indian Financial System is Desirable

The Narasimham Committee on Financial Sector Reform has recommended the opening up of the Indian financial system to the entry of foreign banks. But discordant voices are heard even from responsible quarters that the entry of foreign banks would thwart the progress of the Indian banking system as the foreign banks with their superior customer service, sophisticated operations and computerization would wean customers away from the Indian banks and would adversely affect their deposit mobilization programme, reduce their profitability further and erode the already thin capital base. These apprehensions are overly exaggerated. At present there are only 150 foreign bank branches operating in India and their aggregate assets are less than 5 percent of those of the Indian banks put together. Even if, under the Narasimhan Committee dispensation, the number of foreign bank branches are doubled, there is unlikely to be any threat to the Indian banking system. But, instead, the positive gains are many and they should be considered while examining the issue of entry of foreign banks to India.

All said and done, the Indian banking system is a byword for inefficiency. Quite apart from diversion of funds to priority sectors at concessional interest rates, the loan mela and loan waiver schemes have landed the Indian banking system in doldrums. There is overstaffing in banks, there is unrestrained opening up of branches in areas which are not bankable; in an area where there is not enough business even for a single branch there are 5-6 branches of different banks with the result that administrative expenditure is on the rise. The bank employees are opposed to computerization of banking operations as it is likely to displace labour. The quality of customer service is very poor. In the absence of alternative abode for their deposits the customers have, per force, to go to these banks to deposit their savings. The banks, therefore, are continuing their inefficiency in the thought that their supremacy is unchallenged and they are not under any pressure to improve their operations or the quality of customer service rendered by them.

The objective of the policy of liberalization is to expose the Indian economy to the bracing winds of competition in order to enable every sector of the economy to be cost effective in the global environment. The financial sector is an important segment of the Indian economy and unless this sector is liberalized the programme of liberalization would be incomplete.

The foreign banks presently operating in India have been rendering quick and efficient customer service with the help of sophisticated electronic gadgets. Their deposit mobilization and lending operations are a model for Indian banks to emulate. The computerization of their operations enables them to attend to customer problems and needs with efficiency and quickness. They are highly profitable entities and they are free from labour troubles. These virtues make them attractive to Indian customers. The capital adequacy of these banks renders them safe abodes for the deposits. It is these that are held to constitute a danger to the viability of the Indian banking system. To think so is to make the Indian banks lead to ostrich-like existence.

The Reserve Bank of India has asked the public sector banks to get themselves rated by a credit rating agency. The credit rating of banks is necessary to prepare them to mobilize funds from the market in order to reach the prescribed capital adequacy ratio. Those which are rated high have no problem at all except that they have to improve on the present satisfactory credit rating. But those which are rated low have to make strenuous efforts to enhance their credit rating to be able to convince the lenders that they are solvent in the strict financial sense. This advice of the Reserve Bank of India is in the best interests of the Indian banks. Excessive protection accorded to the Indian banks has made them lethargic and to remain in a state of perpetual inefficiency rendering the financial sector unable to meet the challenges posed by the on-going economic reform measures. When they are exposed to the competitive forces emerging from the foreign banks operating in India they get into an atmosphere of challenge and opportunity and make efforts to reach the standards of efficiency attained by the foreign banks. Seen in this light, the entry of foreign banks into the Indian financial system is desirable and the recommendation of the Narasimhan Committee has to be implemented.

Admittedly, the loan mela and loan waiver schemes have to go for good. But the concessionary lending to the priority sectors has to remain for some more time. The Narasimhan Committee recommends a reduction of this lending from the present 40 percent to 10 percent in stages. But this reduction should be gradual. However, it is a moot point whether the foreign banks could be persuaded to toe the line of Indian banks in the matter of concessionary lending to priority sectors. If they agree there will be homogeneity in lending operations. But if they do not agree there will be two parallel systems. This does not augur well for the progress of the financial sector and the financial sector reform will have no meaning. But the foreign banks operating in India have to be governed by the law of the land. It is a reasonable surmise that they will abide by whatever regulations are applicable to Indian banks considering the imperative need to ensure a competitive atmosphere the entry of foreign banks to the Indian financial system is highly desirable.

5

Independence for the Reserve Bank of India

For thirty months since the introduction of economic reforms in July 1991 when the Government borrowed from the IMF under the structural adjustment facility the Finance Minister spoke of fiscal consolidation. The fiscal deficit was brought down from 8.4 percent in 1991 to 5.7 percent in 1993. Then again the revised figures show that in 1993-94 the fiscal deficit is 7.3.percent of GDP and that the fiscal deficit for 1994-95 is fixed at 6 percent of the GDP. The IMF must be unhappy about the decline in fiscal restraint. But who cares? The fiscal deficit in 1993-94 rose to 7.3 percent of GDP because there was a decline in customs revenue by Rs. 5,000 crore and a decline in excise revenue by Rs. 3,000 crore and a rise in Government expenditure by Rs. 12,500 crore. Even so, the Finance Minister in his budget speech spoke of a "historic step which will in due course contribute to a significant improvement in fiscal and monetary discipline..."

In making this statement the Finance Minister was referring to the decision to stop financing the deficit merely by printing new money. Instead, he proposed to phase out the use of adhoc Treasury Bills over three years and limiting them to Rs. 6,000 crore in 1994-95. In order to underline the significance of this intent he said that the Government of India and the Reserve Bank had "agreed........that the net issue of adhoc treasury bills should not exceed Rs. 9,000 crore for more than ten continuous working days at any time during the year".

The Government is the master and the Finance Minister, as head of the Finance Ministry, represents the Government and the Reserve Bank of India (without meaning disrespect to its knowledgeable Governor) is the servant. The talk of an "agreement" between the master and the servant sounds odd considering the fact that the Finance Minister can implement his intention without an "agreement with the Reserve Bank of India. Mere statement of an intention does not make an earth-shaking event. But there is more to it. The Finance Minister also spoke about giving the Reserve Bank "greater scope for effective monetary management". It must be said unless the Central Bank is really autonomous no Finance Minister is willing and prepared to confer so much freedom on the central bank in any country. Can the Finance Minister of India succeed in giving the Reserve Bank such independence?

The Finance Minister has not been able to hold the budget deficit below Rs. 10,000 crore for even a few days at a stretch during the year barring the window dressing exercises undertaken on June 30, September 30 and 31st December 1993. In the light of this experience, where is the guarantee that the year 1994-95 will be any better ? In 1993-94 there was lack of revenue buoyancy as the customs and excise collections considerably declined by over Rs. 8000 crore. There was also a rise in Government expenditure by over Rs. 12,500 crore and a rise in interest payments on Government debt. If the Reserve Bank of India sells adhoc treasury bills if the level exceeds Rs. 9,000 crore for 10 continuous working days the Government's interest expenditure will rise further. This generates the need for frequent auctions considering the fact that the Government has not been able to hold the budget deficit below Rs. 10,000 crore for any period of ten consecutive working days. Considering the inflexibility of interest expenditure when reduction of borrowing is not on the agenda it may not be possible to bring the adhoc treasury bills down to zero by 1997-98.

However, this scenario can be averted if (a) there is an expected revenue leap and (b) if the public sector shares are put on the sales window and the proceeds are used to retire public debt. The Finance Minister has budgeted for receipts of the order of Rs. 4,000 crore from disinvestments though it is possible to realize Rs. 10,000 crore by an imaginative strategy.

If the Finance Minister succeeds in controlling the issue of treasury bills he has to face trouble in the matter of giving the Reserve Bank freedom to frame and implement monetary policy. The Finance Minister himself said that if the Government fails to keep control over its deficit the Reserve Bank would be free to dump adhoc treasury bills on the market at the going rate of interest and making the Government pay the market related interest on the outstanding debt. This means a rise in interest expenditure and a further rise in the fiscal deficit. But this does not mean that the Reserve Bank of India is fully free in formulating and implementing monetary policy. There are two reasons for this. In the first place, the banking system has to adhere to the policy of mandated lending and the structure of administered interest rates; in the second place, there is not yet legislative backing for guaranteeing the independence of the Reserve Bank as is the case with the US Federal Reserve Board (the FED) and the West German Bundes bank (BUBA).

That the structure of administered interest rates dominates the Indian banking sense is too obvious to need emphasis. The Finance Minister in the course of his Budget Speech on 28.2.1994 stated that the lending rate would be reduced by 1 percent from 15 percent to 14 percent to boost growth. Admittedly the decision to reduce the interest rate by 1 percent is a wise decision as this step is expected to raise investment and consumption so necessary to remedy the on-going recession and to raise the rate of economic growth. But the point to note is that if monetary policy is the responsibility of the Reserve Bank of India the decision to reduce the rate of interest should have been taken by the Reserve Bank and not by the Government. All that the Governor of the Reserve Bank said was to bring down the interest rate the following day in pursuance of the decision of the Finance Minister. What the Reserve Bank would have done if it was allowed, freedom in the matter of monetary policy is anybody's guess. The fact is that the Reserve Bank Governor is taking instructions from the Finance Ministry. The Finance Minister's decision to keep the average level of adhoc treasury bills down to the level of the projected budget deficit of Rs. 6,000 crore in 1994-95 is to acknowledge his awareness of the inflationary consequences of the huge fiscal deficit which was projected to be 7.3 percent of GDP at the end of March 1994. This quantum of fiscal deficit is not far below the figure of 8.4 percent at the start of the reform programme.

The independence of the Reserve Bank holds the key to effective monetary control. An independent Reserve Bank can hold out the threat of a high interest rate on Government borrowing if the Government indulges in fiscal excesses. As the high interest rates retard the rate of economic growth and make nonsense of the Government's claim to accelerate growth and adversely affect the chances of the politicians reelection they behave more responsibly than they otherwise would. The idea of an independent Reserve Bank should be put through the cabinet and the parliament. An independent Reserve Bank is an effective safeguard against the fiscal profligacy of the Government.

A careful perusal of the Budget Speech of the Finance Minister reveals lack of agreement between his assurance to give the Reserve Bank "greater scope for effective monetary management" and his unilateral decision to cut the lending rate by 1 percent from 15 percent to 14 percent expecting the Reserve Bank implicitly to obey his decision. The Finance Minister in the course of his reply to the debate on the General Budget in the third week of April 1994 will do well to clarify his position in the matter.

The Economic Survey of 1993-94 calls for a cut in the size of the fiscal deficit. But the fiscal deficit correction is off-target. At the end of 1992-93, the fiscal deficit had been brought down to 5.2 percent of GDP and the target for 1993-94 was 4.7 percent. India has missed the target by a wide margin. This has an impact on inflation. The rate of inflation which had come down to 7 percent by the end of 1992-93 has crept back to 9 percent. GDP growth in 1993-94 is estimated at 3.8 percent which is less that the growth rate of 4.0 percent achieved in 1992-93. The Finance Minister eminently aware of both the problem and the solution. The problem is, to use the words of the Economic Survey, "Pressures for fiscal laxity and business as usual". The solution is to crack the whip in the same way as the Finance Minister did in the first 18 months.

The success of the South East Asian Tigers is attributed to three factors: low fiscal deficit, low inflation and keeping the markets open. Low inflation is also the best way not to cause alienation among the very poor, that is, those who will not reap immediately the gains of an economy that has embarked on reforms. The growing sense of alienation among the lower middle class and the poor in India can be attributed to their disillusionment with the Government's capacity to check prices. There are also other side effects. As a result of high fiscal deficits the Government has to borrow both from the Reserve Bank and from the market thus pre-empting resources from real investment. A further consequence is that interest rates continue to remain high. Low levels of investment and high interest rates act as a damper on industrial recovery and economic growth. The Economic survey has the correct prescription for growth. It says that rapid growth is possible "if the macro economic environment is stable" inflation is low and fiscal deficits are in check".

The move towards full convertibility of the rupee on capital account has been wisely deferred. It should be a long term aim and should not pursued till fiscal adjustment, tax reform and financial sector reform are further advanced. A high fiscal deficit leaves the economy in an inflexible position with regard to possible shocks, fiscal pressures which may arise from the reform programme itself and possible inflationary pressures due to foreign inflows. The foreign inflows are to be sterilized and the Government could borrow these inflows instead of from the Reserve Bank of India. But there is a negative aspect to its. High inflows reduce the export competitiveness of Indian goods. Countries like Malaysia, Thailand, Taiwan and Indonesia have high foreign exchange reserves without inflation because they have a flexible fiscal policy. Fiscal tightening and continued control over inflows are necessary to offset the inflationary pressures. Fiscal tightening is possible if the Reserve Bank of India is allowed independence in the matter of monetary management, if debt financing of the fiscal deficit is brought under control not just to reduce the direct inflationary dangers involved in it but also to reduce the indirect inflationary dangers emanating from the fiscal deficit caused by the high interest payments. Inflation control is the prime need of the hour. To this end fiscal deficit however financed must be brought down. If the Reserve Bank of India is given independence it will itself place a cap on monetary financing and the parliament must put a constitutional ceiling on Government borrowing. This along with tax reforms will achieve fiscal consolidation.

6

Are Subsidies the Cause of Fiscal Deficit and Inflation?

When the Government of India approached the International Monetary Fund for a loan facility over two years ago, it made certain irrevocable commitments and gave the assurance that they would be honoured and that all efforts would be made to honour them. These commitments, inter alia, are the reduction of the fiscal deficit in a proportion of GDP and the reduction of the rate of inflation. Because of certain extenuating circumstances these commitments have remained unhonoured. The fiscal deficit as a proportion of GDP has been rising and, along with it the rate of inflation has also been rising generating macroeconomic instability, acute distress to the common man and rendering the target of poverty alleviation unattainable.

The Finance Minister said in New Delhi on November 25, 1993 that India's target of reducing fiscal deficit to 4.7 percent of GDP in the current year "looks difficult" because of the rise in some subsidies due to " the Government's preoccupation with the election in the Northern states. He told the American television network CNN in an interview that "once the elections are over, we will come back to the problem of introducing necessary corrections". Evidently this means that the fiscal deficit rose because of the rise in Government expenditure because of populist programmes adopted by the Government. While saying so, the Finance Minister has categorically held the subsidy exercise responsible for the rise in the fiscal deficit.

But an important cause of the rise in the fiscal deficit is sidelined. Revenue collections from income tax and customs and excise duties have continued to fall upto September 1993 causing concern to the Government. While the fall in income tax collections, including corporation tax, decreased by Rs. 60.78 crore in September 1993 as compared with that in the corresponding period in 1992-93 the fall in customs and excise duties was 15.44 percent and 1.7 percent respectively during this period. A summary of the monthly revenue collections report states that gross income tax, including corporation tax collected during September 1993 was Rs. 5,990.67 crore. The customs duty collections upto September 1993 was Rs. 10,086.61 crore and the excise duty collection was Rs. 14186.87 crore representing a 7.9 percent fall in the overall collections of indirect tax in September 1993 as compared with that in September 1992. The monthly statistics show that collections of customs duty upto September 1993 formed 36.38 percent of the budget estimates of Rs. 27,727 crore for the whole of 1993-94. In the case of central excise it was 42.22 present of the 1993-94 budget estimates of Rs. 33,600 crore while in income tax it was 29.95 percent o the budget estimates of Rs. 20,000 crore. The arrears of central excise duties at the end of August 1993 were about Rs. 2050.95 crore as against about Rs. 1961.35 crore at the end of July 1993. The arrears of customs duties at the end of August were around Rs. 130.56 crore as compared with Rs. 125.82 crore at the end of July 1993 showing an increase of Rs. 4.74 crore in the arrears. As many as 411 cases involving evasion of duty amounting to Rs. 984 crore were detected during September 1993. The seizure under customs Act during the period amounted to Rs. 11.05 crore in value. The importance of a decline in revenue collections and the mounting tax arrears cannot be minimized as a factor contributing to the rise in the fiscal deficit and the rise in the rate of inflation. This has rendered the attainment of the fiscal deficit of 4.7 percent of GDP difficult. But the Finance Ministry has overemphasized the importance of subsidy payments in causing a rise in the fiscal deficit and rise in the rate of inflation.

The rate of inflation displays a drastic fall and a significant rise. The trend is not always a declining trend. A slight decline is followed by a steep rise indicating a rise in the trend. This rise in the trend is due partly to the raising fiscal deficit and partly to the enhancement of procurement prices of rice, wheat and other articles of food. Payment of subsidies plays a part and not the whole part in the inflation process. Subsidies are a non-plan expenditure and, admittedly, they help to widen the fiscal gap. But the consequences of abolition of subsidies are to be put in the right perspective in order to assess their role in the inflation process. Fertiliser subsidies are an important item of the subsidy aggregate. Some economists and politicians strongly recommend the abolition of fertilizer subsidy on the ground that it would reduce the fiscal deficit and help to reduce the rate of inflation. This is admitted. But they ignore the side effects of abolishing fertilizer subsidies. Abolition of fertilizer subsidies raises their price. If the demand for fertilizers is price-elastic, the demand for fertilizers and their input fall causing a fall in per acre yield of crops. If the crops are food crops, the yield of food grains falls. The demand for food being the same a fall in the supply of food causes a rise in food prices. A rise in food prices raises the cost of living index. As the wages are tied to the cost of living index, the wage rates rise occasioning cost push and demand pull inflations. If, on the other hand, the demand for fertilizers is in elastic, the demand and input of fertilizers remains constant. This will not cause a fall in the per acre yield of food crops. But a rise in the price of fertilizers causes a rise in the cost of production and in a situation where costs determine prices, the prices of food articles rise. This causes a rise in the cost of living index, a rise in wages and a generation of cost push and demand pull inflation which get entwined and become difficult to disentangle. This means that the abolition of fertilizers subsidies causes a rise in the rate of inflation despite a reduction of the fiscal deficit by means of a reduction of the fertilizer subsidy. A similar line of argument can be employed in respect of abolition of food subsidies also. Empirical research has shown that the demand for fertilizer is price elastic so that a rise in the prices of fertilizers caused by the abolition of subsidy causes a fall in the demand for and input of fertilizers and through this causing a fall in crop yield, fall in food output and a rise in food prices which occasion demand for higher wages and wage induced inflation. Thus, if the fertilizer subsidy is retained there will be a rise in the fiscal deficit which generates inflation; if it is abolished the fiscal deficit is reduced but the consequent rise in fertilizer prices causes a fall in the demand for and input of fertilizers, a fall in food output and a rise in food prices which exacerbate the rate of inflation. In view of this it is a safe presumption that inflation occasioned by the rise in the fiscal deficit due to the retention of fertilizer subsidy is preferable to inflation caused by the abolition of fertilizer subsidy. Another side effect of the abolition of fertilizer subsidy must be noted. It is the small and marginal farmers that are going to be adversely affected by the abolition of fertilizer subsidy. The demand for fertilizers on their part is more elastic than the demand for fertilizers on the part of the large farmers. This means that the demand for fertilizers and the input of fertilizers on the large farms falls less than that on the part of small and marginal farmers. It can be assumed that the demand for fertilizers on the part of small and marginal farmers falls completely so that the yield on these farms falls to the barest minimum. This renders the distribution of income within the farm sector more unequal and causes acute distress among this section of the farm sector more unequal and causes acute distress among this section of the farm population. It is true that the small and marginal farmers are poor and a reduction of income of this sector pushes them below the poverty line rendering poverty alleviation programmes ineffective. A fall in their income causes a fall in their demand for industrial goods and aggravates the recession in the industrial sector. A reduction in the lending rate may stimulate investment in the industrial sector and increase industrial output but in a situation of falling demand for them the industries have to hold unsold stocks which are evidence that recession is a reality. Furthermore, the reduction in the lending rate will not encourage the small and marginal farmers to borrow more and spend more. As their income prospects are bleak and as their repaying capacity gets impaired they will be reluctant to borrow and spend. Thus despite a reduction of the lending rate there will be no increase in borrowing and spending on the part of this sector. All these factors point to the need to maintain the fertilizer subsidies.

There is another factor which renders the reduction of the fiscal deficit and the reduction of the rate of inflation difficult. India's rising oil bill is an important factor contributing to inflation. The OPEC countries have come out with a proposal to raise the price of oil. The 12 important OPEC countries which met in Vienna on

24.11.1993 feel that the price of oil is dangerously low at present and demand the adoption of measures to raise it significantly. On Monday 22.11.1993 the price of oil per barrel (42 gallons) in the world market had fallen to $14.70 and this is said to be the lowest in the past three years. They demand that the price of oil should be raised to $ 21 per barrel. If the price of oil is raised to $ 21 per barrel from $ 14.70 the oil bill of India will rise by 50 percent. As India's oil bill at present is Rs. 16,000 crore a rise in the price of oil by 50 percent will take India's oil bill to Rs. 24,000 crore unless domestic production of oil is stepped up significantly. This will exacerbate domestic inflation and the balance of payments crisis. In view of this it would not be correct to blame the subsidies for the rise in the fiscal deficit and the rise in the rate of inflation.

In a fully marketised economy subsidies have no place. But India is not a fully marketised economy though it is moving ahead along the road to a market economy. Even in countries which boast of mercerization, like the USA and the EC countries, farm subsidies are being paid in order to sustain agricultural sector. When this is the case it would not be correct to argue for a reduction/removal of subsidies. At the present stage of evolution of the Indian economy, and the farm sector in particular, subsidies are necessary and they should be continued. Fiscal correction has to be attempted in other areas and not in the area of subsidies. In particular, as explained above, vast arrears are due from the income tax, corporation tax, customs and excise duty assesses and efforts should be made to recover these arrears expeditiously. At the same time, inessential Government expenditure has to be drastically slashed. Interest payments on the public debt do not admit of any reduction as they are committed payments; expenditure on defence is in need of stepping up owing to deteriorating security environment in the subcontinent. Subsidies can, of course, be reduced but they should not be reduced. The proposed Value Added Tax (VAT) will help streamline the indirect tax structure and to contribute to revenue yield in a significant measure. The revenue yield from all these measures is far more than the subsidy payment. Thus, why talk of subsidy reduction?

7

The Problem of the Rupee

In the context of the slide of the rupee indicating depreciation and generating speculation about the possible devaluation it is necessary to study the behaviour of the rupee in the foreign exchange market to see whether the slide in the rupee is transitory or permanent and whether the rupee is going to slide further forcing its devaluation.

The rupee stood its ground for two years with the rate of exchange being Rs. 31.37 per US dollar. But at present the rupee appears to be giving in. It was expected that the demand for dollars which moved up in August would go down towards the end of August. It may be recalled that the quotation of rupee remained stable at Rs. 31.37 per US dollar since the foreign exchange market switched over to the direct quotation system in August 1993. But at present the dealers are prepared to bet on a new range of Rs. 31.70-32.50 per dollar in the days ahead.

The rupee survived two attacks in the past. The first was in March 1993 soon after the presentation of the Union Budget for 1993-94. At that time it went down to Rs. 33.50 per dollar. This slide was attributed to uncertainty about the unification of the rupee. But soon it rose back to Rs. 31.50. In March 1995 before the presentation of the Union Budget for 1995-96 the rupee went down to Rs. 32.15 on rumors of capital account convertibility. But within a few days it rose back to Rs. 31.40. Though the possibility of a further slide of the rupee cannot be ruled out it is unlikely as the slide in the rupee is due to excess demand for dollars.

On both the occasions i.e., March 1993 and March 1995 the rupee slided due to panic in the market caused by uncertainty about the unification of the rupee and rumours about capital account convertibility respectively. The rupee recovered easily as the transition from the dual exchange rate system to unification or single exchange rate system turned out to be a smooth affair. In a similar manner, when the rumours about capital account convertibility turned out to be untrue in March 1995 the rupee rate was restored to its original level without any difficulty.

At present the rupee has slid because of excess demand for dollars. Since the middle of July 1995 the supply of excess demand is on the decline. This is because of the rise in the current account deficit. In the first four months of 1995-96 imports went up by 40 percent while exports registered a rise of 28 percent. In addition there is a decline in the inflow of foreign funds and funds through the GDR route. This mismatch in the inflow and outflow of dollars has its impact on the exchange rate of the rupee.

It became known in the second week of August that the market was short of dollars. Immediately, the rupee hit a low of Rs. 31.57/58. In the third week of August it hit a low of Rs. 31.65 and in the fourth week it slid to Rs. 31.85. Due to the continuous rise in the demand for dollars on August 30, the rupee fell to 32.10.

During the earlier declines of the rupee the market was optimistic that the rupee would recover. But this time the rupee failed to recover. On September 3, the rupee started sinking and before the close of the day it hit a low of Rs. 32.52 per dollar. Quotations also went up to Rs. 32.57. It is not known whether any deals were struck at Rs. 32.57. The majority of deals were at Rs. 32.52. There was a large spread between a buying and selling quota. In a normal market the spread will be about a paisa or two. But in the first week of September it was about 10 paise.

There is confusion about the identity of the buyers of dollars also. It was the State Bank of India which used to buy dollars. The buying was caused by debt repayment. Earlier the responsibility of debt repayment was that of the Reserve Bank of India. But since June 1995 the State Bank of India has been shouldering this responsibility. The fall in the rupee is attributed to rise in the demand for dollars by the public sector units like the Indian Oil for oil imports. It is reported that on September 5, 1995 the State Bank of India bought $ 250 million for ONGC and $ 50-$ 60 million for Indian oil. The State Bank of India was also buying dollars to meet the

Government's debt repayment obligations. Since September 5, the rupee has begun to recover its lost ground. It was quoting at Rs. 32.20/2 on September 8. Having done this the rupee is expected to stabilize at Rs. 32 and in the long run it is likely to move in the range of Rs. 31.50 and Rs. 32.50. There may also be alternate bouts of buying depending on the periodicity of debt repayments.

The Reserve Bank of India has in its vaults about $ 20 billion which it bought for Rs. 31.37 per dollar. It is now buying dollars at Rs. 32.52/55. In doing this, the Reserve Bank of India is incurring a loss of Rs. 1.18 on every dollar it buys. Indeed this defies logic. The remedy for this situation seems to be for the Reserve Bank of India to meet the demand for dollars by drawing on its dollar accumulations. If the supply of dollars increases on the market, the excess demand for dollars which is causing a slide in the rupee will disappear removing the mismatch between the supply and demand for dollars and eliminating the loss caused by the higher price of dollar. The volume of business is estimated at between $ 300 and $ 400 million per day on spot basis and about $ 1.0 billion including swap deals. This means that if the dollar is purchased at the price of Rs. 32 the loss will be of the order of Rs. 68 crore per day—a colossal amount indeed. This loss can be avoided by the Reserve Bank of India releasing the officially accumulated dollars to meet the growing demand for dollars. A moderate decline in the rupee is considered necessary to boost exports up to the point where the exports and imports match thus eliminating the current account deficit which is one of the causes of the slide in the rupee.

During April-July 1995 the trade deficit was of the order of $ 1525.89 million against $ 593.78 million earlier. This was due to the exceptional rise in imports in May-July 1995. But because of the improved outlook for food and cash crops in the current agricultural season it will be possible to export fairly large quantities of fine cereals, cotton and sugar. At the same time imports may not be of the order reached in April-July and the trade deficit for the whole year should not be more than $ 2 billion. This is because exceptional imports of cotton and sugar can be eliminated and additional foreign exchange resources also secured through the export of the same products in the coming months. This explains why the Union Finance Minister has not taken a pessimistic view of the developments on the foreign trade front. In fact, he has been advocating the use of forex reserves for importing even consumer goods and other goods in short supply for ensuring the availability of quality products to Indian consumers and also bringing down the inflation rate to below 7 percent. If the trade deficit does not turn out to be more than $ 2 billion the current account deficit may be manageable.

The Finance Minister has made the observation that the balance of payments position will remain comfortable and that foreign exchange reserves will not disclose any significant net decline, even with larger repayment obligations and no sign of uptrend in forex reserves lately. There may be an exaggeration in this rupee value of exports and imports for some weeks as there has been an unmerited decline in the external parity of the rupee vis-à-vis the dollar to Rs.32.20 from Rs. 31.37 in the past few weeks.

With heavy purchases of dollar in the open market by the IOC for meeting its requirements and no large floating supplies the rupee deteriorated to Rs. 32.56 per dollar at one stage. As the Finance Minister has ruled out capital account convertibility of the rupee in this immediate future and has also expressed confidence that the balance of payments position will not be deteriorating, there is no justification to the aberration in the rupee value of the dollar. This might be welcomed by exporters though the repatriation of their foreign exchange earnings and the fresh inflow of invisible receipts might get delayed if the impression gains ground that the rupee will depreciate further against the dollar.

At present exports have been showing up well and non-oil imports may not continue to be at the same rate with replenishment of inventories and greater availability of the required inputs from indigenous sources, as unmerited depreciation of the value of the rupee should be avoided. The Reserve Bank of India could effect sales of dollars, if need be, for a short period especially when exceptional imports are involved.

It is encouraging to note that the behaviour of the economy is continuing to be satisfactory and the GDP will be rising by 6 percent.

If the shortage gets relieved in many directions and exports also rise at the rate of 28-30 percent in the whole year larger imports can be afforded. But care has to be taken to see that the unnecessary imports of products which can be secured from indigenous sources are eliminated.

With the improvement of the current account deficit the outflow of dollars on this account is on the decline. The other item of outflow continues though in a reduced form. These two outflows which get reduced in volume will be a source of relief for the rupee as the strain on it is mitigated. This checks the slide of the rupee below Rs. 31.37 per US dollar. If a slight slide is indicated this will not constitute any problem as this will give a boost to exports and increase export earnings. At the same time this will increase the prices of imports and add to the import bill. Even this is no problem considering the fact that a rise in import prices to the extent that the demand for imports is price elastic will reduce the import volume. The inputs for exports which account for 45 percent of total imports may be price inelastic and the rise in their prices will increase the prices of exports and this will remove any price advantage depreciation of the rupee may confer on exports. This can be mitigated by reducing the customs duties on imported inputs for exports. This strengthens the forces which cause a rise in the supply of dollars and a fall in the demand for dollars and the two reduce excess demand for dollars which is the cause of the slide of the rupee in the foreign exchange market. Any small excess demand for dollars can be met by drawing on the accumulated dollar reserves if the slide goes beyond a certain limit.

Even here there is a problem. The Reserve Bank of India purchased dollars at the price of Rs. 31.37 per dollar. If because of the slide of the rupee the Reserve Bank has to pay a higher price than Rs. 31.37 it is bound to incur a loss. The rise in the price of dollar is due to excess demand for dollars. The reduction in the current account deficit will to that extent reduce the excess demand for dollars. The demand for dollars to pay for oil imports and for meeting debt repayment obligations will remain. But if the Reserve Bank of India releases dollars from its reserves and begins to sell them on the foreign exchange market the supply of dollars rises and this reduces the excess demand for dollars which is the cause of the slide of the rupee. In this case, the exchange rate of the rupee will move towards Rs. 31.37 per dollar and this is great relief for the rupee.

This will prevent uncontrolled slide of the rupee. The apprehension that the depreciation of the rupee is imminent will turn out to be unfounded. The expectation that the rupee is in for devaluation will not be realistic. In fact, the occasion for devaluation of the rupee will not arise at all. The transfer of foreign funds by the foreign investors. NRI's and even domestic investors outside India following the Mexican experience will not take place. The rupee remains strong and stable and will not pose any problem for the authorities.

8

Is India getting into the Debt Trap?

The detractors of the structural adjustment policies and economic reforms in India have lost no time in alleging that India is getting fast into the classic debt trap. It is admittedly true that India has been borrowing from the I.M.F., the World Bank, the Asian Development Bank and other financing agencies but it is maintaining solvency in regard to external debt transactions. The recent developments in the Indian economy are, of course, encouraging engendering guarded optimism that India is making a breakthrough in its domestic economic policies and for that reason in its international economic policies as well.

There is cautious optimism that with the considerable easing of the foreign exchange reserve position and downtrend in the annual rate of inflation the economy should register a growth rate of 4 percent in 1992-93. The annual rate of inflation which was 16.7 percent in August 1991 fell to 11.5 percent in mid-June 1992 and at the end of July 1992 it was 10.9 percent—close to the single digit rate. The Finance Minister is not overoptimistic when he says that by March 1993 the annual rate of inflation will decline to 8 percent. The foreign exchange reserves which were uncomfortably low a year ago have registered a rise to Rs. 19,000 crore though it must be said that this is not enough considering the enormity of India's external obligations. Under the liberalized import policy large quantities of essential imports for better supply management and market intervention to defeat inflationary expectations besides some $ 5 billion of debt servicing would bring the reserves under pressure before long.

The current account deficit of the balance of payments steeply declined to $ 2.2 billion in 1991-92 because of severe import compression measures and tight credit policy and to some extent because of devaluation of the rupee. But it is estimated to rise to $ 6 billion in 1992-93. The Finance Ministry has been able to tie up the requirement of $ 3 billion of " exceptional financing " with the Aid India Consortium meeting and the I.M.F release of $ 647 million out of the $ 1.6 billion to be drawn in 1992-93 under the standby credit arrangements. Though the Aid India Consortium pledged $ 7.2 billion for 1992-93 the quick disbursing amount would only be $ 1.8 billion excluding the IMF assistance, as against $ 2.3 billion in 1991-92. Bilateral creditors, having their own budgetary problems, are averse to increasing the quantum of fast-disbursing aid and take the view that India's reserves are relatively improving. In view of this multilateral disbursements have necessarily to be larger.

There is the dire possibility of India encountering balance of payments difficulties over the next three years—up to 1995 even assuming an export growth of 10 percent in dollar terms. As the commercial lending on a significant scale can be ruled out because of the reluctance of the lenders on account of low credit rating, the existing standby arrangement with the IMF which runs up to March 1993 is about to be converted into an Extended Fund Facility (EFF) which would have longer repayment terms. The EFF is likely to be combined with the Enhanced Structural Adjustment Facility (ESAF), which is a more concessional conditionality assistance, so that India can cover its exceptional financing needs of the order of $ 6 billion till 1994-95. This medium-term arrangement (1992-95) will be on the basis of the Eighth Plan policy projections. Negotiations for EFF are expected to take place before November 1992 by which time, it is assumed that India's performance in fiscal tightening, lowering inflation rate and trade flows would have improved significantly. The balance of payments projections envisage actual flows of foreign investment, both direct and portfolio, of the order of $ 500 million in 1992-93 rising to $ 700 million in 1993-94 and to $ 900 million by 1994-95. It is hoped that by mid-1990s there will be an inflow of $ 1 billion a year at least.

On the domestic front there is a distinct improvement in the situation. The Government has succeeded in reducing the gross fiscal deficit from 8.4 percent of GDP in 1990-91 to 6.5 percent in 1991-92. Total receipts increased by 13 percent, aggregate expenditure increased by only 7 percent during 1991-92. The budget deficit at Rs. 7032 crore was thus Rs. 687 crore lower than budgeted. The 1992-93 budget has projected a further decrease in the gross fiscal deficit to 5 percent of GDP. Broad money (M_3) increased at a much higher rate of 18.6 percent during 1991-92 as compared with the 15 percent increase in 1990-91. The credit policy for the first half of 1992-93 envisages a sharp reduction in the pace of monetary expansion to 11.3 percent.

India's trade in dollar terms declined in 1991-92. Exports and imports, both declined compared with the performance in the preceding year. Trade deficit declined from $ 5929 million in 1990-91 to $ 1584 million in 1991-92. As tariff and non-tariff barriers to trade are reduced under the liberalized import policy imports are likely to increase. It thus follows that exports have to increase correspondingly. This requires a new and functional export strategy. The current account deficit as a percentage of GDP is estimated to have declined sharply from 2.6 percent in 1990-91 to 0.90 percent in 1991-92. This is projected to increase to 2.1 percent in 1992-93. The eighth plan has maintained that the current account deficit as a percentage of GDP should not exceed 1.6 percent in the plan period. Given the overambitious size of the Eighth Plan this may be a chimera.

The foreign investment approvals had risen to Rs. 1528 crore between August 1991 and May 1992. Large proposals cleared by the Foreign Investment Promotion Board total more than Rs. 500 crore. These investments would substantially cover all outflows of foreign exchange by stimulating export earnings.

The outflow of NRI foreign deposits amounted to $ 1716 million in 1991-92 against an inflow of $ 229 million in 1990-91. The outflow has not yet been totally reversed. In April-May 1992 such outflow amounted to $ 264 million. With access to international capital market restricted, India had to bring down its borrowings from $ 1242 million in 1990 to $ 239.6 million in 1991 and to $ 114.4 million in the first four months (January-April) of 1992 by way of medium and long term bank loans.

The Government is committed to reducing the fiscal deficit to 5 percent of GDP in 1992-93 and to 4 percent of GDP in 1993-94. But the Government has to grapple with the problem of payment of subsidy on food and fertilizers. If these subsidies cannot be cut (and they should not be cut) cuts in unessential expenditure are inevitable. There may also be the need to cut down capital expenditure also to some extent. Despite the cuts in personal income tax rates and reduction in customs tariff, tax collections in the current year are reported to be encouraging. Total collections of customs and excise and income tax were Rs. 14,276 crore in April-June 1992 against Rs. 10,503 crore in the corresponding period of 1991.

In view of all these factors the Government is hopeful of an upturn in the economy in 1992-93 after the crisis of the previous year. The distinct improvement in the foreign exchange resources and the decline in the rate of inflation are positive indicators. Budgetary position is not uncomfortable though fiscal discipline will have to be vigorously pursued.

India's external debt is of the order of $ 74.7 billion. Total debt service payment in 1992-93 is expected to be $ 7.2 billion, equivalent to 29 percent of exports of goods and services including $ 3.4 billion in interest payments and $ 3.8 billion in amortization payments. Fresh borrowings from the IMF will make the debt burden larger. There is a limit to which external borrowing can keep financing imports and help meet repayment obligations on old loans. While the IMF credit may be cheaper than commercial borrowing more has to be paid elsewhere. The IMF delayed the release of the second instalment of the $ 2.2 billion loan as it was not happy with India's performance in some areas, especially the failure to meet the target for money supply growth. In the Memorandum that the Government submitted to the IMF in June 1992 it has promised to tighten performance.

The experience of several Third World countries has made some journalists and economists conjuring the horrifying spectacle of the debt trap for India. Every big country with a debt burden which has approached the IMF for help has had the bitter experience of having the loan tap closed as they had not met some of the targets prescribed by the IMF. This was the experience of Mexico, the Philippines, Argentina, Brazil and many smaller countries. Their demands for loans being turned down by all creditors, official and commercial agencies, these countries had to go back to the IMF on their knees. But the burden in the intervening period was a very heavy one. Pessimists and detractors of the structural adjustment reforms say that India will have to meet the same fate getting deeper into external debt.

The Indian economy has made much headway during the past 12 months. The Finance Minister in his Memorandum to Mr. Michel Camdessus, Managing Director of the IMF, has highlighted the progress India has made and has made commitments of meeting the targets prescribed by the Fund. The fiscal deficit will be brought down to 5 percent of GDP in 1992-93 and to 4 percent of GDP in 1993-94, the annual rate of inflation has declined to 9.28 percent on 25.7.1992 and it is expected to fall to 8 percent before March 1993; the rate of monetary growth has been brought down to 11.5 percent. These are not mean achievements. India will be able to honour all its external obligations as per schedule. It is true that India's credit rating is low and the commercial lenders are wary of lending to India. The Managing Director of the IMF has called for support for India. As the economy experience an upturn the credit rating agencies have to upgrade India and the commercial lenders will be enthusiastic about lending to India. With the adoption of the new export strategy exports will register a faster rate of growth and avert the balance of payments crisis. In the attempt to encourage the inflows of NRI investments the Governmenι of India has introduced variations of the Foreign Currency Non Resident (FCNR) bank schemes. It is expected that these schemes will not only encourage an inflow of NRI funds but will also reverse the existing outflow. The Export-Import Bank of India in its annual report for 1991-92 has stated that through economic liberalization the country has demonstrated its willingness as an international borrower to honour on time its international obligations notwithstanding the stresses and strains to reach a market economy environment.

These are some of the silver linings on the horizon and India does not have to fear being forced into the external debt trap. India has overcome the incipient recession and is poised for accelerated growth which will enhance India's solvency as a debtor.

The IMF's structural adjustment programme requires a large inflow of foreign exchange over a fairly prolonged period to finance a large outflow on imports of capital goods, components and raw materials—all meant to make Indian products more competitive in world markets. But the foreign investment inflows, inflows of NRI deposits and assistance from the IMF and the commercial lenders who find India's economic performance satisfactory—all these will help manage the show without falling into the external debt trap. If there is any debt trap at all, it is far away from India. It is a bogey which should not scare us. But, at the same time, it is necessary to exercise care not to go near the trap. The spectrum of a debt trap arose because there was a dip in foreign exchange reserves from $ 2236 million in March 1991 to $ 1100 million in November 1991 coupled with an outflow of $ 330 million per month and this led to external borrowing. These signals are not there at present.

The Government's determination to liberalize and integrate the Indian economy into the global system and the commitment that the on-going economic reform measures are irreversible have infused confidence in industry, trade and finance circles. The OECD study feels that the drive to liberalize is comparatively weak. The policy makers are under tremendous pressure to ensure that the liberalization programme does not destabilize the existing economic and political structures. Thus, according to the OECD Report, India's current economic reform is deliberately moderate because of the powerful constituency which is in favour of retaining the conservative and protective inward looking character of the economy. Admittedly, the Indian policy makers are in a somewhat circumspect and cautious mood influenced not the least by the recent securities scam whose total dimensions at a conservative estimate are of the order of Rs. 3500 crore. Undeterred by this scam the Government is determined to persist with liberalization of the Indian economy even as it takes measures to prevent the distortion of reform.

India has been borrowing and it has to pay interest on it and repay the loan itself as per schedule. A certain measure of fiscal discipline is necessary for the purpose.

In Europe, there is the European Monetary Union. The entry of members into the Union is governed by the Maastricht Treaty. The conditions of entry stipulate that the member's budget deficit must be less than 3 percent of GDP, its public debt should be less than 60 percent of GDP and its rate of inflation should be within one and a half percent points of the lowest individual country figure in the European community. These conditions are regarded as general principles to ensure good financial housekeeping. The European countries trying to enter the Union are endeavouring to discipline themselves to satisfy the conditions of entry. It is obvious that these conditions are stiffer than those imposed on India. But these countries do not complain of surrender of sovereignty. India's fiscal deficit had to be reduced from 8.5 percent of GDP to 6.5 of GDP in 1991-92; from 6.5 percent of GDP to 5 percent of GDP in 1992-93. The inflation rate had to be brought down from 16.7 percent in July 1991 to a single digit figure now. These general principles of fiscal discipline which are not stiff on any reckoning are of great importance to India which is seeking assistance from the IMF under the Enhanced Structural Adjustment Facility. Interest rate on this facility is only 0.5 percent against about 9 percent under the Extended Fund Facility (EFF). India should not regard these conditions as unduly burdensome and should instead regard them as principles of good financial health. With these conditionalities, India will be able to pay interest and amortization and repay its debt without default. Just because India borrows from the IMF, it cannot be regarded as surrendering its sovereignty to the Fund Bank Combine. India needs the debt and is able to repay it. There will be no debt trap.

Many observers of Indian economic reforms hold an optimistic view of India's economic progress. The Asian Development Bank in its Report "Asian Development Outlook, 1992" has predicted that the Indian economy, after touching the rock bottom in 1991, is expected to make a visibly significant recovery in 1992 and 1993. The former world Bank President, Mr. Barber Conable stated in the first week of June 1992 that India can achieve an overall growth rate of 10 percent if it takes advantage of its "very sound industrial base." This confidence is understandable if one views the immense domestic market in the country whose consumption rates are increasing much further than even those of industrially advanced countries like Britain or the USA.

Given such an immense potential for growth, it would be an exercise in growth pessimism to predict a slow or even a stagnant growth rate for the Indian economy. The acceleration of growth rate will generate resources which will enable India to clear its foreign obligations and to ward off the danger of the debt trap, if there is any, as feared by the opponents of structural adjustment policy and economic reform measures underway for the good of the country. When the structural adjustment policy is completed India will land itself on the path of self-sustaining growth and the Eighth Plan targets will be easy of realization.

9

Structural Adjustment: Human or Brutal

The structural adjustment policies initiated by the Government of India in July 1991 at the instance of the International Monetary Fund which made the implementation of these policies a condition precedent to the grant of structural adjustment facility has come in for a good deed of criticism. The Finance Minister has gone on record, albeit rightly, that the structural adjustment has a "human face". But the detractors of these policies take pride in underlining what they call a "Brutal side" to it. The issue needs to be examined and put in the right perspective.

The new industrial policy aims at modernisation and technological upgradation of Indian industry in order to make it internationally competitive. Its objective is to unshackle the industrial system from bureaucratic controls and licensing procedures and to allow foreign participation. Technological upgradation results in unemployment of course, but this unemployment is transitory. The Government has provided a safety net in the form in a National Renewal Fund which would be used to provide compensation to those rendered unemployed by technological upgradation to retrain them and to redeploy them in areas where newly acquired skills will be useful. Unemployment resulting from it is only temporary and this is the price the country has to pay for the benefits of industrialisation.

According to the workshop about 1-3 million workers in 1992-93 and about 4-8 million workers in 1993-94 would be thrown out of employment. The workers thrown out of employment in the organized industrial sector would swell the rank of those working in the unorganised industry and in other areas. This would increase the incidence of poverty in India. At the same time, the workshop observed that the structural adjustment, when completed, would result in increasing the growth rate of the economy from the 5.5 percent achieved during the seventh plan period to 7-8 percent. The workshop declared a consensus" in favour of the programme to help the "National Economy to pick up in the long run". The laudable objective to make the organized segment of the Indian industry "efficient, modern and internationally competitive".

What is called the brutal side of the programme is not brutal at all when it is remembered that a safety net in the form of this National Renewal Fund (NRF) is established to retrain and rehabilitate those who are rendered unemployed by technological upgradation. It is admitted that the NRF is to start with inadequate resources to provide succour to all those who are unemployed. The ILO-UNDP workshop notes with concern the slackening tempo of the ongoing poverty alleviation programmes and recommends that the Government should earmark more funds for the programme. According to an estimate this has to be of the order of Rs. 3,500 crore in 1992-93 and Rs. 4,700 crore in 1993-94 to take care of the problem of only the additional unemployment structural adjustment.

In the attempt to cushion the poor from the impact of structural adjustment programme there is revamping of the PDS. But the revamped PDS is tracing grave problems: the need to import wheat from abroad by paying twice the price of domestic wheat, the demand of the farmers to raise the procurement prices of wheat and rice and the enormous subsidy to be paid on food supplied through the PDS.

The Government of India placed orders with the Canadian Wheat Board for the import of over 10 lakh tonnes of wheat at a price of Rs. 546 per quintal while the price of domestic wheat is Rs. 246. The subsidy on imported wheat will have to be about Rs. 300 per quintal. How much of this subsidy reaches the poor? This has got two aspects to it, the aspect of leakage. According to estimates about 37 per cent of the subsidy on wheat and rice is lost through leakages the figure for edible oils being 55 per cent and that for sugar being 39 per cent. The actual quantum of subsidy that reaches the poor is Rs. 1500 crore the total subsidy on food being Rs. 2500 crore. The second aspect concerns targeting. According to bodies conducted on the problem, the poorest 40 percent gets only 48-50 percent of the food grains that reach the poor people the balance going to the richer sections of society. This means that the quantity of the subsidy that reaches the poor people is Rs. 700 crore 750 crore only. Even if the food subsidy is kept below Rs. 2850 crore it is possible to enlarge the coverage of the scheme for the really poor by making sure that there are no leakages and that the top 60 percent of the population is denied access to the benefits of PDS. But this is indeed a difficult task.

Various suggestions have been made to solve the problems of leakage and targeting. The Agricultural Prices Commission recommended in December 1989 that the Government should start distributing coarse grains through the PDS. This scheme is claimed to have two advantages: (1) since only the poor would like to consume coarse grains, the rich would voluntarily abstain from consuming them (2) this would cut down the incentive for pilferage from the system. This involves the problem of storing coarse food grains but if this problem can be solved this is a worthwhile suggestion. But inferior varieties of food grains are less productive and if the farmers are to be induced to grow inferior varieties of wheat and rice, they will have to be paid higher procurement prices which exacerbates inflation. This is unavoidable.

The distribution of food articles bristles with formidable difficulties. No system can be perfect or foolproof. What is necessary is to devise a scheme which is least imperfect.

Only coarse varieties of food grains should be sold through the PDS; the superior varieties should be sold through the market. The poor will then derive benefit of subsidies. Those who want to purchase superior varieties of food articles can do so in the open market by paying a higher price. In this case they will not have the benefit of food subsidies. As the inferior varieties of food grains cannot be stored for long without their determination only enough stock of them lasting for a year should be held in stock. As and when the stocks are depleted, fresh stocks must be purchased and held for short period only. As the productivity of coarse food grains is low research should be undertaken to increase the productivity of coarse food grains and the farmers should be given the incentive to devote more and more land to the production of coarse food grains. A part of this saving on subsidies could be used to provide incentives to them. The Pakistan experiment of selling wheat flour rather than wheat through the PDS could be tried in India. The rich and the middle class consumers may also buy wheat flour but this is only an exception. It is generally believed that wheat flour sold in the ration shops is not as clean as wheat flour freshly ground in the mills. This makes the rich sections of society, by and large to purchase wheat in the open market rather than purchasing wheat flour from the ration shops.

The question of identifying the poor is fraught with formidable practical difficulties. An income limit could be fixed and only those who income is below it should be entitled to ration cards. Special offices could be opened manned by accredited authorities to issue income certificates any fraud in this respect being made a punishable offence. Special squads could be appointed to ascertain the income of those who claim to be poor on a random basis any under declaration of income being made a punishable offence. If some who underdeclare their incomes with the object of getting ration cards are caught and punished, this will act as a disincentive to such underdeclaration and only those who are really poor will be able to get the benefits of food subsidy. This involves the appointment of special staff for the purpose and the expenditure involved can be met by the budgetary savings in subsidy. For this purpose, the income limit should be fixed at a level higher than the per capita monthly expenditure recently fixed by the planning commission while defining the poverty line; it is Rs. 50 for the rural section and Rs. 57 for the urban sector. These figures are ridiculously low considering the fact that the per capita daily expenditure for the urban dwellers is fixed at Rs. 1.66 which has to cover his lodging and transport expenses also. Therefore, the per capita monthly expenditure limit for both the rural and urban dwellers has to be raised. If this is done, the number of people below the poverty line will increase. The food articles supplied to them will have to be subsidised. This is one way of alleviating the poverty engendered by the implementation of the structural adjustment policies. Otherwise, the structural adjustment will have a brutal face rather than a human face.

India is an integral part of the global system and to be able to survive in the global economy it must make the economy really competitive. This means that the economy as a whole and all it parts must be exposed to the bracing of competition. It is only then that India will be internationally competitive. But this process involves costs unemployment and poverty which are only transitory. Action should be taken to mitigate the incidence of these costs. This memorandum adumbrates these actions and the mechanics of their working.

The structural adjustment policies are expected to yield results slowly. There are many imperfections caused by structural and institutional rigidities which are inherent in the economy; these imperfections impede the working of the reform measures and for this reason the response is slow. This should not make one conclude that the structural adjustment measures have a brutal face. Far from it. Already, the inflation rate has declined from 12.2 per cent to 10.9 per cent and it is now close to the single digit. With the progress of the measures it is expected to fall further. There is also a marginal decline in the balance of payments deficit. In 1991-92 the economy grow thought just above the rate of population growth despite import curbs, devaluation and foreign exchange crisis. Recession in the economy is receding, there are indications that the human face will project itself to belie the fears of the pessimistic detractors.

10

Holding down the Fiscal Deficits of the Centre and the States

The Tenth Finance Commission chaired by Shri. K.C. Pant is facing a delicate task of requiring the state Governments to reduce their fiscal deficits. It is necessary to remember that the fiscal deficit is a cause of inflation. The IMF in its conditionalities has prescribed a reduction of the fiscal deficit as a means of inflation control. Accordingly, the fiscal deficit of the Central Government which was 8.5 percent of GDP in 1990-91 was brought down to 5.7 percent in 1992-93 and it was expected to be brought down to 4.7 percent in 1993-94. But the chances of the fiscal deficit being brought down to 4.7 percent in 1993-94 are not bright. Infact, it may remain at 5.7 percent. The reduction in customs and excise duties causing a drastic reduction in revenue and the burgeoning expenditure jointly militate against the expected reduction of the fiscal deficit. In addition, the hikes in procurement prices of rice, wheat and barley and the expected rise in the prices of petroleum products which generate additional demands on Government revenues are sure to increase the fiscal deficit exacerbating fresh inflation in the economy.

In a tri-fiscal system, the fiscal deficits of the state and Local Governments are as much inflationary as the fiscal deficits of the Central Government. This calls for a reduction of the fiscal deficits of the State Governments and of the Local self Governments. Many State Governments have been running fiscal deficits in order to meet their expenditure programmes. Therefore, while computing the quantum of permissible fiscal deficits, mere concentration of attention on the fiscal deficits of the Central Government will not do. The fiscal deficits of the State Governments should also be taken into account and the aggregate fiscal deficit should be determined for each year. This is what I have already recommended in my Memoranda to the Prime Minister and the Finance Minister.

While the reduction of the fiscal deficits of the State Governments is necessary, there are doubts about the possibility of this reduction being brought about. In fact, the State Governments are as helpless as the Central Government in this matter. The Tenth Finance Commission is scheduled to meet the representatives of the State Governments specifically to ask them to reduce their fiscal deficits and to assist the Central Government in its difficult task of fiscal consolidation. But this part of the agenda is expected to be a major irritant in the talks. The discussions between the Tenth Finance Commission members and the State Government representatives will serve as the basis for the award of the States' share of central taxes for the next five years. The main plank of the agenda is the states' role in the reduction of the fiscal deficit. Already the Finance Commissioner has taken the view that all the State Governments should reduce their fiscal deficit. It must be noted that several state Governments have expressed reservations on this issue. And their reservations are understandable.

The Reserve Bank of India, on October 11, 1993, reduced the Statutory Liquidity Ratio by 2.5 percent from 37.25 percent to 34.75 percent in order to help the banks to lend liberally to the industrial sector which is faced with a serious recession. This has made most of the States face severe financial constraints considering the fact that the reduction of the SLR has reduced the banks' need for Government securities. As a result, the State Governments find it difficult to obtain funds from the banks by means of floating securities.

Furthermore, in the Union Budget for 1993-94 the Finance Minister drastically reduced the excise duties with intent to stimulate demand in order to ward off the ongoing recession and required the industries to pass on excise duty reductions to the consumers in the form of lower prices of industrial goods. This caused a drastic fall in excise duty revenue to the Government. The excise duty revenues being sharable between the Centre and the States; the share of the states in excise duty revenue has fallen. The Government of India has been announcing income tax reliefs every year as it feels that the economy is overtaxed. The fall in tax yield affects the states adversely as lower yield means a lower share of states.

According to the Ninth Final Commission's award, the States' share of taxes was fixed at 4.9 percent in the case of income tax. 5.9 percent in the case of additional excise duties and 4 percent in the case of Union excise duties. The Finance Commission, for its reasons which are prima facie valid, has criticised the State Governments for their inability to bring down their fiscal deficits. The State Governments, for their own reasons which are understandable, express their inability to reduce the fiscal deficits to the level required in order to bring down the rate of inflation. This is bound to emerge as a point of controversy between the representatives of the State Governments and the members of the Tenth Finance Commission. It will not be a surprise if this proves to be an irritant in the intergovernmental fiscal relations in India at present.

It needs no emphasis that the Government expenditure at all levels is burgeoning. Both the Central Government and the State Governments have adopted several unmeaning populist measures which involve heavy Government expenditure. This is financed by borrowing and drawing down of accumulated balances which have inflationary consequences though the mechanics of inflation is different in each case. These populist measures at all levels of Government are part of the electoral strategy meant to appease the electorate. The Central Government is partly to blame for this. This strengthens the case for exercising strict economy in expenditure. It is true that the revenues of the Government in absolute terms are rising but the Government expenditure is rising faster than revenue enlarging the fiscal deficit. It will not serve any purpose to blame the State Governments for their failure to bring down their fiscal deficits. The Central Government should first set its house in order and preach economy to the State Governments, on their part, should make it a policy to cut the coat according to cloth. This means that they should not overstretch their expenditure programmes necessary though they appear to be. The demands of the State Governments should be viewed with sympathy and understanding. There are already frictions in the federal financial relations in India. These frictions should not be allowed to cascade into a major breakdown. The Gadgil Formula governing federal financial transfers is found to be unscientific and several States have expressed themselves in favour of revising the Gadgil Formula and designing scientific criteria of financial allocations to states. The Tenth Finance Commission should design a formula which would be to the advantage of the poor and backward states. This will soothe their distress, agony and resentment.

As a method of inflation control the aggregate fiscal deficit has to be brought down. The Finance Minister has to bring it down to 3 percent of GDP by 1995-1996. This 3 percent figure relates to the Central Government fiscal deficit. If the State Governments too run fiscal deficits the aggregate fiscal deficit of the States and the centre will be more than 3 percent of GDP. If the aggregate fiscal deficit is to be brought down to 3 percent, the State Governments should also collectively bring down their fiscal deficits to a level at which the aggregate fiscal deficit is not more than 3 percent. It is therefore, necessary to aim at an aggregate fiscal deficit required to bring down the inflation rate to the pre-determined level envisaged in the conditionality prescriptions of the IMF.

Both the centre and States are going on a spending spree as part of the election strategy and also to keep the vote satisfied that the money is being spent for their welfare projects which can wait need not be implemented and only those projects which are of urgent necessity and which add to nation's productivity can be undertaken and pushed through. Unless expenditure is productive, it raises the rate of inflation.

In this connection it is pertinent to invite attention to the letter of May 31, 1993 written to the World Bank President Mr. Lews Preston by the Finance Minister. The annexure to this letter describes "the medium term programme of the Government to liberalise India's external sector and investment regime."

"The 1993-94 Budget aims at further reducing the Central Government fiscal deficit from about 5.7 percent of GDP in 1992-93 to 4.7 percent of GDP in 1993-94. Because of the rising cost of interest payments on the Central Government debt. The contractionary effect of the 1993-94 Budget on aggregate demand is much sharper than suggested by the reduction in the fiscal deficit."

This statement only means that if the interest burden cannot be made less heavy and the fiscal deficit has to be cut at the same time, the axe has to fall on other items of expenditure. In his letter to Mr. Preston, the Finance Minister says that non-interest expenditure of the Central Government is budgeted to decline by 5 percent in real terms to 11.5 percent of GDP in 1993-94 from 12.9 percent of GDP in 1992-93 and 15.2 percent in 1990-91. Over the four years since the beginning of the nineties, the reduction in non-interest expenditure is very steep. This only means that expenditure on development activities has been forcibly contracted. As a consequence, the overall levels of demand, investment and production in the economy have come down. There are authoritative reports to confirm that certain core industries such as steel and cement are in the midst of a recession and face the rising inventories of finished goods. These and other industries are heavily dependent on Government orders and on economical activity spurred by Government spending. With the expenditure cuts, their markets have shrunk and hence they are unable to sell as much of their goods as before. This is what the Finance Minister means when he says that the "contractionary effect of the 1993-94 Budget on aggregate demand is much sharper than suggested by the reduction in the fiscal deficit".

The Finance Minister is, of course, committed to bringing down the fiscal deficit in sharp stages. If expenditure cannot be cut because it will cause recession and contraction of aggregate demand, what is the way out? The Finance Minister, in his letter to Mr. Preston offers the way out. He is eminently aware of the dangers of indiscriminate cuts in Government expenditure. In the letter he says that "continuation of this trend (of declining non-interest expenditure) in the future is not feasible however in view of the large expenditure needs for human resources and infrastructure". He then contemplates the desirable route to fiscal deficit reduction. He say: "Further reductions in the fiscal deficit will have to rely primarily on improved resource mobilisation. Since this will have to be achieved during a period when customs tariffs will be progressively reduced, it is essential to ensure that reforms in tax policies and tax administration are implemented at a pace which ensures improvement in tax revenues, thus reconciling the Government stabilisation and structural reform objectives .... through improved tax performance, the Government intends to reduce the fiscal deficit to four percent of GDP or less in 1994-95 and lower levels in subsequent years". The logic of the Finance Minister is, of course, impeccable, but it must be noted that heavier taxation meant to reduce the fiscal deficit takes the spending power away from the people causing a reduction of aggregate demand and sending the economy in a recessionary spin and thus a low growth path which will affect the incomes and livelihood of the poor. This danger can be avoided if the extra resources mobilised are used to finance development expenditure. Concurrently, interest and other non-developmental expenditure like Government servants' salaries has to be reduced in order to reduce the overall spending so that the fiscal deficit is brought down without pain to the economy.

This view is endorsed by Professors J. Bhagwati and T.N. Srinivasan two NRI economists working in the USA. They have found that development expenditure is taking the brunt of the efforts at fiscal deficit reduction and this would adversely affect the rate of economic growth. They add, "Developmental expenditure links directly to the long term health of the economy. The reduction of developmental expenditure is likely to reduce the growth rate and therefore haunt us in the shape of further pressures to resume excess spending through the Budget as in the 1980s".

"The cuts in (real) development expenditure by the Government may well affect adversely the private investment expenditures in the economy, creating deflationary impulses in addition to those that the Government had intended. Because the crucial infrastructure activities are in the public sector and private investment finds its returns dependent on the availability of these infrastructure inputs (such as power), private investment has traditionally been crowded in rather than out by public investment in these infrastructure sectors. Thus, the Government must make every effort to ensure that despite predictable political pressures, the reductions in developmental expenditure are brutally selective. Sparing areas where the infrastructure bottlenecks are currently quite severe".

The foregoing views lead to the conclusion that following the dictates of the market or of the IMF will not do. There is a lot to learn from the economics of development. What matters is not the dictates of the market or the action of the Government but the efficiency of Government intervention in the running of the economy in each of its sectors and as a whole. If this view is accepted, fiscal deficit as a percentage of GDP is to be reduced without cutting down development expenditure which is so necessary to accelerate the rate of economic growth.

Spending wisely is the need of the hour. In order to identify the projects which are at present unnecessary and which can be postponed to a later date and those which are of urgent necessity and which raise the productivity in the sectors where they are promoted an authoritative body is necessary. This is the Expenditure Commission. This body should be vested with authority to scrutinise every project proposed by the state or the Central Governments and to approve only those that are urgent important for the development of the economy. This body is necessary to hold down Government expenditure and to reduce the aggregate of fiscal deficits of the State Governments and of the Centre. This will go a long way in holding down the price multiplier and the rate of inflation. In the matter of public expenditure programmes it is highly desirable to employ the cost-benefit calculus and to allow only those projects which satisfy the rigorous requirements of this calculus.

Reduction of the fiscal deficit is, of course, important but more important than this is the instruments employed to reduce it. Extra tax effort yields larger revenue which is necessary for fiscal reduction but this instrument by reducing purchasing power in the hands of the consumers reduces aggregate demand aggravates the recession. Therefore the instrument of expenditure reduction can be used but it must be so used as not to affect development expenditure both at the Centre and in the States. Given this criterion the task of the Expenditure Commission is rendered easy.

11

Prohibit the Import of Gold and Silver

India has acquired the unenviable name as a voracious absorber of gold. Its appetite for gold is insatiable. Gold is acquired for two reasons: (a) Gold jewellery is an externally visible symbol or affluence commanding high social esteem; (b) Gold is acquired and is held idle as it appreciates in value conferring a windfall gain on the owner. The demand for gold is, for these two reasons on the rise, the rise in its price notwithstanding. The domestic supply of gold is inadequate to meet the surging demand and in consequence India imports gold in large quantity spending considerable quantity of foreign exchange. The demand for gold is increasing and it has become necessary to import 450 tonnes of gold in a year which is roughly 50 percent of the total absorbed by India and West Asia. The large imports have necessitated the expenditure of forex reserves both regular and clandestine of the order of $ 5.37 billion or roughly Rs. 20,000 crore. This is equal to the oil import bill. But the requisite foreign exchange is not obtained directly. There is a large quantum of clandestine import of gold financed by foreign exchange obtained through the hawala route.

The holders of gold benefited due to the rise in the price of gold consequent on the prohibition of gold prior to February, 1992. But the Budget for 1992-93 introduced the scheme of import of gold by the NRIs and eligible Indians on payment of duty in foreign exchange. The quotation for gold in June 1991 was Rs. 3735 per 10 grammes against the world price of $ 366.10 per troy ounce. At that time the exchange rate was Rs. 21.01 for a US DOLLAR. In June 1992 the price of gold rose to Rs. 4068 for 10 grammes as there was a decline in the value of the rupee to Rs. 30.50. This despite the fall in the world price of gold to $ 343.50 per troy ounce.

With the slide in the external value of the rupee since August 19 the rupee price of gold has risen. Though the world price of gold has remained unchanged, the slide in the rupee and the payment of import duty on an advalorem basis have enhanced the price of gold and silver. The rupee exchange rate was Rs. 35.50 per dollar early in September having risen from Rs. 31.94. This has raised the import price of gold by 10 percent. In consequence the price of standard gold has risen from Rs. 4710 for 10 grammes on September 1, 1995 to Rs. 5028 in Bombay. The price of gold in Newyork which is $ 380.10 per troy ounce now fell from $ 382.83 in the same period. Thus there has been a rise in the rupee price of gold by 6.75 percent. The future price of gold depends on the exchange value of the rupee in the currency market and the advalorem duty imposed on its import.

At present there is a scramble for buying dollars for various purposes including the expectation of an appreciation of the dollar in the currency markets. The Reserve Bank of India has been selling dollars to meet the rising demand for them but the sale of dollars is too inadequate to meet the rising demand for them. The Reserve Bank of India wants the Government to obtain dollars to meet its demand in the open market. At a time when the trade deficit is getting larger and larger and the forex reserves are getting depicted the Reserve Bank decision to require the Government to obtain dollars from the open market has led to a decline in the external value of the rupee. There is demand for the Reserve Bank intervention in the currency market to prop up the sagging rupee. Even if it is propped upto Rs. 35 per dollar this represents a decline in the value of the rupee by over 6 percent. To that extent there will be a rise in the import price of gold and the import duty being on an advalorem basis the import duty commitment will rise. These two fall in the external value of the rupee and the rise in the import duty on gold will cause a rise in the price of gold.

It is necessary to reiterate that the value of imported gold is of the order of $ 5.17 billion or Rs. 20000 crore. This is not a small amount. Even if the inflow of capital into India is of the usual magnitude the import of gold of this value will cause a severe drain on the dwindling dollar reserves. If the net decline in forex reserves is large the mark operators will lose faith in the stability of the external value of the rupee. The Reserve Bank of India, in that event, will not have the reserves to enable it to sell dollars when the rupee slides beyond the outer limit of the band. The rupee will then have to depreciate further with horrendous consequences on the macroeconomic stability of the economy. The appreciation of the value of gold is already over 15 percent. If the gold import continues without restrictions, the depreciation of the rupee causes a depletion of forex reserves of more than Rs. 20,000 crore per year. The depreciation of the rupee is already of the order of 13.5 percent. If the rupee depreciates still further the value of gold import rises. The prices of gold are unlikely to fall. They are, infact, going to rise. Expecting a further rise in the price of gold the imports will import more gold by spending forex reserves. This, indeed, is a dangerous situation which should be avoided.

Prior to February 1992 the import of gold and silver was prohibited in the context of the balance of payment crisis of 1990-92 and the danger of a default on external commitments. A similar policy initiative is necessary at present. The Government will do well to prohibit the import of gold and silver. Those who import gold and silver by expending scarce forex reserves make a windfall gain when the gold prices rise. They reap the windfall gain at the cost of the nation. This is to be avoided. The burden of this song is: *Prohibit the import of Gold and Silver*.

12

The Basu Committee on the Norms for Regional Rural Banks

In the wake of the nationalisation of 14 commercial banks in July 1969 these banks were expected to pen their branches in the rural areas with authority to disburse loans to farmers for agricultural development and other allied activities. But the impression gained ground that these banks would not be able to reach out adequately to the rural population. In order to get proper guidance in the matter of helping the rural sector the Government appointed a Banking Commission under the Chairmanship of Dr. A.M. Khusro in 1969. This Commission submitted its report in 1972 expressing doubts about the capacity of the commercial banks to spread the banking facilities in the rural areas. This suggested the establishment of a new class of rural banks in the alternative ways: (a) some selected viable primary agricultural credit societies could be converted into rural cooperative banks and (b) subsidiaries of commercial banks in rural areas could be established or Primary Agricultural Credit Societies be organised as a subsidiary of commercial banks. Until 1975 the recommendations of this Commission could not be implemented. A scheme was unveiled to provide credit to the weaker sections in rural society. Accordingly the Government appointed a Working Group under the Chairmanship of M. Narasimham in July 1975 to suggest ways and means of providing alternative means of finance for the weaker sections of rural society landless labourers, rural artisans and small and marginal farmers. This working Group suggested the establishment of Regional Rural Banks. This suggestion was accepted by the Government and the "Regional Rural Banks" ordinance, 1975 was issued by the President of India on 26 September 1975. After some time this ordinance was replaced by the Regional Rural Banks Act, 1976.

The main objective of this bank was the spread of banking facilities in rural areas and to provide institutional credit to the weaker sections of rural society. The RRBs are sponsored by the commercial banks. At present, there are 196 RRBs sponsored by 26 commercial banks, 50 percent of the share capital is contributed by the Union Government, 15 percent by State Governments and 35 percent by the sponsoring commercial banks. At the end of September 1993 there were 14546 branch offices of the RRBs. As regards the banking facilities in the rural areas the position of the RRBs is fairly satisfactory. However, the viability of most of the RRBs is not satisfactory as most of them are incurring losses.

In the light of the performance and unviability of the RRBs several committees were constituted to suggests ways and means of rendering them viable. These committees have suggested the modes of improving the working of these banks. The most important of these committees have been the Agricultural Credit Review Committee under the Chairmanship of Dr. A.M. Khusro which submitted its report in 1989 and the Narasimham Committee of 1991. The recommendations of the Narasimham Committee have not yet been accepted by the Government. However, it is expected that the National Rural Bank of India (NRBI) would soon be established and all the RRBs would be merged into this bank. In the Budget speech of 1994-95 the finance minister declared that 50 percent of the loss-making RRBs were selected for comprehensive restructuring including the cleansing of their balance sheets and infusing fresh capital. In the Budget speech of 1995-96 he announced that another set of 50 RRBs would be selected for restructuring. In July 1995 the Reserve Bank of India appointed an expert group under the Chairmanship of Dr. N.K. Thingalaya in order to examine the major policy issues regarding managerial and administrative restructuring of RRBs selected for the purpose between 1994-95 and 1995-96. But if the NRBI is established it should be allowed to work as an autonomous body free from Government interference.

It is in the area of recovery of loans that the RRBs face insuperable problems. In 1982 the recovery of loans was 42 percent. In 1990 this improved to 51 percent. This means that 50 percent of the loans remain unreturned. This dismal recovery scenario is due to lack of supervisory staff to monitor the end-use of credit, wrong selection of families use of credit for inefficient productive purposes, inadequate marketing facilities and the policy of waiver of loans. The total outstanding advances of RRBs at the end of September 1993 was Rs. 4682 crore. This calls for the appointment of efficient supervisory staff who would monitor the end-use of credit and to provide guidance to the borrowers in the optimum use of credit. This will enable the 100 percent recovery of loans. If any borrower becomes a willful defaulter stringent action needs to be taken against him so as to serve a lesson to other borrowers.

The RRBs are incurring huge losses at present. The recovery of loans is poor, the productivity of the staff is low, the service is limited to target group only, the rate of interest on loans is less than the rate charges by the other financial institutions, the deposit mobilisation capability of the staff leaves a lot to be desired as most of them are untrained in the art. They have not recruited the personnel residing in the nearly rural areas. This is causing inefficient working of the staff. The overdues are mounting and the cost of service is very high. It appears necessary to close down the loss-making branches of the RRBs or to reorganise their working. The branches need to be merged with viable units and their area of operation needs to be expanded. The staff appointed need to be given adequate training in the art of recovery of loans, efficient use of credit and if these steps are taken the RRBs would become viable.

In the beginning the functions of the RRBs were to help rural artisans small and marginal farmers and rural entrepreneurs. But under the changed circumstances they have to provide credit facilities to the rich farmers and non-farm sectors in order to increase their earning capacity. The rate of interest charged by them should be on par with the rate charged by the commercial banks. Timely credit supply should be made available to the small farmers who now complain of inadequate credit supply which makes them approach the village moneylenders who charge a high rate of interest, some times more than 30 percent. The rate of interest charged by the banks could be 20 percent. This will increase the earning capacity of the RRBs. At the same time attractive rate of interest on deposits should be offered in order to strengthen the savings habit of the rural people and the deposits made by them should be transferred to urban centres and the funds so transferred could be used for investment in industrial development and these industries could create employment opportunities for the unemployed rural youth. Introduction of the system of effective supervision of the end use of borrowed funds would help the rural families to use the funds for the purpose for which they were borrowed. If this is done the overdues will fall and recovery of loans will be an easy task.

The working of the Gramin Bank of Bangladesh should make our RRB managers to open their eyes to the need to follow its example. This bank is working very well and is successful in realising the social objectives. This is due to the fact that loans are granted only for productive purposes and to those families who are identified to use the credit more effectively and productively so that nobody can misuse the funds borrowed by them. The recovery of these loans is 75 percent and almost all the banks are earning profits. The Indian RRBs will do well to emulate the example set by the Gramin Bank of Bangladesh.

Lately there is a welcome change in the organisation and functioning of the RRBs. The Report of the Basu Committee on revamping RRBs has recommended the introduction of prudential norms with immediate effect in all the 196 RRBs. The report is expected to the submitted to the National Bank for Agriculture and Rural Development (NABARD) shortly. Earlier the Bhandari Committee had recommended the introduction of prudential norms in the 49 RRBs taken up for comprehensive restructuring in a phased manner from 1995-96. It was the view of the Committee that as in the case of the commercial banks the RRBs should also classify their assets into four categories, namely, standard assets, sub-standard assets, doubtful assets and loss assets. This committee feels that the norms prescribed by the Reserve Bank of India for classifying an asset as a non-performing asset (NPA) for commercial banks were harsh when applied to more RRBs whose financial health is poor. Instead the Committee feels that the credit facility in respect of which interest or instalment of principal has remained due for a period of four quarters or two seasons of harvest of Kharif and Rabi (covering two half years) may be treated as NPA. According to this committee the amount should be considered past due when it remains outstanding for 30 days beyond due date. At present the period to declare an asset as NPA is four quarters for commercial banks. According to the Committee a loan should be treated as NPA if interest instalment remains past due for four quarters. In the case of agricultural term loans four quarters may be replaced by two seasons of agriculture corresponding to two half years. An overdraft account will be treated as NPA if the account remains out of order for four quarters. This norm is fixed at two quarters for commercial banks. No reversal of interest or provision for unrealised interest of earlier years has been suggested for the RRBs. The cut-off point to classify loans and advances based on the above criteria has been suggested at Rs. 7500. The Committee has taken this view because the average amount of loans disbursed by the RRBs during 1993-94 was of the order of Rs. 6000. The Committee has also recommended four slabs based on the period for which the advance has been considered doubtful for the purpose of provisioning as against the three slabs prescribed by the Reserve Bank for commercial banks. Under provisioning norms for loss assets, it has been suggested that 100 percent of the outstanding should be provided for DICGC claims received or receivable may be considered within the provision. In the case of doubtful assets provisioning of 100 percent of the extent to which the advances are not covered by the realisable value of the security (including DICGC cover) to which the bank has a valid resources be made. In addition to this, depending upon the period for which the asset has remained doubtful 10-15 percent of the secured portion will also have to be provided for. A general provision of 10 percent of the total outstandings has been suggested for sub-standard assets. The report says:

"For loans below 7500, the bank may make provision to the extent of 7.5 percent of the aggregate amount outstanding in respect of such advances. While making provisions to the extent of 7.5 percent, amounts guaranteed by DICGC should not be deducted from the amount of advances. Also, value of security in any form including term deposits NSC, surrender value of life policies etc, should not be deducted from the aggregate advances under this category".

The Committee feels that the provisioning requirements should be gradual.

A flat rate of 7.5 percent of the aggregate amount outstanding in respect of loans below the cut-off point has been suggested for RRBs as against 10 percent of the outstanding suggested for commercial banks.

Credit facilities backed by Government guarantees though "past due" should not be treated as NPA. In the case of advances guaranteed by DICGC provision should be made only for the balance in excess of the amount guaranteed by the corporation.

The Government of India made a provision of Rs. 300 crore in each of the years 1994-95 and 1995-96 to clean up the balance sheets of 50 RRBs during these years. An equal amount was required to be contributed by State Governments and sponsor banks in the ratio of 15:35.

The Report of the Basu Committee is an indepth analysis of the problems faced by the RRBs in India and it offers several far reaching recommendations for the improvements of their operational efficiency. Admittedly at present the RRBs, by and large, are overburdened with non-performing asset and unless their burden is reduced and also unless in future care is taken to avoid the accumulation of these NPAs the future of the RRBs looks bleak.

13

Precautions against a Rise in the Rate of Inflation

The rate of inflation in the Indian economy is refreshingly on the decline. The report on January 8, 1995 showed a decline to 6.38 percent. This is attributed to the decline in the rate of monetary growth to 14 percent from the projected growth of 19 percent and to the tight money policy in vogue which has sent the rate of interest to higher levels. With the Rabi crop turning good the rate of inflation may well decline further. But one cannot be sure.

But the tight money conditions in the economy are set to affect the rate of industrial growth and this may land the economy in a recession. Quite apart from the tight money conditions, there are other factors which cause a decline in the rate of industrial growth. They are the inadequate supply of power especially in the South and the truant monsoon. In consequence, the rate of industrial growth in the second half of 1995-96 is unlikely to be above 8.5 percent. The effect of the present liquidity crunch is likely to be felt in the first half of 1996-97. The Finance Ministry is not open to it many choices. The present credit squeeze adopted to control inflation will have other side effects which are not conducive to higher industrial growth. The high interest rates have already affected the industries at the fringe as they are crucially dependent on loans and lease finance. The growth in this sector had attained 57 percent in July 1994 and May 1995. But it slumped to 6 percent in October 1995. It was these industries which in December 1993 spearheaded the economic boom. It is the acceleration effect of the growth of this sector that sparked off the industrial boom. In 1992-93 the output of capital goods had fallen by 0.1 percent. This was due to the fiscal stabilization programme adopted in 1991-92 following the implementation of the conditionality prescriptions of the IMF. There was also a further decline by 8.8 percent in the first seven months of 1993-94. But due to the relaxation of the programme of fiscal consolidation in 1994-95 it grew by 20 percent. If the liquidity crunch continues unabated the capital goods industry will slip back into slump depressing future investment plans of the corporate sector. If the downward acceleration effect is sharp the resultant recession will make the corporate sector postpone the investment plans. The evidence of this is already visible in the 37 percent decline in fresh capital raised by the corporate sector. This is added to by the existing political uncertainty. The drop in the capital goods sector will reinforce the decline in the rate of growth of the industrial sector. The resultant recession will make the fiscal imbalance worse. A slow down in industrial growth will be accompanied by a slow down in the rate of growth of tax revenues. This means that a reduction in the rate of monetary growth and the reduction in bank credit to industry will be offset by the enlargement of the fiscal deficit. As the Government has to cover the deficit by means of borrowing, it will create a base for generating more high-powered money. This will add to the fires of inflation which will come to coexist with recession the phenomenon of stagflation will reassert itself. Thus, attempts to hold down the rate of inflation might result in stagflation. India's attempts to raise the rate of economic growth to over 6 percent are likely to be frustrated.

The Government finds it difficult to reduce the fiscal deficit by reducing the expenditure on populist programmes in an election year. At the same time, it has tried to moderate the rate of monetary growth by borrowing Rs. 40,000 crore from the banking system against the expansion of bank credit of only Rs. 23,000 crore. The Government can think of reducing the fiscal deficit by selling vast stretches of prime urban land need by the railways, the defence establishment and by itself. The Government can realise Rs. 5,000 - 10,000 crore by selling this land and using the proceeds to cover the fiscal deficit. If this is done, the liquidity position in the economy can be ease by enhancing bank credit to the non-food sector by allowing the multiplier accelerator mechanism to operate to raise the rate of economic growth. This will serve to increase output which will serve as an antidote to inflation. Inflation thus has to be fought from the side of demand and also from the side of supply. The fight against inflation from the supply front is more efficacious than the fight from the demand front.

The Government seems to be concerned with controlling inflation rather than with accelerating the rate of economic growth. A higher rate of growth generates larger output which counteracts the inflationary pressures. This calls for a policy of easing the liquidity crunch which, though imposing inflationary pressure in the short run, promotes economic growth which enlarges output which counteracts the ongoing inflation. Therefore, preference should be for a higher growth rate instead of a lower rate of inflation.

14

A Mechanism of Curbing States' Deficits

Ever since the Finance Minister presented his budget for 1994-95 on 28.2.1994 assuring that the fiscal deficit would be brought down to 6 percent of GDP in 1994-95 from 7.3 percent in 1993-94, public attention has been focused on how the Union Government will conduct its financial affairs. In his Budget speech the Finance Minister admitted in the preceding year, the deficit had overshot the Budget estimate. Even at 6 percent of GDP the fiscal deficit would be looming large but the finance minister expressed confidence that it would be brought down to 4.7 percent in 1994-95.

In the target of fiscal deficit little attention has been paid to the behaviour of State Governments. Almost every state in the Indian Union has run up huge deficits: the aggregate amount for all the states comes to Rs. 1,25,000 crore. This figure should be worrisome because it adds upto 4.1 percent of GDP. In a tri-fiscal system the deficits of the State Governments are as inflationary as the deficits of the Central Government. Unless the deficit of the State Governments are reduced mere reduction of the fiscal deficit of the Central government will not be of much avail in the task of inflation control. For even if the fiscal deficit of the centre is brought down to 4.7 percent, if the deficits of the State Governments, in their aggregate remain at 4.1 percent the total fiscal deficit will be 8.8 percent of GDP. This was the position of the Central Budget in 1990-91 when the inflation rate ruled at 17.5 percent. Luckily, the inflation rate has come down to 9.75 percent. It is pertinent to remember that the Finance Minister had assured the nation that the rate of inflation would be brought down to the single digit figure by October 1994. If the decline in the rate of inflation continues it is expected that by October 1994 it will be around 8 percent. This will show that the Finance Minister has redeemed his pledge. If the deficits of the State Governments are also brought down the rate of inflation is likely to fall to 6 percent. Can we expect this to happen?

The problems of State finances are highly complex. The Central government has greater powers to raise resources and to increase its revenues than the States. In the event of financial crises the Central Government has borrowed from the multilateral financial agencies to fill the gap. This avenue is constitutionally closed to the States. Besides this the revenues of the States are not as buoyant or as elastic as those of the Central Government. Some choose to hold this as a justification for the fiscal behaviour of the States. Constitutionally, the States may not be left with enough room by way of taxes to raise revenues. The Seventh Schedule of the constitution lists the division of taxes between the Centre and the States. A number of taxes coming under the States' jurisdiction do not generate any revenue mainly because the States do not think it worth their while to levy them or because they yield a paltry sum like the power rates because of subsidisation for agricultural consumers.

It is held by many that too much power rests with the Centre and too little power rests with the States. On the face of it, this may seem valid. The Centre can raise foreign loans while the States cannot. In fact, the extent of their internal borrowing is limited by their repayment of earlier loans. As almost all the States are indebted to the Central Government, their capacity to raise internal loans is severely limited. The States have traditionally relied on such loans for capital expenditure than on market borrowings. In view of this the reduction of internal loans has a severe impact on capital expenditure.

If, for example, there is a greater devolution of financial powers to the States without evolving a mechanism for monitoring capital usage, it will create more problems. If the Seventh Schedule of the constitution is modified to allow States the exclusive or partial revenue from corporate taxes, or if the States are permitted to raise revenue through market borrowings or if the Planning Commission and the Finance Commission become more generous than at present in their awards to States, can there be any assurance that the States will use the capital resources more prudently?

It is not necessarily so. During the past 15 years transfers from the centre have remained constant at around a percent of central expenditure. Even so, the indebtedness of State Governments is growing. In 1993-94 gross transfers from the Centre increased by 38 percent but net transfers were no more than 30 percent because the rest went into servicing of debt.

Recently, Shri S. Venkataramanan, a former Governor of the Resever Bank of India, proposed that an Inter-State Monetary organisation be set up to deal with the finances of the States. This organisation could monitor the finances of every state, organise a rational allocation of resources and even help to raise money from the market. This is an eminently sensible proposal whose details need to be elucidated and implemented in the interests of fiscal balance in the country.

The Indian union is made up of several states each being independent of the others in many respects. Thus the Indian macrocosm is divided into a multitude of microcosm which are a crazy quilt of patches with no warm sense of unity. There are many unresolved riparian disputes, border disputes and disputes of a similar nature. These disputes have intensified inter-state rivalry and even discord. Some years ago some states had planned to secede from the union to form an independent nation founded on ethnic uniqueness. These criteria do not satisfy many of the states. They raise the bogey of inequity in the matter of allocation of federal resources. The endowments of resources, the rates of economics growth vary from state to state. Each state has its own planning commission which prepares a plan fixing the growth target unmindful of the ground realities. The states seem to feel that the rate of economics growth is a function of expenditure. For this reason each state plans for expenditure which it can hardly meet from out of its revenues and transfers from the centre. Labouring under severe resource crunch each state stands like Oliver Twist with a bowl in hand. The more it is given, the more it needs. Its thirst for resources is insatiable. But the centre's resource position does not allow it to meet all their insensate demands. The states spend a considerable part of their resources on non-plan items like administration, interest payment on the debt and profligacy of the ministers and their staff. Given the need to meet capital expenditure they have to run deficits to meet the current non-plan expenditures. These deficits, in their totality, fuel inflation. It is not enough if the Central Government reduces its fiscal deficit. It is equally necessary for the state Governments to reduce their fiscal deficits in order to reduce the rate of inflation.

As averred above, the Central Government can borrow from the international financial institutions to fill the fiscal gap agreeing to abide by the conditionality prescriptions of the lending agencies. This helps to hold down the fiscal deficit of the center. An inter-state monetary organisation functioning more or less like the IMF is necessary to help the State Governments to reduce their fiscal deficits. Four decades of Centre-State relations have engineered futile debates on financial devolution. Even so, no light has been thrown the mode of monitoring the finances of the States. There is pressure from outside on the Centre to arm at fiscal consolidation. In a similar manner the States need for pressure on the State Governments from a new institution to use their capital resources productivity.

The States have exclusive jurisdiction over their respective finances. As their resources are not elastic any increase in their current expenditure will be at the expense of their capital expenditure or by increasing their market borrowings. This leads to their deficits with inflationary consequences. The Inter-State Monetary Organisation (IMO) has to call for the revenue and expenditure statements of each State and prescribe the targetted deficit for each State which should be adhered to in letter and spirit. The IMO should have the authority to borrow from the market and to obtain assistance from the Centre and to constitute a fund from which it should make loans to be repaid from them as per the prescribed schedule. Of course, the interest charged will have to be equal to the market rate of interest. The States should be required to adhere to the deficit prescribed by the IMO. In exceptional circumstances like natural calamities when the assistance offered by the Centre from the Calamity Relief Fund (CRF) is meagre, the State can be allowed to exceed the limit of deficit prescribed by the conditionalities of the IMO. But in ordinary circumstances the limit of deficit should be strictly adhered to. At the same time, the Fiscal Commission should revise the criteria of allocation so that the criteria conform to the requirements of fiscal equity. In the matter of fiscal transfers in a federation the roots of wealth lie elsewhere and not at the point of collection. The States where they are collected should not gloat over the fact that their contribution to the kitty is significant and for this reason they should get a larger allocation. All the States in the federation have contributed to the kitty and it is by accident that the points of collection are located in certain States like Bombay. Until recently the Gadgil Formula and then the revised Gadgil Formula and then the re-revised Gadgil Formula were there to govern federal fiscal transfers. Even they are found wanting in several respects. A set of new criteria is to be devised to meet the emerging challenges. What these criteria should be is for the Fiscal Commission to evolve. The Fiscal Commission (The Pant Commission) which is grappling with the task of fiscal transfers should appoint a sub-committee just to evolve a set of progressive criteria to govern fiscal transfers. These criteria should be forwarded to the States for their comments. In the light of their comments they should be revised. It is true that no criterion or no set of criteria is satisfying to the States. Justice is always rough. This should be borne in mind by the State Governments. This is the only way in which the fiscal deficits of the State Governments can be brought under control.

One may be tempted to argue that this mechanism erodes the sovereignty of the State Governments in the management of their public finances. If this argument is valid, the arguments of the opposition political parties in the country that the Central Government borrowing from the IMF accepting its stiff conditionalities would erode the sovereignty of India should also be held to be equally valid. But this is to stretch the sovereignty argument too far. The IMF which advances loans to sovereign nations has to make sure of the safety and security of its loans as otherwise the loans may become unrepayable in which case it will accumulate bad debts. In a similar manner the IMO should make sure that the loans it makes to the States are safe and secure and that they do not degenerate into bad debts. This should not be taken to involve surrender of the sovereignty to a supra-state monetary organisation. Seen in this light, the institution of the IMO is eminently desirable. Otherwise there will be no check on the profligacy of the States which sows the seeds of macroeconomic instability. The Centre should keep its house it order by ensuring fiscal consolidation and set an example to the State Governments to emulate. The burden of this elucidation is that fiscal deficits should be brought down at all levels of Government in order to maintain macro-economic stability.

15

Exchange Rate Bank, Import Liberalisation and Full Convertibility of the Rupee on Current Account

The Reserve Bank of India has been following a policy of intervention in the forex market in order to prop up the sagging dollar. In consequence, the rupee-dollar exchange rate is kept constant at Rs. 31.37 per dollar. Early in July 1994 the foreign exchange traders trained their guns on the almighty dollar. But now despite an abortive attempt by European central banks to support the US dollar, it has crashed below the 100 Yen level and has also slipped against the deutsche mark. Through this turbulence the Reserve Bank of India has not let up its support for the sagging dollar. It has continued to maintain the dollar at Rs. 31.37 as it has done since July 1993. Therefore, despite a dollar deluge, primarily the result of a low trade deficit and unprecedented capital inflows, the rupee has remained steady against the dollar, the official intervention currency. The reason is that the dollars that have poured into India has been gobbled up by the Reserve Bank. Eventually even the Reserve Bank seemed to be tired of the dollar constant and allowed it to fluctuate in a slightly wider band than before. It is felt that this is only a prelude to allowing the scope to appreciate a little after which the Reserve Bank would intervene to maintain the rupee in a wider band at a higher value.

The Reserve Bank of India at present is reported to be formulating an exchange rate band for the Indian rupee. This would allow the rupee to fluctuate against the dollar within a certain band. The introduction of the new mechanism will pave the way for the Reserve Bank to withdraw gradually from the exchange market. The Reserve Bank will intervene in the exchange market only when the exchange rate touches the ceiling or the floor. The exact levels the ceiling and the floor rates are yet to be decided. The absence of intervention so long as the exchange rate is within the band should indicate the real strength or weakness of the rupee. The foreign exchange market is agog with rumour of the impending introduction of the exchange rate band and exporters are in a frenzy to sell their receivables forward. This has resulted in a crash in the forward premium on the dollar which had persisted ever since current account convertibility was launched. At present, the forward premium on the dollar has reached its record low of 1.9 per cent against 3 per cent towards the end of July 1994. Earlier, the forward premium had remained at a steady 6 percent for a long time. Besides, the conspicuous absence of importers in the local market is taking the premium down. The eventual withdrawal of the Reserve Bank of India from the local exchange market has become inevitable because of the heavy costs involved in such operations. Thus, the reported decision of the Reserve Bank to fix a band on the exchange rate is welcome.

A long and sustained debate has gone on the virtues of fixed and flexible exchange rates. Under the traditional gold standard the exchange rate was fixed and gold flows would cause inflation or deflation depending on whether there was a gold inflow of gold outflow. Further, under the gold standard fixed exchange rate led to the international transmission of trade cycles. Flexible exchange rates were stated to generate exchange rate instability and through it to generate domestic instability as well. For these reasons the founders of the Bretton Woods Institutions opted for an adjustable peg system. Experience showed that even the system was not free from pitfalls. In the course of the debate on the planning of the international monetary system several proposals were preferred by economists about the kind of exchange rate regime that would free the domestic economy from the instability emanating from the exchange rate. One of the them is the band proposal made by Professor George Halm during the 1960s when the debate on the refurbishing of the international monetary system was taking place. According to this proposal the exchange rate would move within a band which would have an upper limit and a lower limit. If the country has a deficit in the balance of payments indicating an excess supply of the currency, the currency would depreciate making exports cheaper and imports dearer. This would stimulate exports, discourage imports until the trade balance was restored. If, on the other hand, the country had a favourable balance of payments indicating an excess demand for the currency the currency would appreciate and appreciation would make imports cheaper and exports dearer. This would discourage exports, stimulate imports until the trade balance was restored. Thus, the exchange rate would move within a band. It is only when the exchange rate moves outside the limits set by the band the Central Bank would intervene in the foreign exchange market in order to pull the exchange rate back to the band. Thus, if the exchange rate goes above the upper limit indicating absolute appreciation, the Central Bank would increase the supply of the currency and purchase foreign currency. The demand for foreign currency would reduce the degree of appreciation and bring it down to inside the band. If on the other hand, the exchange rate goes below the lower limit indicating depreciation the Central Bank would sell foreign currency and this would reduce the degree of depreciation and bring it upto inside the band. This policy has to be supported by monetary policy. The monetary target should also move within a band. Professor Milton Friedman suggested a monetary growth rate of 3 percent per annum. This is a rigid rate of growth of money supply which does not adjust to changes in other variables. Thus, in the event of the exchange rate moving outside the upper limit, the monetary growth target should move towards 5 percent; in the event of the exchange rate moving outside the lower limit the monetary growth target should move towards 3 percent. These monetary growth movements will help to steady the exchange rate. The upper and lower limits of the band for exchange rate movements and for monetary growth movements proposed here are not sacrosanct or unalterable. They are indicated here only for illustrative purposes. What the width of these bands should be is an empirical question and the width of these bands is to be determined pragmatically in the light of the actual exchange rate movements.

In my writings on the balance of payments I have held the view the band proposal holds the key to domestic stability, infact in my Memorandum forwarded to the Dr. C. Rangarajan Committee on the Balance of Payments in October 1991. I strongly advocated the adoption of the band proposal and its adjunct, the monetary growth rate. This combines the virtues of the flexible exchange rate mechanism as the exchange rate moves up and down within the band and of the fixed exchange rate mechanism as the exchange rate cannot move outside the limits in the band. If the exchange rate moves outside the limits set by the band, changes in the monetary growth rate act as a corrective mechanism. In view of this, I welcome the reported decision of the Reserve Bank of India to adopt the band scheme in respect of exchange rate movements.

There is a massive inflow of dollars into the value of the Reserve Bank of India. At present the forex reserves stand at $ 17 billion and they are expected to go up to $ 20 billion by the end of the fiscal 1994-95. This is a major cause of inflation in the Indian economy. Until 1992-93 net Reserve Bank credit to Government accounting for the major chunk of money supply (M_3) expansion but in the past two years, the scenario has changed. Now it is the increase in the forex reserves that is the major contribution to M_3 expansion. Its share increased from 7.8 percent during the period from 1987-88 to 1991-92 to 40-42 percent during the two subsequent years. Indeed the increase in the net foreign exchange reserves of the Reserve Bank of India in 1993-94 was more than the total increase in reserve money. To some extent this was neutralised by the Reserve Bank's open market operations but no one questions that the increase in forex reserves is a direct and important contribution to inflation. This has generated a vicious circle. To help exports the Reserve Bank maintains the rupee-dollar rate constant. But in buying up dollars it puts rupees into the system. In so doing it adds to money supply and fuels inflation thereby pushing up the real exchange rate of the rupee. If the Reserve Bank reduces the purchase of dollars the rupee would appreciate gradually and more towards the upper limit in the band. This money to some extent affect exports adversely, but the consequent slowing down of the rate of inflation would compensate to some extent. Furthermore, an appreciation of the rupee would make imports cheap. This would also encourage exports by reducing the cost of imported inputs. In this way a movement of the exchange rate towards the upper limit is beneficial.

India's imports during 1993-94 amounted to $ 23.19 billion which was roughly a tenth of the country's GDP during the year. Allowing the rupee to appreciate by 10 percent (by making it move towards the upper limit along the band) would reduce prices of 10 percent of the GDP by 10 percent in rupee terms. In other words, it would reduce overall inflation by 1 percent. At a time when the prices of all essential commodities are rising, a 1 percent drop in the rate of inflation would bring it down to 9.25 percent from the present 10.25 percent. This should be regarded as a perceptible fall in the rate of inflation. In this way the adoption of the band proposal would reduce the rate of inflation and would also stimulate exports to some extent, other things being equal.

It must be admitted that though the favourable impact of a slight appreciation of the rupee on the trade balance may be there in the medium term in the short run it might depress exports and stimulate imports. At present, the trade deficit is there though its magnitude is very small and is easily manageable. Normally appreciation of the currency is adopted in the context of a favourable balance of trade. The question may arise whether it is advisable to appreciate the rupee, however gently, when there is a trade deficit. Over two years ago when non-debt capital inflows were very meagre India had to look towards exports to pay for imports which were surging. When exports fell India had to cut down its imports with adverse effects on the rate of economic growth.

It is necessary to consider the trade prospects of India in the short run. The growth in exports was helped considerably by partial and then full convertibility of the rupee in 1992-93 and 1993-94 respectively. However, the price advantage on account of convertibility tends to get exhausted after a while. Exports are more demand-driven rather than supply-driven and they cannot be sustained unless there is a change in the composition and unless they are in demand in the importing countries. India's anti-export bias has now yielded place to pro-export bias. This will be successful if India's exports are in demand in world markets. Besides, the rupee being held at a higher rate than the market would support, exports may find it difficult to rise substantially. Furthermore, any widening of the inflation differential between India and other trading nations is bound to undermine the competitiveness of Indian exports. Some of the recent developments in the world outside India cannot be considered to be helpful. The industrialised countries are keenly interested in the market-driven reforms in the Asian developing countries mainly because these reforms open up vast markets for them. But market-driven reforms are also making Asia's economics including India's highly effective players in the world market. This, the industrialised countries cannot relish. So exports from India will find road blocks all the way. While India is opening up to the world, the world is indulging in protectionism and in erecting tariff walls and non-tariff restrictions in the name of social dumping, human rights, environmental control or technical factors. There will be temptation to use the very GATT mechanism to restrict the entry of our competitive high-quality products into their own markets. India, like some other countries in Asia, will then be left to find that it is deprived the full benefit of its natural comparative advantages like abundant manpower and rich natural resources to penetrate the world markets. India may even find that the grievance redressal machinery of the new World Trade Organisation (WTO) is tiresomely slow moving. However, it is hoped that the Marrakesh trade accord will open up world markets to India's exports in the medium and long run.

The behaviour of imports presents a dual image. Lower imports do help to alleviate the balance of payments problem. However, if the rate of growth is low despite convertibility it also means that industry is not importing the quantum of goods which one would have expected, given that the customs duty rate has been lowered continuously, from 85 percent to 65 percent in the Union Budget for 1994-95. This means that capital investment is lower which would have long-run consequences on the growth process. These developments in the export and import sectors have led to a marginal improvement in the balance of payments situation. The current account deficit which was $ 9.6 billion in 1990-91 fell to $ 230 million in 1993-94 and the trade deficit declined from $ 5.93 billion to $ 1.04 billion.

The Finance Minister is in favour of liberalising consumer goods imports as an anti-inflationary measure. Though this may stem inflation it will create a trade gap. An increase in consumer goods imports will increase competition for domestic producers. It will thus provide a stimulus to domestic consumer goods industries to bring about much needed improvements in efficiency and quality. Therefore, the policy of liberalisation has passed these industries by. Through the effects of current partial liberalisation of trade, they have even received higher protection than before. Imports of machinery, equipment and intermediate goods have been freed and the duties on them have been lowered, while imports of consumer goods have remained restricted and are even now subject to high duties. Therefore, domestic consumer goods industries now receive higher protection than before. This imbalance in the effects of liberalisation must be rectified. Greater competition will put Indian consumer goods industries on their mettle. It should prepare India for the export of new classes of sophisticated consumer goods. This policy of import liberalisation will add to the trade gap though it will help to bring down the rate of inflation.

The shortage in the output of cotton, sugar and oil seeds in the 1993-94 season is proving to be costly at a time when it was expected that the performance on the trade front will again be encouraging in 1994-95 and so the trade gap will not be rising even with dearer crude and petroleum products. However, imports of 8-10 lakh tonnes of sugar alone will involve an expenditure of Rs. 1300 crore in foreign exchange while purchases of cotton may also be costing Rs. 500 crore. The shortfall in availability of edible oils from indigenous sources is more pronounced than visualised earlier as the summer groundnut crop in Tamil Nadu and Andhra Pradesh is affected by unfavourable weather conditions while the decline in the yields of soyabeans and the availability of cotton seed has been more than earlier calculations. The demand for edible oil can be met only if the imports of 2-3 lakh tonnes can be secured in the coming months. These imports may cost Rs. 600 crore. Thus the expected outgo of forex reserves on the import of three products in short supply may be Rs. 2500 crore. If the oil bill also costs additionally Rs. 2000 crore even with no significant increase in quantum there will have to be a faster growth of exports especially as other imports also have been increasing in volume due to a higher level of industrial production. If there is a cut back in imports of cotton and edible oils due to the improvement in the yield of cotton crop and oil seeds in the 1994-95 season it will provide some relief. But at present no definite view of the prospects of cotton and oil seeds production can be taken. With the import liberalisation programme to absorb the forex reserves and to act as an antidote to inflation the trade gap is likely to be bigger than anticipated.

This raises the question of whether a trade surplus is evidence of strength or a trade deficit evidence of weakness of a country's economy. The US economist Paul Krugman points out in a recent seminal article: "In both theory and practice, a trade surplus may be a sign of national weakness, a deficit a sign of strength". He cites the case of Mexico which, in the 1980s, was forced to run huge trade surpluses in order to pay the interest on its foreign debt since international investors refused to lend it any more money. It began to run large trade deficits after 1990 as foreign investors recovered confidence and began to pour new funds. Krugman queries: "Would any one want to describe Mexico as a highly competitive nation during the debt crisis era or describe what has happened since 1990 as a loss of competitiveness"? This question needs to be put about India also. India seems to be paying far too much attention to the trade balance to the neglect of the capital account flows of the development variety. A gently appreciating rupee within the prescribed band can attract capital inflows. Foreign investors would remain satisfied with smaller return on their investment if there is no risk of a depreciating rupee and they stand to gain from an appreciating rupee provided the appreciation is within the upper limit of the prescribed band. The foreign direct investors and foreign portfolio investors are concerned not so much with the exports which are less than a tenth of the GDP as with the giant and expanding domestic market. If profits from domestic investment are high they will invest enough funds which will finance imports. At the same time, the Government is of the opinion that more imports are not a bad thing after all for two reasons. (a) The Finance Minister wants to liberalise imports in order to contain inflation directly. (b) Larger imports mean more customs revenues so necessary to reduce the fiscal deficit. This will again help to reduce the rate of inflation. At the same time it will make more capital available to industry at lower interest rates thus reducing the cost of production and also cost inflation. In view of this, an upward movement of the exchange rate towards the upper limit within the prescribed band appears desirable.

There is ample evidence to show that the foreign investors are coming to India with euphoric expectations despite the discouraging credit rating given by the international rating agencies. Standard and poor whose services were commissioned by Government of India a few months ago is reported to be likely to rate India one notch below the investment grade, a rate first arrived at in February 1991 that is, before the current reform programme was initiated. The reasons for the non-upgradation are, however, changing. Earlier, high level of foreign debt relative to export receipts, inefficiencies in the industrial sector and large investment requirements in social and physical infrastructure were some of the reasons professed. In the S & P's most recent study, political instability is reported to be the most important reason. It must be mentioned that the earlier reasons have lost some of their validity. Foreign inflows, particularly of the non-debt creating variety, have been increasing rapidly. Foreign direct investment which was $ 148 million in 1991-92 rose sharply to $ 550 million in 1993-94. FDI approvals, since the reforms began, are close to $ 5 billion. A recent comparative study concluded that the FDI environment in India is comparable to that of South Korea, Taiwan and Indonesia and is more open than that of China and Malaysia. Exports, notwithstanding their recent downturn have been growing steadily. Moreover, optimism is written large over virtually every study on India's growth prospects. In view of this, the refusal to raise India's credit rating by the S & P agency has given rise to the suspicion that there is a deliberate attempt at arm twisting. In view of this, the credit rating by the S & P agency which is suspect, is not to be taken seriously.

Gradual appreciation of the rupee upto the upper limit in the band will mean a slow inflow of foreign exchange reserves which, to that extent, cause monetary expansion. This is to be absorbed in order to mitigate the pressure on the price level. The Finance Minister in his budget for 1994-95 held out the promise that the rupee would be made fully convertible on current account. This exercise is to be undertaken within "the next few weeks". This makes foreign currency freely available to those who can afford foreign travel. This and the proposed import liberalisation will enable the siphoning off of the rupees injected by the Reserve Bank. Importers, like travellers abroad, would then pay the banks rupees thus reducing the money supply to buy foreign currency to pay for the goods bought from abroad. This would increase the supply of goods in the economy and thus help to reduce the rate of inflation. Besides encouraging the expenditure of foreign currency, full current account convertibility will also mean a squeeze on the inflow of non-resident deposits with the banks. FCNR(A) deposits which are of the order of $ 10 billion will lose the exchange rate guarantee from the Government as under the band, exchange rate guarantee cannot be given. This combined with the reduction in interest rates offered for these deposits will slow down the growth of FCNR(A) deposits. There is also the possibility of these deposits being withdrawn. Besides this, with full current account convertibility other non-resident India deposits amounting to $ 6 billion will be entitled to repatriate freely the interest accruals. This causes a change in the pattern of non-resident deposits. This results in a decline in the growth of non-resident deposits. In this way, getting the rupee Article VIII status of the IMF will involve free use of foreign exchange and the withdrawal of extra-market management of non-resident foreign currency deposits. This will slow down the rate of accumulation of foreign exchange reserves. This will mitigate the pressure on the rupee to appreciate. However, if foreign institutional investors continue to send money to India in the same way as they did in 1993-94 reserve accumulations might pickup. But with the gradual appreciation of the rupee upto the upper limit the inflow might slow down. However, if the appreciation goes beyond the upper limit, the Reserve Bank of India has to intervene to purchase foreign currency in order to keep the exchange rate at the upper limit or within the band. This will inevitably cause monetary expansion. With full current account convertibility of the rupee and the liberalisation of imports the money supply will be absorbed and this will hold down the rate of inflation. Thus, the adoption of the exchange band, liberalisation of imports and full current account convertibility will free the economy from the inflationary consequences of foreign exchange reserve accumulations.

It is contended in certain quarters that instead of liberalising consumer goods imports the Government should liberalise the import of capital goods and advanced technology. At present aggregate investment in the Indian economy remains on the low side. Of course, investment needs to be given a fillip to increase the capacity of the economy to import advanced technology with foreign exchange. The Union Finance Minister has proposed a further liberalisation of consumer goods imports in view of the rising forex reserves. He has stated that the strategy of liberalising imports is by no means out of line with the current policies being pursued by the Government. Moreover, the neighbouring South Asian Countries have a more liberal regime. Unless India moves in tandem with its neighbours, smuggling of banned items could again become a menace, with its attendant ill-effects on the country's economy.

The current comfortable forex reserves position has to be considered in the context of the emerging trends in the balance of payments situation and flow of external payments. Undoubtedly the current level of forex reserves of around $ 17 billion can be considered healthy. But if there is a surge in imports under the liberalised import regime and also as a result of the pickup in economies activity in general and in the industrial sector in particular this level may turn out to be small. It has been noticed that open economies show their economies strength by having a reasonably high level of reserves. For example, a small country like the Republic of China (Taiwan) has foreign exchange reserves of around $ 70 billion, which have been accumulated over the years and which indicates the economic strength of the country.

In order to prevent the expansion of aggregate demand fiscal policy has to be employed. In many countries this route has been tried. It can therefore be argued that if the Government is successful in keeping under control the budgetary and fiscal deficits, the rising forex reserves at a reasonable accretion of 3-4 billion per year should not pose any problem. For this will push the exchange rate gently towards the upper limit in the band. If, however, the exchange rate goes above the upper limit, the Reserve Bank intervenes to purchase it and this will not allow the exchange rate to move above this upper limit. This will increase the stock of forex reserves. But this will be taken care of by rising imports and the full convertibility of the rupee on current account.

Neither a stable exchange rate nor a floating exchange rate is necessary for India in the present situation. The maintenance of a stable exchange rate over time would depend largely on the achievement of a sustainable balance between exports and imports. In this the exchange rate itself will play an equilibrating role. However, there will be an increasing link between exchange rate and the stance of monetary policy and the overall price situation. Thus, to maintain a reasonably stable exchange rate it would be necessary to have a stable domestic price situation. But the domestic price situation at present is far from stable.

If capital flows into the country, in a regime of floating exchange rates, there will be a nominal appreciation of the rupee. The extent of appreciation necessary to eliminate the excess supply of foreign exchange will depend on the elasticities of exports and imports. It is generally believed that such an appreciation may be undesirable from the point of view of export promotion. In view of this, uncontrolled appreciation of the rupee will adversely affect the trade balance.

In view of the foregoing analysis, adoption of the exchange rate band combined with liberalised imports and full convertibility of the rupee on current account will free the economy from the danger of inflation. Of course, the fiscal deficit which is a major source of inflation needs to be brought down. The Finance Minister has assured the nation that the fiscal deficit would be brought down to 6 percent of GDP before long. This should help to bring the rate of inflation down to the single digit figure. Of course, what the width of the band should be is left to the Reserve Bank of India to determine. This is purely an empirical decision. It must be said that the exchange rate band will free the economy from the danger of unbridled appreciation of the exchange rate caused by a policy of non-intervention in the forex market. This has to be tried in India.

16

The Problem of Inflation Management

As the date of presentation of the Union Budget for 1995-96 is fast approaching, the problem of reducing the fiscal deficit assumes unprecedented significance. The rising rate of inflation compels a reduction of the fiscal deficit which is said to be one of the causes of double digit inflation; at the same time, the compulsions of maintaining subsidies undiminished and incurring social expenditure on the eve of the elections to the Lok Sabha in 1996 have to be reckoned with. This has made the task of reducing the fiscal deficit difficult despite the buoyancy of tax revenues though fiscal deficit is just one of the many causes of a rising rate of inflation.

There are two ways in which the rate of inflation can be brought down: Supply Management and Demand Management. Despite the accumulated stock of 31 million tonnes of food in the Government warehouses the food prices are rising. There is a severe shortage of cotton, edible oils and pulses and this shortage has led to a rise in prices. Though imports have been arranged for in order to increase the supply of these commodities in the domestic market, the fact that the prices of these goods in the world markets are high, the imported prices have per force to be high too despite the increase in their supply. The prices of non-ferrous metals, petro-chemicals and heavy chemicals have also been higher because of the rising import prices. The domestic producers of the related products have raised their selling prices in the domestic market. They also export large quantities which, in turn, accelerate the rise in domestic prices. If the output of cotton, edible oils and pulses increases and if the world prices of these goods also decline, there is likely to be a decline in the domestic prices of these commodities. But nothing definite can be said about until the 1995-96 Kharif season. In the meanwhile the Finance Minister has to take note of the special factors responsible for the upsurge in prices in some directions. Efforts have to be made to convince the weaker sections of society that action is being taken to reduce the cost of living index. This may necessitate an increase in food subsidies and subsidies on fertilisers. This means that the Finance Minister finds it difficult to minimise the burden of subsidies however much he may wish to reduce it. At the same time there will be the imperative need to increase the allocation for social welfare expenditure. The Finance Minister can afford to increase these expenditures if the present uptrend in revenues continues in 1995-96 also. It is expected that with the expectation of a rise in industrial output and the sale of this output bearing excise duties and also the increase in the import of dutible non-oil imports there will be an increase in tax revenues. This may help the Finance Minister to reduce the fiscal deficit in percentage terms, if not in absolute terms. If it is possible to borrow the required sum, the overall deficit can be reduced to Rs. 6,000 crore. This is possible because of the fact that an assurance has been given to the Reserve Bank of India that borrowing through the issue of adhoc treasury bills will be discontinued in three years.

The fiscal deficits in the years 1991-95 when aggregated will be of the order of Rs. 1,89,964 crore. This covers the overall deficit of Rs. 34,047 crore. The fiscal deficit in 1991-92 was Rs. 36,325 crore; in 1992-93 it was Rs. 40,173 crore in 1993-94 it was 58551 crore in 1994-95 it was Rs. 54915 crore. (BE). In 1995-96 the size of the fiscal deficit needs to be reduced. Even if it is around Rs. 50,000 crore, borrowing in various forms may be difficult in the absence of a big increase in investible funds of the banking sector, and also additions to the resources of the LIC. Provident funds and other institutional investors. In the earlier years the fiscal deficits were covered by obtaining market loans, special credit in provident funds etc. Later as the scope for increasing borrowing from the institutional investors expanded, the Government was able to obtain substantial amounts through 91 days and 364 days treasury bills. The same pattern of borrowing may be continued in 1995-96 also though some difficulties may be experienced if there is no decline in discount rates or if there is no improvement in investible resources. The Government has also to decide on the desirability of borrowing on dearer terms in which case there will be a rise in the interest cost of the public debt and hence a rise in the fiscal deficit. This, of course, calls for financing the deficit by borrowing from the Reserve Bank of India instead of from the market. It is held in recent fiscal theory that while both monetary financing and debt financing of the deficit are inflationary, debt financing is more inflationary than monetary financing considering the fact that the former adds to the fiscal deficit on a continuing basis while the financing of the deficit by money creation has an inflationary effect once and for all. Therefore monetary financing of the deficit is one of the methods of reducing the fiscal deficit. With a reduction in the fiscal deficit and an increase in the domestic output of supplies in 1995-96 the rate of inflation can be halted even if it cannot be brought down to the single digitzone.

But what of the demand side of the inflation management? The Reserve Bank of India was blaming the excess liquidity in the economy as a cause of inflation. But ironically enough it was under pressure to pump Rs. 2000 crore into the market on a single day to ease the liquidity crisis. There is also a reversal of policy in the case of interest rates. Despite the surging inflationary pressure, the Reserve Bank of India in mid-October 1994 announced the busy season credit policy deregulating the interest rates. The lending rates were lowered in the hope that the banks would compete among themselves to lower the interest rates and supply low cost credit to industry and business. It was thought that this would counter the inflationary pressure. But within less than three months the lending rate was raised by one percent taking the prime rate to 15 percent and the real rate to 10-19 percent. The busy season credit policy has virtually collapsed. There is also a reversal of the inflation management strategy of the Reserve Bank of India which wanted to mop up excess liquidity from the system. The Reserve Bank also was expected to offload dated securities in the open market and to absorb liquidity. But contrary to expectations the Reserve Bank could offload securities worth Rs. 1,600 crore in 1994 instead of Rs. 9,000 crore worth of securities in 1993. In the process the Reserve Bank injected Rs. 2000 to Rs. 2500 crore in order to ease the liquidity crunch in the money market, in order to hold down the rate of rise in lending rates.

There has been a change in the strategy of the Government to go in for market borrowing to finance the fiscal deficit. This has made the Government one of the largest borrowers in the market pushing out industrial borrowers. The Reserve Bank has cautioned the banks to be more prudent in the matter of fund management. In a recent function in Delhi the Reserve Bank Governor pointed out:

"......banks need to equip themselves to operate in a more deregulated interest rate environment. They should be able to fix the rates of deposits and loans depending upon the overall liquidity conditions, demand factors and their impact on profitability. The call money market rates remained subdued during the greater part of the year. However, in recent periods, the rates showed a substantial volatility with the rates rising sometimes as high as 40 percent. Some tightening of the call money market during a period of rapid expansion in credit is to be expected. However, sharp swings may be due to temporary factors such as withdrawal of funds for tax purposes etc".

Continuing the Governor went on to say "While the call rates in the market can always be moderated by supply of additional funds by the RBI as was done recently the RBI can provide liquidity only to tide over temporary situations. Banks need to take appropriate action to forecast adequately the liquidity requirements and minimise liability mismatches. Excessive dependence on the call money market for expanding credit must be avoided".

The temporary factors listed by the RBI Governor, as causing liquidity crisis are:

1. The bulk deals in borrowings of some Rs .11000 crore taken out of the system in November and December.
2. Rs. 1600 crore in RBI open market operations.
3. Rs. 1000 crore in new Government securities by banks.
4. Subscription to UTI Unit '64 rights issue estimated to be Rs. 3600 crore.

5. Public sector disinvestment of Rs. 2500 crore.
6. Advance tax payment due in December placed between Rs. 2,500 crore and Rs. 300 crore.
7. The shooting up of bank credit to the commercial sector.

Thus the liquidity crisis in the market is more to do with the availability of lendable resources than the liquidity in the system which is, of course, at a high level. The Reserve Bank is not able to intervene effectively in the matter of controlling liquidity in the system.

Apart from liquidity, the prime cause of continuing inflationary pressure is the monetary impact of capital inflow. There has been a flow of foreign institutional investment into the Indian capital market. This is aided by the raising of capital in the European capital markets by the Indian corporate sector which started in December 1993 and continued up to September 1994. This inflow had the effect of appreciating the external value of the rupee. In order to keep the exchange value of the rupee stable the Reserve Bank had to intervene in the market to buy up the incoming dollars. In consequence the exchange rate of the rupee stands stable at Rs. 31.37 per dollar. This caused the monetary expansion which was the prime cause of inflation. While announcing the busy season credit policy in mid-October 1994 the Reserve Bank Governor said that the source of reserve money expansion in 1994-95 till September 1995 had been through the increase in net foreign assets of the Reserve Bank which showed an increase of Rs. 15,596 crore as against a rise of Rs. 3,933 crore in the same period in 1993. The Government took steps to announce that money raised abroad by the Indian corporate sector should be parked abroad till the need for these funds in the country arises. This eased somewhat the pressure on the Reserve Bank to buy dollars.

In the meanwhile the inflow of dollars through the FIIs dried up it fell from $ 230 million in September 1994 to a paltry $ 10.1 million in November 1994. However, the inflow continued at a diminished rate.

A section of the Indian economic community feels that the Government should have opened up the Indian capital market after pushing the process of fiscal consolidation to completion. However in 1993 the fiscal restraints became extremely lax and the fiscal deficit ended up at 7.3 percent of GDP. The process of fiscal consolidation has been halted as the Government has failed to prune the subsidies. Besides this, the Government also finds it difficult to profitably disinvest public sector equity in order to mobilise resources. Thus at a time when there was substantial liquidity in the economy with great potential for inflationary pressure the Government invited liquidity from abroad through portfolio investments and added to the problem. At present foreign direct investment is a trickle and as such it does not pose much of a problem. But if it swells in the future it might create problems for the authorities.

The rate of inflation which was 11.55 percent has marginally fallen to 11.33 percent. A marginal decline in the inflation rate is a cause for official exhilaration and a marginal rise is a cause for concern. The inflation rate is playing a truant and is a cause for concern for the common man. The Finance Minister expressed the hope that the rate of inflation would fall to 7 percent by the end of 1994. After having dipped to 7 percent in the middle of 1993, the inflation rate started its upward climb in the second half of 1993. The rate went up in early 1994 after the hike in administered prices leading to an inflationary build-up in April 1994. Since then the rate has been fluctuating sometimes rising and sometimes falling. The fact to remember is that substantial inflation continues in the economy for the fifth consecutive year. The Government's hopes of controlling inflation are a fond dream. Earlier it was expected that the release of food stocks of the order of 31 million tonnes with the official agencies would increase market supply and would reduce the inflation rate. Besides, this the imports of sugar and edible oils would also help the supply side management in controlling the rate of inflation. The decision to import sugarcane too late and the initial reluctance to subsidise imports of sugar had to be abandoned. Ultimately, the imports of sugarcane to the country and the quantum of subsidies also rose. However, the entire affair became a scandal with the proceedings of the parliament being halted by the opposition and the Minister losing his job.

The foregoing narrative goes to show that the inflation management strategy was not a success. The supply management did not succeed as the anti-inflationary effect of enormous stocks of food grains and imports of sugar and edible oil was too little and came too late. The demand side management was blatantly inflationary undoing any anti-inflationary effect of supply side management. Both fiscal and monetary policies were procyclical i.e., they both added to the inflationary pressure. The subsidy element in the budget added to the fiscal deficit and proved to be inflationary. The pumping of liquidity into the economy by the Reserve Bank of India through its monetary policy and through the inflow of dollars added to the inflationary effect of the fiscal deficit. Consequently, the inflation demon continues to haunt the economy. The high inflation rate makes India's exports uncompetitive in world markets and slows down the export promotion efforts. The higher prices and incomes in the economy encourage imports and thus widen the current account deficit. Thus we witness the emergence of the inflation crisis and the balance of payment crisis. The tyranny of the twin deficits fiscal deficits and balance of payments deficits continues unabated.

China is facing the inflation crisis of great magnitude. The official rate of inflation is said to be 28 percent while the unofficial figures put the rate at 40 percent. India, fortunately, has not reached this stage as the inflow of foreign capital is not as large as that into China. However, care has to be taken to keep the inflation rate in India at no more than 7-8 percent. The World Economic Forum in 1994 stated that India is facing two problems fiscal deficit and inflation. This means that fiscal deficit has to be reduced. But given the political compulsions to keep the subsidies undiminished, reduction of fiscal deficit is an almost impossible task. The fiscal deficit has to be reduced by means of revenue buoyancy. This is the task for the Finance Minister who has to present the budget on 15.3.1995.

17

Conditions Favouring a Reduction of the Rate of Inflation

India's growth process is caught between the two blades of the growth scissors: the inflation blade and the balance of payments blade. These two jointly have impeded the growth process. It appeared as though these blades are unavoidable. But under the Finance Minister dispensation their sharpness is blunted for good. The rate of inflation which was 17.4 percent in 1991 was brought down to 7 percent in 1993-94 and again it went up to 12 percent towards the middle of 1994. The Finance Minister asserted that this rise in the rate of inflation was a seasonal phenomenon and before October 1994 the rate of inflation would fall to the single digit zone. Fortunately even before October i.e., as on 27.8.1994 the rate of inflation was 9.01 percent and it is expected to fall as the rain-god is favourable.

The balance of payments reached the crisis stage in July 1991 when the deficit was $ 9.0 billion. The Government which was faced with the problem of financing the deficit had to pledge its gold stock and to borrow from the IMF by agreeing to abide by the conditionality prescriptions. But at present, the balance of payments deficit is of the order of just Rs. 700 crore. This is not a cause for concern because of the expected surge in exports and the accumulation of forex reserves of $ 17.8 billion which is a comfortable situation. This is expected to reach $ 20.0 billion before the end of this year.

While the monetary policy is operating to reduce the rate of inflation and the fiscal policy, because of the buoyancy of tax revenues, is working in the same direction, the vast accumulation of forex reserves is acting as an expansive force stimulating monetary expansion to exacerbate and feed the ongoing inflation. This problem is not there is the other countries which are in possession of larger stocks of reserves than India. Even so, the Reserve Bank of India had to take quick measures to absorb the unexpected inflow of reserves. Thus, the forex reserves in the other countries are as under:

Brazil	$36.7 billion
South Korea	$20.8 billion
Singapore	$50.4 billion
China	$20.6 billion
Taiwan	$100.0 billion

When compared with these countries the forex reserves of India are only $ 17.8 billion. India's forex reserves are in for a further rise. The export growth rate is expected to rise to 15 percent by the end of 1994 due mainly to industrial recovery. This would further swell the inflow of forex reserves. At present the foreign exchange reserves including gold and special Drawing Rights are of the order of $ 22.3 billion. There is also improvement in the pace of direct foreign investment. The Government has already approved FDI Rs. 20,585 crore in value terms since the initiation of liberalisation over three years ago. The actual inflow stands at Rs. 4,000 crore. Of the total forex in value terms the foreign institutional investors brought in Rs. 7,979 crore since April 1992 and Rs. 11,484 crore from Euro issues and global depository receipts. At the same time, the considerable debt servicing by the Government in September is a source of relief as this will reduce the forex level. This is likely to be offset by the rise in exports due to further industrial revival resulting from the removal of restrictions on licensing and other relaxations which has induced the industrial sector to undertake modernisation and technological upgradation.

Admittedly, the upsurge in forex reserves has resulted in monetary expansion which is not restrained by a balance of payments deficit, however small. Under the traditional gold standard, a deficit in the balance of payments would cause an outflow of gold which would reduce the supply of money and the price level as the price level is determined by the supply of money is consonance with the assumptions underlying the Classical Quantity Theory of Money. A fall in the price level would increase exports and reduce imports until the trade balance was restored. But in the India case, a rise in the balance of payments deficit has not caused a fall in the rate of monetary growth. Instead, the inflow of foreign exchange reserves has led to an expansion of money supply. Thus, the rising forex reserves has had an offsetting effect on the supply of money. The remedy for this is to be found in the liberalisation of imports of consumer goods which, by increasing the availability of goods, reduce the rate of inflation. This strategy was devised by the Finance Minister who has underscored the need for removing quantitative restrictions on imports and reducing customs duties on consumer goods in a phased manner in order to counter inflation, to make Indian industry more efficient and to ensure its smooth integration with the World economy. At present Indian industry is, or feels, safe behind a high tariff wall. The height of this wall has to be reduced in the context of the Marrakesh Trade accord signed by India. All the countries with which India has trading relations, the developed countries in particular, insist that India should reduce customs duties. This insistence cannot be regarded as interference in the affairs of India as some political parties in the country seem to regard it. Furthermore, the present trend the world over is towards lower import duties. This is the most important way of increasing efficiency without which globalisation is very difficult. If globalisation is attempted with this outfit, the industrial sector will get into trouble. The days of protection or discriminating protection are gone for good. In a regime of globalisation protection has very little place.

Liberalisation of consumer goods imports exercises an anti-inflationary effect and counters the inflationary forces let lose by the surging forex reserves. The reduction of import duties exposes the Indian industry to the bracing winds of foreign competition which makes it improve its efficiency and to raise it to world levels. The reduction of import duties may be held to reduce customs revenue and to widen the fiscal deficit. But the increase in the volume of imports will, on balance, improve revenue yield. Even though the unit rate of customs revenue falls, the aggregate customs revenue rises rendering any threat of a widening of the fiscal deficit a sham threat.

With the projected reduction in the forex reserves caused by the repayment of external debt in September and the payment for consumer goods imports under the policy of import liberalisation, the inflationary effects will be mitigated. With the expected increase in revenues there will be a reduction of fiscal deficit below the targeted 6 percent of GDP in 1994-95. So, there will be a further reduction in the rate of inflation. The stage is thus set for an easy path to macro-economic stability.

18

Easing the Liquidity Crunch

At the start of the economic reform programme, India had to grapple with a balance of payments crisis, increasing account deficit, low forex reserves and a low economic growth. Thanks to the forward-looking measures and competent macro-economic management of the economy, there was a resurgence of economic growth, rising exports, controlled increase in imports and an unexpected swelling of forex reserves. But this buoyancy did not last for long. Within three years the stock of forex reserves began to dwindle. There was an excess demand for dollars causing a depreciation of the rupee.

An inflow of forex reserves had in inflationary impact. The rising reserves led to an appreciation of the rupee. In addition, rising exports also had their impact on the external value of the rupee. Appreciation had the effect of reducing the competitiveness of exports. The Government had to take corrective measures to stem appreciation. The Reserve Bank stood ready to purchase the inflowing dollars with intent to prevent appreciation. But soon another problem was created. The inflow of foreign capital dwindle and the demand for dollars led to a depreciation of the rupee. This called for another intervention by the Government and the Reserve Bank of India. And intervention to stem depreciation generated liquidity crunch. The rising inflation rate compelled the Reserve Bank of India to adopt a tight money policy which reduced the rate of inflation to 6.2 percent. The rate of monetary expansion was moderated despite the failure of the Government to reduce the budget deficit. The rate of monetary growth which was 20 percent was brought down to 14.28 percent. This reduction was due, in large part, to the decline in the rate of accretion of foreign exchange assets of the banking system. For the week ended December 5, 1995 the rate of growth of credit to the Government increased by 12 percent against the 9 percent recorded for the same period in 1994. At the same time bank credit to industry has increased by 18.58 percent as of December 8, 1995, compared with that in December 23, 1994. The growth rate of bank credit is far in excess of the growth rate of bank deposits which grew by only 7.96 percent. Despite this growth of bank credit the industrial sector complains of shortage of funds. Given the accelerated tempo of industrial activity and production during the first half of 1995-96 and the rising cost of imports due to depreciation of the rupee since September 1995 there is an accelerated increase in the demand for bank credit. The Reserve Bank of India made attempts to increase the availability of credit by reducing the Cash Reserve Ratio in two stages from 15 percent to 14 percent in November and December 1995. These measures increased the lendable resources of the banks by Rs. 4,000 crore. Even so, industry, especially the small scale sector, complains of inadequate availability of bank credit.

The liquidity crunch has reached such proportions that industrial production will be gravely affected during 1996-97 if the present trend continues. Even so the Government is optimistic about achieving a growth rate of 10 percent. The Indian Banks Association (IBA) has proposed selective lending restrictions to assist member banks in combating the problem of liquidity. As the banks in general have almost run out of funds the IBA has called for a kind of rationing system rather than a total halt to disbursements. The Reserve Bank of India has already relaxed credit controls for NRI deposits. Though this is expected to provide some improvement to the overall liquidity problem those which are likely to benefit are the public sector banks and foreign banks operating in the country. Credit relaxation on NRI deposits is expected to release an aggregate of Rs. 2,475 crore. The banks have to lend to industry and also to the Government during the last quarter of 1995-96. The public sector banks have been complaining to the IBA about slow deposit growth and the intense pressure on liquidity generated both by industry and Government.

The problem of Liquidity Crunch had its origin in December 1994 as there was a shift in the Government's priorities inflation management came on the top of the agenda. Tight money policy was considered necessary to bring down the rate of inflation which was expected to soothe the betrayed feelings of the electorate. Money supply during April-October 1995 grew by 4.5 percent against an increase of 11.5 percent during the corresponding period of 1994-95. The industry began to feel the pinch after a lag of 6 months in mid-1995. The Associated Chambers of Commerce brought out a note to establish the existence of a liquidity crunch on the basis of the call money rates which were rising and a rise in the deposit and lending rates/there were defaults on repayments, there was a slow down in disbursements by financial institutions. There was a poor response to the Government paper compelling the Reserve Bank to create money. As the stock market was not in pink health the financial institutions had switched over to holding Government bonds which were free from risk. There was also a reduction in the inflow of foreign investment funds and this also aggravated the liquidity crunch.

While there was an accelerated rise in the demand for credit, there has been a decline in bank deposits. According to the data supplied by the Reserve Bank of India the demand deposits declined by 8.3 percent during April-October 1995 while time deposits increased by 5.9 percent against an increase of 11.5 percent during the same period of 1994. The data supplied by the Planning Commission are supportive of this observation. According to it the savings rate declined reflecting a sharp turn towards consumerism which increased after the reform programme was initiated. The household savings declined from 20 percent GDP to 16 percent of GDP by 1993-94. It is possible that they have declined further since 1993-94. This was due to the withdrawal of the major tax incentives to savings and the shift of policy towards rewarding risk-taking investment in the context of the booming stock market. The savers shifted their savings to mutual funds and to other stock market related instruments. Another reason for the decline in bank deposits is the tax deduction at source on bank deposits. Those with resources shifted to other means of investment. This accounts for the rise in the price of gold and real estate.

The Government claims that there would be a growth rate of 10 percent in the current fiscal year. As a rule industrial recovery picks up in the second half of the fiscal year and the index of industrial production has shown a growth rate of 10.7 percent during April-October 1995. The consumer goods categories have a 24 percent weight in the index of industrial production. A steep growth in this sector means a higher overall industrial growth. Consumer durables recorded a growth rate of 23.7 percent during the first five months of 1995-96 while non-durables registered a growth rate of 10.8 percent. The capital goods sector has registered a growth rate varying from 27.8 percent to 12.8 percent. The Government is concerned with stability in this area as the output fell sharply during the first three years of reform. This is the present industrial scenario.

At a time when the banks are struck by liquidity crunch 13 private sector banks have formed a Private Sector Banks Association (PBA). These banks, in contrast to public sector banks, have not suffered much on account of the liquidity crunch. Their average rate of growth of deposits is higher than that of the public sector banks. At the end of March 1995 their aggregate deposits amounted to Rs. 26,430 crore while their advances amounted to Rs. 13,980 crore and their profits stood at Rs. 359 crore. The villain of the piece is the slow growth of deposits.

This calls for a rise in the savings ratio. An increase in the savings ratio above the current rate of 20.21 percent will increase the deposits which in turn will increase the flow of credit to agriculture, industry and the service sectors. The Finance Ministry projects a rate of growth of 6 percent and above. This requires a rise in the volume of savings in order to bridge the savings investment gap.

This has to be done by increasing the savings ratio through the offer of various tax incentives and through tackling the problem of tax evasion which is the source of black money. Measures need to be designed to eradicate black wealth and black money. Tax incentives need to be given for investment in the capital market and the amount invested in public issue needs to be deducted from taxable income.

Attempts need to be made to increase the inflow of foreign equity and to increase its stake upto 74 percent in order to increase such investment maintaining a balance between foreign and domestic investments. This inflow will remedy the existing liquidity crunch in the economy to a great extent.

If the foregoing measures are adopted, there will be an increase in the flow of funds in the economy. This will have a positive impact on economic growth. Of course, this may occasion inflation in the economy. But this does not matter because it helps to make the economy grow and to increase output which counteracts any inflationary pressures emanating from the increase in liquidity. A trade-off between higher growth rate and lower inflation rate is considered necessary. A higher growth rate is preferable to lower rate of inflation which may retard growth. The rate of inflation has fallen to 6.03 percent. Attention should be shifted towards accelerating the rate of economic growth by easing the liquidity crunch.

19

Oil Prices and Inflation

At present India is faced with the twin dangers of domestic inflation and balance of payments deficit. The oil prices and oil imports hold the key to both of them.

The import of petroleum products costs about one-fourth of India's export earnings. The drastic fall in the domestic production of these products coupled with the full convertibility of the rupee is likely to add to the country's import bill. The oil bill is bound to rise with the passage of time. The rise in oil bill can be checked by an increase in domestic production. But no immediate increase in domestic output is in sight as the Oil and Natural Gas Commission (O.N.G.C.), the central organisation continuing over 90 percent of India's crude oil production, has shut down some of its key off shore oil wells in Bombay High following their deterioration due to over exploration. In the past 15 years of its operation, the Bombay High has yielded about 200 million tonnes of crude. According to the O.N.G.C. officials, a progressive closure of 16 more Bombay High Wells is expected, in addition to the closure of 29 wells in May-June 1992. The O.N.G.C. has already reduced its planned production of crude by two million metric tonnes with the crude production in 1992-93 standing at 24.32 million metric tonnes. Besides the closure of oil wells the militancy in Assam, which accounts for 54 lakh tonnes output per year, also contributed to the fall in crude production. The O.N.G.C. sources hope that the falling oil output of O.N.G..C. would be arrested by the middle of 1993-94 and the trend could be reversed in 1995-96. To improve the production profile the O.N.G.C. has drawn up a plan for additional development of existing oil fields like Bombay High, Ravva, Panna, Mukta, Neelam, L-2, L-3, (Northwest Bombay offshore) which are expected to yield 31 million metric tonnes of crude in the Eighth plan. Besides, another 2 million metric tonnes is envisaged from three joint venture projects (Mukta, Ravva and Panna) making it a total of over 33 million metric tonnes for the period 1992-97.

It is estimated that while the domestic output of oil and petroleum products will stagnate at 44 million tonnes at the fag end of the Eighth Five Year Plan (1996-97) the demand for these products in the country will be 81 million tonnes. The level of oil imports is expected to see a 27 percent rise over the next five years.

As regards the financial year 1993-94 the official figures indicate that the import of oil and petroleum products which was 33.8 million tonnes in 1991-92 and 39.89 million tonnes in 1992-93 would go up to 44.2 million tonnes in 1993-94. Government figures show that the import bill for petroleum products will rise to $ 8.87 billion during 1993-94 from $ 6.18 billion in 1992-93. The declining trend in domestic production, the increased domestic consumption of petrol, oil and lubricants (POL) and the unified exchange rate mechanism are sure to push up further the import bill for petroleum products in the country in 1993-94 supported by monetary expansion.

At present the international oil prices exhibit a soft trend. This may soon turn out to be temporary if the OPEC decides to slash output by more than one million barrel per day at the forthcoming meetings. According to industry sources a one million barrel per day cut has already effected a $ 1.5 rise in crude prices in the United States. An adjustment of domestic petroleum prices in line with international trends will have to be done under the unified exchanger rate system. If and when the adjustment is carried out the burden will necessarily be passed on to consumers.

It must be mentioned here that the efforts of the O.N.G.C. will only marginally bridge the yawning gap between demand and supply in the oil sector and are unlikely to help reduce its huge imports and avoid the consequent negative impact on the country's economy.

The oil pool account surplus will be drying up soon following the rupee's full convertibility. Oil imports have become dearer for the Indian Oil Corporation (IOC), the main channelising agency since the announcement of full convertibility considering the fact that it used to import certain petroleum products like diesel and kerosene at the official rate which was lower than the market rate. The budget estimates put the surplus in the oil pool account of the Oil Coordination Committee (OCC) at about Rs. 1045.58 crore which forms the basis of the Government's assumption that the prices of petroleum products would not rise immediately after the switch over to the unified exchange rate mechanism. But this surplus will be wiped out before June 1993 as the Indian Oil Corporation will now pay more for its oil imports leading to a rise in the prices of these commodities.

India has contracted oil supplies for 1993-94 at an average price of about $ 15.5 a barrel and with an estimated oil import of about 30 million tonnes, the oil import bill will work out to $ 7 billion. This means that the country will finish with an oil import bill of Rs. 15,000 crore in 1992-93 itself. This bill will jump to Rs. 22400 crore in 1993-94 assuming an exchange rate of Rs. 32 to the U.S. dollar. The international price is about Rs. 15-16 a barrel. The OPEC wants to stabilise oil prices at $ 18-19 a barrel immediately and freeze prices at about $ 20-21 in a year or so. The redeeming feature is that the United States would not like the oil prices to go up. But how far the United States will be successful in checking the rise in the international oil prices is anybody's guess as most of the petrodollars earned by OPEC members are deposited in the U.S. banks. In this scenario world prices of crude will rise to around $ 17-18 a barrel in the immediate future. This would mean an additional burden of about $ 1-2 per barrel. A rough calculation shows that India would have to pay about Rs. 600 crore more every year for every dollar increase in the price of crude. For a $ 2 increase it would be Rs. 1200 crore more. An extrapolation of this figure shows that India would ultimately end up paying Rs. 7,000-9,000 crore more if international prices increased between $ 1-2 per barrel. This figure is based on a conservative estimate of the exchange rate of about Rs. 30 to the dollar.

About the inflationary impact of the unified exchange rate the Finance Minister said that "there will be no oil-fed inflationary impact. There is a cushion in the oil industry account so that even if it buys foreign exchange at the market rate it does not have to raise prices".

The Finance Minister's categorical statement is based on several assumptions:

1. There is already a cushion in the oil industry account which absorbs the inflationary impact of the higher exchange rate without passing it on to the consumers in the form of higher prices.
2. Oil prices are pretty soft and they will remain soft.
3. Rise in money supply does matter in the medium turn as there is a close relationship between money supply and prices. But in the short run there is no rigid relationship.

These assumptions are far removed from reality.

In the first place, the surplus of 1,045.58 crore in the oil pool account will be wiped out before June 1993 as the IOC has to purchase oil at the higher market rate of exchange. This will necessitate the passing on of higher oil prices to the consumers.

In the second place, at the recent meeting of the OPEC it was indicated that there would be a production cut back to 22-23 million barrels a day. This will obviously cause a rise in the international price of oil from $ 15-16 a barrel to $ 18-19 a barrel immediately and the OPEC wants to stabilize prices at $ 20-21 in the coming year. This means that the oil prices are not "pretty soft" as the Finance Minister assumes but are firm and will firm themselves up even more.

In the third place, the relationship between the supply of money and the price level is in consonance with the mechanism underlying the Quantity Theory of Money though we have to provide for a lag between monetary expansion and price rise. We have also to provide for a two-way cessation. Just as a rise in the supply of money causes a rise in the price level directly a reverse cessation is also possible, a rise in the price level necessitating a rise in the money supply. Quite apart from good harvests checking the rise in prices engineered by monetary expansion, there is need to restrict monetary growth to check the rise in the price level unleashed by the rise in petroleum prices. The following model will make the position clear.

Assume a situation of full employment beyond which any excess demand causes a rise in the price level; assume that the supply of money is held constant; assume further that the price of oil rises. In this situation there will be inflation of course. But if we analyse the problem with the keynesian framework we will arrive at an entirely opposite conclusion. A rise in the price level caused by a rise in the oil price, the supply of money being constant, causes a fall in real balances. If we assume that consumption demand is a function of real balances, this demand falls. Again a rise in the price level, the supply of money being constant, causes a rise in the transactions demand for cash. As the supply of money is held constant, the transactors have to obtain the required cash balances by selling their bonds in the bond market. This causes an excess supply of bonds, a fall in bond prices and a rise in the interest rate. To the extent that investment is interest elastic there will be a fall in investment. Furthermore, the consumers under the influence of "money illusion" incur the same amount of money expenditure. At a higher level of prices, this causes a fall in real expenditure. In this way both the constituent parts of aggregate demand consumption and investment fall causing a fall in the prices to the old level. In this way, with a constant supply of money, higher oil prices bring about their own fall. But if the supply of money is expanding at the rate of 16 percent as at present the contractive effects on consumption and investment will not be operative and the prices rise unchecked. Higher oil prices will be inflationary even with favourable harvests. The remedy is to keep the stock of money constant and still better to reduce it. When the supply of money is expanding, it would not be correct to say that higher oil prices would not be inflationary as the above model makes it clear. What is necessary is to include the monetary variable in the model. The Finance Minister is right in elucidating the classical Quantity Theory mechanism. But that is not enough.

It must be realised that the demand for oil and the price of oil are not constant. With a rise in the consumer demand for oil and a shortfall in the domestic production of oil the demand for oil imports rises. The price of oil is left to be determined by the OPEC which causes a rise in the price of oil suo moto the supply of oil being constant or makes the price of oil rise by reducing the supply of oil.

India and other oil importing countries have no control over oil prices as the OPEC is a carter having full control over prices. The production of oil in the Bombay High and other oil fields which are already over-exploited causes a rise in the cost and in price. As the production of oil in these wells is subject to the operation of diminishing returns/increasing cost, further exploitation inevitably leads to a rise in unit cost and in prices. Thus whether it is oil imports or domestic oil production the price of oil is bound to rise. Unless the consumption of oil is strictly controlled, there is no way in which the oil bill can be controlled. This calls for a plan of action to control domestic consumption. Price mechanism cannot control it as the recent experience has made it so distressingly obvious. The demand for oil is price-inelastic. Therefore, the Government should resort to strict rationing of oil as is done in Japan. This provides a partial solution to the inflation problem and the balance of payments problem. Tinkering at the periphery will not do.

20

Privatisation of Insurance Business

India is going fast on the road to structural reforms despite the initial halting and hesitant progress. At present, it has taken up the task of privatising the insurance sector and of allowing foreign companies to undertake insurance business. The Government has taken the Report of the Narasimham Committee on Financial Sector Reforms with due seriousness. It has already introduced certain reforms in the banking sector. It is the turn of the insurance business now. In April 1993 the Government appointed a committee under the Chairmanship of Shri. R.N. Malhotra, a former Governor of the Reserve Bank of India, to suggest ways and means of reforming the insurance sector. In the course of his budget speech in February 1993 the Finance Minister had adumbrated the idea of privatising the insurance sector. After the industrial sector, banking sector and the trade sector were exposed to the winds of economic reforms the insurance sector had to take its chance.

In the recent past public sector was considered to be the sacred cow. It was thought necessary to protect the society against the rapacious instincts and operations of the private sector; it was also considered necessary to keep the foreigners at a distance. The need to foster the rate of economic growth was considered imperative. This required a large amount of capital. This capital was the outcome of the savings of the rich sections of society. The need to direct this capital into productive ventures in order to maximise output was thought urgent and imperative. In order to collect the savings of million of savers and to utilise it for plan purpose, the Government nationalised life insurance as early as 1956. At that time there were 244 private insurance companies. The Government made all of them come under its control. It was then that the Indian Life Insurance Corporation came into being.

Its capital was just Rs. 5.0 crore. The entire amount was Government's capital. In 1971 the Government took general insurance under its control and in 1973 it nationalised it. The General Insurance Corporation incorporated into its fold four companies: New India, Oriental, Fire and General and United India Insurance Companies. This establishment initiated the insurance business in the country.

It cannot be said that all the private insurance companies were functioning satisfactorily. It was a collection of good and bad companies working in unison. The policy holders of some companies were bestowed with great security and were provided facilities. The policy holders of other companies were left almost uncared for. Undoubtedly, nationalisation of insurance was of great benefit to the policy holders. Uniformity of premium payment, enhancement of bonus, timely payment, the insurance facility to those who did not have this facility so far were the benefits accruing from nationalised insurance business. The insurance business expanded by leaps and bounds and it was also diversified.

But any system should change and is subject to change with the passage of time. The old belief that under nationalisation, the policy holders would derive benefits of unprecedented dimensions came to be belief. The nationalisation phobia came to be increasingly questioned. In the absence of competition several defects in insurance business came to be built into it. It was therefore considered necessary to expose the insurance sector to the bracing winds of competition. Globalisation of insurance, opportunities for competition, privatisation of insurance all these were considered to restructure the insurance business. The Malhotra Committee has inclined towards privatising the insurance business. It has argued for putting the public sector insurance companies on the road to privatisation and for opening up insurance business to private insurance companies and for allowing the foreign companies to the insurance sector.

During the past 20 years the life insurance business has expanded twenty times; the general insurance business has expanded by over 150 times. But there is urgent need to have plans of removing losses.

Further the insurance business is yet to touch the rural sector completely. There is also the need to focus attention on profitable investment of insurance premia and to distribute the profits among the policy holders. Profitability and security are antipodes. Wisdom lies in reconciling these two objectives. This requires wide experience. But the present insurance sector is unsatisfactory in this respect. This is not conducive to the public opting for insurance policies. If the insurance agents, employees and others are not exposed to competition, the insurance sector is bound to suffer corrosion. It is in this context that the Malhotra Committee recommends privatisation of insurance. In the capital of life insurance, 50 percent should be owned by the Government and the remaining 50 percent should be owned by private enterprise. In each of the four insurance companies the Government should own 50 percent of the capital; the General Insurance Corporation should give up its guidance of the general insurance companies. In future the General Insurance Corporation should undertake only re-insurance business only. At the same time their capital should be increased to be in consonance with the size of their transactions and their needs. As per the Life Insurance Corporation statute, it must be a company. Its capital has to be raised from Rs. 5 crore to Rs. 200 crore. In like manner the general insurance corporation should become a limited company and should raise its capital to Rs. 200 crore. The capital of the four general insurance companies should be raised to Rs. 100 crore each. Half of this capital should be contributed by the public and the other half by the Government. In other words the Government should contribute an amount equal to that contributed by the public.

It is necessary to usher in an atmosphere of competition in the insurance sector but it should be done so in gradual stages. The new entrant companies should have a capital of Rs. 100 crore. The promoters should not contribute more than 40 percent of the capital. In respect of others nobody should contribute more than 1 percent of the capital. The idea behind this limitation on capital ownership is to restrict contributions to only those who have a clear sense of responsibility to the Corporation. Nobody should be allowed to have monopoly control over the corporation by owning a large chunk of the capital. The foreign companies are allowed to enter the insurance business but they should cooperate with domestic companies. These companies have ample opportunities for investing their capital resources profitably. At the same time recommendations are made for strict control over them.

The Malhotra Committee recommendations have come in for a great many criticisms.

The Malhotra Committee recommendations are in keeping with the on-going economic reforms for structural adjustment and the thrust towards liberalisation and globalisation of the economy and opening up of banks and mutual funds to the private sector. The proposal of public participation in the Life Insurance Corporation (LIC) and General Insurance Corporation (GIC) equity is in line with Government's policy to disinvest part of its stake in select PSUs. This would generate additional funds for the Government which could use it for productive purposes. The Malhotra Committee's recommendation to reduce LIC and GIC low interest rate mandated investment in Government securities would mean better return on investment. The stipulation of minimum paid-up capital of Rs. 100 crore for new entrants will prevent indiscriminate entry of parties into the insurance business. The opening up of the insurance sector to private enterprise will help to expand the insurance business in rural areas and result in keen competition and all round efficiency. It will benefit the consumers in terms of the range of insurance products, lower premium, better services and customer-friendly approach which is so essential in insurance business.

The object of the Malhotra Committee recommendations is to ensure better service to the insuring public. The opposition political parties have alleged that the Malhotra Committee Report was drafted at the instance of the United States and the World Bank. This is the bogey which the opposition parties are prone to dangle at every reform measure. There is, however, the danger of private companies flooding the insurance sector. But this danger can be averted by controlling the entry of private companies. Some apprehend the danger of the private and foreign companies forming cartels and to checkmate the forces of competition. This can be checked by instituting a regulatory authority which would prevent cartelisation. This authority could be given powers like the SEBI. This authority would guard against cartelisation and supervise the investment of funds by the insurance companies in order to safeguard the interests of policy holders. In order to give autonomy to the LIC and GIC the Committee recommends disinvestment of equity of the existing companies by 50 percent. The foreign companies cannot enter the insurance sector by setting up branches in India as in the case they would not be subject to the law of the land. If the foreign companies float Indian companies with Indian partners they would be subject to the same regime as the Indian companies under the Companies Act. The idea behind recommending private sector participation is to inject competition in the insurance sector considering the fact that in a competitive market no one would survive if his performance is not satisfactory to the clients. The recommendation as regards the private companies having a minimum of Rs. 100 crore capital is to ensure that there were only serious players in the field.

The recommendations of the Malhotra Committee are of far reaching consequences. They are in consonance with the on-going reforms and are meant to further the reform process. The Government which set up this Committee cannot afford to shelve the report if it means business by its commitment to the reform process.

21

Forecasts about the Indian Economy

In the post-budget months this year the predictions made by the western agencies about the future course of the Indian economy and the business behaviour are both optimistic and pessimistic. There are two think-tanks and they have predicted opposite growth paths for India. The US think tank WEFA an off-shoot of the Wharton Econometrics has recently predicted that India's real GDP will grow at 6.3 percent in 1995-96 and 6.5 percent in 1996-97. In their opinion growth rate will be fuelled by a rise on private consumption of 6.5 percent in 1995-96 and there would be an inflow of foreign direct investment of $ 2 billion. The picture this agency predicts is rosy and cheering.

But there has been a recurring reference to political uncertainty in the media. This has lately come to be perceived as the single most important determinant of the goings-on in the stock market or the halting progress in the inflow of foreign direct investment. The latest in the series is the growth forecast by the London based Economist Intelligence Unit in its latest quarterly report. This anticipates political instability in India as a damper of the investment scenario. It also predicted in its last quarterly report that India's risk rating is lower than that of China even though it rated Indian economic policies to be more risk conducive than those of China and Pakistan. But they emphatically pointed out that political risk was higher in China. In the latest quarterly report they have warned against the growing political risks in India.

The Finance Minister has gone on record predicting a growth rate of 5.5 percent. But the Economist Intelligence Unit (EIU) for the first time predicts a less than 5 percent growth rate. This is sweet music to those who have been warning about the slow pace of economic reforms. According to the EIU growth will be constrained by the slow growth in consumer demand as a result of higher interest rates, disruption to production caused by the 1996 elections and devaluation of the rupee. It warns about the rupee reaching a level of Rs. 42 to a US dollar (as against the current rate of Rs. 31.37). It also predicts the possibility of current account deficit increasing due to a deluge of imports and a large outflow of funds if the current political stability persists. If these predictions materialise the warning could become a relief.

The Prime Minister and Finance Minister had long ago initiated a counter-refrain ruling out any reversal of economic reforms, or slowing down of its pace even if the Congress were out of power. Many corporate leaders and heads of business organisations kept echoing the refrain for some time.

The EIU predicts a decline in private consumption as a result of higher interest rates, disruption to production caused by the forthcoming 1996 elections to the Parliament and devaluation. This prediction needs close examination. This examination holds a mirror to the grave pitfalls in the forecasting made by the EIU.

Growth Prospects

The emphasis of the Finance Minister this year on the two-track strategy reflects the desire to reach out directly to the 700 million people who are outside the purview of the market. But he is constrained by the existing system. Having raised social spending and anti-poverty programme allocation in the last two years the Finance Minister has concluded that simply increasing budgetary allocation for social sectors and poverty programmes is not enough. Instead, the requirement is to revamp delivery systems and administrative structures for such programmes to make them much more accountable and responsive to the beneficiaries for whom the schemes are intended. But the fiscal deficit comes in the way of doing more than this on the second track. Containment of the fiscal deficit is the only anti-inflationary tool. The other track of the two-track strategy of accelerating growth, investment and modernisation continues without any let or hindrance. The budget continues with the process of lowering excise and customs duties aimed at making the Indian industry competitive and growing. The expected higher levels of industrial production are expected to contribute more revenue for the Government and help it to reduce the fiscal deficit. There is optimism that this would be the result of the taxation exercise. Many changes have been made in the excise rules and regulations aimed at plugging the loop holes in revenue. The expectation of buoyancy in tax revenues depends on this also.

The benefits of reforms have not spread evenly among the 250 million of Indians who constitute the upper middle class and who are supporting the ongoing economic reforms. Within this group there are those who grasped the early opportunities provided by the market economy and who have improved their living standards. The others feel that the benefits of reforms are bypassing them. It is necessary to respond to their feelings and to devise policies meant to improve their lot.

The Indian economy is looking up and the rate of economic growth is bound to grow. In July 1991 when the economic reform programme was initiated the London Economist published a report captioned "The Tiger Unchained" meaning thereby that the economy was unshackled by bureaucratic controls and licensing procedures. The *Economist* of January 1995 was a special on India Titled "The Tiger Steeps Out" it mirrored India very comprehensively. It said "After four decades of suffocation and a couple of years of post adjustment gloom, Indian business is bouncy. The business confidence index compiled by the National Council of Applied Economic Research, went from optimistic to ebullient in 1994. Corporate projects in the first half of 1994-95 were up by 102% .....". The Asian Tigers are leaping forward on the high road to economic growth. The Indian Tiger more buoyant and more dynamic will leap forward faster.

The Budget for 1995-96 assumes that the income and corporation taxes would rise by 20 percent. Since prices are assumed to rise by 8 percent growth is assumed to be 7 or 8 percent. Union excise duties are assumed to rise by 16 percent after taking changes in rates into account. In other words, a real growth of at least

8 percent is assumed. In the case of customs duties, import growth of 17 percent seems to have been estimated assuming that there is no devaluation. Thus all these figures point to a GDP growth of 7 to 8 percent i.e., a rise from the 1994-95 figure of 5.3 percent. Such a rise implies an industrial growth rate of 12 percent. The budget is expected to provide the stimulus for the rate of growth to rise to this level.

A lot depends on agricultural growth which in turn depends on favourable monsoons. It is estimated monsoons this year will be favourable so that the rate of agricultural growth will rise generating higher incomes for the farm families. This higher income is to be used to improve their standard of living, healthcare, sanitation and the housing facilities and the consumption standards in general. This provides an added stimulus to growth through the acceleration mechanism. The prophets of doom have blinkered view of the future of the Indian economy. All evidence points to a buoyancy economy brimming with dynamism. This is as it should be after the initial years of the economic reform programme.

Decline of Foreign Capital Inflow

Statistical evidence, of course, shows that there is a decline in the inflow of foreign capital into India. The forex reserves had started dwindling because of the reduced capital inflow after November 1994. This had started putting pressure on the dollar rupee exchange rate of late. Between April 1994 and November 1994 the foreign exchange reserves excluding gold and SDR s increased by around 30 percent from $ 15.073 billion to $ 19.496 billion. But during the next four months the reserved increased by only around 2.3 percent to $ 20.954 billion infact during the current financial year the reserves had taken a further dip. On April 21, 1995 the reserves had depleted by around $ 460 million. This put pressure on the dollar exchange rate which went up sharply in recent days. In April 1995 the rupee had depreciated to the average rate of Rs. 31.60 per US dollar. The market circles feel that with the widening trade deficit the rupee would depreciate further.

Until 24th May 1995, the Government was reluctant to give permission to repatriate Euro-Issue proceeds to India as it would increase the money supply which would give a further upward push to the rate of inflation. But in a move to book the sagging forex reserves the Ministry of Finance decided on May 24, to permit Indian companies to bring their Euro-Issue proceeds back to India as foreign currency deposits with banks and public financial institutions. This was required to give a boost to the stock market which has remained continuously at a bottom level because of the prevailing liquidity crunch in the country which would affect industrial growth this year. It was argued that if the repatriation of the Euro-issue proceeds could help in ameliorating the situation the Government must permit the same. It is said that if the rate of inflation came down to less than 8 percent and remained at that level for four consecutive weeks the Government would allow the repatriation along with conversion into Indian currency. The Ministry further said that the repatriated money would only be converted into Indian rupee as and when the expenditures for the approved and uses are incurred. This decision would help to boost the dwindling forex reserves.

The prediction of reduction in the inflow of foreign capital is not invalid. It is likely to slow down in 1995-96 for several reasons: (a) national elections are due early in 1996 and there is a perception in international capital markets of a political uncertainty; (b) devaluation of the rupee is expected since havala market premium has risen and this creates the fear of a capital loss; (c) the international climate is not conducive to inflow of foreign capital after the collapse of the Mexican Peso and the rising interest rates in the US. The last factor is reinforced by the warning administered by the IMF Managing Director Mr. Camdessus. Speaking to the representatives of the co-financing institutions in Washington on May 26, 1995 he said that world growth has now close to its long term trend rate and he expected most industrial countries to experience sustained growth and developing countries to maintain 6 percent growth a year if policy improvements are maintained. But he mentioned two key risks the instability and misalignments of exchange rates among currencies and "a sharper than expected slow down in capital flows to emerging market economies" India is among the major emerging market economies today. He said that the IMF's projections include a further weakening of these capital flows following their rapid growth in the early 1990s, partly as a result of the recovery in the industrial economies. "But the risk is that there could be a much sharper fall-off, perhaps triggered by financial crisis in one or two countries but threatening growth prospects much more widely". Mr. Camdessus said. He emphasized that this risk was vividly illustrated by Mexico's financial crisis and its spill-over effects which reached many countries in the Western hemisphere, he further said. This risk as well as the exchange rate instability were partly the result of globalisation of financial markets. But he warned that the answer to this situation is not reversion to exchange rate controls or less open markets but in improving economic policies at the national level as well as stronger international monetary cooperation at the global level through the IMF. Mr. Camdessus noted that a number of policy lessons could be drawn from the Mexican experience vis-a-vis capital flows. The Mexican crisis displayed all too clearly how suddenly market assessments of a country's situation can turn around when a country lowers its guard and allows its economic policies to weaken.

Mr. Camdessus referred to the market economies in general that too those whose policies are weak and not at all to India. It would be wrong to draw a parallelism between Mexico and India. The Mexican crisis is the country's own making, having devalued the Peso contrary to its earlier promise and not having been in a position to take suitable follow up action. Some economists have gone to the extent of attributing the London bank failure to adventurism, both unwanted and unwarranted, in globalisation. If what they say is correct, nationalised or communist economy must be better. But that is not to be. It has caused the disintegration of an entire nation a super power at that.

Be that as it may, it would be idle to pretend that what happened in Mexico will happen in India and to blame the "useful toils of the Finance Minister. The investments in Mexico were of a short-term variety liable to shift without notice. These investments were made mostly in consumer goods industries. Mexico had a massive current account deficit of a 8 percent of GDP. The rate of inflation was high and surging. The weakness of the fiscal-monetary policies made the foreign investors shift their capital abroad. In about two weeks the foreign exchange reserves declined from $ 27 billion to 7 billion. This in sharp contrast with the situation in India; the rate of inflation is 8.5 percent at present and is expected to fall further; the current account deficit is 0.5 percent of GDP and even if it goes upto 1.0 percent of GDP because of the surge in imports there will be no danger to the economy. The credit rating agencies have rated India very high.

Need to Attract Direct Foreign Investment

With the opening up of the economy India has emerged as an attractive destination for foreign direct investment from all over the World. Since July 1991 India has attracted $ 7 billion in terms of foreign equity. There are now 300 foreign institutional investors registered with the SEBI. Their net investment as on March 1, 1995 stood at $ 3179.5 million.

If the country has to get out of its present economic difficulties and reach a higher growth path, its annual export growth must rise to 20-25 percent level in dollar terms and FDI should increase by 6-8 billion dollars per annum. As a result of India's efforts its exports grew by 20 percent in 1993-94. Similarly, FDI approvals reached $ 2.6 billion in the same period. USA, Japan and Germany together accounted for three-fifths of the FDI approvals in the post-reform period. At present USA tops the list of foreign investors in the country followed by the UK and the Netherlands. However, the gap between the need and inflow of FDI is disconcerting. The FDI stock in the Asian region, as per the document released by the UNCTAD has more than doubled between 1988 and 1993 and an estimated $ 53 billion in 1994. India's share in this remains low at $ 7 billion in 3 years since 1991. Compared to this China remained successful in attracting FDI with $ 28 billion in 1993 and $ 30 billion in 1994.

The Finance Minister has warned against depending too much on foreign investments for the country's ongoing reform programme, especially in the Mexican context. The lessons contained in China's success story are worth considering. A recent UN study in FDI found China to be the largest recipient of FDI among the developing countries. It concludes that the attractions in China are high growth rate, rising income and large domestic market. As labour is cheap in China some firms are using China as a production centre for exports. These are precisely the attractions for India as well. Given the low cost and high skilled labour, India too is rated high by transnationals. Yet the high differential between FDI flow to China and India highlights the shortcomings in policy measures which need to be changed to make India an attractive investment destination.

The Japanese and German investors have proposed the following pro-investment measures. They include:

1. the reduction in the number of channels to process the FDI proposals.
2. a shift from the "positive list approach" to "negative list approach" at the entry level.
3. removal of restrictions on equity holidays, and
4. a liberal exit policy.

Under the prevailing political climate this Government should not implement these measures to please the investors at the cost of the voters. However, "middle path" is to be adopted in order not to repel investors.

A better climate for FDI is the stimulating domestic private investment. Increase in domestic savings is a step in this direction. The policy import liberalisation contained in the recently announced EXIM policy is an added incentive. A lot has also to be done to improve the administration, tardy legal system and poor infrastructure. What is urgently needed is a rational orientation to the whole concept of FDI in India. In this way the inflow of foreign investment can be increased and speeded up in order to promote economic growth. At a time when domestic savings are inadequate to meet the investment demands for accelerating economic growth foreign savings become inevitable. Hence the need to attract direct foreign investment.

Will the Consumption Demand Decline?

Will there be a decline in consumer demand? Economic growth in India is dependent on the performance in agriculture. Last year saw the seventh good average monsoon in a row after 1987 and the third good one since 1992. This along with sharply higher procurement prices since 1992-93 has pumped purchasing power into the rural areas.

Cyclical factors have led to increased demand after three years. The upturn seems to be based on the demand for consumer durables because of easy availability of lease financing, the wealth effect of the sharply higher share and real estate prices and increased incomes of the upper middle class families. The rise in the fiscal deficit and the fall in the current account deficit as a share of GDP in the last two years added to consumer demand.

The Budget for 1995-96 needed to give a boost to growth by stimulating the long run factors. Officials argue and it actually does so by (a) cutting in direct taxes so as to stimulate consumer demand by lowering prices (b) giving tax holiday to infrastructure investments and (c) giving a fillip to the small scale sector. All these are supposed to boost private investment. To talk about consumer demand it is necessary to examine the influence of cuts in customs and excise duties on consumer demand. The customs duties are reduced in order to expose Indian industry to the competitive forces coming from abroad and to enable them to improve their efficiency. At the same time customs duty reduction will make imports cheaper and increase demand for them. In a similar manner the reduction of excise duties, if passed on to consumers in the form of lower prices will stimulate demand for them. Hence price elasticity of demand and income elasticity of demand work to increase consumer demand. When the prices are reduced, income remaining constant, the demand for these goods rises, again, when income rises, even if prices are held constant the demand for these goods rises. But in the instant case a fall in prices causes a rise in demand for the goods. Also a rise in income causes a rise in the demand for these goods. Thus, the influence of price elasticity and income elasticity of demand on consumer demand are addition. The effect is to increase consumer demand. It must be mentioned here that 45 percent of imports are to serve as inputs to exports. A reduction in the prices of imported inputs will reduce the prices of exports and promote export growth. There is also the influence of fiscal deficit on consumer demand.

Admittedly lower levels of foreign capital inflow, ceiling on monetised deficit and impact on the banking sector due to the poverty schemes will keep interest rates high. It is argued by the EIU forecast that higher interest rates will reduce consumer demand. This is so on the assumption that the demand for consumer goods in interest elastic. If the demand is interest inelastic higher interest rates fail to reduce consumer demand. There are factors which help to increase demand. Consumerism has invaded the middle income group households. The demonstration effect works to increase the consumption standards of those lower in the income scale. These factors help to stimulate consumer demand despite higher interest rates. This will stimulate industrial growth. In the rural sector the affluent sections who are gradually drawn to the market system increase their demand for modern gadgets under the influence of higher agricultural growth and higher income. In fact there is likely to be surfeit of demand rather than a decline. If goods are not produced in sufficient quantities to meet the surging demand there will be a rise in prices. The increase in consumer demand causes a rises in investment through the acceleration coefficient and the interaction between the multiplier and the accelerator will take India upto a higher growth path. Therefore, there is no ground for apprehension of a decline in consumer demand.

The EIU mentions two other factors which are alleged to reduce consumer demand. They are (a) disruption to production during the 1996 elections and (b) devaluation. The general elections are a normal democratic process which normally take place once in five years and it is difficult to see how the elections disrupt the production process. There may be booth capturing and violence during the elections but they cannot be held to disrupt production process. If anything general elections help to stimulate demand. During the elections enormous sums of money will be pumped into the economic system both by the Government and the party candidates and their supporters. If anything this should help to increase consumer demand and to stimulate productive activity.

The EIU forecasts devaluation of the rupee in the context of the rising current account deficit and it asserts that it will depress consumer demand. Their logic is based on the fact that devaluation makes imports costlier and this reduces the demand for imports and the consumption of imports. But there is another side to it. If imports become costlier the consumers take to the consumption of domestic substitutes for imports. In consequence the fall in the consumption of imported goods will be made good by the rise in the consumption of domestic substitutes. Furthermore, devaluation through the price effect may reduce the demand for imports. This assumes that the income remains constant when devaluation is undertaken. If the fiscal deficit rises as it does, and if the wage rates rise as they are bound to consumer income rise and this through the income effect causes a rise in the demand for imports. In this case the price effect on the demand for imports will be swamped by the income effect of rising incomes. We have to take into account the influence of exports on consumer demand. Devaluation makes exports cheaper and thus stimulates exports. When exports rise the export incomes rise and they generate demand for imports of consumer goods. There is a factor on the export side which may cause a fall in the demand for consumer goods. It is expected that under devaluation the terms of trade of the devaluing country deteriorate i.e., a given volume of exports fetches a smaller volume of imports. Even this depends upon the elasticity of demand for the country's exports. The terms of trade may turn adverse to the devaluing country but not necessarily. If the terms of trade turn adverse to the country real income will be less than real output and this might cause a reduction in the demand for imported goods. Even so, the possibility of a rise in export income stimulating import demand cannot be ruled out.

In the Indian case devaluation will not be undertaken. The Government spokesman have ruled out the possibility of devaluation as a method of correcting the balance of payments deficit. The current account deficit at present is 0.5 percent of GDP. Even if it rises to 1.0 percent under the impact of rising imports there will not be a balance of payments crisis warranting devaluation. Forex reserves are there in plenty to meet any current account deficit especially when it is within manageable limits.

Is Devaluation Necessary?

The EIU predicts a surge in imports. This is true as the EXIM policy has made it abundantly clear. In 1992 the Government announced a five year EXIM policy. For the next two years the Commerce Ministry tinkered with it announcing amendments every March end. But the Ministry did not steer the policy in a radically new direction. In March 1995 the Commerce Minister broke with a two-year tradition. In far reaching amendments to the EXIM policy he opened up the consumer goods sector and reduced the levels of protection for businessman. The Ministry put 32 mass consumption items on the open general license (OGL) list, thereby trying to address the problem of inflation. A host of products can now be freely imported. Indeed the OGL list has been expanded from 43 to 75 and restricted import list has been pruned from 114 to 65. The Commerce Minister had made his intention clear even before the latest changes in EXIM policy were announced. He had said that the Government would allow consumer goods to be imported but according to its time-table. He declared that "in that time-table mass consumption goods will get the highest priority. This is indication that the walls of protectionism are crumbling. Apart from mass consumption goods it will be easier now to import items like uninterrupted power supply systems and even capital goods. The special import licence (SIL) shopping list has been expanded from 42 to 75. These items have been chosen with the small scale sector in view.

Last year imports surged by about 20 percent thanks to the revival of industrial growth. The Commerce Minister believes that this year's deficit will over around last year's level (roughly $ 2 billion or Rs.6,200 crore) although the revised EXIM policy has made it easier to import several items. The Minister has argued that exports in 1994-95 grew by over 17 percent to top $ 25 billion imports grew to under $ 27 billion leaving a difference of $ 2 billion which is the trade deficit. But the Finance Ministry on the other hand predicts a deficit close to $ 4 billion with imports touching $ 34 billion and exports roughly $ 30 billion. The Finance Ministry is worried about the rising current account deficit and the narrowing capital account surplus. However, with the economy picking up, imports are growing and the domestic market is increasingly becoming more attractive to businessmen. The slowing down of capital inflows explains the Finance Ministry's worries.

The surge in imports and the current account deficit has made the EIU predict a devaluation of the rupee. Devaluation was effected in July 1991 when there was a balance of payments crisis of unprecedented magnitude because of the surge in imports and a decline in the rate of growth of exports. Devaluation was to some extent successful though it caused a rise in the external debt in rupee terms in the same proportion. But the current account deficit persisted though in a smaller measure. This is because of the fiscal deficit and wage escalation which exercised an expansive effect on import demand. But, at present, there is no need for devaluation for the current account deficit which is less than 0.5 percent of GDP does not justify devaluation. In fact imports are surging as the policy of the Government is to liberalise consumer goods imports in order to counter the inflationary pressure. The Finance Minister has, in fact, advocated a policy of liberalisation of consumer goods imports as a counter-inflationary move and it is intended to finance them by drawing on the accumulated forex reserves. If the fiscal deficit is brought down; if the rate of monetary growth is brought down to the target rate of 16 percent from the present rate of 20 percent and if the food supply rises on account of the good monsoons this year the rate of inflation will be brought down. If this happens, as it is likely to happen, liberalisation of consumer goods imports is not necessary. In this case the current account deficit poses no problem for the Government. This renders devaluation unnecessary. In view of this the EIU prediction of devaluation of the rupee goes wrong. In fact devaluation is a desperate remedy applicable to the balance of payments of countries suffering from "fundamental disequilibrium". There is no evidence that Indian balance of payments displays symptoms of fundamental disequilibrium. In this situation devaluation is not necessary and if it is undertaken it does more harm than good. There is a direct variation and causal connection between fiscal deficit and the current account deficit. If the fiscal deficit is brought down the current account deficit falls and renders devaluation of the rupee unnecessary.

Conclusion

Economic forecasting is highly scientific and sophisticated exercise. Its reliability depends crucially on the accuracy of the statistical data made available to the forecaster, the trends in the economy over a period of years in the past the factors governing the future trends in the economy and the predictability of the economic behaviour of the strategic variables. That the two think-tank agencies have reached diametrically opposite finding about the prospects of the Indian economy cannot be easily explained. On the basis of available evidence the forecasts of EIU are unduly pessimistic and this renders the forecasts about the rate of growth the exchange rate, import and export behaviour highly suspect. The forecast made by the WEFA of the Wharton Econometrics appear more reliable and point to the future course of events in the Indian economy. The growth prospects, the consumption demand, investment trends and the balance of payments appear closer to reality and therefore the forecast made by it can be trusted. There is, therefore no need for the authorities to be unduly concerned about the pessimistic forecasts made by the EIU. The EIU seems to be overwhelmingly influenced by the Mexican crisis and the possibility of the Mexican type crisis brewing in the case of India is at the back of the minds of the forecasters though they have not stated it in clear terms. But there is no need for the Indian authorities to be unduly concerned about any crisis brewing in the case of India. The WEFA forecast is reliable and policy adjustments need to be made to realise it.

22

The Liquidity Crunch in the Indian Economy

Liquidity crunch has become a serious problem in the Indian economy in recent months. In the context of rapid industrial growth the demand for bank loans has risen. But the deposit accretion at the banks has not come upto expectations. The banks are short of resources to meet the every-growing demand for non-food credit. In order to overcome the cash crunch the banks themselves are found to be raising loans. In consequence, the call money rates rose to unprecedented heights. Neither the Government nor the Reserve Bank of India has taken steps to increase the supply of liquidity to match rising demand for it. What the Reserve Bank has done is nothing more than reducing the Cash Reserve Ratio (CRR) in two stages: from 15 percent to 14 percent. Even so, the liquidity crunch has not abated to any noticeable extent. In short, there is a shortage of liquidity in the economy at present impeding economic growth.

The RBI injected funds of the order of Rs. 5,070 crore with a reduction of CRR on two occasions by 0.5 percent each time and with a lowering of the CRR to 7.5 percent from 14.5 percent in respect of deposits in external accounts. An amount of Rs. 2,000 crore was released from the impounded cash balance of banks on November 10 with the lowering of CRR to 14.5 percent with a further lowering of the CRR by half a percentage to 14 percent and to 7.5 percent in respect of deposits in external accounts an additional amount of Rs. 3,070 crore was made available to banks on December 10. A further rise in deposits and additions to cash balances have been helpful in easing monetary stringency somewhat. The inter-bank call rate has been fluctuating around 15-16 percent lately. The payments against advance tax dues in the third week of December 1995 have not been reflected in a significant tightening of monetary conditions. But industrial circles are worried that a cautious attitude on the part of the banks while extending additional credit even to worthy borrowers may have an inhibiting effect industrial production. While the full impact of the release of Rs. 5,070 crore eased the monetary situation somewhat the intensification of the borrowing programme of the Government has had a neutralising effect partially. Any fresh investment by banks in new loans will reduce the availability of funds for lending purposes. This may call for the increase in net Reserve Bank credit above the Rs. 11,904 crore reached on November 24, 1995. Short-term measures to increase liquidity are called for.

As the deposit mobilisation has not been a complete success the banks are unable to lend the required quantum of finance to the borrowers. But this is not the only reason for liquidity crunch. If the loans advanced by the banks are repaid as per schedule the liquidity status of the banks will be satisfactory. The loans advanced by the banks are, for the most part, short-term loans. If the loans are repaid quickly the deposits will increase. But this is not happening at present. In 1994-95, by November the rate of growth of deposits was 22 percent. But this year (upto December 1995-96) it is a meagre 11.6 percent.

The money lent by the banks, the bank deposits etc constitute M3 money supply. In 1994-95 this rose by 21 percent. This year (1995-96) uptill now it has risen by 14.96 percent. In the context of on-going inflation it was felt that a rate of growth of M_3 need to be only 15.5 percent in order to meet the demands of a growing economy. But it is unlikely that the money supply would grow even at this rate. It is expected that the GDP in 1995-96 would grow at the rate of 6.2 percent. If the rate of growth of money supply is such as not to meet the demands necessitated by this rate of growth of GDP, this will impede the rate of growth of GDP itself. It is felt in some circles that the rate of economic growth cannot be more than 3-4 percent. It is natural to apprehend that the rate of economic growth might decline to this level because of liquidity crunch. If this happens this amounts to demonstrating the failure of the liberalisation programme. Achieving rapid economic growth is the objective of liberalisation. But the Reserve Bank does not seem to be contemplating the expansion of liquidity. Since 1993 and upto the middle of 1995 there was a massive inflow of dollars to India. The foreign institutional investors evinced interest in the shares of Indian companies. Foreign bonds were flowing to India in order to take advantages of the higher interest rate prevailing in India. This was welcome as India needed foreign exchange. But this had an expansive monetary impact and led to monetary expansion, leading to a rise in the rate of inflation. But by the middle of 1995 the inflow of foreign capital has dwindled. The rupee began to depreciate in terms of the US dollar. In order to alleviate excess demand for dollars the Reserve Bank has began to sell dollars and to obtain rupees in exchange. This step is deemed necessary in order to reduce the rate of monetary growth and to hold down the rate of inflation. The liquidity crunch is caused by the absorption of rupees by the Reserve Bank of India. In spite of this step the rate of inflation has not fallen significantly. Now it is 6.96 percent. The Reserve Bank's policy has not made any major impact on the inflation rate which needs to fall in order to strengthen the competitiveness of India's exports.

We have to find out why the bank deposits have not registered a significant growth and why the liquidity is not adequate. The household savings are the main source of bank deposits. Recently when the deposit rates were reduced the savers began to shift their deposits to institutions outside the banking system to reap the benefits of higher interest rates offered by them. There is no dearth of institutions which offer attractive interest rates. Urban real estate and urban housing area an attractive source of income. Investments in these areas are considered better than holding deposits whose real value is being eroded due to inflation. The savers are shifting their savings towards assets which yield a higher interest income and which appreciate in value year by year. In addition, black markets and black money dealings are flourishing. Those who purchase urban property do not indicate the actual price paid in the sale deeds. What is indicated is far less than what is actually paid. The difference constitutes black money. This does not come to the banks as deposits. Many invest this money in havala transactions. There is also difference between the actual money received and the money recorded as received in the foreign trade transactions. This is due to under-invoicing of exports and over-invoicing of imports. The foreign exchange earned in this manner is not indicated in writing and this is not returned to the banking sector. As these transactions yield a higher return in real estate and urban housing, this money is attracted to these areas. The political uncertainty in the country also has aggravated these trends. All the political parties have to spend colossal sums of money to finance the election expenses of their respective candidates violating the Seshan dictate. This cannot be done through the banking system. The Seshan effect is emerging very strong on the Indian political horizon. The money spent by the political parties and by the candidates themselves has to be outside in the economy. These does not seem to be any immediate remedy. The coming days are anxiety-ridden. How to abate this anxiety is a problem for the authorities and to the Finance Ministry in particular.

In 1995 the financial sector witnessed several adjustment problems which were the outcome of an immature market being thrown open to market forces with the deregulation of interest rates both on deposits and lending the RBI has completed a major part of the process of interest rate de-regulation as recommended by the Narasimham Committee four years ago. The freeing of interest rates and the persistent liquidity crunch have prompted banks and financial institutions to behave in an arbitrary manner. This has caused the hiking of lending rates by atleast 2 percentage points since the deregulation of interest rates in November 1994. The cost of bank funds has also turned dearer due to the freeing of term deposit rates above two years of maturity.

The term-deposit rates of nationalised banks have risen to 13 percent while the foreign banks and the private banks have started offering upto 14 percent. Similarly the cost of borrowing from banks and financial institutions have gone up substantially. Nationalised banks have raised prime lending rates to 16.5 percent and foreign banks to 17 percent. At the same time, the supply of funds in the financial system declined sharply towards the end of October 1995 due to many unfavourable factors as the RBI withdrew over Rs. 2500 crore resulting in severe pressure on the system. Besides this, the flow of funds receded sharply over a period of time as the mutual funds were low on funds. They floated very few schemes compared with 1994-95 due to the sluggish trends in the secondary market. As the two previous credit policies were aimed at containing inflation through credit squeeze. The availability of funds has shrunk over time. It is clear that the RBI is determined to bring down the rate of inflation to a reasonable 6 percent to 7 percent to make financial liberalisation more meaningful. As the credit crunch persisted, the RBI took several measures to ease the situation. Even so, the liquidity crunch continues.

The Government of India seems to prefer low inflation rate to high growth rate. Obviously high rate of growth needs the facility of adequate financial flow from the banks at reasonable interest rates. But the liquidity squeeze and the high lending rates are bound to hold down industrial growth, though they may reduce the rate of inflation. As the targeted rate of inflation is 7 percent and as the inflation rate has fallen to 6.93 percent the target is more or less achieved. There is no need to give precedence to high rate of growth. For even though there may be a slight spurt of inflation immediately, after a time lag this will be countered by the rise in supply made available by a high rate of economic growth. Growth theorists advocate a gently rising price level as an inducement to a higher rate of growth.

The Government directed the Reserve Bank of India to tackle inflation on a priority basis and this has been on top of the agenda. The Reserve Bank tightened money supply growth in 1995 and, in consequence, the annual rate of inflation fell to 6.93 percent by early December. This was due to the check on money supply. Between March 31, 1995 and October 13, 1995 the growth in money supply was only 4.5 percent compared to 11.1 percent growth during the corresponding period of 1994-95. This in itself restrained growth in liquidity. In addition more money has gone to the Government than to the commercial sector which complained of a credit squeeze. While growth in net bank credit to Government was at 8.5 percent in 1995 the figure for 1994 was 4.4 percent. Even the RBI credit to the Government increased by 14 percent in 1995 against an increase of 4.2 percent in 1994. Bank credit to the commercial sector increased by 4.2 percent in 1995 only against an increase of 6.6 percent in 1994. This slow increase in the commercial sector credit coupled with the fact that capital mobilisation from the stock markets has also been low has constrained the industrial sector growth as a whole. This calls for easing the liquidity situation by means of reducing the CRR by another 1 percent from 14 percent to 13 percent which would release Rs. 4000 crore and allowing Indian corporate entities to raise capital abroad and to bring back the amount immediately. These measures would ease the inflow and create productive capacity.

Considering the fact that the targeted inflation rate has been achieved, there is need to take steps to accelerate economic growth. This calls for easing the liquidity position in the economy. At the same time, there is need to keep vigil on the fiscal deficit and to reduce unnecessary and wasteful expenditure leaving alone the on going populist measures adopted on the eve of the impending general elections.

The GDP continued to grow during 1994-95 forcing the Planning Commission to revise it to 6.2 percent from the projected 5.3 percent earlier. The Central Statistical Organisation has projected a 7 percent growth for the current year (1995-96). Its optimism is based on the 13 percent industrial growth achieved in the first quarter itself with a sustained growth in agriculture at 4.8 percent. If this rate of growth of the economy is to be sustained and the growth rate is to be accelerated, the economy needs the lubricant of sufficient supply of money. This may cause a temporary rise in the rate of inflation. But inflation caused by supply of money to accelerate economic growth has a back wash which tends to expand the supply of output and this is why inflation carries with it the seeds of its own destruction. Therefore, instead of sacrificing growth to check inflation the Government should sacrifice price stability for a while to achieve a higher rate of growth. This calls for reordering the priorities.

The monetary authorities appear to be in an uncomfortable dilemma as the liquidity in the banking system has to be improved for enabling borrowers in industry and trade to get their genuine requirements and facilitating also the mobilisation of resources by the Government and avoiding the enlargement of the overall deficit. At the same time it is feared that there should not be any accentuation of inflationary pressures. The Government has lately expressed its preference for price stability at the cost of growth if necessary. It is true that inflation hurts but it needs to be borne in mind that low growth or zero growth hurts more. A slight rise in prices is the necessary price to pay to realise the benefits of a higher rate of growth. There is a trade-off between inflation and growth. A high rate of growth with a gently rising price level is preferable to slow or zero growth with price stability. This dimension of the growth-inflation trade-off controversy needs to be borne in mind while formulating economic policy. The people need to be enlightened on the benefits of a higher rate of growth accompanies temporarily by a higher level of prices.

23

Focus should Shift from Social Banking to Commercial Banking

Under the Bank Nationalisation Act of 1969 social purpose was injected into the operations of banking. This social purpose involved concessional lending to the priority sectors which consisted of agriculture, small scale industry and exports. The banks were required to earmark 40 percent of their lendable resources to the priority sectors. But many public sector banks have failed to reach the 40 percent target of the 28 public sector banks as many as 22 fell short of the target by a substantial amount. The State Bank of India could reach only 29.7 percent of the target while its associates averaged 31 percent. The Syndicate Bank with 750 branches with rural bias could manage only 30 percent of the target. The average priority sector lending of the 28 public sector banks in only 36 percent. The down trend is likely to continue. During 1993-94 the total bank credit disbursal was Rs. 13,000 crore. Only a fraction of this had reached the priority sector. The Reserve Bank of India is dismayed at the downtrend in priority sector lending and to achieve the prescribed target of 40 percent it has laid down the following targets:

1. Every bank should reach a minimum level of 40 percent of the total advances to the priority sector;
2. Out of this 40 percent not less than 18 percent shall go to agriculture. Indirect agriculture finance shall not exceed 25 percent of this sub-target;
3. Weaker section advances shall have a sub-target of 10 percent of net credit. In order to improve matters the Reserve Bank of India has made certain relaxations in March 1994 so that banks may re-classify their advances and show a

higher percentage. Even so, the banks have failed to reach the target. Estimates for March 1994 show that priority sector lending of public sector banks would be around only 34-35 percent.

Several factors explain this failure of banks to reach the target lending of 40 percent to the priority sector. In the first place, since March 1993 banks are required to take into account only the income realised and not the income accrued on paper. Banks also have reduced the interest for 1992-93 and 1993-94 on non-performing assets. This has reduced the total amount of credit outstanding. After 3 years, the balance of an average priority sector advance is expected to have about 25 percent as unrealised interest. As the banks debit interest only on the basis of actual realisation, balances stand reduced. In the earlier years the banks reached the 40 percent target due to the then prevailing accounting policy. Though the actual disbursals were low they were made good by the increase by way of interest debits. If the 40 percent target was fixed considering this aspect the Reserve Bank should consider reducing it under the present changed circumstances.

Rural debt recovery is only 54 percent. The balance is accounted for by default. This level of default is not conducive to the healthy functioning of the banking system. This degree of default is due to the following factors;

1. The scheme introduced in 1990 of waiver of weaker section loans upto Rs. 10,000. The Union Budget set apart Rs. 1,000 crore to compensate the banks for this waiver but in actual fact the demand made by the banking system has crossed the Rs. 7,500 crore mark. A major part of this is yet to be reimbursed by the Government.
2. Borrowers came to regard bank loans as largesse from the Government which they being in the weaker sections need not repay. In consequence the recovery percentages dropped. The Revenue Recovery Act has been made applicable only in a few states and these states, in consequence, have shown good recovery performance. As this Act is not in force in many States has loan recovery programme is adversely affected.

3. Many Government sponsored schemes involving bank loans are not viable as regards income generation. The objective of these schemes was to help the weaker sections with self-employment schemes and to raise their incomes above the poverty line. But the overdues in 9 out of 10 loans would be about 80-90 percent. The only scheme which has realised a reasonable degree of success is the IRDP which continues to be the major poverty alleviation programme. Poor recovery is also due to lethargy of the bank staff who do not take any rigorous follow-up action. As the bank staff usually reside in cities they do not have contact with the rural sector borrowers and this has made the recovery programme less than a complete success. Furthermore, a document gets time-barred after three years of execution. The bank manager has to revalidate it within that time failing which he has to face disciplinary action. Tracing the borrower to get revalidation of the document is difficult. To be on the safer side the bank managers desist from advancing loans.

Profitability is the criterion for evaluating the performance of a bank. As such banks have become extremely cautious in their lending programme. The banks have to get interest if they are to consider their asset as performing. The banks are reluctant to take up assets which are non-performing. They consider it better to invest in zero risk assets like Government bonds at 12.5 percent interest. This accounts for the increase in bank investments in Government bonds above the SLR requirement of 34.75 percent. This can be checked if the Government reduces the interest rate on its bonds to 7-8 percent.

A healthy banking system subsists on profitability. The banks are shifting their focus from social purpose to viability. The Regional Rural Banks which were once considered to be agents of rural transformation are in trouble because of the losses they have suffered during the past two decades. They have become unviable from the point of view of profitability. If the banks are to survive they have to satisfy the criterion of profitability. But priority sectors are not considered to be profitable avenues for lending as they are beset by recovery problems. In the present context profitability and priority sector lending appear to be incompatible. If the targets of priority sector lending are to be realised the banks should not be allowed to bear the losses. If they are to continue to be healthy and viable institutions they should not be subject to controls about the deployment of their funds. They should be free to invest their funds in avenues which yield the greatest percentage of profits.

The Narasimham Committee Report on Financial Sector Reform recommended the reduction of priority sector lending from 40 percent to 10 percent. Large agriculturists and road transport operators were excluded from this definition. Priority sector included only the real "weaker sections" who needed bank credit to sustain their activities. This recommendation was not accepted; instead, the definition of "priority sector" has been expanded. But it must be borne in mind that the extension defeats the very concept of priority sectors.

The public sector banks have about 20,000 branches in the rural sector and these branches have per force to lend to the priority sectors in the absence of other avenues for the deployment of their funds. But the banks are not free to identify the solvent borrowers, approve the viable schemes and fix the quantum of credit for each activity. They are there to follow the instructions laid down by the Reserve Bank of India. They function only as intermediaries and the borrowers recognise them as such. If the priority sector has to survive their targets for lending must go. The banks should not be pressurised to reach fixed targets of credit. The banks should be made to realise the profit potential in their lending and they should be assisted in their recovery operations. Banks should be free to identify solvent borrowers and viable proposals. In this scenario the banks would be able to lend to priority sectors and to satisfy the interim of profitability. Bank lending under the loan mela schemes which involved lending to ineligible borrowers caused great damage to the banking system. The unsavoury effects are felt by the real weaker sections who find bank credit closed to them. The banks which have accumulated non-performing assets have become reluctant to lend to them. At present banks are flush with funds but the needy sectors are starved of credit. This situation is unlikely to improve despite penalties and bank-specific actions contemplated by the Reserve Bank against "erring" banks. The answer lies not in tightening controls over bank operations but in relaxing them and in allowing banks to take decisions for which they alone are responsible and accountable.

Despite the declining trend of profitability of the nationalised banks due, inter alia to the priority sector lending at concessional interest rates, the Governor, Reserve Bank of India, announced on June 18, 1994 that the present policy of providing 40 percent of bank credit for the priority sector would be continued. Referring to the controversy that has arisen about the sanctity of the 40 percent credit allocation for the priority sector he stated. "We have decided firmly to continue the same allocation". In the light of the declining profitability of the banking sector and the accumulation of non-performing assets the Narasimham Committee had recommended the reduction of priority sector lending from 40 percent to 10 percent in a phased programme. As the priority sectors have been attuned to concessional borrowing of 40 percent of bank funds the sudden reduction of this volume to 10 percent would be too drastic. There is need to reduce it in stages to 10 percent and even to zero. It must be realised that with the entry of private and foreign banks into the banking sector not committed to concessional lending of 40 percent of their lendable resources, they will be in a better position to compete successfully with the public sector banks. The introduction of provisioning norms, income recognition norms and capital adequacy norms makes it incumbent on the public sector banks to earn sufficient profits. With the continuance of concessional lending of 40 percent of this lendable resources to the priority sector the banking sector will be hard put to it to satisfy these norms. In view of the above it appears necessary to reduce the concessional lending below 40 percent and even to zero in the near future. In the immediate future the Reserve Bank of India could consider the adoption of one of the following options: (a) the allocation of 40 percent of the lendable resources of the banking system could be continued at the going market rate of interest; (b) if concessional lending is considered imperative, it could be brought down successively to the zero level of the which lending could be at the market rate of interest. The priority sector cannot have it both ways.

Social banking since 1969 has eroded the profitability of the banking sector, has led to the accumulation of non-performing assets and bad debts and has put the banking system on the verge of a collapse. Banks are profit making institutions and to be able to earn adequate profits they must be allowed to be run on commercial lines. Their balance sheets should be framed on the principles of liquidity and profitability. But the present social banking is in violation of these two principles. They are not adequately liquid as they have accumulated bad debts and they do not earn adequate profits because of the existence of non-performing assets and concessional lending. If banks are to remain vibrant there should be a shift of focus from social banking to commercial banking.

24

The Prime Minister on Foreign Investment

It is common knowledge that the rate of economic growth depends crucially on investment in infrastructure. The rate of economic growth in India is slow at 3-4 percent though it is expected to rise to 7 percent in the next 2-3 years while the Chinese rate of economic growth is 12.5 percent. The slowness of India's growth can be attributed, in part, to inadequate infrastructure. This means that if the rate of economic growth in India is to be speeded up the rate of investment in infrastructure should be speeded up too. But India is labouring under shortage of domestic investible resources. Unless foreign investment is encouraged India will not be able to afford sufficient infrastructural investment so necessary for accelerated economic growth.

During the last three years i.e., since the economic reforms were initiated in July 1991, the climate favourable to foreign investment has been built up. Due to persistent efforts on the part of the Government to attract foreign investment it has just started picking up. The foreign investors are more than willing to invest in India especially after the credit rating agencies the Moody's and Japanese Bond Research Institute (JRBI) have upgraded India's credit rating. This will enable India to enjoy the benefits of a larger foreign investment inflow at cheap interest rates. However, the Prime Minister while addressing the 67th Annual Session of the Federation of Indian Chambers of Commerce and Industry (FICCI) in Delhi on December 9, 1994, dropped a hint that India has been getting too much of investment from abroad and quoted his colleagues as having told him that the foreign investment flow was, infact, a torrent. He said. "How much can I take from outside? There are limits. If, I do not recognise the limits future generation will never forgive me".

It goes without saying that there is an element of exaggeration in this observation. What India gets is just a trickle when compared with what Thailand which came to the scene hardly a decade ago or China a decade and a half ago gets. In all India has so far received $ 8 billion (Rs. 24,000 crore) by way of investment and by way of promises and the flow has risen to roughly about a billion dollar per year from around $ 400 million a year earlier. This certainly is not a torrent especially in view of the wide gap between the available domestic resources necessary to provide adequate infrastructural facilities. The Indian leaders have spoken at home and abroad that they would need investment in infrastructure such as energy, transport, telecommunications, mining and so on. As the Prime Minister's observation represents going back on this commitment, it is bound to send wrong signals to the foreign investors. The position therefore needs to be clarified without loss of time.

The Prime Minister is of the opinion that there is a limit beyond which the inflow of foreign investment should not be allowed to go. This is for the reason that "the future generations would not forgive me". According to him some curbs on foreign investment are necessary. But curbs on foreign investment flow are not necessary when the country has just recovered from a setback it suffered three years ago when there was industrial stagnation. At that time the Moody's had downgraded India's credit rating. But India's credit rating has been upgraded now by the Moody's and JBRI. To talk of the necessity to curb foreign investment inflow at this stage is to discourage the foreign investors if not to scare them away. The foreign direct investment has not even started steadying properly. In a situation like this the talk of slowing down the momentum generated by the overall favourable investment climate does not appear to be in order.

There is imperative need to stick to the present policy for a reasonable period of time. There has to be continuity and consistency in the declared policy of the Government for the world to take it seriously. The Prime Minister's compulsion in changing horses midstream seems to follow a rather cautious approach in view of the second batch of six states going to the polls in February 1995. Then the country has to gear up for the next general elections in 1996 unless the Prime Minister decides to advance the date.

The people were agitated not about the economic reforms but about the rising prices. The rate of inflation was, of course, brought from 17.5 percent in 1991 to 7 percent in August 1994. But it has started to rise gently in recent months. The argument that the rate of inflation has been brought down to the single digit zone is a poor consolation to the harried consumer who is greatly agitated over the continuous rise in the prices of essential commodities. Therefore, care has to be taken to maintain reasonable prices of essential commodities. The market economy concept is good but it should not be taken to mean an unadulterated laissez faire economy.

The Prime Minister has expounded the strategy of the "middle path" in the pursuit of economic policy. The mixed economy concept represented a mixture of the private and the public sectors a mixture in which the public sector was given the dominant role in the organisation of the economic structure. But the "middle path" expounded by the Prime Minister is not the same as the mixed economy of the Nehruvian conception. It is a path between a market economy and a State managed economy with emphasis being laid on the former which should gradually expound its scope of activities But the "middle path" concept has to be spelt out clearly in order not to allow multiple interpretations. The "middle path" should not be a form of mixed economy. If mixed economy could last for four decades, is it not possible to give the market economy experiment a little more time to settle down? But the electoral compulsions warrant that the market economy be tempered by concern for the poor who are groaning under the weight of rising prices. If this is done, there is no need to cry halt to the inflow of foreign direct investment which is so necessary to develop infrastructural facilities in India.

The Prime Minister expressed the apprehension that if foreign investment is allowed without any check "the next generation would not forgive us". This apprehension is unnecessary. In the past many countries which are at present developed were financed by foreign investment. This investment was used productively to build permanent assets which were able to redeem the foreign debt. China has opened its doors to foreign investment and is experiencing double digit rate of economic growth. In a similar manner the Asian Tigers have welcomed foreign investment and they are brimming with confidence that they will be able to redeem the debt before long. If foreign investment in India is diverted to channels where it does not increase productivity and efficiency it becomes deadweight debt to be borne by the future generations which will not forgive the present generation. As stated already foreign investment is to develop infrastructural facilities which help to accelerate the rate of economic growth which in turn will enable the Government to pay interest and repay the principal without any difficulty. The assets built by foreign investment remain permanently yielding benefits to the future generations even after the debt is redeemed. The future generations will have cause to thank the present generation. For this reason foreign investment should be welcomed and it should be diverted to channels which increase the productivity and efficiency of the economy.

The gaps in infrastructural facilities are daunting. The enormity of the gap was indicated by the finance minister on the fifth anniversary of India an Indian Government publication focusing on economic issues before the nation. The Finance Minister said: "Our policies aimed at reducing infrastructural imbalance in the economy and making India internationally competitive have been in the right direction but a lot of ground is still to be covered. "India has vast infrastructural gaps. It has to add 10,000 new MW of power capacity in the next ten years. It has to upgrade, both quantitatively and qualitatively, telecommunications network. It has to upgrade its roads and ports network to move rapidly expanding volumes of merchandise. It has to tap large reserves of hydrocarbons to meet its energy requirements".

Welcoming US businessmen to India the Finance Minister said: "India is committed to creating a profitable and hospitable climate conducive to the growth enterprise".

The publication India pointed out that according to the Commerce Secretary Ron Brown, between now and the year 2000 new infrastructural projects in India could amount to $ 100 billion (Rs. 3,10,000 crore). Unless this done, the much needed increase in private investment and growth on which the success of economic reforms depends will fall well below India's potential. In view of the need to develop infrastructure which is possible only with the help of foreign investment it is imperative to allow free flow of foreign investment into the infrastructure and allied sectors.

25

Relaxing the Rigid Stance about Monetary Growth

Liquidity crunch caused mainly by the reduction of money supply growth from 20 percent to 13 percent has hit the industrial sector land and has retarded its growth. The easing of the liquidity crunch is possible if the rate of monetary growth is raised. It was feared earlier that a rise in the rate of monetary growth would exacerbate inflation. Stability of prices which was hailed as the objective of policy required a reduction of the rate of monetary growth even below 13 percent as per the monetarist logic. The adverse effects of this on the rate of economic growth were not given due recognition. Price stability took precedence over economic growth. However, Dr. C. Rangarajan, Governor of the Reserve Bank of India in his Presidential remarks at a lecture of the IMF Executive Director for Germany, Mr. Stefan Schoenberg in Bombay, on February 19, 1996 said that India and other developing countries had not wholeheartedly accepted the growing consensus in European countries and the United States that price stability is the dominant exclusive objective of Central Bank's monetary policy. Sustained increase in prices is not possible without an increase in money supply and hence monetary supply had to be integrated in the policies. India is facing a dilemma growth. It is the considered view of many that economy growth should be given precedence over price stability. If that is so, there is need to relax a rigid stance adopted thus far about the stability of prices. In fact, prices can be allowed to rise generally if that ensures a higher rate of growth.

The latest official figures indicate that the Indian economy is sound with inflation well under control at 4.71 percent, industrial growth being robust and exports showing a rising trend. The forex reserve, excluding gold and SDRs, having shrunk to $ 16.412 billion (as at the end of January 1996) from the recorded high of $ 20.06 billion recorded in May 1995 and the rupee sharply depreciating by 20 percent since August 1995 the Government can take comfort from the fact that the "dragon of inflation" has been tamed. The rate of inflation which had reached a record high of 17.5 percent at the stance of economic reform programme in June,1994 has been brought down to 4.71 percent. Though the rupee's depreciation against the US dollar reached a historic low of Rs. 38.50 on a single trading session early in February, 1996, it rallied round to settle at Rs. 36 to a dollar following the adoption by the Reserve Bank of India or a four-point strategy to stem the speculative ride on the rupee. The Finance Minister stated that the current value of the rupee was in tune with the tune economic fundamentals of the economy and advised industry to adjust itself to the phenomenon of fluctuations which is natural to an economy integrating itself with the global economy. This will not adversely affect the economy and the current account deficit would not be more than $ 3.5 billion or 1.5 percent of GDP. The rupee is unlikely to depreciate further in the near future as the supply of dollars has increased following the Reserve Bank package which has made repatriation of Export proceeds denominated in US dollars quicken and imports costlier to check draw down on reserves. The rate of domestic savings has risen from 20 percent to 24 percent and has helped to close the Saving-Instrument Gap.

Not many in India have noticed the fact that during the past 30 months since August 1993 though the rupee had remained stable at Rs. 31.37 per U.S. dollar, the dollar itself had been depreciating speedily against the major European currencies and especially against Yen. This suited the Reserve Bank of India because it helped to partially offset the 5 percent higher inflation rate in India than the OECD countries. But in February 1995 the fall in the dollar suddenly accelerated. From buying 98 Yen in January 1995 it was able to buy only 81 Yen in April and 82 in May. The rupee slided with the dollar. In July the dollar rose to 99 Yen and the immediate impact was a fall in the value of the rupee to Rs. 34 or by about 8 percent. By

January 31, 1996 the dollar was buying 106.9 Yen. A further depreciation of the rupee to Rs. 35 per dollar was to be expected. By now the bear sentiment had gripped the Indian Stock market and the rupee was driven even lower. The U.S. had come to have second thoughts about the higher interest rates. On February 1, 1996 the Federal Reserve Bank lowered the interest rate in order to ward off recession and to stimulate economic growth. The European countries followed suit with a competitive interest cut regime. This would stop the rise in the value of the dollar. In turn, this would check the depreciation of the rupee. If the Federal Reserve Bank again raised the interest rate there will be an appreciation of the dollar which means depreciation of the rupee. Even then the depreciation of the rupee can be halted by mobilising dollar resources by means of eradicating overinvoicing of imports and underinvoicing of exports and by banning the import of gold. The dollar reserves to be mobilised in this matter are of the order of $ 12 billion. All these indicate due strengthening of the macroeconomic fundamentals of the Indian economy.

In this situation, priority has to be given to accelerated economic growth. The countries of South East Asia which are called Asian Tigers and China have achieved over 10 percent economic growth. The rate of growth in India is 6 percent and it is expected to rise to 8 percent in the immediate future. But this depends on the raising of the liquidity crunch. At present, the rate of monetary growth has been brought down from 20 percent to 13 percent and this has caused a fall in the rate of inflation to 4.71 percent. This is achievement enough. But this has caused a retardation of economic growth. A rise in the rate of monetary growth above the present 13 percent to about 15-16 percent will ease the liquidity crunch to a great extent and help the rate of economic growth to rise to 8 percent. This may cause a rise in the rate of inflation initially but this is a small price to pay for a higher rate of economic growth. Thus, there will have to be a trade-off between price stability and economic growth.

The Governor of the Reserve Bank of India, until recently, was harping upon price stability as the aim of monetary policy even if it meant some retardation of the rate of economic growth. But on February 19, 1995 he has relaxed this rigid stance and has said that price stability is not the only aim of monetary policy. Monetary policy has got several objectives, price stability being the major aim. The developing countries have not wholeheartedly accepted the growing consensus in the European countries and the United States that price stability is the dominant, exclusive objective of monetary policy. In this context it is a good thing that the Reserve Bank Governor has relaxed the rigid concern for price stability. A rise in monetary growth which causes a temporary rise in the level of prices, accelerates economic growth and causes a rise in the volume of output which serves as an antidote to inflation. In view of this, there is a strong case for raising the rate of monetary growth to 15-16 percent from the present 13 percent.

The monetarists argue that a rise in the rate of monetary growth causes a rise in the level of prices. This is admitted but they do not take into account the rise in the value of output occasioned by a rise in the rate of economic growth which has a backwash which in turn causes a fall in the level of prices. Seen in this light, the case for a rise in the rate of monetary growth above the present rate of 13 percent is strong and unassailable. The Reserve Bank of India and the Finance Ministry have to ponder seriously over this proposed (which may not be ingenious) and take action to raise the rate of monetary growth appropriately.

Easing of the liquidity crunch and the fostering of economic growth are dependent on a higher rate of monetary growth. India is burdened by the rising incidence of poverty. Unless there is a sharp rise in the rate of economic growth it is unlikely that there will be a perceptible reduction in the poverty levels. The rate of economic growth that will be required is not 5-6 percent but 8-9 percent, East Asian Tigers like China are experiencing now. The poverty reduction in these countries has been made possible by the extremely high growth in their economies. This also adds strength to the argument for raising the rate of monetary growth to ease the liquidity crunch and to promote economic growth.

26

Need to Re-constitute the Audit Committees of Public Sector Banks

It is common knowledge that the Reserve Bank of India, in consultation with the Ministry of Finance, has issued fresh guidelines to the banks in the matter of furnishing accounts to the Reserve Bank every six months. There is in addition, the need for an Advisory Committee of the Board of Directors (A.C.B.) which has to perform the duties mentioned herewith. The composition of the ACB and its functions are as under :

The ACB attached to every public sector bank has five members who are :

1. Chairman and Managing Director.
2. Executive Director of the Bank (and in the case of State Bank of India a whole time director)
3. Two Official Directors—one of them being a nominee of the Government and the other being a nominee of the Reserve Bank of India)
4. Two non-official, non-executive directors, one of them being a Chartered Accountant.

The meetings of the ACB are to be chaired by any one of the non-executive directors.

The Audit Committee has to perform the following functions: Providing directions to the banks and overseeing the total audit function. Total audit function comprises organisation, operationalisation and quality control of internal audit and inspection within the bank. This has to be followed by the statutory external audit of the bank and inspection by the Reserve Bank of India. As regards the internal audit the ACB has to review the internal audit function including the quality and effectiveness of the audit. It has to review the inspection reports in respect of specialised and large branches and of all branches with unsatisfactory ratings. In particular, it has to focus on the following functions:

1. inter-bank adjustment accounts.
2. unreconciled long standing entries in inter-bank accounts.
3. arrears in the balancing of books in various branches and the funds if any.
4. all other major areas of house keeping. The banks usually transfer the big account to loss-making branches in order to enable them to earn profits. The Reserve Bank of India has levelled serious objections against this practice.
5. Obtaining and reviewing the half yearly reports from the banks as per the instructions of the Reserve Bank of India.
6. As regards the statutory audit the ACB has to follow up the issues raised in the Long Form Audit Report (LFAR). It has to interact with the external auditors before finalising the annual/ semi annual financial accounts and reports.
7. The ACB has to be concerned with all the issues raised in the inspection reports of the Reserve Bank of India.

The Audit Advisory Committee of any nationalised bank is an important Committee constituted as per the Reserve Bank guidelines. This committee consists of the following members.

1. Executive Director
2. A Government nominee
3. A Reserve Bank nominee
4. A Chartered Accountant

It is suggested here that an Advocate should be a part-time Director in order to enable the effective functioning of the Audit Committee. This suggestion gains relevance in the context of the large number of waivers of loans taken by both the genuine and bogus defaulters the latter being in large number.

In the year 1994-95 the waiver of the loans ran to a hefty Rs. 1,000 crore as stated by Shri Talwar, Deputy Governor of the Reserve Bank of India. If this is shared by 20 nationalised banks the share of each bank on an average will be Rs. 50 crore. This is in addition to the non-performing assets of the order of Rs. 4,000 crore.

The Reserve Bank introduced this scheme in order to clear up the balance sheets of the nationalised banks. However, the scheme was misused both by the bank officials and the borrowers acting in collusion. In consequence, the depositors' money was wrongfully appropriated by the wilful defaulters in collusion with the corrupt bank officials. The benefits of write-offs have gone to willful defaulters rather than to genuine defaulters. If an advocate is made a member of the Committee, as suggested above, he will exercise vigil over the inclusion of willful defaulters and take care to eliminate them from the benefit of write-off. Some may raise the objection that even the advocate member might get into collusion with the bank officials, willful defaulters and make a gain in the process. But this venture is risky for him for, in the event of an enquiry by the CBI or by any other agency he will be caught as his notings will be on record in the files. This risk deters him from getting into collusion with the bank officials and the willful defaulters. Therefore, the presence of an advocate whose opinion has to be obtained in all cases of write-offs is felt imperative as he serves as a watchdog keeping vigil on the write-off exercise.

The presence of an advocate on the Committee will lend credibility to the bank operations. This will brighten the image of the Government on the eve of the elections to the Lok Sabha scheduled for early 1996. If the existing committee (without an advocate on it) is allowed to continue, the burden of write-off is likely to escalate into Rs. 2,000 crore. The public is raising the question: Whose money is being written-off? In order to avoid the willful defaulters misusing the write-off provision the appointment of an advocate on the Committee is a categorical imperative.

27

A Case for Additional Food Subsidy

India's food economy presents a paradox of poverty in the midst of plenty. The food stock is mounting but the poor have to remain half fed and half nourished. At the end of June 1995 against the buffer stock norm of 14.5 million tonnes the food stock held by the Government reached the 37 million tonnes mark. This was against the food stock of 31.31 million tonnes at the end of June 1994. The off-take through the public distribution system is 1.2 million tonnes per month or 14.5 million tonnes per year. Given the prospect of another good year of food grains production it is expected that the current agricultural year may end up with a food stock of 40 million tonnes.

Though a good harvest is likely to lead to a crash in food prices, the Government, in view of electoral compulsions, is not likely to compromise on the policy of supporting the farmers. About a third of the food stock held by the Government is stored in the open exposed to the ravages of wind and weather and with no safeguard against the deterioration of the quality of food stock. The Southern States, of course, hold stocks in protected locations but they have to face the problem of prompt movement of food grains due to paucity of railway facilities to move them. Holding food stocks also create financial problems. For the week ending August 4, 1995 the total commercial bank credit increased by 26.88 percent. Advances for food procurement stood at Rs. 15,159 crore which increased by 20 percent. How this situation will change during the remaining part of the financial year depends on a complex mix of variables including the policy of the Government towards the mounting food stock. Export of food grains is a solution to the problem of surplus food stock but the prospect for export of food grains are not very bright.

The Government has to choose between two alternatives. Of the total food stock of 37 million tonnes about a third i.e., 12 million tonnes is held in the open without any safeguard against deterioration of the quality of food grains. If this food is held in the present location with no safeguards there is the hazard of incalculable loss of public funds arising from the decaying of food stocks. The second option is to use this food stock for the benefit of the poor who are half-fed and undernourished. Given the two hazards the latter hazard appears to be a rational choice. The Ministry of Food has proposed that the issue price of both wheat and rice should be reduced and these food articles should be channeled through the Revamped Public Distribution System. During April-June 1995 the offtake stood at 3.4 million tonnes against 2.8 million tonnes in April-June 1994. This is a distinct improvement. If the issue price of wheat is reduced the offtake will register further improvement. The issue price of wheat could be lowered from Rs. 4.22 a kg to Rs. 3.50 a kg and of rice could be reduced from Rs. 6.90 a kg to Rs. 4 a kg. This will remove the glut in the Government store thus removing the hazard of deterioration in quality of food stock and will also benefit the poor who will be enabled to consume more food. The extra food subsidy will be of the order of Rs. 400-500 crore. But the Finance Ministry which is grappling with the problem of reducing the fiscal deficit does not seem to be in favour of the proposal to reduce the issue prices of wheat and rice. The Finance Ministry is being accused of discriminatroy treatment towards the food subsidy.

The Fifth Pay Commission is bound to enhance the scales of pay and dearness allowances of Central Government employees. The salary scales demanded by the employees stagger the comprehension of the human mind. When implemented they will be implemented anytime now the extra expenditure of the Government will be over Rs. 1,500 crore. This being the case, it does not appear prudent to cold shoulder the proposal to allow additional food subsidy for the poor. The Government which delivers pro-poor rhetoric will do well to allow this additional food subsidy which will, on the one hand, reduce the mounting food stock and avoid deterioration in quality and, on the other hand, help the poor by providing easier access to food at lower prices.

The rate of inflation at present is just over 8 percent and it shows an upward slant. It is obvious that in India it is the food prices that govern the general price index. When the food prices rise even though the budget is in balance or in a surplus the general price level rises. If the food prices fall the general price level falls even though the budget is in deficit. If the additional subsidy of Rs. 400-500 is granted the fiscal deficit will rise by that amount and will exacerbate inflationary forces in the economy. If this additional subsidy is not paid, the issue prices will not be reduced, the food prices remain high and this causes a rise in the general price level. Both the courses are inflationary but the inflation caused by the fiscal deficit due to the payment of additional subsidy is more tolerable than the inflation caused by the rise in food prices. The inflation caused by the fiscal deficit is general while the inflation caused by the higher food prices is specific to the working class who demand higher wages which occasion cost push and demand pull inflations. In view of this it is necessary to hold down the food prices by reducing the issue prices of wheat and rice and through it to hold down the rate of inflation. The Government is not weary about raising the subsidies for producer-farmers. Why should it be weary about raising food subsidies which will benefit the poor and will also help the Government in holding down the food stock and in holding down the cost of storage and the hazard of deterioration of food stocks.

I appeal to the Finance Ministry and in particular, to the Hon'ble Minister of Finance to re-examine the whole issue of meeting the additional cost of reducing the issue prices of wheat and rice by the grant of additional food subsidy of the order of 400-500 crore and view the case for additional food subsidy with sympathy and understanding.

28

Exit Policy is an Immediate Necessity

In July 1991, the Government of India announced the adoption of a New Economic Policy meant to tigerise the Indian economy. This policy envisaged the deregulation of industry, liberating it from bureaucratic controls and licensing procedures. This appeared necessary to attract direct foreign investment in Indian industry. An adjunct of this policy was the EXIT Policy. Under this policy the sick and unviable industrial units were to be closed down and the labourers removed from these units had to be retrained and re-deployed. There was a sort of safety net in the form of the National Renewal Fund to take care of the temporarily unemployed labourers. This Fund received liberal contributions from the World Bank.

In the theory of the firm founded on neoclassical economic theory both the entry into and exit out of the industry are free. Any firm which makes subnormal profits or even losses leaves the industry sub-normality of profits is a sign of disequilibrium which can be corrected by the exit of the firm from the industry; conversely, if firms in the industry make supernormal profits, others are attracted into the industry. Supernormality of profits is a sign of disequilibrium which can be corrected by the entry of new firms into the industry. If the profits are normal there is neither entry into nor exit one of the industry exit policy announced by the Government as part of the new industrial policy has its bearing in the neo-classical theory of the firm whose aim is the promotion of competitive efficiency.

The exit policy announced by the Government is the most controversial aspect of the new industrial policy. Some attack it on the ground that it leads to large scale unemployment in the industrial sector and this adds to unemployment existing already.

The Fund-Bank duo which have advised the adoption of this policy do not, of course, mean that India should opt for enhancing unemployment. It is necessary, therefore, to understand the longer term implications of the exit policy which is yet to be adopted. What is the experience of the other countries which have implemented the exit policy?

In the United states of America many companies suffering sustained losses close down their plants throwing workers out of jobs. The leading American companies like General Motors and IBM are going through this process. Over the past two decades the majority of the Fortune 500 companies have undergone this kind of a restructuring process. If the exit policy in the USA were to reduce job opportunities on a long-term basis one would expect a decline in the total number of people working.

The exit policy in Western Europe is not as free as in the United States of America. Even so, the experience of these countries is similar to that of the United States though additional job creation was at a slower rate. The total industrial and service employment increased from 88 million in 1973 to 94 million in 1990. In Japan the policy of life time employment was given up long ago. In 1992 alone as many as 14000 Japanese companies were closed down. Even so job creation in Japan is very high. As the domestic labour supply is limited immigrants from Brazil and other countries have to be brought in to fill the vacancies. In Communist China the policy of guaranteed life-time employment has been given up under the reform programme adopted in 1988. Though a number of industrial units were closed down China is experiencing an unprecedented boom. Industrial production is growing at the rate of 20 percent per annum. Exports are rapidly rising and foreign investment inflow is over 40 times that of India.

In the first half of the present century in India entry and exit of industrial units were free. There was large-scale investment in labour intensive units of both foreign capital and domestic capital. The tea estates, jute mills, cotton mills, coal mines were the main industries set up between 1900 and 1950. They had huge employment potential; they were also substantial exporters. Sick units were allowed to close down; even so there was growth in industrial employment. The same trend continued even during the dark days of the Great Depression of the 1930s. In 1950 India was the tenth largest industrial power in the world controlling 2 percent of world trade. It had substantial foreign exchange reserves and had no external debt commitments. But between 1950 and 1990 the Indian economy came under stringent regulations and India slipped from the position of 10th to 27th in industrial production, its share of world trade slipped from 2 percent to 0.4 percent and the foreign exchange reserve position deteriorated necessitating the accumulation of huge external debt. There has been hardly any employment generation in the organized industrial sector. The following Table shows the index of organised employment in the private sector and registered unemployment.

Year	Organised Unemployment in the Private Sector (in Lakh)	Registered Unemployment (in Lakh)
1991	67	51
1976	68	97
1981	76	178
1986	74	301
1989	75	327

During the past 20 years the total unemployment in the organised private sector industry has remained constant at 7 million while the registered unemployment figure shot up from 5 million to 33 million. The small scale industrial sector which is not subject to the rigours of labour legislation has shown a much better growth of employment. Employment in this sector has grown from 5 million to 12 million in the past 20 years. This is in sharp contrast with the static employment situation in the organised private sector. The small scale industrial sector enjoys the flexibility required under the exit policy. Unviable units are closed down and labourers are provided Jobs elsewhere. Employment in this sector has increased by 250 percent during the past 20 years. In the organised industrial sector where there is no exit policy there is a total stagnation of employment.

Empirical evidence available with respect to India, China, Japan, Western Europe and the USA indicates that exit policy does not reduce employment but, instead, increases it. There is, therefore, the imperative need to frame a well-conceived exit policy in order to place the Indian industrial sector on a sound footing.

The trade unions through the country supported by the left parties in the parliament and the state legislators are opposed to the exit policy under the misapprehension that the labourers would be thrown out of jobs and would have to face destitution. They should be made to realise the exit policy is necessary in order to make Indian industry internationally competitive and to promote Indian exports. Under the liberalized import policy imports into India are surging at the rate of 18 percent while exports are rising at the rate of 4 percent. This is causing acute concern for the authorities who are faced with a yawning trade deficit and the need to obtain external finance to meet it. As a result India is accumulating external debt of vast dimensions. India's total external debt : long, medium and short term is currently estimated at \$ 85 billion and the year-wise amortisation and interest is \$ 9.85 billion for the fiscal year 1992-93, \$ 8.95 billion for 1993-94, \$ 9.25 billion for 1994-95 & 8.5 billion for 1995-96 an average of \$ 9.0 billion a year from this year to March 1996. The balance of trade deficit for the year ending March 1993, on an annualisation of the performance for the first eight months will be around \$ 4.6 billion : \$ 17.4 billion exports and \$ 22.0 billion imports. The two (capital and current account) together will give a balance of payments deficit of \$ 15 billion for this year. If the current account keeps producing a deficit of \$ 3 billion to \$ 5 billion a year the annual deficit will be \$ 12 billion to \$ 14 billion and the total cumulative payments deficit inclusive of this year upto fiscal 1995-96 will be a \$ 48 billion to \$ 56 billion. If India is unable to close this gap through exports it will have to borrow in one form or another. By the end of fiscal 1996 India will have a debt burden of around \$ 137 billion thereby emerging as the largest debtor among Third World countries well ahead of Brazil.

The remedy for this dismal situation is export promotion. There are two reasons why export growth is sluggish (1) Indian GDP growth is slow and it must grow at the rate of 8.3 percent to ensure that exports close the gap. (2) India has to sell more of the same products at cheaper prices. Considering the commodity-cum-low technology nature of Indian exports there is a limit to their demand by the developed countries for such products. The world does not need Indian exports beyond a point because India is largely de-linked in terms of technology from the products and services of the developed countries. Such a linkage can take place only if there is a fundamental technological restructuring of the Indian industry in order that it may produce quality goods and services. The world Competitiveness Report which ranked 10 countries in 1991 gave the tenth place to India. India's industrial policy has to be a trade instrument. This must be the first step towards "tigerisation". Japan adopted this policy in the mid-fifties and Korea, Taiwan, Hong Kong and Singapore in the mid-seventies. Such a policy will have to focus on industries with high income elasticity of demand, high rates of growth in productivity and have high value-addition, in order that high wages can be paid.

If the industrial sector is to be made an instrument of trade, Indian industries are to be tigerised in the same way as industries in Japan, Korea, Singapore and Hong Kong. The adoption of the exit policy is the first step in that direction. Technological upgradation is a categorical imperative if Indian industries are to become internationally competitive. This is possible if the sick and unviable industries are allowed free exit. The apprehensions of trade unions and their political mentors are to be effectively allayed and they should be assured that under the exit policy employment will increase rather than diminish and in the long run labour will stand to gain in terms of increased employment opportunities, higher productivity, higher wages and higher standard of living. If the labourers are educated on the benefits of exit policy accruing to them and to the nation, they will co-operate with the Government and the industries and make the industrial policy a success. The Government has to undertake this task before implementing the exit policy. There is no time to lose. India is characterised as a "caged tiger". It must be uncaged to enable it to emerge as a King Tiger of Asia. It must be realised that without a remarkable export growth, India has no way of avoiding the debt trap. Unless it becomes a King Tiger of Asia export growth cannot be augmented. It cannot be a King Tiger of Asia unless a well-conceived EXIT Policy is formulated and implemented with the cooperation of labourers and the political parties supporting them in opposing the EXIT policy. The exchange rate mechanism could assist export growth and so it would be desirable to change the conversion ratio from 60:40 to 80:20. Devaluation has to be ruled out as it enhances the burden of external debt.

29

A New Dimension to the Mexican Crisis

The Mexican currency crisis of December 1994 began to haunt the developing countries experiencing fiscal deficits, inflation and capital outflows. It did not leave India untouched. Many knowledgeable persons in India apprehended the danger of India facing the Mexico-type crisis. In my Memoranda submitted to the Hon'ble Prime Minister and the Hon'ble Finance Minister, I emphatically brushed aside this danger as the macro-economic fundamentals of the Indian economy were strong. However, this apprehension persists even now though it is not of any serious nature.

The Mexican crisis and the reactions to it from the centers in the North and the international financial institutions underline the case for rethinking the current orthodox policy advice tendered to the developing countries: a uniform development model, complete withdrawal of the State from the economy and financial liberalization. This was a major topic of discussion among the panel of economists of UNCTAD and other participants in a recent seminar on "International Finance : From Globalisation to Crisis".

The participants in the Seminar were of the view that the IMF World Bank advice changed in the late 1980s and early 1990s and the developing countries were pressurised to open up their financial sectors and capital markets to suit the interests of the US and European countries where the later find that the 'rescue' operations as for Mexico would involve asking the tax payer to meet the bills. In order to avoid this situation there might be a reversal of policy advice and the developing countries would be asked to regulate their capital markets and impose restrictions. UNCTAD Officer-in-Charge Carlos Fortin who chaired the Seminar in his brief opening comment noted that in 1994 when the Trade and Development Report had raised some of the issues about global finance and role of the State in the economy the Wall Street Journal had called the UNCTAD economists Rip Van Winkles but it has now published a story about how the economists had been warning for years about the likelihood of the kind of crisis that overtook Mexico.

Shaheen Abrahamian heading the Global Inter-dependence Division of the UNCTAD (and one of the Principal authors of its annual Trade and Development Report) said: "Mexico did not go out to attract short term capital. The inflows were the result of its was economic policy and till the crisis Mexico was being held out as 'exemplar'. The question that has to be asked is how did the 'exemplar' policies result in a serious flaw in the economy? How did the 'rewards' of the market become the 'seeds' of crisis?... The real question to be asked is whether the current orthodox paradigm is right, whether the pendulum has swung too far over the State role in the economy and whether the current paradigm needs to be corrected".

Mexico is said to have got into a crisis not because of wrong policies or mismanagement, but because it succeeded so well in following the orthodox policy line and advice. Mexico had cut its public deficits, had brought inflation under control (annual 9 percent rate in November 1994) and undertook trade liberalisation including the financial sector.

The conventional analysis is that if the public sector deficit is taken care of, the deficit of the private sector does not matter because the market knows what to do and that capital is scarce in developing countries and provides a high rate of return. Therefore, if the developing world opens up its capital account and encourages investment from abroad, capital would come into the country. The countries would get into trouble only if there are problems elsewhere high budget deficits, high inflation and unliberalised trade, if they were right all problems and difficulties would disappear.

The Fund Bank duo have advised the Government of India to aim at fiscal consolidation meaning a reduction in the fiscal deficit, gradual withdrawal of the State from economic activity and financial liberalisation. This policy has been, by and large, followed. The fiscal deficit which was 8.5 percent of G.D.P. in 1990-91 was brought down to 6.5 percent in 1995-96; the rate of inflation which was 17.5 percent has been reduced to 8.5 percent; the current account deficit which was 3 percent of G.D.P. has come down to over 1 percent of G.D.P.

The foreign exchange reserves in 1991 were $ 1.2 billion enough to finance 15 days imports. The Government adopted financial liberalisation and opened up the financial market to foreign finance companies. This led to an inflow of foreign capital through debt and non-debt channels. By July 1995 the forex reserves were of the order of over $ 20.0 billion. The rupee-dollar exchange rate was Rs. 31.37 per $ 1.

But by September 1995, the exchange rate began to slide and in fact it slid to $ 34 per dollar. In the beginning the Government thought that this was a technical correction to the ongoing inflation rate and so the Reserve Bank of India adopted a policy of non-intervention. But as the exchange rate slid to Rs. 36 per dollar the Reserve Bank intervened to check the slide in the external value of the rupee and at present it stands at above Rs. 34 per dollar.

But there are areas which cause much anxiety. There is a steady growth in agriculture and the industry getting into an upswing. It is on the strength in the productive sectors that the Central Statistical Organisation (CSO) revised the G.D.P. growth estimate for 1994-95 from 5.3 percent to 6.2 percent and has projected a 7 percent rise in 1995-96. It would thus be seen that the country is poised to achieve, if not exceed, in average, the Eighth plan target of 5.6 percent per annum. The Planning Commission should have no cause for its own reservations atleast of the growth target.

But the industrial recovery which started in 1993-94 and the near boom conditions evidenced in 1995 have not had any positive impact on the stock markets which have been on a bear phase. Meanwhile, the depreciation of the rupee and the rise in the call money rate have created problems for the monetary authorities. This must be seen in the context of the slower deposit growth and credit crunch and the raising of thc primary lending rate partly forced by the higher deposit rate. The boom conditions in industry seem threatened by liquidity shortage in the banking system. With the credit crisis in the banking system the slow down in industrial activity cannot be ruled out. The Reserve Bank is thus obliged to stabilize the rupee and to help the banks to overcome the liquidity shortage by reducing the reservation.

Even the comfortable balance of payments position is becoming open to question. The volatile exchange rate and the import intensity of industry which has to face global competition and of exports is likely to push the trade deficit to around $ 5 billion in 1995-96 and the pressure on the reserves is bound to emerge afresh. The weakening of the rupee and the set-back to fiscal consolidation necessitating continuous borrowing of Government and uncontrolled inflation rate pose serious risks to the growth trend. But the corporate profits should provide relief.

The sluggish stock market might suggest that the corporations are in the red. But corporate fortunes have been building for the past two years. A Reserve Bank study of 1030 companies in the private corporate sector for the year 1994-95 shows that total income recorded a 31 percent rise and post-tax profits an impressive 73.9 percent. Profitability ratios too registered distinct improvement with profits after tax as percentage of sales moving up from 7.4 percent in 1993-94 to 9.9 percent in the following year. The study also points out that of the 1,030 companies as many as 995 registered post-tax profits in 1994-95 against 950 in 1993-94. The good performance was spread across financial and non-financial companies as also across the industry groups. The profit boom has continued into the current financial year (1995-96) if the half yearly results announced by the companies are anything to go by. A number of companies including among others, East India Hotels, Crompton Greaves, India Cements etc. have reported net profit gains in excess of 90 percent. What is more, the contribution of "other income" in company profits a category which had significantly held up company bottomlines in the past few years appears to be falling suggesting a welcome shift in corporate priorities from trading and asset sales to manufacturing and asset formation. As for corporate prospects in the short run, there again seem no less bright. The tight liquidity conditions, with their effect in terms of rising interest rates will no doubt work to reduce profit margins. But demand remains robust in large measure a consequence of rapidly increasing government expenditure and this should more than offset any adverse interest rate effects. However, with emerging infrastructural bottlenecks higher corporate profits may be associated with higher prices of their products. But higher profits also mean larger savings and larger investment in modernisation and technological upgradation.

The Finance Minister was confident of pegging fiscal deficit in 1995-96 at 5.5 percent of G.D.P. But now he has begun to voice concern over the state of public finance as he finds the tax yield despite its buoyancy falling short of expectations, especially in respect of indirect taxes. Though he has called for control over expenditure along with larger tax collections the Government is not in a position to cut down subsidies especially in the election year. The plethora of Social Welfare Schemes however desirable they may be and the interim relief of the employees make up only part of the post budget expenditures which cannot be covered by the expected rise in tax revenues by Rs. 7,000-8,000 crore. In the current year the Government expected to realise Rs. 7,000 crore from disinvestment of public sector equity. The Finance Minister feels that without a massive disinvestment programme the fiscal deficit cannot be brought down to a sustainable level.

The falling share prices are sure to fuel the liquidity crisis. The falling share prices will undermine the capital market; the sluggishness in this primary market will compel corporates to increase their demand on the banking system; interest rates will rise in sympathy in the short and medium term, call money rates will turn volatile, the forex market will be badly affected and the fiscal system will be in jeopardy. They will force the Central and State Governments to pay higher interest rates on their securities. This will add to the debt burden. Less money will be available for development. The stock market crisis may be attributed to the fiscal policy of the Government. The Finance Minister has lamented that he could not streamline the fiscal system because every year between 1992 and 1995 he was constrained by elections in one part of the country or the other.

India's external debt is growing. Until 1980 India's external debt was $ 20.6 billion. By the end of 1990 it stood at $ 82 billion. At the end of 1993 it rose to $ 91.8 billion and in March 1995 it was estimated to be $ 95.2 billion. By March 1996 it is expected to touch $ 97.7 billion. The repayment of external debt is possible by generating a surplus on the current account. The invisible account showed a surplus of Rs. 3655 crore in 1981-82. This rose to Rs. 4,268 crore by 1991-92. In 1992-93 there was a sharp decline to Rs. 1,337 crore. In 1994-95 the surplus on invisibles was almost half of that generated in 1993-94. In view of this invisible are not likely to provide any solution to India's debt problem. Generating trade surplus is an equally challenging task. India's trade deficit in 1994-95 was $ 2.03 billion. During the first half of 1995-96 exports grew at 26.3 percent, while imports grew at 32.8 percent. As invisibles are a small part of the current account the way out to repay India's debt along with interest is to generate a trade surplus. But data over the past two-and-a-half decades reveal a very higher correlation between India's exports and imports. The co-efficient of correlation is estimated at 0.90. This means that whenever exports increased imports also increased, thus creating an obstacle to generating a trade surplus. This calls for making exports cheaper and imports costlier. This was tried by devaluation. Data on devaluation of the rupee and exports for the past five years show that the value of the rupee in terms of the dollar has fallen from Rs. 18 in 1991 to Rs. 31 by 1994 end a decline of 73 percent. As against this, exports grew from $ 18.20 billion in 1991-92 to $ 26.22 billion in 1994-95 an increase of about 44 percent. This gives a price elasticity of India's exports at 0.80 which is less than unity and thus failed to help in an effective way. Therefore, the price competitiveness of India's exports is to be increased to save the situation. Any further downward adjustment will make imports costlier and for this reason prices are sure to flare up. Further, prices in the domestic market rise when exports exceed imports.

The debt problem has already assumed a serious magnitude. The World Bank in its latest report has identified India as a mediumly indebted country. Repayment of this debt has to be done by tightening the belt. A change of policy is needed. The government has to adopt a policy which it imports low value commodities and exports them after value addition. This is possible only in a limited way. On the import side POL and capital goods cannot be made to come under this policy. There is also need to discourage consumerism which is responsible for the import of white goods and which also has caused a fall in the savings ratio. This also calls for a change of policy.

It is the currency aspect that is important. Why did the slide in the rupee occur? It occurred because of the excess demand for dollars. The Government needed dollars to meet its debt obligations in terms of dollars. The Indian Oil Corporation which had to meet its payments in dollars needed them. At the same time, the inflow of dollars to India declined. These factors jointly acted to cause a slide in the external value of the rupee. At present the exchange rate is Rs. 34.60 to a dollar and it is unlikely to slide further. If it begins to slide the foreign exchange reserves can be drawn upon to meet any excess demand for dollars. The foreign investment has begun to pick up. The Reserve Bank of India has relaxed the restrictions on the inflow of commercial borrowing and the GDR proceeds. The Indian companies which raise funds in the European Capital Markets are now free to shift them to Indian banks. They will swell the stock of forex reserves. If the over-invoicing of imports and the under-invoicing of exports are checked there will be an accrual of not less than $ 5 billion to India. Again, if the import of gold is banned this would save $ 6 billion. This will be more than enough to meet any excess demand for dollars. Therefore, there is no danger to the stability of the rupee or no threat of capital outflow threatening its stability. Thus, there is no need for reversing the policy of financial liberalisation.

The rate of inflation is 8.5 percent. This is caused partly by the higher import prices caused by depreciation of the rupee and partly by the higher cost of borrowing. This is also caused by on-going fiscal deficit which, given the macro-economic situation, is excessive. The World Bank and the IMF have cautioned India against increasing the fiscal deficit. But given the buoyancy of revenues the fiscal deficit is likely to come down. Therefore, it can be said with confidence that there is no danger of getting into the Mexican type crisis. The present liberalisation programme is doing well and there is no need to reverse it.

India is well on the road to a market economy with the State gradually withdrawing from economic activity and yielding place to the private sector which expects and gets adequate returns. Many public sector enterprises are running under losses and they need to be replaced by Private initiative. The Prime Minister and the Finance Minister have been saying time and again that the economic reform programme is irreversible and it must be so. There is no danger of the Mexican type crisis occurring in India warranting the reversal of the reform programme.

30

The Spring Meeting of the IMF and the World Bank

The Spring Meeting of the IMF and the World Bank held in Washington in the last week of April 1995 is the first since the outbreak of the Mexican currency crisis. It was held in the context of the decline of the US dollar and the rise of the German D-Mark and the Japanese Yen. The Fund-Bank meeting was concerned with the mode of financing the countries in the crises of the Mexican variety and of stemming the decline of the US dollar. Both were necessary to maintain international economic stability.

The dollar is virtually battered. It opened at 101 Yen on 1.1.1995 but it fell to 80 Yen on 10.04.1995. This is symptomatic of the fact that the world is fast losing its confidence in that currency. While forwarding the Economic Report to the US Congress in February 1994 Bill Clinton had said: "As 1994 begins, out economy is strong and is growing stronger". He asserted that with continued deficit reduction, we can crease the foundations of an even more prosperous America". However, things have not moved that way.

What are the factors that have caused the decline of the US dollar? They are the budget deficit and the trade deficit. The budget deficit was $ 23 billion in 1971 has swelled to $ 254 billion in 1993. In a similar manner the annual trade deficit has been between $ 100 200 billion since the 1980s. It is held in several quarters that the US Government is unable to control its deficits. The balanced budget constitutional amendment has failed. This would have required the US Government to balance its budget in the early part of the 21st century.

Furthermore the US deficits which fuelled inflation in the country led to trade deficits. In 1993 there was an agreement between the

US and Japan by which the USA agreed to "actively pursue the medium term objectives of substantially reducing fiscal deficit, promoting domestic savings and strengthening its international competitiveness". The US has not been able to reduce its fiscal deficit. The US is now constantly appealing to the Japanese and the German Budnes bank to prop up the dollar.

In the normal course, fiscal deficits would lead to inflation. This would create pressure on the policy makers to contain the deficit. The trade deficit, on the other hand, would have led to the devaluation of the dollar. An equilibrium would have been reached at a lower level. But this process of adjustment has been retarded by the heavy purchase of dollars by foreign investors. The deficits, therefore, do not translate themselves into problems for the US economy. As long as the foreign investors believe that the dollar will remain strong, the parity can go on. Consequently the fiscal and trade deficits lead to a burgeoning Federal Debt rather than a run on the dollar.

Between 1982 and 1993 the Federal Debt has grown from \$ 1.1 to \$ 4.4 trillion. This means that the US Government has borrowed to the tune of \$ 3.3 trillion through the sale of US treasury bonds. This money has been used to finance the US deficits. The federal debt is held by foreigners. Out of the \$ 4.4 trillion federal debt in 1993 \$ 1.1 trillion was held by foreign Governments directly. Of the balance of \$ 3.3 trillion, a substantial part was held by foreign investors who felt that the dollar was a safe bet in comparison to their own currencies. The rate of interest is between 3 and 7 percent depending upon the maturity period. If the dollar depreciates the foreigners lose on their dollar holdings. Whatever gain they make from interest rate is eaten away by the loss in the value of the principal investment. It pays the foreign investors to hold on to the dollar so long as it does not depreciate. If they feel that the dollar is likely to depreciate they will sell their dollar holdings and invest the proceeds in the instruments denominated in the other currencies which are stable. This can trigger a run on the dollar in the same way as a run took place on the Mexican Peso.

A decline in the dollar has adverse effects on the foreign exchange reserves held in dollars. India is holding \$ 20.00 billion in its foreign exchange kitty. For example on 1.1.1995 the dollar had traded for 101 Yen. Since then it has been sliding continuously. It recorded a low of 80.15 Yen on 10.4.1995. This means that the Reserve Bank of India would have lost Rs. 10,000 crore on its foreign currency reserves. The same is true of other central banks which are holding their foreign exchange reserves in terms of dollars.

In view of the decline in the dollar the Japanese, the Germans and Indians also want to get out of the dollar. At present there has been a psychological shift away from the dollar. If the foreign investors get out of the dollar in a big way the USA may find itself in a situation like the one in which Mexico found itself. It must be remembered that it was the run on the Peso which brought about the Mexican crisis. It would be premature to predict that the dollar has reached that stage. But the US economy cannot afford to ignore its weak macroeconomic fundamentals.

While Japan is confronted with a recession the other developed countries are experiencing better than expected growth as noted by the IMF. The G-7 communiqué after expressing "concern about recent developments in exchange markets" noted that currency movements had gone "beyond levels justified by underlying economic conditions in the major countries". This refers to the usual pledge of cooperating "closely in the exchange markets". Recent currency cooperation (buying dollars and selling D-Mark or Yen) did not halt the dollar's slide. Intervention in the currency markets by the central banks is of little avail when the macroeconomic fundamentals are not right.

It is one thing for the IMF, a multilateral institution to ask the United States to raise interest rates in support of the dollar. But it is quite another for Germany or Japan to tell another sovereign nation what it should do. This makes G-7 policy coordination difficult. The communiqué talks of "further efforts to raise savings to lower long-term interest rates and thus underpin economic growth". This hints at the need to raise interest rates in the United States where savings are short of requirements. But this is nowhere near the IMF prescription of raising short-term interest rates in the US and thus increasing interest differentials vis-a-vis Germany and Japan which have already cut interest rates. This would drive buying away from DM and Yen into the US dollar.

The G-7 group has indicated what needs to be done in the long term. The focus is on an "Orderly reversal" of unjustified or excessive currency movements. This is indicative of reluctance to push the US hard. One reason could be the uncertainty about the current US economic growth which is seen to be slowing down. At this juncture a rise in the interest rate could push the US economy into a recession. Japan will be unable to hold down the Yen as it sets up production bases in Asian countries with weak currencies. This will mean rising Japanese exports and a growing trade surplus.

The subject which dominated the Spring Meeting of the Fund Bank duo was the method of coping with the recurrence of the Mexican-type crisis in the world. The concern is not new but predates the flight of capital from Mexico at the end of 1994 and the beginning of 1995. The Fund-Bank duo have been suggesting that the volatility of capital flows across national borders the need for mechanism to deal with any sudden outflow of capital from any country. But the governments of the industrial countries were averse to proposals of this kind as it would call for fresh commitment of resources.

The IMF bailed out the Mexican economy with a huge rescue package of $ 17.8 billion. But this decision was taken under special circumstances. The US Government formulated an aid package and persuaded the IMF to contribute substantial resources. Many industrial countries were unhappy that the IMF was stretching its resources too far to help Mexico. However, if the IMF wants to play this role its resources have to be enlarged. There is also an urgent need to set up a special fund to handle volatile capital flows.

The flow of private capital to developing countries is threatening to slow down. The Institute of International Finance in Washington has estimated a significant decline in the flow of private capital to the developing countries in 1995 to the tune of 50 percent. This at a time when the IMF's "World Economic Outlook" has predicted a deceleration of economic growth in the developing world from 6.3 percent in 1994 to 5.6 percent in 1995. The decline in the flow of private capital to the developing world is due to nervousness in the minds of investors following the Mexican crisis. There is also the continuous rise in the interest rate in the US. This makes investment more attractive.

The Fund-Bank meeting did not come out with any new mechanism to handle volatile capital movements. This is because of the opposition by the developed world. Germany has come out with its opposition to any new fund for developing countries. It is held that the package for Mexico should be regarded as a one-time deal and should not be repeated as it will encourage countries to be lax in their fiscal monetary policies.

The IMF, in fact, has come up with various suggestions for augmenting its resources. The Managing Director of the IMF has suggested a doubling of the quotas of members. The other suggestions include enhancing the General Agreement to borrow and selling part of the gold stock held by the IMF. However the prospects of an increase in the resources of the IMF are bleak. Germany has said that global liquidity has been growing by 8.5 percent per year while the annual expansion of world trade is 4.8 percent. In view of this there is no need for any fresh issue of Special Drawing Rights (SDRs). It is also suggested that the IMF should, instead, take upon itself the responsibility of monitoring the policies of the developing countries in order to make the solvent and prevent a Mexico type crisis. This would render any new monetary mechanism unnecessary. But there is a snag. The developed countries do not like to have their macroeconomic policies monitored by the IMF. In view of this the idea of empowering the IMF with powers to monitor the economic policies of the developing countries is unacceptable.

Volatility of short-term capital is disruptive of international monetary equilibrium. It was this kind of inflammatory capital movements that disrupted the exchange rates of the European currencies in the inter-war period and led to the establishment of the Exchange Equalisation Account. The Volatility of capital flows is at present causing havoc in the exchange markets. It is they that occasioned the Mexican crisis. The Tobin Tax has been recommended by some in order to stem the volatile capital flows. But this tax has not found favour with many countries.

The Reserve Bank of India has accumulated $ 20.00 billion of forex reserves. There is the danger of the short-term component of this reserve flowing out without notice. Keeping this possibility in view Mr. Stanley Fischer of the IMF has apprehended the possibility of Mexican type crisis occurring in India. At the same time Michael Mussa while releasing the document "World Economic Outlook" prepared by the IMF has ruled out the possibility of the currency crisis taking place in India. It is premature to predict that the Mexican type crisis would occur in India. The macroeconomic fundamentals of India and those of Mexico are far different and one can rest in the thought that there is no possibility of any kind of crisis occurring in India. The IMF has given the assurance that in the event of the Indian economic reforms getting into trouble because of the crisis, it would come to the aid of India.

The international financial scene is murky and anything is possible. To forestall any eventuallity there is urgent need to institute a special fund to aid countries in distress owing to capital outflows.

However, the attempts of the IMF to boost its capital base primarily required to help the developing countries to deal; with the financial crises were checkmated by the United States and its allies. They also did not allow the creation of a special financing mechanism that could be used to solve the liquidity problem of the type which beset Mexico. A resolution adopted by the IMF's policy setting interim committee on April 27, 1995 said that the Fund's liquidity position was "adequate at present" despite recent large demands on its resources. But it hastened to add that "the Fund liquidity is projected to decline sharply over the next two years". Instead of allowing the raising of resources, as suggested by the Managing Director of the IMF, to deal with the projected liquidity crunch the Committee requested the Fund's Executive Board "to continue to review the adequacy of the Fund's resources". The Committee saw a need "to examine the issues related to borrowing by the Fund from members and, in particular, the role of the General Arrangements to Borrow (GAB) a kind of credit line the Fund may draw in emergencies from the industrialised nations and Saudi Arabia. The Managing Director stated that the British proposal to raise resources by selling off gold reserves of the Fund did not find favour. The IMF Chief drew attention to the inadequacy of the lendable resources of the Fund He said: "We now have the GAB to raise resources". To face the Mexican type emergencies in the short run. The US secretary of the Treasury, Robert E. Rubin was opposed to an increase in quotas. He also asserted that there was little merit in designing a new safety net based on the SDRs. The proposals for the IMF to borrow SDRs require a funding of global need for general SDR allocation which does not exist at present. India and other developing countries lent strong support to the proposal for doubling of quotas and substantial general allocation of the SDRs. However, to prevent the crisis from occurring the Interim Committee agreed that Fund surveillance should be strengthened in "a symmetrical manner and taking into account the lessons to be drawn by member countries and by the Fund itself from the recent crisis in Mexico.

The Committee avoided recommending any specific action to stem the decline in the dollar and instead merely stressed the desirability of orderly reversal of the exchange rate movement for some major currencies which had gone further than warranted by economic fundamentals. It agreed on the need to make strong efforts to reduce internal and external imbalances. Its advice to most of the developing countries was to reduce inflation and to take stronger action to raise growth rates above the rate of population increase.

The Finance Minister explained the rationale of the economic reforms in progress in India and made a persuasive plea for adequate external assistance to make the reform programme a success. He assured the meeting that the economic reform programme in India was irreversible despite political developments in India during the past six months when it was apprehended that the reforms would come to a grinding halt. The meeting expressed faith in the message of the Finance Minister and this is creditable enough.

31

The Impatient G-13 with Economic Reforms

In the early part of February 1995 thirteen "eminent" economists who are referred to as "G-13" published a statement holding the on-going economic reforms responsible for inflation, unemployment and poverty but fortunately they forgot to hold them responsible for the earthquake in Kobay in Japan. It is intended to examine here the extent to which economic reforms are responsible for the growing incidence of unemployment in the country.

The Government has claimed that it would provide employment for all by the year 2002. This claim files in the face of the fact that in the so-called market-friendly economy the trend of employment generation has reversed. The Ministry of Labour in its latest report admits that 94 million jobs would have to be created to achieve a state of full employment by 2002. This necessitates an annual rate of growth of 3 percent in employment. But the rate of employment generation has been declining through time. For instance between 1971 and 1991 the rate of employment generation was only 2.2 percent. This has dropped since the economic reform programme got underway. The Ministry of Labour has admitted that the rate of growth of employment is not elastic to increase in Gross Domestic Product (GDP). Upto the 1970s when the economy achieved a growth rate of 3.5 percent the growth rate of employment was a little over 2 percent. During the 1970s when the growth rate increased to 4 percent the rate of growth of employment declined slightly. In the 1980s the GDP grew at a rate of 5.5 percent but the growth rate of employment is estimated to be 1.8 percent. This was before the economic reform programme was initiated. The declining rate of employment generation is due not to economic reforms but to the technology intensive growth pattern which displaces labour.

Furthermore, the declining rate of employment generation is not peculiar to India. In fact, it is a global phenomenon where employment generation and capital intensity vary inversely. This is true not just of the industrial sector. It is equally true of the agricultural sector. This is evident by the decreasing rate of employment generation in the green revolution areas. It is pointed out by the Report of the International People's Tribunal recently that privatisation of the public sector, application of new technologies and reversal of state discrimination of backward areas threw 6.6 million Indians out of jobs in just one year. In Brazil the after effects of the structural adjustment programme were a drop in the share of income going to labour from 50 percent in the late 1970s to 35 percent by the early 1990s. In Central America after the introduction of economic reforms the situation was similar. "....real wages continue dropping, social spending has contracted and unemployment levels are higher than ever".

It is an accepted tenet of growth theory that the rate of growth is higher with capital intensive techniques of production than with labour-intensive techniques. If employment generation is to increase the country should go in for labour intensive techniques in all the sectors of the economy. The economic reforms initiated in July 1991 were intended to overcome the crisis situation and to stabilise the economy rather than to expand it. The reforms are bound to make an impact on the unemployment situation in the next 2-3 years when many investments will yield results. Estimates are that direct foreign investment will lead to a substantial number of jobs all over the country both directly and indirectly by increasing and stimulating economic activity.

The decline in the rate of employment generation in the first three years of economic reforms was in part due to recession in Indian Industry. Now that the recession has ended, there should be an impact on the unemployment situation as production increases. Production will also rise with the commissioning of new projects in the private sector which are expected to rise. This will also help the employment market. The increase in industrial activity as a result of the boost in private investment will also improve the problem of educated unemployed, the numbers of which are increasing every year with the increase in education and literacy all over the country.

After the decline in employment in the period of stabilisation (1991-1993) employment generation increased to 6 million in 1992-93 as against 3 million jobs in the previous year. According to the Finance Minister employment generation has taken a quantum jump during 1994-95 since all the growth indices like GDP and industrial production have gone up substantially.

The Government has reneged on its assurance to use the National Renewal Fund (NRF) as a safety net by retraining workers and starting new industries to employ the displaced employees. But at present NRF has been used to pay for voluntary retirement schemes of public sector units. If the slogan of employment for all by 2002 or even by 2010 is to materialise, a careful strategy of creating distinct sectors of the economy both in industry and agriculture which will be labour rather than capital intensive is needed. But again this reduces the rate of economic growth. There seems to be a trade off between economic growth and employment generation. Unemployment is the consequence of capital-intensive technique of production. Unemployment can be alleviated by adopting labour intensive techniques but this step involves a reduction in the rate of economic growth. This is a problem facing the planners.

Quite apart from this, unemployment is also the consequence of population growth which adds to the labour force. The rate of labour absorption is more than the rate of labour addition. The difference between the two rates is net addition to the unemployed labour force. The sovereign remedy for unemployment is the reduction of net addition to the labour force which requires a reduction of the rate of population growth.

The G-13 attributes poverty to the economic reforms. The poverty syndrome has remained unmitigated since 1947. If India has to come out of the poverty trap the growth rate must rise to 7-8 percent. The only States where there has been an appreciable impact on poverty eradication are those where growth has been significant. Punjab and Goa are good examples. The story is identical in the international sphere. The East Asian miracle of Taiwan, South

Korea and South East Asian countries like Singapore, Malaya is clearly linked to their high growth rates sustain over a couple of decades. They have eradicated poverty by sustained high growth rate. If India had achieved a 7-8 percent growth rate in the 1980s poverty would have been alleviated considerably. The economic reforms must aim at this objective. A growth rate of 8 percent is by no means difficult for India. The countries of East and South East Asia with much less resource endowments have already shown that this can be done. Growth rate can be raised by means of additional investment. But this requires a rise in savings. But the savings ratio is low. Therefore India needs additional investment from capital-rich countries. Therefore, the Government must attract foreign investment so as to raise the investment rate from the present 25 percent to 30 percent. China, Malaysia, Thailand, South Korea are all maintaining an investment rate of over 30 percent with admirable results on their growth rates. Most East Asian countries have long ago eradicated their basic poverty. Their per capita income has crossed the US $ 10,000 as against India's $ 350.

Ensuring a growth rate of 8 percent is not just a matter of investment. Efficiency and effectiveness of these investments depend on the reforms in the financial sector, fiscal system and administrative system, etc.

The poor have waited long enough since 1947 to see better days. They have not felt any significant improvement though the poverty levels in 1995 are less than they were in 1947. Even so, the G-13 has attributed poverty to economic reforms. Poverty has been there since times immemorial and it is the task of economic reforms to alleviate it. But it cannot be alleviated in a short period of 4 years. The two-track strategy adopted by the Finance Minister in his 1995-96 Budget will go a long way reducing the incidence of poverty.

The G-13 attributes inflation to economic reforms. The rate of inflation in 1991, before the introduction of economic reforms, was 17.4 percent. It was brought down successively to 7.5 percent. Subsequently it started rising. It rose to 12.5 percent and since January 1995 it has started to decline. The critics argue that the

Government has failed to bring the rate of inflation down to 6-7 percent. But the facts have not been understood by the critics. There was delay in increasing the import of sugar, edible oil, cotton and other materials. This gave an upward push to the rate of inflation. The vast accumulation of forex reserves which presently stand at $ 20 billion had its monetary impact which led to the monetary expansion of 20 percent against the targeted 15 percent. Though the food stock is of the order of 30 million tonnes it was not released to the open market. All these factors led to a rise in the rate of inflation. The Finance Minister does not deserve the blame for the escalation of prices.

Apart from the supply factor its is the government's fiscal policy or the slippage in fiscal corrections which have had a decisive bearing on inflation. The money supply (MS) surged during 1994 at an average of 20 percent compared to 1993-94. Although there was a contraction of RBI credit to the Central Government practically throughout 1994 the Bank credit to the commercial sector showed a 14.3 percent increase at the end of December 1994 compared to the previous year. What really triggered monetary expansion is the pronounced increase in foreign exchange assets of the banks from Rs. 53,727 crore at the beginning of April 1994 to Rs. 70,103 crore at the end of December 1994. The present indications are that the rate of accretion of capital inflows is coming down although the damaging impact on prices already became a fact to live with. In view of this the inflation cannot be attributed to economic reforms. It can be attributed to the failure of the Government to act in time. It is a matter of great relief that the rate of inflation has come down to 8.74 percent. It is expected that it will come down further. This calls for the adoption of the following measures:

1. Moderate increase in the procurement prices during the next crop seasons.
2. Moderating the rate of growth of money supply so that it does not go above the target of 15 percent.
3. Liberalisation of consumer goods imports.
4. Reduction of fiscal deficit.
5. Release of food stocks to the open market.

6. Adoption of wage freeze in all the establishments public and private.

What about the behaviour of the current account deficit. In 1993-94 the current account deficit was $ 300 million; but it was as much as $ 8 billion in 1988-89, $ 4.87 billion in 1985-86 and $ 2.80 billion in 1980-81. Even in 1989-90 the deficit was $ 6.84 billion and as much as $ 9.68 billion in 1990-91. The big deficits were mainly due to huge trade gaps, these being $ 1.04 billion in 1993-94, $ 5.53 billion in 1988-89, $ 7.16 billion in 1980-81, $ 4.61 billion in 1989-90 and $ 5.93 billion in 1990-91. At present India's current account deficit is 0.5 percent of GDP. Thus there is a gradual decline in the size of the current account deficit in the reform period.

The G-13 are overly impatient about the results of the economic reforms. They fail to realise that the reforms take some time to yield results. In July 1991 The Economist published a Report titled: "The Tiger Unchained". This was in the aftermath of the announcement of economic reforms. The Economist of January 21, 1995 was a special on India titled, "The Tiger Steps Out", it mirrored India very comprehensively. It said: "After four decades of suffocation and a couple of years of post adjustment gloom, Indian business is bouncy. The business confidence index compiled by the National Council of Applied Economic Research, went from optimistic to ebullient in 1994".

India is an ambitious country these days. There is more hope but there is more frustration too. If Indians can stop turning their anger on each other and use it instead to demand the kind of government they need they will be on the way to getting an economic system that works better. Then there will be no stopping the new tiger. The Tiger has stepped out after it was unchained. When it was chained the limbs of the Tiger were in disuse. It takes some time for them to get active and buoyant. The G-13 will do well not to be impatient.

One feels heartened to note that China which once looked down on the Indian economic progress is today amazed at the development and is increasingly trying to draw lessons from the Indian economic reform process. Recently a team of Chinese economists visited

India and is understood to have submitted a report on the plan of action based on the Indian experience. Chinese economists are believed to be of the view that the progress India has achieved since the liberalisation of the economy was remarkable and the over 5 percent growth rate was "commendable". Regarding foreign investment flow to China, the report indicates that it is mostly by way of loan and from nonresident Chinese. In the case of India more of the foreign direct investment is in the form of equity besides sizeable amount from nonresident Indians. At the same time the Japanese investors are lately interested in investing in India rather than in China in view of the political stability and economic liberalisation that the Narasimha Rao Government has embarked upon. The impatient G-13 will do well to note this.

32

How to Structure the Union Budget for 1995-96

The Union Budget for 1995-96 is important for several reasons:

1. The rate of economic growth is below the expected figure and the object of policy is to accelerate the rate of economic growth.
2. The rate of inflation is hovering around 10 percent after a decline from 17.4 percent in 1991 to 7 percent in August 1994. The object of policy is to bring it down to 6 percent and below in order to provide relief to the harried consumers especially the poverty-stricken ones. This means that the Budget should be pro-pro-poor without being populist.
3. The fiscal deficit is large and is growing fuelling inflation. The object of policy is to mobilise revenues in order to reduce the fiscal deficit.
4. The trade deficit is widening despite export growth. This poses the problem of financing it. Though India has acquired over $ 20 billion of forex reserves which can be drawn upon to finance the deficit, the continued inflow of forex reserves has its impact on money supply and the rate of inflation. The recently formulated guidelines regarding the inflow of money raised by means of Euro-issues goes part of the way in stemming the rate of inflow of forex reserves but it does not fully solve the problem. Ways and means have to be found to mitigate this problem. The hands-off policy by the Reserve Bank of India will not do for this policy has the effect of causing the appreciation of the Indian rupee which will have adverse effects on export growth and the balance of payments.
5. Unemployment and poverty are on the increase making the beneficial effects of economic reforms highly suspect.

6. The incidence of both domestic debt and external debt is very high and rising holding out the threat of debt-traps. The decision of the Government to shift from monetary financing to debt financing of the deficit has aggravated the problem as this shift adds to the magnitude of the debt and to the non-plan expenditure of the Government and thus to be fiscal deficit.
7. The Finance Minister has called for a national debate on the economic reforms and has asserted: let the people of this country decide which way they would prefer to go". The Finance Minister agreed that the liberalisation process lacked a human dimension and failed to make an impact on issues like social security for the poor, farm sector and rural development and the duty concessions did not benefit the consumers as the industry did not pass them on to consumers in the form of lower prices. But he believes that the liberalisation process has restored the macro-economic stability of the economy through a strong industrial recovery. But there are apprehensions that the economic reform programme may be diluted if not dropped altogether. Much depends on the results of the elections to the State Assemblies in February-March 1995. It is against this back-drop that the Union Budget for 1995-96 has to be formulated. The following pages contain ideas to be taken into account in order to accommodate the feelings and sentiments of all sections of society and to save the economic reform package from dangerous dilution. It is hoped that the Finance Ministry will find them useful in restructuring the Budget so as to enable it to realise the objectives of inflation control, external solvency and accelerated economic growth.

Fiscal Deficit

The Finance Minister identified the large fiscal deficit as the villain behind the economic malaise. In the first two years he succeeded in bringing it down but it slipped badly in the third year. As against a target of 4.7 percent of GDP, the fiscal deficit rose to 7.3 percent in 1993-94. He gave up what he himself called the contractionary policy and set a fiscal deficit target of 6 percent of GDP for 1994-95. But this target is likely to elude his grasp because of the large subsidies and the high interest burden on the carry forward stocks of food grains.

But inflation is likely to make the realisation of the fiscal deficit target easier though it is part of what economists call the money illusion. The GDP for this year had been estimated at Rs. 9,00,000 crore. With the inflation rate of 10 percent against 8.4 percent last year the GDP at current prices should be up by Rs. 15,000 crore. This is called "money illusion". The larger GDP is monetary terms makes the task of limiting the fiscal deficit to the targeted level easier. Higher the inflation rate the larger the revenue receipts. This is because excise duty and sales tax are collected ad valorem. This partly accounts for the revenue buoyancy this year. The total revenue collections from customs and central excise during April-October 1994 have been placed at Rs. 34,024 crore, a 17.96 percent increase over the collections during the corresponding period of 1993. This time lag enables the Finance Ministry to use figures to show a lower fiscal deficit. The rising import boosted customs collection during this period in 1994 to Rs. 13,882.26 crore is up by 16.91 percent from the collection during April-October 1993. Industrial production has been going up since May this year and it is 8-9 percent at present. This will mean higher excise revenue. Central excise collections during April-October 1994 stood at Rs. 20,141 crore registering a 18.68 percent increase.

Inflation pushes up not only revenue but also expenditure. But expenditure catches up with a time lag. For instance, DA due for employees is announced after a time lag of three months. This time lag enables the Finance Ministry to use figures to show a smaller fiscal deficit. But when, after the delay, the DA arrears are paid with retrospective effect they exacerbate inflation in the economy. But money illusion apart the fiscal deficit is larger than anticipated. Unless it is brought down through thoughtfully designed fiscal measures it is bound to aggravate the inflationary pressures with harmful consequences all-round.

The root cause of the present inflation is the fiscal deficit. The budgeted massive deficit of Rs. 55,000 crore in 1994-95 is on top of another massive Rs. 58,000 crore deficit in 1993-94. This conceals many worrisome features. During 1993-94 the Finance Minister budgeted for a deficit of about Rs. 37,000 crore. It shot up by Rs. 21,000 crore in the course of the year. This way because the Government was compelled to finance State elections and thus throw away the fiscal discipline. The August 15, give aways and the MP development fund amounting to nearly Rs. 800 crore are other examples. Due to the elections early in 1995 there will be a repeat performance and 1995-96 will again be another repeat because it is the pre-general election year.

With heroic efforts and partly under the advice of the IMF the Government did bring the deficits under control and initiated the reform process. It is now a great relief to the Government which was already acquired $ 20 billion as foreign exchange reserves that it does not have to go to the IMF for a loan and is thus spared the IMF conditionality rigours to reduce the fiscal deficit.

High fiscal deficits cannot be separated from inflation. They may not be the only cause of inflation but undoubtedly they are the most important and at the root of it all. If high fiscal deficits can be avoided inflation will be within moderate limits even with other factors present. But if high fiscal deficits persist high inflation will persist too even if other factors are not present. There is a one-year time lag between deficits and inflation. The present high rate of inflation is the result of the Rs. 58,000 crore deficit incurred in 1993-94 and the massive Rs. 55,000 crore deficit for 1994-95. This is bound to result in high inflation in 1995-96 also.

The Economic Survey for 1993-94 laid down the good intention of inflation. It declared that "inflationary pressures can be said to have been purged out of the system only after inflation has been brought down to no more than five to six percent per year for two years". On this definition the earliest two years could only be 1996-97 and 1997-98. Therefore, the claim of politicians regarding inflation control need not be taken seriously. The Finance Minister in his Budget speech on 28.02.1994 placed before the nation the stark risks when he said: "Unless the deterioration in fiscal deficit witnessed in 1993-94 is speedily reversed, there is a serious danger that we may slip back into a position where large Government deficits fuel inflation, widen the current account imbalance and push up interest rates, making it impossible to bring about the rapid economic growth we need to raise living standards and create productive jobs in adequate numbers".

But the fiscal deficit can be reined in. There has been a buoyancy in tax revenues. The vigorous drive for two collections and revival of economic activity since September 1993 have been responsible for a smart rise in tax revenues. Larger sales of various products bearing excise duties have been effected. There has also been an improvement in profit margins of the manufacturing units in the face of rising costs. The pick-up in the off-take of commercial vehicles, passenger cars, consumer electronic products, cement, blended fabrics and petrochemicals on which the incidence of excise duty is fairly heavy is facilitating the improvement of tax receipts. As there has also been an increase in imports of dutiable items with higher values of industrial production in many directions the customs revenues have also risen above the budgeted estimates. The revenue from indirect taxes is up by 18 percent compared to the revenue in 1993. Likewise, the revenue from direct taxes has more than doubled (107 percent). The increase is, of course, exaggerated to a significant extent as advance tax dues were payable on June 15, 1994 from this year. However, even allowing for collections earlier than usual the adjusted receipts are larger than the budget estimates.

The drop in total tax revenue in 1993-94 from Rs. 84,867 crore to Rs. 76,750 crore was mainly responsible for the increase in the fiscal deficit to over 7 percent from 4.7 percent (budget). The uncovered debts also rise to Rs. 9,060 crore from Rs. 4,314 crore (budget). The enlargement of the overall deficit took place inspite of heavier total borrowings of Rs. 29,692 crore against only Rs. 9,700 crore (budget). These adverse developments in 1993-94 are unlikely to be repeated in 1994-95. Instead, there is the likelihood of the budget estimates for tax revenues being considerably exceeded when the revised estimates are presented to the parliament.

The receipts from both direct and indirect taxes in 1994-95 have risen significantly. There will also be an increase in non-tax revenues as the performance of public sector enterprises in 1994-95 will be much better than in 1993-94. Larger dividend payments may thus be made by many of these PSEs. While receipts from other sources too may be higher than in 1993-94. Furthermore, the scope for borrowing has improved as the target of Rs. 3,700 crore for market loans has been exceeded. Total borrowing has thus surpassed the estimates considerably. The Finance Ministry will not have any difficulty on this score as the banking system is flush with funds and fresh investments in treasury bills and terminable securities are being effected in increasing volume. Infact, borrowings in all forms may have to be increased only to contract the deficit. Much will depend on the success in preventing the increases in non-plan expenditure as there will be no reduction in the burden of subsidies. This is because the Government may not be inclined to raise the selling price of essential commodities in future as there will have political implications. Furthermore, the reduction of fertilizer subsidy will have to be maintained.

The source on which the Government depended considerably for reduction of fiscal deficit has come out to be not much helpful. The current exercise of disinvestment in public sector enterprises for the purpose of reducing the fiscal deficit has given a clear signal to the Finance Ministry that this route of raising funds for meeting Government expenditure is drying up fast. However, the sky would be the limit if the Government decides to privatise the PSUs by bringing down its equity stake in them to no less than 50 percent which is not possible at the moment particularly because of the unmanageable unemployment situation that would be an inevitable emergence of such degree of privatisation. The Government, thus faces a dilemma, Disinvestment next year has to be on a much larger scale than Rs. 4,000 crore that might be somehow collected in the current year. The Government will have to find an additional Rs. 10,000 crore if the fiscal deficit as a percentage of GDP is to be brought down to 5 percent next year as against the current year's budgetary target of 6 percent which has been far exceeded by the time. A situation is fast emerging in which the Government might be compelled to implement the recommendations of the Rangarajan

Committee which wanted that the percentage of equity to be disinvested should be 49 percent in industries reserved for the public sector and 74 percent in other cases.

The Finance Ministry has said that the budget deficit is limited to two-thirds of one percent of the expected GDP or Rs. 6,000 crore in 1994-95. This has been sought to be achieved by limiting the creation of adhoc treasury bills to Rs. 6,000 crore at the end of the financial year 1994-95. The Ministry signed an agreement with the Reserve Bank of India under which the net issue of adhoc treasury bills would not exceed Rs. 9,000 crore for more than ten continuous working days at any time during the year. If it does exceed this limit, the RBI would automatically sell treasury bills in the market to reduce the level of adhoc treasury bills. This would mean that the onus on paying higher interest rates would shift to the Government of India.

The Finance Ministry will progressively reduce recourse to adhoc treasury bills and by 1997-98, the Government of India will cease to have recourse to the Reserve Bank for financing its deficits. The Ministry has introduced new instruments to borrow and raised Rs. 17,149 crore upto September 1994 through its market borrowing programme as against Rs. 10,946 crore in the corresponding period of 1993. The check is higher interest rates which will automatically make the Government think twice before borrowing at high interest rates as the higher interest cost will widen the fiscal deficit.

The Finance Ministry says that fiscal deficit which reflects the net borrowing requirement of the Government was Rs. 23,003 crore upto the end of September 1994 which was 41.9 percent of the Budget Estimate for 1994-95. This is against Rs. 29,832 crore in September 1993-94. The Budget Estimate provides for a fiscal deficit of Rs. 54,915 crore for the current financial year which is 6 percent of GDP. This represents a considerable scaling down of the fiscal deficit though it does not reach the target. Action is necessary in the realms of taxation and public expenditure to raise tax revenue and to reduce public expenditure in a manner which enhances the quality of life of the people and raises productive investment.

The Finance Minister is busy with the arduous task of fiscal planning for 1995-96. He has held discussions with the economists, industrialists, businessmen, labour leaders, farming lobbies and consumer interests and has elicited their views on the kind of budget each of these groups would like to have. He has to accommodate their views without sacrificing the supreme task of fiscal consolidation. In the present context of yawning fiscal deficit and growing inflation this is an important task. But unless there is a drastic cut in Government expenditure the talk of fiscal consolidation sounds hollow despite the buoyancy in revenue collections. Considering the present political situation in the country there may not be much scope for reducing non-plan expenditure. But there is a lot of flab in the area of administrative expenditure. This needs to be cut drastically. There is also urgent need to adopt the deferred payment scheme and to freeze the new salary scales and DA rates for the time being. This step will reduce the fiscal deficit and will also help to reduce the rate of inflation.

Taxation

In the fourth year of the reform process the object of fiscal policy is to consolidate the gains of the previous years in order to give confidence to savers and investors to step up the rate of growth and to carry forward the reform process further. The focus of the 1995-96 budget should be on achieving these results.

During the past three years there has been a consistent trend towards reducing the rates of tax on person and corporate incomes in the hope of increasing the revenue yield. It was hoped that lower tax rates would induce voluntary compliance and increase tax yields. This is in conformity with the Laffer Curve Analysis. The lower tax rates have infused confidence between the tax assessees and tax administrators and this has caused an improvement in the revenue yield. There has been a 50 percent increase in direct tax collections between April and October 1994. Upto September 22, 1994 total tax collections amounted to Rs. 8,394.80 crore compared to Rs. 5,605.29 crore in the corresponding period of 1993.

On the income tax side the Chellaiah Committee had recommended that 40 percent of tax be made applicable to income of Rs. 2 lakh. The Finance Minister adjusted the tax slabs and rates for individuals and the maximum tax of 40 percent was made applicable to income of about Rs. 1,20,000 as against Rs. 2 lakh recommended by the Chellaiah Committee. It now appears desirable to reduce the maximum tax rates further on different slabs and raise the exemption limit to Rs. 50,000 from the present Rs. 35,000 in keeping with the erosion of the value of the rupee.

The corporate tax rates were brought down from 51.5 percent to 40 percent in the 1994-95 budget the effective tax incidence being 46 percent. The corporate tax revenue registered a rise of 78 percent during April-October 1994 to touch Rs. 4,524.45 crore compared to Rs. 2,535.95 crore in the corresponding period in 1993. This also reflects the fact the recessionary tendencies in the industrial sector has slackened. Due to the flowing in of advance tax payments the target of Rs. 26,090 crore in direct taxes is bound to be achieved.

In the order progressive countries of the World Corporate Tax rates have come down to 30 percent. There is a strong case for dropping the surcharge of 15 percent on corporate tax assesses as in the case of individual assesses. The reduction in corporate tax rates is necessary to enable the corporation to accumulate internal sources of investible funds for further growth of the corporate sector.

The general rate of depreciation on plant and machinery has been reduced to 25 percent. Due to rapid technological obsolescence, the necessity of continuous modernisation and technological upgradation of plants has to be admitted. This requires larger sums at the disposal of industry. The replacement cost of machinery is higher than the historical cost. Therefore depreciation at the rate of 33 1/3 percent which existed earlier should be restored. Infact, the L.K. Jha Committee on Economic Administrative Reforms had recommended this rate.

In the context of ongoing competition intensification the industrial sector is in the process of restructuring. This may take the form of amalgamations, de-mergers and reconstruction. These are considered necessary for survival and expansion in the context of economic reforms. The Chellaiah Committee recommended that no capital gains tax should be levied in the case of demerger and reconstruction. Furthermore, in the case of reconstruction depreciation should be computed on the same basis as in the hands of transferor companies. Capital gains tax is imposed in other areas without justification. Section 45(4) of the Income Tax Act was brought forthwith the intention of taxing income that arises as a result of distribution of capital assets on the dissolution of a firm. In the process of conversion of a firm into a company the partners of the firm become the shareholders of the company. In this case there is no capital gain or profit. By under Section 45(4) an illusory gain is construed merely because conversion involves dissolution of the firm. This is a case of taxing imaginary gain. Again, in the case of a widely held company being acquired by a company in which the public is not interested the losses to be carried forward are disallowed under section 79 of the Income Tax Act. The Finance Minister has made the tax rates uniform for all categories of companies. But anomalies of this type render it difficult for companies to restructure themselves and become viable.

The expenditure on R&D is dismally low. In the context of globalisation Indian industry has to attain international competitiveness. The goods produced must enjoy cost and quality competitiveness. This required the innovation of new products or new varieties of products. This is possible if the industry is modernised and technologically upgraded at frequent intervals. At present technology is, for the most part, imported. What is out of date in the West is uptodate in India. It is necessary for India to be self-dependent technologically. For this reason, indigenous research and development is necessary. A R&D Fund needs to be set up to finance research into new technologies. Every company has to be made to pay a cess at a certain rate which will be a proportion of the capital investment. This Fund should be used to finance technological research. This should be called the R&D cess.

There is an urgent need to impose two taxes wealth Tax and Gift Tax. At present black money culture is all pervasive and a good part of wealth is made up of black money and black assets. These assets are overly undervalued whether they are held in the form of buildings, landed assets etc. At a time when the value of these assets especially in the urban areas is rising without check there is need to impose a wealth tax by a scientific assessment of the market value of these assets. This meets the requirements of intersectoral equity and justice besides yielding sizeable revenue to the Government. Hence the case for a Wealth Tax. Tax on shares and stock holdings also need to be taxed at steep rates for the same purpose.

A large part of the gifts made by the individuals is made up of black money and black assets. These are bequeathed to their relations either when they are alive or at the time of death. Gifts are also made on important occasions. Gifts made in the form of money cannot be identified, ascertained or assessed and this reason gifts in the form of cash cannot be taxed as they are clandestine operations. But gifts in kind can be identified. They are to be assessed at the market value and they are to be taxed at steeply rising rates. These gifts are part of unearned income and there is every justification for so taxing them.

The service sector is a fruitful source of revenue. In the 1994-95 Budget the Finance Minister for the first time extended taxation to the service sector based on the recommendations of the Narasimham Committee Report. His proposal to levy a 5% tax on the telephone bills, the net premium charged by non-life insurance companies and the commission charged by stock brokers is expected to yield about Rs. 600 crore this year. The Finance Minister should explore other areas in the service sector, to garner more revenue. They are advertising, architects and interior decorators. There are high cost services and taxing this area is expected to yield substantial revenue. The age of consumerism has dawned in India. All the products are sought to be advertised in order to create maintain and expand the markets. Taxing this sector will yield large revenue. Every household in the urban and semi-urban settlements desires to have houses which are an architectural wonder. They seek the services of architects and interior decorators to give a posh look to their houses. As a consequence architects and interior decorators are having a roaring business and the income earned by them goes untaxed. Taxing these area: advertising, architecture and interior decoration will yield a large revenue which will help to reduce the fiscal deficit.

At present direct foreign investment is a must for India which has to reach the projected growth rate of 5.5 percent per annum. The rate of economic growth depends crucially on the availability of infrastructure. The Asian Tigers have been attracting foreign investment in the area of infrastructure like ports, highways, telecommunications, power generation, satellite townships, circular railway around mega cities and the like. They are therefore in a position leap forward. In a similar manner India should give appropriate incentives to foreign investment in the area of infrastructure. Infrastructural bottlenecks have impeded India's growth mechanism. Foreign investors have expressed faith in the policy of liberalisation and globalisation being pursued by the Union Government and they are sure that the economic reforms are irreversible despite the clamour of the anti-reform brigade in the country. Appropriate tax incentives to foreign investors in the area of infrastructure are to be given besides counter guarantees of capital but not profit for guaranteeing profits leads to inefficiency. Therefore, counter guarantees of capital need to be given by the Government.

There are several other segments of the service sector which can serve as a fruitful source of revenue. Several private buses are playing especially in the rural areas. At present they enjoy a monopoly positions as they are free from the competition of Government owned buses. The fares they charge are out of proportion to the cost of service. In the urban sector hundreds of taxis and tempo vans are plying carrying passengers. Free from competition they charge fares which are again out of proportion to the cost of service rendered by them. It is not possible to levy a tax on the income of private lorry, or taxi or tempo owners for the payment made by the users of these services does not go on record. As their income is unidentifiable tax on their incomes cannot be imposed. Instead a tax on each lorry, taxi or tempo can be levied. This is income tax pure and simple and the State Governments cannot claim to tax these incomes. This should be the area to be reserved for the Union Government. There are million of lorries, taxis and tempo vehicles throughout the country. A service tax at suitable rates can be levied. This is in addition to the road user tax paid by them to the respective State Governments.

Indirect Taxes

It is expected that indirect tax collection might show an increase of Rs. 1,500 Rs. 2,000 crore over the target by the end of March 1995. This trend is indicative of the correctness of the policy being pursued though marginal adjustments to set right the anomalies in specific sectors may seen necessary.

The Finance Minister in his Budget speech presenting the Union Budget for 1994-95 laid down the principles of restructuring the excise duty. They are:

1. Extension of modvat to capital goods and petroleum products.
2. Shift in the bulk of excise taxation from specific to advalorm rates which will ensure built-in buoyancy of tax revenue.
3. Reduction in the total number of advalorm tax rates to about half the existing number which will be a major step towards simplicity and transparency.
4. Continuing the process of lowering rates when they are unduly high.
5. Application of uniform rates for similar commodities to the extent possible. This will reduce classification problems, scope for misuse and widespread litigation.
6. Removal of the complicated price list procedure.
7. Reduction of the number of specific exemption notifications by about half.

While 3, 5, 6 7 are concerned with the details of tax administration 1, 2 and 4 are concerned with the scheme of lowering tax rates and shift from specific to advalorem taxes. The Laffer Curve Analysis made applicable to direct taxation with advantage can be made applicable to indirect taxes also. A reduction of indirect tax rates lowers the market prices of goods and increases the demand for them on the assumption that the demand for them is elastic. Lower tax rates on a larger number of goods will increase tax yield.

Furthermore, in a period of rising prices of goods a shift to advalorem taxes will yield a larger revenue than specific taxes. In view of this reduction of tax rates and the shift to advalorem taxes will enhance the tax yield. In a similar manner modvat will also increase tax yields. The scheme needs to be continued and the number of goods subject to modvat has to be increased. Furthermore the number of goods subject to advalorem taxation should be increased. At the same time the tax administration needs to be streamlined so as to free the tax payers from the harassment of tax authorities.

The latest trend has been for the Finance Ministry to take a bold view of the response through better compliance at lower rates. Recent figures which show an increase of 20 percent of excise collections in the first six months of 1994-95 would appear to bear out the Finance Minister's optimism.

There is need to get away from the high peaks of excise taxes. Such peaks do lead to inducements to tax evasion. A lower peak and more effective measures at compliance will help elicit tax payers' cooperation. The 1995-96 Budget should make a bolder move to advalorem, lower peaks, more commodities under modvat and removal of anomalies and nuisance excises which do not contribute to higher revenues. The Finance Minister has already tried to clean up the thicket of rates. He should complete this exercise of tax reform in the coming Budget.

A few lines on the monetary effect of reduction of consumption taxes are necessary. Ordinarily a reduction of consumption taxes is said to reduce the market prices of the goods in question. This is the classical version. But we have to analyse the problem within the Keynesian framework. A reduction in consumption taxes, the supply of money being held constant, causes a fall in the prices of these goods. As the supply of money is held constant, the real balances rise. On the assumption that the demand for goods is a function of real balances, the demand for goods must rise. Furthermore, a fall in the price level causes a fall in the demand for transactions cash balances. The excess cash balances are used to purchase bonds causing a rise in bond prices or a fall in the rate of interest. This stimulates investment. Thus the two components of aggregate demand consumption and investment rise. This causes a rise in the prices to the old level. This means that if the reduction of consumption taxes is to result in a fall in the final prices of goods, the stock of money should be reduced in the same proportion as the decline in goods prices. The policy implication is that there should be a reduction in the stock of money if reduction in consumption taxes is to result in a reduction of the final market prices.

Agricultural Income Tax

The case for taxing agricultural income is strong indeed. If the tax GDP ratio is to be improved agricultural income has to be taxed. Gross farm income is put at twice that of the industrial sector and yet it remains untaxed. A few years back the K.N. Raj Committee supported taxing agricultural income. The World Bank also recommended agricultural taxation as an important source of resource mobilisation. It said; "Taxation of affluent farmers offers possibilities in the long run despite the obvious political and administrative difficulties". Only a small percentage of farmers will be affected by this levy. It is not intended to support the case for taxing the income of each and every farmer. What is advocated here is the taxing of affluent farmers. In the combined actual tax revenue of the Union and State Governments the contribution of the farm sector is hardly 1.6 percent. Thus 80 percent of the population makes a contribution of 1.6 percent to the exchequer against a contribution of 98.4 percent made by the remaining 20 percent of the population. An additional tax revenue of Rs. 150 crore could be raised from agriculture involving a modest amount of Rs. 400-500 on each household whose income is taxable. The Government should seriously consider the necessity and desirability of bringing farm income under the purview of the central income tax. The farmers should also be motivated to contribute by way of investment in bank deposits, life insurance, unit trust, Government and other securities. This will contribute Rs. 500 crore per annum.

The Agriculture Ministry wants the subsidies on farm inputs not only to continue but also to be raised but it does not want the agriculture income to be taxed. At the same time the Ministry wants the system of support prices to continue. And now it wants the agricultural sector to be treated on par with the industrial sector but at the same it also wants all these concessions to continue in favour of the agricultural sector. The kind of agricultural sector we are building up is bound to be a pain in the neck in the long run. When the GATT agreement becomes operational India would have been supporting one of the agricultural systems which can survive only on the crutches of subsidies and tax-free incomes. This does not go well with the spirit of liberal economic reforms. If this agricultural system continues for some more time we will have a situation where we will have a competitive industry and an uncompetitive agricultural sector. The moment one talks of doing away with subsidies on farm inputs or taxing farm incomes one is branded anti-farmer. By not taxing farm incomes the whole burden of direct taxation falls mainly on business, professionals, salaried classes and corporate entities. In order to subsidise farm inputs the Government is forced to keep both the direct and indirect taxes at high levels. We have also distorted the distorted price structure of the farm products. The Government must take a tough decision on this. But it would not be proper to dismantle the antiquated structure overnight but the Government should make it clear that it will be dismantled over the next 5-6 years so that the farmers can get enough time to reorient their responses to the new system.

Social Expenditure

The Government has been progressively reducing the expenditure on social services. The Budget for 1994-95 showed that actual spending on areas such as health, water supply and sanitation, labour employment and social security registered a minus growth of 3.4 percent. The continuation of this process considered to be part of economic reforms will have a direct impact on the States' spending on poverty, literacy and health.

It has become clear that the new economic wisdom of the Government in the course of economic reforms was suppressing the productive capacity of the economy. The capital expenditure in the Union Budget, that creates lasting assets and adds to productive capacity has fallen from 6.0 percent in 1990-91 to 3.6 percent in 1993-94 (revised estimate). However, considering the 8 percent average inflation, the actual capital expenditure has fallen almost by 22 percent since 1990-91. Such a cut in capital spending by the Government means that very little fresh productive capacity would be injected into the economy and hence the requirements of infrastructural development would not be adequately addressed. This would result in drying of Government orders for industries and resultant changes in their performance.

Need to Step up Productive Investment

There is urgent need to step up capital expenditure to increase the productive capacity of the economy and the rate of economic growth. Between 1981-90 the economy grew on an average by 5.5 percent of GDP accompanied by an inflation rate of 7 percent. As against this between 1990 and 1995 the growth rate was 4 to 4.5 percent of GDP with inflation averaging 10 percent. However, the Finance Minister is confident of achieving more than 5 percent economic growth an industrial growth of 8 percent with a capital formation of 8 percent. While the Centre for Monitoring Indian Economy (CMIE) has forecast a GDP growth at 4.5 percent the Reserve Bank Governor is confident of achieving 5.5 percent growth in 1994-95.

According to the World Development Report China has shown an average growth rate of GDP at constant prices of 9.1 percent over the period 1980-81 to 1991-92. During the same period India has shown a growth rate of 5.2 percent. In more recent years China's growth rate is believed to have been around 13 percent. In 1990-91 India had a growth rate of 1.8 percent, 4 percent in 1992-93 and possibly about the same in 1993-94. In 1994-95 it is expected to be 5 percent. The question is : Can India reach the Chinese rate of growth? The rapid growth of China's GDP growth during the past 15 years has been attributed to the ability of a totalitarian State to take decisions and get them implemented speedily, the rapid growth in demand, to China having reformed agriculture first, to its excellent record of health and education, to the vast inflow of foreign investments from overseas Chinese when such investment was permitted, to laying emphasis on labour intensive production and focusing on village industries. For these reasons China had spectacular economic growth and appears set to continue it. Nobody has predicted such high rates of growth for India. Even the Finance Minister talks of 7 percent growth towards the end of the century. One view has been that very rapid growth could lead to high levels of inflation as in China. But there are instances of countries having achieved high rates of growth with modest levels of inflation. But this requires continuing reductions in the deficits of Government.

In view of this the deficit reduction exercise assumes great importance. In this connection it is necessary to see that public sector must improve the returns on Government investments. Invest in public enterprises yields a return of 2.4 percent or less while the interest paid by the Centre on its total debt is 8.33 percent. Disinvestment of Government holding has been slow and the market shows perfunctory interest in the purchase of shares of public enterprises for reasons of meagre returns. Nationalised Banks and postal services are inefficient and overstaffed. There are also serious distortions in the pricing of Government services and products controlled by the Government. The high prices for oil seeds with protection from imports, distortions in power pricing, higher education all add to Government deficits.

The Government is found to be suppressing productive capital expenditure though it is a source of growth. The capital expenditure in the Union Budget that creates lasting assets and adds to productive activity has fallen from 6.0 percent in 1990-91 to 3.6 percent in 1993-94 (RE). However, considering the 10 percent inflation rate actual capital expenditure in real terms has fallen almost by 22 percent since 1990-91. Such a cut in capital spending by the Government means that very little fresh productive capacity would be injected into the economy and hence the requirements for infrastructural development would not be adequately addressed.

The Centre for Monitoring Indian Economy (CMIE) has estimated that during 1993-94 the Indian corporate sector had raised Rs. 30,930 crore from the domestic capital market in addition to the $ 2.6 billion raised from European markets. Now it has been proved that the money raised are not being used for setting up new plants or financing expansion projects. There is thus a strong case for increasing capital expenditure especially in the area of infrastructural development as this is necessary to raise the rate of economic growth.

The high inflation rate accelerates the process of transferring income from the working class to those who earn from profit, rent, interest, dividends and trading margins. Besides, the tendency to raise indirect taxes rather than direct taxes such as income tax and corporation tax would further expedite the process of upward transfer of income between classes. This undesirable redistribution of income not only takes place through the pattern of raising revenue but it can also be seen in the pattern of expenditure. For example, in the 1994-95 budget the largest single item in budgetary expenditure was the interest payment component. The percentage of interest payment against the total expenditure was 30.3 percent in 1994-95 against 14.3 percent in 1985-86. At the current rate of growth it is estimated that the figure will rise to 46.1 percent in 1999-2000. It is a fact that the higher payment of interest means greater flow of money from the Government exchequer to private coffers, especially to those who have investible surplus and the financial intermediaries. Against this, the Government is progressively reducing the expenditure on social services. The Budget for 1994-95 showed that actual spending on areas such as health, water supply and sanitation, labour, employment and social security registered a minus growth of 3.4 percent. The continuation of this process considered to be apart of economic reforms will have a direct impact on the States spending on poverty, literacy and health.

The emphasis in recent years is shifted from GNP to quality of life. GNP as an objective of growth policy has been dethroned from the high pedestal it occupied in earlier years and it is substituted by the quality of life as an ideal. Growth of GNP per se is meaningless if there is illiteracy, poverty, malnutrition, ill health, infant mortality and insanitary living conditions as of which have reduced the quality of life. For this reason there is need for the Government to increase expenditure on improving the quality of life besides raising the rate of growth of GDP. The Budget has to make adequate expenditure in this direction.

Subsidies

Subsidies are an important item of non-plan expenditure. The Union Finance Ministry is busy financing the budget estimates of expenditure before proceeding to formulate estimates of revenues. The Ministry desires to finalise proposals for additional taxation after the results of the election to the five Assemblies in February become available. Since no important changes can be made in the quantum of subsidies on food grains, sugar, edible oils and fertilisers additional provisions will have to be made under various heads in 1994-95 and in 1995-96.

The Finance Ministry had hoped earlier that definite steps would be taken for minimising the expenditure on subsidies with upward adjustments in issue prices for food grains and increases in pooled selling prices for nitrogenous fertilisers. Because of the elections the issue prices of food grains have not been raised though the procurement prices of wheat and rice have been raised moderately. The adjustments in issue prices have to take account of the outgo on account of the carrying and interest charges with bulging buffer stocks.

The expenditure on subsidies relating to nitrogenous and phosphatic fertilisers will increase significantly as imports of urea are being effected at prices which have risen sharply in recent months with imports becoming dearer, it has become necessary to raise selling prices which the Ministry of Agriculture desires to avoid. With larger sales of complex nutrients, the fixed subsidy of Rs. 1,000 per tonne will necessitate an increase in disbursements.

In 1993-94 the revised estimates of fertiliser subsidy rose to Rs. 4,400 crore from Rs. 3,500 crore (Budget). The actual disbursements were higher than the revised estimates inspite of there being inadequate payments against arrears. As an amount of Rs. 500 crore has been provided in respect of imported fertilisers and retention prices of urea to the new entrants had to be revised the total fertiliser subsidy will have to be higher by atleast Rs. 1,500 crore in the revised estimates. The increase in total subsidies might thus be by Rs. 3,500 crore in the revised estimates for 1994-95.

It is likely that there will be an increase in other subsidies and in non-plan expenditure under the remaining heads. For this reason the revised estimates for 1994-95 may have to provide for an additional expenditure of Rs. 5,000 crore.

As the fertiliser imports will have to be in larger volume with no likelihood of a big rise in domestic production, the subsidies will be even higher. In this sense, the expenditure estimates have to be formulated liberally as sugar imports will have to be sizable and the subsidy element will be more pronounced as the bulk of imports will have to be on Government account. The net rise in total expenditure may not get reflected in a larger fiscal deficit because of the buoyancy of tax revenues. It can be anticipated that the growth in indirect taxes noticed in 1994-95 will be sustained as the uptrend in industrial production and imports may remain in evidence in the absence of expected developments. In any case the government has to provide for increases in subsidies and higher cost or social welfare programmes as the farmers and weaker sections of society and others will have to be satisfied and there should not be any undue exertion of inflationary pressures. A further rise in food subsidies can be prevented if the buffer stocks of food grains which are now over 30 million tonnes do not rise further. While India is on the high road to a market economy some sort of State intervention is required in some basic areas which will affect the poor. There is need to continue subsidies and protection in areas where their withdrawal will directly affect the poor.

The Fifth Pay Commission

The Fifth Pay Commission is in session at present. The Terms of Reference of the Commission constituted in April 1994 are significantly wider in their ambit and scope than those of its predecessors. Apart from determining their appropriate salary structure and pensionary benefits for Central Government employees the Commission has also been asked to examine the terms and conditions of service of Armed forces personnel and to recommend the reforms necessary to bring about desirable changes in work methods, environment and attitudes aimed at promoting efficiency in administration and optimising the size of the Government machinery.

Many employee associations have pitched their demands high on this occasion because of the high expectations generated by economic liberalisation, the free plans of market forces and the rise of consumerism combined with the removal of ceilings on private sector managerial salaries. There is now an increased demand for parity with the commercial undertakings in the public and private sector. The progressive increase in the size of the Government machinery over a period of time and its adverse impact on the Government's ways and means position are a cause of concern. Besides public dissatisfaction with the performance of the Government machinery is more discernible now than ever before. It is probably on these considerations that the Government have for the first time asked the Pay Commission to suggest methods for its optimisation.

There is a thinking that the compensation packages and "invisible" benefits available to Government employees are even now excessive in relation to their job demands and responsibilities and in contrast to the million who live below the poverty line. There is also a feeling that the country can ill-afford the luxury of extending further concessions to its employees in the overall context of the mounting fiscal and revenue deficits of the Central and State Governments and of their inflationary impact.

However, given the militant stance adopted by the employee associations the pay commission cannot brush aside the demands of these associations. Its recommendations regarding pay enhancement will have a cascading effect on the State Governments, the public sector, autonomous institutions, local bodies etc. These demands which will be conceded will in their collectivity have an inflationary impact on the economy.

It is the prime task of the coming Budget to hold down the size of the fiscal deficit and through it to rescue the rate of inflation in order to provide relief to be common man who is being harried and to increase the competitiveness of India's exports. But the additional salaries and dearness allowances to be granted the Central and State Pay Commissions and those to be granted by the private organisations will pump in purchasing power into the economy and this is to create excess demand which escalates the price level. In order to accommodate the new pay scales the supply of money has to be expanded with the inevitable consequence of fuelling the flames of inflation through the demand-pull and cost-push effects. Under the traditional gold standard under which the supply of money depended on the stock of gold there be no money to meet the higher wage demands. But in a situation where the monetary system is permissive the supply of money is expansible to accommodate higher wage demands. In consequence the monetary system, in the words of Professor J.R. Hicks, has gone on the "Labour Standard". The point to note is that the recommendations of the Central and State Pay Commissions which will be implemented will have inflationary consequences and makes nonsense of the claim to reduce the rate of inflation.

This calls for effective action in the sphere of inflation management. The Government should announce a wage freeze so that the labourers and others will not be paid additional wages and dearness allowances for some more time. In the alternative the Government should announce a deferred payment scheme, under which the payment of the difference between the present wage and dearness allowance and those recommended by the pay commissions is deferred to a future date when the economy is able to absorb this purchasing power without generating inflation.

Expenditure Commission

The new economic policy aimed at imposing fiscal discipline which, of course, was a good idea. The Finance Minister had made a commitment that the fiscal deficit would come down from 8.6 percent of GDP to 6 percent of GDP and further down. The deficit could be brought down by reducing expenditure and raising revenue.

The World Bank way of cutting down expenditure was by abolishing subsidies and raising the prices of public articles and services. In pursuing this policy the Finance Minister abolished the sugar subsidy, reduced the food subsidy and raised the railway fares and the prices of petroleum products and cooking gas successively and these measures had a cascading effect. The banks also have started charging for their services in order to reduce their deficits Essential goods and services have become costlier for the common man.

While there is a significant increase in revenues there is no reduction in public expenditure. The burgeoning expenditure is sustaining the ongoing inflation. There has been no comprehensive exercise for curbing public expenditure of the sort undertaking by Raja Chellaiah for reforming the tax structure.

The non-plan expenditure is consistently on the rise—subsidies, interest payments and defence. In the context of the deteriorating security environment the defence expenditure does not admit of reduction. If anything there is a strong case for stepping up defence expenditure in real terms. But there is a heated controversy regarding the reduction of subsidies. The market oriented gentry want the subsidies of all kinds abolished while those with acute concern for the poor want subsidies on food, fertilisers and other essential commodities to continue as they are believed to be a source of relief to the common man groaning under rising prices. The interest payments are also a cause of rising fiscal deficits. But the interest payments can be brought down by reducing borrowing. This necessitates the imposition of a constitutional limit on Government borrowing and restructuring the maturity schedule of debt. But while subsidies should have no place in a market-oriented economy, their continuation in India is necessary for some more time and their rate needs to be brought down in gradual stages. At what rate it should be brought down cannot be determined a prior. It has to be decided on the basis of several factors including the rate of inflation and the resource availability with the Government. In a similar manner the extravagant expenditure of the Government needs to be pruned drastically. There is urgent need for an authoritative study of the Government expenditure in all directions and the directions in which it has to be pruned without hurting the economy and the economic well being of the people. This calls for the appointment of an Expenditure Commission which should undertake the task of suggesting the rationalisation of public expenditure in all directions. This commission needs to employ the cost-benefit calculus in permitting/cutting down public expenditure. The Expenditure Commission should consist of eminent economists, representatives of the farm lobbies, legal experts and trade unionists. Unless there is drastic pruning of public expenditure the possibility of reducing the fiscal deficit is remote.

Inflation management is a part of the Budget exercise. It must be said to the credit of Dr. Manmohan Singh that he brought down the rate of inflation from 17.5 percent in 1991 to 7.5 percent in the middle of 1994. The present trend of inflation is an average of 10 percent this year and it is generally accepted that it will hover round that figure next year also. The important factor causing inflation in the fiscal deficit. But there are several other factors also at work: the annual increases in the procurement prices of food grains, a high rate of import duty on imported edible oil which does not allow lower world prices to be reflected in domestic prices; excessive regulations and controls on sugar at all stages keeping sugar prices high; lack of growth in investment in agriculture and the consequent poor growth of farm production; delays in the execution of projects leading to income generation because of investment expenditure but no results in respect of output; distortions caused by interference in the prices of farm inputs like water and electricity rates causing distortions in cropping patterns and land use patterns and resulting in high-cost production. Along with these there have been sharp increases in administered prices especially fuel and power.

Monetary factors are also important. Money supply is increasing at a rate of 13.4 percent during March 31 November 11, 1994. The increase in the rate of inflation is being ascribed to the expansion of money supply since other parameters are positive. The Khariff crop is good and there is a pick-up in industrial production. But the monetary growth is 13.4 percent between March and November 1994 against 10 percent during the same period 1993. Currency with the public has gone up by 15.4 percent and bank credit to the commercial section as shot upto Rs. 16,886 crore between March and November 1994 against Rs. 5,762 crore in 1993. The fiscal deficit of the Government was at a level of Rs. 23,003 crore in the first six months of 1994 though it is on expected lines. Another contributory factor is the net foreign exchange assets of the banking sector. While these assets were placed at Rs. 5,680 crore during March-November 1993, during the same period in 1994 these assets were worth Rs. 18,451 crore. This increase is due to the massive inflow of foreign exchange into the country compelling purchases by the banking sector and corresponding release of rupee funds into the economy.

What has the Government done to reduce the inflation rate in the monetary sector? The Finance Ministry's inflation management strategy has been based on market borrowing to avoid deficit financing. The Government, in the process, raised Rs. 1,714 crore from the market upto the end of September 1994 against Rs. 10,946 crore during the same period in 1993. The Reserve Bank of India also planned to mop up liquidity from the market by offloading some of the earlier Government stock in its possession. Another measure to contain the inflow of foreign exchange into the country is the permission for Indian companies which raise loans through Global Deposit Receipts to park funds abroad under the new guidelines issued in this connection. The Finance Ministry expects to peg the inflation rate at 10 percent by the close of the fiscal 1994-95. But this depends on expenditure over-runs.

The lack of control over expenditure and inadequate improvement in the sphere of Government performance can be identified as major constraints. There are political constraints on improving public sector efficiency by cutting over staffing and improving returns on investment. This applies to public sector enterprises and to other Government department undertakings like the Railways etc.

At present, the Government is selling public sector equity and is using the proceeds to finance Government expenditure. This does not contribute to inflation control. Instead the proceeds can be used to reduce the public debt and thus to reduce the interest cost which is an item of non-plan expenditure. The Finance Minister has switched over from monetary financing of the deficit to debt financing. Both these methods of financing are inflationary but debt financing is more inflationary than monetary financing. Debt financing involves interest payment. The interest cost is an item of non-plan expenditure which fuels inflation. Furthermore it enhances the burden of debt on future generations. It also causes a shift of income from the tax payers to bond holders and intensifies inequality of income distribution calling for corrective measures.

The inflation in India is partly due to the payment of remunerative prices to farmers during the past three years. This had the effect of raising the prices of food articles which engendered inflation. It is possible to argue that if remunerative prices were not given the farmers would have reduced food output because of disincentives and higher food prices would have engendered inflation. But this is a different matter.

Money Supply

Excessive money creation is a cause of inflationary pressure. It was assumed that the curb on the primary creation of money through reduction of deficit financing would tame the secondary increase in money supply. But the experience is contrary to the assumption. The M3 increased at 15.7 percent during 1992-93. In 1993-94 it went upto 18.2 percent. The total quantum of M3 as on March 31, 1994 was Rs. 4,33,566 crore as compared to Rs. 3,17,046 crore on March 31, 1993.

The Reserve money registered an increase of 9.3 percent in the last quarter of 1993-94. This spurt was caused by an increase of Rs.18,431 crore in forex reserves showing an increase of

29 percent. The money stock would have gone up had not the policy of automatic monetisation of budgetary deficit been reversed. The volume of monetised debt was reduced from Rs. 14,746 crore in 1990-91 to Rs. 260 crore in 1993-94 (RE). The Reserve Bank also resorted to large scale open market operations for reducing the volume of created money. During January-March 1994 the rate of Bank credit also declined from 6 percent to 3.6 percent. But the accumulation of forex reserves added to the money stock.

Inspite of these measures the expansion of money stock could not be contained. The SLR, CRR and open market operations were deployed extensively. Even so, the total M_3 increase since 1991-92 exceeds 14 percent. There is excess liquidity of 30 percent. The present monetary - fiscal policy measures are unable to mop up this excess liquidity.

The Finance Minister has assured the nation that monetary, fiscal and international trade policies would be applied to reduce the rate of monetary growth. But the modus operandi of the scheme is not made clear. The existing fiscal-monetary policy apparatus can absorb 7-8 percent of excess liquidity. The balance of 22-23 percent has to absorbed. The policy of import liberalisation which would increase the supply of goods in the economy would absorb a part of the excess liquidity. A hike in the interest rates on savings instruments including those on post office savings certificates would divert money from consumption to savings. A resort to monetary targeting relating to money supply growth of between 3 and 6 percent would reduce the rate of monetary growth by half and reduce addition to liquidity. These measures would reduce the liquidity overhang and bring down the rate of inflation.

Black Money

The inflation management strategy should include the strategy to check the black money menace. There is a colossal stock of black money in the country. This money is not held in the banks but is held privately. The existence of this black money has rendered ineffective contractive fiscal and monetary policies when a contractive monetary policy is adopted with intent to check spending and to reduce the rate of inflation the borrowers who find bank borrowing costlier go to the parallel economy where they borrow and spend. In consequence, despite a contractive monetary policy spending and aggregate demand will not fall and inflation becomes immitigable. A similar situation arises even if a contractive fiscal policy is pushed. At present the inflation generated by the fiscal deficit is compounded by the inflation generated by the expenditure of black money. Therefore, even if the fiscal deficit is brought down to the targeted level there will be no relief on the inflation front.

In the past several measures were adopted to unearth black money but they did not meet with any success. The amount unearthed was only paltry and this was not of much consequence. An effective strategy is to be designed to control the black money menace. I have elucidated a scheme to control the black money menace in my book : Eradication of Black Wealth and Black Money. This scheme could be examined and, if found acceptable it could be implemented. This is an antidote to inflation.

Balance of Payments

India is faced with the balance of payments crisis varying dimensions since 1957-58 when the Second Year Plan was half way through. It is these crises which led to the rapid accumulation of external debt. The balance of payments deficit is the external manifestation of the fiscal deficit as the Cambridge Economic Policy Group (CEPG) has established. The balance of payments is a function of two variable exports and imports. The rate of growth of imports exceeds the rate of growth of exports and this is the crux of the problem. Despite the new export- import policy of 1992 and its modified version of 1994 the trade gap persists. At what rate are exports and imports growing?

India's exports in the first eight months of 1994-95 are estimated at $ 15,941.05 million as against $ 13,839.55 million during the corresponding period of the fiscal year 1993-94 signifying a growth of 15.18 percent. Imports during the same period are estimated at

$ 17,603.01 million against $ 14,372 million against during the corresponding period in 1993-94. The trade deficit during April-November 1994 is $ 1,661.96 million compared to $ 532.57 million during the corresponding period in 1993.

According to the Commerce Ministry release the continuing two-digit export growth during April-November 1994 reflects the expected "positive effects" of the steps taken by the Government while the continued growth of imports reflects the openness of the economy. Due to the point-to-point inflation rate having risen above 10 percent, the favourable effects of devaluation of the rupee are eroded given the much lower rates of inflation in the trade-partner countries.

The continuing monetary expansion fuelling inflationary forces in the economy continues to counteract optimism on the price front. Despite the surge in foreign exchange assets of the Reserve Bank of India the growth of money supply (M3) has more or less been kept around 18 percent, thanks to the 11 percent reduction in net Reserve Bank credit to Government and the near stagnation in bank credit to the commercial sector. If the surge in forex reserves continues at the present rate it could put the Reserve Bank under test as there are limits to the process of sterilization of such inflows through immobilisation of commercial bank resources. In the event of imports not gathering pace this factor of forex flows could itself aggravate the inflationary process. This is the logic behind the argument of the Finance Minister for a policy of import liberalisation. But the Commerce Ministry is opposed to import liberalisation on the plea that it would adversely affect the small scale industrial sector as the demand for its products would fall. This plea cannot be taken seriously. Imports and the goods produced by the small scale sector cater to the needs of two different groups of consumers. Those who were formerly consuming the goods produced by the small scale sector do not regard the imported goods as substitutes. For this reason the inflow of imports will not change the consumption pattern of consumers. For this reason it would be too far fetched to hold that import liberalisation would adversely affect the small sector. Imports are necessary to hold the price line.

The Union Commerce Ministry has come out with a sharp attack on the Government's policy of steeping up GDP growth through increased foreign investment and imports. It says that the critics of import led growth would be vindicated by the growth of imports since liberalisation. The Finance Minister who is concerned with the task of reducing the rate of inflation generated by the inflow of forex reserves advocated a policy of liberalising imports which would increase the supply of goods and serve an antidote to inflation. But the Commerce Ministry is opposed to this policy on the ground that it would hurt the small scale industrial sector. It must be remembered that the imports are not perfect substitutes to the products of the small scale industrial sector. There is a well defined market for these goods and the imports will not cut into the market share of the goods of the small scale industrial sector. In view of this it is not correct to hold that the imports will hurt the small scale sector in any significant way. Considering the need to fight inflation the policy of import liberalisation is well conceived. The trade deficit generated by it is not to be feared as the country has got a large volume of forex reserves which could be drawn upon to pay for these imports.

The trade figurers released by the Commerce Ministry for the first eight months of the fiscal year 1994-95 suggest two developments which may be of long term consequence to the Indian economy; (1) the resilience of exports and a quantum jump in its long term growth rate; (2) a widening trade deficit. The first is borne out by the 26.9 percent increase in exports in a month which was marked by the plague scare that resulted in the imposition of import restrictions by some countries. The average export growth rate of 13.9 percent is above the 7-8 percent average the country saw in the pre-reform period. This figure has been rising since August and the average for the year may be higher still. Together with the 20 percent export growth achieved in 1993-94 this is definite evidence that India has made some advance on the reforms objective of a major step up in export growth.

Imports during this period increased by 19.8 percent non oil imports by as much as 30.6 percent. These imports are feeding industrial recovery and there is little cause for complaint. With forex reserves touching $ 20 billion and expected to touch $ 25 billion by the end of March 1995 with their monetary implications greater imports are welcome. But the difference in the export and import growth rates is leading to a widening of the trade deficit one is reminded of the second half of the 1980s when a similarly widening trade deficit led to a balance of payment crisis. With external debt servicing likely to peak in 1996, with a significant portion of forex reserves composed of volatile portfolio investments and with Foreign Direct Investment not picking up adequately, the Commerce Ministry is understandably worried that unless exports increase commensurately with imports India would be in trouble again. There is legitimacy in this concern. A variety of measures to increase exports further are necessary. But the Commerce Ministry which feels that restrictions on imports are necessary has to note that imports are necessary for the following reasons:

1. Imports of capital goods, technology and raw materials are necessary to promote exports;
2. Imports of consumer goods are necessary to reduce the price level in the country caused in the main by the fiscal deficit and the monetary growth caused by rising forex reserves;
3. The reduction in the rate of inflation is necessary to enhance the competitiveness of India's exports in world markets.

Seen in this perspective import liberalisation despite its short run balance of payments implications is necessary not only to reduce the rate of inflation but also to promote the growth of exports.

Some recent developments in the world outside India do not seem to be helpful for export growth though many are euphoric about it. The industrialised economies are keenly interested in the market-driven reforms in the Asian developing countries mainly because these reforms open up vast markets to them. But market-driven reforms are also making Asian economies including India's highly effective players in the World market. This the industrialised countries may not relish. Exports from India will find roadblocks all the way. While India is opening up to the world the world is indulging in protectionism and in building tariff walls and non-tariff barriers in the name of social dumping, human rights, environmental control or other technical factors. They are tempted to use the very GATT mechanism to restrict the entry of India's competitive high-quality products into their own markets. India will then find that it is denied the full benefits of its natural comparative advantage of abundant manpower and rich natural resources to penetrate world markets. India may also find that the grievance redressal machinery of the new World Trade Organisation (WTO) to which India is a signatory is tiresomely slow-moving. The Finance Minister is aware of their emergence and their seriousness. Adequate precautions are necessary for securing speedy redressal of grievance through the WTO.

The Commerce Ministry is blaming the Finance Ministry for not providing subsidies to exports. This reflects the absence of a macro-view of the problem. Exports are a purely commercial activity and there is no reason why subsides should be paid to the exports all the time. Generally speaking export incentives and subsidies are paid when a new product needs to be pushed into the world market and that too for a limited period depending on the circumstances of each individual exporting country. Subsidies or incentives cannot be demanded as a matter of right.

The real meaning of cash subsidy or incentives to exporters is that the Indian tax payer is made to pay so that the foreign buyer can buy the Indian goods for a lower price. The export earnings are already exempt from income tax. Is not this an incentive enough for the exporters? The export sector does not pay tax and yet it demands subsidies as well. The exporters should be asked to cut their costs, become innovative and competitive. The indirect taxes have been cut across the board in the past three years and even then if the exporters cannot compete in the world markets then they should rather close down their shutters.

The Finance Ministry has given enough incentives to exporters by making export earnings tax free and by reducing customs and excise duties. The time has come for the Government to say a firm 'No' to subsidies to exporters.

The question of exchange rate of the rupee is important. For over four decades India is under the tyranny of two deficits the fiscal deficit and the balance of payments deficit. In this context the revival of growth is tardy for fiscal expansion would be reflected in monetisation which in turn would result in a widening of the balance of payments deficit. The economic reforms initiated in July 1991 brought about fundamental changes in the economy. The changes in trade, industrial and foreign investment policies combined with exchange rate reform eased the bind on the balance of payments. The two-step exchange rate depreciation of the rupee in July 1991, the move to a dual exchange rate system in March 1992, the unification of the exchange rate in March 1993 and the steps towards current account convertibility initiated in March 1994 and completed in August 1994 all brought about an appropriate pricing of foreign exchange. The trade policy measures reversed the earlier policy which had an implicit bias against exports.

Owing to the continued commitment to the pursuit of the reform programme the credibility of the policies has been established. With the change in policies relating to capital inflows through foreign institutional investors and Euro-issues have become sizeable. With the substantial improvement in exports, there is the likelihood of a reduction in the balance of payments deficit.

At present the exchange rate of the rupee is stabilised at $ 1 = Rs. 31.37. There is an inflow of forex reserves which the Reserve Bank of India is committed to buying in order to prevent the rupee from appreciating as an appreciated rupee would increase imports, reduce exports and aggravate the current account deficit. This, of course, has had an inflationary effect through the impact of forex reserves on the money supply. Some economists want the rupee to be appreciated unmindful of harmful consequences to the economy.

Certain opposition political parties recommend devaluation of the rupee in the context of the current account deficit on the assumption that devaluation would correct the deficit. But the success of devaluation depends on the fulfillment of certain essential conditions viz.

1. The sum of the elasticity of demand for imports and the elasticity of demand for India's exports is greater than unity.

2. The fiscal deficit should be constant;
3. The wage rates should remain constant.

These conditions are difficult of fulfillment in India. No precise estimates of elasticities are available for India. But it can be stated that the sum of the two elasticities is not greater than units. The demand for imports is inelastic because of the essential nature of the imports raw materials, capital goods and spare parts. The elasticity of demand for India's exports abroad may not be significant unless the prices of India's exports fall more than the prices of goods supplied to world markets by the other countries to which India is a competitor. In view of this the sum of the two import demand elasticities will be greater than unity.

India is grappling with the problem of reducing the fiscal deficit. The actual fiscal deficit is generally more than the targeted fiscal deficit. This generates inflationary impulses in the economy. Furthermore, the wage rates are not constant. The labourers, groaning under the weight of inflation enforce their demands for higher wages and dearness allowances successfully. For these reasons, devaluation as a remedy for the current account deficit may not succeed. Furthermore we have to reckon with the "J Curve Effect" on the deficit. The deficit worsens initially before it improves, if at all. The favourable effect of devaluation on the current account cannot be taken for granted as there are many imponderables working against devaluation.

The effect of devaluation of the rupee on the external debt cannot be ignored. At present the external debt is of the order of Rs. 3 lakh crore. If the rupee is devalued, the rupee value of the external debt rises in proportion to devaluation; added to this rupee value of the interest cost will also rise in proportion to devaluation. This will worsen the capital account of the balance of payments. For these reasons, devaluation of the rupee is an inappropriate remedy for the current account deficit.

After the introduction of current account convertibility of the rupee, the next step in the exchange rate management is capital account convertibility. The Finance Minister has gone on record committing himself to capital account convertibility in due course.

But the time is not opportune for the introduction of capital account convertibility. Given the capital account convertibility the foreign investors and others who are holding capital in India may feel inclined to shift their capital in which India will find it difficult to meet these demands for withdrawal. This will erode investor confidence which is so necessary for the success of the reform programme. For these reasons the recourse to capital account convertibility is untimely.

India's External Debt Profile

As early as 1991 India was facing a debt crisis as there was the possibility of default in meeting its external payment obligations. India obtained IMF financing facility by adopting the adjustment policy so as to be able to cope with the problem of 'liquidity' facing the country. India had for long been one of the largest developing country debtors. But the problems arising out of the debt burden were not considered compelling till the 1991 crisis. This view was held by the Government, international financial institutions and the credit rating agencies. The World Bank in its Annual Report accompanying the 1992-93 World Debt Tables (WDT) acknowledged the existence of a debt crisis in India though India was a problem debtor much earlier in terms of the criteria laid down by the Bank to identify problem-debtors. The Government of India in its Status Report on External Debt published in 1991 put the debt crisis in perspective. The paper gave a comprehensive account of the position regarding external debt which included the defence debt and the rupee debt to the erstwhile Soviet Union. After a large increase in 1990-91 the rate of growth of external debt decreased in 1991-92 and in 1992-93. However, the magnitude of increase was still large. The level at which foreign debt stood was larger at the end of 1993-94 than in 1990-91 and had touched $ 90 billion. At the end of 1990, the total debt stock was $ 69 billion. This went upto $ 71.5 billion in 1991 and by 1992 end it increased to $ 77 billion and at the end of 1993-94 it swelled to $ 91 billion. These figures indicate that India has been accumulating external debt since the launching of the structural adjustment programmes at a rate faster than that recorded for the South Asian region as a whole. At present India is the third largest debtor among developing countries. At the end of 1991 over 90 percent of India's debt was long-term debt. India reached the threshold of the crisis on the external debt front in 1991 when it was forced to seek IMF support. India's debt-service ratio has become worse after the launching of the structural adjustment programme. The debt-service ratio exceeded 31 percent and the total debt stock to export ratio was over 300 percent in 1994. The debt to GDP ratio also increased considerably over the 1991 level.

This gives rise to the apprehension that the debt crisis would get accentuated in the coming years. More than a third of the external debt or about $ 25 billion is due to be repaid in the next four years. According to the Reserve Bank estimates the total repayment of principal and interest on external debt in 1995-96 will be as high as $ 10 billion—a formidable figure indeed. The Budget has to make adequate provision for it. At the same time ways and means are to be found to reduce the debt burden.

India's forex reserves at present are over $ 20 billion and they are expected to swell to $ 25 billion by April 1995. These reserves through their impact on monetary growth are fuelling the fires of inflation. These reserves are, in part, volatile prone to leave the country at short notice, after having caused havoc in the economy. The inflow of such reserves needs to be discouraged by means of the interest rate mechanism. Other reserves of a fairly stable nature can be used to repay high-cost external debt. This will reduce the interest burden of the debt and will avoid the need to provide for their repayment as per schedule from out of current export earnings. This will provide some relief on the balance of payments front and will go a long way in ensuring external solvency. This will also mitigate the impact on monetary growth and ultimately on the rate of inflation. At the same time, resort to further external borrowing needs to be minimised in order to hold down the burden of debt and to be free from the opposition charge that the Government is bowing to the dictates of the Fund-Bank duo. But the reduction of external borrowing is conditional on fiscal consolidation. India has for long been under the tyranny of twin deficits. The Budget should free India from this tyranny.

India's Internal Debt Profile

In the fourth year of reform the World Bank talks of the "risks of falling into a domestic debt trap". New annual borrowings now leave little after debt servicing. In 1990-91 48 percent of the Centre's borrowings (fiscal deficit) went into interest payments. In 1992-93 the proportion rose to 77 percent and in 1994-95 it will be 84 percent. Borrowing to pay for borrowings can lead to a situation where new borrowings fall short of debt servicing requirements. This is the feared debt trap.

Initially reforms worked. Borrowing was brought under control. In 1990-91 the fiscal deficit was 8.4 percent of GDP. The fiscal deficit declined with the start of reform: to 6 percent of GDP in 1991-92 and 5.7 percent in 1992-93. But the fiscal deficit spurted to 7.3 percent in 1993-94. It was proposed to reduce it to 6 percent in 1994-95.

The cost of debt is rising. According to the World Bank "The Liberalisation of interest rates has increased interest cost on the Central Government debt from 4 percent of GDP in 1990-91 to 5.1 percent of GDP anticipated in 1994-95". The Government opted to borrow at high market-related interest rates. As the stock of debt rises with new borrowings at high interest rates, so does the interest outgo. Furthermore from this year borrowing from the Reserve Bank at 4.5 percent interest are to be phased out. These are being replaced with borrowing at market interest rates at 13 percent. The World Bank feels that it would be difficult to contain the fiscal deficit to the level targeted this year. The Government has to raise the interest rates to keep annual borrowings ahead of rising interest outgo. This is necessary to induce the market to lend to the Government as in the late 1980s. The Government can sell public sector units. But this is not current revenue. But the sale of PSU shares results in a transfer of assets but not in an increase in aggregate investment. At present India is labouring under a severe deficiency of investment. This is due to the absence of a level playing field for domestic industry. A second factor is the high level of interest rates. Investment deficiency is at the bottom of low Government revenues. This has increased the need to borrow. Because of low investment import, demand is weak. This is the cause of excess money supply which is a cause of inflation. This makes it difficult for the Government to lower the interest rates. There is thus a vicious circle of high inflation, low investment low growth and low revenue. This requires a step up in investment.

There is need to restructure the debt. At present the internal debt. of the order of Rs. 2,43,000 crore and the interest cost is enormous and this adds to the fiscal deficit. A shift from monetary financing to debt financing of the deficit is inflationary as the increase in interest cost adds to fiscal deficit which generates inflation. The object of policy is to reduce the interest cost. This can be done in the following manner.

1. By imposing a constitutional limit on borrowing.
2. By shifting from debt financing to monetary financing of the deficit.
3. By changing the maturity pattern of debt. If the maturity pattern is shifted in favour of long-term debt it is less inflationary than short term debt as it reduces the liquidity of the debt but it involves higher interest payment considering the fact that long term debt carries a higher rate of interest. If it is shifted in favour of short-term debt it increases the liquidity of debt and is inflationary but the interest cost falls. It is necessary to effect a balance between these two kinds of debt.

These measures would mitigate the inflationary pressure emanating from the debt segment of the Budget keeping in view the need to reduce liquidity and the interest cost.

Is the Mexican Experience Relevant?

In the letter addressed to the Finance Secretary on 4.1.1995, the Indian Executive Director to the IMF K.P. Geethakrishnan has warned of the adverse consequences of liberalisation. According to him "in a free market politics there is no place for compassion or sympathy" for the poor. He has suggested that India should learn from the turmoil in Mexico due to free market policies. He has pointed to the demands being made in Mexico that some of those who pushed for liberalisation be tried for reason.

The reason for this turmoil in Mexico is the relentless rise in prices of essential goods which has rendered the lives of the poor miserable. It is true that the prices of food in India are rising due to inflationary pressures but food subsidy is being continued to rein in the rate of price rise. India is not yet a fullfledged market economy though it is on the road to it. It is the continuous sufferings of the people since the late 1980s that is the cause of the Mexican turmoil. But the Indian inflation rate is no match to the Mexican. It stands to the credit of the Finance Minister that he brought down the rate of inflation from 17.5 percent in July 1991 to 7 percent in August 1994. But since then the rate of inflation is fluctuating between the marginal double digit and the marginal single digit. But there is no higher inflation of the Mexican variety. Admittedly the poor are hurt by whatever price rise that has taken place. But the people have to make certain sacrifices at the present time to ensure a prosperous future. The rising prices hurt not just the poor but the entire community. Poverty can be mitigated by means of raising the incomes of the poor and not by means of doles to them. Income can be increased by means of employment generation. But in India employment opportunities are not being generated in sufficient volume. According to the Governor, Reserve Bank of India "Even agriculture has been showing declining employment elasticity in the aggregate primarily because of geographically concentrated growth in agriculture". He said that elasticity has been as low as 0.01, 0.07 and 0.19 in Punjab, Haryana and U.P. respectively. The figures are generally higher than 0.7 in most States in the Eastern, Central and Southern India. A special thrust on agricultural growth in the latter States can raise the aggregate elasticity in agriculture significantly. The Eighth Five Year Plan has assumed an employment elasticity of 0.5 for manufacturing. It should be possible to achieve this elasticity with suitable sectoral composition combined with an efficient small scale sector. This calls for a diversified strategy for employment generation as the problems are different between the rural and urban sectors and between the educated, the skilled and the uneducated. In order to accelerate employment generation encouragement should be given to those sectors which are labour-intensive. Nearly two-thirds of the work force is engaged in agriculture. Therefore, the overall growth of employment depends on agricultural growth. A faster and geographically diversified approach is crucial in any scheme of employment generation. Mere growth of medium and large scale industries which are mainly capital intensive may not generate employment to the requisite degree. But the growth of these sectors can favourably affect the growth of labour intensive sectors like small scale industries, transport, construction and the informal sector.

In the short run it is necessary to hold the price line to give relief to the harried consumers who have begun to voice their protest against price rise. This requires the rationalisation of the Public Distribution System (PDS) and the continuation for some more time to come the subsidies on food and fertilisers. The recent hikes in the prices of fertilisers have generated resentment in the minds of the farmers who are up in arms against them. Empirical studies have shown that the demand for fertilisers is price-elastic causing a rise in their prices to reduce the input of fertilisers. This has the effect of reducing the farm yield and farm output which consists of food output and output of raw-materials for domestic consumption and exports. In a country like India where food prices govern the general price level and the rate of inflation it is necessary to hold down the prices of food. This is possible if there is a rise in food output. The fertiliser subsidy which reduces the price of fertilisers increases the fertiliser input in the farm and increases food output which helps to reduce food prices. Seen in this perspective the continuation of fertilisers subsidy is absolutely essential. At the same time food subsidy needs to be continued to help the poor to purchase food at subsidised prices. These measures are pro-poor without being populist.

It is contended that the subsidies increase the fiscal deficit which is inflationary. This is admitted. But the withdrawal of subsidy raised the prices of food articles, raises the cost-of-living index and generates demands for higher wages which in turn give rise to cost-push and demand pull inflations which get entwined and become difficult to disentangle. This is also inflationary. Inflation caused by the fiscal deficit is less dangerous than inflation occasioned by the withdrawal of subsidies.

The Mexican experience cited by Geetha Krishnan is relevant for India. The situation in India is not as grave as it is in Mexico; Poverty in India is not as pervasive or as intense as poverty in Mexico. Mexico is fully fledged market economy while India is yet to be one. Mexico had a current account deficit equal to 8 percent of GDP whereas in the Indian case it was brought down from over 3 percent in 1990-91 to less than 1 percent GPD in 1994.

Therefore, what is bad for Mexico is not necessarily bad for India i.e., what is bad for the goose is not necessarily bad for the gander. It thus appears that citing the example of Mexico and asking India to change its course is irrelevant.

It is held that the reforms are anti-poor. Poverty alleviation depends on economic growth. The growth rate has, of late, picked up under reforms. Pravin Krishna and Dvashish Mitra of Columbia University have analysed firm level data in several industries to show that trade liberalisation which is part of economic reform package is followed by increased growth of productivity. It is held on the basis of perverse logic that growth cannot effect poverty. It must be admitted that growth through economic reforms is an anti-poverty strategy. It provides gainful employment to the poor. By increasing tax revenues it enables the Government to spend more on poverty alleviation. This means more and not fewer reforms.

Conclusion

The Union Budget has to be formulated keeping in view the need to provide immediate relief to the people who allege that the economic reform package is anti-poor and to ensure long-term prosperity for the nation. It will not serve any purpose to blame the people who are unable to comprehends the long-term implications of the reform programme. The expect immediate gains in the belief that in the long run we are all dead. But the Government has to keep the long run interests of the nation in view in its policies and programmes. But it cannot afford to ignore the immediate gains expected by the people for to do so would be politically disastrous as the results of the recent Assembly elections in the South have made it so distressingly obvious. To balance the immediate needs of the people and the long-run interests of the nation is an extremely delicate task and this task has to be performed, however arduous the exercise. The Finance Minister has reaffirmed India's firm commitment to the economic reforms with a "human face". While conceding that the structural adjustment programme may result in "undue hardships" to the people if implemented unimaginatively. In saying this the Finance Minister has understood the delicate nature of his task.

The Budget is an important policy tool to realise the goals which the Government has placed before itself. The goals are both short-term and long-term. They have to be realised without sacrificing the one for the other. The foregoing thoughts on the Union Budget for 1995-96 are intended to enable it to realise these goals. Political expediency and high principle have both to be followed to enthuse the people into involving themselves in the task of unchaining the Indian Tiger to leap forward on the road to accelerated economic growth.

The present economic reforms programme has become a bull of criticism. This criticism is not without political overtones. For long India has remained a backward country despite its natural endowments and abundant manpower. India remained a chained tiger in the cage. The economic reform has now unchained it. But it is yet to take the forward leap because of many and varied structural and institutional rigidities. It is the task of economic statesmanship to remove these rigidities. The on-going economic reform programme is doing just that. One cannot expect instant miracles. What is necessary is patience. The detractors of the reform programme cannot be allowed to have their way. If they are allowed to have their way, the country will revert to the colonial stage when Indians were hewers of wood and drawers of water. This should not be allowed to happen.

33

Problems of Food Storage

The task of procurement, storage and distribution of food grains bristles with formidable problems. The Food Corporation of India has taken upon itself the responsibility of paying minimum support prices for good grains to the farmers at the harvesting season and storing it in order to prevent the food prices from falling; it has also taken upon itself the responsibility of maintaining stable prices in the open market in order to help the poor and the needy. However, ever since this scheme was initiated there have been far reaching changes in the scheme. Not long ago, India was depending on foreign supplies of food grains. The decades of the 1950s and the 1960s were years of acute shortage of domestic supplies. In the decade of the 1950s India had to import 29 lakh tonnes of food grains per annum; in the decade of the 1960s this figure escalated to 58 lakh tonnes. In 1966 India's dependence on foreign supplies reached its peak. In that year, India imported 103 lakh tonnes of food grains. In the subsequent years there was a change for the better in the food scenario. The Green Revolution increased the supply of wheat manifold. Even so, there was need to supply food grains to the weaker sections of society at fair prices. In order to prevent the rise in prices in the years of scarcity it was considered to prevent the rise in prices in the years of scarcity it was considered necessary to purchase food grains, store them and to distribute them through fair price depots. This led to stability in prices and fairness in the distribution of food grains. However, this system was not completely satisfactory. The benefits of this scheme are yet to reach the weaker sections in the remote villages. Over half the number of villages do not get the benefits of distribution of food grains even now. It is alleged the benefits of this scheme are appropriated for the most part by those who are not in need to these benefits. The burden of food subsidy is also mounting. The restructuring of the public distribution system in order to restrict these benefits to the weaker sections is yet to be initiated in right earnest. This is one facet of the problem. There is another facet. This has to do with the Food Corporation of India.

At one time the Government had to collect food grains from the farmers at a predetermined quantities. Though this system became a subject of criticism it was absolutely necessary to store a certain minimum stock of food. When there was surplus food production the situation changed. In order to prevent the prices of food grains from falling because of excess supply and to distribute food grains this scheme came in handy. The emphasis was laid on paying minimum support prices to the farmers. This took away the bitterness involved in compulsory levy. In the determination of minimum support prices to be paid to the farmers political elements crept in and the authorities determining these prices came under intense pressures from all directions. It is alleged that the hike in support prices caused the hike in open market prices. As the prices in the fair price depots rose in conformity with the hikes in minimum support prices there was not much differential between the prices charged in the fair price depots and those prevailing in the open market. It was believed that the food grains available in the open market were better in quality than those available in the fair price depots. For this reason there was a reduction in the outflow of food grains from the public distribution system.

For this reason the Food Corporation of India is confronted with an intricate problem. Its storage activity has gone on briskly. But the amount it has to spend for this purpose is colossal. As on 1.7.1994 the food stocks held by the Central Government and the State Governments were of the order of 3.12 crore tonnes. This is unprecedented. This is 50 percent more than the required stock. The stock of rice is 1.45 crore tonnes. If this stock is 92 lakh tonnes it would be sufficient. Furthermore, it is anticipated that the stock of rise to be collected from the Khariff crop would be of the order of 1.36 crore tonnes. Even if we deduct the rice to be distributed nearly 40-50 lakh tonne of rice would be added to the existing stock imposing a burden on the Food Corporation of India.

In recent years many high-yielding and quick-yielding varieties of crops are being used. The Food Corporation is embarrassed by the fact that it does not have finance to purchase the food grains and does not have storage facilities to store it. Furthermore, the stock of food grains cannot be held for more than 30 months. If it is held for more than 30 months the rice deteriorates and becomes unfit for human consumption. It has to be sold before it gets spoiled. But who is there to purchase it?

The Food Corporation of India has appealed to the Government to allow it to sell the stock of food grains at prices below the market prices. But this involves the danger of the prices of food articles crashing. In view of the forthcoming elections, the Government may not venture to concede the appeal of the Food Corporation of India. Even if 5 percent of the present stock is considered inferior in quality; For this reason about 10 lakh tonne can be written off as lost. This is older than 2 years in stock. It has cost Rs. 74 crore to the Government. In addition to it there is the burden of food subsidy. The cost of storing a quintal of food including the interest on the borrowed funds, and rent of premises for storing is estimated to be Rs. 140. It is estimated that if the stock is held for 1 ½ years instead of 1 year the cost per tonne of food so held would be Rs. 1,400 crore.

The Government claims that after it signed the Marrakesh Trade Accords on 14.4.1994 the foreign markets are open for India's exports of food. If the claims is tenable the Government can export the stock help by the Food Corporation of India to the needy countries. But there is no demand for out food outside. India is not able to export even high quality rice (Basumathi) in a significant quantity. The prices of other varieties of food articles in India are 45 percent higher than the international prices. Excess stock holding, cost of the stock held, the irritation of the consumers, rising burden of subsidy and the anger of the farmers have in their collectivity created formidable problems for the Government. The immediate solution of these problems is the primary task of the Government.

It is obvious from the foregoing that the Government in a dilemma in its policy of food procurement and storage. If it does not procure adequate food the prices of food grains crash adversely affecting the interests of farmers. If, as at present food is procured in quantities necessary to hold the food prices stable the cost of storage and distribution and also the risk of deterioration of quality of food grains will be enormous. A way has to be found to avert the dilemma.

At present food subsidy which includes consumer subsidy and the cost of building buffer stocks is enormous. Its rapid risk from Rs. 6 billion in 1980 to Rs. 22 billion in 1988 and further to about Rs. 30 billion in 1992-93 is a drag on the resources of the Government. This can be avoided by increasing the quota allowed for the poor under the Public Distribution System. The food availability in India is low. China has already reached a production level of over 300 million tonne according to a US estimate. This for a population of 1,100 million represents a gross per capita availability of around 330 kg per annum against only 200 kg in India. Those who are euphoric about the harvest of 180 million tonne of food grains should remember that the harvest should have been higher by 100 million tonne to match the Chinese achievement. India should aim at a per capital availability of 300 kg. This requires a production level of 300 million tonne.

At present the per capita consumption of food grains in India is too low to meet nutritional standards. The per capita off take of PDS card holders is far less than they should consume.

There is a continuous upward revision in the procurement prices of food grains. This is a result of the persistent demands by the influential rich farmers lobby which the Government seems unwilling to antagonise. The galloping procurement prices are one reason for the rise in the prices at the PDS level. Higher issue and procurement prices for rice and wheat have more negative fallouts. The vulnerable sections of society do not meet their requirements through the PDS. They purchase the residual requirement at higher open market prices which follow the Government's price policies. For example, as per the NSS information the bottom 20 percent of the rural and urban population purchase merely 16 and 21 percent of their rice requirement respectively from the PDS. The corresponding figures for wheat are even less at 10 and 15 percent. The rest of the requirement bought in open markets in thus nearly 4-5 times of the PDS purchases. Thus the PDS has failed in one of its primary objectives, that of acting as a price stabiliser. There are other irregularities like substandard quality of grains, illegal price mark ups etc.

This calls for increasing the per capita allotment of good quality food grains to the consumers holding ration cards at affordable prices. Furthermore, care should be taken not to raises the procurement prices at the behest of the risk, influential farmers. The procurement prices should be cost-determined. The Commission on Agricultural costs and prices is the to recommend any hike in the procurement prices of food grains. The Government decision to raise prices should depend on the recommendation of the CACP and not on the whims of the rich farmers.

Storing food grains for more than 30 months renders them unfit for human consumption besides increasing the cost of storage. If the per capita availability of food allotted to the card holders under the PDS is increased, the stock is bound to fall significantly. The problem of deterioration of quality of food grains will be minimised considerably. If the stock of food remains unsold, it could be exported on the basis of an export subsidy. The amount spent on storage could be paid as export subsidy.

It is rice that has created the problem. Obviously, there is an excess supply of rice. All varieties of rice produced cannot be exported. The importing countries need high quality rice. Land should be switched over from the cultivation of inferior varieties of rice to the cultivation of superior varieties like high grade basumathi. Furthermore as there is excess demand for sugar causing a risk in sugar prices and occasioning sugar imports at considerable expense of foreign exchange the land devoted to the cultivation of rice could be switched over to the cultivation of sugarcane. This will reduce excess supply of rice, reduce the cost of storage of rice and also deterioration of its quality if the stock is held for more than

30 months. This will also increase the supply of sugar and help to reduce its price and the need to import it. This task will be rendered easy if the sugar industry is deregulated.

The food stock held by the Food Corporation of India is nearly 50 percent above the normal average stock of food grains. This shows two things: (1) the export competitiveness of food grains is less than what the Government claims it to be; (2) the incentive structure for farmers is all wrong. As the Government has imposed minimum prices for exports do not sustain the optimism of the Government. The principal constraints on food exports are the high domestic prices compared to global market prices. These are compounded by poor transport and export loading facilities. The first requirement is to remove the present restrictions on the movement of food grains both within the country and across international borders. This should be followed up by improving the infrastructure of grains transport and loading. These measures together will have a significant downward impact on domestic prices. This cure will be incomplete without the abandonment of the officially sponsored price incentive system for farmers.

Periodic hikes in procurement prices which is the Government's answer to falling agricultural returns is one of the reasons for the Food Corporation of India's 31.3 million tonne problem. They also cause the open market prices to rise. Higher procurement prices add to the food subsidy the proper use for of which is targetting the poor consumers. The present price incentives need to be replaced by a combination of better facilities such as irrigation and encouragement of more innovative cropping patterns and the abolition of restrictions on food grain movements. This will ensure that the farmers are not left high and dry and that the subsidy burden and export potential receive a better deal. These changes will not happen fast as the bureaucratic and political obstacles impede their progress. The Food Corporation of India which, at present, is holding excess stock of food grains can lessen its burden by selling its stock at reduced prices. Fears of a sudden lowering of these buffer stock need not haunt the Government because its large foreign exchange reserves can be used to book advanced buying deals in the global market. If harmful controls are removed and the existing resources are used cleverly the worrisome food stocks pose no problem at all. But as the Food Corporation has to sell its stock at reduced prices i.e., prices below the procurement prices paid by it it will have to incur a loss. But the Government has to bear this loss if it has to get rid of the surplus stock. If this is not done, there is the danger of the food stock held beyond 30 months deteriorating and proving useless for human consumption. The entire food stock will go to waste and impose a greater loss on the Food Corporation of India. The only way to minimise the loss is to sell the stock at reduced prices.

Surplus production of food is not an unmixed good. It generates it own problems and the Government has to bear the brunt of stock holding and avoid deterioration of quality of the food stocks held. In particular, the Government should desist from hiking procurement prices for political considerations. This will help in reducing the burden of subsidy. The Government will do well to ponder over the suggestions elucidated above.

34

India's Foreign Exchange Reserves

India's foreign exchange reserves have been rising for sometime and have now reached the $ 10.2 billion mark. The anxiety that prevailed three years ago is disappearing. The reserves at the time were too inadequate to finance imports of even the essential requirements. The days when foreign suppliers of goods were reluctant to supply goods to India are gone for good. Foreign investing companies have begun to purchase shares in the Indian stock market. They are showing interest in the purchase of new shares floated by the Indian companies. In consequence, foreign exchange is flowing into India. Our imports are rising at a slow pace while our exports are rising fast. For these reasons, the foreign exchange reserves have touched the $ 10.2 billion mark.

There is another reason for the rise in India's foreign exchange reserves. As the foreign investors and investment companies are interested in the shares of Indian companies the value of the rupee is prone to appreciate. Those who buy Indian goods have to spend more of their money than before. This has also got the effect of reducing our exports. The appreciation of the rupee in the currency markets is unfavourable to India's trade. This necessitates the adoption of prompt action to adjust the external value of the rupee. The appropriate measure is the purchase of foreign exchange by the Reserve Bank of India. This policy helps to prevent the value of the rupee from appreciating and to stabilise it.

Thus far, the Reserve Bank of India has purchased $ 600 crore of foreign exchange. If this was not done, the actual value of the rupee would have been higher than its realistic value. This would have adversely affected India's export prospects. But the Reserve Bank cannot afford to purchase dollars without limit in the attempt to stabilise the external value of the rupee. Though the stabilisation of the external value of the rupee is encouraging to exports, it prevents the undue growth of imports as they become costlier in terms of foreign currencies. As the Reserve Bank of India is using rupee to purchase foreign currency, the supply of money in the country rises causing a rise in the level of prices and the rate of inflation. The rate of inflation in India is higher than that in the foreign countries. For this reason it is easy to import foreign goods. But this discourages exports. In this manner several contradictory forces have been working and this has made the situation extremely complicated.

This situation is likely to continue in 1994-95 also. As the foreign investors are stepping up their investment in Indian companies, and as the foreign investment companies are buying old shares in the Indian stock market and as they are keen on buying new shares floated by them a sum of $ 500 crore is expected to flow into India. Furthermore, as the production of oil is expected to increase due to new oil exploration and due to the exploitation of existing oil wells a sum of $ 60 crore is expected to be saved in the oil bill. As India's exports are rising her trade deficit may decline. For these reasons there is the likelihood of India's foreign exchange reserves rising. This obviates the need to approach the IMF for assistance.

While this is an encouraging trend, there is another trend which is a cause for concern. From 1994-95 onwards, India's debt servicing obligations increase. During the next three years, the obligations will be of the order of $ 500 crore. Afterwards, they will decline. This is a peculiar situation where though the foreign exchange reserves are rising the necessity of raising a loan is imperative.

At present, a large amount of money is flowing into the Indian share market from foreign sources. All on a sudden, the foreign investors and investing companies have begun to evince interest in the India stock market. This is the effect of the policy of liberalisation. This has made it possible to get foreign funds without having to obtain foreign loans. Though this trend is prima facie good, it is bound to generate certain problems. The Reserve Bank of India has to device appropriate remedies for them. It is certainly good if the foreign investors buy the new shares floated by the Indian companies. This money will be the capital of the companies. It becomes possible to purchase capital goods and technology without having to raise any foreign loan. But if they purchase existing shares the capital will not flow into the companies directly. The capital will flow into the hands of those holding these shares. As the rupees are to be created in an amount equal to this foreign capital, the supply of money in the country rises. The reason why foreign exchange holders keep their reserves here is the possibility of making profits. But this is not the money which will remain stable in India. As they purchase shares of Indian companies the share prices rise and create a situation where the Harshad Mehta type of scam may emerge. The foreign money invested in India will not remain permanently here. In the event of political instability in the country and in the light of attractive profit prospects elsewhere, the shares held by them will be sold and the sales proceeds will be transferred there. This is the case of hot money flow which upset international monetary equilibrium and caused fluctuations in exchange rates in the inter-war period. India should take care to see that it is free from the disturbing influences of volatile capital movements which render the full convertibility of the rupee exercise difficult indeed.

India's balance of payments, despite the comfortable level of foreign exchange reserves, has not been a source of comfort to the authorities. If the full convertibility of the rupee is to be undertaken the Government should have at its disposal an adequate quantum of foreign exchange reserves to be able to counteract the baneful influence of foreign currency outflows. It thus appears necessary to acquire foreign exchange reserves through export promotion. The Governor of the Reserve Bank of India C. Rangarajan, has stated that the country has to be vigilant against the international investors who are the "fair weather friends". The ease with which financing requirements could be met from different sources should not become the basis for incurring current account deficits. This mode of financing is very often deceptive. In fact international capital flows which are fair weather friends begin to reverse and flow back the moment the trouble spots appear. In this case, the foreign exchange reserves plummet as the foreign investors will pull out in search of safe pastures. This is what makes the economy, its external account vulnerable. The policy maker cannot risk a reserve depletion in support of import liberalisation. The current account deficit should not be allowed to go beyond one percent of GDP. This may appear to be too cautious but only to those who have forgotten the foreign exchange crisis of 1990-91. The present foreign exchange reserve position is vulnerable and so it should not be a cause for comfort.

35

Integrated Approach to Poverty Alleviation

The Government recently admitted in the Rajya Sabha that 32.2 percent of the World's poor live in India. This is double the corresponding statistical figure for share of population since Indians form about 17 percent of the world's population. The UNDP in its latest development report has mentioned that 410 million people in India were poor according to the poverty data for 1990. At the time India's population was 850 million and this implies that in 1990 nearly 50 percent of the Indians were below the poverty line.

The Planning Commission has recently drawn the poverty line. According to it those with a per capita expenditure of Rs. 50 per month in the rural areas and Rs. 57 per month in the urban areas are poor and these people and those with a per capita monthly expenditure of less than this are below the poverty line. According to this line about one-third of the population are poor in India. The per capita monthly expenditure fixed to determine the poverty line is too low. The per capital expenditure per day in the rural areas is Rs. 1.66 and in the urban areas it is Rs. 1.90. How can a man/woman subsist on Rs. 2.00 per day in the urban areas? This sum includes his food, clothing, shelter, water, electricity and transport and other amenities including medicines and hospitalisation charges. It is thus necessary to raise the per capita monthly expenditure to Rs. 100 in the rural areas and to Rs. 120 in the urban areas. If this is done, the percentage of people below the poverty line doubles to 60 percent. This means that not less than 500 million are below the poverty line.

It is claimed in official circles that the number of people below the poverty line is dimishing and that India is on the high road to affluence. This is to make a cruel joke at the people who are wallowing in poverty without even a square meal a day, with only rags to wear and unhealthy huts in the slums where life is miserable. India has a long way to go before it sees a reduction in the number of people who are poor and destitute.

The structural adjustment policies under way in India for the past 14 months are intended to alleviate poverty. But it takes a long time for them to do it. In the meanwhile poverty persists and this is the price the country has to pay for progress. It is said that the main antidote to poverty is a high rate of economic growth coupled with stable prices. But it is doubtful if both of them can be attained. The Eighth plan aims at a rate of growth of 5.5 percent assuming several things constant, one of them being the price level. Whether the price level will remain constant is a moot point.

The annual rate of inflation has fallen to a single digit at the end of July 1992. After months, it seems that sterner fiscal and monetary policies are finally beginning to deflate demand induced inflation. While the Government has not been completely successful in reducing the budget deficit and has failed to sterilise monetary growth arising from higher foreign exchange reserves, it has indeed controlled net Reserve Bank credit to the Government sector. This helped to keep in check both demand and inflation.

However, the possibility of the Government taking decisions in the near future that will push up prices has to be reckoned with. The Government may have to slash the fertiliser subsidy and this will push up prices. Full convertibility of the rupee on trade account will require the raising of petroleum prices with multiplier effect on the economy. The issue price of wheat has to be raised by Rs. 60 per quintal to offset the increased procurement price. The procurement price of rice will also have to be increased. These factors will have the effect of raising the inflation rate. As a consequence, the Government has to monitor the food sector closely. The terms of trade which had shifted in favour of agriculture are gradually shifting in favour of industry. As the food items have a larger weightage in all price indices than manufactured items, improved terms of trade for agriculture meant accelerated inflation. In view of the shift of the terms of trade in favour of industry the ordinary consumers will get a better deal. Under the new Export-Import policy import compression has ended. These factors have caused a mitigation of the supply side causes of inflation. There is, therefore, the need to increase production since the economy cannot depend on rising imports alone to improve the supply-side. All this means that emphasis should be laid on increasing production and productivity. This comes to the point stressed earlier that a higher rate of growth is the effective antidote to inflation and poverty.

The most important cause of all the problems the country is facing is the high rate of population growth. The family planning programme is yet to make headway in the rural sector and in the urban poverty sector. Despite misery and starvation the rate of population growth especially in these segments of the population is very high—higher than the national average. Greatest weightage has to be given to population growth for the poverty in the Country. The Government should aim at zero population growth (ZPG). The high rate of population growth has retarded the rate of growth of per capita income defined as GNP divided by population. Paul Erlich, in his book, "The Population Bomb" (1968) has analysed the harmful consequences of population explosion. He advocates zero population growth as soon as possible. The annual increase in population in India is 1.7 crore. If population grows at this rate it would be not surprise if the population of India exceeds that of China. Though India has made remarkable progress in several areas, its progress in the area of population control is unsatisfactory.

It is now obvious that the incentives offered to small families have not yielded the expected results. The number of people who underwent surgical operations in 1975-76 was 70 lakh but in 1988-89 it declined to 45 lakh. The South Asian Regional Conference on population recommended that the incentives currently being offered to those who agree to restrict population should be stopped. There are allegations of misuse of funds meant for family planning purposes; there are also allegations of manipulation of figures of those who underwent surgical operations. It is necessary to educate the woman folk about the advantage of small families. Expanding female literacy is an important step in this direction. The rapid growth of population in the rural sector has created problems of migration of people to urban centres generating the demand for food, shelter and employment. There is need for a population policy which is not general but area specific. The family planning programmes should be enforced on all sections of people. There can be no exceptions in this vital area. Poverty alleviation, population control, adequate food supply, employment generation and growth with stability all these must be interconnected prorammes. If poverty alleviation is the end we must adopt an integrated approach and not a piecemeal one as has been the practice heretofore. Poverty is a curse and it is the mother of all crimes. It is mainly responsible for all the social evils that plague Indian society. Time was when poverty was sought to glorified. Now poverty needs to be eradicated at all costs and at all hazards.

36

A Case for Deferring Payment of Additional Salary and Dearness Allowances

The National Development Council (NDC) at its meeting on Monday April 5, 1993 adopted several far reaching decisions regarding the economy which is facing the inflation crisis and the balance of payments crisis. In the wake of the adoption of the unified exchange rate for the rupee the exchange value of the rupee appears to have held its head high. But the money market watchers and foreign exchange dealers are positive that the rupee's present strength is only transitory and before long the value of the rupee will slide indicating a devaluation. It is an empirically established fact that domestic inflation and balance of payments crisis are causally related indicating that the remedy for the balance of payments gap is a reduction of domestic inflation.

The rate of inflation in India is said to have come down to 6.8 percent. But the market reality is different. The prices of essential articles of consumption are on the rise thus believing the official claim of a reduction in the rate of inflation. It is true that the fiscal deficit as a proportion of GDP is brought down to 5 percent. This will, of course, have a salutary effect on the rate of inflation but the reduction in the bank lending rate from 18 percent to 17 percent will have the opposite effect. The reduction of the bank lending rate is considered necessary as an anti-recession measure.

One of the factors that should be held in cheek is the burgeoning DA payment. There is a statutory connection between the rise in prices and the payment of DA to employees in Government service and in private establishments. The DA for Government employees alone is growth at a staggering rate of 40,000 crore during the Eighth Five year plan period. The Prime Minister rightly said that the Eighth

Plan would crash if the dearness allowance for the Government staff alone grew at this rate during the five year period of the Eighth Plan. The Prime Minister said:

"We have to come to grips with this (DA) problem and cannot possibly go into the figure of Rs. 40,000 crore in one five year plan 10 percent of the (Public Sector) plan outlay. I can understand 10 percent on salary, D.A., everything combined. It just battles me and I am sure it will baffles any one who takes the plan as a whole".

"This is the kind of thing that we have to spend on the spenders. If it comes to this kind of staggering figure, I do not think any plan will prosper".

The Eighth Five Year Plan with its plan outlay of 7,98,000 crore is overambitious judged by any standard and as such it has a built-in inflationary bias. The DA payment alone is of the order of Rs. 40,000 crore. This is 10 percent of the public sector outlay. With the progress of inflation this is bound to rise as a DA instalment is to be paid for every 8 point rise in prices. In this case the DA payment will be more than 10 percent of public sector outlay. This is bound to strengthen the inflationary bias of the Eighth Plan.

In this connection the Report of the Austerity Committee headed by Shri Biju Patnaik is relevant. Though there was a general endorsement of the recommendations of the Austerity Committee at the NDC meeting it was felt that there was need for wider consultation on the issues, especially the one relating to DA for Government employees.

The revenue deficit of the Union Government is of the order of Rs. 16,000 - Rs. 18,000 crore. The State Governments also had been showing larger deficits in their revenue expenditure over their receipts while the Eighth Plan required the Centre and the States to show substantial surpluses to finance the Plan. The Prime Minister said:

"The way our non-plan expenditure is growing, we will soon be using Government resources only to pay the salaries of Government employees, and I am afraid that the people will not accept such a situation".

"In fact, I learn that in some states even paying the Government employees has become a question mark and I really do not know how these States or this country can prosper or progress with this kind of horrendous situation staring us in the face".

The Prime Minister regretted that there was shortfall in the States' performance in additional resource mobilisation saying that against an expectation of Rs. 7,000 crore they had achieved only Rs. 700 crore. The Prime Minister said :

"This is something which will take us no where and it is this extreme seriousness of the matter that the Chief Ministers, the Central Government, all of us will have to realise".

After saying this the Prime Minister called for a consensus on matters such as dearness allowance.

As averred above against the additional resource mobilisation by the States in the first year of the Eighth Plan of Rs. 7,000 crore, the 13 states had mobilised only Rs. 700 crore. The Eighth Plan envisages a total public sector outlay of Rs. 4,34,100 crore at a 1991-92 prices while the total of the States had been fixed at Rs. 1,79,985 crore. Latest estimates show that the balance from current revenue (BCR) of States alone was Rs. 2,940 crore. A substantial improvement in BCR amounting to almost an annual average of Rs. 7,000 crore for the Centre and the States taken together during the Eighth Plan period was required.

The Austerity Committee underlined the need to bring down the ratio of non-plan expenditure to total revenue of States. From the base year, all states should bring down this ratio, on an average by five percentage points during the Eighth Plan Period. Such a reduction was implicit in the plan size of states already agreed to with the planning commission.

The Government expenditure on salaries and dearness allowances has been relentlessly rising. The demand for higher wages and higher rates of dearness allowances stems from the rise in prices. The payment of higher wages and dearness allowances provides an upward thrust to the price level. There is thus a vicious circle in operation. When the Central Government appoints a pay Commission to revise pay scales and to evolve a new DA formula, the employees of State Governments demand the appointment of pay Commissions with the same purpose. The employees of the

Central Government and of the State Governments get the benefit of new pay scales and revised DA formula immediately and with retrospective effect. The payment of arrears constitutes a hefty injection of money into the economic system. It must be admitted, following the Keynesian logic, that the wage earners and salaried employees have a high propensity to consume and a low propensity to save. A sudden hefty injection of money into the economic system causes an upward spurt in the price level generating demand for wage and salary revision and revision of dearness allowances. This occasions monetary expansion which fuels inflation. As Professor said, in the good old days of the gold standard wages would not be increased at all for there would be no money to pay wages. But under the present permissible monetary system monetary expansion has to take place to accommodate a higher wage bill. Therefore, it is the higher wage bill that occasions monetary expansion and it is the labourers who cause the wage bill to rise. Therefore, the monetary system comes to be on what Professor J.R. Hicks calls the "Labour Standard". India is fast moving in that direction.

During the Second World War when inflation was on the ascendant in Britain J M Keynes formulated the Deferred payment scheme. The adoption of such a scheme in India at present appears imperative. As an experimental measure pay revision should be held up for a year and the DA and bonus should be freezed. These steps would help to improve the fiscal balance of the Centre and the States and to reduce the price level directly and also indirectly by reducing the cost-push and demand pull inflation generated by wage escalation. It is an accepted principle of macroeconomic balance that in a period of inflation there should be shift to profits so that the marginal propensity to save out of profit income is higher than that out of wage income. This is necessary to hold down the rate of inflation. This theoretical prescription warrants the adoption of a policy of deferred pay and allowances scheme in India at present in order to hold down the rate of rise in prices. At the end of the year the question of paying additional DA and wages could be revised. If the situation warrants they may be paid. Otherwise the deferred pay and allowances scheme could be continued.

One gets the impression that the policy of the Government is overly permissible. The labour unions clamour for higher wages unmindful of the productivity movements. The bank employees have already given notice of holding demonstrations and rallies unless their insensate demand for higher wages and dearness allowances are met in full. They should be told in a mood of sweet reasonableness that their cooperation is necessary to save the country from the demon of inflation. They should be told that their pay would not be cut but its payment is only deferred and this constitutes compulsory saving which is to their advantage. In this manner the rate of inflation can be brought down further.

The reduction of the rate of inflation is necessary to avert the balance of payments crisis. India's exports have to grow at the rate of 22 percent in dollar terms failing which the payments crisis would ensure. Latest figures released by the Commerce Ministry show that India's export growth during April to January 1992-93 has been a poor 2.2 percent in dollar terms much below the year's target of 9 percent. This has serious implications for debt-servicing. Import of new technologies and capital goods would mount in the next three or four years because of the need to modernise industry and create export dynamism. Import of capital goods in 1993-94 could be in the region of $ 2 billion. This calls for adopting measures to make the revised EXIM Policy a success. What is necessary at present is the infusion of export culture work ethic in respect of costs, quality delivery and assured long-term supplies which are pivots in international trading need to be rigorously implemented. The reduction of wage costs is an important ingredient of this strategy. The deferred payment scheme will help to reduce the inflation rate and the cost of production of goods for the domestic as well as for the export market. The deferred payment scheme has to be viewed in this perspective. The report of the Austerity Committee deserves to be taken with due seriousness. The Committee set up by the NDC to examine the deferring of the pay and dearness allowances should take a decision with no loss of time.

37

Economy in Public Expenditure

There has been a heated controversy during the past one year about the mode of reducing Government expenditure and restraining the escalating budget deficit. The Government has placed itself under the obligations of the IMF and the World Bank which have been administering sermons about reducing the budget deficit as a method of bringing down the rate of inflation. Some are acceptable and the others are not.

Do these sermons apply only to the Union Government or to the State Governments also? Yes, they do. In a tri-fiscal system the deficits in the budgets of the State and Local Governments are as inflationary as the deficits in the budgets of the Central Government. This necessitates the three layers of the Government to work in unison in order to bring down the deficits in the budgets of each layer.

It is beyond dispute that if the financial crisis of the country is to be resolved the Government expenditure should be subject to economy requirements. The sub-committee of the National Development Council made an in-depth examination of the issue and offered several useful suggestions about the modality of reducing Government expenditure. These suggestions should have been examined by the National Development Council. One of the suggestions was the need to withhold, for a year, the payment of dearness allowances. The non-plan expenditure of the State Governments should not exceed their revenue, the consumers of electricity, water and higher education should pay the full cost of these facilities; restricting the benefits of the public distribution system to the weaker sections of society—these were some of the important suggestions of the sub-committee. But even before the National Development Council examined the feasibility of these suggestions, the Central Government announced the payment of another instalment of dearness allowance. It also postponed the meeting of the National Development Council. This policy of the Central Government caused acute embarrassment to the State Governments. The State Government employees quite justifiably asked for the payment of dearness allowance to them also. This is an additional burden on the precarious finances of the State Governments. If the Central Government had to pay dearness allowance to its employees at all, it could have waited till the National Development Council examined the consequence of this payment, the resource availability and the effects of this payment on the State Government employees. But this was not done. During the balance of the present financial year the payment of an instalment of dearness allowance to Central Government employees costs the Government a sum of Rs. 850 crore. If the State Governments follow suit their budgets will get into deeper deficits in a situation where their financial position is overly precarious.

The monthly statistics published by the Reserve Bank of India (RBI) provides enough evidence to show how the financial position of the State Governments is precarious. Of the 25 States in the Indian Union as many as 19 states are in budget deficits of varying dimensions. The aggregate deficits of these States is of the order of Rs. 2,526.2 crore. Of these States only 11 states have given indications of mobilising additional resources. Their total resource mobilisation is of the order of Rs. 891 crore. Of them Karnataka Kerala and the Punjab are important. These three States in the aggregate are able to mobilise Rs. 474 crore of resources. The remaining States show yawning budget deficits.

When the budgets of the State Governments for the year 1992-93 are analysed several interesting facts surface themselves. The Chairman of the Economy Committee of the National Development Council was the Chief Ministeı of the State of Orissa. Dissatisfied with the extravagance of the Central Government, he resigned his position as Chairman of the Economy Committee. Nobody can point an accusing finger at the Orissa State in the matter of the budget. There is no deficit in the Orissa State Budget. The States which have taken measures to mobilise additional resources to meet additional expenditure are Bihar, Gujarat, Karnataka, Kerala,

Madhya Pradesh and Haryana. The states which have designed measures of additional resource mobilisation are Assam, U.P., Mizoram, Rajasthan and West Bengal, the States which despite yawning budget deficits, have not taken any action to mobilise additional resources are Kashmir, Himachal Pradesh, Meghalaya, Maharashtra and Andhra Pradesh. As a consequence of the fiscal profligacy of these States the inflation rate has received an upward push. The measures of additional resource mobilisation which some States have adopted are the routine measures of additional taxation. The imposition of these taxes has adversely affected several industries which find their internal resources depleted rendering them incapable of undertaking development programme. These taxes by raising the price level have frayed the tempers of the general public who are on the verge of an incipient revolt.

Several State Governments have adopted populist measures and have not been levying the reasonable prices for the services rendered by them; they have also been incurring unnecessary and avoidable expenditure in order to earn popular goodwill. These two are dangerous policies which help to aggravate their fiscal crimes. No attention is being paid to the returns on investment in power generation and irrigation facilities as the rates charged for these services are far below those that should be charged on strict economic grounds. As a consequence, the burden of arrears to be paid by the users of these services is greater than the benefits of the services utilised by them. No action is taken to improve the efficiency of these services. However, it is satisfying to note that the revenue obtained by the State Governments from the non-tax sources has risen by 36 percent this year. This trend should be strengthened for good.

In the budgets of the State Governments there are two parts: Capital account and revenue account. In the capital account the revenue of the State Governments is 40 percent of total revenue; but the State obtain the balance of 60 percent from the Central Government. This year the State Governments get more revenue by way of their share in Central taxes, grants and loans. But as the current revenue expenditure of the State Governments is increasing by leaps and bounds, the income under capital account is being transferred from the capital account to the revenue account. As a consequence the development programme are hard hit. This year the State Governments have to spend 28 percent on plan expenditure. The States which are in unmitigated financial distress are unable to incur this expenditure on plan programmes. This makes it difficult for the country to realise the targeted rate of growth. The Union and State Governments should thrash out a plan of action meant to exercise effective control over the escalating non-plan expenditure.

The Union Government finances its expenditure partly by domestic borrowing and partly by money creation. Both are inflationary but debt financing is more inflationary than money financing as debt financing involves the payment of interest charges which widen the budget deficit. The Reserve Bank of India has called for a legal ban on Government borrowing from all sources "beyond a certain ceiling" with a "sub-ceiling on borrowing from the Reserve Bank. This is a good piece of advice to a country made aware in the last five years of the deleterious consequences of deficit financing in support of fiscal extravagance. But public expenditure should be slashed in such a way that it does not adversely affect the growth-promoting public investment-health and primary education, agriculture and extension and start-up investments in infrastructure on which is dependant investment by both the private sector and the commercialised public sector. The first two are covered by transfers to the States. The States, on their part, must gradually reduce subsidies and do away with some altogether. But it is unreasonable to expect them to achieve this quickly and deny them needed central resources. If such reform is adopted discontent will surge froth. The better-off States which will benefits from market friendly investment will be irked by disturbed conditions in large parts of the country. This in turn may strain inter-state relations at a time when the Indian federal structure is overly fragile.

The need to control Government expenditure is undisputed. Expenditure in excess of revenue is financed by borrowing and money creation. Borrowing of money which would have been saved by the private sector and spending it is inflationary as it leads to a rise in the income velocity of money; borrowing of money which would have been spent by the private sector is price-neutral for the

Government spends what the private sector does not spend and so there is no net rise in expenditure. But borrowing of any sort involves the payment of interest on it and this is a non-plan expenditure which widens the budget deficit and is inflationary. Money financing of the deficit causes a rise in the price level in consonance with the mechanism underlying the Quantity Theory of Money. Thus, borrowing which does not involve the reduction of private expenditure and money creation are both inflationary. This calls for a reduction in Government expenditure.

The reduction of Government expenditure cannot be arbitrary. It has got to be on the basis of certain criteria. What these criteria should be are to be determined by an authority body. This body is none other than the Expenditure Commission which should undertake an assessment of the revenue accruals. The criteria of expenditure control should be scientifically designed so as to minimise any welfare loss. Expenditure reduction involves a welfare loss; at the same time increase in expenditure which results in inflation also involves a welfare loss as it imposes an inflation tax on the community. That policy which involves minimum welfare loss should be preferred.

There should be an Expenditure Commission for each State. This should also adopt the same criteria. There should be harmonisation of the expenditure policy of the Central Government and the expenditure policies of the State Government. In a tri-fiscal system such harmonisation is a necessity. For expenditure reduction by the Central Government unless accompanied by the expenditure reduction by the State Governments will not by itself ensure a non-inflationary situation. If expenditure is to be incurred in excess of current revenue it should be financed more by money creation than by market borrowing for the former is less inflationary than the latter as it does not involve interest payment which widens the budgetary gap. It is necessary for the Government to apply a tight rein on its expenditure if it is serious about inflation control. If the Central Government sets an example of economy in expenditure the State Governments emulate its example and there will be an overall reduction in Government expenditure at all levels.

38

Whither the National Renewal Fund?

The 30th Indian Labour Conference (ILC) which concluded its two-day session on 7th September 1992 resolved to draft a Bill on industrial rotations on the basis of the G. Ramanujam Committee recommendations. It further resolved to discuss the draft Bill on an appropriate forum before it was presented to the Parliament. The views expressed by the ILC would be adopted in the Bill to be formulated.

The main area of concern of the ILC is the impact of the incipient industrial revolution in the country on labour and its welfare. The Narasimha Rao Government announced its New Industrial Policy with intent to increase the price and quality competitiveness of Indian goods in world markets by means of modernisation and technological upgradation of industry. The Government has sought to allay the fears that industrial restructuring would result in large scale layoffs and unemployment and described such apprehensions as exaggerated. But admittedly retrenchment as a fallout of the new policy cannot be ruled out. The Government made it clear that closures and retrenchments would be only a last resort after all means of reviving the sick enterprises were exhausted. While a liberal industrial policy is necessary for the organised sector, the Government is fully committed to protecting the interests of labour by equipping them to deal with the inevitability of technological changes.

The Indian Labour Conference called upon the Government to provide a detailed blueprint for the redeployment and retraining of surplus labour. The Government which is committed to protecting the interests of labourers has not yet come out with an Exit Policy. The Government has not yet realised that without an Exit Policy there cannot be a redeployment policy. If there are problems associated with formulating an Exit Policy, then those associated with redeployment and retraining are likely to be even more severe. In the Indian Labour Conference, the Government did not provide any clear guidelines about its labour policy. Instead the Government used this opportunity to fridge the issue further. In fact, what the Government did was to send conflicting signals to industrial labourers in the country. On the one hand the Prime Minister gave the assurance that the new industrial policy, dictated by the structural adjustment programme will not lead to "any human distress; on the other hand the Labour Minister admitted to the Labour Conference that the new economic policies will in fact result in the dislocation of labour and that the situation called for "some sacrifice by the present generation". The Labour Minister is closer to the truth because exit would mean dislocation of labour. Amidst this confusion what appears clear is that the Government has placed itself in a tight spot in formulating a labour policy in keeping with its commitment to the World Bank and the IMF. The Government is well aware that it will not be able to contain the political fallout of large scale retrenchment. It is generally agreed that there is overstaffing in the public sector. At the same time there are no plans to demonstrate that after getting rid of the excess labour employed there, these industries will suddenly go on to the growth path. If the economy is not growing and, even if it is growing if the employment potential of the Eighth Plan is not satisfactory, it is difficult to provide employment to the surplus labour force. The Government should share with the labourers its assessment of the sectors of the economy which it thinks are likely to experience growth in the near future so that the labour unions can help their members to seek retraining for redeployment. Apart from the mechanism for identifying the workers for retraining, the process of identifying the growth industries of the future is not yet in sight. In the case of some public sector industries like the National Textile Corporation, the Government has identified the surplus labourers who should be given a "golden handshake" so that they can start their own self-employment schemes. But self-employment does not amount to retraining or even meaningful redeployment. The question at present is whether these workers are to be de-skilled by leaving them to their own devices and some money or re-skilled through a well-thought out retraining programme. But there is no satisfactory as yet.

Apart from retrenched labour the need to provide employment to labourers entering the labour market is imperative. The labour force in the country was projected to grow by 35 million during the Eighth Plan period from 1992 to 1997 and by another 36 million during the five years thereafter. A ten-year perspective plan to achieve the goal of near-full employment would require that employment opportunities grow by 9.4 million per year on an average over the decade 1992-2002. This is, indeed, a stupendous task the achievement of which depends on many imponderables. This is for the medium run.

The short-run requirement is to redeploy labourers retrenched due to technological upgradation. The Finance Minister, Dr. Manmohan Singh, in his budget speech in July 1991 announced the formation of the National Renewal Fund (NRF) and said that it would provide more than a safety net protecting workers from the adverse consequences of technological upgradation of industry. It was expected "more importantly" to retrain workers "so that they are in a position to remain active partners in the process of modernisation". The Government spokesmen maintain that the NRF would operationalise the policy objectives of the Government of minimising the human costs of readjustment in the public, private, organised and unorganised sectors. The NRF would meet the costs of retraining and redeployment of surplus labour, compensation to employees of closed units and funds for employment generation. This could be done by identifying the needs of different groups of workers, by categorising them into age-groups and skills levels.

The NRF is, at present, seen as a corpus to finance Voluntary Retirement Schemes (VRS) for workers in sick public sector units. But the NRF is too small to even cover the demands of the VRS in sick public sector units of the Central Government leave alone, meet the needs of the private sector and public enterprises of the State Government.

Initially the NRF will be of the order of Rs. 2,200-Rs. 2,500 crore. The Union Government in its budget for 1992-93 provided Rs. 200 crore to it. Of the total proceeds of the second round of public sector disinvestment Rs. 1,000 crore will be provided for the NRF. The International Development Agency of the World Bank announced last year that it would subscribe $ 400 million (Rs. 1,200 crore) to the Fund. The administration of the Fund is to be governed by the draft operational guidelines. These draft guidelines seem to have drastically pruned the scope of the Fund. The "concept paper" on the NRF circulated by the Ministry of Industry in the early part of 1992 the idea was to have three components: (1) The first and biggest was the National Renewal Grant Fund which would provide compensation to workers in units that would have to be closed down or reduce them in size as well as retrain them in new skills; (2) the second component was the Employment Generation Fund which would provide loans and grants to the self-employed and workers in the unorganised sector; (3) the third component was the Insurance Fund for Employees. This would receive contributions from employers and labourers and would provide a cushion against future changes in technology and market conditions that could adversely affect individual industrial units.

It now appears that the Government has abandoned the Insurance Fund for Employees on the ground that at present it would be difficult to organise it. The Employment Generation Fund will, of course, be operationalised to meet criticism that the unorganised sector is being ignored. The scope of the National Renewal Fund is being pruned.

The National Renewal Fund has aroused suspicious in the minds of the labourers that it is a mechanism to ease labourers out of employment rather than as a way to prepare them for new jobs. This suspicion will be strengthened if the Fund merely hands out compensation for workers opting for voluntary retirement. However, there is something which would be likened to retraining. This is a plan to open counseling centres to workers to help them decide on what they can do with the compensation they receive.

In the initial stage of the institution of the NRF it was thought that the Fund would provide retraining to labourers eased out of employment. But on closer examination it appears that retraining in not an easy task. Even the industrialised countries have largely succeeded only when individual firms have taken up schemes to prepare their employees for new in-house jobs that would replace the old. The Government retraining programme can work when there is identification of those skills that will be in demand and can be utilised by the retrenched workers. Ever since the plan for the NRF was prepared not much attention seems to have been paid to this aspect. At a time when the economy is not growing fast the chances of labourers moving from industry to another or from one skill to another are not bright. In a situation like this counseling centres are not of much help. They may warn the labourers against spending away the compensation amount they receive but in an economy registering only slow growth the workers cannot do otherwise. The first claim on the compensation amount is the repayment of debt. The balance will be utilised by the workers for setting up roadside service establishments.

The National Renewal Fund is too inadequate to meet the needs of the situation. The Fund of the order of Rs. 2,200-Rs. 2,500 crore may appear large in an absolute sense but when compared with the number of workers to be covered it is inadequate.

Originally the idea was to cover the private sector and the State Public sector units. This idea seems to have been given up. The contributions from the private sector and the State units would have enlarged the size of the Fund. But unless the Central Government contribution Rs. 1,000-Rs. 1,500 crore per year the NRF has little chance of covering even voluntary retirement schemes. However, the Government at present, appears to be unconcerned about the operational details of the NRF and its components. It simply prefers to get it going in the thought that things will take care of themselves in the future. But this attitude of the Government will be unhelpful to labourers facing the prospect of unemployment due to modernisation schemes.

It is a commitment of the Government to fulfill the elementary responsibility of assuring the feelings of the labourers. Along with the announcement of the New Industrial Policy, the Government should have announced a Labour Policy for labours and capital are the two partners in progress. The absence of a Labour Policy has generated genuine apprehensions in the minds of the labourers that the NRF would not provide a trustworthy "safety net" in the event of their being thrown out of employment consequent on the modernisation and technological upgradation of industry. This apprehension is not conducive to industrial peace and industrial harmony. It is, therefore, incumbent on the Government to formulate a Labour Policy and to provide assurance to labourers that their interests would be safeguarded. As the same time the size of the National Renewal Fund must be enlarged keeping in view the size of the labour force that the Central Government, from the World Bank and from the industries undergoing modernisation and technological upgradation. At the same time employment potential of the Eighth Five Year Plan should be increased so as to make the rate of employment match the rate of growth of labour force. An adjunct of this policy should be a population policy aimed at achieving Zero Population Growth (ZPG). These policies adopted simultaneously will enable the New Industrial Policy to proceed without frictions and impediments. The Government should ponder over these suggestions. Otherwise there will be no industrial harmony and industrial peace.

39

The Wheat Import Scandal

As the wheat output fell below the estimated target this year, the price of wheat started rising pushing up the inflation rate. In the attempt to increase the supply of wheat in the market in order to hold down the wheat price and through it the inflation rate the Government of India thought of importing of wheat from Canada and Australia. The Prime Minister permitted to import of wheat is violation of all prescribed norms Lo and Be hold; the quality of imported wheat is very poor and constitutes a hazard to health.

As per the food control regulation has imported food articles should be of prescribed quality. Furthermore, the Union Cabinet and the Planning Commission should accord permission for the import of food articles. However, the Prime Minister issued a green signal for the import of 1.25 million tonnes of wheat from Canada. The Central Food Department stated that the imported wheat is of poor quality Even so the fact that the Prime Minister issued a green signal for the import of substandard quality wheat has given rise to suspicion.

The wheat imported is said to contain the poisonous microtoxin. For this reason, there is reason to investigate the extent of microtoxin in the imported wheat. However, the officials of the Food Department aver that no such investigation took place. If there is excessive microtoxin and aplotoxin content in the wheat flour, it will be hazardous to health. There should be investigation atleast before the import of wheat. In the beginning, the Canadian Wheat Board had investigated the toxin contents of the wheat exported from Canada. This investigation conclusively proved that the wheat contained excessive microtoxin. For this reason it had declined to award export guarantee certificate. However, it is stated that the State Trading Corporation of India had pressurised the Canadian Wheat Board to issue the export guarantee certificate in order to enable the Canadian wheat exporters to export wheat to India.

Why did the Prime Minister bypass the other agencies which should have been consulted before giving a green signal for the import of wheat? Many interpretations, some unsavoury are possible and they are all vented in the newspapers. This calls for a probe.

Though the wheat imported from Canada was infested with aflotoxin, official certificates, saying that it was free from toxin, was obtained by the Commerce and Food Ministries. This toxin affects the limbs of the human body and also leads to cancer. Under the law the Food Ministry had earlier refused to import this wheat. After this the State Trading Corporation was directed to invite tenders. However, this corporation did not do it. Instead it tried hard to obtain letters stating that the Canadian wheat was toxin-free and was fit for consumption. Before the wheat was imported the experts of exporting country had to examine the quality of the wheat to be exporting but this was not done. There was no pre-shipment test. As per law in any imported food article the toxin element in any imported food should not be more than 30 PCB. It was stated that the aflotoxin and microtoxin content in the wheat imported from Canada was not more than 30 PCB.

Earlier it was agreed to import 2 million tonnes of wheat. But later on it was reduced to 1.25 million tonnes. This wheat had to land in India before march 1997. But it is not likely to land in India before March.

If the consumers of imported Canadian wheat which is toxin inflected get their limbs damaged and get even cancer who is to be held responsible? The Prime Minister? The Commerce and Food Ministry officials? The Food Corporation of India? The matter needs investigation and the responsibility has to be fixed on the guilty whoever be/they might be. When the matter went to the Court under Public interest Litigation, the petition was dismissed.

This is not the first time that he bypassed the appropriate agencies before taking decisions. Two of them can be cited. The transfer of Shri Romesh Bhandari from Goa to UP as Governor was not without the knowledge if not the concurrence, of the Home Minister. Again the extension of service of Shri Padmanabaiah as Home Secretary was against the will of the Home Minister. The Home Minister a decent parliamentarian, should resign in protest against the humiliation meted out to him.

40

Supply-side Economics: Its Relevance to India

The inauguration of Ronald Reagan as President of the United States in 1980 witnessed the revival of interest in Supply-side Economics. Since then there is a growing consensus that the macro stabilization policies emanating from the Keynesian doctrines are not of much use in solving the current economic problems; there is also the belief founded on mounting evidence that the Keynesian economic policies have greatly contributed to current economic problems of inflation, unemployment, low rate of capital investment reduced economic growth and a rapid rise and expansion of the "underground economy". This disenchantment with Keynesian macroeconomics in the late 1970s has turned the attention of policy makers towards supply-side economics which, therefore, has occupied the centre of the stage. Reaganomics, which is the offshoot of supply-side economics has been hailed as the cure all for the economic ills afflicting the US economy. The fiscal policy adopted by Ronald Reagan with emphasis on tax incentives, reduced Government expenditure, deregulation and market-oriented economic behaviour on the part of consumers and corporations has been interpreted by supply-side economists as a return to classical economic principles and Reaganomics has been hailed as ushering in "an American renaissance".

The economic policy measures adopted by the Government of India are claimed to represent a "departure from the past" and they are believed to promote growth through efficiency and technological upgradation. Its emphasis is on maximising production rather than on creating employment though one would wish to see equal emphasis being placed on creating employment in the context of abundance of labour. However, the pronouncements made by the Government of India and its spokesmen bear eloquent testimony to its commitment to go all out in the pursuit of policies which have their roots in supply-side economics. The long-term fiscal policy to be announced by the Finance Minister in September, obviously grounded in supply-side economics, is expected to usher in an Indian renaissance. The adoption of this policy in India despite its structural and Institutional rigidities, pervasive unemployment, sluggish response to market forces, the preponderance of the agricultural sector with its semi-feudal characteristics and abject poverty deserves close examination.

Supply-side economics stresses tax rate incentives rather than growth of the budget to stimulate productivity and economic growth but this emphasis rooted in the ideas of Adam Smith James Mill, David Ricards and J.S. Mill underlined the importance of positive incentives for saving, investment and capital formation. The classical writers accepted Say's Law of Markets—supply creates its own demand—and laid emphasis on production and supply. Say's Law is founded on the premise that people produce in order to consume and since increased output will increase purchasing power and create demand of equal value, it was held that any deficiency of demand would be temporary. The classical writers also emphasized that high tax rates generate an "underground economy" through tax evasion, fraud and smuggling. Jack Kemp and Arthur Laffer in the United States have contributed to the revival of the supply-side movement which was downplayed for a generation after the Keynesian Revolution of the mid -1930s which emphasized that "demand creates supply". The Keynesian doctrine was formulated on the premise that unemployment involuntary unemployment exists because the demand for goods and services is not adequate to make use of all the resources available. From this followed the prescription that the remedy for unemployment is to stimulate demand through expansive fiscal monetary policies. Keynes proposed tax reduction and deficit financing in order to stimulate aggregate demand which would call forth increased supply through increased demand for labour and utilisation of excess capacity in industry; conversely the remedy for inflation is a reduction of excess demand through restrictive fiscal-monetary policies—higher tax rates budget surplus and higher interest rates. The Governments of the industrialised countries of the West adopted these policy prescriptions to remedy for unemployment and deficiency of demand and restrictive fiscal-monetary policies to remedy inflation. This policy came to be known as "fine tuning" the economy. However, in the 1960s and 1970s this policy could no longer work as it had to encounter a new phenomenon—the co-existence of inflation and unemployment. Expansive policies to stimulate demand and reduce unemployment exacerbated inflation while restrictive policies to depress demand and remedy inflation aggravated unemployment. A new policy which would meet the requirements of the new situation was called for. Policy prescriptions founded on supply-side economics were offered to meet the new situation. These policies aim at increasing production, reducing unemployment and promoting non-inflationary growth. The main instrument of policy is the budget-low tax rates, larger tax yields resulting from expanded production and enlargement of the tax base and larger Government expenditure without occasioning budget deficits. The mechanics of the new type of fiscal operation is rationalised in what is known as "Laffer Curve" after its author Arthur Laffer who has advanced the hypothesis of an inverse relationship between tax rates and tax yields.

Higher tax rates and the disincentives created by them reduce production in a number of ways : (1) they make tax payers substitute leisure for work in several ways including longer vacations, less over time work and earlier retirement; (2) they make people reduce the amount of productive effort by engaging themselves in domestic work instead of engaging others to perform it; (3) they make people to devote resources to the tax shelter industry by engaging tax consultants to suggest ways and means of reducing tax liability; (4) they make the tax payers substitute tax-deductible items of expenditure for non-tax deductible items which results in reduction of tax yields; (5) high marginal tax rates erode the moral basis of the tax system and increase the incentive to evade taxes. In the United States, Italy and Sweden there is a co-variation between increasing tax rates and rate of growth of the underground economy" where transactions are off the books and not subject to taxes speaking about Sweden Gunnar Myrdal says: "The tax system is turning Swedes into a gang of hustlers .... the present tax system is making nine out of ten Swedes criminals". In Italy about 30 percent of national income is produced in the underground economy. In the United States unreported transactions are estimated to be growing rapidly.

In the supply-side approach high tax rates are regarded as barriers to production and a key idea is the relationship between changes in tax rates and tax yields. When the tax rates are near zero necessary public services cannot be provided and output will be low. As tax rates increase to provide essential public services economic activity expands and tax yields increase. At low levels of taxation increases in productive efficiency outweigh any disincentive effects of higher tax rates. As tax rates increase the disincentive effects become more important and at some point the loss in revenue due to disincentives as well as the increase in tax evasion overwhelms the increase in tax rates and consequently tax revenues peak and then begin to decline. Thus, when tax rates are high lower tax rates stimulate business activity and shift income from underground to taxable activity and therefore tax yields increase. The conclusion is that the effect of tax rate reduction depends critically on the current level of taxation and can lead to either decreases or increases in tax yields. It is impossible to predict the effect of a reduction in tax rates on tax yields in India but the Finance Minister contends that tax yields will increase and reduce the need for a large budget deficit. In fiscal parlance, this is called a "tax paradox" lower the tax rates smaller the budget deficit. In India, a progressive reduction of tax rates in the previous years has not resulted in higher tax yields: Pranab Mukherjee admitted that "lower taxes have only marginally improved tax compliance" but argued that "we need more time to see the effect of lowered taxes". Figures show that taxes as a percentage of GDP have been falling. According to a recent estimate, in 1977-78 central taxes accounted for 11 percent of GDP and this has fallen steadily since then to between 10 and 10.5 percent. In view of this it would be too optimistic to expect lower tax rates to result in higher tax yields. It is held by supply-side advocates that the largest amount of tax revenue is the point at which the electorate desire to be taxed. However, the pattern of tax rates which results in maximum revenue to the Government which is enabled to increase its expenditure is inconsistent with the classical view of limited role of Government in the economy.

Professor Colin Clark, an Oxford economist, stated as early as 1945 that no democratic Government in peace time can collect more than 25 percent of national income by way of taxes without causing inflation. He held that taxation above this limit will greatly discourage saving and work and will induce tax payers to evade taxes and to increase wasteful expenditure. In India taxes which are about 10 percent of national income are far below the Colin Clark limit. Even so, there is inflation. This means that taxation perse is not the cause of inflation though indirect taxes which are added to the prices of taxed commodities do contribute to inflation. It is the expenditure side of the budget that is to blame for inflation. Supply-side enthusiasts maintain that inflation can be solved easily and painlessly. In their view the budget can be balanced and deficits can be avoided through a renewal of economic growth achieved by tax cuts. It is generally agreed that a reduction in the rate of growth of money supply will be required to reduce the rate of inflation though there is no consensus about the nature of the adjustment process. Some supply-siders argue that reductions in tax rates, Government spending and the rate of growth of money supply can reduce inflation without serious disruption of economic activity. Professor Hayek, a neo-Austrian theorist, contends that Government spending must be reduced to reduce budget deficits which are a cause of monetary expansion. In 1981 the Reagan Administration contended that the proposed 30 percent cut in income tax rates over three years would provide incentives sufficiently so that the tax yields would increase; it also maintained that the attainment of the goal of non-inflationary growth would be facilitated by reduction in Government regulation.

Implicit in the policies emanating from supply-side economics is a concern with the saving rate. In the literature on "stages of growth" an increase in the saving rate was seen as the motive force for the take off into self-sustaining growth. In all models saving was given a central role as the source of the investment funds necessary for growth and for increase in productivity. Income distribution and welfare considerations were deemphasized and it was argued that the best form of social security was a rapid expansion of productive employment opportunities to all through the creation of sufficient capital by some. This became the rationale for income inequality if it raises production for all and not consumption for a few. It is also held that "the road to eventual equalities may inevitably lie through initial inequality".

The World Bank sponsored studies relating to the countries of the Third World agree that the economic policies adopted by them, based as they are on supply-side economics, were successful in attaining the desired results. GNP grew and at rates higher than historical experience. Bill Warren who made a detailed study of the Third World countries adopting supply-side economics has said "The period has witnessed titanic strides forward in the establishment, consolidation and growth of capitalism in the Third World, with corresponding advances in material welfare and the development of the productive forces". This would, of course, seem to be proof of supply-side economics and its effectiveness.

Assuming that supply-side economics will be effective in accelerating economic growth in India we have to examine whether our objective should be growth perse or growth with equity. It is argued that rising growth rate is no guarantee against worsening poverty, that divorce between production and distribution policies is both false and dangerous and that distribution policies should be built into the very pattern and organisation of production.

In the Third World countries which registered high growth rates income distribution became more skewed towards the wealthy. Evidence from African and Asian countries indicates that the incidence of absolute poverty generally measured by numbers of percentage of population below the poverty line increased with the growth of GNP. Unemployment and underemployment in these countries were also a continuing problem. Dr. Haq noted that the literacy rate in Pakistan fell from 18 percent to 15 percent during 1950-70 period. Malnutrition grew and diseases began a resurgence. Thus, the awareness of the costs of supply-side development has made several development economists reject the growth strategy based on it. The increase in supply under these policies came at the expense of the poor and the powerless as income was distributed in favour of the rich. The costs now seem too high, the type of development which occurs too skewed, the loss to the poor who are left behind is too great. This is not to opt for stagnation. Countries like Taiwan, Cost Rica or Singapore were able to achieve relatively high growth rates without maldistribution of income. They have adopted "growth with equity strategy" of development. Their success with this type of development strategy is due to several factors: (1) They welcomed government involvement in economic development as they felt that private sector will not be able to do it alone; (2) They incorporated the poor directly into their plans. This meant providing the small farmers prices which were remunerative and they adopted policies to aid small businessman. (3) They adopted a variety of techniques of production not relying solely on the large-scale and capital intensive techniques. These policies were eminently successful in achieving high rates of growth and equality of income distribution.

The supply-side enthusiasts lay emphasis on the tax side of the budget and advocate tax cuts to provide incentives and they do not lay equal emphasis on the expenditure side. Most supply-siders would agree that tax cuts lead to lower government revenues. The opposite argument based on the Laffer Curve-that tax cuts will lead to growth in tax yields has few staunch partisans. Furthermore, Government spending has a tendency to "crowd out" productive investment by the private sector and should be limited, if necessary, by balancing the budget. Transfer payments have a negative effect on productivity and on the incentive to work and they become prime candidates for reduction. This case is even stronger when the country is faced with external threats which requires increases in defence expenditure. When these strands of thought are woven together, they lead to a policy of substantially lower government expenditure and transfer payments.

If these propositions are adhered to influence policy, cutting of transfer payments and particular government programmes aimed at certain groups of recipients becomes inevitable. If these programmes are stopped the distribution effects will be much more profound. This has two lessons to offer. The first lesson is that if these policies are successful in raising GNP in the other Third World countries, they will be equally as successful in India. The second lesson is that the question of income distribution cannot be assumed away. If supply-side economics is in euphemism of changing income distribution in favour of this rich this should be spelled out. Of course, not many Indian economists are prepared to deal with these issues. When the proposed policies and the probable manner of their implementation are examined it is possible that they will tend to greater inequality in the distribution of income and contribute to the growth of absolute level of poverty.

Supply side economics advocates free market economy on the ground that it promotes competitive efficiency. Profitability becomes the magnet that pulls resources into their most productive uses. Thus, in the competitive market place economic self-interest becomes an engine of social welfare.

The incentive system of the market place confers rewards on some and imposes heavy penalties on the loses. The Unmitigated verdict of the market place condemns million to deprivation. Small farmers are exposed to serious deprivation at the whim of nature. Technological progress extracts its toll and renders many workers jobless; vast disparities in living standards, income and wealth inevitably create serious inequalities of opportunity that represent arbitrary handicaps. In an unmodified market-dominated society poverty becomes a vicious circle. The children of the poor are handicapped in many ways their nutrition, their education, their inability to get funds to start business and homes. Any commitment to a reasonable degree of equality of opportunity requires some correction of the glaring inequalities which an unmodified market place would decree. Even more fundamental poverty cannot be ignored by a society that proclaims democratic values insisting on the worth of all its citizens and equality of their political and social rights.

In India, 40 percent of the people are below the poverty line. Those who spend less that 65 rupees per month in the rural areas and 75 rupees per month in the urban areas are said to be poor. Their poverty is to be eradicated and they should be enabled to rise above the poverty line by means of transfer payments and anti-poverty programmes. The successive Five Year Plans are committed to eradication of poverty though full success in this task is not achieved. Supply-side economics with its faith in the "magic of the market" and its advocacy of eliminating transfer payments is bound to increase poverty and deprivation. Furthermore, the earmarking of funds to uplift special groups of the population will not allow any reduction of government expenditure. If any reduction is attempted it is bound to provoke violent protests compelling the government to restore the original expenditure. Redistribution of income is thus necessary to temper the harsh edges of competition.

Subsidies of any kind are incompatible with supply-side economics. In the current year budget the Union Government has retained the subsidy on food as an anti-inflationary measure and the subsidy on fertilisers in order to increase agricultural productivity. The subsidy on food is kept at Rs. 1,100 crore and the subsidy on fertilisers is kept at Rs. 1,200 crore. The supply-siders Professor A.K. Khusro among them demand the abolition of subsidy. However, it must be remembered that in India it is the food prices that govern the general price level. The subsidy on fertilisers is intended to enable the farmers to increase the input of fertilisers to their farm so as to increase farm yields. An increase in agricultural production is expected to serve as an antidote to inflation, and to increase the taxable capacity of the farmers. In view of this the Government expenditure does not permit any reduction.

Supply-side economics which advocates the operation of market forces presupposes high degree of flexibility of the economic structure. India is a dual economy with the advanced industrial sector co-existing with the backward rural sector, the latter being predominant. While the industrial sector is fairly responsive to market influences the rural sector is most unresponsive governed as it is by custom, tradition and cultural factors. Price incentives and disincentives do not, for the most part, influence human behaviour in the way expected by supplys-siders. There is considerable unemployment in this sector. Unless efforts are made to develop this sector the rural economy is bound to remain backward. In its active concern for high-tech production in the industrial sector, the Government does not seem to have any worthwhile plan for accelerating the development of the rural sector apart from pronouncing pious platitudes about integrated Rural Development. Unless this sector is developed and the purchasing power of the rural people is enhanced there will be no demand for the goods produced in the industrial sector with the help of advanced technology. The goods produced in the industrial sector have to find markets only in this sector. There will thus be a perpetuation of the dualistic economic structure with no integration of the two sectors. When the rural sector which is the base is weak it will not be able to sustain the advanced industrial sector. The interdependence of the sectors calls for special measures to develop the rural sector but these measures are not consistent with the prescriptions of supply-side economics.

The burden of the song is that Government spending is not an item that should be pruned. It goes on increasing making budget deficits inevitable and these deficits increase with the passage of time.

Supply-siders advocate balanced budgets as an antidote to inflation which is causing concern to the Government. But budget deficits themselves are not a problem as far as inflation is concerned. The problem is different: How is the deficit financed? If it is financed by printing of more money, the deficit is likely to be inflationary; if it is financed by borrowing, it may crowd out private investment. However, supply-siders want budget balancing as a means of enforcing efficiency in the operation of the bureaucracy. But a balanced budget is not particularly useful as a symbol of the fight against inflation or as a guide for whether we are operating the macro-economy appropriately. Budget deficits of moderate dimensions may be necessary as a method of helping supply groups and of alleviating poverty by providing basic needs to them. However, they are not consistent with supply-side economics even if they are financed by borrowing. In the first place, they crowd out private investment and in the second place they necessitate higher taxes in order to meet interest payments on the debt. This is inconsistent with tax rate reduction which is the core of this philosophy.

Tax cuts alone will not result in lower inflation and steady growth. According to Professor P.A. Samuelson there is not much scientific basis for a large part of "supply-side moonshine". Repeated tax cuts meant to provide incentives along with new tax giveaways to stimulate good causes means a more expansionary fiscal policy and bigger budget deficits unless there are cuts in non-military spending. And cut in non-military spending are hard to achieve as they are essential in our socio-economic milieu.

The pursuit of the goal of non-inflationary growth enjoins on the Government to pursue a mix of fiscal and monetary policies. Monetary policy affects inflation through the pressure of demand on the economy. With inelastic supply and easy credit sharp price rises can be initiated in particular markets experiencing excess demand and they feed on themselves with pronounced effects on general inflationary expectations and hence on wage bargaining and pricing divisions in the economy. Public announcement of targets for the rate of growth of money supply may provide one of the best ways of giving concrete expression to the Governments' intention not to accommodate high rates of inflation. Those targets have to be brought down overtime as inflation is brought down. There may arise occasions when the authorities fail to meet their monetary targets. This approach should be adopted in a pragmatic and flexible manner with a upper and a lower limit rather than a fixed point for these permissible rate of monetary expansion.

Budget deficits are normally associated with inflation. Advance legislation that increases or decreases in taxation will be terminated on a given date can help to shift private expenditure in the way desired. Operating on the expenditure side has a quicker and more certain impact on the economy and when the need is for restrictive action, it has the enormous advantage of not raising costs or prices. There may also be a case for automating fiscal policy by legislative trigger mechanisms which set off tax or expenditure action if, for example, inflation rises above a certain rate. In certain cases resort to a wage stop and / or price freeze on a voluntary or statutory basis may be justified as an emergency measure so long as it is accompanied by appropriate demand management policies.

The policy prescriptions based on supply-side economics may operate effectively in the United States but it would be wrong to assume that they do operate equally effectively in India with its large rural sector not responsive to market incentives in the manner depicted in the literature on the subject. The effect of a tax cut on savings, investment, output and tax yields will vary between countries and overtime within the same country for various reasons including and overtime within the same country for various reasons including cultural factors, level of current tax rates, expectations regarding inflation and the investment climate. Relationships among economic, political and social developments change over time in unpredictable ways. Past relationships cannot be assumed to provide a good prediction of future events and the conclusion that tax cuts will result in increased tax yields is matter of inference and judgment. Furthermore, removal of controls and regulations is not practicable in India though it is held in certain quarters that controls occasion corruption and Government regulation stifles economic activity. Adam Smith warned over two hundred years ago the Government regulation of economic activity gives rise to "underground economy". According to a recent estimate the GNP in India in 1985 is of the order of Rs. 1,92,000 crore and the black money is 40-50 percent of GNP. It cannot be argued that black money of this magnitude is due to Government regulation of economic activity. There are many other factors that account for this phenomenon. India adopted planning within a mixed economy framework where the role of the private sector was limited and its activities were brought under control and surveillance. Planning could not be left in the hands of the Private Sector as it did not have the resources to undertake "big push" investment to build up the necessary infrastructure with its long gestation period and uncertain direct returns. The Government had to undertake "big push" investment to build up the necessary infrastructure with its long gestation period and uncertain direct returns. The Government had perforce to subject the activities of the private sector to regulations so that the growth process may proceed in the desired direction. However, it would be wrong to associate the emergence and growth of the parallel economy with government regulation of economic activity. It is the lack of honesty on the part of the politicians in power and the bureaucracy and the absence of fear of any sort on the part of offender that should be held responsible for the parallel economy. If supply-side economics can get rid of the parallel economy there is every justification for adopting it as a basis of policy. However, one can be categorical that it cannot do it. The Indian economy is too inflexible to permit the market forces to operate effectively and to yield desired results. The argument that it has operated in the United States and so it will operate in India too is most inconvincing. The policy-makers in India have to realise that what is good for the goose is not necessarily good for the gander. Where markets encounter inertia, frictions and resistances government is often substituted for the market in accordance with the theory of the second best assuming, of course, that the market conforms to the theory of the first best. Supply side economics with its across the board, tax cuts, balanced budgets, market mechanisms, deregulation and reduction of transfer payments is at present not relevant to India.

41

Union Budget, 1985-86

From this emerges a new concept of growth which is urban-oriented and which is based on capital intensive structure of production. In the two sector models of economic growth developed by Ragnar Nurkse and Arthur Lewis, Gustav Ranis and Fei for adoption by the labour, surplus economies like India, the institution of labour-intensive technique of production was recommended as the surest way of absorbing redundant labour from agriculture. According to the Prime Minister the industrial sector is not necessarily the best sector for employment generation, the industrial sector has to maximise production rather than generate employment. This philosophy becomes obvious from his statement "out textile policy is not targeted at producing jobs but at producing clothes". A major plank of this philosophy is the policy of liberalisation. The Finance Minister made this abundantly clear when he said; "many a time short term revenue considerations cloud our vision for economic growth; infact growth and revenues are complementary. A growth-oriented revenue environment is what we should aim at to achieve over the years". An environment of this type can be achieved by eliminating restrictions and controls which stifle production and by reducing the tax burden on industry and trade. This marks a departure from the kind of policy pursued heretofore. It is in this context that the Union Budget for 1985-86 is to be analysed.

The budget is indeed a "departure from the past" in more senses than one. It envisages a net uncovered deficit of Rs. 3,349 crore after taking into account additional tax revenue accruing to the Government through new imports of Rs. 311 crore. In the year 1985-85 the budget estimate of deficit was of the order Rs. 1,773 crore while the revised deficit turned out to be Rs. 3,985 crore. The overall deficit for 1985-86 was Rs. 3,660 crore and this is brought down to Rs. 3,349 crore as a result of additional tax revenue of Rs. 311 crore. The budget deficit is becoming bigger and bigger as the years pass by and it appears as though the Government cannot do without it. In an inflationary situation a budget deficit is bound to exacerbate inflation through monetary expansion and demand generation which it makes possible. In the western economics the Governments adopt a policy mix to mitigate inflation. An expansive fiscal policy is combined with a tight monetary so that the laxity of one can be mitigated by the severity of the other. However, in India while the Finance Minister envisages a budget deficit of Rs. 3,349 crore there is no indication that a tight monetary policy will be pursued. Infact, the Reserve Bank of India has announced a reduction of lending rate from 18 percent to 17.5 percent. As a consequence, there is a combination of expansive fiscal policy and an expansive monetary policy which reinforce one another in exacerbating inflation though the officials of the Finance Ministry in their customary post-budget elucidation of the official position have maintained that the budget deficit and the new levies "will not have any inflationary impact in the macro sense". Such a massive budget deficit is said to be motivated by two major factors: the high level of food stocks available with the Centre (22 million tonnes) and the comfortable level of foreign exchange reserves with the Reserve Bank of India.

It is in the sphere of personal income taxation that the Finance Minister displays his talent for fiscal innovations though these innovations however appreciated by the tax payers are bound to generate additional demand for goods. By raising the exemption limit from Rs. 15,000 to Rs. 18,000 the Finance Minister has reduced the number of tax assesses by about a million. Each one of them is left with Rs. 3,000 of untaxed income. Furthermore, by reducing the rates of income tax on personal incomes on every slab and by reducing the tax liability to 50 percent of income he has left the assesses with more disposable income. These assesses being those in the low and lower-middle income groups have a higher marginal propensity to consume. The loss to the Government due to the proposed rationalisation of Income Tax structure will be Rs. 200 crore on account of income tax and Rs. 197 crore on account of abolition of surcharge on income tax. The abolition of tax on interest income accruing from bank deposits, the abolition of excise duty, reduction of Wealth Tax and abolition of compulsory deposits will leave a considerable amount of tax-free income in the hands of the tax payers. If this income is saved and invested the task of resources mobilisation for the Seventh Five Year Plan would be rendered easy. In a situation of rising prices when money is losing value people would rather spend this money than save it and this adds to inflation. The result of these reliefs is to increase the marginal propensity to consume on balance. In an inflationary situation the effect of a higher marginal propensity to consume is to raise the value of the money income multiplier and to cause a rise in the price level. The Finance Minister is hopeful that with lower levels of taxation there will be honest compliance on the part of the tax payers and that tax yields will increase. This idea seems to be motivated by the Laffer Curve hypothesis which maintains that the tax rates and tax yields vary inversely. The validity of this hypothesis is as yet untested in the U.S. economy. It is therefore hazardous to rely on it as a basis of policy formulation in India. A progressive reduction of tax rates in the previous years has not resulted in higher tax yields. Even Pranab Mukherjee admitted that "lower taxes have only marginally improved tax compliance" but argued that "We need more time to see the effect of lowered taxes". Figures show that taxes as a percentage of GDP have been dropping. According to a recent estimate in 1977-78 Central taxes accounted for 11 percent of GDP and thus has fallen slowly since then to between 10 and 10.5 percent. In view of this one cannot be too sure that lower tax raters will result in higher tax yields. The Finance Minister expects tax revenues to keep pace with economic growth. But the Finance Minister's optimism is unfounded. The abolition of licence fee on radio, T.V. sets and VCRs will benefit their users who are normally rich not in need of this relief at all. The sympathy for this class of people coming on top of several income tax reliefs is grossly misplaced.

The Government has been imposing a surtax which, in reality, is a tax on efficiency. Greater the profitability the higher is the incidence of this tax and so the less is the incentive to be efficient.

For this reason expert committees like the Boothalingam Committee and the Wanchoo Committee had advocated its abolition.

The Finance Minister has taken new steps to create an environment wherein both small and big industries can invest in capacity expansion. Some industries are to be delicensed and they are to be encouraged to set up new units. The upper limit of investment by selected small scale industries has been raised from Rs. 20 lakh to Rs. 35 lakh and Rs. 40 lakh. The assset limit for MRTP companies has been raised from Rs. 20 crore to Rs. 100 crore. The maximum interest payable on convertible debentures of non-MRTP companies has been raised from 13.5 percent to 15 percent is order to improve their market availability. There is a reduction in the basic rate of corporation tax by 5 percent. This tax relief in the absence of abolition of surtax is hardly the incentive to the Corporations to invest in capacity expansion. This is at variance with the announced policy of industrialisation. The only redeeming feature is the reduction in the bank lending rate from 18 percent to 17.5 percent. This is too poor an incentive to investment activity. The Seventh Five Year Plan lays emphasis on increase in productivity. There is no certainty that the fiscal incentives to industry are powerful enough to realise this goal. Industrialisation of a developing economy like India needs several incentives like accelerated depreciation allowances and investment allowances to attract investment. However, abolition of additional depreciation and gradual phasing of investment allowances would adversely affect the cause of industrialisation. Incentives to invest in high-tech industries are necessary if the new strategy of growth is to be successful.

Indirect taxes present an interesting mixture. Those taxes which can be shifted forward to consumers in the form of higher prices and which push up the rate of inflation are enhanced and those taxes which do not show up in a higher rate of inflation are either constant or are reduced. Thus the auxiliary duty on crude petroleum is raised from Rs. 100 to Rs. 300 per tonne and this is expected to fetch a revenue of Rs. 620 crore, the basic duty on printing, writing and craft paper is increased by Rs. 200 per tonne, basic excise duty on cement is raised from Rs. 205 to Rs. 225 per tonne the duty on kerosene has gone upto 65 paise per litre. Similarly the duty on soap, medicines has gone up considerably. These duties have an inflationary effect without any countervailing effect coming from the abolition or reduction of taxes on several commodities like computers, black and white T.V. sets, and commercial vehicles etc., as they are not taken into account while computing the cost of living index. It will thus be seen that the inflationary effects of indirect taxes are too strong to be overcome by the disinflationary effects of tax reduction/abolition on certain items. The rise in the price of crude oil may to some extent reduce the demand for oil on the part of the vehicle owners; to this extent it will reduce the volume of oil imports. However, the extent to which the oil imports will come down depends on the elasticity of demand for oil. In a situation where the ownership and use of vehicles are a matter of status and snobbery the demand for oil may not come down at all despite a rise in the price level.

Added to this are the inflationary effects emanating from the Railway Budget which envisages a 12.5 percent surcharge on all railway passenger fares and a supplementary surcharge of 10 percent of freight of all commodities beyond 50 kilometers. These imports are expected to yield an additional revenue of Rs. 495 crore. These imports not only impose a burden on the common man but in addition result in cost inflation as the cost of transporting commodities and inputs to industry and agriculture rises; the prices of final output will be higher not just by the amount of the additional cost of transport but by even more as the producers feel confident that in an inflationary situation the prices of final output can be enhanced by more than the cost of transport and can successfully be passed on to final consumers. In a regime of permissible monetary policy allowing continuous monetary expansion rise in the price level is bound to occur.

Monetary policy in 1984-85 was permissive being formulated against the background of a high rate of growth of both money supply and reserve money in the previous year. Efforts were made to reduce the rates of expansion of these monetary aggregates to more acceptable levels. They included a two-phased increase in the statutory liquidity ratio, maintenance of the incremental cash reserve ratio of 10 percent on additions to deposits imposed in November 1983 and the raising of the cut off point for food credit beyond which 100 percent refinance is made available. These restrictive monetary measures notwithstanding the supply of money grew at a slightly higher rate, 15 percent, in the current year upto January 25, 1985 than in the corresponding period in the previous year. This has been attributed to an unexpectedly higher increase in net bank credit to the Government and an improvement in the net foreign assets position of the banking system.

In an economy like India where the impact of money supply on the price level is in consonance with the monetary mechanism underlying the Quantity Theory of Money, it is necessary to exercise tight control over the supply of money. Milton Friedman of the university of Chicago advocates monetary expansion of not more than 3 percent per annum to maintain a stable economy. This rate of expansion may be too restrictive for India which is a growing economy desirous of being free from monetary constraints. However, monetary growth at the rate of 15 percent a year is too permissible. That the rate of inflation has decelerated in the current year despite monetary growth at the rate of 15 percent may be advanced to justify monetary growth at this and even higher rates. This argument overlooks the fact that the deceleration of the rate of inflation in the current year is due to higher than expected growth rates in agriculture and industry and the overall growth rate of the economy at 5.2 percent. If the monetary growth was less than 15 percent the rate of inflation would have been less than 5.2 percent thus ensuring a situation of "growth with stability". It is necessary to allow the rate of monetary growth to be not more than 7-8 percent per annum so that any monetary requirements may be taken care of by velocity adjustments.

The Balance of payments position in comfortable despite a deficit. According to the latest statistics for the period April November 1984 exports totalled Rs. 7,058.6 crore which were 22.9 percent higher than exports during the corresponding period of the previous year. Imports were Rs. 10,075.2 crore which were also higher by

14.2 percent than imports during the corresponding period in the previous year. There is thus a marginal reduction in the trade deficit from Rs. 3,080.1 crore to Rs. 3,016.6 crore. The Finance Minister is optimistic that the export target of Rs. 11,127 crore for 1984-85 would be attained.

It would be unrealistic to hold such an optimistic view of the balance of payments. The Economic Survey notes that certain special factors which operated to make the balance of payment position comfortable would not operate. Furthermore, the flow of net invisible which strengthened the balance of payments during the past few years are likely to slow down along with the remittances by non-resident Indians. These misgivings are corroborated by the U.N. Economic and Social Committee for Asia and the Pacific (ESCAP) in its report for 1984 where it is said that though India has been successful in making adjustments to external payments constraints in recent years, it will not be easy to ensure a continuation of the sanguine performance in the years to come. It ascribes two reasons for this pessimistic forecast : (1) India's successful external adjustment thus far has been helped by its ability to increase domestic crude oil production in the Sixth Plan period. Though oil production will continue to increase, the rate of increase is expected to be lower in the Seventh Plan period; (2) in the past few years India has encountered a shift in the structure of external financing away from long-term concessional flows towards medium term non-concessional flows. Debt servicing payments arising out of these flows are likely to be high during the rest of the decade. According to the World Bank data India's debt service ratio which was 13 percent in 1984 will increase to 20 percent by 1989-90. Data by other agencies show a possible increase to 30 percent by that year. All these factors in the balance of payments situation have been admitted by the Finance Minister.

Debt servicing of such a colossal magnitude requires massive efforts on the export front. However, these efforts are bound to encounter formidable difficulties. According to C. Fred Bergsten of the Institute of International Economics, Washington, the domestic policy mix and hands off policy of the U.S. Administration towards the exchange rate have engendered overvaluation of the dollar which taxes exports by 40 percent and subsidies imports by the same amount leading to an increase in the U.S. deficit on current account from $ 100 billion in 1984 to $ 300 billion in 1990. Making it necessary protectionist measures. This will certainly hit India's exports to the United States. Furthermore, industrialised countries of the OECD are expected to have low growth rates in the next few years and this will have a negative impact on India's exports.

In a situation like this the budget makes special provision for promoting exports. The Finance Minister has announced abolition of export duties on 12 commodities to serve as an offset to the protective tariffs imposed by the importing countries. He would like to place emphasis on the concept of 'net foreign exchange' in future policy formulation. The idea behind this concept is that in giving export incentives the net foreign exchange earned should be taken into account. Accordingly, exports with larger domestic content would be entitled to more incentives. The strategy is to maximise export earnings. However, the problem is one of identifying items which have a smaller import content. Besides this emphasis is to be laid on reducing the import of edible oil and food by increasing domestic production of these items. Importables which could be produced domestically ought to be produced by means of imports substitution. However, there is no assurance that all these measures would bring about equilibrium in the balance of payments. In the first place, the economy has according to a U.N. Report, limited scope for contractionary adjustment even if it were possible; in the second place, in a situation where expansive fiscal monetary policies are vigorously pursued it is impossible to reduce imports unless import controls are imposed. In the context of import liberalisation import controls would not be in order. The one commodity on whose restriction the fate of the balance of payments depends is the oil import. Though the production of oil in the country increased three-fold in a decade from 36.27 million tonne in 1970-75 to 103.26 million tonne in the Sixth Plan period the oil import bill is rising as the domestic consumption of oil is increasing by more than domestic production. Although the OPEC reduced the price of Arab light crude from $ 29 a barrel to $ 28 a barrel the import price of crude in terms of rupee has gone up from Rs. 2,140 a metric tonne in June 1983 to Rs. 2,750 a metric tonne representing an increase of 29 percent. The Government claims that this has happened due to the continued upswing in the value of the dollar resulting in an adverse impact of Rs. 1,000 crore on the oil companies which import 14 million tonne of crude oil and petroleum products annually. The raising of auxiliary duty on crude petroleum from Rs. 100 to Rs. 300 per tonne may not lead to a reduction in domestic consumption of oil and therefore in the import bill. The balance of payments will therefore continue to be a source of anxiety to the Government.

The Economic Survey states that in the early part of 1984-85 there was heavy pressure on the price level though this pressure eased in the later part of the period. This is attributed to the effectiveness of several anti-inflationary measures adopted by the Government and to the impact of two good harvests coming in succession. By February 9, 1985 the annual rate of inflation in terms of wholesale Price Index had come down to 4.6 percent against 10.8 percent in the corresponding week of 1983-84, in terms of consumer price index also the annual rate of inflation declined to 5.2 percent in December 1984 compared with 12.5 percent in December 1983.

The deceleration of the rate of inflation in the current year should not lull the Government to a mood of complacency. A massive budget deficit of Rs. 3,349 crore and a permissible monetary policy are bound to administer an upward thrust to the rate of inflation. There are also several factors in the budget which have an inflationary impact: the rise in the auxiliary duty on crude petroleum, rise in the duty on paper, kerosene, soap and other articles of daily use have a price raising effect. It is true that a growing economy benefits from gently rising price level which provides incentives to producers by increasing the profit margin. But inflation of the present magnitude, not to speak of the one that is bound to emerge in the near future, cannot be characterised as a case of gently rising price level. A rise in the price level that is bound to occur generates clamorous demands for higher wages which when granted generate both cost inflation and demand inflation which before long get entwined and become indistinguishable. A higher price level necessitates monetary expansion to accommodate it and this in turn gives an upward thrust to the price level. At a time when it is imperative to promote exports by making them competitive in world markets higher domestic prices are in conflict with the country's export policy. With imports pouring in under a scheme of liberalisation the balance of payments situation is bound to deteriorate reducing the foreign exchange reserves to uncomfortably low levels.

The Finance Minister has retained the subsidy on food as an anti-inflationary measure and the subsidy on fertilisers as a measure meant to increase agricultural productivity which is one of the objectives of the Seventh Five Year Plan. The subsidy on food is kept at Rs. 1,100 crore and that on fertilisers is kept at Rs. 1,200 crore. In India it is the food prices that govern the general price level and therefore food subsidy is meant to stabilise the food prices and to prevent the food sector from imparting inflationary impetus to the general price level. The subsidy on fertilisers is intended to enable the farmers to increase the input of fertilisers to their farm so as to increase farm yields. An increase in agricultural production is expected, and rightly too, to serve as an antidote to inflation and to increase the tax-paying capacity of the farmers. In these respects the retention of subsidies is in consonance with the objectives of the Seventh Five Year Plan.

There is considerable black money constituting a parallel economy in the country. No authentic estimate of its magnitude is available. However, the research wing of the International Monetary Fund estimated that in 1981 the amount of black money was 50 percent of national income. In that year the national income was estimated to be Rs. 1,20,000 crore and this implies that the amount of black money was Rs. 60,000 crore. Since 1981 its magnitude must have grown bigger.

The raids on black money undertaken in recent months by the Income Tax authorities have led to a spurt in the prices of bullion and real estate as black money has moved into those markets in a bid to escape the attention of the authorities. There has also been a hectic demand for bearer bonds which, in consequence, are being sold at a premium. The bearer bonds are of the value of Rs. 1,000 crore giving an opportunity for black money barrons to buy them when the raid is expected and to sell them when the raid is over or when it did not come off. The existence of bearer bonds enables black money to remain black. Therefore, a more drastic remedy is necessary viz., the demonetization of Rs. 100 notes and the exchange of new ones with different colours and designs to those who surrender the old ones with genuine and acceptable reasons for keeping them a ceiling being placed on the total number of notes each person can surrender. If the period of surrender is limited to one week hardship to the public will be mitigated. If this is not done the parallel economy continues to grow financing all illegal transactions and administering a perpetual upward thrust to the price level and rendering all anti-inflationary measures futile. The institution of special courts to try tax evaders will not tackle more than a fringe of the problem.

The Finance Minister has introduced several social security schemes to help the families of workers who die in accidents and those of small and medium farmers; he has stepped up the allocation for upliftment of scheduled caste people and has envisaged rural water supply schemes. These measures are intended to increase social welfare by mitigating the hardships of the poor and the downtrodden sections of society. According to the Seventh Five Year Plan nearly 30 crore people in the country are below the poverty line and has been given an allocation of Rs. 4,900 crore in 1985-86 as against Rs. 4,141 crore in the previous year. It is hoped that increase in productivity and production will take care of those below the poverty line.

The Union Budget which is claimed to be a departure from the present Government. The industrialists who were protected from foreign capital and technology during the past three decades were able to strengthen their financial and production base. They are now prepared to have collaborative arrangements with multinational firms regarding the supply of capital and sophisticated technology and to restructure the industrial sector so as to accommodate new technology. The development which the new philosophy warrants is based on profit maximisation and cost-benefit calculus. The idea is to maximise production rather than to generate employment. This philosophy makes it unnecessary to have any special concern for 30 crore people below the poverty line by means of Integrated Rural Development Programme and the Rural Employment Schemes. The Finance Minister has not made it clear how demand for goods in the rural sector can be generated by increasing the production of capital intensive goods in the urban sector; there is also no strategy for generating employment. A massive budget deficit, imposition of surcharge on passenger fares and freight rates, reliefs and concessions in personal income tax and the enhancement of indirect taxes on several essential commodities combine to accelerate the rate of inflation. Fiscal policy is claimed to foster economic growth as the GNP is expected to increase by 10 percent this year; at the same time it exacerbates inflation as well despite routine annual protestations to the contrary by the officials of the Finance Ministry. There may be growth but not with stability.

42

Dash to High-tech Production: Problems and Prospects

The Government of India, has designed a spectacular scenario in which India will launch itself on the high road to economic growth which clearly represents a "departure from the past". The pace and pattern of economic growth thus far have not been satisfactory. According to the Prime Minister, the major problems of the economy today are low productivity, high costs and technological stagnation. The new strategy of economic growth, based on supply-side economics, is expected to revitalise the economy and to give fresh impetus to development at a time when economic conditions in India and abroad are both complex and difficult.

The pace of economic growth in India has been mellowed down by unrelenting inflation, high oil prices, severe balance of payments problems, gnawing uncertainty about the availability of concessional aid and its eventual reduction making, commercial borrowing inevitable, heavy debt burden, slower growth of markets due mainly to recession in the industrialised world and the growth of protectionism in the advanced countries despite impressive rhetoric about "trade, not aid" in the official reports on international development. Political turmoil and hostile neighbourhood have made it necessary to divert scarce resources from development to defence. The necessary synthesis between traditional values and the imperatives of modernisation in a world of rapid technological change has grown more difficult under the impact of accelerating change. The country which is at the parting of the ways has to choose between two futures: a future of self-sustaining growth, an expansion of trade and reduction of poverty or a future of economic stagnation, declining trade and the spread of poverty. The former alternative should certainly be our choice. The international economy can help us to pursue this alternative course with unabated vigour by making the necessary resources available to us. As the Brandt Commission on international development points out: "Above all, the achievement of economic growth in one country depends increasingly on the performance of others". The Prime Minister has rightly said that in solving the challenges facing the country "we except help from our foreign friends". It is on strategy of growth should be designed. But this strategy must be informed by the lessons of the past and realities of the present. Such lessons, extracted from hard experience, offer the basis for principles to guide us in executing a new policy of growth in a troubled environment.

India is in the midst of "information explosion". The Government of India and the Indian people are keen to catch up with the West. The post-war technological revolution is impressive in range and impact. Thanks to the vision and imagination of successive prime ministers, India lost no time in realising the importance of scientific research and its technological fallout. The emphasis on promotion on science and technology was vigorously pursued by Lal Bahadur Sastri. Ever since independence the Ministries of Atomic Energy as well as Science and Technology (and later Electronics, Space, Environment Ocean Development) have been presided over by the successive Prime Ministers acted as a Catalyst to spread the scientific temper and helped to build modern "temples of technology". As a result, India can pride herself as one of the countries caught up in the technological revolution sweeping the western world.

India is on the threshold of a new era. The Government's emphasis on new management culture and technological progress augur well for the future. Development without destruction should be our aim. To be sure, as the Nature magazine report, "Science in India" emphasized: "The Government seems to be taking the empirical view that what has been spent has returned social, economic and intellectual benefits and that spending a little more can only yield more of the same. That is good approximation to a strategy". India has plenty of splendid achievements to its credit but the existing charm between high technology and pervasive poverty must be bridged and abridged too. Failure to demolish this dichotomy will be a sure recipe for national disaster.

In the pursuit of a new strategy of growth India seems to be guided by the experience of the United States. President Ronald Reagan has been imbued with a deeply felt belief that reliance on the free market represents the surest road to economic progress. In his view departure from this path in the direction of steadily greater emphasis on Government involvement in the economy was the cause of much of the economic malaise inflation combined with slow growth that afflicted both the developed and developing countries in recent years.

Determined to restore an era of non-inflationary growth to the US economy, Ronald Reagan, in his first term in office, pushed through a multi-faceted programme that emphasized creating increased incentives for individuals and businesses and deemphasized reliance on Government involvement in economic matters. He obtained the Economic Recovery Tax Act of 1981 (E.R.T.A.) which reduced income tax for the average working American by 25 percent over three years, indexed the tax system so that wage earners will not automatically be swept into higher tax brackets by inflation and included tax measures to encourage business investment. E.R.T.A., though somewhat modified by later tax legislation, was the centerpiece of the supply-side economic programme that has come to the known as "reaganomics". Accompanying this crucial fiscal policy step was the Federal Reserve's Monetary policy which emphasized the maintenance of a steady non-inflationary money supply growth.

First troubled by a slide into recession in 1981-82 the US economy, under the stimulus of the new economic measures, rebounded briskly in 1983-1984 with consumer spending, business investment and productivity all registering impressive recovery. Towards the end of 1984 economic expansion had become one of the most vigorous of the post-world war II era creating about 6 million new jobs for Americans. The fact that the US inflation rate had dropped from 12 percent in 1980 to 4 percent in 1984 contributed to a new spirit of confidence in the US prospects and to a strong dollar in exchange rate markets. The booming US economy helped pull many economies out of stagnation. Global trade showed signs of recovering from a period of decline. This was of particular benefit to debt-ridden developing countries that desperately needed to increase their exports. In his address to the Fund-Bank meeting in Washington in September, 1984 Ronald Reagan referred to these achievements as "an American renaissance". However, Reagan's goal of balancing the budget by 1983 proved elusive despite the reduction of Government spending. The US budget deficit grew from about $ 60,000 million in 1980 to $ 1,75,000 million in fiscal 1984. By election time in 1984 how to balance the budget had become a contentious element in economic policy making discussions the democratic candidate advocating a rise in tax rates. Reaganomics which induced "an American renaissance" seems to have inspired the present government to adopt a package of similar economic measures meant to promote an Indian renaissance.

The essence of Government is the promotion of growth through efficiency and technological upgradation. The Prime Minister has elucidated a new concept of growth based on capital intensive structure of production. This means a gradual departure from the labour intensive techniques of production advocated in the models of growth designed for labour surplus economics like India. He is deeply interested in modernising the industrial sector by applying sophisticated electronic systems and high technology which are expected to do away with the feudal structure of the agricultural economy and modernise it so that it may cater to the needs of the new industrial system. The objective of the new economic order is to maximise production rather than to maximise employment. This is evident from his statement on textile policy: "Our textile policy is not targeted at producing jobs but at producing clothes". The Finance Minister who is said to be a "market minded" and has made it clear that economic growth and revenues are complementary and that the object of fiscal policy is to create a growth oriented revenue environment by eliminating restrictions on production and reducing the tax burden on industry and trade. Mr. L.K. Jha, Chairman of the Economic Administration Reforms Commission has reinforced the philosophy underlying the new economic policy when he says: "There should be complete freedom to produce to the maximum installed capacity and even more. Then only will there be domestic competition, improvement in quality of the products and higher revenues from higher production." This philosophy is rationalised by the Minister of Industries who enunciated the new industrial policy in the Lok Sabha on 19 April. This presupposes a radical restructuring of the industrial sector on the model of free enterprise economics by means of modernisation and technological upgradation governed by economics of efficiency and measured by cost-benefit calculus. The criterion governing production is one of profit maximisation which is the classical test of success of any business venture. The private sector with faith in the "magic of the market place" is also prepared to co-operate with the Government in the adoption of new model of growth. All that it demands is the grant of fiscal concessions and liberation of the economy from the multitudinous restrictive measures which stifle growth. The Government has expressed its readiness to respond favourably to the demands of the private sector. It has already adopted policies to throw open the entire field of electronics, automobiles, telecommunications and a few priority segments to the private sector which, so far, had been barred from such ventures, the private sector has also been permitted to import capital goods, high-tech machines, electronic equipment and computers which would update the technology of the industrial sector. These liberalisation measures were adopted earlier by the Government of India as part of its commitment to meet the conditionality clauses governing the grant of a $5 billion loan by the International Monetary Fund. The Prime Minister has gone further in this direction and has offered several incentives to the electronics industry and has held out the assurance that he would free the industrial licensing system from administrative and ideological restraints. The Government is also contemplating the liberalisation of the Foreign Exchange Regulation Act meant to induce the industrialised countries to invest their capital in high-tech industries. The Indian companies governed by the MRTP Act are also allowed entry into the production areas which were till now the exclusive preserve of the public sector. The Union Minister of State for Science, Technology, Electronics and Ocean Development, has stated that the Government would welcome foreign collaboration for high quality and high technology in electronics components industry. Inaugurating the national symposium on the "Growth of Electronics" at the Central Scientific and Instrumentation Organisation in Chandigarh on 3.4.1985 he stated that the new electronics policy of the Government aims at issuing industrial Licences for entertainment electronics, tests and measuring equipment, computer peripherals and semiconductor devices. He expressed the confidence that the country would not require or depend on foreign technologies during the Eighth Plan Period by which time it would have built its own electronic base. He also assured grant of concessions from the MRTP Act and exemption of excise duty on a number of electronic equipment. The Government has also set up an 18-member working group to prepare a project report for establishing a technology data bank covering imported and indigenous technologies with direction to submit its report by 30 September 1985. Such a technology information base is expected to enhance the possibility of obtaining favourable terms in the acquisition of foreign technology. Plans are afoot for establishing regional computer centres in different parts of the country as an integral part of the nation wide computer network. On 12 April the Union Government announced a new EXIM policy liberalising the import of capital goods, raw materials and components easing import procedures by decanalising 53 items of imports and simplifying the licensing system. This policy gives incentives to the electronics sectors especially computer systems. The main sectors which benefit from this policy of capital goods imports are automobiles, electronics, oilfield service, leather and jute manufacturers. The object of this new policy, according to the Finance Minister is among other things to impart continuity and stability, to make all possible savings in imports and to accelerate technological upgradation and modernisation. This policy has a three year life span and this is intended to provide a more stable environment for trade and industry. The new policy will come into effect on

10 October. The Government will employ the concept of "net foreign exchange" earned in evaluating the performance of export and trading houses and encourage the production of goods with a smaller import content. There is a two-tier policy concerning the import of computers and compute-based systems. Those costing below Rs. 10 lakh (CIF) will be allowed to be imported by all persons for their own use. The duty will be less if such items are imported after obtaining clearance, of the Department of Electronics. For imports under OGL a minimum specified configurations would have to be imported. The object of these policy measures is to free the industries from the shackles of past development policies and to give a new direction to growth.

The new design of non-inflationary growth and the prescription of a new growth path founded are undoubtedly attractive. If they succeed in realising the goals set before the country, they will constitute a model for other developing countries to adopt. However, the new package of measures representing a "dash to high technology" are fraught with formidable complications which the country can ignore or underestimate at its peril.

High technology requires considerable capital investment in industries adopting capital intensive techniques. The Prime Minister has invited foreign investors to come to India and help build a "new dynamic and self-reliant economy". The incentives and concessions offered to foreign investors to invest in India are no doubt attractive but at a time when there is competition among the developing countries to obtain capital resources the incentives offered by India have to be stronger than those offered by others. The response of foreign investors to India's appeal for help is to be watched. It would be hazardous to depend on the fluctuating moods of foreign investors. Though the savings ratio may pick up in course of time its present magnitude 22 percent of GNP is too small to permit extensive adoption of high technology. Technological revolution in the west is taking place at a breathtaking pace. A machine which is uptodate at present may become absolute it reaches its technical age limit. Competitive market situations demand that these capital goods should be thrown to the scrap heap and that the latest ones be installed in their place to ensure cost competitiveness and this entails heavier capital expenditure. The capital-output ratio in the Indian economy is 7-8:1. There are vociferous demands that it be brought down to 4-5:1. However, with the adoption of high-tech production which requires heavy capital investment the capital output ratio will go up. Furthermore, in the absence of adequate concessional aid the country has to take resource to commercial borrowing. In the past few years, India has encountered a shift in the structure of external financing from long term concessional flows towards medium term non-concessional flows. This year it will be still more as the IDA assistance to India will be cut by $ 200 million. Debt servicing payments arising out of these aid flows will rise in the rest of the decade. According to the latest statistics India's debt-servicing liability will reach the peak during the Seventh Plan period amounting to a little over Rs. 13,950 crore at the current exchange rate. According to the explanatory Memorandum on the Union Budget for 1985-86 the outstanding external debt which amounted to Rs. 16,857.22 crore in 1984-85 is expected to rise to Rs. 19,001.39 crore in 1985-86. Apart from this India is planning to resort to foreign commercial borrowing to the tune of Rs. 1,500 crore in 1985-86 to finance ambitious programmes of modernisation of industry and the imports of electronic and telecommunications equipment and other capital goods. The Deputy Governor of the Reserve Bank of India Mr. Amitabh Ghosh has said that the debt servicing ratio would go up to 16 percent by the end of the 1980 as against 14 percent at present. UN economic and Social Committee for Asia and the pacific (ESCAP) in its report for 1984 has come to the conclusion that "the external payments position will pose problems in the years ahead'. In 1984-85 Indian exports were of the order of Rs. 11,000 crore. The projected slowing down of the rate of growth in the industrialised countries and the trend towards protectionism there would make things difficult for India. In view of this, plans are afoot to cut down the Seventh Plan outlay of Rs. 1,80,000 crore by Rs. 13,000 crore and thereby reduce the resource gap of Rs. 40,000 crore to a manageable level. The massive programme of technological upgradation with cost escalation will create further problems widening the resource gap and further pruning of the plan inevitable. The Seventh Plan is likely to meet the same fate as the Second Plan did in 1958-59. When the inflationary gap and the balance of payment gap compelled its pruning.

High-tech structure of production presupposes the existence of personnel possessing the skills required to man the sophisticated equipment. India cannot at present claim to have adequate manpower and managerial skills necessary for the new technology culture. This underlines the need for investment in skill formation and restructuring of the Indian education system giving it a technological bias from the start. Obviously this takes time. In the meanwhile India has to import technical personnel from abroad and utilise foreign consultancy services at considerable expenditure of scarce foreign exchange. The technological manpower is bound to prove to be a limitational factor slowing down the growth mechanism.

Adoption of high-tech equipment which is energy-intensive presupposes adequate supply of energy, particularly petroleum. In the field of oil exploration India's thrust for self-sufficiency is commendable. Prospecting for petroleum calls for sophisticated frontier technology. Per capita consumption of oil in India is very low. According to a survey conducted by the Energy Policy Committee in 1979, energy consumption is linked with economic progress. There is a direct correlation between energy consumption and per capita income. The per capita oil consumption in the USA in barrels per annum is 51.7 while that in India is a measly 0.9 which is much less than the world average of 6.0. Obviously India is keen on expanding the offshore operations where, according to the geologists, atleast 45 percent of the crude reserves remaining to be discovered will be found. Oil production increased threefold in a decade from 36.27 million tonnes in 1970-75 to 103.26 tonnes in the Sixth Plan period. During the Seventh plan period the ONGC has planned to increase oil production to 155 million tonnes. It is obvious that though oil production will increase in absolute terms, the rate of increase will be much lower. Consequently, the import of more oil to meet the requirements of new technology becomes inevitable. At present India is spending Rs. 3,000 crore per year on oil imports. As import substitution in oil has reached the saturation point the expenditure of foreign exchange on oil will rise. The foreign exchange reserves now stand at Rs. 6,961 crore, but the trade deficit which in the first ten months of 1984-85 was Rs. 3,864 crore is expected to be Rs. 5,000 crore in the full year. Considering the fact that the OPEC raises the price of oil at frequent intervals that the price of oil is expressed in terms of the US dollar whose value is rising in the foreign exchange markets in terms of rupees and that the demand for oil is price-inelastic as high technology is energy-intensive, the rupee value of imports will rise beyond all reasonable expectations creating balance of payments problems, increasing the debt liability and pushing India perilously close to the doors of the debt trap. It is doubtful whether exports will rise enough to avert this contingency. According to a World Bank sponsored study poor quality of coal, local in-puts, difficulties in getting imported inputs, power shortage, transport bottlenecks, unreliable delivery dates have reduced India's international competitiveness. These are bound to hinder the growth of exports.

The deficit in the Union Budget for 1985-86 is of the order of Rs. 3,493 crore, the budget deficits of all the States is likely to be more than Rs. 2,000 crore. This colossal deficit along with the several concessions in the income tax and the enhancement of commodity taxes and the increase in passenger fares and freight rates announced in the Railway Budget are bound to generate inflation despite official protestations to the contrary. In the first week after the presentation of the budget the wholesale price index (base 1970-71) rose from 340 to 342.8, in the second week it rose to 344.8 and in the third week it rose to 346.2. There are no signs of inflation abating. Already inflationary expectations have taken hold of consumer psychology. This makes non-inflationary growth an unattainable goal. Furthermore, the compatibility of high-tech production with the parallel economy fed by black money of the order of Rs. 60000 crore is to be examined.

The institutes of higher education and research have to reorient their activities in the direction dictated by the skill requirements of high technology, robotics, computerisation, microelectronics and programmable automation which constitute technological culture. India can boast of a number of institutes and laboratories which were established in the post-independence era. The Government is spending one-third of the higher education budget on expanding the activities of the institutes and laboratories. However, the research undertaken and turned out in them are only initiative and not innovative. These laboratories make a poor show of their achievements. The researchers have to work in an environment uncongenial to creative work. The junior research staff of high research, capability have to labour under several handicaps like unhelpful bosses, shortage of materials and equipment required for research, lack of promotional opportunities, frustration, base politicking and all the circumstances which impede creative research activity and encourage brain drain. Perpetuation of the same conditions in altered circumstances will be inimical to technological progress. Therefore, the planners have to redesign the educational curriculum at all levels provide incentives for creative research and redefine the responsibilities of the research laboratories so as to make them serve as a catalyst for the technological revolution underway. India should not depend on imported technology for ever. Its laboratories should be assigned the task of devising fuel-efficient technology appropriate to its needs and transfer it to other developing countries which need it. In the context of computerisation of every sphere of activity a nationwide programme of training school children in the use of home computers and manned by highly trained technicians should be adopted. Microcomputer sets are inexpensive and they have to be manufactured on a large scale. Unless this kind of an educational infrastructure is built the technological culture cannot flourish.

India is a labour surplus economy and it is pertinent to examine whether the adoption of high technology on an extensive scale will not add to existing unemployment. The Government is optimistic that the demand for labour will increase in many occupations and industries, not just those undergoing technological changes. Because the new jobs will not be limited to the changing sectors, employment in those sectors may fall even as total employment increases. This raises the possibility of structural unemployment. Although the total number of new jobs may in certain sectors exceed the number lost to technology, some workers will have difficulty making the transition to new employment. Geography may stand in the way. If the activities in which technology is reducing the demand for labour are concentrated in a particular region, the job growth in other industries in that region may not be sufficient to absorb all the displaced labourers. Other regions may experience labour shortages. Furthermore, the skills required in the expanding activities may not mesh with those of the workers who have lost their jobs. The problem is not that displaced workers cannot satisfy the skill requirements of the new jobs. Rather, many of these workers have specialised skills or experience for which they were paid relatively high wages; these skills are no longer valued and to achieve the same wage level a different set of specialised skills is required. Unless they acquire these skills they remain unemployed.

There is another view regarding the effect of technology on employment. It is argued that the narrow view of equating the technological advances with the use of computers and to see the office and industrial automation as the primary purpose of computers ignores the computer's potential for lowering costs of production by improving quality control. Permitting more precise inventory management and reducing energy use and waste. It ignores the computer's role in such diverse activities as diagnosing disease, directing the country's defence systems and providing education and entertainment at home. It also ignores technological advances in other fields such as biotechnology and communications. However, these benefits can accrue only after computerisation attains full maturity.

This preoccupation with the labour-displacement possibilities of computers and future technological advances is perhaps inevitable. The adverse effects of technology are often highly visible. Those who are displaced tend to be vocal. Those who find employment because of technological change are unlikely to sing the praises of technology. Unless they actually work for a computer or electronics company they may not even recognise its role in creating their jobs. Even then they may be apprehensive of displacement in the near future because of a more sophisticated technological change. If automation results in a labour saving that enables a firm to compete more effectively in world markets, workers see only the jobs lost to technology and not the larger losses that would have resulted had the firm not become more competitive.

Our knowledge of the impact of new technology on white collar jobs is sketchy and imprecise. Moreover, hard data on the number of jobs lost, created or changed solely because of new technology are hard to find or to estimate. Many other variables usually come into play: changes in consumer preferences, interindustry competition worldwide, altered economic conditions, industry restructuring, new legislation, government regulation or deregulation, and so on. Even so, it is possible to isolate the technology factor and assess its impact on employment. This requires several in-depth studies of the problems industry by industry. However, the impact of new technology on office jobs can be assessed easily and this impact is expected to be adverse. The office jobs dwindle creating unemployment there. The advocates of high technology are yet to prove that computerisation will actually increase employment in the service sector. It is for this reason that the employees in the banks and the Life Insurance Corporation of India oppose the introduction of programmable automation and their apprehension is understandable. Unless alternative jobs are provided for them they are bound to resist computerisation of office work. Many labour organisations have begun to voice protests against "indiscriminate computerisation".

High technology is intended to enable the producers to increase their market share. By enabling firms to underprice their foreign competitors, technological change may result in large export gains and therefore employment increases that more than offset the reduction in labour input per unit. It is this opportunity, together with the fear that failure to introduce cost-saving changes will enable foreign producers to make inroads into the domestic market, that causes many who take pessimistic view of the labour market effects of technology to support efforts to encourage the adoption of technology. However, it all depends on the extent of cost reduction and quality enhancement which would increase the demand for domestic goods in preference to imported goods. On balance it can be said that the demand for labour will fall, in the industries adopting new technology. The result will be a "skill-twist" in which the demand for low-skill jobs will decline while the demand for high-skill engineering and other jobs will rise. This calls for retraining the displaced labourers to enable them to perform new jobs requiring new skills. The possibility of adaptation to new and changing strategies of production depends on the flexibility and resilience of the economic system. Given the rigidity of the structural and institutional framework it would be too much to expect the requisite degree of flexibility and adaptability in the short run. This makes it necessary to cultivate, a stoic preparedness to put up with unemployment. However, through the fiscal mechanism of income redistribution it is possible to mitigate the hardships of those who lose jobs by taxing the beneficiaries of technology and transferring the proceeds to the unemployed. However, the magnitude of such transfer is too colossal to the practicable. Even if it is practicable, the frequent introduction of fiscal innovations for the purpose militates against the idea of stable fiscal planning under contemplation.

The Wall Street Journal of the United States in an editorial of India's new growth strategy has hailed the Governments economic policy crediting it with bringing the economy into the "Maruti Age". It has commended the Prime Minister for launching a vigorous attack on controls, taxes and State paternalism which, in its view, have smothered the economy for forty years. It concludes with the statement that "if these policies succeed" they would "jolt India out of its low growth age and into the ranks of the world powers". This appreciation obviously emanates from its ideological commitment to the free market economy. Given the shortage of capital resources, abundance of labour, inadequate infrastructural facilities, shortage of energy, substandard education general and technological structural and institutional rigidities, unsympathetic bureaucracy, inflationary fiscal monetary policy mix, the need to protect certain genuinely infant industries against foreign competition which is at variance with the projected policy of import liberalisation and eradication of unemployment, one wonders whether the euphoric dash to high-tech production and supply-side economics will find a hospitable environment. Euphoria should not lead us to apply Euclidean remedies to a non-Euclidean world. That way lurks danger. We cannot build castles first and then put the foundation under them. High technology, computerisation, liberalisation and the exposure of the economy to the free play of market forces are undoubtedly necessary to meet the challenges facing the country, but their introduction, all at once, with startling suddenness without preparing the base to nurture them is bound to generate shocks and problems inimical to stable fiscal monetary environment and to social cohesion. Not to adopt high-technology in a world of rapid technological change would be disastrous, to adopt it extensively all of a sudden despite infrastructural constrains would be catastrophic. Prudence dictates progress by discreet steps.

43

Wheat Imports to Restrain Inflation

The Government of India has taken an unexpected decision to import 1 million metric tonne of wheat from the United States of America. This is indication that the war against inflation is yet to be won. The Government had previously agreed to import wheat from the United States. At that time the United States refused to supply wheat to India on the pretext that India was supplying rice to Cuba with which its international relations were not cordial. When the Indian delegation led by the Minister of Food, Government of India, went to Washington to negotiate the wheat deal, George Bush, the U.S. President readily agreed to supply wheat to India. It is possible to argue that the decision of George Bush to supply wheat to India and the forthcoming Presidential election are not unrelated. There are 15 lakh Indian voters in the United States and George Bush and the Republican Party Presidential nominee Mr. Bill Clinton have started wooing the Indian voters. This explains the change in US attitude to the supply of wheat to India. Whatever the reason, it can be said that the import of subsidised US wheat is an anti-inflationary measure and, viewed in this perspective, it is a welcome step.

The Indian delegation signed the agreement on 7.10.1992. The Equity Grains, Louis Drefus and G. Aron & Co to supply 5 lakh tonnes of wheat. The balance of 5 lakh tonnes will be supplied by Kangil International and continental Grain Company. Of the tenders submitted by 24 good exporting companies the tenders submitted by the above companies were accepted. In accordance with the Export Enhancement programme the US Government pays a subsidy of $ 33.45 for every tonne of wheat supplied to India on account of this subsidy. India is able to obtain wheat at the competitive price of $ 110.50 - $ 112.50 per tonne. A few months ago India entered into contract with Australia for the purchase of 5 lakh tonnes of wheat at a price of $ 137.5 per tonne and with the Canadian Government for the purchase of 1 million tonne of wheat at a price of $ 147.50 per tonne. But it is learnt that the Canadian and Australian wheat is better in quality than the US wheat. However, as the price of US wheat is lower than that of Canadian and Australian wheat, US wheat can be purchased. In the subsidy scheme applicable under the Export Enhancement Programme it is held that India can purchase another 5 lakh tonnes of wheat from the United States. A decision will be taken after an assessment of the food requirements and food availability in India.

Is the wheat import from the United States inevitable? Even though the rain-god has been generous for the past three years and the crops have been bountiful the food prices have maintained their upward trend. Experts advance several reasons for this situation. The farmers and merchants have held stocks of food grains in the expectation that their prices will rise in future. If this artificial scarcity is to be remedied food grains should be available in plenty in the market. It is for this reason that the Government decided to import wheat, edible oil and cotton. The idea seems to be the expectation that those who have held stocks of these commodities might put them on the market in the fear that the prices may decline causing a loss to them. In the meanwhile the reason for the Agricultural costs and prices commission deciding to fix the wheat support price and purchase price for the 1993-94 season might be to check the artificial scarcity of wheat in the year 1993-94 and through it to check the rise in food prices. Anyhow the import of wheat from abroad is meant to check the rise in wheat prices and through it to check the rate of inflation. If this could materialise, well and good.

The United States is prepared to supply subsidised wheat to India. In the 1991-92 wheat marketing season wheat procurement was low and wheat procurement in the next season beginning in April 1993 has prompted the Government to take advantage of the offer of subsidised wheat. Since July 1992 India has entered into import contracts for a total of 2.5 million tonnes of wheat. The US wheat, favoured by Indian consumers was the first choice for imports. The United States Government which wants to please the farmers on the eve of the election included India among the 30 countries entitled to price subsidy under the US export enhancement programme. For India, the price of imported wheat is 30 percent less than the cost of wheat purchased from Canada in July 1992. India has, of course, gained in price and the presently available foreign exchange reserves enable India to take advantage of this offer.

The wheat stock with the Government is about 9 million tonnes. This is well below the norm. The procurement of wheat in the last season was 20 percent less than the target despite a 25 percent increase in the procurement price. The wheat stock at present is just adequate to meet the needs of the public distribution system until May 1993 when the rabi crop starts arriving in the market. There is not enough scope for the Government to use its stocks to restrain the price rise. Wheat imports will, to some extent, enable the Government to do it but this is only a temporary expedient. For the past three years procurement has fallen short of the target as the farmers held back stocks and sold them in the market when prices rose. The situation may not be different in the next season. A substantial increase in the rabi crop will reduce the prices and persuade the farmers that it is profitable to sell wheat to the Food Corporation of India. But even this does not seem to be likely as the Kharif harvest this year is expected to be marginally smaller than the targeted amount.

The import of 2.5 million tonnes of wheat of which the Canadian and Australian wheat is of the order of 1.5 million tonnes and the US wheat is of the order of 1 million tonne is just enough to make up for the shortfall in procurement of wheat in the current year. But if the Government is serious about expanding the Public Distribution System (PDS) the level of food stocks needed for the purpose would have to be raised. The expansion of the PDS to 1,700 uncovered blocks in backward regions as announced by the Government means that it needs another 2 million tonnes of good grains. Seen in this perspective the food stock position does not seem to be comfortable even after the import of 2.5 million tonnes of wheat. To be able to meet the requirements of the PDS the

Government will do well to import more wheat. India can take advantage of the US Government offer of subsidised wheat. The gain to India is evident from the fact that the US wheat is 30 percent cheaper than the Canadian wheat imported in July 1992.

Importing subsidised US wheat is, of course, good. But the final price of wheat after including the cost of transportation and handling would be higher than the support price paid to Indian wheat farmers. It might be argued that instead of paying a higher price to US farmers the Government of India can as well pay a higher support price to Indian wheat farmers to enable them to grow more wheat. As the supply of wheat is elastic to its price it seems necessary and worthwhile to raise the support price in order to stimulate domestic production. But this increase has to be based on domestic economics of wheat production and the need to ensure an adequate return to the farmers rather than on the price trend in foreign markets. The comparison with foreign prices is misleading since the Indian farmer not only gets farm inputs at cheaper prices but also pays much lower wages to labourers than the farmers in Europe or the United States. The abysmal poverty of the India consumer especially in the rural areas is the reason for the introduction of the revamped PDS and the payment of subsidy on food grains. At a time when inflation is raging in the country and the rural and urban poor are undergoing untold hardships it is necessary for the Government to adopt all measures to supply food grains at reasonable prices. Seen in this light the import of wheat is a necessary step.

Control of inflation is the aim of official policy. Already in the aftermath of the hike in petroleum prices, the rate of inflation which had declined to 7.4 percent has begun to rise to belie the official claim that the rate of inflation will decline to 5 percent by March 1993. The rise in food prices will occasion a rise in the cost-of-living index and set the stage for wage escalation which further engenders a rise in the rate of inflation. This will also have adverse effects on the already uncomfortable balance of payments position as a rise in wages and other costs will reduce the payments position as a rise in wages and other costs will reduce the price competitiveness of Indian exports in the global market. All these considerations justify wheat imports at present and in future also. In the meanwhile, all incentives should be provided to farmers to increase food supply like subsidised fertilisers and remunerative prices. At the same time when the food supply is short of drastic requirements it would be injudicious to export food to foreign countries like the export of rice to Cuba and the export of Wheat to Jordan. The price of domestic wheat is lower than the price of imported wheat even if it be at subsidised prices for the cost of transportation and handling will make the market price of imported wheat higher than the market price of domestic wheat. Furthermore, the import of wheat at a higher price and the export of wheat at a lower price means that the differential between foreign exchange income and outgo will be to the disadvantage of India. Therefore, until the good stock position is comfortable it would be injudicious to export food which is cheaper and to import food which is dearer. The countries to which India exports food can well be asked to import food from countries which have surplus food and which they are eager and ready to sell. All these policy ingredients should be included as integral parts of the food supply strategy that should be adopted in the Eighth Plan Period.

44

Disinvestment in Public Sector Equity

In March 1990 there were 244 public sector units owned by the Central Government of which 11 were under construction and 233 were in operation. Of these, 133 PSUs were in the manufacturing sector and 73 were providing services of various kinds. The total investment in PSUs at the time was 99,315 crore. Net profits made by all the PSUs after allowing for losses totalling about Rs. 1,959 crore made by the loss making units were Rs. 3,782 crore. Net profits on investment thus work out to a poor 3.9 percent. However, on a total paid-up capital of Rs. 35,580 crore (excluding Rs. 3,777 crore of the paid-up capital of units under construction) net profits work out at 10.6 percent. While, on an overall basis, this is not too unsatisfactory, one has to take note of the fact that (1) a significant number of PSUs have been chronically making losses, some of them quite substantial in relation to their operations requiring budgetary support and (2) one of the original objectives of PSUs that they would generate surpluses for financing the future growth of the economy has clearly not seen realised.

It is necessary to take note another parameter about these units. Of the 257 PSUs under production in 1989-90, the operating results of which have been published by the Bureau of Public Enterprises, 53 percent (or 136 units) were operating at more than 75 percent of capacity, 23 percent (or 58 units) were operating at between 50 and 75 percent of their capacity; and 24 percent (or 63 units) were operating at less than 50 percent of capacity. Of these, 12 units were brought on stream during 1989-90 and one should not expect satisfactory utilisation in the first year of operation.

The operations of the PSUs have come under a good deal of criticism and they can be summed under 4 broad heads: (1) PSUs are generally inefficient, overmanned and high cost; (2) require budgetary support for this expansion at a time when they should be contributing to public exchequer and to the growth of national savings; (3) they have not contributed adequately to Research and Development, that they have not developed indigenous capability, that they have stuck to outmoded technology and that they have not contributed adequately to the growth of exports (4) their need for budgetary resources inhibits the use of these scarce resources for meeting other developmental needs. What is true of PSUs is equally true to private sector enterprises.

The foregoing charges point to a malady common to the Indian Industrial Economy, namely, the general absence of dynamism, R&D effort and improvement in process technology. The problems of PSUs have in the past been studied by a number of high-level committees. The most notable of them is the Economic Administration Reforms Commission under the Chairmanship of the late L.K. Jha which came out with four reports. The Jha Commission recommended that the Government should present a comprehensive white paper to Parliament. Though three white papers were prepared by successive Governments in 1988, 1990 and 1991 none has so far been presented to Parliament. Instead what has been presented to Parliament is a list of chronically sick PSUs which are proposed to be referred to the Board of Industrial and Financial Reconstruction (BIFR) for a decision as to their future. However, the Government of India in the attempt to reduce the fiscal deficit has found it expedient to engage itself in a programme of disinvestment in PSU equity.

The Government of India has adopted a policy of disinvestment in public sector units for the simple reason that it is not able to bear the dead weight of these units and it is not prepared to keep them going by bearing the losses they incur. The IMF has suggested disinvestment in these units in order to reduce the burden of losses they incur. For these reasons the Government has adopted the policy of disinvestment in public sector units.

In 1991-92 the Government sold a percent of the shares of 30 public sector units and got Rs. 3,000 crore. This made it possible for the Government to reduce the fiscal deficit to 6.5 percent of GDP as committed to the IMF. This year the Government has proposed to sell 20 percent of the shares of 20 public sector units and to obtain Rs. 3,500 crore. It is proposed to use Rs. 2,500 crore of this amount in order to bring down the fiscal deficit to 5 percent of GDP. This will continue next year also. It is planned to realise Rs. 2,500 crore next year. But this amount will not be used to reduce the fiscal deficit. A sum of Rs. 1,000 crore realised from the sale of shares this year and sum of Rs. 1,500 crore to be realised next year will be used to increase the size of the National Renewal Fund to which the Government has already remitted Rs. 200 crore.

The disinvestment in public sector units and the National Renewal Fund are closely related. There is another objective of disinvestment. The Government feels that the public sector units will be able to operate profitably when the private share holders enter them as partners. At present many PSUs are top heavy; their production techniques are not modernised; their machinery and techniques of production are traditional; the number of labourers are more than necessary for them. Some of them are not able to be profitable. It is considered necessary to close down those units which cannot survive; it is desirable to cut down surplus manpower. Those who want to retire can be retrenched by giving compensation; others can be retrained and re-employed in industries requiring the newly acquired skills. All these require finance. It is for this reason that finance is to be supplied from the NRF which has to use it for retraining and re-deployment of labourers, modernisation of enterprises these are being considered by the Government as interlinked programmes. These programmes are dictated by the IMF. It is for this reason that the Government has to earmark a part of the funds it realises from the sale of shares of the PSUs.

The IMF is not agreeable to using the funds realised from the sale of shares for closing the fiscal gap. It feels that it is indiscreet on the part of the Government to use the assets built up by the Government over the years in this manner. If the IMF agreed to this last year and this year it is because of the need to help the Government which had to face a critical fiscal situation. The IMF feels that Government should be enabled to maintain fiscal balance. It feels that the Government should transfer Rs. 2,500 crore to the NRF. The task of reviving the sick PSUs should start immediately and the golden handshake should start now. If there are no adequate funds for this purpose there will be furore in the labour front. These are the problems facing the Government at present and these problems are to be successfully sorted out.

In the previous year 8 percent of the shares of 30 PSUs were sold and this year 8 percent of the shares of 20 PSUs are slated for sale. The extent to which these sales are successful has to be assessed. The Government claimed that due to the sale of the shares of these enterprises they are not being privatised and that they are part of the capital is being sold to financial institutions and mutual funds. But the institutions which bought these shares sold them immediately for a price 10-20 times higher. Some of them bought these shares on behalf of private institutions and private brokers. This policy of thc Government generated extensive criticism.

This year the Government invited bids from private individuals with intent to sell the shares to the highest bidders. But it made it clear that it would not receive bids of less than Rs. 2.5 crore. For this reason the small investors could not bid for shares in the market. The same person offered many bids. Though bids of the aggregate value of Rs. 2,091 crore were made it was possible for the Government to accept bids of the value of only Rs. 682 crore. As only a few were permitted to bid there was a tendency to quote a lower price. It must be admitted that not all companies are profitable. There is no clear picture about the value of their property, profitability, the rate of return on investment etc. It is necessary to modernise some companies. In view of this it is not clear how the Government could reach its target of Rs. 3,500 crore. It is believed that the Government shares can command a higher price only after voluntary retirement of labourers, closure of sick and inefficient units and the modernisation of the remaining units. The objective of the Government can be realised only when it adopts a business like attitude in handling the affairs of the companies.

Certain comments are in order about the sale of shares of PSUs. The 1992-93 Budget has proposed a disinvestment of the equity of PSUs this time by calling for bids in the open market. Three points need to be made in this context: (1) the sale of equity is undertaken merely to reduce the fiscal deficit of the Government of India nothing being done to address the specific problems of the PSUs. (2) the PSUs get nothing out of the transaction. It would be a different thing if they are allowed to invite fresh equity from the market at a premium and thereby raise new capital for their expansion, modernisation and technological upgradation. (3) the price at which these assets are sold has no relation to the real value of these assets. Even in the sales through bids there arise two problems; the bids are likely to be manipulated, also the private sector does not have the capital required to pay a reasonable price for these assets built up over long years and the present procedure is likely to end up with valuable assets built up over long year being sold at an incredibly low price. The reference of the sick PSUs to the BIFR is mystifying. Each PSU has its own specific problems to which specific solutions have to be found. The BIFR lacks the expertise necessary to suggest solutions to the problems faced by them.

The advantage of disinvestment is that it generates ready cash for the treasury which can be used to retire debt but it is being used to reduce the fiscal deficit. Apart from this public share holding will enforce public scrutiny and accountability which will enhance efficiency of the enterprises. It will broaden the share holding base in the stock market and open up a new source of funds. All this is based on the hope that the funds thus raised will not be squandered by the Government on unproductive current expenditure.

Prudence demands that the sale of public sector assets should be used to reduce the internal debt which at present is of the order of Rs. 2,60,000 crore. One of the main causes of the current fiscal deficit is that over 1/3 of Government revenue is used to pay interest. A reduction of the size of internal debt will restore fiscal stability. One way of doing this is to reduce the quantum of public borrowing and replace it by the sale of public sector equity. But this is to be accompanied by efforts to eliminate the deficit on the revenue account so that resources mobilised from the capital account are not squandered on current expenditure. Thus both the sale of public sector equity and debt reduction should go hand in hand.

Closing the fiscal deficit by resorting to disinvestment can hardly be called sound management of the public finances. For another, while it is true that there has been compression of expenditure all-round, it is capital expenditure that has borne the major brunt of the economy measures. The adverse long-term impact of this on the growth of the economy that is in the throes of a recession in recent years cannot be overemphasized. Hence the suggestion that the proceeds of disinvestment should be used to retire public debt and through it to reduce the interest payments which are a committed expenditure of the Government.

To sum up, the proceeds of disinvestment in PSU equity should not be used to reduce the fiscal deficit directly but should be used to reduce the size of the public debt which, in turn, has the effect of reducing the fiscal deficit through reducing the interest payments. It is hoped that the Government will reconsider the present action in this area of economic policy.

45

Enhanced Support Prices for Food Grains

Recently the Government of India has enhanced the support price of food grains to facilitate the transfer of Rs. 335 crore to the farmers. As a consequence the prices of rice and the price of wheat the two food grains used in the public distribution system are to rise by Rs. 40 and Rs. 50 per quintal respectively. The Minister for Agriculture, has maintained that the support prices of rice and wheat have been raised in order to reduce the financial burden imposed on the farming community by the rise in fertiliser prices consequent on the reduction of fertiliser subsidy. This means that the burden which would rest on the farmers is shifted on to the shoulders of the consumers.

The IMF and the World Bank insist on the removal/reduction of subsidies of all hues as they feel that subsidies are anathema to a market oriented economy. The consequence of implementing, albeit partially, the conditionality prescriptions is to impose a burden on the common man. When the fertiliser subsidy was reduced, the Government had molified the farmers who were sore with the policy. But it had not given any assurance that it would take action to prevent a rise in prices. Even so, it had given the assurance that it would check the rise in the rate of inflation. Now that the prices of rice and wheat have risen this assurance has been falsified. In November and December 1992 the price of rice was falling. This was due mainly to the removal of zonal restrictions on the movement of rice. But now as a consequence of the enhancement of the support price for rice the price of rice in the open market has begun to rise again. The Government of India had earlier raised the support price. But it had not raised the support price by Rs. 40-50 per quintal. This rise appears to be steep indeed.

It was possible for the Government to shift the burden of Rs. 335 crore to the fertiliser industry itself. It was also possible for the

Government to reduce the price of fertilisers by making the subsidy payment for production and holding of fertiliser conditional on not raising the price of fertilisers. This is not a difficult task if only the Government takes measures to streamline the distribution of fertilisers. Without doing any of these things the Government has only shifted the financial burden from one sector to another as it if is not its concern. In future whenever the Government takes action to reduce the subsidy or to remove it, the harried consumer has inevitably to bear the burden of the price rise in consequence.

It must be remembered that it is the food prices that hold the key to the rate of inflation in the Indian economy. On the one hand, it takes measures like the reduction of the fiscal deficit and the reduction of the rate of monetary growth with intent to reduce the rate of inflation to a level specified in the fund's conditionality prescription; on the other hand, it takes measures that would raise the rate of inflation. These two sets of measures are mutually contradictory.

The Fund-Bank combine is underwriting India's transition to a market economy and the transition is fairly rapid. But this should not make the Fund-Bank combine insist on the removal of all subsidies on the ground that subsidies are inconsistent with a market-oriented economy. The American and the European economics are more market oriented than the Indian economy. Even so, subsidies are mainly of American and European agriculture. When this is the case there appears to be no reason for the Fund-Bank combine to prescribe the removal of subsidies as a condition of making the loan available to India.

Removal of the fertiliser subsidy cause a rise in fertiliser prices. As the fertilisers are an essential farm input, the cost of production rises. To be able to meet the higher cost of production, the Government has to enhance the support prices of food grains so far so good. But what are the further consequences. The market prices of food grains rise. The consumers have to buy food grains by paying the higher market prices. This causes a rise in the cost-of-living index which governs the wage rate. The labourers enforce their demands for higher wages. If they are not granted there will be strikes and lockouts which through a reduction in mandays reduce output and through supply deficiency raise the price of output. On the other hand, if higher wages are granted, as they have to be granted they generate both cost-push inflation and demand-pull inflation which get intertwined and become difficult to disentangle. Thus, a removal of the fertiliser subsidy may help the Government to reduce the fiscal deficit but the rise in the support prices of food grains at the farmers' level causes a rise in the prices of food-grains at the market level and generates inflation. This can be checked by offering food subsidy. But what is saved on fertiliser subsidy is lost on food subsidy so that there is no net saving to the Government to enable it to reduce the fiscal deficit and through it to reduce the rate of inflation.

This means that the removal of fertiliser subsidy, by reducing the fiscal deficit, reduces the fiscal deficit induced inflation rate but it engenders the cost-induced and demand-induced inflation due to the enhancement of the support price. In either case there is no relief from inflation.

India is not yet a free market economy through it is on the road to reach this goal. For some more fertiliser subsidy is necessary. When the fully market-oriented American and European economics are offering fertiliser and other kinds of subsidies to their agricultural sectors it would not stand to reason to demand the removal or even reduction of the fertiliser in the Indian economy. Fertiliser should, of course, be phased out in stages. Agreed, but at the present stage of the evolution of the Indian economy fertiliser subsidies are a necessity. To remove them at present is to cause a social upheaval in the agricultural sector and also to dye at the Government's efforts to reduce the inflation rate. At the end of December the rate of inflation reigned at 7.84 percent. But the consequence of a spurt in support prices for food grains due to the reduction of fertiliser subsidy is to provide an upward thrust to the inflation rate. Therefore, the reduction of the fiscal deficit, the reduction of the rate of inflation and the removal of fertiliser subsidies are not a coherent package of measures.

The burden of this song is that the fertiliser subsidies must be retained as an antidote to inflation for some more time. The support prices can be enhanced if warranted by the rise in other input costs so as to provide incentives to farmers to step up production.

46

Modifications of the Loan Waiver Scheme

The Indian banking system is in urgent need of reform as recommended by the Narasimham Committee. As it is, the profitability of the banking system is eroded with a few banking institutions having become sick. This for three reasons: the Loan Mela Scheme, Priority sector lending and the Loan Waiver Scheme. The Loan Mela Scheme was intended to help the unemployed and the destitutes to become self-employed. The Loan Waiver Scheme was intended to bail the debtor farmers out of the loan morass into which they had fallen. The priority sector lending more is the most important reason for the erosion of bank profitability. The lending is of the order of 40 percent of bank resources. The three priority sectors are: agriculture, small scale industry and the export sector. Fortunately, the Loan Mela Scheme has been discontinued. The Narasimham Committee has recommended the reduction of lending to priority sectors from 40 percent of bank resources to just 10 percent.

This recommendation has generated an acrimonious controversy. The recommendation is well taken but its implementation bristles with formidable practical difficulties. Under the bank nationalisation scheme financial assistance to the priority sectors was envisaged in order to help the farming sector to improve its operations so that it may increase farm output; to help the small scale industrial sector to improve its viability and to help the export sector to increase exports to bridge the balance of payments gap. The lending to the priority sector, of course, has reduced the profitability of the banking system. It is to help the banking system that the Narasimham Committee recommended the reduction of concessionary bank lending to the priority sector from 40 percent of bank resources to just 10 percent.

Admittedly, concessionary bank lending is anathema to a free market economy. But India is not yet a free market economy though it is on the road to it. For this reason the drastic reduction of lending to the priority sector from 40 percent to 10 percent of bank resources is fraught with grave economic consequences quite apart from the social unrest it causes in the farming community. Thus, while the reduction of lending to the priority sector from 40 percent to 10 percent of bank resources, it should be done in a phased manner in order not to antagonise farmers. Therefore the lending to the priority sector should be reduced not at one go but in gradual stages. This means that for the present priority lending should be retained.

It is the Loan Waiver Scheme that is in need of a review by the Government and the banking sector. The Government has lost Rs. 25,000 crore in 1992 as a result of Waiver of loans upto Rs. 10,000 to borrowers who did not pay any instalment in the last five years. The loan waiver scheme is a bigger tragedy than the securities scam. This has eroded the credibility of the banking system as to whether the securities scam was due to the liberalisation of the Indian economy or due to the system failure. The indication of the ill effects of the loan waiver scheme were demonstrated by the fall in loan recovery from an average of 55 percent to 30 percent during 1992. The banks were facing severe financial crisis because of the stoppage of repayments from the borrowers which directly affected the re-cycling of funds. Furthermore, the unprecedented boom in the stock market upto April 1992 gave a major set back to the banking system as huge funds were diverted to the share market by the depositing public as well as the borrowers. This dried down the deposit growth and led to acute shortage of funds with the banks. This occasioned the Reserve Bank of India imposing a ban on bank finance to all sectors. The large scale mushrooming of funds and finance companies administered a severe blow to the deposit growth. These mutual funds and finance companies used all kinds of methods to mislead the public and to give exaggerated commitments to secure more public deposits which were used to speculate in the stock market.

A section of the banking community feels that the securities scam was the consequence of the policy of liberalisation which gave freedom to the Government undertakings, mutual funds and finance companies to raise enormous funds for speculating in the stock market. This was aggravated the Reserve Bank's decision to permit Government undertakings and financial institutions to deal in securities which was not permissible earlier. But the Reserve Bank of India which did not foresee this untoward development in the financial sector did not consider it necessary to monitor and control and entire financial sector. These problems were compounded by the partial implementation of the recommendations of the Narasimham Committee especially in the areas of reorganisation and restructuring of banks, capital adequacy, rural banking, branch expansion, interest rate structure, competition, accounting procedures and practices, supervision and privatisation.

The Government of India was obliged to make good the amount of Rs. 25,000 crore to the banking system which had earlier advanced loans to the farmers to enable them to undertake/improve farm operations. At a time when the Government was hard put to it to mobilise resources to reduce the fiscal deficit to 5 percent of GDP this year the need to make good the colossal amount of Rs. 25,000 crore in 1992 was a very heavy burden on the exchequer. If the loan waiver scheme is done away with, there would be no difficulty in meeting the fiscal deficit target. But the farm lobby is vehemently opposed to the abolition of the loan waiver scheme.

The loan waiver is demand in cases when the farmers are unable to repay the loans. The farmers borrow money from the banks ostensibly in order to invest in farming operations. Sometimes the borrowed funds are so invested; in many cases funds borrowed for farm operations seep into unproductive channels through an osmotic process. In the latter case the farmers are totally unable to repay the loans. The funds invested in farm operations may be invested in legitimate farm operations but because of floods or droughts the investment may turn out to be bad investments. In this case either the standing crops are submerged in water because of floods or they get dried up before they yield grains because of droughts. In these cases the investment turns out to be unfruitful and the farmers are rendered incapable of repaying the loans. The loan waiver scheme is employed to waive both kinds of loans. This imposed a financial burden on the Government.

The Government has to distinguish between waiving loans used for genuine farming operations and waiving loans borrowed for investment in farm operations but not used for this purpose. The loans which are invested in farm operations but which cannot be repaid because of the failure of crops under flood and drought conditions can be waived and the loans which are used for consumption purposes should be recovered in full along with the interest accruing on it. This will discourage the borrowers from misusing the loans. In fact, a penalty can also be imposed on those using the loans for consumption purposes. This will reduce the burden of loan waiver on the Government by at least Rs. 10,000 crore. This is not a small sum.

The Government should constitute a monitoring cell in each State with the specific objective of monitoring the use of the borrowed funds. This will prevent the diversion of loans from productive to consumption purposes. It is necessary in the interests of the banking system to discontinue waiving loans used for consumption purpose. The loans borrowed for legitimate productive purposes but which because of floods and droughts cannot be repaid can, of course, be waived and the Government should reimburse this amount to the banking system. This scheme will not starve the banks of funds and will, in fact, help them in their deposit mobilisation efforts.

Even when the loans used for productive purposes but which cannot be repaid are waived. The waiving should be on a selective basis. Some farmers are well to do, especially the big farmers but the small and marginal farmers are penurious. The former category of farmers should be made to repay their loans fully or partially depending on circumstances as they are not totally unable to repay the loan. But the small and marginal farmers who do not have any reserve of funds should be exempted from repaying the loan. A scheme of this type will reduce the burden on the exchequer and also enhance the viability of the banking system.

The main suggestions of this Memorandum are:

1. The Loan Mela Scheme which was grossly misused by the borrowers and the middlemen and which rendered many banks sick and unviable has been stopped and it should not be revived for any reason.

2. The concessionary lending to the priority sector should be continued for the time being and should be phased out in gradual stages as a sudden cessation/reduction as recommended by the Narasimham Committee is bound to generate disaffection in the farm sector and cause social unrest.
3. The Loan Waiver facility should be given only to those who make investment of borrowed funds in the farm sector but who become unable to repay because of natural calamities. Even here a distinction should be made between the farmers who are able to repay despite the natural calamities and the farmers who are unable to pay. The former category of farmers could be asked to repay the loans while the loans advanced to the latter category of farmers could be waived. A Standing Committee should be constituted for each State/District to monitor the utilisation of the borrowed funds so that the funds borrowed for legitimate agricultural purpose are not diverted to consumption expenditure of the farmers. The loans used for consumption purposes should not be waived.
4. The funds currently used to waive farmers' loans could be used to reduce the fiscal deficit without having to enhance the tax burden on the community.

47

Partial Privatisation of Banks is Dangerous

The Government of India is said to be contemplating the partial privatisation of the banking system. The commercial banks in the country were nationalised in 1969 in order to fulfill social objectives. Prior to this the banks were under "social control". But the social control did not meet the requirements of social purpose. For this reason the banks were nationalised and they were obliged, under the law, to fulfill the social purpose. This was to lend funds to the three priority sectors at concessional interest rates. They were: Agriculture, small scale industry and the export sector. These sectors took away 40 percent of the bank lending. This was one of the causes of low profitability of the banking system. Besides this, the loan waiver scheme introduced by the National Front Government in 1990 in a spirit of competitive populism cost the banking system about Rs. 8,000 crore. The banking system, for this reason, was in doldrums as its capital base was inadequate when compared with international norms of adequacy. The last two schemes for the most part, turned out to be notorious for corruption and mismanagement.

The Narasimham Committee Report has underlined the need for Indian banks to move towards international capital adequacy norms as otherwise they would not be able to compete in the global financial system. In this context the Government is reported to have debated three options : (1) provision of funds by the Government to the banks by way of budgetary support: (2) raising of money by the banks in the market; (3) a policy mix wherein the Government provides some money and the banks raise some equity by offering shares to their employees and the public in a very limited way.

The Government in its budgetary allocation in 1992-93 has earmarked some amount to the banks. But it is unwilling to make any more allocation than has been done already in 1992-93 for the augmentation of the banking sectors equity base.

The International Monetary Fund has advised the Government to introduce financial reforms in order to strengthen the capital base of the banking system. At present the Government is negotiating the conversion of its stand-by credit from the IMF into an extended fund facility (EFF) for the over $ 8 billion loan and is trying to tie up another $ 500 million sectoral adjustment loan for the financial sector. In view of this the financial sector reforms have acquired a sense of urgency for the Government. The Fund-Bank team is currently in Delhi examining the progress of economic reforms. It is, therefore, suggested in some quarters that if the announcement of financial sector reforms is made now the Government has to encounter the charge that the announcement was made under the Fund-Bank pressure. They, therefore, advise the delaying of the announcement. However, the Government is likely to announce its moves towards partial privatisation of the banking sector.

Under partial privatisation the banks would have to continue under "social control" through the Government. Banks which were under private ownership were brought under social control and were then nationalised ostensibly to fulfill the social purpose. The fulfillment of the social purpose has led to a fall in productivity, fall in profitability and fall in efficiency of the banking system. It is for this reason that the Narasimham Committee Report recommends the reduction of priority lending from the present 40 percent to 10 percent in stages. If the banks come under partial privatisation the Government may insist on the banks fulfilling the social purpose while the banks may refuse to undertake priority sector lending anymore. The two positions may become irreconcilable with the result the priority sectors suffer. The anxiety of the banks is understandable. If the loans made to these sectors become irrecoverable the banking system will come to trouble and when it comes to trouble the Government will not come to its rescue and provide relief. In a situation like this, it would not appear to be reasonable for the Government to insist on the partially privatised banks fulfilling social objectives. If the idea is to make the banks fulfill the social objectives they should not be privatised; if they are privatised they cannot be pressured into fulfilling the social objectives. If, with limited private ownership, the banks would continue to be under social control through the Government there is bound to be clash to jurisdictions between the Government and the private ownership. The policy of liberalisation demands that the banks be privatised and not be left in public ownership. If the banks continue to be in public ownership as at present they will be under an irrevocable obligation to fulfill the social obligations priority sector lending at concessional interest rates, loan melas and loan waivers all of which have had disastrous consequences on the banking system. Therefore, the right course would be to privatise the banks abolishing the disastrous loan meals and loan waiver schemes but retaining the priority sector lending which should be reduced in a phased manner. The dual control over the banks envisaged under the scheme of partial privatisation will create more problems than it solves. Full privatisation of banks with adequate safeguards to the priority sectors is the need of the hour.

Ensuring capital adequacy of the banking system is necessary to make it solvent. This can be done by allowing the banks to raise money in the market. Under full privatisation where the profitability of the banks is ensured the private sector will be more than willing to buy the shares offered by the banks. Therefore, full privatisation permitting the banks to raise money in the market to strengthen their capital base appears to be a better alternative than partial privatisation which involves clash of jurisdiction and interests between the Government and the private banks with deleterious consequences on the progress of banking capital adequacy norms should be met first for those banks which are operating internationally.

Privatisation of the banking system will enhance efficiency of its operations and lead to cuts in expenditure. At present the employees of the nationalised banks are opposed to computerisation of banking operations. This has rendered the Indian banks incapable of competing with branches of foreign banks which have installed sophisticated electronic gadgets for the efficient operation of customer services. This has attracted the clientele to them. If the Indian banks are to reach the level of operational efficiency of the foreign banks, they must render customer service of the type and quality which the foreign bank renders. This is not possible with nationalised banks where the employees are militant and do not allow any policy measure meant to improve efficiency. Their militancy has led to the enhancement of their wages out of proportion to their productivity. But under privatisation where market forces have free play this is not possible. This means that privatisation results in efficiency of customer service, cut in administrative expenditure and a rise in the rate of profitability and solvency of the banking system in general. Seen in this perspective privatisation of the banking system is a desirable more. But privatisation should be total and not partial. Partial privatisation involving dual control over banks creates confusion and impedes their healthy development.

One of the ingredients of financial reforms is the reduction of the Statutory Liquidity Ratio (SLR) and the Cash Reserve Ratio (CRR) in a phased manner. These reforms would free resources which were hitherto preempted by the Government and would thus ease pressure on the banking system and allow banks to increase the flow of credit to all sectors. This would also increase the profitability of the banking system. But under nationalisation the banks are prone to come under powerful political pressure and extend credit to unviable schemes which ultimately lead to disaster. However, if the banks are fully privatised this danger would not exist. The banks would extend credit only to bankable schemes and would not advance any uneconomic and unviable loan to anybody. In short, under privatisation the banks will give themselves good management for which there is no substitute. The banks will also maintain transparency in accounting procedures which would make it impossible to conceal losses. It must be admitted that it was the absence of good management, effective internal control and vigilant supervision and absence of transparency in accounting procedures that were responsible for the recent securities scam which rocked the financial sector and the economy in general. Under full privatisation of the banking system scams of this type which are due to the "failure of the system" will be a thing of the past and the banking system will register healthy growth. Seen in this perspective financial sector reforms are necessary to root out scams in the system in future.

48

Ceiling on Borrowing to Reduce the Fiscal Deficit

The International Monetary Fund which advances loans under the structural Adjustment Facility and the Extended Fund Facility prescribes several conditionality prescriptions which the borrowing countries have to implement. The ceiling on the fiscal deficit is one of them. The idea is to make its loans solvent and recoverable as per schedule. Nobody can find fault with it. The IMF does not invite the member countries to borrow. As a prudent creditor, it has to ask the borrower to abide by certain prescriptions. This is in the interests of both the lender and the borrower. When India borrows agreeing to abide by the IMF prescriptions it would be uncharitable to allege that India surrenders its sovereignty to the IMF. They why do you borrow? You can as well keep off the IMF and the IMF will keep off India leaving it to fund for itself.

When India borrowed in July 1991 it put a ceiling on fiscal deficit as a proportion of GDP. In accordance with it the Government cut down the fiscal deficit as a proportion of GDP from 8.5 percent in 1990-91 to 6.5 percent in 1991-92 and to 5 percent in 1992-93. In 1993-94 it should have been 4.7 percent. But in actual fact it has turned out to be 7.3 percent and in 1994-95 it is targeted to be 6 percent of GDP. The reason for the unexpected rise in fiscal deficit in 1993-94 was the decline in indirect tax revenue collections by Rs. 8,000 crore and the rise in Government expenditure by Rs. 12,500 crore. The Finance Minister expects the fiscal deficit to fall to 6 percent of GDP in 1994-95. The earlier fiscal deficits were financed by the Government taking recourse to monetary financing which, of course, had inflationary consequences.

The deficit reduction in 1991-92 was effect on paper at the year-end. These deficit reduction exercises are committed in respect of public investment which promote growth. Any cut back in public investment will retard the rate of economic growth. In 1993 the Reserve Bank of India called for legal ban on Government borrowing from all sources "beyond and certain ceiling" with a sub-ceiling on borrowing from the Reserve Bank". This is sane advice as its has the effect of holding down the fiscal deficit, reducing the rate of inflation and achieving macroeconomic stability.

Out of a given level of gross fiscal deficit, net of foreign debt servicing, the bulk of the residual will go for domestic debt servicing. In consequence, the Government will be left with little to meet essential expenditure. This is hardly necessary, of course, to finance the other items of expenditure which are essential for growth. The proponents of enlarged fiscal deficits argue for removing the ceiling or sub-ceiling on Government borrowing and are accusing the Reserve Bank of India of obeying the dictates of the IMF which has a clean policy regarding fiscal deficit targets.

Their contention is that the fiscal deficit exercise cuts into public investment which is so essential for economic growth. Nobody in his senses would advocate a policy of cutting down public investment. But is that the only items of expenditure which has to be cut by a policy of fiscal deficit reduction? The first charge on the budget is the servicing of domestic and external debt. Since debt is continuously incurred, it follows that Government's expenditure is in excess of revenue. The servicing of the public debt will require to be met out of the fiscal deficit in future i.e., through borrowing (besides external borrowing) borrowing from the market and others and also from the Reserve Bank. The first charge is a mind-boggling one equivalent to 4.9 percent of GDP for 1993-94. If the fiscal deficit is limited to that prescribed by the IMF, an impossible situation is, of course, bound to arise. The debt-servicing liability of the Government is slated to grow in the coming years. This is inevitable because of the increased reliance on market borrowing in 1994-95. The Government has been borrowing at successively higher interest rates and borrowing rates are likely to continue to rise in future. If the rate of growth of GDP flags as in 1991-92 the ceiling on borrowing has to be pierced. In a year of inadequate income growth implying a fall in real per capita income, the Government will not be able to borrow enough as the economy lacks funds for lending. In this case it will have to piece the sub-ceiling of borrowing from the Reserve Bank if, for example, it is prescribed at say 1.5 percent of GDP.

The fiscal deficit target for 1994-95 is 6 percent of GDP which is higher than the one prescribed by the IMF. This is needed to cover besides debt servicing, other essential expenditures the three principal ones being those on health and primary education, agriculture and extension and start-up investments in infrastructure on which is dependent investment by both the private sector and the commercialised public sector. The first two are covered by transfers to the States and the squeeze on them is getting severer by the day. The last one was cut in the Union Budget for 1992-93. The Bhagwati-Srinivas a Report on economic reforms has objected to the cut in public investment. There are economists who want the Government to negotiate with the IMF for a bigger fiscal deficit as it is necessary to meet all expenditures including the transfers to States to meet their subsidy requirements and other essential expenditures.

Given the rising rate of inflation and the deficit in the balance of payments the case for holding down the fiscal deficit is strong indeed. The case for reducing borrowing is even stronger as this would reduce the debt servicing and help to bring down the fiscal deficit. The raising of the fiscal deficit will encourage fiscal profligacy of the Government. There is considerable scope for reducing expenditure. There is no question that excessive expenditure to keep the bureaucracy and public sector employees in clover must be ruthlessly eliminated. This is necessary to roll back fiscal deficit. But public investment should not be slashed as this is necessary to accelerate the rate of economic growth and through this to raise tax revenue which is necessary to reduce the fiscal deficit.

Wage escalation is the bane of the Indian economy. Under the good old good standard wages could not be raised as there was no money to pay the enhanced wages. But in a situation of permissive monetary policy the Government resorts to borrowing from the

Reserve Bank to be able to meet higher wage claims. One cannot accuse the labourers of enforcing their demands for higher wages. In a period of rising prices wages have to be raised to compensate the labourers for the rising prices. Rising prices are the cause of rising inflation rate which is the consequence of the rising fiscal deficit. If the multitudinous macro-economic linkages are understood the case for reducing the fiscal deficit becomes incontrovertible. Seen in this light the suggestion made by the Reserve Bank of India for imposing a legal ban on Government borrowing from all sources "beyond a certain ceiling" with a "sub-ceiling on borrowing from the Reserve Bank" is sensible. It is high time that it is implemented.

49

Fiscal Consolidation, Inflation, Balance of Payments and the Exchange Rate

Fiscal deficit is the main reason for domestic inflation and balance of payments deficit. The growth of Reserve Bank Credit to the Centre is an item of fiscal deficit. The growth of Reserve Bank credit since March 31, 1995 to the Centre was Rs. 16,999 crore as on July 28, 1995. According to the latest Reserve Bank figures this declined to Rs. 13,317 crore on August 25, 1995. In a similar manner, the growth of adhoc treasury bills which was Rs. 13,415 crore on July 28, had fallen to Rs. 10,990 crore on August 25. The level of borrowing by the Centre from the Reserve Bank is higher than that budgeted for the entire financial year. This moderation in the growth of adhoc treasury bills is due to the increase in the Centre's borrowing from the market. According to the Annual Report of the Reserve Bank of India for 1994-95, of the Rs. 6,585 crore that the centre borrowed as long and medium term loans until the middle of August 1995, as much as Rs. 5,000 crore has been raised since the end of July. The success of market borrowing has added to the stock of internal debt. At the same time due to the switchover to market determined interest rates the burden of interest payments has gone up. This has increased the importance of market borrowing in the financing of the fiscal deficit and has led to a bunching of repayments. The following table shows the gross fiscal deficit and the market borrowing:

Years (In Rs. Crore)	Gross fiscal deficit (In Rs. Crore)	Market Borrowings
1989-90	35632	7404
1992-93	40173	3676
1995-96	57634	27087

The place of adhoc treasury bills has been taken up by costly borrowings from the market. The trend is towards costly market borrowing to finance the fiscal deficit. Even if the size of the gross fiscal deficit is brought down in future, the debt financing of the deficit at higher interest rates will adversely affect Central Government finances. As per the Reserve Bank Annual Report (1994-95) the repayment schedule for Central Government market loans is as under:

Year	Repayment (Rs. Crore)
1995-1996	5556
1996-1997	7921
1997-1998	2903
1998-1999	5892
1999-2000	8799
2000-2001	10928
2001-2002	12464
2002-2003	10165
2003-2004	13143
2004-2005	3435

The table makes it obvious that the repayment schedule of market loans is rising except in 1997-98 when there will a relief. But in 1998-99 the situation changes. Till 2003-2004 there will be an extreme burden to be borne by the Government. If the market borrowing is not controlled, the "hump" in repayment will be worsened causing embarrassment to the Government.

One of the consequence of rising fiscal deficit is inflation. Inflation which was 17 percent in July 1991 is at present down to just over 8 percent. This is indeed a creditable achievement. But the fiscal situation being what it is, the rate of inflation is not likely to fall any further. If anything, there will be a rise in the rate of inflation not to the double digit zone as feared but above the present 8 percent. This is due to the expanding fiscal deficit. The fiscal deficit which was 8.4 percent in 1990-91 was brought down to 6 percent in 1991-92. Encouraged by its success in reducing the fiscal deficit, the Finance Minister chose a figure of 4.7 percent as the fiscal deficit for 1993-94. It was mentioned that the fiscal deficit would be lower but a higher figure was provided in order to re-heat the economy which had cooled down in the previous year. It was proudly claimed that the fiscal deficit could be brought down to 2-3 percent in the coming years. Most unexpectedly, there was a slippage that very year. The fiscal deficit which was targeted at 4.7 percent ended up with 7.7 percent. The main reason was the easing up on fiscal discipline because of elections in the northern states. The Finance Minister who felt embarrassed at the rise in the fiscal deficit announced a return to fiscal consolidation and promised to close the year 1994-95 with a fiscal deficit of 5.5 percent. But what happened was a fiscal deficit of 6.7 percent. In a recent report the IMF stated: that ..... " the stabilisation of the *Indian economy owed much to the initial fiscal adjustment at the Central Government level, which increased the credibility of the macroeconomic policy. In view of the subsequent fiscal slippage at the Central Government level, however and a deterioration of the States fiscal position, the consolidated public sector deficit in 1994-95 remained close to its level in 1990-91"*.

The IMF goes on to voice a common concern: *"The continuing large deficits and high level of public indebtedness raise concerns about the sustainability of fiscal policy. Increasing pressures on real interest rates have already emerged and these threaten to crowd out private investment. These fiscal pressures underscore the need to strengthen State finance given the risk that fiscal adjustment at the Central Level could be undermined by expansionary policies by States"*.

Another reason for the increase in the size of the fiscal deficit is the shift from monetary financing of the deficit to debt financing. Borrowing at higher interest rates has been resorted to. Money which could earlier be borrowed at 6 percent interest is now being borrowed at 13-14 percent interest. This has led to a rise in the interest cost of public debt. In the fiscal year 1995-96 the interest cost is expected to be Rs. 52,000 crore or 52 percent of the revenue receipts.

There is an uncontrolled rise in Government expenditure. The introduction of welfare package has cost the Government Rs. 5,000 crore. This is expected to push up the deficit by 0.5 percent of GDP. There is the apprehension that food and fertiliser subsidies would go beyond the targets, because of the carrying cost of the rising food mountain and the cheaper sale of food through the revamped public distribution system. Furthermore, because of the high cost of production of fertilisers, the final market price of fertilisers is likely to rise. In order to hold down the market price of fertilisers subsidy has to be enhanced. The higher subsidy outgo on these counts will push up the fiscal deficit. The expenditure of Rs. 1,650 crore on account of the interim recommendations of the Fifth Pay Commission will add significantly to the fiscal deficit. These additional expenditures can be covered if the Government is able to get more revenue. But the accrual of additional revenue is unlikely. The excise revenue is not showing the required degree of buoyancy. The income tax and customers revenues are higher but there are several loopholes in the excise revenue system because of the extension of the Modvat system to more items and this has caused a leakage of excise revenue. In view of this the mobilisation of additional revenue is difficult. In consequence, the fiscal deficit will remain high fueling the fires of inflation. This calls for energetic efforts to reduce the fiscal deficit. But because of burgeoning expenditure it has become virtually impossible.

The Reserve Bank of India in its Annual Report for 1994-95 has focused on the fiscal situation and has expressed itself strongly in favour of pruning the deficit. There are, of course, encouraging reports of the performance of the economy. The overall growth rate has picked up aided by better performance in both agriculture and industry. The balance of payments situation has remained under control with the current account deficit remaining below 1 percent of GDP. But these creditable indicators are likely to be offset by the fiscal deficits which have an impact on the inflation rate. According to the Reserve Bank of India there are two concerns at the macro-economic level and the trade-offs would require delicate balancing in order to achieve a target of sustainable growth with price stability. The economic reform process itself pre-supposes fiscal consolidation which implies a reduction in the fiscal deficit in the short term and medium term. The Reserve Bank rightly expresses alarm over the increase in the gross fiscal deficit to 7.7 percent in

1993-94 and to 6.2 percent in 1994-95. During 1991-92 and 1992-93 it was at more manageable levels of 5.9 and 5.7 percent respectively.

The marks adopted by the Government to bring down the fiscal deficit have not worked in the way they were intended to work. A shift to debt financing of the deficit at market-determined rates of interest was meant to indicate a correct measure of its cost. This, alongwith the decision to limit the Government's access to adhoc treasury bills, was expected to ensure fiscal discipline. At the end of 1994-95 the increase in adhoc treasury bills was Rs. 1,750 crore against a budgeted estimate of Rs. 6,000 crore. These advantages seem to have been lost from the beginning of 1995. The interest cost of Government debt has risen sharply and even at higher interest levels the response of the market is inadequate. In consequence, the Reserve Bank had to provide support to the Central Government. During the first four months of 1995-96 there has been a share rise in the holding of adhoc treasury bills by the Reserve Bank.

Having regard to the fact that the target for borrowing in 1995-96 is large than is imperative need to contain expenditure. Recent experience has shown that there are limits to Government borrowing at an affordable cost. The Reserve Bank of India has offered very valuable suggestions for grapping with the problem of fiscal deficit. They are the reform of the tax structure to increase the revenue buoyancy, the setting up of an mortisation fund for debt redemption including a sinking fund which would be accumulated through revenue receipts every year.

The monetary policy aspect has to be considered in the context of the ongoing inflation. The Central bank of any country has to devise its monetary policy in order to maintain price stability. The Central banks of the industrially advanced countries have a long established tradition of independence and they implement the monetary policy to achieve price stability. In India monetary policy is seen as the most appropriate means of achieving stability of prices. But monetary policy creates a dilemma for the authorities.

Price stability is one of the objectives of economic policy. The attainment of this objective may conflict with other objectives. There is therefore the need for balancing so that there is no fundamental conflict between objectives at the macro level. Price stability is a matter of several factors and not of just a monetary factor. The Reserve Bank of India has this to say on the subject:

"Prices are a result of a complex set of factors operating on the supply and demand side. The level of output and more particularly of essential commodities, imports and the distribution system, all have a bearing on the price situation".

As inflation cannot occur without a continuous rise in money supply, controlling overall monetary demand is pivotal to any programme of combating inflation. Both the change in output and the rise in money supply are to be seen together to determine their impact on the price situation. According to the Report there cannot be a trade off between economic growth and inflation and therefore over the medium term price stability is a since qua non for a growth-oriented environment. The monetary policy for 1995-96 has two faces: to bring about a substantial reduction in the rate of inflation and to enable the flow of credit in sufficient quantity to stimulate real output.

According to the Report, the monetary growth during 1994-95 was very strong with broad money M3 rising by between 19 and 22 percent. The objective of monetary policy for 1995-96 is one of "moderating monetary growth so that demand pressures are contained and inflation rate brought down substantially". At the same time there is need to supply sufficient credit to assist growth of real output. Therefore, monetary policy has aimed at a targeted increase of 15.5 percent in money supply and 16.8 percent increase in deposit growth.

Monetary policy is a part of economic policy. Its efficiency depends on how effectively other economic policies are administered. The fiscal situation has a decisive say on how effective monetary policy would be. The Report makes a strong indictment of the Government's fiscal imbalance. Even at the beginning of 1995-96 the Reserve Bank is not very happy about the state of public finances. There has been a large increase in net Reserve Bank credit to the Centre. As on 4.8.1995 it stood at Rs. 18,479 crore. Also, the increase in adhoc treasury bills has been well above the limit of Rs. 9,000 crore agreed to between the Government and the Reserve Bank of India. The Government's market borrowing at the market interest rate has become expensive imposing a heavy interest burden correcting the fiscal imbalance is an urgent task. Without this correction the good performance of the economy will be nullified. The Report points out that the rate of growth of credit is far in excess of the rate of growth of production. The Reserve Bank has advocated moderation in the rate of growth of credit supply.

During April-July 1995 exports were buoyant by 29.86 percent. It is another matter that import growth too is at a high of 39.20 percent. But the bulk of imports was for industrial production which shows buoyancy in the production front. The higher import growth is not yet a matter of concern as the import growth is likely to be checked by the depreciation of the rupee. It is expected that both imports and exports would go up but there is no need for alarm. Import payments are covered by export earnings to the tune of 90 percent since 1992. In the 1980s the coverage used to be around 52.4 percent and 70 percent by the end of the 1980s. The higher level of imports has caused a rise in the current account deficit of the order of 0.6 percent of GDP in 1994-95. But the situation is not causing concern as long as the invisible earnings are good-net invisible earnings amounted to $ 1.8 billion last year. There is an increase in foreign direct investment commitments. There are indications of a revival of foreign institutional investment though it is not more than $ 250 million.

The developments in the foreign exchange market since March 1995 have become a cause for concern. The forex reserves had to be utilised to the tune of $ 1.8 billion for meeting debt servicing obligations and other payments. The trade deficit for April-May has widened to $ 1.53 billion from $ 593.78 million in the corresponding period in 1994-95. It is possible that the total deficit for 1995-96 may rise to around $ 3 billion assuming that a more pronounced rise in exports and a less significant rise in imports in August-March 1995-96 will prevent the trade deficit from being higher than $ 3 billion. If net invisible receipts continue to rise in 1994-95 which are likely with a larger inflow of tourist traffic, freight income of shipping companies and other receipts, the current account may be manageable.

The Reserve Bank of India has expressed the confidence that the rupee-dollar exchange rate may not get significantly disturbed. Even so, heavy purchases of dollars by the State Bank of India, IOC and other corporates have led to a sharp depreciation of the rupee as the Reserve Bank of India did not come out as a seller of dollars. In the absence of any intervention by the Reserve Bank and fears that there may not be any large net inflows of foreign exchange resources during the period of confusion panicky buying of dollars led to the exchange rate depreciating to Rs. 35.20 when the exporters with dollars in their possession came forward to sell them the rate dropped to Rs. 33.70 at the cost of September 15, 1995.

The Reserve Bank could not intervene for technical reasons but it raised its reference rate which was higher at Rs. 34.15 on September 15, against Rs. 33.16 on the previous day. The decline in the rupee has made the market operators to view the rupee bearishly. What is surprising in the concentrated buying of dollars by the public sector enterprises though it is feared that a further rise in the current account deficit may not be fully offset by the balance of payment surplus as in 1993-95 and there might have to be a net drawing down of forex reserves for meeting commitments. As the rupee has been declining with the dollar it is reasonable to expect that the rupee will move up concurrently with the dollar and even reduce the rate of depreciation against the other currencies recorded earlier. But the recent increase in the inflow of NRI funds will give a boost to the external value of the rupee and it is likely to settle between Rs. 31.37 and Rs. 34.15 per dollar. The Finance Minister has given the assurance that there will be no capital account convertibility of the rupee in the near future and the economic fundamentals are fairly strong as undue depreciation of the rupee in terms of all currencies should be avoided.

The fall in the value of the rupee is not due to the deliberate act of the Reserve Bank of India. Ever since India, along with the rest of the world, abandoned the fixed rate system in 1971 it is not possible for any monetary authority to deliberately change the part value of its currency through an administrative fiat. Devaluation and revaluation are obsolete expressions in a floating rate system while depreciation and appreciation are relevant today.

The Finance Minister has done well in pointing out that the movement of currencies either way is a natural happening in the international currency markets and India should get used to them. The official view point is right in maintaining that for purposes of exchange rate comparison the weighted real effective rate of the rupee (REER) is relevant rather than a comparison with any currency. A conclusion based on the trends in the former, according to a Reserve Bank study, does not lead to an alarmist view point. The adverse inflation differentials of 2.5-3 percent between India and the rest of the world were more than offset by a nominal depreciation of the rupee in real terms between March 1994 and March 1995. The fall of the rupee against the dollar in the second week of September 1995 has to be seen against the backdrop of a few other major currencies also losing in relation to dollar. Furthermore, the Indian economy is seen to be performing well especially in the export sector though a better performance is necessary to reduce the current account deficit.

But the importers are upset by the rise in the prices of imports caused by the depreciation of the rupee especially those goods for which the demand is price inelastic. The importers of these goods have to pay more for these imports in terms of rupee if they are invoiced in dollars. But exporters stand to benefit. Depreciation of the rupee will also spur export competitiveness.

India has to contend not just with depreciation of the rupee but also with the volatility of the foreign exchange markets. The sudden slide in the rupee after a period of stability has induced knee-jerk reactions in both importers and exporters. In consequence they are prone to book their transactions at rates which need not have been the most favourable. It is not clear how the foreign financial institutions, the Indian stock market and the NRIs would be affected by the volatility of the rupee. A cheaper rupee draws in more investment but problems arise when servicing them. The lesson offered by the rupee is that it should be rendered stable. This is not to be understood merely in terms of Reserve Bank intervention. The users of the system need to be educated to enable the country to reap the benefits of integrating with the rest of the world for, otherwise, India's chances of making a mark will be remote.

The Finance Minister has rightly argued the case for freeing the rupee in order to enable it to find its level without any support from the Reserve Bank. In this case the rupee exchange rate may slightly decline. But this should be no cause for alarm. It will boost exports by making them cheap. At the same time it will restrict imports by making them costlier. The extent to which the imports will be restricted depends on the price elasticity of demand for imports. Restricting in essential imports of all varieties is welcome as it will help to reduce the current account deficit. But it will also raise the prices of imports which are inputs for exports and also those which accelerate industrial growth. But in this case the reduction of customs duties is necessary to hold down the market prices of these goods. The rate of Rs. 31.37 per dollar was an artificial rate maintained by the Reserve Bank intervention. If intervention is stopped the rupee will find its own level. This should not be construed as a case for a freely fluctuating rupee. This certainly is dangerous as it is bound to unleash speculative activity and cause a withdrawal of the foreign funds amounting to $ 20 billion in the vaults of the Reserve Bank of India. This will also render the capital account convertibility of the rupee at a future date dangerous. It is expected that the rupee in a free market will settle down at a rate between Rs. 31.37 and Rs. 33.00. This is tolerable and needs to be allowed. India cannot remain in isolation from the international community. It has to be integrated with the world economy and this calls for withdrawing Reserve Bank support from the rupee in the foreign exchange market. This step will help India's trade to grow at a rate higher than the one witnessed at present.

It is universally acknowledged that the reduction of fiscal deficit is necessary to reduce the rate of inflation and to strengthen the rupee. The present slide in the rupee is due partly to the rise in the inflation rate and partly to the excess demand for dollars caused by the purchase of dollars by the State Bank of India and the Oil Corporation of India and by the need to meet external debt obligations. When excess demand for dollars is stemmed the rupee will recover and provide a stimulus to India's trade. This calls for imposing a constitutional limit on external borrowing. The Present quantum of external debt of the order of $ 95 billion is too burden some for the economy. There is a strong case for reducing it to manageable levels.

A large part of the external debt is of the short-term variety. This calls for frequent repayments as and when repayments fall due and they fall due at frequent intervals. The need to repay the debt calls for fresh borrowing. This can be solved by converting short-term debt into long-term debt. Though the long term debt carries a higher rate of interest this is welcome for this saves the botheration and anxiety of frequent repayments. If the debt is of the long-term variety this anxiety will not be there. India can keep the foreign exchange and use it to repay debt when repayment falls due and repayment does not fall frequently. The high interest rate imposes a higher cost but this is the price India has to pay for freedom of manoeuvre.

Fiscal deficit has to be reduced in order to save India from inflation and balance of payments crises. There are two methods of financing the fiscal deficit: monetary financing and debt financing. The Government in recent months has shifted from monetary financing to debt financing. It is true that both types of financing are inflationary but debt financing is more inflationary than monetary financing. While monetary financing results in a rise in the price level in the same proportion as the rise in money supply debt financing which causes a rise in the interest cost expands the fiscal deficit by the amount of the interest payment and generates inflation. So long as the debt remains unrepaid the interest payments have to be made and they add to the fiscal deficit every year causing the inflation rate to rise. Seen in this perspective the recent shift to debt financing is more inflationary than the earlier monetary financing of the deficit. This calls for a return to monetary financing of the fiscal deficit which is less inflationary than debt financing. At the same time there is need to change the maturity structure of the public debt. It is a familiar proposition in monetary theory that short-term debt which has a high degree of liquidity is more inflationary than long-term debt which is less liquid and so less inflationary. It is true that long term debt which carries a higher rate of interest is costlier than short-term debt which carries a lower rate of interest. But the higher interest cost of long term debt is the price the country has to pay for a lower rate of inflation. Therefore, it is suggested that the composition of the debt should be changed in favour of long-term debt. These measures along with the measures to enhance the revenue buoyancy of the tax system will help to reduce the rate of inflation. A reduction of the inflation rate will enhance the competitiveness of India's exports in world markets, will help to promote India's exports and to reduce the current account deficit. These will have a salutary effect on the exchange value of the rupee.

The credit policy for the forthcoming busy season will be announced on September 29, 1995. This policy will have to take into account the increase in the requirements of borrowers in industry and trade and the need to borrow heavily by the Central and State Governments and other privileged institutions. However, with slower growth of deposits in the First five months of 1995-96 and a keen demand for funds from borrowers in different segments of the economy because of rising industrial production.

50

Stabilisation of Coffee Prices

"Coffee Cheers but does not inebriate" so goes the admiration for the cheering hot beverage. Coffee is popular throughout the world. Coffee enjoys the first preference and tea enjoys the second preference. But in recent years the coffee prices have been raising the eyebrows of the harassed consumers. What is ironical about the coffee prices is that when they ought to fall in the years of bumper harvest they have maintained an upward trend. Between January 1993 and January 1994 the average retail price of coffee witnessed a 14 percent rise. The current spurt in coffee prices has coincided with a regime of liberalised trade in coffee. The liberalised coffee trade regime has benefited the coffee growers who get better prices for the coffee they are directly marketing. The coffee growers point out that the spurt in coffee prices is the consequence of the poor harvest of coffee over a year ago when production was a poor 1.61 lakh tonnes as against the current year's production of 2.8 lakh tonnes. If poor coffee crop causes a rise in prices of coffee it follows that a bumper crop of coffee should cause a fall in coffee prices. But this has not happened.

Under the liberalisation of trade in coffee the domestic prices of coffee reflect the international prices. Earlier the Coffee Board and the private auctioneers followed the practice of holding separate auctions for domestic and export markets. At present this practice is discontinued. The single auction system has led to the elimination of price differences between international and domestic prices of coffee.

Before July 1993 the production of coffee had stagnated and the prices of coffee were falling. But since July 1993 the international prices of coffee have become buoyant. The coffee growers are of the view that with the arrival of South American Coffee the lean period comes to an end and the prices may ease. But this depends on the quantum of coffee arrivals. The quantum of arrivals is unlikely to be significant. The coffee growers in the other countries can hold back a large part of the coffee they grow under the retention scheme in order to keep the prices of coffee pegged at a high level. In view of this possibility, the expected fall in coffee prices may not materialise.

It is true that the higher auction prices in the liberalised trade regime have put pressure on the retail prices of coffee. But it is not certain that a fall in international prices would have a reverse effect on the retail price level. It is admitted by the growers that a slide in retail prices is a remote possibility. This is disheartening to the coffee consumers.

Another aspect of the price rise has to be taken into account. The growers of coffee were allowed to market a part of the coffee output. Under the internal sales system it was 30 percent; but under the new free sale quota system, this has been raised to 50 percent. But the quantity which the growers would like to keep would be much higher. It is believed that the Coffee Board would handle just 25 percent of the coffee produced or 50,000 tonnes out of the 2 lakh tonnes of coffee produced. This means that the Coffee Board would not be in a position to play the role of a stabiliser of prices and supply. The private sector will be in a position to influence both supply and prices of coffee. If the international prices of coffee are higher than the domestic prices, there will be a diversion of coffee output to the export market. In consequence, the domestic supply of coffee falls causing a rise in domestic prices. This is bound to hurt the domestic consumers of coffee. The coffee growers believe that there is no need to subsidise the price of coffee in the domestic market. The argument they advance against subsidy is that about 90 percent of the coffee growers in the country are small growers. If they are getting a higher value realisation for their produce it would mean that the consumers were so far being subsidised at the expense of the fair return to the small growers.

Whatever merit this argument may have, the fact remains that in the context of the rising rate of inflation the consumers are further burdened by the higher prices of coffee. With the continuing rise in prices the consumer is sure to be hard hit. The wholesale prices of coffee have come under pressure and therefore the trend of a continuing rise in prices is a certain possibility.

Coffee was an essential beverage till recently only in the urban and metropolitan centres. But in recent years it has deeply penetrated into the rural sector. There is practically no rural household where coffee is not prepared for family consumption. Furthermore the men folk who work outside go to restaurants for coffee. If the prices of coffee rise the family budgets of the households in the rural and urban sectors experience an expansion. The prices of coffee along with the prices of other essential food articles determine the cost-of-living index which govern wage determination in the industrial sector and in the rural employment sector. The wage rates rise around and this generates cost-push and demand-pull inflations. This demands the stabilisation of coffee prices. The Coffee Board has to play an important part as a stabiliser of coffee prices. The Board should hold sufficient stocks of coffee which could be released in the market in the event of a rise in coffee prices. Export of coffee, of course, results in larger forex reserves. The country has to choose between forex reserves and lower prices of coffee in the domestic market. As the reduction of the rate of inflation has to be given precedence over accumulation of foreign exchange reserves, the export of coffee has to be reduced and the stock of coffee has to be held by the Coffee Board.

51

Can a Strong Rupee Deliver Goods

One of the causes of the present inflationary surge in India is undoubtedly the persistent inflow of capital. The forex reserves in the vaults of the Reserve Bank of India have increased from $ 9.8 billion in March 1993 to more than $ 16.5 billion at the end of June 1994 and they are expected to keep rising till they reach between $ 25 and $ 30 billion by the end of the fiscal 1994-95. This situation, despite its inherently inflationary bias, appears to be comfortable seen in the context of the emergency assistance India obtained from the IMF in July 1991 to meet its foreign repayment obligations. This vast accumulation of forex reserves has caused a debate about whether the policy of intervention by the Reserve Bank of India to hold the rupee dollar exchange rate steady at Rs. 31.87 per US dollar. The justification for holding the rupee dollar exchange rate stable was that it would boost India's exports. But the trade data about the apparently poor performance of exports has given rise to the demand, for a review of the Reserve Bank policy of intervention.

It is the nature of the foreign exchange holdings that has given doubts about the utility of such a large volume of forex reserves. This accumulation is not due to export earnings considering the fact that the trade gap persists even now, though in a smaller dimension. It is not even due to the inflow of long-term foreign capital known as Foreign Direct Investment. These two sources of foreign exchange reserves are generally considered beneficial as the country's foreign currency spending places can be confidently based on them in the medium term. The cause for concern emanates from the fact that the bulk of forex reserves consists of capital raised by Indian companies abroad, portfolio investments by foreign institutional investors and NRI deposits. These deposits are highly volatile and they are likely to shift outside the country if they can get higher rate of return elsewhere. Indian companies are reported to have raised over $ 2.5 billion from the Euromoney market and have used this to retire debt within the country obtained earlier at higher rates of interest. Portfolio investments are estimated to be about $ 3 billion and they are confined to the capital market. They are liable to shift in the event of the rates of interest falling below those obtainable abroad. As for the NRI deposits, it is officially admitted that the higher interest rates offered to them have hardly benefited India. A large part of these deposits are shadow deposits kept in India to take advantage of the interest rate differential. The official policy is now to reduce this category of deposits by reducing the interest rate offered to them. In the light of this instability the present policy of official intervention in the forex market to keep the rupee dollar exchange rate stable has come in for criticism.

One of the grounds for criticism is the decline in exports below the target; at the same time, it is also held that imports have become expensive and that it would be unwise to pay higher prices for imported industrial raw materials. In view of this a strong case has been advanced against continuing the present policy of official intervention in the foreign exchange market and for letting the rupee take its own course depending on the supply demand relationships. This case is strengthened by the fact that the higher interest rate offered in India has not attracted the kind of funds that India needs to hold and to develop its industries. It is held that a stronger rupee may affect exports but this is only transitory. In fact, the case of the Japanese Yen and the German Mark has been cited to prove that the strength of these currencies has not priced the export of these countries out of world markets. In fact, it is held that the positions of these countries have become stronger. Furthermore, a stronger rupee would make imports cheaper and this would help to lower the domestic costs of industrial goods. On these grounds it is argued that the route through a stronger rupee is sustainable in the long run. This means that the present rupee-dollar exchange rate is depreciated and that policy should aim at appreciation of the Indian rupee by desisting from intervention in the foreign exchange market.

The fact that exports are flagging despite a depreciated rupee is the main ground for advocating an appreciation of the rupee. This requires an examination of India's export trends and performance vis-a-vis those of other countries in the Asian region. According to the figures released by the Commerce Ministry exports stood at $ 11,806.97 million during April-May 1992, went down to $ 10,832.08 million during the same period of 1993-94. The rate of growth of exports was thus 9.7 percent. In the context of the export growth of 20.37 percent in 1993-94 and the targeted growth rate of 25 percent for 1994-95 the 9.6 percent export growth rate achieved in April-May 1994 is disturbing. It is held that the devaluation of the rupee undertaken in July 1991 took care of the rising rate of inflation and the present stability of the rupee-dollar exchange rate is alleged to have affected the competitiveness of exports. If the rupee depreciates, it is easy to accommodate the rise in input cost but the rupee has remained stable and this has affected exports further.

It must be noted that the export growth in April-May 1994 has not really come down for it is compared to export growth which, during April-May 1993, was very high. This was due to the fact that large export shipments which could not clear the Indian shores during the first quarter of 1993 because of the communal riots and bomb blasts in Bombay came to be cleared in April-May 1993. It must be noted that the rupee-dollar exchange rate has not really affected the export growth. In the case of value added exports from imported goods the steady exchange rate is beneficial. If the rate depreciates, the cost of imports will go up generating pressure on the profit margin. Having regard to the fact that the export growth rate has been rather erratic in the last few years and fall in the export growth rate in April-May 1994 does not appear to be very relevant. For instance, exports grew by 9.4 percent in 1986-87, by 24 percent in 1987-88, by 15.6 percent in 1988-89, by 19 percent in 1989-90 and by 9 percent in 1990-91. During 1991-92 there was a negative growth of 1.5 percent. In 1992-93 there was only a marginal positive growth and in 1993-94 the growth rate was 20.37 percent.

It is admitted that India's exports should grow at a faster rate than at present. India's share in world trade was about 0.5 percent during 1989-91. The other Asian countries have done well in world trade. China's Share was 1.6 percent, South Korea's 2.2 percent, Malaysia's 1 percent, Taiwan's 2 percent, Singapore's 1.8 percent and Indonesia's 1.5 percent. Other figures are interesting. India's exports were 8.2 percent of GDP in 1993-94. It had never been more than 7 percent during the period since Independence, compared with this, China's exports constitute 13 percent of GDP. In 1991-92 China's exports were of the value of $ 72 billion against India's $ 17.8 billion. In 1993-94 India's exports totalled $ 22.17 billion while China's exports were $ 91.3 billion.

There are several hurdles India has to face in her export promotion efforts; inadequate infrastructural facilities, high local taxes and the persistence of recession in the USA, the EC countries and Japan, the resistance to imports from the non-member countries by the regional trade blocs, emphasis on eco-friendly goods and observance of certain human rights conditions. These factors are more important for export promotion than mere price and quality competitiveness of export goods. Also important is the stability of the policy regime.

Quite apart from these essential pre-requisites for export growth the impact of the exchange rate should also be taken into account. In the year following the devaluation of the rupee in July 1991 exports registered a steady growth. Infact, the declining trend in the Indian export scenario evident since the 1990s has been reversed and during 1993-94 it reached $ 22.17 billion exceeding the target of $ 22.13 billion. The performance registered a dollar growth of 20.37 percent against the 1992-93 performance when the total exports value was $ 18.4 billion. This reversal has been attributed to the Government's new export-import policy (1992-97) which deregulated licensing and quantitative restrictions and regulatory and discretionary controls. In fact, in the years ahead, exports are expected to grow further.

In view of this, the cases for appreciating the rupee exchange rate against the US dollar loses its relevance. The averment that a stronger Japanese Yen and stronger German Mark have not caused the exports of these countries to be priced out of international markets does not hold good for India. It must be understood that what is good for the goose is not necessarily good for the gander. A stronger rupee will make exports more expensive and imports cheaper causing a fall in exports and a surge of imports. It is not just the industrial raw materials that become cheaper in the regime of an appreciated rupee but all goods and all varieties of goods including consumer goods. In a regime of liberalised trade they cannot be kept out by means of import restrictions. In consequence, the current account deficit will be bigger. Devaluation of the rupee would have been more effective in promoting exports and reducing imports if the fiscal deficit was maintained at the targeted level, the rate of inflation had remained at the single digit level and if the wages and salaries had remained constant. The rise of all these variables reduced the effectiveness of devaluation in promoting exports. This cannot be a case for appreciation of the rupee dollar exchange rate. If anything, the case for maintaining stability in the exchange rate is stronger than even before. Appreciation is not the remedy for trade imbalance; infact, it makes it worse.

52

Fears about a "Dollar Trap" Unfounded: Adequate Dollars can be Mobilised to Overcome Dollar Shortage

India's balance of payments has remained a source of concern since 1956 when the Second Five Year Plan was inaugurated. What the successive Governments did was to adopt adhoc measures of alleviating the crisis situations. One of them was to take resource to the assistance from the international financial institutions leading to the accumulation of external debt which in turn, has contributed to the balance of payments problem. In the context of the dip in the foreign exchange reserves from $ 20.8 billion to less than $ 17 billion at present and the impending dip further and the slide in the exchange value of the rupee there is the accentuation of the apprehension of a balance of payments crisis in 1996. The seriousness or otherwise of this apprehension needs to be examined.

In 1987-88 Michael Camdessns, Managing Director of the IMF, was ready to offer to India a safety net of around $ 2 billion. His officials had forecast serious balance of payments problems for India. Most Indian economists and officials also agreed with the forecast. But political sensitivities generated resistance to the safety net. Perhaps, such a safety net, if it was accepted, might have mitigated the severity of the 1990-91 crisis. The IMF is an institution which the politicians and bureaucrats in the developing world dislike though they need it. The senior officials of the African nations oppose IMF intervention but, at the same time, they welcome it albeit with reluctance. While they oppose interference, they feel that without the IMF they cannot keep their profligate Governments in check. Indian politicians and bureaucrats always felt superior that they did not need IMF conditionalities. But tables were soon turned when the crisis of 1991 broke out. Even after the Government obtained the structural adjustment facilities agreeing to abide by the conditionality prescriptions "suggested" by the IMF the opposition political parties in the parliament characterised this as a "sell out" to multinational financial institutions refusing to realise what a grave predicament the country would have been in without the IMF assistance.

At present the forex reserves stand at $ 17 billion. The Government is spending between $ 1.0 billion and $ 1.2 billion every month to hold the external value of the rupee stable. If the dollars are spent at this rate, by June 1996 when the new Government will be in office, the outflow would cross $ 7 billion. Even if there is no other outflow caused by any other reason India's forex reserves would fall to $ 10 billion. Of this $ 10 billion, $ 7 billion consist of foreign institutional investment funds. Their stability cannot be taken for granted. They can come under pressure unless a stable Government takes office in June 1996. This may cause a flight of capital. This is predicted on several assumptions: viz; there will be no inflow of capital and there will be political uncertainty after the general elections. Even though there is no cause for concern on account of these assumptions Indian policy makers need to be alert to the seriousness of the problem. Having experienced a severe balance of payments crisis in 1991 the Government needs to take every possible precaution against such a scenario reemerging in the middle of 1996, unless preventive measures are taken the rupee may have to undergo a drastic depreciation by the middle of 1996.

What has been the behaviour of forex reserves? In the recent past the forex reserves went up at a steady rate and created concerns about inflation management because of the monetary impact of capital inflows. The document prepared by the IMF lists out the sequence of events in the early 1990s. Prior to 1991 capital inflows were mainly aid flows, commercial borrowings and NRI deposits. Foreign direct investment averaged a mere $ 220 million a year on the average over the period 1985-91. In 1991 when a more open approach to foreign investment was adopted under the economic reform programme, the scenario changed for the better. In the first place, the Government made automatic approvals for direct investment participation upto 51 percent in priority areas and it also liberalised the criteria for general foreign investment approvals. In the second place, it was announced in February 1992 that the Indian firms with good record would be permitted to raise funds through equity and convertible bond issues in foreign markets. In September 1992 registered foreign institutional investors were allowed to purchase both equity and debt securities directly on local markets. In the third place in the 1993 budget several incentives were announced to encourage the inflow of these funds further. They were that the tax on interest and divided income on FII holdings was set at 20 percent while the capital gains tax was set at 30 percent on investment held for less than one year and 10 percent in the case of holding of over one year. This acted as a lock-in period. According to the IMF, after an initial delay, the response to these liberalisation measures was strong. Total foreign direct and portfolio investment rose from $ 148 million in 1991-92 and $ 585 million in 1992-93 to $ 5.1 billion in 1993-94. There was some slowdown in November 1994. Even so that total inflow during the year 1994-95 reached $ 4.8 billion. There was a similar response in respect of GDR issues. In 1992-93 the total GDR inflow was $ 241 million despite the restraining influence of the stock scam of 1992. In 1993-94 GDR issues and foreign currency convertible bond issues totaling $ 1.0 billion were floated. During the first eight months of 1994-95, 25 GDR issues raised $ 1.8 billion while the two floating rate note issues raised $ 300 million. However, the demand for the Indian GDRs weekend even before the Mexican crisis of mid-December 1994 due mainly to the unsettled conditions in the international financial markets. The new GDR issues came out at high discounts. Due to market situation a number of issues were cancelled. Foreign direct investment rose to $ 344 million in 1992-93, to $ 620 million in 1993-94 and to 1.3 billion in 1994-95. The actual inflow of $ 1.3 billion was smaller than the approved investments of $ 6 billion between August 1991 and March 1995.

In contrast to this build up there has been a steady decline in forex reserves since April 1995 on account of various trends in the economy like the telecom imbroglio which cautioned the foreign investor to wait till the political dust settles down, the mismatch between exports and imports necessitating the utilisation of dollars to pay for the trade deficit and the holding back of repatriation of export earnings and the consequent depreciation of the rupee though the last one is disputed by the Finance Ministry.

Since the middle of 1993 there was a massive inflow of capital into India. This held out the threat of the rupee being appreciated in terms of the dollar. Any appreciation would have adverse consequences on the current account of the balance of payments by increasing imports by making them cheap and by reducing exports by making them costly. In order to avert this danger the Reserve Bank of India began to intervene in the foreign exchange market by buying the inflowing dollars in order to hold the exchange rate stable at Rs. 31.37 per US dollar. But in the later part of 1995 there was an excess demand for dollars and the rupees were in excess supply. This led to a depreciation of the rupee. Initially the Reserve Bank of India allowed the rupee to depreciate. The Finance Secretary emphatically brushed as idle any threat to the rupee. The Governor of the Reserve Bank of India stated that the depreciation of the rupee represented a technical correction to the inflation differential between India and the other countries with which India had treading relations and that the depreciation need not cause any worry. The Finance Minister stated that the depreciation of the rupee was market ordained and the market forces were allowed to determine the exchange rate and as soon as the exchange rate reaches its true value the rupee would stabilise itself in the currency markets. But when the rupee began to slide further the Reserve Bank of India was compelled to intervene to hold the rupee stable by supplying the dollars in great demand. The slide of the rupee was checked from October 30 onwards through a series of interventions including the pumping of precious dollars from the stock of forex reserves. The Reserve Bank announced a series of measures on October 30, 1995 to stabilise the rupee level. But the impending elections have made the task of rupee management difficult. If the foreign inflow was forthcoming as scheduled the

Reserve Bank would have had no difficulty in propping up the rupee by paying out dollars at the rate of $ 1.0 billion per month for some time but it is feared that period would be more than six months in which case there will be a depletion of reserves. The currency market experts point out that the purchase and sale of foreign exchange reserves is the main method of managing the exchange rate. But there are two reasons why this should be done with great caution. In the first place, selling of reserves means withdrawal of liquidity from the market. If this happens, the shortage of liquidity in the market raises the interest rates further. This would impede growth and the pace of industrial recovery. In the second place a large withdrawal of reserves in a span of six months would lead to a loss of confidence in the stability of the rupee. The Government has to manage the rupee without occasioning a large depreciation in the election year. A slow depreciation can be allowed without triggering volatility. But this entails the danger of risking the image of the Government.

The forex reserves are expected to decline to $ 7 billion by June 1996 when the new Government will be in office. Some pessimists pictured the "worst case scenario" and have gone on to paint a Mexico-like situation where the declining reserves would lead to panic withdrawal of foreign institutional investment and even NRI deposits resulting in another balance of payments crisis by the middle of 1996. But there are enough indication to show that the Mexico-type situation is unlikely to take place in India a situation where the Mexican Peso collapsed leading to the shaking of investor confidence and the consequent capital flight.

An objective analysis of the problem confirms the unlikelihood of the emergence of a "dollar trap" and a balance of payments crisis. This for the following reasons:

1. The Reserve Bank of India has been making purchases of dollars since November 1, 1995 and did not allow the depletion of forex reserves though it intervened occasionally.
2. There are expectations of fresh inflows of reserves in the coming months as the committed foreign aid for specific projects had matured and disbursements for $ 300 million were expected soon and the installments of the Asian Development Bank loan

for the petroleum sector and those of the World Bank loan for the financial sector were due towards the end of December and they would be of the order of $ 200-300 million.

3. Foreign institutional investments are positive on balance and they indicate fresh inflows.
4. Companies floating Euro Issues are allowed to freely remit funds into the country in anticipation of the use of funds for approved and uses; companies are allowed to raise funds from Euro Issues without having to show three-year good track record; the Euro Issue scheme has been extended to include Foreign Currency Convertible Bonds (FCCBs) and a part of the approved GDR can now be raised through FCCBs. All these provisions relating to GDR issues will lead to a substantial inflow of forex reserves.
5. The inflow of foreign direct investment has become slow and sluggish. Whatever foreign direct investment has taken place is in the areas of telecommunications and some consumer goods for the relatively affluent sections of society. It is feared that this does not add to the productive capacity of the country and, in consequence, the country's dependence on imports will increase and will mount pressure on the country's balance of payments. But the World Investment Report, prepared by the United Nations Conference on Trade and Development (UNCTAD) states that in future foreign direct investment will rise leading to acceleration of the globalisation process and, as a result, foreign direct investment will be increasingly prominent on the agendas of international policy makers. The World Investment Report outlines the measures to be adopted to accelerate the inflow of foreign direct investment. If they are adopted there will be a substantial inflow of foreign investment.

All these factors underline the unlikelihood of a collapse of the forex reserves. The depreciation of the rupee in September-November was the market-ordained correction of the inflation differential in India vis-a-vis the competing countries in the global markets, so as to maintain the competitiveness of India's exports. In fact, of late, the Reserve Bank of India has begun to purchase dollars and in consequence there has been no net depletion of forex reserves. It is true that at present imports are increasing. At the same time there is a substantial export growth as well. In consequence, exports can cover 90 percent of imports. The trade deficit has started narrowing while the inflow on invisible account is positive. Due to these factors the current account deficit is expected to be around 1-5 percent of GDP which is sustainable. All these factors confirm the continued strength of the balance of payments and rule out the possibility of a balance of payments crisis.

The pessimists fear a liquidity crisis as well as they argue that the sale of reserves amounts to withdrawal of liquidity from the market which might raise the interest rates further and this would dampen growth and industrial recovery. But the perception of the Indian Investment Strategy Report of November 23, 1995 prepared by Lehman Brothers, an international investment bank is different. It has predicted an increase in liquidity in the short-term for the Indian financial system as the Government tries to achieve its growth targets. This is expected to be accomplished by lower loan-to-deposit ratio. It attributes market movements primarily to liquidity in the financial system over the past two years and it expects the sentiment factor to be significant in determining short-term volatility. It has, therefore, listed liquidity and equity market sentiments as the main concerns in determining longer-term portfolio decisions. The equity market sentiment is expected to improve after the general elections early in 1990. Lehman Brothers has recommended a neutral stance for investors through the first quarter of 1996 with an emphasis on cautious stock selection in anticipation of a market upturn in the second quarter of 1996. The market is expected to reach the 3,650-3,850 level on the Bombay Sensitive Index by December 1996 due to the high negative correlation between loan-to-deposit ratios and market movements. These suggest that with the increased liquidity in the financial system and consequent decline in the loan-to-deposit ratio the stock market should benefit.

The behaviour of the rupee vis-a-vis the US dollar and other major currencies lately gives room for the impression that the rupee-dollar rate may get stabilised around Rs. 35 rather than Rs. 34.50.

For its part the dollar has not been strengthening significantly after the recent recovery against the Yen and D-Mark. The Reserve Bank has not been intervening in a big way of late and it is being speculated whether there will be a further weakening of the rupee and those having to honour the commitments towards interest charges and repayments against foreign currency loans will have to cover their requirements even with payment of a fairly high premium. The Governor of the Reserve Bank of India has pointed out that the decline in inflows on account of FIIs and GDR issues will be partly offset by larger direct investment of $ 1.97 billion in the current year and there may also be additions to the NRIU deposits. If the trade deficit is eliminated in the first quarter of 1996 it will be possible to proceed with greater confidence especially.

The economy has been performing satisfactorily and the GDP may be rising by 6.2 percent in 1995-96. Merrill Lynch investment bankers have predicted that India will register a fast growth in 1996-97. As the rupee has depreciated drastically it needs to be examined how there can be corrections of the undervalued currency in particular directions after various uncertainties are out of the way. The depreciation of the rupee since June 1991 has been pronounced and it is not justifiable to maintain that the pronounced drop in two months is due to the appreciation of the US dollar against other currencies.

During the past 50 months the rupee has dropped against the dollar by 34.3 percent, against the pound sterling by 27.7 percent, against the D-Mark by 44.5 percent against the Swiss franc by 47.1 percent, against Yen and Singapore dollar by 47.1 percent, against the French franc by 43.9 percent. In a little over 10 weeks the cumulative drop in rupee is 40.2 percent, sterling 33.3 percent, D-Mark 50.2 percent, Swiss franc 53.4 percent, Yen 55.9 percent and Singapore dollar 51.9 percent. The dollar Yen rate was 138.13 on May 31, 1991 and Rs. 9,745 on September 4, 1995 or a drop of 29.4 percent. It was around 101.96 on December 18 or a drop of 26.2 percent. This means that the rupee has lost ground against all currencies mainly due to recent developments. But this down trend needs to be arrested in the manner outlined below. The primary step to be taken is the reduction of the rate of inflation.

One of the factors that is cited by the pessimists is the high rate of inflation and the large fiscal deficits. Inflation, said the Finance Minister in Parliament recently would be brought down in a few weeks time. He had earlier assured the World Economic Forum gathering that the fiscal deficit a strong source of inflation and other imbalances in the economy, would be effectively controlled. But inflation has come down to 7.3 percent on December 20, 1995, but the fiscal deficit is in the neighbourhood of 6.5 percent of GDP. The recent survey by the IMF (September, 1995) of its experiences with conditionality shows that the IMF programmes in recent cases do emphasize the impact of adjustment on the poor and the need to mitigate it. The reviewers admit that initiative for mitigation of poverty seem to have outstripped resources. Such actions include "subsidies", price controls on essential goods and services and enhanced social spending". It is this that has helped to sustain the fiscal deficit at 6.5 percent of GDP though it needs to be brought down to not more than 3 percent to GDP as promised to the IMF by the Finance Minister in his first letter to it seeking a structural adjustment loan. But political compulsions have come in the way.

Certain political parties hold the spectre of a Mexican-type crisis occurring in India though international experts visiting India deny any similarity between the Mexican crisis and the problems India is facing today. The Mexican crisis happened on December 20, 1994. In Mexico since December 1994 GDP growth rate is falling and the interest rates are sky-rocketting. Unemployment is on the rise and many businesses have collapsed under heavy losses. The rescue package of $ 50 billion has failed to restore the health of the Mexican economy or the confidence of the foreign investors. High interest rates have left the foreign investors happy but high interest rates have retorted industrial growth and economic recovery. The Peso reached new lows recently and the worst is not yet over. But as compared to Mexico in 1994 India's forex reserves are at $ 17 billion and more is to flow in. At the same time India's external debt during the past four years has grown: from $ 82 billion in 1990-91 to 1997-99 billion at present. It is pointed out that most of it is on concessional terms and non short-term debt as in Mexico. Therefore, there is no danger of capital flight. The Government has decided not to go in for capital account convertibility and also it has not been borrowing abroad to finance current account deficit. Mexicos dollar-denominated Government bonds were the source of its troubles and the Government went on borrowing through these instruments when the current account deficit reached the unsustainable figure of 8 percent of GDP the overvalued Peso could not be sustained. When the Peso was devalued the foreign creditors wanted their dollars back. The reserves which stood at $ 24 billion in February 1994 fell at a fast rate: $ 3 billion in March, $ 8 billion in April, $ 4.5 billion in November and $ 6.5 billion in December. There was a balance of payments crisis. In contrast, India's forex reserves are comfortable. They were $ 20.8 billion in March 1995. But the rapid depletion of reserves since October 1995 has made several politicians conjure up the Mexican type crisis. The Reserve Bank of India had to use over $ 1 billion in a matter of four days to support the sliding rupee. The current account deficit is expected to $ 5 billion in 1995-96. The net capital inflows are expected to reach $ 3.7 billion. The rate of growth exports is expected to be 13 percent in contrast to the projected import growth rate of 17 percent. The total exports are expected to be of the value of $ 31.2 billion the total imports are expected to be of the value of $ 35.2 billion. To complicate the matter the oil import bill is projected to rise Rs. 23,000 crore from Rs. 19,000 crore. But the investor confidence is at a low ebb because of the depressed stock market and the uncertainty of the post-election political scenario. They lost money when the rupee depreciated to Rs. 35 per dollar. This has caused a decline in the FII inflow recently. The total FII investment in October 1995 stood at $ 4 billion and NRI deposits stood at $ 10.1 billion. Thus out of a total forex reserve of $ 17 billion about $ 14 billion are "volatile" money. If this reserve stays well and good and if more capital flows in it would be better for by the end of June 1996, the Government has to make a payment of $ 3.9 billion. This will put pressure on the rupee. The World Bank is apprehensive about India being able to mobilise $ 40 million in the next four years in order to meet interest and debt repayments and the enhanced oil import bill.

There is the view that it is not so much the foreign investors who moved their capital outside Mexico but domestic investors. It is held that the foreign buyers are not guided by rumours and impressions unlike the domestic investors. The Mexican crisis was triggered by domestic players who were better informed about local developments and were quick to react to adverse news and rumours. According to statistics compiled by the IMF direct investment as well as purchases of Peso-denominated debt and equity by foreign investors in Mexico in 1994 amounted to $ 9 billion. Following the scare created by the devaluation of the Peso between November 30 and December 19, 1994 the net sales of foreign investors amounted to $ 326 million in debt securities while they had net purchases of equity. In the entire month of December 1994 the sales of equity and debt by foreign investors was $ 370 million. The foreign exchange reserves of Mexico fell from $ 6.7 billion to $ 1.7 billion suggesting that most of the out flows was caused by sales by Mexican investors. Foreign investors did not begin to sell large amounts of securities till February 1995 by which time the crisis had occurred. According to survey published recently by the *Economist* some players had access to inside information about the impending devaluation and had taken advantages of it. Clearly the hot money problem of Mexico was caused by its peculiar political system in which a single party ruled the roost for many years and their cronies derived undeserved benefits. Much of the volatility in capital markets was due to local factors which discouraged investment among long term foreign players.

The Reserve Bank of India and the Finance Ministry hold the view that current account deficit is under control during the past few years. In 1991-92 it was as high as 3.5 percent of GDP and in 1992-93 it fell to below one percent. This was aided by the import squeeze in operation at the time. Once the imports were relaxed in order to counter inflation the current account deficit rose to 1 percent and is expected to go up to 1.5 percent in 1995-96. In contrast Mexico had a current account deficit of 3 percent of GDP in 1991 and then it allowed the deficit to expand to over 8 percent of GDP by 1994 when the crisis hit the economy. Capital flight from India, if any, is no problem. In contrast to Mexico capital account convertibility of the rupee is not permitted and what could go out in panic is only foreign institutional investment. At present this investment is just 24 percent of reserves. Any pull out of this money need not cause a collapse of the reserves. But when the new Government takes over early in 1996 the inflow will increase. However, precautionary measures are the need of the hour not just because of any impending crisis but because the economy need to be stabilised.

This calls for accelerating industrial growth and export growth. The industrial growth is expected to be only 10 percent because of the liquidity crunch and the high interest rates. The fiscal deficit is high and the Government savings are zero. If the rupee depreciates the Reserve Bank will have to support it by selling dollars for rupees in which case there will be a liquidity shortage. Though the danger of this is not imminent, it is time to arrest any decline in industrial growth by easing the liquidity situation. The Government has to reduce its spending as the rupee needs to be bolstered by a low rate of inflation.

The example of Pakistan is revealing. It is pleased with the late November (1995) agreement with the International Monetary Fund on a $ 600 million stand-by loan. It has its eyes on a further loan under the Extended Structural Adjustment Facility of $ 1.5 billion programme begun in 1994 that stood suspended this year on the ground that Pakistan had failed to hit targets for reducing inflation and budget deficits. The Government set targets lower than those demanded by the IMF cutting the budget deficit from 5 percent of CDP for 1995-96 to 4.5 percent instead of 5.7 percent and reducing maximum tariffs from 70 percent to 65 percent compared with the IMF target of 45 percent.

This is not to suggest that India should adopt a "Killer Budget". But it is meant to highlight the imperative necessity of bringing the fiscal deficit to at least 5 percent of GDP from the present level of 6.5 percent of GDP. This calls for stopping the give aways under the populist programme put into effect in the election year. But political compulsions come in the way. However, after the elections, these political compulsions give way and enable the Government to reduce the populist programmes, the resultant fiscal deficit and the rate of inflation. These measures on the fiscal front combined with the inflow of foreign capital after the present political uncertainty has ended will strengthen the reserve position and render the rupee strong and stable making any apprehensions about a balance of payments crisis and a "dollar-trap" unnecessary psychological inhibitions.

There is another reason why the fears of a "dollar trap" and of a balance of payments crisis are grossly unfounded. According to a study made by the economists of the Florida University, the under-invoicing of exports and over-invoicing of imports by the Indian traders in 1993 resulted in the accumulation of about $ 4.5 billion on their account in the US banks. If in the two following years the same practice persisted the accumulation of dollars in the U S banks by the Indian traders in the aggregate would be around $ 14 billion. If these traders are directed to repatriate this amount of dollars to India, the dollar reserves which are $ 17 billion at present would swell to $ 31 billion. Furthermore, if the import of gold into India is barred there would be a saving of $ 6 billion. If this is added to the stock of forex reserves, they would rise to $ 37 billion. This will be in addition to the inflow of foreign institutional investment, foreign direct investment and NRI deposits. These calculations point to the non-existence of a "dollar trap" and rule out any balance of payments crisis. But, at the same time, all possible measures should be taken to hold down the fiscal deficit and the rate of inflation which are necessary to make the rupee strong and stable in currency markets. If the rate of inflation is brought down any technical correction of the exchange rate in terms of depreciation would be unnecessary.

The rupee touched a low of 35.14 December 27, 1995 and thanks to RBI intervention it was stored up to the level of Rs. 35.10 subsequently. The earlier depreciation of the rupee since September had to do with the launching of debt repayment and the large scale acquisition of dollars by the ONGC and the State Bank of India are an old story. But at present the rupee has come under pressure for several reasons. (a) During April-November 1995 the current account deficit has reached $ 3.29 billion. (b) net capital inflows upto September 1995 declined to $ 1.7 billion as compared to $ 3.1 billion during 1994, (c) market expectation of a further slide in the rupee has led to a parking of dollar proceeds abroad. (d) the unwillingness of the RBI to intervene in the market so long as the depreciation of the rupee does not go beyond the correction of its overvaluation. Though the rate of inflation has sunk below 7 percent the existing rate is higher than the rate prevailing in the USA, UK, Germany and Japan. This has relevance to the exchange rate. The question arises whether in view of the rise in the current account deficit to $ 4.5-5 billion and the net receipts on capital account expected to be less than $ 3 billion the rupee can be maintained at Rs. 35 per dollar. But considering the strong economic fundamentals the decline in the rupee is not warranted. Even so there is the likelihood of a slightly overheated demand for dollars. This might generate expectations of a further depreciation of the rupee. This could cause a capital flight causing a rise in the demand for dollars.

The question arises whether India should adopt a fixed exchange rate system or allow some flexibility in it. The days of fixed exchange rates are gone for good and a flexible exchange rate system will usher in instability and speculation. There is need to adopt an exchange rate target zone under the surveillance of the IMF. The present system has generated macro-economic and trade crisis including the recent currency crisis in Mexico and prolonged departure from the equilibrium exchange rate. These crises would have been averted had the countries adopted policies based on 'standard macroeconomic policy', namely, aiming at internal and external balance. Internal balance cannot be achieved only by monetary policy. Fiscal policy must be given a central place in the scheme of macroeconomic management. Maintaining external balance requires setting internationally consistent current account targets rather than letting the market decide it. The determination of a sustainable current account target would lead to the achievement of the exchange rate needed to achieve the current account target under conditions of fiscal balance. This would yield a fundamental equilibrium exchange rate and the Government should not allow the exchange rate to deviate from it. Expect outside the 10 percent of it either way. The authorities should prevent the exchange rate going beyond these target zones through sterilised intervention. This could be backed by changes in interest rates when such action is not necessary to the needs of the domestic economy. The authorities should not insist on hard margins around the target zones but there could be soft margins. The rate could be kept within the target zone as far as possible and to push it back to equilibrium. But the Government should not feel obliged to compromise monetary policy to the point of guaranteeing that the exchange rate would never go beyond the limits of the target zone. This requires multilateral surveillance of the policies of the country required to maintain internal and external balance. A stability of this nature in the exchange rate mechanism will assure the foreign investors that the exchange rate would not deviate normally from the target zone and would not cause any capital flight which has the potential for a currency crisis. This kind of exchange rate arrangement needs the support of the International Monetary Fund which should be empowered to engage itself in the task of enforcing the maintenance of internal and external balance. A proposal of this type has been made by John Williamson of the Washington based Institute of International Economics.

53

The Planning Commission on Devaluation of the Indian Rupee: The Case Rebutted

Finding that the real exchange rate of the rupee has appreciated quite significantly, the Planning Commission has revived the earlier aborted debate on a possible devaluation. In its midterm appraisal of the Eighth Five Year Plan, the Commission has underlined the inevitability of an active exchange rate policy by the Reserve Bank of India for two main reasons : (a) an effective exchange rate policy is the only direct intervention that the Government can undertake to promote exports over and above the present export growth rate of 18 percent; (b) if the real exchange rate of the rupee continues to appreciate, there is a real possibility of havala trade in foreign exchange re-emerging in a big way with consequent fall in official remittances. This would generate a balance of payments crisis.

The Planning Commission, in the context of the trade scenario, states that the policy options available to the Government today for raising or even maintaining the absolute level of profitability of exports beyond what is determined by market forces are much more limited than they were earlier. As part of the reform process, the Government gave up almost all discretionary export incentives leaving only the Special Import License (SIL) scheme which is likely to lose its incentive value with the progress of the import liberalisation regime. The Commission holds that as the import growth is of the order of 22 percent in 1994-95 export growth has to keep pace with it. "If the process continues for the next two years, India's import bill would be of the order of $ 42 billion by 1996-97. Even if exports continue to grow at the target rate of 18 percent per year, which in itself is quite optimistic, the trade deficit will rise from the current level of about $ 3 billion to $ 6 in 1996-97 which was level that prevailed in 1990-91. Exchange rate management again appears to be a major, if not the only available, instrument to forestall such a possibility". The Commission holds the view that the exchange rate grows beyond just trade issues. According to it, "One of the primary reasons for the low current account deficit during the past two years has been the spurt in the inward remittances which have gone up from the $ 2.5 billion level that had persisted for a long period to over $ 4 billion in 1994-95. This has been ascribed to a shift in remittances from the havala route to legal channels".

According to the Commission, the explanation for the spurt in remittances is to be found in the correction in the gross overvaluation of the rupee which existed in the past primarily through two devaluations in July 1991 and the subsequent shift to market determined exchange rate of the rupee. This correction led to a dramatic decline in the havala premium and the process was supported by the growing confidence in the strength of the Indian economy. In view of this, the Commission has warned that "if, however, the exchange rate gets misaligned, the havala premium may go up again and if expectation builds up for exchange rate depreciation, the flow of remittances may suffer a serious setback, putting substantial pressure on the current account balance".

The Commission holds that given the fact that the exchange rate management is central to the management of the external sector than ever before, though the Government has managed to maintain a constant parity between the rupee and the dollar through foreign exchange market intervention, the real exchange rate has appreciated quite significantly during the past two years and if this trend continues problems are likely to arise.

The latest trade figures appear to be supportive of the fears expressed by the Planning Commission. The spurt in imports during the first quarter of 1995-96 (April-June 1995) is a warning signal. Imports during these three months increased by 38 percent over the first quarter of 1994-95. This is 25 percent more than the projected growth rate for the current year. If the trade trends continue in this manner the foreign trade deficit will increase proportionately to \$ 5 billion which is one billion dollars more than the anticipated level. This huge increase in imports has taken place at a time when the country's exports have grown at 28 percent, 11 percentage points above the prescribed rate of 17 percent. Thus despite a commendable rise in exports the situation at the end of the first quarter is that the economy has been unable to manage its imports. Hence the trade deficit.

However, the increase in the trade deficit should not cause much worry as long as the inflow of foreign investments continues. The inflow has been strong enough this year to ensure that the balance of payments is not under too much pressure. Reports on investments by foreign financial institutions and the foreign direct investments show that they have been the highest since last year.

At present, the economy is becoming more dependent on imports. Recent studies suggest that the import intensity of exports i.e., the import content of exports has been increasing. This means that the country has to import more and more to keep its exports increasing. Devaluation of the rupee has the effect of raising the prices of these imports and the cost of production and the prices of these exports which contain imported inputs. The higher prices of exports reduce the volume of exports and undo the favourable effect, if any, of devaluation on exports.

In recent weeks the market has come to determine the exchange rate based on demand and supply of foreign exchange. In fact, intervention in the foreign exchange market by the Reserve Bank of India has come down drastically and the market is determining the rupee value. This has caused a slide in the value of the rupee. The rupee value of the US dollar crossed the Rs. 32 mark in the last week of August 1995 for the second time in recent months indicating a fairly consistent pressure with banks and financial institutions including the FIIs seeking to pick up large volumes of dollars for one reasons or the other. The assessment in the money market a few weeks ago that the Government would declare capital account convertibility of the rupee might have been one reason for the slide of the rupee but the substantive reasons for the pressure on the rupee are clearly the increasing trade deficit and the inflationary pressure which has reemerged at home. This situation is just the reverse of that which prevailed last year when the price line was relatively stable and India's trade performance was better despite the liberalisation of consumer goods imports. This caused a decline in the trade deficit in 1994-95. This resulted in a pressure on the dollar compelling the Reserve Bank of India to buy up dollars in the money market to keep up the demand for this currency and thereby tightly control the possible appreciation of the rupee against the US dollar.

This policy of the Reserve Bank of India had occasioned some controversy because not many agreed with the Bank's logic that an appreciation of the rupee would jeopardise export prospects by making them more expensive. What the Reserve Bank was doing was a minor devaluation by preventing an appreciation of the rupee through market intervention. In consequence, the true market value of the rupee could not be realised because of the Reserve Bank's dollar purchases. The impact of this action was short-term. The trade gap is widening this year despite a good export performance and this coupled with inflation is tending to push down the relative value of the rupee in the international markets. The question now is whether the Government should go in for an open devaluation to prop up exports and to make imports more expensive. The choices before the Government are not easy, especially since the inflationary pressures within the economy are bound to increase in consequence. Moreover the benefits of devaluation wear out beyond the short run so that the hard decisions on the export front will have to be faced all over again during 1996-97. The major imperative is to control inflation and to keep the exchange value of the rupee stable.

The rupee has depreciated by 1.38 percent during August 1995 recording an annual slide of 33.12 percent. This is due to the Reserve Bank of India abandoning its market intervention policy on the one side and the demand for dollars rising on the other. When the rupee began to fall against the dollar the reason given was the rise in the demand for dollar primarily from the State Bank of India on behalf of the Indian Oil Corporation and Oil and Natural Gas Commission, defence payments of the Government and lately from Diamond

Trading Corporation. The amount which the State Bank of India purchased from the market is roughly $ 1.75 billion in August. Even at the rate of Rs. 31.80 and around the State Bank of India is reported to have purchased dollars.

The Reserve Bank forex reserves fell drastically by $ 769 million in three weeks between July 29 and August 18. It is felt that $ 0.77 billion is a big fall in such a short time which was not seen in the recent past. This has raised the question: Did the Government buy dollars from the Reserve Bank in addition to buying them from the market. Only the Government can buy dollars from the Reserve Bank and major Government purchases are for repayment of external debt and payments for defence equipment. The FII inflow in July was $ 250 million. In August, it is expected not to go above this level. The sentiment is not bullish for the rupee.

On the forward market there is evidence of the rupee strengthening. The six month forward premium came down from 5.05 percent to around 4.75 percent. Exporters sold the dollars in the forward market bringing the forward premium down. Even the importers cancelled the forward contracts booked by them. When there is a rise in the supply of forward dollars, the forward premium has to come down. Now everything depends on the demand for dollars from the Government sector. If the Government purchases of dollars stop, it will go back to the earlier level. Even so, it might continue in the 31.60/31.65 range. When compared with the earlier rate of 31.37 per dollar this is a decline in the exchange value of the rupee indicating hidden devaluation.

The authorities have to choose between this hidden devaluation caused by depreciation of the rupee and devaluation proper. The implications of devaluation have been examined in the pages that follow and the case is made against it for the reasons elucidated there. This hidden devaluation, if moderate, can be allowed to remain to serve as a booster to exports. The rise in the prices of imports can be mitigated by reducing the customs duties. If the hidden devaluation is immoderate the foreign exchange reserves which are of the order of $ 19.5 billion can be used to purchase rupees in order to mitigate the slide.

The Planning Commission attributes the spurt in forex reserves to the shift in foreign remittances from the havala route to legal channels. This shift is attributed to the correction of the gross over valuation of the rupee that existed in the past to two devaluations undertaken in July 1991 and the subsequent shift to market-determined exchange rate of the rupee. This shift led to a decline in the havala premium. The Commission feels that in view of the present overvaluation of the rupee the havala market may become reactivated and the flow of remittances may shift from the legal channel to the havala route causing a reduction in the flow of remittances at a time when the reserves are necessary for the economy.

The main question is : What is the magnitude of forex reserves shifted to the havala route? If it is substantial it is no problem. At present the forex reserves are high and are rising though at a diminished rate. A country needs a certain minimum level of reserves to cover day-to-day fluctuations in external receipts and payments as well as to meet large unexpected needs for foreign exchange. However, when reserves rise far above this level and keep rising they create serious problems.

As is obvious, excess foreign reserves create inflationary pressures in the economy. They occasion rapid monetary growth. They also imply large lending to other countries. They represent a failure to use available resources though they are badly needed to accelerate economic growth. There are three ways in which the Government can deal with excess forex reserves. It can take measures to offset the expansionary monetary impact of these reserves. It can take external measures to moderate the pace of growth of these reserves. It can also take measures to increase the utilisation of these reserves for investment purposes.

The forex reserves can be used to increase investment in the economy. This generates the need for increased imports of machinery and equipment. It also requires the relaxation of current restrictions on consumer goods imports. These steps slow down the growth of forex reserves. It is necessary to remove the constraints which check or slow down investment. Relaxation of import restrictions on consumer goods results in increased imports which result in a trade deficit. But the increase in the domestic availability of consumer goods will also stem the inflationary pressures directly. For this reason, the relaxation of controls on consumer goods imports is justified. Furthermore, an increase in the imports of consumers goods increases competition for domestic producers producing similar goods. This induces the domestic producers to improve efficiency and quality. Despite liberalisation these industries are enjoying a great degree of protection. Liberalisation will enable India to produce and export new classes of sophisticated consumer goods. At present the stock of forex reserves is excessive and they have resulted in monetary growth feeding inflation. The purchase of the inflowing dollars by the Reserve Bank of India has helped to hold the exchange rate stable. This means that it has prevented the rupee from appreciating. The contention of the Planning Commission is that it has led to an overvaluation of the rupee. If, as the current thinking in the Finance Ministry runs, this leads to a shift of the inflow into the havala route, so much the better as this would reduce the rate of accumulation of forex reserves and would render the purchase of dollars by the Reserve Bank less necessary. This would check the degree of overvaluation of the rupee. The Government has rightly maintained that a theoretical devaluation of the rupee would be quite impractical as the market would determine the exchange rate based on demand and supply of foreign exchange. In fact, intervention by the Reserve Bank has come down quite drastically and the market is determining the rupee value. This renders the devaluation of the rupee unnecessary. The market determined exchange rate corrects the overvaluation resulting from market intervention and this automatically reduces the flow of foreign exchange through the havala route.

The Planning Commission holds the view that the low current account deficit is due to the inflow of remittances from abroad: "One of the primary reasons for the low current account deficits during the past two years has been the spurt in inward remittances... due to shift in remittances from the havala route to legal channels". There is no relation between the inward remittances and the current account deficit. The low current account deficit was due to factors other than the inward remittances. The current account deficit being given it might be financed by drawing on the forex reserves which increase due to inward remittances. But these remittances cannot by themselves cause a reduction in the current account deficits. The fall in current account deficits was due to the reduction in the fiscal deficits, the reduction in the rate of inflation and the growth of exports under the new EXIM Policy and the growing strength of the Indian economy. All that can be said is that the rising forex reserve caused by inward remittances, were used to meet the current account deficits.

The Commission holds the view that the real exchange rate has appreciated due to the maintenance of the constant parity between the rupee and the US dollar through exchange market intervention by the Reserve Bank of India. This appreciation in the view of the Commission, will further aggravate the balance of payments crisis due to the misalignment of the exchange rate. This statement was made before the Reserve Bank of India let the exchange rate be determined by the market forces. In actual fact, the rupee has slid in the exchange market and is sliding further to reach the purely market determined rate. Therefore, the question of misalignment of the exchange rate does not arise. The threatened appreciation of the exchange rate will not come about. The slide in the rupee in the foreign exchange market is sure to serve as an incentive to export growth, quite apart from other incentive schemes designed by the Government to promote exports. Therefore, the need for devaluation of the rupee does not arise.

Even so, it is necessary to examine the mode of operation of devaluation of the rupee of exports, imports and the balance of trade and the existence or otherwise of the conditions necessary for the success of devaluation as a remedy for the balance of payments deficit in India.

Devaluation, as a remedy for the balance of payments deficit, is undertaken in the context of a "fundamental disequilibrium" in the balance of payments as defined by the International Monetary Fund. The main task is to find out whether there is fundamental disequilibrium in the case of India's balance of payments. One indicative factor is the existence of inflation. At present the rate of inflation in India is 8.51 percent while it is 2.5-3 percent in Europe and the united States of America. There is thus price disparity and cost disparity as well. But given that the fundamental disequilibrium exists warranting devaluation, the next question is to consider whether the conditions necessary for the success of devaluation exist in India. They are:

1. The sum of the elasticities of import demand in each country is greater than unity; this is the celebrated Marshall Lerner condition;
2. The wage rates remain unchanged after devaluation;
3. The fiscal deficit remains constant after devaluation.

There are no precise estimates of elasticities of demand and supply of goods in the case of India to enable us to draw firm conclusions regarding the effects of devaluation on the trade balance. There was a considerable body of opinion in the years after 1945 that depreciation should be avoided as the elasticities were so low that the balance of payments would not be helped much. This general opinion was dubbed "elasticity pessimism". This was a strong element in the negative reaction to devaluation. However, there is a school of thought that rejects the elasticity pessimism argument against devaluation. It is held that long run elasticities are higher than short-run elasticities so that devaluation which seems to have little impact in the short run, may turn out to have a great effect on the balance of payments a few years later. Another point against elasticity pessimism is that although statistical measures of elasticities based on price and quantity trends over a period of several years typically show that elasticities of demand either for total imports or for individual commodities are quite low, of the less than 1 in absolute value, various downward biases in the statistical techniques make it plausible that as a matter of fact the elasticities are fairly high.

There are in general terms : There are no precise estimates of elasticities for imports in the aggregate or of individual commodities. For this reason no precise conclusions can be drawn about the impact of devaluation on imports and exports. It is a fair presumption that the elasticity conditions are not favourable. Even if they are found to be favourable, the ultimate effect of devaluation on the trade balance depends on the other two conditions.

Can wage rates be kept constant? On account of the ongoing inflation the cost of living is rising. This engenders demands for higher wages and higher dearness allowances. The demand for higher wages in all the sectors of the economy is strong and insistent. The workers go on strikes of their demand for higher wages and higher dearness allowances is not met. If higher wages are granted it generates cost-push and demand-pull inflations which combine to push up the rate of inflation. It becomes difficult to disentangle the two inflations. Higher wages mean higher spending; at the same time higher wages mean higher cost of production. These two push up the rate of inflation and offset any favourable impact devaluation may have on the trade balance. The Fifth Pay Commission award injects income to the income stream and weakens the effectiveness of Marshal-Lerner conditions.

The fiscal deficit is not constant. The actual fiscal deficit is far larger than the targeted fiscal deficit. This is due to subsidies of all varieties, the expenditure on the Prime Minister's welfare package and enhanced social sector spending. These factors help to inject income to the income stream and add to aggregate demand. A rise in aggregate demand causes a rise in imports, a decline in exports and a further deterioration of the trade balance. Thus, even if the long run elasticities are found to be favourable their effect on the trade balance will more than offset the favourable effect, if any, in the long run. In the short run one has to encounter the "J-Curve Effect" which causes a deterioration of the trade balance only to improve it in the long run. This on the assumption that the conditions (b) and (c) are favourable. But the wage rate and the fiscal deficit cannot be held constant under the conditions prevailing in India. Thus, in the short run, the "J-Curve Effect" militates against any improvement in the balance of payments and in the long run the wage escalation and burgeoning fiscal deficits do the same. Therefore, devaluation is unlikely to have a favourable effect on the trade balance. At the same time it will increase the burden of external debt and of its serving in proportion to the degree of devaluation.

The two-stage devaluation of the rupee in July 1991 increased the country's debt servicing payments by 33 percent each year. This is exclusive of the service charges payable to the IMF on drawals made under the Stand-by Arrangement and Compensatory and Contingency Financing Facility. The Controller and Auditor General (CAG) in his report 1 of 1992 on "Union government Civil" pointed out that the annual debt service payments were expected to comply 71 percent from Rs. 7,627 crore in 1989-90 to Rs. 11,476 crore in 1995-96 at the rate of exchange prevailing at the end of March 1991. The total debt service payments for 1995-96 at the exchange rate on 8.7.1991 (after devaluation) was estimated at Rs. 15,239 crore marking an increase of 127 percent over 1989-90. The report said: "The downward adjustments of exchange rates in July 1991 have increased the projected debt service payments by nearly 33 percent per year". At that time the country's cumulative external debt amounted to Rs. 1,00,425 crore (1990-91). The debt servicing during 1989-90 required funds in excess of the foreign exchange reserves i.e., 135.4 percent of the reserves. At present the amount of external debt is $ 92 billion ie., Rs. 2,88,300 crore and the service charges will also rise in the same proportion. If the rupee is devalued by 10 percent the burden of debt will rise by 28,830 crore. This is a burden which the country is unable to bear given the current account deficit. This also points to the inadvisability of devaluation of the rupee at present.

Devaluation also has the effect of causing a deterioration of the terms of trade. According to Joan Robinson, the terms of trade deteriorate if the product of the supply elasticities exceeds the product of the demand elasticities. According to Harry Johnson when the terms of trade deteriorate income will be less than output for a larger amount of domestic output has to be surrendered in exchange for a given amount of imports. This causes a fall in domestic income. All these complications can be avoided and devaluation can be made effective by reducing domestic absorption. This will reduce the demand for imports and increase exports and helps to improve the trade balance by assisting the effects of devaluation. This is conditional of keeping the wage rates and the fiscal deficit constant. But, at the present juncture, they cannot be held constant. Therefore, they serve as reversal factors offsetting any favourable effect devaluation may have on the trade balance even assuming that the Marshall-Lerner condition is satisfied. In view of this it can be concluded that devaluation fails to improve the trade balance or to improve the terms of trade. Infact, by raising the prices of imports, it will give a further fillip to the ongoing inflation rate which adversely affects export growth. There is another way in which it adversely affects export growth. About 45 percent of imports consist of inputs for exports. If, following devaluation, their prices rise, the cost of production export goods rises causing a rise in export prices. This offsets any price advantage which devaluation may confer on exports. All these factors go to show that devaluation is not the right remedy for a deficit in the balance of payments at present. The right remedy is the reduction in absorption which is not possible on the eve of the general election. But absorption can be sought to be reduced through a tight monetary policy and reduction of the rate of monetary growth from the present 20 percent to the targeted 15 percent or even less. Devaluation is a text book remedy for a deficit in the balance of payments but a close examination of all the ramifications of devaluation on the macro-economic fundamentals of the economy at present should warn us against any dash to devaluation.

At present the rupee is sliding in relation to the US dollar because of the widening trade gap. The Reserve Bank of India has allowed the market forces to determine the exchange rate. In a regime of floating exchange rates the deterioration of the current account of the balance of payments will lead to a depreciation of the rupee. But this depreciation in a regime of floating exchange rates may not exercise a self-correcting influence. When the economy is globalised a depreciating rupee may inflict more harm through cost-push inflation than promote exports through enhanced price competitiveness for exporters. However a deterioration of the current account of the balance of payments need not necessarily cause a depreciation of the rupee. The capital account can offset the current account deficit if the authorities allow it. At present the indications are that the inflows of direct foreign investment as well as portfolio funds would be at a lower level as compared to 1994-95. The estimates of capital flows made by the CMIE are that they would be $ 1.8 billion through GDR and FII and that the overall balance of payments surplus would be of the order $ 3.5 billion. These estimates can be dismissed as unrealistic. These estimates assume that direct foreign investment which was $ 700 million in 1994-95 would rise to $ 2 billion in 1995-96. The scrapping of the Enron contract and the political uncertainties created by the pre-election atmosphere are likely to dampen the inflow of FDI funds. In April-May 1995 the inflow on GDR account has declined to $ 86 million compared to $ 230 million during the corresponding period of 1994-95. FII inflows have also diminished in recent months from $ 422 million (net) in April-May 1994 $ 123 million in April-May 1995.

If the current account deficit reaches $ 3 billion and more and if capital inflows are not enough to meet this deficit and to service the external debt, estimated at $ 8 billion the rupee will suffer a depreciation. As the forex reserves at the vaults of the Reserve Bank of India are of the order of $ 19.5 billion (at the end of July 1995) the Reserve Bank of India can intervene in the market by selling dollars to prevent a slide in the rupee. The prevention of the slide of the rupee may have an adverse impact on export growth. What is to be done under the circumstances is left to the wisdom of the authorities the Reserve Bank of India and the Finance Ministry. If the slide is moderate it can be allowed to stay there without market intervention. But if the slide is considerable the Reserve Bank of India will do well to intervene in the market, sell dollars and return the rupee exchange rate to the old level of Rs. 31.37 - $ 1. This will prevent a rise in import prices caused by depreciation. If the depreciation is moderate it can be allowed to serve as a booster to exports. The rise in the prices of imports can be mitigated by a reduction in customs duties.

The US dollar moved in narrow ranges against all the major currencies on the international foreign exchanges markets in the later half of August 1995. On the domestic front the rupee fell sharply in dollar terms though the forward premia remained steady. The rupee fell to a low of Rs. 31.98 per $ before ending the month of August at Rs. 31.84 per $. The demand pressures which had commenced in mid-August failed to abate probably due to holidays in various centres. The movement in the rupee-dollar rate has been around 2 percent. This may seem high in relation to the remarkable stability of the exchange rate over the preceding two years, but on the international markets such a degree of volatility is hardly rare. Indeed, over the past one month—August 1995 the dollar's gains vis-a-vis the Japanese Yen, the German Mark and the British Pound have been much more than its gains against the rupee. Interestingly, the forward premia have not flared up despite the rupee's weakness indicating that corporates with payables continue to wait and watch in the hope that the weakness of the rupee is only temporary. In view of this undue anxiety about the future rupee-dollar exchange rate is overly exaggerated.

The question that is uppermost in the minds of the authorities at present is whether the rupee will hold against the US dollar in 1995-96. In 1994-95 and before there were apprehensions in the minds of the authorities that the rupee would appreciate against the US dollar because of the large inflows of foreign investments, particularly in the portfolio segment. But, at present the indications are that the rupee is persistently weakening against the dollar. At the beginning of the financial year 1995-96 the rupee-dollar exchange rate was Rs. 31.37 = $ 1.0. This was sustained for over three years by the Reserve Bank of India standing ready to purchase the incoming dollars in order to prevent the appreciation of the rupee which would have adverse consequences on exports. But in recent weeks the dollar has tended to appreciate. At present the rate has been hovering at Rs. 31.85/31.90 per US dollar. This is due to the widening of the trade deficit without there being any dramatic turn around in 'invisibles' particularly tourism insight. This suggests that the current account deficit may increase causing a further slide of the rupee against the US dollar. However, this can be abated by drawing on the forex reserves to pay for the deficit. As the slide in the rupee is temporary, the devaluation of the rupee is considered unnecessary.

The Planning Commission suggests devaluation of the rupee in order to correct the present overvaluation which has the effect of making the inflow of foreign funds shift from the legal channels to the havala route and to promote exports. This they call "the effective exchange rate policy which it is not". At present the case against the devaluation of the rupee is strong indeed and is also incontrovertible. Therefore, devaluation of the rupee has to be ruled out. The depreciation of the rupee can be mitigated by the Reserve Bank of India drawing on the accumulated forex reserves of $ 19.5 billion to buy the rupee and to maintain stability of the exchange rate if the depreciation is immoderate. If it is moderate this can be left as it is and this can help export promotion. The rise in the prices of imports can be held in check by reducing the customs duties on imports. The burden of this song is that devaluation of the rupee at present is unnecessary, unwarranted and is also harmful.

54

Banning the Movement of Essential Goods to the Neighbouring States

The rate of inflation in India is hovering around 10 percent and is poised to go higher as the days advance. The prices of several essential commodities used by the masses who are poverty-stricken have been rising. The neighbouring States of Andhra Pradesh and Maharashtra which have announced overly populist measures to sell rice, oil and other food articles at incredibly low prices are in need of these articles for supply to the expectant people. The rise in their prices in those States has induced the merchants in Karnataka to move their stocks to the other states where they intend to make a huge profit. In consequence, there is a shortage of these commodities in Karnataka. The rise in the prices of these commodities in Karnataka is phenomenal staggering the comprehension of the human mind. The harried consumers who have to purchase these commodities by paying unconscionably high prices, the demand for them being inelastic, have found it difficult to make both ends meet.

In this situation the Government has decided to import sugar and to reduce the prices of other commodities issues through the public distribution system. This decision is understandable. However, these measures are difficult to implement given the tight budgetary position. The Government in Karnataka has announced the sale of rice at Rs. 3.20 per kg and this is an irrevocable commitment. As the Union Government is not in a position to extend subsidy to the State Government, the burden of the subsidy falls on the State Government. The movement of food articles outside Karnataka to take advantage of higher prices prevailing in the neighbouring States will create a shortage of these commodities and will push up their prices. The higher these prices, the greater the burden of subsidy on the Government. This will increase Government expenditure. This has to be met by increasing tax revenue and/or reducing expenditure in other directions. The reduction in expenditure on social services will reduce the quality of life; the reduction in expenditure on public investment will reduce the rate of economic growth and this will reduce the per capita income of the people. In view of this the Government has to raise revenue through additional taxation. But the Minister of Finance in Karnataka has gone on record stating that no new taxes would be levied or that the rates of existing taxes would not be raised. In view of this official commitment, raising revenue through the tax route can be ruled out. In order to meet the subsidy burden the Government has to borrow heavily. This will add to the debt burden and the burden of interest payments. Interest payment will widen the budgetary gap which will have to be bridged by means of further borrowing. Hence the vicious circle.

If the prices of essential commodities are allowed to rise because of the export of these commodities to the neighbouring States, the Government will have to subsidise more heavily the difference between the procurement price and the final market price. Furthermore, there may also be a demand for raising the procurement price itself in which case there will have to be a rise in the final market price. The increase in subsidy will itself be a cause of further inflationary pressure through an increase in the budget deficit. Furthermore, higher subsidies will need to be maintained or further increased indefinitely if the inflation rate is to be held down. The reduction of subsidy on fertilisers leads to an increase in the procurement prices of food articles as the higher cost of production has to be covered. It is suggested that the adoption of a prices and incomes policy which has been on the Government agenda for many years. The present inflationary context can be used to reopen this question.

This, of course, is a measure for the medium run. But, for the immediate present, when the export of essential commodities to the neighbouring States has reduced their availability in Karnataka causing a rise in their prices, the remedy is to stop the movement of these commodities outside Karnataka. This may go against the spirit of liberalisation but a temporary lull for it in the present context appears inevitable. This will help to hold down the rate of rise in prices of essential commodities in Karnataka and will go a long way in relieving the sufferings of the poor masses. The Government of Karnataka will be well-advised to stop the movement of essential goods outside the borders by merchants with intent to make a windfall gain. The Karnataka consumers should not be made to pay a price for the benefit of the consumers in the neighbouring States which have thoughtlessly announced populist schemes only to get a political mileage in the process but upsetting the economic apple cart.

Will the Government of Karnataka act in time to save the harried consumers? Will the Government stop the movement of goods to the neighbouring States for a short while?

55

Alternative Guarantee Proposals in the Power Sector

In the monsoon session of the Parliament Minister of Power, moved a motion in the Rajya Sabha regarding the grant of counter guarantee to the foreign investors in the power sector. This was considered necessary as the foreign investors were not satisfied with the guarantees granted by the SEBs which are in the red. This move was opposed by the opposition in the Rajya Sabha. Subsequently even the Finance Ministry expressed reservations about this move. There were also widespread criticisms of the counter guarantee proposal. In order to meet these criticisms the Minister of Power has announced seven sets of incentives to entrepreneurs. But these incentives do not meet the demand of the foreign investors in the power sector to provide guarantee to them.

For the eight power projects involving foreign investment, the Government proposed to provide counter guarantees as well as foreign exchange cover for dividends. The Government considered this step necessary to attract foreign investment to the capital intensive power sector. This has come under criticism on the ground that it would serve as an incentive to inflate capital costs and that it assures returns in dollar terms as the dividends enjoy foreign exchange cover. In the light of these criticisms the Government has decided to do away with the counter guarantee for foreign investment. But the question is : how will the Government deal with future investment proposals in the power sector.

The alternative proposals concern the replacement of sovereign guarantees with a different kind of guarantee or linking the power generating agency with the consumers. The guarantees proposed will not involve the Union Government but will involve the intervention by the State Governments, the Reserve Bank of India and the banks. Under these proposals there will be an "escrow account". The revenue of the concerned SEB will flow into the escrow account and the first charge will be to meet the revenue demands of the power generating agency. The Financial institutions will stand guarantee for the escrow accounts or the Reserve Bank of India will deduct the revenue proceeds from the State's share of Central Government taxes in the event of the SEB defaulting.

These arrangements are guarantee of a certain kind though they are not sovereign guarantees. They are intended to assure to them that their investments are safe and secure and that the poor financial health of the SEBs will not prevent them from meeting the costs of power generation. It is the very same sense of insecurity that made the foreign investors demand sovereign guarantees for the earlier proposals. Though these guarantees induce a sense of confidence that their investments will be safe, they will not address the problems faced by the SEBs. At present the SEBs have to bear the financial burden of supplying power to the agricultural sector at subsidised prices and also of the colossal theft of power which causes enormous losses. These problems will worsen the financial health of the SEBs considering the fact that the power companies revenue becomes the first charge on the State bodies. In fact, if the financial health of the SEBs is improved there will be no need to provide guarantees to the foreign power companies.

The remaining proposals do not involve the sovereign guarantees and so they are not likely to be favoured by the private power companies. It is, therefore, suggested that the private companies should directly supply power to the high tension consumers. This avoids the necessity of the SEBs evolving their pricing practices. But this suggestion will work in the case of small power generating companies. The large companies generate more power than what the high tension power consumers require. If the distribution of power is separated from generation of power there is need to make investment in the distribution segment also. This will enhance the cost of power supplied by the private or foreign power companies to the consumer.

The foreign and private power companies are to enter into an agreement with the Power Grid Corporation of India for transmitting power from the surplus to the deficit areas. In this case, the power companies have the fear that they will not be able to make their collections. This calls for improving the financial health of the SEBs.

The best way to safeguard the financial health of the SEBs is to reduce the power subsidy initially and to do away with it ultimately and also to eliminate the theft of power in the process of transmission. The pruning of subsidies has been put on hold and the farmers' lobbies are up against any move to reduce or remove the subsidies on power. As a result, the SEBs are required to sell power to the farmers at a price below the cost of generation. This has considerably damaged the financial health of the SEBs. They can be restored to pink health by removing power subsidies, not at one go but in gradual stages. There are also complaints of theft of power during transmission. This theft reduces the revenues to the SEBs. There are also complaints of under-billing of power supply by a clandestine understanding between the power consumers and the officers preparing electricity bills. If these practices are eliminated, the SEBs which are running under loss will become profitable in which case the guarantee of the type envisaged by the Minister seems unnecessary. The SEBs experience revenue buoyancy which is a source of confidence to the foreign investors that their investments will be safe and secure. The revenue of the SEBs will flow into the suggested escrow account which will be able to meet the revenue demands of the foreign investor. If the escrow account is viable there would be no need for the financial institutions to stand guarantee for the escrow accounts or for the Reserve Bank of India to deduct the revenue proceeds from the States' share of Central Government taxes in the event of the SEBs defaulting for there will be no occasion for defaulting. The main thing to do is to restore the financial health of the SEBs in all possible ways which do not rule out hikes in electricity tariff sufficient to meet the cost of power generation and the rate of return expected by the foreign investors.

56

Capping of Coffee Exports is Necessary

"Coffee cheers but does not inebriate" goes the saying. But of late coffee has ceased to cheer those who are fond this beverage. The sudden upsurge in its price has made several consumers avoid it altogether. The coffee price increased from Rs. 90 per kg to between Rs. 150–Rs. 180 has forced many to abandon this brew. Coffee sales have, in consequence, fallen by 25 percent since June when the prices started rising.

The most important cause of the spurt in coffee prices was the damage to coffee crop caused by the frost in Brazil. Till recently, the price of coffee was falling. But the fall in the supply of coffee reversed the downslide causing a rise in the international prices of coffee. They rose from Rs. 9.50 per kg to Rs. 60. Today it stands at Rs. 63 and the price predicted for December 1994 is Rs. 65.4 per kg. The coffee growers say that the rise in the price of coffee is no problem and what according to them is the source of the trouble is the introduction of the Free Sale Quota (FSQ) for coffee. In earlier years coffee growers were handing over their entire produce to the Coffee Board for marketing. But since January 1994 they have been allowed to sell 50 percent privately to any one whether exporters or domestic dealers. The other 50 percent goes to the Coffee Board. Before this the Coffee Board held separate auctions for exporters and domestic dealers. The export auction prices had nothing to do with the domestic auction prices. At present joint auctions are held where the determining factor is the international price. The prices at the coffee auctions determine the price at which the FSQ is sold by the coffee growers. As exporting turned out to be more profitable, a large part of the coffee began to go to exporters. This has reduced the domestic availability of coffee, rise in its price and has generated misery to the coffee lovers.

In August 1994 the Government issued a directive capping coffee exports to 1.10 lakh tonnes out of the total predicted coffee output of 2 lakh tonnes and the complete halting of exports of secondary grades of coffee have not been of much help. As long as the international prices of coffee continue to rise, the domestic producers feel encouraged to raise the price of coffee in the domestic market.

It is argued by the coffee planters and exporters that capping exports is not the solution to the higher price of coffee. Planters had suggested that the Coffee Board should channel 5000 tonnes from the pool quota into the domestic market through the Public Distribution System at Rs. 30 per kg. But the proposal did not catch the imagination of the exporters who have not yet agreed to underwrite the costs. The planters also demand that they be allowed 100 percent FSQ which will allow them to sell their produce to customers of their choice for maximum profits. The coffee drinkers in India consume 60,000-70,000 tonnes of coffee annually. They are anxiously watching the movement of coffee prices.

The Finances Minister while in Bangalore on 25.9.1994 assured the Coffee Planters Association that a decision on the 100 percent PSQ would be taken shortly. He cautioned the Association that the marketing department of the Coffee Board may have to be dismantled if 100 percent FSQ was introduced. But the coffee growers oppose this move for several reasons:

1. If the marketing department of the Coffee Board is dismantled, there is no provision in the existing Coffee Act for fixing support prices in the event of a price crash in the domestic or international markets.
2. The introduction of the FSQ in a phased manner is not practical as there are a large number of small holdings where coffee is grown.
3. Several cooperative marketing societies had been established both at the district and state levels to help small and marginal growers to market their produce.

If 100 percent FSQ is permitted it is bound to lead to a rise in prices far above the existing level which is already high. The international price of coffee is higher than the domestic price. The exporters will then be inclined to export more coffee than they are doing at present. This will reduce the availability of coffee in the domestic market. The demand for coffee remaining constant, there will be an excess demand for coffee causing a rise in its price. Thus allowing 100 percent FSQ is not conducive to price stability. Nor will it help the coffee growers. The higher price of coffee will go to swell the profits of the exporters. In view of this it does not appear desirable to allow 100 percent FSQ. Whether the number of small and marginal farmers is large or small, the introduction of FSQ even in a phased manner appears undesirable unless there is surplus production of coffee.

The demand for the dismantling of the marketing department of the Coffee Board is legitimate. The objection to it on the ground that there is no provision in the existing Coffee Act for fixing support prices in the event of a price crash in the domestic or international markets does not hold water. If the support price for coffee is deemed necessary, a provision to this effect can be incorporated in the Coffee Act by a legislative enactment.

The existing arrangement capping exports of coffee is in order. If there is no such capping the exporters may export a large part of the coffee produce leaving very little in the domestic market thus helping to raise the price of coffee. Thus the exporters who sell the produce at the higher prices in the world market and who sell the produce at the higher prices in the domestic market stand to make a double gain the benefit not being allowed to go to the coffee growers. Therefore, capping exports is necessary and as and when the output of coffee rises, the cap can be moved upwards.

57

Economics of the Power Sector

In a developing economy like India infrastructure lays the foundations for accelerated economic growth "power" is an important component of infrastructure. Power is necessary for almost every sector of the economy : industry—small, medium and large agriculture, services, domestic consumption for lighting and cooking purposes etc. Therefore adequate supply of power is the sine qua non of economic growth.

At present the Government is acutely concerned about power supply. It is agitated by the possible shortage of power in future years. Recently, the Prime Minister while speaking in the conference "India Electricity 1994" has expressed concern about the shortage of electricity. This conference discussed the question of investing adequate capital in power generation and to increase the power generation capacity. The Prime Minister has underlined the need to ensure adequate supply of power on which is dependent industrial progress. But the Government is not in a position to invest capital in adequate magnitude. The Government has to make adequate investment in areas to which the private capitalists do not wish to enter. They are: education, primary health drinking water, welfare schemes. These are the responsibility of the State. This requires large investment. If the domestic private investors and foreign investors are prepared to invest in the power sector the Government will be free to invest more and more in the sectors mentioned above.

The Government has provided many incentives to those who wish to invest in the power sector. The foreign investors need not have any apprehensions about the failure of their investment programme as the Government has given the assurances about the capital investment. In order to attract capital into this sector the Government in the Union Budget for 1993-94 announced several concessions: reduction in the import duty on imported capital equipment, reduction in excise duty on the electric accessories, tax holiday for new enterprises establishment to generate power etc. Even before this the Government had provided for the 100 percent investment of foreign capital. They had the facility of getting four times the loan of the share capital and the assurance of 16 percent profit. Furthermore, the private electricity generating centres were allowed to own their own coal mines.

It is not without reason why the Government is virtually pampering this sector. This situation in the power sector is so disturbing that the Government is prepared to give up its monopoly control over power generation and supply. The power shortage is of the order of 10 percent of power requirement. In the years of peak requirement of electricity this shortage goes upto 22 percent. The demand for power is rising at the rate of 8-9 percent. The present power generating capacity is 70,000 MW. By 2005 it must be raised to 1.4 lakh MW. Even if the financial institutions in India supply finance, the power supply can be increased by only 1,000 MW per year. Even at a liberal estimate the power supply can be increased by 10-12 thousand MW. Even then it is not possible to meet the demand for power fully. For this reason inviting private sector companies and foreign companies to undertake the task of power supply has become inevitable.

The investors domestic or foreign expect adequate return on their investment. The Minister for power has so thoughtfully stated that the private companies are not Charitable institutions. Their tariff may appear to be a bit high. But this is far better than there being no power at all. The power tariff in India is said to be the lowest in the world and for this reason enhancement of power tariff may not be unreasonable. At the same time the interests of the users of power cannot be ignored. It is uncontrovertible that the need for augmenting power supply is urgent and important. Thus for about 70 units in the private sector have reached the stage of approval. The aggregate investment in these units is Rs. 1,000 crore. They can generate 3,000 MW of power. But their operationalisation is not easy. It is not yet clear as to how many private entrepreneurs will come forward to set up power generation units, as per the guidelines prescribed by the Government. There are said to be several complications.

It is difficult to take decisions about approving them after getting bids from the intending investors. It is generally felt that it is desirable to accord approval only after satisfying about the stability, prestige and efficiency of the units. As power generation is the responsibility of both the Centre and the States a proposal has to pass through 42 departments. This naturally results in delayed decisions. Thus it is necessary to make arrangements for examining all aspects of the case in just one place.

As to power sector is a public utility there is need to determine the power tariff at a reasonable level. This has to be determined in the light of the investment and the rate of return on it expected by the investors. In this respect there is divergence of perceptions of the private investors and the Government. The private investors have to wait for a long period before their investment starts yielding returns. Power generation cannot yield returns in a year or two. The private investors have to take into account this time factor also. Even if the investment yields as internal return of 25 percent it is not an attractive rate of return for the private investors. The Government assures 16 percent return on investment. It is reasonable for the private investors to ask why should we invest in low return enterprises while there are several avenues for investment which yield a higher rate of return and in which the risk of loss is minimum.

Even assuming that power is generated in adequate quantity, the question of its disposal looms large before the Government: Should the Government sell the power to the electricity boards of the State Governments? Can anybody obtain the contract to dispose it of ? If there is excess supply of power, how should it be disposed of ? Should the return be based on power generating capacity or on the power actually generated? The question of this type are really complex and cannot be answered easily.

It was earlier expected that the private investors would come forward to invest in the power sector if the power generated is 63.5 percent of the installed capacity thus assuming 16 percent return, it was hoped that for every 1 percent rise in power supply 0.7 percent increment in return would be assured. But the question is whether the private investors domestic and foreign will find these assurances attractive. The expected response of the private investors was not forthcoming. The power sector in India is in doldrums. In the countries of the west the power generated is 70-90 percent of installed capacity. During transmission about 20 percent will be lost. The power tariff is not scientifically determined. There is the question of who should bear the burden of free or concessional supply of power; there is further the question of whether the consumers can bear the electricity tariff prescribed by the private sector. These are questions for which answers cannot easily be found.

However, these questions confront the Government after the power supply is expanded. But the expansion of power supply requires adequate investment in this sector. The Government which is acutely concerned about power shortage has been frantically inviting the foreign investors. Despite the liberal economic scenario the response of the foreign investors is less than enthusiastic. As the Government is openly admitting that the power problem is serious the foreign investors are biding time hoping for a more liberal assurance about the return on their investment. The incentives offered to foreign companies has not enthused the hard bargaining multinationals to invest in the Indian power sector. The lukewarm response of foreign investors was evident from the Prime Minister's recent call to MNCs to invest in power projects fearlessly. There was the announcement that an investment of $ 25-30 billion would flood India from the USA and that the power sector would get a major share of this investment. This sort of announcement is being made in respect of other developing countries. But it is yet to be seen that this assurance will be operationalised.

In the last year of the 8th plan period (1996-97) the anticipated power shortage is of the order of 14 percent (energy) and 28 percent (peaking). The sloppy approach to the power sector during the previous years has led to a situation where the country would need twice the present available capacity of 70,000 MW during the next 10 years to escape a major power crisis. The Minister for power has admitted that the country would be able to have only 20,000 MW of new generation capacity during the 8th Five Year plan. The plan target has already been sealed down to less than 30,000 MW due to the non-availability of investible resources. In the private sector at present only 1,340 MW of new capacity is under construction. Of the 75 proposals already received by the Government 35 are from foreign companies. They plan to put up a generating capacity of 32,662 MW valued at Rs. 1,04,152 crore. However, these proposals have come in the form of expressions of interest and have not reached the stage of completion. The long gestation period involved in power generation will not allow an early improvement.

The State Electricity Boards owe to the National Thermal Power Corporation (NTPC) huge dues. The Government has agreed to give counter guarantee to the foreign investors to ensure timely payment from State Electricity Boards. Most of the State Electricity Boards are in the red because of cheap supply of power to consumers, particularly to the farmers, non-payment of tariff by the consumers and theft of electricity. In fact most of them do not qualify for counter-guarantee. Despite the existing power crisis some critics have charged the Government with extending a more favourable treatment to the foreign investors in preference to Indian investors. They argue that private entry on such favourable terms would lead to a rapid rise in power tariff and affect the interests of domestic consumers adversely. Unless timely action is taken to resolve the power crisis the crisis is bound to persist for many years to come. This can be resolved by timely action.

The growth mechanism can be speeded up or impeded depending on the availability or otherwise of infrastructural facilities. The Indian economists have been warning the Government time and again that unless adequate infrastructural investment is provided for the growth mechanism will be impeded. The Planning Commission is aware of it. But it is helpless in the matter. Power being an important part of infrastructure it must be generated in adequate measure in order to help all the sectors depending on it for their efficient performance. This calls for the following measures to be adopted to resolve the power crisis.

In the domestic sphere the following measures need to be adopted: The State Electricity Boards are suffering losses on account of the concessional tariffs charged by them for the various classes of users. Concessional tariffs are anathema to a market economy or to an economy moving fast on the road to marketisation. Concessional tariffs reduce the revenue of the SEBs and make them depend upon subsidies which enlarge the fiscal deficit and contribute to inflation. The big landlords who are the largest beneficiaries of concession tariff are the ones who make profits but their income is going untaxed. It is thus necessary to charge tariffs which enable the SEBs to recover the cost of production and to realise a reasonable rate of return on investment. The domestic consumers are alleged to be hit hard by any enhancement of power tariffs. But it must be realised that middle class consumers of power are able to pay the enhanced tariffs. It is those who are below the poverty line that cannot afford to pay even the concessional tariffs. But it must be borne in mind that this class of households use kerosene for lighting and fuel for cooking. Any enhancement of power tariff will not affect them adversely. Therefore the case for avoiding concessional tariffs is not strong. Moreover there is theft of electricity. The households and industries are in an unholy nexus with the staff of the electricity department and they manipulate the transmission of power to the industries or to the residential houses in order to reduce the electricity bill. In consequence power is consumed but the revenue to the SEBs declines. This contributes to their losses. Effective supervision of the flow of electricity must be undertaken in order to check theft of electricity.

At the same time the fear that privatisation of power generation and the inclusion of foreign companies in the power sector will enhance the tariffs is grossly unfounded. The efficiency of the operation of these units will result in reduced tariffs. Even if the tariffs cannot come down this will ensure adequate supply of power and mitigate the power crisis. There are several countries in the run for entrusting the sphere of power generation to foreign companies. In a market economy, other things being equal, the foreign companies divert their investible resources to those countries where they earn reasonable returns. India should take note of this factor and assure the foreign companies reasonable and even competitive rates of return for them. No price is too great to ensure adequate supply of power. The Chinese economy achieved a rate of growth of 13.5 percent in 1993 because of adequate supply of power to all the sectors. The Asian Tigers like South Korea, Taiwan, Singapore, Malaya and others are leaping forward as they are enjoying the facility of adequate power supply. The rate of economic growth is targeted at 5 percent per annum. Even this appears to be difficult to realise. Therefore the foreign companies should be encouraged to make investments in the power sector and this can be done by assuring them adequate rates of return. Surrendering to foreign multinationals must be laid to rest for good.

58

Monetary Financing and Debt Financing of the Fiscal Deficit

The fiscal deficit for 1994-95 does not take into account the loss of revenue caused by many tax concessions, however desirable they may be in a recessionary situation. Further the Finance Minister provided for Rs. 5,700 crore in the 1993-94 budget and Rs. 5,600 crore in the 1994-95 budget to help the banks to meet the capital adequacy norms prescribed by the Basle Committee. These provisions do not enter the budget figures. They are proposed to be in the form of Government bonds and therefore will not involve an immediate cash outgo. But interest payments and amortisation will be a charge on the future budgets. Though the Finance Minister has condemned the waiver of loans to farmers he has not hesitated to cover the bad debts of urban commercial interests and of the industrial sector. The public sector undertakings and nationalised banks are required to raise equity and bonds which will have to be serviced outside the budgetary provisions. It is also proposed to sell equity of public sector undertakings to raise as much as Rs. 4,000 crore next year to cover the revenue expenditure of the Government. In consequence the revenue, budget and fiscal deficits next year will therefore be larger than shown in the budget estimates. Side by side the burden of interest payments on the budget is proposed to swell next year and in the years following. The interest payment as a non-plan expenditure of the Government will increase compared to that in 1993-94 by as much as Rs. 8,000 crore in 1994-95.

The deficits uncovered in the budget for 1994-95 are claimed not to fuel inflation. This is because the Finance Minister has agreed with the Reserve Bank of India that the net issue of adhoc Treasury Bills during the year should not exceed the estimated Rs. 600 crore budget deficit. This is contingent on recouping the loss on account of tax concessions from higher realisations of revenue at reduced rates of taxation by widening the tax base. It must be admitted that covering of revenue deficit by resort to the issue of adhoc Treasury Bills is inflationary as the created money to cover the revenue expenditure of the Government swells demand without generating matching supplies to meet the demand. But it is decided to phase out the issue of adhoc Treasury Bills over a three year period. Besides the decision to restrict the issue of adhoc Treasury Bills to one and half times the budget deficit for not more than ten continuous working days at any time during the year is welcome. This will reduce resort to the Reserve Bank for money.

This, by itself, is insufficient in wiping out the revenue deficit which is already as much as 40 percent of the revenue expenditure. This is due to the interest payments on the accumulated interest bearing debt of the Government. Borrowing from the market for covering the revenue deficit and even the fiscal deficit when such borrowing is used to meet revenue expenditure or even if productively spent does not result in revenue yield higher than the rate of interest on borrowing may not pump created money into the economy and therefore cannot have a direct and immediate impact on inflation as the Quantity Theory of Money makes us believe. But it is inflationary all the same for two reasons: (a) such borrowing forecloses available resources for the Government to be used for non-productive and non-profitable purposes and adds to interest burden on the budget. This makes it difficult to balance the revenue budget and generate surpluses for productive investment in economic development. (b) it is held in recent fiscal theory that while money financing and debt financing of the deficit are both inflationary, debt financing is more inflationary than money financing. While money financing raises the price level once, debt financing raises it year after year. Debt financing results in interest payments which are an item of non-plan expenditure. This widens the deficit and is inflationary. As the interest burden is to be borne as long as the debt remains unrepaid it adds to the deficit every year and raises the prices level every year during the pendency of the loan.

The Government has been borrowing from the market in the form of interest bearing dated securities, 364 days Treasury Bills and so on to cover the revenue and fiscal deficits. This merely postpones the day of reckoning and is unhelpful in keeping the inflationary forces under effective control which is the ostensible purpose of phasing out recourse to adhoc Treasury Bills. The recourse to borrowing imposes a severe burden on the future generation besides exacerbating, inflationary pressures in the economy.

The Finance Minister's proposal to put a cap on Government borrowing from the Reserve Bank of India is welcome for two reasons: (a) if there is a limit on Government borrowing from the Reserve Bank of India, the Government will be compelled to manage its finances better; (b) indiscriminate borrowing from the Reserve Bank hampers efficient conduct of monetary policy since such borrowing leads to the creation of high-powered money which fuels inflationary fires in the economy. Therefore, the limit and subsequent phasing out of Government's recourse to the Reserve Bank will instill much needed fiscal discipline in Government expenditure and enable the Reserve bank to frame its monetary policy over a longer time period. However, if the imposition of a limit on Government borrowing from the Reserve Bank causes a shift in the source of borrowing from the Reserve Bank to the public without tackling the problem of mounting fiscal deficit, the proposals, from the point of view of inflation control is not of much use.

The idea of imposing a limit on Government borrowing from the Reserve Bank is not new. In fact, it has been a long-standing demand of the Reserve Bank of India. The Finance Minister has conceded the merit of this demand and has placed a limit of Rs. 9,000 crore on the net issue of Treasury Bills at any point of time. The arrangement is that if this limit is exceeded for more than 10 continuous working days the Reserve Bank will automatically sell Treasury Bills in the market to bring down the level of outstanding adhocs. Over the subsequent three years, recourse to the Reserve Bank is to be progressively reduced. By 1997-98 direct recourse to the Reserve Bank is to cease altogether and in subsequent years the entire Government requirement is to be met through Government borrowing from the market.

The impact of this proposal has to be gauged when viewed in the context of the sheer volume that will have to be mobilised from the market if the fiscal deficit continues unchecked. Currently, the deficit is financed partly by borrowing and the balance is automatically covered by the issue of adhoc Treasury Bills. The issue of adhoc Treasury Bills which began as a temporary arrangement in the mid-1950s to enable the Government to tide over short-term mismatches in its funds flow has, over the years, degenerated into something quite different—into a routine recourse to adhocs. This arrangement had its effect on the management of the Government finances. The budgetary deficit rose from Rs. 6,858 crore in 1991-92 to Rs. 12,312 crore in 1992-93, and though it declined to Rs. 9,060 crore in the revised budget estimates for 1993-94 the figure was much higher during the greater part of the year.

Correspondingly, there has been phenomenal increase in the total outstanding Treasury Bills. Until 1955 the outstanding was well below Rs. 500 crore. Subsequently it rose to Rs. 2,518 crore by March 1971 and further to Rs. 12,851 crore by March 1981. The profligacy of the Government in the 1980s saw the figure rise to Rs. 19,266 crore a decade later. In fact, but for the funding of Treasury Bills to the tune of Rs. 71,000 crore during the 1980s the actual outstanding as at the end of March 1993 would have been Rs. 90,266 crore. A large part of these Treasury Bills was held by the Reserve Bank of India resulting in the monetisation of the budget deficit. Thus the outstanding reserve money created by the Reserve Bank as at the end of March 1993 stood at Rs. 1,10,943 crore, of this the Reserve Bank credit to the Government accounted for 87 percent. In such a situation a ceiling on Government borrowing from the Reserve Bank marks the beginning in controlling a situation that was threatening to go out of control.

With the gradual closure of an easy route to financing the fiscal deficit market borrowing will have to fund an increasingly larger part of the fiscal deficit. This entails a greater danger than monetary financing.

However, in this part market borrowing posed no problem as the banks were compelled to hold Government debt through the imposition of the Statutory Liquidity Ratio (SLR) which ensured a captive market for Government securities at low rates of interest. As long as the SLR could be raised funding an ever increasing volume of Government borrowing was not difficult as any shortfall could be bridged by the issue of adhoc Treasury Bills. But such fund raising had a price attached to it. A high SLR reduced bank profitability. After a while SLR borrowing were bound to plateau. This has happened at present. At present any attempt to improve bank profitability is linked to a reduction in the SLR. This reduces the extent of the captive market for Government debt. Thus the success of such a borrowing programme depends on the pricing of such debt.

The average rate of interest on internal liabilities rose from 8.2 percent in 1990-91 to 9.1 percent in 1992-93. For 1993-94 it is well in excess of 10 percent. According to the budget documents interest payments for the coming year are estimated at Rs. 46,000 crore or 53.4 percent of revenue receipts. With newer loans raised at higher interest rates, interest payments will account for an overwhelmingly large share of the total revenue receipts. Ideally the higher interest cost should restrain Government borrowing in order to bring down the fiscal deficit by restraining the Government expenditure/raising its revenue receipts. But the impact of costly borrowing will be felt only after a lapse of time. As a result the willingness to reduce such borrowing is weak in a democracy. In this situation the burden of future servicing of the debt may assume astronomical proportions. This is bound to reduce the availability of funds for financing developmental expenditure.

As averred above there are two methods of financing the deficit: (a) monetary financing and (b) debt financing. Monetary financing is inflationary in the short run but it does not impose any burden of debt on future generations. Debt financing of the deficit is inflationary in the medium and long run as it involves payment of interest which widens the fiscal deficit. The Government has chosen to reduce its dependence on monetary financing and to increase its dependence on debt financing. It must be borne in mind that the market is no longer captive to lend to the Government at a reduced rate of interest. The reduction of interest rate involves a raising of the SLR which involves the erosion of profitability of the banking system. Restoration of profitability of the banks and their observance of the capital adequacy norms involve a reduction of the SLR and a raising of the rate of interest on market borrowings. This imposes a burden on future generations besides enlarging the fiscal deficit which would have inflationary consequences greater than those involved in monetary financing of the deficit. Both types of financing are to be brought down. The imposition of a cap on adhocs Treasury Bills has the effect of reducing monetary financing. At a time when the rate of monetary growth has jumped from 11.5 percent to 14.5 percent, this is a welcome step. But this has to be followed by a ceiling market borrowing involve in debt financing of the deficit. I propose the imposition of a constitutional limit on Government borrowing relaxable only by parliamentary approval. If, at any time, borrowing becomes inevitable to meet the budget deficit, monetary financing, subject to a ceiling, should be resorted to, as it does not involve an accentuation of the fiscal deficit or a burden on the tax payers.

59

Need for an External Economic Strategy

In the context of the rising rate of inflation (10% in the first week of April 1994) and the threat of a burgeoning balance of payments deficit there is imperative need to devise a thoughtful external economic strategy. The policy makers seem to be overconfident that the forex reserves of $ 14 billion will stand the country in good stead. But their vulnerability of the forex reserves cannot be ignored.

The forex reserves do not represent only the export earnings, remittances and other invisible receipts but are also made of borrowings and external assistance. As per estimates, export earnings account for 30 percent of forex reserves and the balance made up of borrowings accounts for 70 percent. What is noteworthy is that this level of reserves has been achieved despite a steady outflow of deposits from non-resident Indian accounts. According to figures available, between April and August 1993 there was a net outflow of over $ 500 million from Non-Resident External Rupee Account and Foreign currency Non-Resident Accounts. During the same period of 1992 the outflow was only $ 175 million. The credit rating agencies like standard and poor had pushed the country below the investment grade and the NRIs just did not feel it safe to keep money in Indian Banks. In fact, on this reckoning there was a net outflow of $ 1.6 billion of deposits from NRI accounts during the whole of 1991-92. As of July 12, 1991 the country's foreign exchange reserves had gone to as low as $ 975 million which would have taken care of barely one week's imports. But the trend was reversed once the Government initiated its economic reform programme.

From $ 975 million in July 1991, the reserves rose to $ 7.6 billion, a rise about $ 7 billion achieved in a matter of little over two years. Against the background of this commendable performance, the fall in NRI deposits in 1993-94 is somewhat confusing. One theory is that it was the Governor of the Reserve Bank of India who initiated action to get rid of short-term deposits and the fall in NRI deposits was a sequel to his actions.

One of the main factors responsible for the rise in forex reserves is the convertibility of the rupee of trade account effected from March 1993 with convertibility, there was virtually no incentive for exporters to keep their earnings in foreign countries. Additionally, it also helped devalue the rupee further from what it was when the rupee was only partly floated. This increased the profitability of exports. The Reserve Bank statistics suggest that in April 1993 alone, the forex reserves rose by a whopping $ 1.0 billion as a sequel to full float of the rupee.

In the first five months of 1993-94 exports went up by 24 percent in dollar terms and this reflected favourable on the reserve position; on the other hand, the rise in imports was not very high. There were also good prospects of foreign exchange accrual from direct foreign investment as also investment in the capital market from foreign institutional investors. On account of all these factors the reserves at present stand at $14 billion.

The question is : Is the country's external account any less vulnerable than in 1990-91? The question was cautiously raised by Dr. C. Rangarajan, Governor of the Reserve Bank of India in the Govind Vallabh Pant Memorial Lecture in New Delhi in January 1994. There are several good reasons for this poser and not only because the heavy (and rising) debt servicing associated with the country's very large external debt has a prior claim on reserves. The other reasons are best summed up in the question: Is the current rise in forex reserves based on export earnings? Only partially and not so firmly: that is the uncomfortable answer.

The trade deficit in the current year (1994-95) has shrunk to a comfortable low 0.5 percent of GDP. But the rise in exports-19 percent will have to be sustained at 15 percent a year in dollar terms. This will not be easy. Since agricultural surpluses fluctuate (as seen from the recent flare-up in domestic prices of cotton, and the consequent ban on its export), their exports cannot be sustained in the medium term. There has been a slippage in infrastructure investment on roads, railways, petroleum and coal mining. Both the generation of an export surplus and their movement are heading for retardation. The slow down in imports 2.2 percent below last year's level has also contributed to the squeeze on this year's deficit. But imports will have to rise by 10 percent a year to make production for exports feasible. Import growth will have to be largely in non-oil goods. This requires domestic oil production to register a smart recovery. However, no major oil discovery has so far been made. Economic growth will boost oil imports (and there is no knowing when oil prices abroad will rise). Aggregate import growth may rise by well over 10 percent. It is highly likely that there will be slippages in the areas of both imports and exports. If this happens there will be a wider trade deficit; not only that; a substantial part of the non-debt creating inflows (namely foreign investment, notably in the share markets), will turn into outflows. The foreign exchange reserves will fall considering the fact that the fair weather friends will pull out in search of safe pastures. This makes the external accounts vulnerablc. The country cannot afford to risk a reserve depletion in support of policy of import liberalisation. The current account deficit at present is 0.5 percent of GDP; it should on no account be allowed to go above 1.0 percent of GDP. This is imperative though, for those who have forgotten the crisis 1990-91, the limit may appear to be over cautious.

The main burden on the forex reserves is the servicing of external debt. This has been growing with unabated vigour. There are two ways of bringing it down. (a) by imposing a constitutional limit on borrowing, both external and internal and (b) by effecting appropriate adjustment of the exchange rate. The Reserve Bank paper on external debt suggests that the exchange rate of the rupee should be adjusted with the repayment obligations of the country in mind. This is a timely warning to those who hold the view that keeping the rupee value depressed with respect to hard currencies as a profitable strategy. This warning is administered by a senior Economist of the Reserve Bank Mr. D. Anjaneyulu in a staff paper. He notes that while this is a short-term tactic to benefit exports, this could also increase the rupee value of the country's debt obligations thereby adding to the debt-burden at home. Ever since the rupee was put on free float in March 1993 the large inflow of US dollars from abroad as remittances and fund transfers shot up sharply and this has pushed up the value of the rupee against hard currencies. The Reserve Bank has so far purchased over $ 4 billion in accordance with the official strategy to keep the value of the rupee at about Rs. 31.37 to the dollar so that Indian exports could retain their price advantage in world markets. The study shows that for every one percent downward adjustment of the rupee, the rupee value of external debt will rise by as much as 0.39 percent. This clearly negates a significant part of the immediate gains of exports. It also points out a similar limitation about using imports to shore up domestic production. Contrary to the view that a certain buoyancy in imports is necessary to keep domestic industry going, the study has found that for every one percent increase in imports, domestic output increases by 0.20 percent at the maximum and at that level there is a 1.01 percent increase in external debt. It is, therefore, necessary to work out an optimum level of imports. According to the study, if imports were to increase by 20 percent, then if the debt burden were to be kept at the same level, either exports must also increase by 20 percent, or domestic productivity should increase by at least 9 percent. In the light of the experience of the 1980s, when reckless short-term commercial borrowings caused the debt-repayment crisis of 1991-92, policy makers have to make the necessary medium term adjustments of the country's external economic strategy.

Depressing the external value of the rupee may be advantageous to exports but its disadvantage in raising the rupee value of the external debt obligations has to be taken note of in which case the advantage of a depressed exchange rate loses its attraction. The massive inflow of dollars into India has the effect of appreciating the external value of the rupee. But this will render India's exports uncompetitive in world markets. The Reserve Bank of India has stood ready to buy the inflowing dollars in order not to allow the exchange rate to appreciate. This tactic will preserve the competitiveness of Indian exports but there is no guarantee that exports would rise to meet the targets. Imports are necessary to increase exports as the exports are import-intensive. But the gain in forex reserves emerging from the rise in exports may be offset by the loss of foreign exchange reserves caused by the rise in imports. There are thus several facts to the issue. While the exchange rate is held steady by the Reserve Bank purchasing dollars the exchange rate is artificially held rigid. This will not do much to increase exports. Exports can be increased by increasing the productivity of factors of production employed in the export industries. This will enhance price competitiveness of India's exports in international markets and promote them. The export surplus achieved by the USA in the period 1945-55 resulting in dollar shortage was due to higher productivity of factors in industry. Exchange rate cannot be depressed as it increases the value of external debt and the debt service obligations; it cannot be allowed to appreciate as it would adversely affect export performance and increase the volume of imports. There is thus the need for (a) adopting a realistic exchange rate and (b) raising the productivity of factors. The convertibility of the rupee on capital account should be held in abeyance pending the settlement of these issues.

60

Is the Decision to Appreciate the Rupee Desirable

India is caught between the two blades of the "growth scissors" the inflation blade and balance of payments blade. These two blades hold down the rate of economic advance. The inflation is caused by several factors of which two are important the growing fiscal deficit and the massive forex inflow both which have the effect of increasing the rate of growth of money supply. The fiscal deficit was 7.3 percent of GDP in 1993-94. The Finance Minister expects it to come down to 6 percent of GDP in 1994-95 on account of increased revenues realisation. This is expected to bring down the rate of inflation to a single digit figure before this calendar year is out. With the favourable turn of monsoons and the rise in food output this may be a possibility. But the matter is complicated by the massive inflow of forex reserves which push up the rate of monetary growth which is a source of inflation. This means that even though the fiscal deficit as a proportion of GDP is brought down to the targeted level of 6 percent or even less there can be no let-up in the rate of inflation brought about by the capital inflow. Under the traditional gold standard the stock of gold determined the stock of money. The stock of money would vary directly with the stock of gold. A favourable balance of trade occasioning an inflow of gold would cause an expansion of money supply and an unfavourable balance of trade occasioning an outflow of gold would cause a contraction of money supply. In the former case there would be inflation and the latter case there would be deflation. The country which wanted to avoid inflation emanating from the inflow of gold would adopt a policy of sterilisation of gold and this would not cause a rise in money supply. Many countries on the gold standard resorted to this expedient even though this was violative of the rules of the gold standard game.

India's exports are expected to reach a growth rate of 15 percent in 1994-95 while imports are expected to rise by 13-14 percent. This will result in a trade deficit of around $ 1 billion. It is expected that the trade deficit may be less if foreign exchange earnings on account of tourism rise. At the same time foreign exchange inflows are expected to rise in 1994-95 on account of foreign investment, especially portfolio investment. All this is expected to raise India's forex reserves to $ 25 billion by the end of 1994-95. At the same time, there is not much of a counter force. There will be a lower outflow of foreign exchange on account of interest on foreign borrowings, dividend repatriation and debt amortisation. With rising foreign investment and growing external debt these figures are substantial. It is believed that the trade deficit will not rise abnormally and will be contained at around 1.1 percent of GDP which is a manageable figure.

The Government and the Reserve Bank of India are in a dilemma. If the Reserve Bank of India continues to purchase incoming dollars the rupee is prevented from appreciating. This will have a favourable effect on the trade balance but, by causing an expansion of money supply, it exacerbates inflation in the economy. Though the fiscal deficit is reduced to the targeted figure of 6 percent of GDP and the inflation emanating from this source is brought under control, there will be no check to inflation emanating from the monetary growth caused by the inflow of dollars. If, on the other hand, the Reserve Bank of India does not intervene in the foreign exchange market and allows the rupee to find its own level, the rupee appreciates and this will adversely affect the trade balance by reducing exports and increasing imports. The rate at which the Reserve Bank wants to maintain the rupee-dollar exchange rate is Rs. 31.37 per dollar. If the rupee is now allowed to appreciate it could rise to as high as Rs. 28 per dollar and this would mean a sharp fall in export earnings. The Reserve Bank of India has adopted a decision not to intervene in the foreign exchange market in order to keep the rupee's exchange rate stable. This decision is prompted by the embarrassing accumulation of $ 16 billion which is creating inflationary pressures. The decision to intervene in the foreign exchange market to hold the exchange rate stable was taken in the belief that the exchange rate of the rupee needed to be kept depreciated to make India's exports competitive in international markets. Part of the reason for this rise in forex reserves was the Reserve Bank's purchase of dollars, the exchange rate of which was weakening against the major currencies. If now, the Reserve Bank stops its policy of intervention, the rupee will appreciate causing a rise in imports and a fall in exports which become less competitive. Though several economists hold the view that the trade deficit will not go above $ 1.1 billion the possibility of a rise to over $ 2 billion cannot be ruled out. This means that the decision of the Reserve Bank of India not to intervene in the foreign exchange market may reduce inflation emanating from accumulation of forex reserves but it will enlarge the trade deficit. This is a dilemma in which the authorities find themselves caught.

The inflow of dollars are volatile in character and their stability cannot be taken for granted. With a change in market sentiment they are sure to take a flight. If these reserves are used in any other manner, the Government will be put to embarrassment in the event of their flight. It has to borrow to meet this demand. Therefore, only those inflows which will be held stable in India for a specified period could be welcome. These reserves can be used in of two ways: (a) they can be used to purchase gold whose value is expected to appreciate; (b) alternatively, they can be used to retire high interest external debt. This will reduce the burden of external debt and of interest cost. The Reserve Bank of India can continue to purchase dollars keeping the exchange rate at the present level and use the capital inflow in one of these ways. This will reduce the risk of inflation while having a favourable effect on the trade balance.

In the light of the above, it is hoped that the Reserve Bank of India will reconsider its decision to let the rupee appreciate.

61

Will the Rate of Inflation Decline?

The Finance Ministry has been making herculean efforts to hold down the inflation rate and with some degree of success. In the main the narrow fluctuations in the rate of inflation between 7.65 percent in the week ended July 22 and 8.12 percent on October 7 are due to favourable developments on the agricultural front. It is possible that the inflation rate would have risen above 9 percent had it not been for the favourable impact of a high level of agricultural production of both cereals and pulses. These have led to a significant fall in the wholesale prices of these commodities which have compelled even hoarders to bring out their hoarded stock in the expectation of a further fall in prices. These have led to an actual fall in the prices of these commodities with a salutary effect on the rate of inflation. With good monsoons this year leading to a bumper crop of many of these commodities there is likely to be a further slide in the inflation rate.

But there have been several counterveiling forces offsetting the favourable impact of larger agricultural production. The fine cereals have not been cheaper than before because of the conflicting policies pursued by the Union Ministry of Agriculture in respect of procurement prices for wheat and rice and minimum statutory prices for sugarcane. Though the issue prices for these cereals have not been changed, the effect of higher procurement prices has been to push up open market prices. The difficulties relating to the transport of wheat from the surplus Northern States to the deficit Southern States have distorted open market quotations. The Union Ministry of Food and Civil Supplies is keen to prevent a rise in issue prices of both wheat and rice supplied through the fair price shops in order to make them available to the poor sections of society at unchanged prices. The Government has begun to implement several social welfare programmes including the mid-day meal scheme for school children by using food grains on a heavily subsidised basis. The selling price of sugar has not been raised despite an increase in retention prices. This is bound to cause a rise in subsidies which are estimated to rise to over Rs. 6,900 crore during 1995-96. The decision not to increase the price of sugar is due to the bumper crop of sugarcane which will lead to surplus of sugar. Due to favourable monsoons and the rise in agricultural output the prices of farm produce will fall. This is the positive aspect of the current economic scenario.

As against this we must take note of the other developments in the Indian economy. The current account of the balance of payments has begun to widen. This has led to fall in the quantum of forex revenues to just above $ 19 billion from about $ 20.5 billion. This has occasioned a sharp depreciation of the external value of the rupee by about 9 percent despite a sale of dollars by the Reserve Bank of India. Even so there has been an excess demand for dollars which has caused a depreciation of the rupee. The rupee has slightly recovered in recent weeks due to the market intervention policy resumed by the Reserve Bank of India.

The price of petroleum and petroleum products is likely to rise generating a cascading effect on the inflation rate. The Finance Ministry is worried about the rising incidence of subsidy on diesel oil, kerosene and other imports. There is a rising domestic demand for the POL (petroleum, oil and lubricants). This has to be met by means of larger imports on a dearer basis. This will increase the burden of subsidies. Any upward adjustment of the prices of POL will have a cascading effect on the inflation rate making it spiral upwards. If the prices of cereals and of sugar are kept unchanged the expenditure on subsidies will increase. Furthermore, the rise in the prices of imports caused by the depreciation of the rupee will cause a further rise in the rate of inflation. If the subsidy is enhanced to counter this development, the fiscal deficit will enlarge to uncomfortable levels causing a rise in the rate of inflation. But the favourable impact of rising output of commodities will have a salutary effect on the inflation rate. This is bound to tone down the impact of costlier imports caused by a depreciated rupee. But this effect will be strengthened if the subsidies are allowed to continue.

The rising cost of imports is a significant factor in the inflation process in the Indian economy at present. It is feared that imported raw materials and components will become costlier as a result of the significant depreciation of the rupee. There is also the need, following depreciation, to pay larger amounts towards import duties as these are levied on ad valorem basis on higher landed cost. Without a downtrend in world prices of petrochemicals and heavy chemicals and other products, the imported inflation would have been felt more acutely.

Admittedly the slide in the external value of the rupee is due to excess demand for dollars. The Reserve Bank of India intervened in the currency market to check the slide in the rupee but its intervention has not been effective. Psychological factors fuelled the panic in the forex market and these factors will be there for some more time to come. For the first time the dealers had to face the downslide of speculation. After the Liberalised Exchange Rate Mechanism was implemented the market had grown accustomed to a long period of inactivity low spreads, thin volumes and the preparedness of the Reserve Bank to stabilise the market at a particular level. But this situation got two jolts : (1) in the busy season credit policy announced by the Reserve Bank early in October 1995, the earlier tight control it had placed on the overnight levels which authorised dealers could maintain was eased signalling that it would permit a more active forex market. Subsequently when the rupee started fluctuating as market forces caused a demand surge it failed to intervene letting the market find its own level. This stimulated speculative activity in which many made money and some lost. The players were confident that if things went out of hand the Reserve Bank would step in. But the Reserve Bank did not or could not intervene effectively. In consequence panic set in. Some currency experts point out that the Reserve Bank has had no previous experience in interventions to support the rupee unlike Central Banks on the developed countries. The urgent need is to announce a rate and to give a commitment to support it. This will encourage an inflow of foreign funds. Furthermore, billion of dollars can be obtained by eliminating under-invoicing of exports and over-invoicing of imports. These factors will lend stability to the rupee, arrest its decline and check imported inflation by bringing about a reduction in the prices of imported consumables and imported inputs for domestic goods and exports. For the moment the inflation rate has to be brought down not by reducing the fiscal deficit by reducing/ eliminating subsidies but by reducing wasteful expenditure of which there is a lot. If these are not done the rate of inflation is bound to rise despite a rise in agricultural output. This will aggravate the current account deficit which is expected to be of the order of $ 5 billion in 1995-96 and will lead to the postponement of capital account convertibility which has been on the agenda for over two years now.

62

No Devaluation, Please

Just on the eve of the presentation of the Union Budget for 1995-96 on March 15, 1995, the talk of devaluation of the rupee has cropped up only to agitate the minds of those concerned with economic management. Many leading lights in the sphere of trade and industry have begun to demand that the rupee be devalued. The demand for devaluation is promoted by a desire to contain non-oil imports which have risen by 32 percent. Further, the rising rate of inflation has reduced the international competitiveness of India's exports and this requires the correction of the exchange rate.

There are two avenues to devaluation : pushing down the value of the rupee and outright devaluation of the rupee. Under the former, the Reserve Bank of India has to mop up massive quantities of dollars and create a shortage to make the people needing dollars to pay more in terms of rupees. This avenue would increase the liquidity in the economy with all its inflationary effects. In the alternative the Reserve Bank of India can devalue the rupee by temporarily closing the forex market and come out with a new indicative exchange rate. But the sustainability of the devalued rupee would depend on the acceptability of the devalued rupee and this would depend on the supply and demand for dollars in the market. In the event of there being an excess supply of dollars few would be willing to pay the higher rupee rate for the dollar. Furthermore, the effectiveness of devaluation would depend on the conditions that:

1. the sum of the two demand elasticities is greater than unity.
2. the fiscal deficit is constant.
3. the wage rates are constant.

There are no authentic calculations of the import demand elasticities in India. The rising prices and incomes are likely to make the sum of the two demand elasticities less then unity. Again, despite the buoyancy of revenues there is likely to be a rise in the fiscal deficit due mainly to the increase in expenditure on food and fertilisers which are necessary to please the voters. This again causes a rise in prices and income which engender a rise in the demand for imports. The wage rates will not remain constant. The Fifth Pay Commission is in session. It has received a large number of Memorandum from several sections of the Government employees making out a strong case for enhancing the scales of salaries and dearness allowances. The Pay Commission is likely to award compensatory wages and dearness allowances which increase incomes of the salaried employees. When these awards are announced the State Government employees demand similar benefits which have to be granted. All these add to the purchasing power and to aggregate demand. These will in turn cause a rise in the rate of inflation with adverse effects on the current account deficit. Thus the devaluation of the rupee will be frustrated in its effect on imports, exports and on the trade balance. The trade imbalance is likely to be larger despite devaluation. In addition one has to take note of the "J-Effect" of devaluation on the trade balance. The trade balance worsens before improving. What happens in the medium run is in the realm of imponderables but in the short run the trade balance will worsen. These effects of devaluation and its side-effects have not been adequately noted by those who support devaluation of the rupee.

The current account deficit which was $ 1.0 billion at the end of 1993-94 is estimated to be $ 2 billion in March 1995. This is not a cause of concern as the figures for imports and exports are rising lately and as the inflows on invisible account are said to be satisfactory. The Governor of the Reserve Bank of India stated recently that the exchange rate of the rupee against other currencies was satisfactory reflecting the strength of the current account balance and added that the rupee was able to hold its level purely on the basis of satisfactory export-import performance and satisfactory inflows on the invisible account in terms of remittances and tourist arrivals. In 1993-94 the Reserve Bank intervened in the forex market to mop up $ 13 billion to keep the value of the rupee stable at Rs. 31.37 per dollar. In 1994-95 purchases were stopped after a level of $ 9.4 billion but these were not net purchases.

There are important differences of approach to the question of devaluation of the rupee. The confederation of Indian Industry (CII) has called for a "gradual and cautious" approach to the issue but has stated that this should be left to the market. But the Federation of Indian Chambers of Commerce and Industry (FICCI) has categorically stated that devaluation of the rupee was not desirable. It must be remembered that 45 percent of Indian imports were used for production of goods for exports and devaluation would raise the cost of production of exportable commodities.

At present, devaluation of the rupee is inopportune. It will occasion fresh inflationary bouts which have the effect of worsening the current account deficit. It is necessary to stay away from any step to readjust the exchange rate and to leave it to be determined by the market forces. This has, infact, happened to some extent. The rupee has marginally depreciated against the pound sterling, the D-Mark, the French franc and the Japanese Yen in January while it appreciated against the US dollar in the same month. These movements were purely market-determined.

We have to reckon with the other dangers of devaluation India's external debt is $ 92 billion. If the rupee is devalued the value of external debt will rise in proportion to devaluation and enhance the debt burden and the burden of servicing. Again, when the rupee is devalued, the forex reserves of the order of $ 20 billion are likely to be shifted outside by the holders of these balances. This is bound to cease the Mexico-like situation which it is necessary to avoid. While these are the dangers, the beneficial effects of devaluation are in doubt. For these reasons, devaluation of the rupee has to be ruled out for good. The remedy for the external imbalance has to be sought in setting right the domestic economic fundamentals. I repeat: No Devaluation Please.

63

Reducing the Interest Cost of Public Debt

Though the fiscal deficit appears to be under control, this is one of the major reasons for the ongoing inflation which has displayed an upward trend. Three major reasons for inflation today are the recent rise in the prices of some commodities like food grains, steel, the high level of forex reserves which have unleashed a rate of monetary growth of over 20 percent against the targeted 15-16 percent and the fiscal deficits of the Central and State Governments a phenomenon which keeps coming back with nagging regularity every year. The factor causing concern to the Government and the monetary authorities is not so much the direct budget deficit but the fiscal deficit which is a more comprehensive indicator of the health of Government finances. An increase in the fiscal deficit has a bearing on future Government expenditure because of higher repayment liabilities and interest payments. The importance of this indicator is such that today just the interest obligations on the past borrowings of the Government make up 35 percent of the Centre's revenue expenditure. This is the major reason why the Government is unable to reduce its non-plan expenditure. Even if the deficit is brought down the Government cannot remain content with that. With every year that the Government piles up huge debts, its control over its future finances slips away. This is happening because the interest payments on its mounting debt eat up an ever larger part of its revenues.

In 1993-94 interest payments swelled 49 percent of the total net revenues of the Centre. In 1994-95 the ratio of interest payments to revenues was 54 percent. This does not leave much over to meet the cost of administration, defence subsidies and non-plan social and economic programmes.

In 1995-96 interest payments will rise by another Rs. 7,000 crore to Rs. 53,000 crore. Unless total revenues rise by more than

Rs. 14,000 crore (against the projected Rs. 9,988 crore in 1994-95) the ratio of interest to total revenues will continue to rise. The centre for monitoring the Indian Economy (CMIE) estimates that the fiscal deficit in 1994-95 would be not just Rs. 54,000 crore by Rs. 66,000 crore. Even if it comes true when interest payments in 1995-96 will rise by Rs. 8,300 crore. The total revenues will have to rise by Rs. 16,500 crore to keep the ratio of interest to revenues from rising further. This is a tall order indeed, given the existing buoyancy of tax revenues.

This is the Brazilian/Latin American type of debt trap. When once the country gets caught in it, it cannot easily get out of it. The extent to which India has entered the debt trap can be seen by comparing the ratio of the increase in revenues to the increase in interest payments. In 1993-94 total revenue increased by Rs. 2,038 crore but interest liabilities increased by Rs. 8,500 crore. This, of course, is understandable. The year 1993-94 was an unusual year characterised by sluggish industrial growth. This coincided with the rationalisation of the tax structure and a sharp fall in tax incidence. The year 1994-95 turned out to be a normal year. Even so, the rise in interest payments Rs. 8,500 crore is slated to swallow all but Rs. 900 crore of the rise in total revenues. The year 1995-96 cannot be expected to be far different with a further rise in the volume of debt and a rise in the interest payment.

Several ways have been suggested to reduce the ratio of the increase in interest payments to the increase in tax revenues but they are unlikely to work. They are:

1. Inflation. As Inflation rises tax revenues also rise. But this causes a rise in Government expenditure which widens the fiscal deficit.
2. Reduction of subsidies and other non-plan expenditure. The need to reduce the fiscal deficit strengthens the case for reducing non-plan expenditure. But this is bound to become unpopular besides inducing cost inflation as the cost of formerly subsidised items rises. Furthermore, defence expenditure cannot be reduced in view of the deteriorating security environment. If, anything, the case for increasing defence expenditure is strong indeed.

3. Reducing the size of the plan. If the capital component of plan expenditure is cut it will dampen industrial revival and reduce the rate of economic growth. This will further slow down the growth of tax revenues. A reduction in revenue will adversely affect poverty alleviation and employment generation programmes and create social unrest. What is necessary is to accelerate the rate of industrial growth so necessary to increase the buoyancy of tax revenues in order to increase revenue accruals at a rate faster than the rise in public debt and the interest payment on it.

This necessitates consideration of the handling of the issue from the side of the capital account. As the cause of the rise in interest payments is the burgeoning national debt, the solution to it lies in slowing down its growth drastically. It is suggested that the Government could do this by selling capital assets of the PSUs worth atleast Rs. 20,000 crore. This is defended on the ground that the Government borrowed funds from the public to build capital assets. These have appreciated by 10-15 times in some cases. Some of these could be sold back. The World Bank is opposed to this on the ground that the sale proceeds of these assets are not current revenue.

In the current fiscal year it is proposed to raise Rs. 7,000 crore by selling part of the assets of the PSUs. This is called disinvestment. But the prevailing market conditions and the political environment have created a stalemate. In 1994-95 total realisation from disinvestment amount to Rs. 4,843 crore against the target of Rs. 4,000 crore. In 1991-92 and 1992-93 the Government had mobilised Rs. 4,950 crore. Owing to unfavourable market conditions and procedural factors no disinvestment could take place in 1993-94. At present, the issue is confounding. The methodology of valuation of and modus operandi of disinvestment posed formidable questions. The assertion made by Industry Minister, that the funds raised through disinvestment can be diverted to reduce the Central fiscal deficit is disturbing. This will only fuel the controversy over the use of capital receipts to meet revenue deficits. There is no unanimity of views on this issue even among the senior members of the Government. The External Affairs Minister and the Deputy

Chairman of the Planning Commission has questioned the wisdom of disposing of capital assets to meet revenue expenditure and has thus voice the concern of the World Bank. In view of this not much relief can be expected from disinvestment in PSUs though the Cabinet has cleared the programme of selling the equity of 14 PSUs at the "appropriate time". The process of disinvestment has been confounding ever since the Government announced its intention on July 24, 1991 as part of its new economic policy. The new policy envisaged offloading a part of the equity of a select bunch of the PSUs to mutual funds and public financial institutions to raise non-inflationary resources. As the PSUs were unknown entities in the marketplace pricing their equity has not been an easy task considering the risk of over or under-pricing at a time when the entire disinvestment programme had become a politically sensitive issue. In the event, the Government's decision to "offer randomly structural bundles of shares" was flayed by the Public Accounts Committee (PAC) for the alleged "glaring acts of omission and commission". The PAC demanded a probe to fix responsibility for the alleged lapses. The audit review had held that the cut in reserve prices results in under-realisation of receipts totalling Rs. 3,441.71 crore. It also commented on the other "inadequacies" and "disquieting features" in the implementation of the disinvestment process like delays in the selection of PSUs and failure to generate investor enthusiasm. Some PSUs had been selected for disinvestment even when their administrative ministries had pleaded for their exclusion.

These were the problems faced by the disinvestment programme since July 1991 and the problems are existing even today. The tendentious argument that the Government is entitled to use the funds for budgetary purposes contravenes the spirit of the programme. In view of this, not much can be expected from the disinvestment programme. Either the revenue has to be raised or the expenditure has to be cut to reduce the fiscal deficit.

If the revenue is to be increased the revenue buoyancy of the tax structure has to be increased. This requires a thorough rationalisation of the entire tax structure and the discovery and operationalisation of new sources of taxation. At the same time there is imperative need to reduce inessential expenditure drastically. An Expenditure Commission has to be appointed to suggest ways and means of reducing Government expenditure. In every expenditure programme cost-benefit calculus has to be applied so as to realise the maximum productivity from it. This will go a long way in reducing Government expenditure and increasing the productivity of the expenditure undertaken.

Quite apart from the above measures, the quantum of public debt itself has to be reduced. This calls for imposing a constitutional limit on the quantum of public debt. If the quantum of debt is prescribed the annual borrowing will automatically have to be reduced. This will reduce the interest cost of public debt. The deficit has to be taken care of by monetary financing rather than by debt financing. This will save India from the danger of the debt trap. It needs to be noted that monetary financing of the deficit is less inflationary than debt financing of it.

64

A Note on Railway Finances

The railways in any country are an important infrastructural facility so necessary to promote economic growth. Professor North a Nobel Laureate in Economics has explained the role which the railway played in the opening up of the U.S. economy in the initial years of the industrial revolution there. Before an industry is established in a region railways are to be established as they are necessary to transport raw materials and labour to the region and to transport the manufactured goods to the neighbouring and distant markets in the economy. As the new area becomes the hub of industrial activity human settlements come up in the region and passenger services are to be opened up to transport people. At the same time the railways have to compete with the road transport in transporting goods and people. To be able to compete successfully, the railway freight structure and the passenger fare structure should be competitively fixed. If the fares and freight rates are overly high there will be a shift to road transport causing losses to the railways and if the railways are to continue in business they have to be subsidised by the Government.

Under the policy of liberalisation there is a growing competitiveness in the transport sector. This has caused worry to the Railway Ministry. As it is, the railway equipment is inadequate to meet the growing demands made on it. The demographic projections forecast an increase in urban population. This is bound to impose tremendous pressure on the railway network. At present the railways are facing tough competition from the road transport. The freight tariff is based on the principle of cross subsidisation. This is bound to cause a rise in the freight rates which render it difficult for the railways to face competition from the road transport. Cross subsidisation is done between profitable and non-profitable activities. This will go soft on rescheduling passenger fares. In this even there will be no choice for the Government but to raise freight rates which are the main source of revenue for the Railways. Though the authorities do not wish to let this situation continue for long there is very little it can do in the matter.

Some knowledgeable persons argue the case against cross subsidisation which is heavily weighted against the freight rate component. In the Railway Budget for 1996-97 there is the possibility of a major hike in the freight rates. If this happens there is likely to be a shift of freight traffic from the railways to road transport. In the 1995-96 railway budget there was a 7 percent hike in freight rates. This led to a diversion of freight traffic from railways to roads. If the railways are to earn adequate profits by attracting sufficient freight traffic, they have to rationalise the freight rate structure. The Railway ministry has been trying to devise marketing strategies in order to attract more traffic and to become customer-friendly. But these steps, desirable as they are, cannot have a lasting impact unless the fare structure is rationalised and is made competitive.

In the regime of liberalisation there is urgent need to step up Government investment in this sector. At the same time the Government has to meet certain social obligations while trying to run on commercial lines. At present no large scale private investment is forthcoming for the railways. In view of this the railways have to depend on the Government or have to go in for market borrowing. But market borrowing is difficult at present when the Government has entered the market to borrow to finance the budget deficit.

The railway finances have to be rendered viable and the railways have to be self-supporting without the expedient of cross-subsidisation. In the matter of freight traffic there are two principles governing freight rate determination: cost of service principle and value of service principle. If the cost of service principle is followed the bulky but low valued articles have to bear a heavy burden while the light and highly valued articles have to bear a light burden. This is grossly unfair. If the value of service principle is followed the highly valued but light weight articles have to bear a heavy burden and the bulky and low valued articles have to bear a very light burden. This is also unfair considering the strain the heavy and bulky articles impose on the rolling stock. A method of reconciling these two principles has to be found. The light but highly valued articles have to pay freight rates in a fixed proportion of their value and the rate has to be higher on these articles as per the principle of fixing "What the traffic will bear". The freight rates on the bulky articles has got to be lower. Within the bulky category a distinction has to be made between less valuable and more valuable articles for a given weight. Thus food articles of a given weight are more valuable than iron ore or coal of the same weight. The more valuable among the bulky articles have to pay a higher freight rate than the less valuable articles of the same weight. In this manner there will have to be a classification of the articles on the basis of their value and weight/bulk and the freight structure has to be designed accordingly.

As per the passenger fare structure a different principle has to be followed. The fare for the upper class travel has to be higher than for the lower class travel. In the case of both classes upto a certain distance, the fare should be fixed and beyond this the rate should decline for every 100 miles so that the per mile fare decreases as the distance increases. The passengers are inclined to carry heavy luggage if the luggage is free of fare/freight. Therefore after exempting a minimum weight of luggage per passenger the excess has to be made to pay freight. The freight charges will supplement the passenger fares. In the matter of passenger fare fixation it is the cost of service principle that should be the basis. As figures prove the revenue from passenger fares is on the decline. This is for two reasons : (a) road transport is less tedious than rail transport as the buses reach the places of destination unlike the railways in the case of which the passengers have to pay for road transport to and from the places of residence. (b) the increasing incidence of railway accidents has made rail traffic risky which the passengers have to avoid. This situation can be avoided by introducing safety measures like avoiding overspeeding, making driving the trains in a state of drunkenness a punishable offence, by perfecting the signal system. At the same time the passenger amenities in the platforms like well furnished retirement rooms, refreshments at reasonable prices, manual services etc. This will attract passengers to the railways and lead to larger revenues and render cross subsidisation unnecessary.

In a liberalised economic environment in which two modes of surface transport road and railway are in competition the passenger and freight rates charged by the railways should be competitive. They should not be more than the road transport rates for in that case the railways lose both passenger and freight traffic, and suffer losses. They should not be lower than those charged by the road transport for it is unnecessary. A policy of this variety is necessary to make the railways earn enough revenue to meet the cost of operation and depreciation of rolling stock.

65

The SSI Sector and Economic Reforms

In a labour surplus and capital shortage economy like India small scale industrial units have a leading part to play. Capital intensive and technology oriented industries are outside the purview of the small entrepreneurs who cannot afford them. As part of the new economic policy initiate in July 1991, industrial deregulation and the promotion of competitive efficiency became the new slogans. Some sections of the small scale units have become apprehensive that the new economic policy may spell the doom of small units which find themselves unable to face the competition of large units. But these apprehensions have been found to be unfounded. The small scale sector has registered impressive growth in output, employment and exports. The small scale sector accounts for 40 percent of industrial production, 80 percent of industrial employment and 35 percent of total exports. The small scale sector which is labour intensive has been promoted over the years by the Government which has adopted special schemes to encourage and vitalise it. It has also contributed to decentralisation of industrial activity among different regions. The small scale industries thrive in different regions making use of locally available labour and raw materials. The future of this sector in the regime of liberalisation can be said to be safe. Even so, many have raised apprehensions about the future of this sector in the context of the unrestricted entry of large firms domestic and foreign endowed with financial and technological lead. It is argued that the role of the small scale sector is complementary to the large scale sector. But this argument confuses between small scale units and ancillary units. The small scale units are independent units which produce goods on their own while the ancillary units serve as ancillaries to the large units by supplying the inputs to them to produce final products. The small scale units are independent units specialising in all the processes of production.

At present, there are more than 20 lakh SSI units in the country producing goods both for the domestic and export markets. If, under the present policy of liberalisation, the SSI units run the risk of being swamped by the large units, existing and prospective, it is natural to expect them to raise objections to the economic reforms. But experience is otherwise. A recent CII survey on "Business outlook of Small Industry" establishes the fact that the small industrialists are not too skeptical about the impact of liberalisation on their own enterprises. The Survey which covers 414 units shows that as many as 82 percent of the respondents lent clear support to economic liberalisation while 23 percent maintained that the economic reform package had not conferred any major benefit on the SSI sector. However, they were all eager to increase output and exports and to generate employment.

The anxiety of the SSI sector is not about the competitive challenge coming from the large scale industrial units but it is about the inadequacy of the appropriate technical, financial and infrastructural facilities. It is labouring under shortage and indifferent quality of power supply, constraints on the uninterrupted supply of good quality raw materials, inadequate supply of working capital and the unhelpful attitude of the banking sector and the persistence of the shadow of the "License permit Inspector Raj". These problems are not the outcome of the economic reforms but they were there even before the launching of the economic reforms programme in 1991 and they persist even now albeit in a less severe form.

Despite the competitive challenge posed by the large scale units the SSI sector does not seem to be under any pressure to restructure their units. This is surprising in view of the technology lag in the SSI units. This is due to two reasons: (a) the capacity additions in large and medium industry are not commensurate with the surge of market demand for their output, (b) the policy of reservation of production in favour of the SSI Units is being continued even in the competitive economic regime. However, the protectionist regime cannot continue for long. As the new capacities are installed in the large and medium industries competition becomes more vigorous. The liberalisation of consumer goods imports in order to counter the inflationary pressure is bound to affect the small scale sector in the areas where the imported goods are in competition with the goods produced by the small scale sector. In the context of a growing economy and surging market demand, the exposure to advanced global technology will necessitate the graduation of the small scale units into medium sized units. This chance cannot be denied to the small scale units in the name of protection against domestic and foreign competition. In the context of global competition and a growing economy it is necessary to introduce modernisation and technological upgradation of the small scale sector. This, of course, requires finance and technology. In this connection the case for foreign currency loans for efficient industrial units for improving the quality of their products so as to match the quality of the products produced domestically and by foreign firms is strong and unassailable. The foreign investors who are permitted to have 24 percent of the equity in an SSI Unit have remained without adequate and expressed response. Their equity participation could be increased to 35 percent in order to enthuse them to investing in the SSI units. Their participation will make advanced technology easily available. This will also help the skill upgradation of the indigenous labour force.

The apprehensions of some SSI units that they might be swamped by the large scale industrial units equipped with advanced technology and endowed with abundant finance are not entirely unfounded. At present Indias share in world trade is 0.6 percent and it needs to be increased to atleast 1 percent if India is to have a decisive say in the WTO. Furthermore, despite the reduction of customs duties the existing duties are said to be high. With a further reduction of the customs duties the products of the SSI units may be unable to face foreign competition in the Indian market. With the present trend towards liberalisation of consumer goods imports in order to counter the inflationary pressure there will be a surge of imports into India. Unless the domestic goods match the imported goods in quality and compete with them in respect of cost, the SSI units will come to grief. In this situation the promotion of quality and price competitiveness so as to compete successfully with the domestic goods produced by the large industries and with imports is a categorical imperative. This calls for foreign currency loans and even foreign equity participation in the SBI units. What the SSI units lack is capital and technology. If these are supplied in adequate quantity they will make a distinct contribution to output growth, employment generation and exports considering its high profile and great potential the SSI sector deserves all kinds of encouragement.

66

Managing India's Food Economy

The Government of India and the Planning Commission have to keep a close watch on India's food economy. India's population is growing at the rate of 2.2 percent per year and a growing population requires larger food production. In India it is the food prices that govern the general price index. In the years when the food prices are held stable a budget deficit does not cause a rise in prices. In the years when the food prices are rising even a balanced budget is associated with a rising price index. Therefore, the success of Government's anti-inflation policy depends crucially on the stability of food prices. Even the success of the policy of growth without inflation depends on the stability of food prices.

The availability and price of food have implications for poverty incidence. Larger availability and lower prices of food lead to larger consumption of food and higher standard of living. While lower availability and higher price of food lead to lower consumption of food and lower standard of living. India has always tried to achieve food self sufficiency in order to avoid a rise in food prices which is inflationary and also to reduce dependence on food imports at considerable expenditure of scarce foreign exchange reserves. But fortunately at present the problem in India is not one of achieving self-sufficiency but a large and growing food stock. India has accumulated over 37 million tonnes of food stock. As the offtake of food for the public distribution system has been falling rapidly from 21 million tonnes in 1991 to less than 14 million tonnes now the food reserves are sufficient to keep the public distribution system going for over two years without further procurement. If food procurement continues at the present rate of 24 million tonnes each year and the off take for the public distribution system remains at the present level of 14 million tonnes the food reserves would grow to over 50 million tonnes in two years.

Despite rising stocks of food the percepita availability of food has declined from 510 grammes per day in 1990-91 to 465 grammes per day in 1993-94. The availability in 1990-91 was unusually high. The average availability over three years before the reforms started i.e, from 1988 to 1991 was 493 grammes per day. Thus, since the reforms started, there is a fall of some 5 percent. It must be noted that the availability of 465 grammes in 1993-94 is still higher than the average availability over the 1980s. Infact, the food grains offtake under the PDS by the States has been progressively falling short of control allocations and the stocks with the Government have been pilling up. The low offtake from the PDS is mainly due to the decreasing differential between the issue and market prices. Between 1991-92 and 1993-94 the offtake of rice declined from 9.8 to less than 9 million tonnes and of wheat from 8.5 to less than 6 million tonnes. This is inspite of the revamped PDS introduced in remote tribal and dry land areas. It is interesting to note that inspite of lower subsidies and smaller offtake from PDS, Government's expenditure on food subsidies in 1993-94 increased possibly due to increased cost of carrying a large stock. Higher levels of output did not result in lower prices due to higher procurement prices. This led to an increase in the prices of primary articles. The inflation rate for primary articles rose from 6.9 in 1993-94 to 9.0 in 1994-95.

Over the years the per-capita availability of food has remained static and it has improved by no more than 25 percent during the last half century. Indeed agricultural production has barely kept ahead of the rate of population growth. Due to the financial transfers into the farm sector in the form of subsidies rather than investment, further growth in food grains production may slow down. This means that the vast food reserve of over 37 million tonnes is not a sign of well fed populace but a case of under nourishment. This, indeed, is a paradoxical situation. The food reserves cannot be exported as the international price of food is lower than in India. Exports therefore would entail a loss. If exports are to be made possible the Government has to give export subsidy.

A large part of food grains cannot be sold in India as the issue prices are raised in order to cut food subsidy. Most consumers prefer to buy better grains in the open market at higher prices. The reserves cannot be held for long as the warehouses are full and as the quality of the stock deteriorates with the passage of time.

It is unfortunate that this paradoxical situation is created by the politicians. By supporting the farm lobby they see to it that the procurement prices are raised periodically. With issue prices keeping pace and open market prices remaining soft because or abundant supply there is not much of a price differential between the prices of grains in the ration shops and the prices in the open market. Even as more and more grain is offered to the official procurement agency less and less is bought by the people. The inefficiency of the Food Corporation of India (FCI) whose operational expenses are said to be 43 percent of the issue price of wheat and 23 percent of the issue price of rice, means that much of the subsidy goes not to benefit the poor who could do with some income transfers but to finance the operations of an inefficient system.

The problem of mounting food reserve is remediable. If it is intended to provide the basic welfare system for the poor where their basic food requirements is met at a reasonable cost, a food stamp system would be administratively simpler and cheaper too. In the alternative an employment guarantee programme would create incomes that become available to pay for food. Even if the public distribution system is to be maintained it can be supplied with food grains bought from the open market for this explicit purpose. If the national grain market is allowed to operate without mandatory procurement or movement restrictions, grains prices will automatically fall to a level where the demands on the public distribution system would be reduced. In this system the support price operations to prevent distress sale by the farmers would be a far more limited exercise than is the case at present. It would also avert a situation where the Indian consumers are paying more for their wheat and rice than most consumers in other countries. It would also not lead to the accumulation of unwanted food stocks with all the attendant maintenance costs and the sure possibility of deterioration in quality rendering the food unfit for consumption.

Through the years there has been a decline in the procurement price of wheat and rice. The following Table shows the movement of procurement prices during 1991-1996.

The assessment that the official food reserve will not decline in the near future must have played a role in the Government opting for the smallest increase in five years in the procurement price of rice for the 1995-96 season. This continues the process that began last year. As the Table shows the procurement prices of both rice and wheat were increased substantially in the early 1990s. It is only from last year that some moderation has been in existence. In both absolute and percentage terms the increase this year is the smallest in recent years for rice.

Increase in Procurement Prices (in percent)

Marketing Year	Rice	Wheat
1991-92	12.2	4.7
1992-93	17.4	22.2
1993-94	14.8	20
1994-95	9.7	6.0
1995-96	5.9	2.9

There were other reasons also for the small increase in procurement prices. The most important is the sharp increase in procurement prices in the earlier years which contributed to generate double-digit inflation. The following Table shows the increase in procurement prices, the wholesale prices of rice and wheat and the overall rise in wholesale prices since 1990-91.

Increase in Prices in Percent (1990-91 to-date)

Procurement Prices	
Rice	75
Wheat	67
Wholesale Prices	
Rice	75
Wheat	53
All commodities	58

It is obvious that the Government's procurement price policy that was a major factor in the maintenance of inflation at a high level and the of sharp rise in food prices. It is this awareness that has made the Government to slow down the pace of increase in procurement prices.

The prospects for Khairff crop are bright this year because of good monsoons. At present the food stocks are uncomfortably high due to the rise in procurement prices of rice and wheat this year albeit at a lower rate the Union Ministry of Agriculture is faced with the problem of procuring large quantities of wheat and rice. This calls for vigorous export effort. Atleast 5 million tonnes of rice has to be exported in 1995-96 contracts are being negotiated with importers in China and Vietnam and other countries and there may be delay in effecting shipments the actual quantity exported may not be more than 3 million tonnes before March 1996. It is therefore necessary for the Government to enter into long term agreement to deliver the food stock till the end of 1996 at prices which will take into account world prices. In recent months world prices have firmed up and exporters of rice are confident that large quantities can be shipped without involving any loss even in the event of the traders getting their supplies from the open market. It may not be possible to export food at prices below economic costs. The expenditure on export subsidies may be lower than it would otherwise be. The output of rice and wheat has risen steadily over the years and is likely to rise this year there will not be a fall in the exportable surplus of food grains despite the emphasis on the execution of programme aimed at improving the standards of living of the weaker sections of society. Having regard to the vast export potential it is necessary to evolve a crop planning laying emphasis on the variety of rice or wheat that is in great demand in the export markets.

With the signing of the Marrakesh treaty last year the stage is set for the growth of export of agro products including food. The food consuming countries i.e., the countries consuming rice are in Asia. While the wheat consuming countries are all the world over. With the application of appropriate agricultural technology the yield per acre of rice and wheat can be increased and the comparative cost advantage can be maintained. This will benefit the farmers producing rice and wheat and will cause a rise in India's export earnings which will help to pay for India's essential imports. Attention needs to be focussed on this aspect of India's food economy.

67

The Proposed Madras School of Economics

The Telegraph of Monday 15th May 1995 published in Delhi carried a report highlighting the keenness of Dr. Raja Chellaiah to start an elite economics centre in Madras from August 1995 called the "Madras School of Economics" (MSE) which would be patterned on the lines of the London School of Economics (LSE) in London. It is here intended to record a few thoughts on this proposed enterprises.

The London School of Economics was established by Sydney and Beatrice Webb in order to provide advanced training in economics initially. With the passage of time other faculties were included like political science, sociology, law, statistics, econometrics, geography and international relations. Each of these specialities got split into sub-specialities providing chance to the students to opt for one of them as their choice. The LSE is not funded by the Government though it gets an annual grant from it. It gets its wherewithal from the Philanthropic personalities who bequeath their liquid and non-liquid assets which yield a stream of income. The student enrolment is on the increase and it attracts students from all over the world. It recruits eminent scholars who as teachers and researchers have extended the borders of discovery and frontiers of knowledge. The LSE runs a Quarterly Journal called ECONOMICA which; at present, contains original articles which are the outcome of prodigious research effort. At times, they are explosively mathematical which many find to be a closed book. Many scholars consider it a prestige to publish their articles in this journal. The articles published in this journal are extensively cited in the articles published in this and other prestigious journals and the scholarly books of eminent scholars. It has a competent editorial staff capable of separating the goats from the sheep with the utmost objectivity. The editorial board prescribes not only high standards of technical substance but also of linguistic perfection. It is a great pleasure to go through the successive issues of this journal; it is an even greater pleasure to possess them. Their possession is a mark of scholastic respectability.

Not all the applications for admission are admitted as a matter of course. Over five decades ago all those who applied for admission to the doctoral courses were admitted but some of them were found to be ill equipped to face the rigours of the course in the subjects and in linguistic ability. The style, syntax and diction of their language were found to be far below the expected standard. It was a problem for the research supervisors to see them through the course upto the point of success. Some who were hopelessly wanting in substantive and linguistic equipment were sent out with polite "regrets". Then came screening. The students who applied for admission to the doctoral course would first be admitted to the Master's Degree course and would be launched on a research career. If, after a while, they were found to be competent, they would be shifted to the doctoral course; otherwise they would be retained in the Master's Degree course where the standard of attainment is not as high or as exacting as that in the Doctoral Course. The doctoral course is exacting in its demands for quality. The dissertations containing original contributions to knowledge would be published by the LSE itself. The authors of these publications were rated very high in the academic arena and they and their works would enjoy a world market. In fact, many universities would compete with each other to acquire their services as they would enhance the reputation of the institutions acquiring them and would attract the best talent from all over the world. In fact, the LSE was a high profile centre of academic activity.

In 1942 Dr. V.K.R.V. Rao of the Delhi University started the Delhi school of Economics (DSE) and structured it on the LSE model. It held out high hopes of emerging as a premier institution of economic research. Dr. Rao obtained fabulous grants from the Ford Foundation, the Rockfeller Foundation and other Foundations which were flush with funds and were overly liberal in their munificence.

He attracted the best talent available in India. He would invite eminent economists from the British and American Universities to spend some time in DSE, give special lectures to the students and the members of the faculty and would hold seminars on subjects of topical importance so that the Indian scholars would learn the method of organising and addressing seminars. It is in these seminars that new ideas would germinate. In the LSE Professor Lionel Robbins would hold weekly seminars in the Graham Wallace room. The seminars would be attended by the postgraduate students and the members of the faculty. Sometimes visiting foreign economists would attend these seminars. In one of his seminars he said that it was in the seminars that he got novel ideas for in the seminars where there is a clash of perspectives, ideas and arguments new sparks emerge and they open up new vistas of economic scholarship. How right he was.

At present, the DSE is bereft of its earlier glitter. Many eminent scholars emigrated to the American Universities where they are serving as expatriate professors on fabulous salaries, perquisites and facilities. It was difficult to find scholars of comparable eminence to take their places. Postgraduate courses are administered, research of some quality is being carried out and research degrees are awarded as a matter of course. And so it goes on.

In 1953, on the occasion of the tenth anniversary of the DSE Dr. John Mathur delivered the decennial address. In the course of his address he lamented the steady deterioration of quality of teaching and research and stated: "At present everybody is called a "Professor" and, in consequence, the word "Professor" has lost its earlier glory. We must restore to the word "Professor" atleast some of its lost glory". How right he was. The DSE is not what it was initially and what it was intended to be by the founding fathers. In 1951 Dr. Rao became a member of the Planning Commission and also a member of the Taxation Enquiry Commission; then he became the Vice-Chancellor of the Delhi University where he had to grapple with a multitude of administrative problems which left no time to devote to the welfare of the DSE. Others took over as its Directors but they were no match to him in matters of academic excellence or administrative acumen or oganisational skill. In 1966 he entered politics and became a Minister. In 1972 he migrated to Bangalore where he established the Institute for Social and Economic Change (ISEC) which had a flying start under his stewardship but has now lost its earlier glitter. The appointment of retired bureaucrats and also persons with questionable integrity as Directors has eroded the credibility of the Institute as a worthwhile entity. The Institute undertakes commissioned research which consists of field surveys and these surveys are, for the most part, money-spinning exercises and not serious attempts at finding the truth. The officer in charge of these surveys appoints investigators whose duty is to go to the field, issue questionnaires to the people, collect information and to forward it to the officer who, on the basis of this information, prepares a report and submits it to the Government which, finding it to be of not much value or relevance, consigns it to the archives. The field investigators who are averse to the drudgery of collecting data are found to invent statistics, write down the information as if it was supplied by the informants and supply it to the officer. The investigators themselves shamelessly say that it is not a DATA collection exercise but a DA and TA collection exercise. The ISEC is not the only one of its kind; there are many in the country which engage themselves in this reprehensible exercise. It is for this reason that the surveys are suspect.

The main objective of narrating the experience with the DSE and ISEC is to caution the proposed MSE against drifting in the same direction. For, in the Indian context, what is expected is far different from what is realised in the pejorative sense. The establishment of the MSE is a categorical imperative but it must have a purpose and a survey direction to move towards the pre-determined academic targets.

Dr. Raja Chellaiah is a noted expert in fiscal economics. He served as fiscal adviser to the Finance Ministry for three years from March 1992 to May 1995. His tenure ended on Friday 12th May 1995. He proposes to start the MSE in Madras in August this year. The MSE of his conception should be a privately funded centre of postgraduate studies in economics which will have to maintain excellent standards in teaching and research comparable to those obtaining in the LSE. He says : "Our aim at MSE will be to provide a refreshingly free academic atmosphere" and added that if the funds are taken from outside the School would be concentrating mainly on technical papers for the Government, though most of its research would be on specialised subjects. The proposed courses in MSE will include macroeconomics, econometrics, mathematical economics, capital market and financial services, industrial and environmental economics as the fields of specialisation.

The recruitment policy is very important for an institution of this kind. According to Dr. Chellaiah the recruitment will be based on merit and only half of the required professional staff would be hired on a permanent basis. The other half would be drawn on a contractual basis for periods ranging from one to three years. This will enable the MSE to avail of the services of scholars from a wide circle of academic institutions in India and abroad. Making the MSE "a centre of excellence in learning" does not mean any denigration of the existing institutions in the country. He wants the MSE to maintain catholicity of outlook welcoming scholars from all parts of the country. Just because the MSE is located in the south it does not mean that the others would be barred from entry into it whether they are teachers or students. The MSE will make it a policy to locate and attract meritorious persons wherever they may be.

The private sector has begun to enter the hitherto prohibited areas like banking, insurance, heavy industries, financial services and infrastructure. The establishment of the MSE in the private sector is in keeping with the philosophy of liberalism which has rightly become the accepted philosophy of the present Government. In order to supply trained personnel to the private sector and to the Government to undertake competent economic management, steps would be taken to restore respectable standards of postgraduate instruction in the areas which the MSE has chosen as the areas of its specialisation.

At present there is a certain degree of parochialism in the Indian academia. The universities and institutes in the North are filled with north Indians while the universities and institutes in the South are manned by South Indians. This means that north Indians are unwelcome in the South and South Indians are unwelcome in the North. This hinders the process of emotional integration for the North-South divide is inimical to the development of the psychology of oneness though oneness is bandied about on the platforms in both the divisions.

Dr. Chellaiah desires to ensure free academic atmosphere. He seems to believe that freedom is curtailed if the MSE accepts Government funding in which case the MSE has to undertake research for the Government. Just because the MSE undertakes research into subjects necessary for it to formulate policy, it does not mean that its freedom is curtailed. Many institutes in the UK and the USA undertake Government sponsored research into problems of national and international importance and the Government foots the bill. The institutes retain the freedom to express opinions based on technical investigations and scientific evaluations and the Government does not expect them to build its prejudices into the findings. In similar manner, the MSE can also undertake research commissioned by the private sector and submit its findings which become the basis of policy formulation. The greater the income of the MSE the greater the scope for expanding the area of its operation. Private benefaction can also be accepted to enlarge its resources without losing its freedom of operation.

Dr. Chellaiah's idea of establishing the MSE is good and the need for an establishment of this kind is a categorical imperative. But its success in realising the dream of Dr. Chellaiah depends crucially on the directors who run the MSE, the quality of the scholars who are appointed and the promotion opportunities open to them and the facilities made available to them for study and research theoretical or applied and on the quality of students selected to undergo training. But the policy of reservation has to be boldly tackled. The scheme of reservation may satisfy the criterion of social equity but it may not satisfy the criterion of efficiency. A lot depends on the modalities adopted in reconciling the two palpably irreconcilable criteria. This task is daunting indeed. The administration of the MSE has to face up to this task boldly. Tamil

Nadu is a state where popular sentiments cannot easily be brushed aside. Any attempt to do it would encounter formidable difficulties which may thwart the progress of the MSE. To concede to popular sentiments would amount to compromising standards. This may make Dr. Chellaiah's golden dream difficult to realise. How to reconcile the two criteria of equity and efficiency calls for a nationwide debate. Dr. Chellaiah has first to tackle this problem successfully. In a situation were the Mandal Revolution is gaining ground slowly and imperceptibly, it has to be tackled with extreme care and circumspection as the people are oversensitive to the Mandal prescription. The Government is unlikely to be of any help as it is disinclined to displease the vote banks which are a source of power and perpetuation in power. This is a challenge to the ingenuity of Dr. Chellaiah and the Governing Body of the MSE. If the criterion of efficiency is given a go by the future of MSE can be written off as lost. Mandalism is a social entity which cannot be accepted or rejected outright. Dr. Chellaiah is thus faced with a grave social problem which gathers momentum with the passage of time and it may render the translation of Chellaiah's golden vision into concrete reality difficult indeed.

The concern of Dr. Chellaiah for an institution of academic excellence is indeed commendable. But its success depends crucially on the organisation of the MSE and the efficiency of the academic staff it recruits and the quality of the alumni it admits. The MSE may provide excellent facilities for research and investigation but if the quality of the researchers is poor the MSE will not be able to deliver the goods. If it is to deliver the goods firmness in dealing with the problems that may arise is a categorical imperative. Where standards are involved there shall be no compromise. The Governing Body needs to be imbued with an academic purpose. This purpose has to be realised if the MSE is to give a good account of itself. It will be able to give a good account of itself if it is able to atleast match if not to excel the LSE in academic excellence and academic performance. The MSE should take upon itself the duty of dispensing knowledge and not of administering grants.

68

Mexican Crisis: A Figment of the Pessimists Imagination

Ever since the Mexican crisis broke out in December 1994 many in India who have got a negative perception about the fundamentals of the Indian economy have been expressing apprehensions, off and on, that India may go the Mexican way. I have underlined the innate strength of the macroeconomic fundamentals of the Indian economy and have sought to allay apprehensions of the Mexican type crisis occurring in India. However, the dramatic slide in the rupee breaking the psychological barrier of Rs. 36 per US dollar and the indications of a further slide in the rupee have strengthened the pessimists in their attempt to revive the fears of a Mexican crisis in India. It is the object of this note to further allay these fears underlining the strength of the macro-economic fundamentals of the Indian economy.

There are differences between the macroeconomic configurations in Mexico in December 1994 and those in India of 1996. Between 1990 and 1993 there was a massive capital inflow to Mexico of the order of $ 72 billion palpably as a result of the structural adjustment policies recommended for adoption by the International Monetary Fund. But in the middle of 1994 the economic scenario of Mexico underwent a radical change for the worse. Mexico's macroeconomic stability cause to be threatened by the rising interest rates in the United States which attracted capital inflow and reduced capital outflow, mounting current account deficit and political instability. These were compounded by the capital account convertibility so thoughtlessly introduced by the Central Bank of Mexico but exuberantly hailed as the hallmark of economic achievement. These factors engineered a massive flight of capital exercising heavy pressure on the Peso.

The Central Bank of Mexico sought to defend the Peso by means of aggressive market intervention by drawing down its forex reserves. These reserves which were of the order of $ 25 billion in December 1993 fell to $ 6.3 billion at the end of December 1994. The Mexican Peso had to be bailed out of the crisis through the US special funding of the order of $ 20 billion and IMF loans amounting to $ 17.8 billion. It is argued by the pessimists in India that India cannot claim to be a candidate for the assistance of this type and magnitude in the event of India going the Mexican way asserting that India has gone a long way along that route.

Mr. Andrew Crocket, the Managing Director of the Bank for International Settlements (BIS), states that the developing countries have to draw the following lessons from the Mexican experience. They are: (a) economic reform measures must be credible and consistent and not be dictated by political exigencies; fiscal correction must aim at reducing the fiscal deficit drastically (b) the balance of payments deficit must be regarded as a potential anger to the macroeconomic stability of the economy rather than as a temporary expedient which causes a rise in the external debt; (c) the move to capital account convertibility of the currency should be regarded as too hasty, premature and ill-conceived; (d) the foreign capital which the developing countries bank on needs to be seen not as a substitute for domestic savings and efforts need to be made to raise the savings rate. (e) the developing countries have to keep adequate forex reserves in order to cope with volatile capital outflows. The burden of his song is that the Mexican crisis was due to large persistent fiscal deficits, large and unbridgeable balance of payments gap, introduction of capital account convertibility which was hasty and premature, heavy dependence on foreign capital to finance economic development and the reduction of the domestic savings rate due to booming consumerism engendered by the demonstration effect of the US consumers next door, inadequacy of forex reserves which rendered the Central Bank of Mexico incapable of coping with a massive capital outflow resulting in depreciation of the Peso by as much as percent.

Mr. Michael Camdessus, Managing Director of the IMF, sees the Mexican crisis from a different perspective. He underlines the inadequacy of the surely economic approach to the problem of a country undergoing rapid change. In the context of political uncertainties the markets of all kinds (money, capital and forex) cannot remain neutral. When there is a policy slippage like the mergence of fiscal deficits, the markets soon detect the policy weaknesses. When they do it, they react sharply to disturb economic stability. The Mexican crisis of December 1994 and the recession following it were caused by the economic policy disarray compounded by political uncertainty which is part of regional political phenomenon in Latin America.

One of the reasons for the Mexican crisis is the substitution of foreign savings for domestic savings which slided significantly. But is not the case in India. The Central Statistical Organisation (CSO), has recently affirms that the GDP grew at the impressive rate of 6.2 percent during 1994-95. Now comes the CSO estimate that the savings rate in the economy has touched an all-time record of 24.4 percent of GDP during 1994-95 and the investment rate has picked up to 25.2 percent. Productivity in the economy has also increased during the last three years along with new investment and technological upgradation. In consequence, the economy has crossed the traditional threshold of a 5.5 percent rate of growth. The improvement in the savings rate is indicated by the overall macro-economic performance of the economy during 1994-95. A remarkable combination of vibrant growth in agriculture and industry and buoyancy in the capital market after the initial bearish sentiment is itself a clear pointer to an improvement in the savings performance and the investment tempo. The rise in the savings rate is attributed to a significant enhancement in the savings of the household sector and a turnaround in the overall financial performance of the public sector enterprises. It can also be attributed to the growth of money incomes made possible by the expanding range of economic opportunities for the upper and middle classes and the cumulative increase in the income of the agricultural sector thanks to the policy of support prices at remunerative levels which have made possible the increase in the savings of the house hold sector. This has happened despite the increasing consumerism of the middle class families. One evidence of this is the rise in deposits. The bank deposits have started to rise. The growth rate of deposits has risen from 1.4 percent as on November 24, 1995 to 13.2 percent by January 5, 1996. The CMIE quoting the latest banking statistics in its monthly review for January 1996 stated that the time deposits which witnessed decelerated growth of 12.64 percent by September 29, 1995 showed a 14.87 percent rise by January 5, 1996.

Thanks to the policy of liberalisation and globalisation, there has been a dramatic transformation of the commercial and financial performance of the companies. Despite the high dividend payouts many companies have increased internal retention through liberal appropriation of profits to reserves. They have all led to a spurt in company savings. The CSO data suggest that private corporate sector savings have marginally grown from 3.41 percent of GDP in 1993-94 to 4 percent in 1994-95. The current savings rate of 24.4 percent compares, but modestly, with savings levels even in other developing countries such as China (40 percent), South Korea (35 percent and Indonesia (31 percent). However, it must be observed that sustained economic growth at more than 6 percent will warrant a much higher level of savings. The fiscal policy has to address itself to this challenge.

Investment is financed partly by domestic savings and partly by domestic savings and partly by capital inflows. Net capital inflows from abroad financed investment to the tune of 0.82 percent of GDP in 1994-95 as against 0.27 percent in 1993-94. This is indicative of the vast potential in terms of foreign investment which awaits to be tapped. The stock market which was permeated by the bear sentiment has now developed a bull sentiment because of the uptrend in the buying by Foreign Institutional Investors (FII). The FIIs have ignored the political uncertainty and some brokers were squaring off their transactions. At the end of the session on February 9, the BSE Sensex gained smartly 90.49 points while the BSE National Index rose by 69.16 points to close at 1,571.03. This is due to the FIIs bringing in large sums of dollars.

Inflation in India which was 17.5 percent in July 1991 has come down to 5.04 percent at present. This is not anywhere near the inflation rate ruling in Mexico at the time of the crisis. Even if it rises by a couple of percentage points above the present 5.04 percent, it will not go anywhere near the Mexican inflation rate. The fiscal deficit which was 8.5 percent of GDP in July 1991 has come down to below 6 percent of GDP. With the buoyancy of tax revenue it is unlikely to rise above the target of 5.5 percent of GDP despite the rise in social expenditure because of electoral compulsions. The fiscal deficit notwithstanding the rate of inflation is not likely to rise above 5.5 percent. There is a reduction in Government expenditure but this is offset by a rise in social expenditure. There may be a slippage of the fiscal deficit but the slippage will be between 0.1 and 0.2 percent which is not much. This slippage from the target of 5.5 percent will be attributable to the rise in social expenditure on health and education. This deviation is a minor one and is easily manageable.

The current account deficit is 1.5 percent of GDP or, in absolute terms, it will not be more than $ 4 billion. The buoyant export growth of 24 percent will help to keep it at that level even if it cannot reduce it. The Reserve Bank of India has $ 17 billion of forex reserves which are sufficient to meet any capital outflow without occasioning a drastic decline in the external value of the rupee. Owing to heavy demand for dollars mounted by the State Bank of India to meet the oil bill, by the corporate sector, by the exporters not repatriating their export earning and by importers accelerating import payments in terms of dollars, the rupee depreciated to below Rs. 38 per US dollar engendering the fear that it may slide further down.

The Reserve Bank of India on February 7, 1996 adopted a four point strategy to stem the slide in the rupee including the stern warning to the banks and other financial agencies against indulging in unhealthy speculation; requiring the exporters to repatriate their dollar earnings which were of the order of Rs. 7,000 crore within the prescribed time limit and making import finance costlier. These steps have already had a salutary effect on the rupee. These measures slackened the demand for dollars and increased their supply. The rupee gained strength on February 9, to touch Rs. 36.90 against the dollar before closing slightly lower at Rs. 36.97/99 against the previous closing of Rs. 37.13/16. The package of measures to check volatility in the forex market has been effective. If there is no reversal of sentiment the Reserve Bank may have to intervene in the forex market in a big way. The Reserve bank should declare the rate at which it will intervene decisively. This will end speculation leaving arbitrage operations to ensure stability. If intervention is necessary and can mobilise resources the Reserve Bank has to defend the rupee against undue depreciation. At the same time efforts are being made to persuade big importers like IOC, MMTC and others to stagger their dollar purchases from the market to soften the impact on the weakening rupee. Big public sector units have begun to borrow from abroad to repay their forex debts maturing within the financial year. Financial institutions like the IDBI, IFCI and ICICI have also resorted to unusually large forex borrowings. This combined with the jump in the portfolio investment by FIIs, should see the situation ease soon. With the clearing of the 100 percent owned foreign venture, foreign direct investment (FDI) flows too are expected to soar in the last quarter of fiscal 1995-96. Together these developments should enhance the dollar supplies and ease the pressure on the rupee. The rupee slide is expected to end with the dollar inflow gaining momentum.

It must be admitted even by those who holding out the scare of a Mexican-type crisis in India, that the macro-economic fundamentals of the Indian economy are strong enough to ward off the danger of a crisis of any magnitude. Foreign funds are flowing into the country despite the alleged political uncertainty; savings rate has picked up significantly and bank deposits have shown an impressive rise. The current account deficit which is only 1.5 percent of GDP is manageable and the Reserve Bank of India has enough reserves to meet any drain on dollar reserves and is in a position to mobilise more dollars. The rate of inflation has come down to 5.04 percent and is unlikely to rise. The fiscal deficit which is targeted to be 5.5 percent of GDP is likely to be stabilised at this level with a possible slippage of between 0.1 percent and 0.2 percent despite the bludgeoning expenditure thanks to buoyancy of tax revenue. The rate of economic growth at 6.2 percent is impressive. While the Mexican Peso depreciated by 68 percent in December 1994 has rupee depreciated only by 16 percent in February 1996. The rupee is nowhere near the danger zone. All these factors attest to the strength of the macro-economic fundamentals of the Indian economy. In view of this the negative perceptions about the Indian economy by the diehard pessimists are unwarranted. It can safely be asserted that there is no danger of a crisis of the Mexican variety. Any crisis is only the figment of their imagination.

69

A Revised Gold Bond Scheme is Necessary

In this budget speech on 29.2.1992 the Finance Minister proposed the issue of gold bonds enabling gold holders to sell gold to the Government in exchange for gold bonds which carry an interest rate, the depositor being free from the obligation of disclosing how he acquired gold. The gold acquired by the Government in this manner will be sold to the Reserve Bank of India with a repurchase obligation. This scheme is expected to have two effects: (1) The money which the Government gets from the Reserve Bank as sale proceeds will help to reduce government borrowing from the market; (2) it will make the economy look healthy as it enhances the country's foreign exchange reserves as the gold reserves held by the Reserve Bank constitute part of the foreign exchange reserves.

The first effect would result in a substantial reduction in the interest payments made by the Government on its borrowings. To this extent it results in a direct reduction in the budget deficit and in a reduction in the rate of inflation. At present, the government raises money in the market to meet its requirements through the sale of dated securities of 5-10 years maturity at interest rates of 12-13 percent. The Government will not have to pay any interest to the Reserve Bank on the amount realised from it through the sale of gold though it will have to pay interest of 2-3 percent to gold bond holders. This payment is more than offset by the reduction in aggregate interest payments on the money realised from the sale of gold is interest free. In addition, the Government will have to take into account appreciation in the price of gold that may take place between the time of gold sale to the Reserve Bank and the repurchase of it.

But there is snag here. The IMF prescribes a reduction in the fiscal deficit to a 5 percent of GDP in 1992-93. But it does not consider the sale proceeds from gold as indicating a reduction in the fiscal deficit since the sale will be with a repurchase obligation. The fiscal deficit will be reduced only to the extent to which the Government is able to reduce interest payments on the total debt. But there is a bright side to it. The addition to the Reserve Bank's reserves of gold will bolster the country's foreign exchange reserves and will improve the overall creditworthiness of the country. The Reserve Bank can also raise foreign currency loans against the gold security at cheaper interest rates or use gold to meet the credit requirements of export-linked projects. The success of the gold bond scheme depends on the extent of liberalisation of the gold regime and quantity of gold mobilised under it.

A provision is also made for the NRIs, resident Indians including infants returning to India to bring into the country 5 kgs of gold each, from abroad. As the NRIs, purchase gold from out of their foreign currency holdings to that extent the flow of foreign exchange to the country will fall. When they bring gold to the country, they will sell it to the black money holders for a premium. The black money holders who purchase gold from the NRIs will buy gold bonds and after the maturity of the bonds retrieve gold and sell it at the appreciated value. In this way black money will be laundered into white money. Furthermore, the gold bond scheme, despite its assured advantages, has the effect of legitimising fraudulent practices. It is true that after the gold bond scheme was announced there has been a substantial flow of gold into the country. It is suggested that the Government should make gold imports more liberal. But this has the unwelcome side effect of causing a reverse flow of capital from India in order to finance gold imports. Thus while gold import per se improves the foreign exchange position and thus improves the balance of payments the outflow of capital deteriorates both.

According to a study undertaken by the Reserve Bank the quantity of gold in the country at the end of 1991 was 7,565 tonnes values at above $ 87 billion or Rs. 2,61,000 crore. Of this the quantum of gold stock held by the Reserve Bank is 351 tonnes. Those who are holding this gold in their private hoards could be induced to part with a part of their gold in exchange for gold bonds carrying a higher rate of interest than the rates attached to the gold bonds under the present gold bond scheme. In this case those who are holding gold will voluntarily surrender their gold holdings to the Government in exchange for the gold bonds. The Government must give them the guarantee that at the end of the maturity period gold would be returned to them so that they themselves can appropriate any appreciation in the value of gold. This does not involve the laundering of black money into white or the legitimisation of fraudulent practices. Furthermore, it does not also involve the use of foreign exchange earned by the NRIs and resident Indians returning to India after a stay for six months in foreign countries, for the purchase of gold to be brought to India. Liberalised import of gold may cause a rise in the stock of gold reserves of the Reserve Bank but at the same time it results in a reduction in the inflow of foreign exchange as it will be used to purchase gold. If the gain in gold reserves and the loss of foreign exchange reserves are equal there will be no net gain in the aggregate foreign exchange reserves.

The gold bond scheme is good but it is in need of modification. The gold bonds should be issued against domestic gold stock surrendered to the Government and not against imported gold. The latter legitimises fraudulent practices in encouraging the laundering of black money into white money, activates idle money into active money and increases the income velocity of money which has inflationary consequences. But the offer of gold bonds in exchange for domestic gold will not have these consequences. It is therefore suggested that the present gold bond scheme should be stopped and a new gold bond scheme under which gold bonds are offered in exchange for domestic gold holding should be introduced.

The revised scheme has several advantages over the present scheme:

1. It causes a net addition to the aggregate foreign exchange reserves of the country as the acquisition of gold by the Government for sale to the Reserve bank of India does not involve any expenditure of foreign exchange as does the presently designed schemes.

2. It does not cause an outflow of capital to finance gold imports and, for this reason, it imposes no strain on the balance of payments.
3. It does not activate idle black cash and does not cause a rise in the income velocity of money with all its inflationary consequences.
4. It results in a reduction in the interest liability of the Government.

But as a repurchase obligation is built into the gold bond scheme the IMF will not consider the sale proceeds from gold as reduction in the Government's fiscal deficit. For this purpose a part of the gold bonds will have to be of long term maturity of 20-30 years. Such a long maturity period will convince the IMF of the effective reduction in the fiscal deficit by 2020 A.D. India will not have the problem of borrowing from the IMF as at present. This modified scheme could be examined and also tried with advantage.

The gold bond scheme proposed by the Finance Minister should have come into effect in May 1992. But it takes some more time for the Government to put it into effect as it is giving the scheme final touches. Before the scheme is finalised the revised scheme could be given due consideration for the benefit of the nation.

70

Foreign Companies in the Power Sector

Many important developments are on the cards in the power sector. It is a matter of opinion whether these developments are revolutionary or harmful. The Government is caught in a dilemma about the power sector. As power is an important infrastructural facility any inadequacy in its supply is bound to retard the rate of economic growth. If the Government wants to increase the supply of power to the required degree it must have adequate investible resources. But it does not have enough resources. The cost of power generation is far higher than the price of power. This is because power is being supplied at concessional rates or free of any price. The State Electricity Boards which are supplying power at a price lower than the unit cost of production have accumulated losses of the order of Rs. 5,000 crore. They find themselves in a position where they are unable to clear the arrears due to the power generating units. They find it impossible either to raise the power tariff or to stop free supply of power. They are also under political pressure to continue the free supply of power or its supply at concessional rates. In addition there is loss of power during transmission. But the loss of power recorded in the books is not the true loss. Those who get power at concessional rates or free use this power for purposes other than the ones for which they obtain this power. Records of these losses are not available. Those who use pumpsets to lift water use power to lift water unnecessarily, the lack of power maintenance of pumpsets which utilise more power than they should, the failure to grow crops in the planned manner in all these ways the supply of power has remained most unscientific.

Quite apart from these which are, of course, remediable the issue of adequate supply of capital is the most important issue facing the Government. In this connection the Government has to invite private sector companies and/or the foreign companies into the power sector and to ask them to generate power, sell it to State Electricity Boards which would sell it to the actual users. Certain private sector companies have, no doubt, come forward in response to the Government's invitation. But even they are labouring under capital shortage, scarcity of appropriate technology and inefficiency. The generation of power in a manner which does not lead to environmental degradation is yet to take roots in India. This also is a problem.

There is another problem related to the pricing of power. The price of power has to be determined on the basis of the cost of production and a reasonable rate of profit. The supply of power at the price current charged by the Electricity Boards is impossible. If the Electricity Boards purchase power from the private sector companies at the price charged by them and sell it at a lower price they and the Governments supporting them will face a financial crisis and the subsidy becomes an unbearable burden for the Governments.

There is only one way out of this predicament. The Electricity Boards cannot be treated as philanthropic establishments. The Hon'ble Minister for power has rightly said that the Electricity Boards have to revise their price policy and fix a price that would be remunerative. This means that the users of electricity have to pay a higher price than at present and this is inevitable.

The private sector companies are facing the same problem as the one facing the Government. The amount of capital to be invested is enormous. There is no assurance that this investment would yield adequate returns. These companies do not have sufficient experience in the area and they are not bold enough to take risks. For these reasons, they are proceeding at a slow pace. But the American companies are, at present, enthusiastic about investing in the power sector in India. This, no doubt, is due to the efforts of the Prime Minister of India during his recent US visit. This is also due to the policy of liberalisation under way in India. The US President, Mr. Bill Clinton has evinced keen interest in US participation in power generation in India. The US power Secretary who visited India has had wide ranging discussions with the Indian officials. These discussions relate to the removal of impediments to the establishment of power generating companies in India, the assurance to be given to these companies, conditions Governing the supply of power etc. There have also been discussions about the use of technology in power generation. There is an agreement relating to the establishment of a commission to oversee the US-India cooperation in this area and another agreement relating to the transfer of technology which is eco-friendly. All these are indicative of the development of cooperation between the USA and India.

This does not mean that the whole process is not without hurdles. Every party to the transaction desires to maximise its gains. If both the parties are of equal strength there would be no problem. No party will yield to the other. The agreement would be equitable. But in the case of unequal partnership the weak party has to submit to the demands of the strong party. This danger is inherent in the power sector. Those who participate in the deliberations may be honest. Even so if there is no transparency in the transactions there will be danger. The Government is entering into agreement with every company separately. While selecting companies the Government should proceed on the assurance that the agreement is on a competitive basis. It should select those companies whose conditions are attractive. There has been a great deal of controversy about the agreement the Government has entered into with the ENRON company of the USA. This agreement relates to the generation of 2,000 mega watts of power in two stages. The Electricity Board of Maharashtra purchases this power. The price of power is already determined. It has agreed to purchase 90 percent of the power generated. The price is determined by taking into account the cost of several items of inputs. The return on capital invested has to be raised by 4 percent each year. In consequence, the price of power also goes up. If the foreign company is not able to supply the power as per the agreement it has to pay a fine. The Electricity Board agrees to purchase the agreed percentage of power generated. So far so good. But if the foreign company declares a higher price for the machinery and technology used in power generation the Electricity Board and the country have to pay an unjust price for power. It is a problem to determine the actual price of machinery and technology. It is alleged that the price quoted by the ENRON company is 20 percent higher than it its actual price. The possibility of the foreign companies cheating the Electricity Board and the Government of India cannot be easily ruled out.

Whether there is need for power or not the Electricity Boards have to purchase power as per the agreement. The need for power is less during nights. The domestic power companies have them to close down their power generating units and purchase power for the foreign companies. The cost of production of power by the domestic companies is less than the cost of production of power by the foreign companies. In this manner there are problems at every stage. The users of power have to pay this higher price. If the price of power rises, all other prices rise and they give a boost to the ongoing rate of inflation.

Admittedly India and USA are unequal partners in the area of power generation or in any other area of cooperation. This does not mean that the USA should dictate terms to India or that India should submit tamely to the dictates of the USA or of any developed country for that matter. Globalisation and liberalisation are the watchwords of Indian economy policy regime, but this should not mean that India should open its doors to foreign companies to come and operate in India. The developed countries should realise that they should assist the developing countries to come up with their assistance. This means that international cooperation should not be exploitative of the developing countries. Seen in this perspective, the USA should not insist on its terms being accepted by India to the latter's disadvantage. Of course, India should welcome competitive bidding and accept those bids which do not appear to be exploitative. The Indian companies should generate power upto their full capacity and the balance of the requirement should be produced by the US companies. It does not make sense for Indian companies to keep their power generating capacity idle while allowing the foreign companies to generate power upto their full capacity and sell it to domestic Electricity Boards. There should be an assessment of the power requirements of India and the difference between the power generated by the Indian companies and the power requirement should be generated by the US companies. The installed capacity of the US companies should be so adjusted as not to leave any spare capacity. This scheme will make the Indian companies viable and contribute to their healthy growth. Of course, the foreign companies should be assured a reasonable rate of return to their investment. Furthermore wastage of power during transmission should be carefully avoided along with the pilferage of power during transmission. It is in this spirit that the foreign companies whether of the USA or of any developed country should be welcome.

71

How to Rescue the Economy from the Inflation Trap

The rate of inflation which reached the dizzy height of 17.5 percent in 1991 came down to 7 percent in April 1993. But during the week ending 23, April 1994 inflation as measured by the provisional wholesale price index shot up by 0.3 percent in a single week to touch a new high annual rate of 11.15 percent. The final data are expected to show an inflation rate of 13 percent. In 1991 a number of factors acted in unison to raise the inflation rate to 17.5 percent devaluation of the rupee, the import squeeze, higher prices of crude oil, a record fiscal deficit of 8.4 percent of GDP and severe economic crisis, etc. But most of these factors have now vanished barring the fiscal deficit which turned out to be 7.3 percent of GDP as against the targeted 4.7 percent of GDP. In the Union Budget for 1994-95 it is targeted at 6 percent of GDP. If the assumptions underlying the new tax proposals turn out to be valid the fiscal deficit may either come down or may remain at that level. This, of course, is a matter of speculation.

Inflation means erosion in the value of the rupee. A rupee of 1993 has now become worth 90 paise given 10 percent rate of inflation. The purchasing power of the rupee in relation in 1960 prices is deflated to the All India Consumer Price Index for industrial workers with 1960-61 as the base, is as follows:

Annual Average	Purchasing power of the rupee
1961	96.2
1971	52.6
1976	33.8
1981	22.7
1986	15.1
1990	10.9
1991	9.6

In other words, a rupee of 1980 was worth less than 10 paise in 1991 and obviously still far less in 1994. It also means that the what a consumer could get for a rupee in 1960 he has to pay Rs. 10 for the same quantity and quality of the goods. In short the rupee is now worth only 10 paise as compared to the rupee of 1980. The Government was able to control prices till 1992-93 by means of a tight money policy. It also curbed the budget and fiscal deficits appreciably. But in 1993-94 there was fiscal profligacy and this has resulted in inflation of 11.15 as on today.

The Union Budget for 1994-95 is said to have a built-in inflationary bias. In the fiscal 1993-94 the fiscal deficit was 7.3 percent of GDP. This was due to two factors : (a) the reduction in customs duties caused a decline in customs revenue yield by Rs. 5,000 crore and the reduction in excise duties on manufactured goods led to a decline in excise tax revenue by Rs. 3,000 crore. Added to this decline in indirect tax yield there was a rise in government expenditure by Rs. 12,500 crore. These two factors led to a rise in fiscal deficit to 7.3 percent of GDP against the targeted 4.7 percent of GDP. In the Budget for 1994-95 the budget deficit is of the order of Rs. 6,000 crore and the fiscal deficit is of the order of Rs. 54,915 crore. As a proportion of GDP the fiscal deficit for 1994-95 is targeted at 6 percent while this should have been 3-4 percent. The consequence is a rise in the rate of inflation to 11.15 percent. This rate is very high indeed. The Finance Minister attributes this to seasonal factors and asserts that when these seasonal factors become weak by September 1994 the rate of inflation would revert to the single digit zone. The Finance Minister also expects the revenue to increase from the reduction in indirect tax rates a la Laffer Curve Analysis. To this extent the fiscal deficit will come down. However, at present the fiscal deficit is massive and the rate of inflation is unduly high.

When the Finance Minister presented the Union Budget for 1994-95 he expressed the hope that given the cushion offered by the comfortable stock of food grains and record forex reserves of $ 15 billion the adverse impact of the fiscal deficit could be mitigated. But the latest uptrend in the wholesale price Index shows that these cushions are not enough. Several new factors have entered the situation and they weakened the positive impact of these cushions.

A study by the Centre for Monitoring Indian Economy (CMIE) shows that inflation is caused by the high rate of price increase of a small number of important items which comprise the wholesale price index. Thus only 11 items account for the 57 percent of the rise in prices. The increases in administered prices of electricity, petroleum products and others have contributed to inflation. This is due to the reduction in subsidies. The study shows that the sharp increases in the administered prices of rice, wheat and the hike in freight rates have contributed to inflationary pressures. If there was a reduction in the subsidies on farm inputs there was justification for increasing the support prices. Furthermore, the forex cushion is weakened by the global rise in the prices of sugar and cotton. Even after the decision to import these commodities to check the rise in prices, the inflation rate has maintained an uptrend. The Finance Minister is optimistic that the rise in prices is due to seasonal factors and when they lose their strength the prices will come down within the next 3-4 months. This optimism of the Finance Minister is not entirely unfounded. But if the Government announced another hike in prices of food articles on election even the price situation is bound to worsen. The Commission of Agricultural Costs and Prices (CACP) has recommended increases of 9-10 percent in the procurement prices of different varieties of rice in the coming season. As the general price index and therefore the rate of inflation is governed by the food prices a rise in procurement prices will raise the rate of inflation. But the remedy for this is to reduce the subsidies on farm inputs for the farmers cannot have the best of both the worlds. If the Government feels that an increase in grain prices to the world level is necessary as an incentive to production, it will do well to reduce the subsidy on farm inputs. If when the procurement prices are raised, the subsidy on farm inputs is maintained, it may not be possible to reverse the price trend despite record production of food grains and the cushion which the forex reserves are expected to provide.

It needs no reiteration that despite a food grain stock of 23 million tonnes, despite forex reserves of the order of $ 16 billion and despite considerable slack in the industrial sector prices continue to limb. The Finance Minister has again sounded optimistic when he announced that the present rise in the inflation rate is due to seasonal factors and that before September there will be a perceptible decline. Recent studies by the CMIE and the NIPEP suggest that the dynamics of inflation in the 1990s is different from that earlier and that it has to do with the hikes in administered prices.

According to the CMIE study, the inflation rate averaged 10.6 percent in the early 1990s as compared to 7.8 percent in the 1980s and 6.5 percent in the entire post-Independence period. Further, only 11 percent of the 447 commodities covered in the wholesale price index accounted for 57 percent of the inflation in the early 1990s. These included rice, wheat, diesel oil, electricity etc whose prices are administered by the State. The inflation engendered by the hikes in these prices was, of course, fuelled by the liquidity overhang caused by the huge fiscal deficits and the rising foreign exchange inflows. The rise in money supply of the order of 18 percent has enabled speculators and black marketers to control supplies and to maintain prices at a high level. Sugar is a case in point. To provide immediate relief the Government should (a) increase the supplies of essential commodities. (b) Put a check on its unproductive expenditure and (c) put a check on procurement price increases or to reduce subsidy on farm inputs.

The IMF in its "World Economic Outlook" published in the last week of April 1994 has drawn attention to the two troubling features of the Indian economy large fiscal deficit and high inflation rate. It issues a call to "restore the momentum of fiscal consolidation in the interests of sustainable growth. The report says that "high real interest rates associated with persistently large budget deficits have contributed to the recent surge in capital inflows which has complicated monetary management". In addition to calling for fiscal consolidation the report suggests that the ongoing "structural reforms" should be continued because they are the only route by which the economy can get on the path to sustainable growth.

The concern expressed by the IMF has been expressed even more clearly by its Managing Director Michael Camdessus who said at the IMF's Interim Committee meeting in Washington that while the progress made by the Indian policy makers is commendable " a lot remained to be done in continuing the liberalising process". Specifically, according to him, India "still needed to establish a sound basis for its public financing with regard to both expenditures and revenues". He also suggested more deregulation and greater incentives to the private sector.

The concern voiced by the IMF and its Managing Director are not out of place as is indicated by the spurt in the inflation rate to 11.15 percent. The potential of this inflationary phenomenon in upsetting the entire economic reform programme has been recognised by the public, the Parliament and by the Government. While this is to be welcomed, there is so far a curious dearth of sensible prescriptions to this malaise. The IMF cannot take credit for throwing light on the inflation crisis gripping the nation and its remedy. It is true that the remedy lies in the area of public finance. But despite efforts to streamline the public financial operations, the problem persists which implies that there is some basic obstacle standing in the way of a solution.

The objective is financial discipline a reduction in Government expenditure and an increase in revenue. This may sound alright in theory but when it comes to the stage of implementation things prove to be difficult. The Managing Director of the IMF has hinted at this lack of correspondence between theory and practice. He says that India "is the biggest democracy in the world" and for this reason the Government has "to convince its people before undertaking major changes in its economic sphere". This might look easy but it is hard on many an honest and sincere politician in view of the embarrassing compromises that have to be made in the face of myriad political pressures.

The outlook for the future is not bright not because of any lack of determination on the part of the Government but because the Government is an integral part of the Indian social milieu and musts abide by the unwritten laws inherent in such a situation. The Finance Minister has been trying hard to forge a new path for the Indian economy which has encountered serious opposition from a section of Indian industrialists. There can be no doubt that the Finance Minister will try his best to fight such pressures which are ideologically oriented. However, even he has to face the troubling reality. His task has been made doubly difficult by the forthcoming elections to the State Assemblies when the Government has to incur colossal unproductive and wasteful expenditure. For this reason alone, fiscal house keeping has to suffer a rude shock in 1994-95. Such systematic obstacles are strong enough to sweep good economic policies aside. The multilateral financing agencies like the IMF and the World Bank have to bear these systemic obstacles in mind before tendering advice welcome though it may be. It is the systemic obstacles in the area of Government expenditure that have frustrated all honest: efforts at fiscal consolidation.

The following Table indicates the Central Government deficits:

Figures in Rs. Crore	1991-92	92-93 B.E.	92-93 Actuals	93-94 B.E.	93-94 B.E.	1994-95 B.E.
Fiscal Deficit	36325	34408	40173	36959	58551	54915
Budgetary Deficit	6855	5389	12312	4314	9060	6000
Revenue Deficit	6261	13882	18574	17630	34058	32737

In 1991 the Government initiated the economic reform programme which encompassed the fiscal reform also. This consisted in cutting down Government expenditure and thus reducing the size of the fiscal deficit over a period from the then prevalent 8.4 percent of GDP. But the efforts were not successful. The process started with promises to reduce the unproductive expenditure but unexpectedly the axe fell on capital and plan expenditure. Consequently since 1991 the non-plan expenditure has risen more than plan and capital expenditure. The revenue expenditure has increased from 70 percent in 1990-91 to 78.32 percent in 1994-95. The capital expenditure has declined from 30 percent to 24 percent. Already there has been a considerable decline in the share of gross capital formation from 40 percent in 1980-81 to 31 percent in 1991-92. A further decline occurred during 1991-92 to 1994-95.

Though the share of plan expenditure increased marginally from 28 percent in 1990-91 to 30.7 percent in 1994-95 but the revenue component in total plan expenditure increased from 43 percent to 60 percent. This means that greater resources are devoted to recurring and maintaining expenditure. The greater decline in the category of capital expenditure has implications for the future interest payments. Interest payments on debt constitute a large share in total expenditure. It has increased from 21 percent in 1991-92 to 30.3 percent of total expenditure in the 1994-95 budget. Also in 1994-95 51 percent of the revenue expenditure is used to make interest payments. It was only 33 percent in 1991-92. In 1993-94 there was a large resort to debt financing of the deficit on account of the reduction in taxes. Keeping a higher revenue target the expenditure under various categories was increased. A similar experience is likely to be repeated in 1994-95 as the Finance Minister holds a similar optimistic outlook while projecting a revenue estimate of Rs. 86,095 crore.

While on the one hand the non-developmental and unproductive expenditure has gone on rising, on the other hand there has been no attempt to improve the quality of Government expenditure. Considering the fact that there is a huge component of administrative expenditure, there is a imperative need to improve the quality of Government expenditure. The existing pattern of expenditure calls for a review against the need and the efficiency of Government expenditure has to be improved. This will help the Government to reduce the unproductive component of expenditure and to divert it to productive channels. The Government should also set a target for the burgeoning revenue deficit. The revised estimates of revenue deficit is larger than the budgeted revenue deficit. For instance in 1993-94 the budgeted revenue deficit was Rs. 17,630 crore but the revised estimate put the figure at Rs. 34,058 crore. In the 1994-95 budget the budgeted revenue deficit is Rs. 32,737 crore. This is less than even the revised estimates for 1993-94. The growing consumption expenditure is eating into the share capital expenditure. In consequence, borrowed fund are devoted to financing consumption expenditure. This is bound to fuel inflation in future.

The Finance Minister's statement that high fiscal deficit does not add to the price hike is a product of his robust optimism.

In view of the foregoing, the concern expressed by the IMF in its Report "World Economic Outlook" and by its Managing Director himself about the fiscal deficit and its inflationary consequences has been rooted in reality. The solution to the present problem lies in (a) reducing the budgetary and fiscal deficits by means of reducing the unproductive expenditure and (b) by improving the quality of the expenditure itself. Stepping up of capital expenditure in the infrastructural areas in particular will enhance the productivity and productive capacity of the different sectors of the economy and enhance output which will be an antidote to inflation. At the same time there is need for an Expenditure Commission to allocate expenditure on thc basis of cost-benefit calculus. At a time when expenditure is galloping, an authority like the Expenditure Commission is necessary to exercise restraint on it. There is a lot of fat in the unproductive expenditure and this needs to be cut. If the Government takes a decision to cut it, an element of arbitrariness may creep into it and render this step unacceptable. But if an authority like the Expenditure Commission does it, the action taken by it will be regarded as scientific. Even here systematic obstacles may come in the way. But given the political will it should not be a formidable task.

Systematic factors are also in operation in the monetary and banking spheres. Inflation is fuelled by excessive liquidity in the economy. The control of liquidity is possible if the Reserve Bank of India adopts one of the following measures : (a) raising of the CRR and the SLR to impound a large part of bank reserves; (b) raising the rate of interest; and (c) raising the bank lending rates. It is feared that the raising of the CRR and the SLR may come in the way of financial sector reform and it is feared that the raising of the interest rates may be resented by the borrowers especially in the industrial sector; it is also feared that this may reduce investment in the industrial sector and deepen the ongoing recession. About raising the CRR and SLR it must be said that inflation is a more dangerous enemy to the success of the economic reform programme underway that the raising of the CRR and SLR could even be to the financial sector reform. About the resentment likely to be caused to the raising of the lending rates it must be said that the demand for borrowing for investment is unlikely to be elastic. The demand effect of reduced indirect taxes on investment will outweigh the cost effect which a higher lending rate is likely to have on investment. The large scale reduction in customs duties and excise duties and hence reduction of production costs will enable the industrial sector to emerge out of the recession and to face competition in the Indian business empire into which foreign companies are venturing to enter. With more money in the hands of the people through expansion of the rural development programme the quantum of consumption will rise and so the demand conditions will be favourable to growth. A rise in consumption demand will, through the acceleration coefficient, stimulate investment. This will swamp any restrictive influence of a higher lending rate on bank loans. For these reasons, it appears necessary to raise the CRR and the SLR and the bank lending rate. The concern expressed in the "World Economic Outlook" of the IMF is real and well founded. A restrictive fiscal monetary policy mix is necessary and desirable to create the environment necessary to rescue the economy from the inflation trap in which it finds itself today. But other measures are equally necessary. What are they?

While a restrictive monetary-fiscal framework is necessary it is not sufficient to reduce the rate of inflation. The reduction of food subsidies has caused a rise in the essential commodities supplied through the PDS; reduction of fertiliser subsidy has caused a rise in the cost of production of farm products and their market prices. This necessitates hikes in administered prices of rice, wheat, sugarcane and others. Even if the monetary-fiscal framework is restrictive, they do not by themselves reduce the rate of inflation. It is for this reason that a case is made out for retaining for some more time food and fertiliser subsidies. This may enlarge the fiscal deficit and may contribute to inflation but the inflation emanating from this source is more tolerable than inflation emanating from the abolition of subsidies. It appears as though inflation is inevitable but the rate of inflation needs to be brought down in successive stages. The Finance Minister has expressed the confidence that by September 1994 the inflation rate would be brought down to the single digit mark. Let us have faith in his wisdom.

72

Final Act of Full Convertibility of the Rupee on Current Account

August 2, 1994 marks a significant milestone in the history of the Indian rupee. It is on this day that the Reserve Bank of India announced that it would be fully convertible on current account. While presenting the Union Budget for 1993-94 the finance Minister announced the convertibility of the rupee on trade account but while presenting the Union Budget for 1994-95 on 28.2.1994 he announced that the rupee would rendered fully convertible on current account. He was encouraged to make this announcement by the surplus of forex reserves in the vaults of the Reserve Bank and the improvement of the balance of payments position. The balance of payments deficit which was over $ 6 billion in 1991-92 had sunk to $ 1 billion at the end of 1993-94 and the forex reserves had increased to over $ 15 billion. During the four months since the beginning of 1994-95 the forex reserves rose to over $ 17.5 billion which occasioned inflation. It was a problem for the Government as to how to deal with the surging inflow of forex reserves. If the Reserve Bank of India had adopted a policy of non-intervention the rupee would have appreciated vis-a-vis the US dollar with adverse consequences on the trade balance considering the fact that appreciation of the rupee would have raised the prices of exports leading to a decline in exports and it would also have reduced the prices of imports leading to a rise in imports. The Government was not prepared to encounter this unsavoury situation. Therefore the Reserve Bank of India was advised to buy the incoming dollars and this maintained stability of the Rupee dollar exchange rate at 31.37 per US dollar. Thus the stability of the exchange rate was maintained at the cost of domestic instability in the form of monetary expansion of the order of 18 percent per annum and a high rate of inflation. As the Reserve Bank could not eschew the policy of intervention in the forex market and allow the rupee to appreciate, the Finance Minister considered it necessary to liberalise imports of consumer goods as an anti-inflationary measure. This would reduce the rate of inflation not only by increasing the supply of goods in the domestic market but also by increasing the customs revenue which would reduce the fiscal deficit. It was also considered necessary to increase the outflow of forex reserves and thus to hold in check the inflationary pressures emanating therefrom.

Even the balance of payments situation with a reduced deficit was also responsible for the decision to make the rupee fully convertible on current account. In the first quarter of 1994-95 the deficit was lower even with less pronounced rise of 9.49 percent in exports to $ 5,613.59 million from $ 5,127.12 million in the corresponding period in 1993-94. But imports have not risen much (7.05 percent) to $ 5,811.53 million from $ 5,428.61 million comparably. The deficit in June 1994 alone was lower at $ 106.94 million compared to that in the same month in 1993-94. The expected growth of exports in the month ahead will be 15 percent though it will be difficult to achieve the target of 25 percent. As there is no likelihood of a rise in the oil import bill as in 1993-94 and the scope for reducing imports of edible oils and cotton later in the year the import bill will not prove problematic. If the increase in export earnings can be around 15 percent the trade gap may be even less than $ 1.04 billion recorded in 1993-94 as importers and actual users may not be in a hurry to replenish their inventories due to the firmness of the rupee. Thus the trade deficit may not be unduly enlarged and get reflected in a bigger balance of payments gap. This expectation may also have been responsible for the decision to permit full convertibility of the rupee on current account. As there will also be a large inflow of invisible receipts on account of a growth in tourist traffic and remittances from expatriates and other factors the current account deficit may be only marginal as in 1993-94 when it was $ 230 million.

The Reserve Bank of India took several steps in this direction. The Reserve Bank's decision to dispense with the exchange cover on foreign currency non-resident (FCNR) accounts was intended to reduce the quantum of volatile capital inflows into India and to enhance the quality of forex reserves by imparting stability into them. Even so, inflows of non-resident holdings will not cease altogether as evidenced by the growing popularity of the other schemes like the (FCNR) banks scheme with the exchange risk being borne by the banks themselves. Admittedly, FCNR deposit inflow boosted India's forex reserves in the 1980s but at a heavy price. Having regard to the fact that the interest rate offered on them was high and the exchange rate protection provided to the deposits under this scheme must be considered to be costly. The volatility of these deposits created other problems as well. They were greatly affected by the foreign exchange crisis of the early 1990s. Their outflow began to gain momentum at the first sign of distress in the early 1990. And they shot up subsequently and contributed significantly to the foreign exchange crisis in the first quarter of 1991-92. The successive devaluations of the rupee in July 1991 pushed up the cost of forex cover to more than Rs. 5,500 crore during the year ended June 1992. Following the improvement in India's reserve position, exchange cover on these deposits has been reduced. Prior to the scrapping of the scheme, cover was available only on three-year deposits and the exchange risk was borne by the Government rather than by the Reserve Bank of India. Furthermore, interest rates on FCNR deposits were progressively reduced. In consequence, the earlier avenues of arbitrage gain disappeared. The withdrawal of cover on the FCNR deposits is a step towards conforming with Article VIII of the IMF on convertibility. The Government had to remove other restrictions on other current account transactions and move towards complete current account convertibility. Article VIII stipulates removal of restrictions on current Account convertibility.

The announcement made by the Reserve Bank of India on 19.8.1994 that from 20.9.1994 the rupee would be fully convertible on current account was meant to remove these other restrictions. The statement by the IMF resident representative in India Mr. Charles Collynes while releasing the IMF Annual Report early in August 1994 had given ample indication that such a measure was round the corner. The measures announced on the 19th August include the introduction of indicative limits upto which the authorised dealers can make foreign exchange available for travel, gifts, studies medical treatment etc and the elimination of restrictions on the repatriation of interest income under non-resident (non-repatriable) rupee deposit scheme (NRNR) and foreign currency (ordinary) non-repatriable deposit scheme (FCONR). It was clarified that authorised foreign exchange dealers were empowered to allow remittances only upto a limit without RBI approval. However, these were only indicative limits and the bank would consider bonafide requests for additional exchange facilities favourably. The NRNR scheme thus far would not allow repatriation of either the Principal or the interest. But under the new dispensation the Reserve Bank allows repatriation of interest accruing on deposits from the quarter beginning October 1, 1994. But the principal would continue to be non-repatriable. As regards FCONR the Reserve Bank has decided that with effect from August 20, 1994 no fresh deposits would be accepted by banks. But interest accruing on existing deposits from the quarter beginning October 1, 1994 will be eligible for repatriation upto the maturity date of the existing deposits.

Under the new dispensation there is an easing of the restrictions on repatriation of investment income by NRIs and overseas corporate bodies owned by NRIs. Investment income upto $ 1,000 accruing in the current financial year and onwards will be remittable annually under a three-year phased programme allowing remittances of the full income by 1996-97. However, remittances will be allowed only after income tax is paid in full. The phased programme of remittances of investment income reflects the cautious approach of the Reserve Bank of India which wants to ensure that there is no large scale capital flight considering the fact that the potential for capital flight is greater in India than in other South Asian countries.

The decision of the Reserve Bank to further liberalise foreign exchange transactions and make the rupee convertible on current account is thus a logical final step in the series of measures initiated by the Government in the recent past. The writing on the wall was clear when on 28.2.1994 the Finance Minister announced during his Budget speech that there would be a movement towards making the rupee convertible on current account and relaxed the limits on releases on foreign currency to Indian travelling abroad for business, education and medical reasons. The Government has now done away with "absolute" limits and replaced them with "indicative limits". In other words, where as in the past a person needed prior approval of the Reserve Bank to obtain hard currency for foreign travel, he can now obtain the funds through an authorised dealer without seeking the Reserve Bank Government has now done away with "absolute" limits and replaced them with "indicative limits". In other words, whereas in the past a person needed prior approval of the Reserve Bank to obtain hard currency for foreign travel, he can now obtain the funds through an authorised dealer without seeking the Reserve Bank mission provided the quantum is within the indicative limits. This means a person can now exceed the limits and draw more foreign exchange but with Reserve Bank approval which would be granted leniently after confirming that the money is required for bonafide reasons. The decision to make interest income on foreign investments repatriable is part of the new outfit. These steps have gained for India the Article VIII status already achieved by the neighbouring countries like Pakistan, Nepal and Sri Lanka. In essence Article VIII stipulated that countries should not have dual exchange rates or impose stringent restrictions on the exchange rate being determined by market forces.

Though the official position is that the relaxation of restrictions on current account transactions would not lead to an outflow of foreign exchange, this is hardly a matter of concern at present. With forex reserves of over $ 17 billion, with gold and SDR valued at $ 3 billion and with the Reserve Bank having to purchase large amounts of dollars to stop the rupee from appreciating, the Government is keen to ensure that spending in forex picks up. However, this does not mean that the Government is in a position to lift all controls on the use of hard currency in the immediate future. So far the Government has moved in this direction in a phased manner. This implies that the full convertibility of the rupee on capital account is some time and distance away.

The objective of current account convertibility is to remove the obstacles in the way of merchandise and invisible trade, obstacles created by controls over foreign exchange transactions and dual exchange rates. In this respect many obstacles are abolished or liberalised since July 1991. On the other hand the steps taken by the Reserve Bank on 19.8.1994 were the minimum necessary to conform to Article VIII of the IMF. The objective of conforming to Article VIII is to signal to the world community that India is now confident of managing its balance of payments and does not need to retain controls over current account transactions.

The elimination of foreign exchange restrictions on current account is important for the IMF since such restrictions preceded the Great Depression of the 1930s. One of the tasks assigned to the IMF was a foster an international exchange rate regime (free of current account controls) which would encourage the growth of world trade. However, the current account convertibility is circumscribed by the continuation of some regulations; for example, dividend balancing requirements in certain kinds of foreign investment and the restrictions on consumer goods imports. But even with more than $ 17.5 billion of forex reserves it may still be too early to remove these restrictions.

The latest decision of the Reserve Bank of India was prompted by a desire to fully meet the Article VIII obligations of the IMF Articles of Agreement before the 50th anniversary meetings of the IMF and the World Bank scheduled for first week of October in Madrid. The Governor of Reserve Bank of India in a communiqué to the Managing Director of the IMF said, "..... with effect from August 20, 1994 India has moved over to Article VIII Status in the IMF".

The full convertibility move is in the right direction. In fact, this should have been done immediately after the announcement made by the Finance Minister on 28.2.1994. But at that time the Reserve Bank had only relaxed the limits upto which foreign exchange was made available. Considering the volatility of a part of the forex reserves the Government had to first reduce or eliminate the volatile component of the forex reserves before launching on full convertibility on current account.

The Reserve Bank announcement says that the limits envisaged are only indicative. In the event of the demand for foreign exchange exceeding the limit, the dealer will have to refer these cases to the Reserve Bank which will then decide on the merits of granting the additional foreign exchange. Taking advantage of this flexibility the applicants for foreign exchange may apply for more foreign exchange than they actually need and make out a case for it and get it. If they get the foreign exchange they might sell it to others who actually need at the black market rate. Furthermore, there is the possibility of the foreign exchange obtained for any purpose seeping through an osmotic process to other purposes not envisaged in the applications. These operations result in an unwarranted drain on the stock of foreign exchange reserves. In view of this, care has to be taken to scrutinise each application and the demand for foreign exchange made in each of them and allow only those which are genuine. Any spurious demand needs to be penalised. Just because there is a surplus of forex reserves the Reserve Bank of India should not be thoughtlessly liberal.

India stands committed to the international financial community that it will not undertake any restriction on current account payments even in the event of a serious foreign exchange crisis. This is bound to instill confidence in foreign investors. So far as many as 93 countries have got Article VIII Status: the Government must discontinue the FCNR deposit scheme where it bears the exchange risk; there should be no absolute ceilings on foreign exchange release for travel or foreign education; the interest payment on non-resident non-repatriable deposits should be allowed to be repatriable. The Government has met these three conditions in principle though their full implementation will take a couple of years more. The convertibility of the rupee is thus almost complete. But it is not blanket convertibility. It is "convertibility with accountability". The Government has to be convinced about the purpose for which the foreign currency is raised. It is obvious that in India all genuine schemes degenerate into rackets. For this reason, the Government cannot permit blanket convertibility on current account. Even in Japan which has attained the Article VIII status such a thing does not exist. The IMF is not averse to keeping limits on certain transactions.

With the surplus of forex reserves of $ 17.5 billion and with the expected upsurge of forex reserves to $20 billion before the end of fiscal 1994-95 it is appropriate that current account convertibility of the rupee is announced. This step is unlikely to result in a substantial outflow of foreign exchange in the short and medium term. However, as nearly 70 percent of the forex reserves are to some extent volatile, the Government should design a package of measures attractive enough to make the reserves remain on a permanent basis. This announcement by the Reserve Bank is preliminary to making the rupee fully convertible on capital account also in the years ahead. However, any "dash to convertibility" on the capital account is to be avoided. In the early 1980s the west European countries had freed all controls on capital account transactions. But soon they found that cross border capital flows too hot to handle and very soon they retracted their steps. India has a long way to go before it can allow unfettered cross border movements of capital. The need is to get the fundamentals of the country right and to complete the financial sector reforms expeditiously. Till then safeguards are necessary. The IMF also has cautioned India against any immediate steps towards capital account convertibility. The Government should constitute an expert committee to examine the time schedule for making the rupee fully convertible on capital account by taking into account the likely withdrawals by the foreign investor the likely inflow of forex reserves and their net accumulations. If, in a mood of euphoria, the Government introduces full capital account convertibility and then finds that it has resulted in a massive and unsustainable outflow of capital, it may come under pressure to retrace this step. This will shake investor confidence in the Indian rupee. Therefore, the expert committee should indicate the timing of the introduction of full capital account convertibility and also the pace at which the economy should move towards it. The present surplus of forex reserves should not lull us into confidence about the sustainability of full capital account convertibility. Even though it may be sustainable, great caution is necessary about the timing of its introduction and the pace of its advance.

73

Economic Growth Holds the Key to the Reduction of Fiscal Deficit

The World Bank has always been generous in its assessment of India's economic reforms and the line along which they are proceeding but it is not happy about the speed with which the reforms are progressing. It arrives at the conclusion that unless the reform process is speeded up, India's development objectives cannot be realised. The factor that is impeding the progress of the reform package is the growing fiscal deficit of the Government. In the 1994-95 budget the Finance Minister targeted the fiscal deficit at 7/3 percent of GDP for 1993-94 against a target of 4.7 percent. For the year 1994-95 the Finance Minister puts the fiscal deficit at 6 percent of GDP. There are doubts expressed in several quarters about the practicability of the fiscal deficit of 6 percent of GDP. The inability of the Government to cut down non-plan expenditure because of political pressure is not the main issue at present. During the past three years, Government expenditures, other than interest on old Government debt, have been cut by 2.5 percent of GDP and there is not much scope for further reduction. Quite apart from this there are other indications that the fiscal deficit target of 6 percent of GDP may not be realised. Due to the enhanced subsidies on food consequent on the rise in sugar prices the extra subsidy bill will be anywhere between Rs. 500 and Rs. 700 crore. The Government has shifted from borrowing from the Reserve Bank of India to public borrowing at high interest rates i.e., there is a shift from monetary financing to debt financing. In consequence, the interest payments on Government debt are likely to be higher. Furthermore, late this year many State Governments are going to the polls and this involves colossal expenditure. While expenditures are prone to rise there does not seem to be any appreciable buoyancy in revenues as a proportion of GDP. In consequence, the revenues are projected to be the same as those in 1993-94. In value terms customs revenues are expected to rise by 12 percent. But due to the decline in the average import weighted tariff by almost a third, imports will have to increase at a much faster pace than targeted. It is estimated by the Centre for Monitoring the Indian Economy (EMIE) that due to revenue shortfalls and higher expenditures there will be a fiscal deficit of around 7.8 percent of GDP against the target of 6 percent. It is now estimated that the customs revenue has increased by 13 percent due to the rise in imports by 12 percent in April-May 1994 over the same period in 1993. This is a welcome relief.

Admittedly, a high fiscal deficit fuels inflation. The rate of inflation at present is in the double digit zone. It is playing truant; it rises marginally in a week and declines marginally in the following week. It is at present on the wrong side of 10 percent. The Finance Minister is optimistic that it would decline to the single digit level within six months i.e., before the end of December 1994.

Quite apart from this a high fiscal deficit financed by public borrowing limits investment. This may retard the rate of economic growth. Money has been raised in the capital market but this money has been used, for the most part for restructuring of old loans. It is true that the number of investment projects has increased in 1993-94 over that in the proceeding year. But about half of these projects are in the proposal stage. The infrastructure in the economy is far from stimulating to investment, though it offers large potential. Due to insufficient infrastructure, the private investment flows are limited. The World Bank Report says that "the sector level policy and institutional framework are not yet sufficiently supportive of private investment". In the case of the power sector only 7 of the 35 foreign proposals with Foreign Investment Promotion Board have been cleared so far. Not much progress is made in the area of roads, ports and the Government is as yet undecided on the issues of returns, pricing, acquisition of land and so on. If the private sector is to play the lead role in the economy public investment should be reoriented to complement private investment. But according to the World Bank Report this process is yet to start. What is necessary is clear out policy of infrastructure and a policy that is simulative of private investment. This means that the Government should create conditions for private investment and help to develop infrastructure in order to lay a firm foundation for growth. But there is the impression that the Government is going slow with reforms. Going slow with reforms does not necessarily mitigate the pain. In the initial stages investments in traditional lines is unattractive but investments in new areas takes time to flow in with entrepreneurs waiting to see if the reforms are there to stay. In view of this the Government has to create conditions conducive to the growth process. The most fundamental issue concerns the need to correct the fiscal imbalance. It must be noted that failure to correct the fiscal imbalance is the main reason for the failure of various reform efforts in countries like Brazil and Argentina. In fact, Brazil had 13 sets of reforms none of which had any lasting success.

The Finance Minister sets the fiscal deficit target for 1994-95 at 6 percent of GDP as he is hopeful that with the economy achieving a high rate of growth the revenue realisations would increase. The CMI predicts that due to the rise in Government expenditure and shortfalls in revenue the fiscal deficit would be as high as 7.8 percent. If the Finance Minister target of fiscal deficit is to be realised there must be a rise in revenues; the rise in revenues is possible if the economy grows. As averred above, the rate of growth depends on the provision of adequate infrastructural facilities and the creation of conditions conducive to private investment activity. Therefore, the Government will do well to focus its attention on this aspect of economic policy in right earnest and to speed up the progress of reforms.

74

The Reserve Bank of India and a Stable Rupee

The foreign exchange reserves in June 1991 were of the order of \$ 1.8 billion enough to finance 15 days imports. During 1994-95 there was a dramatic increase in reserves to \$ 20.80 billion. In 1993-94 itself the increase in forex reserves was much larger at \$ 8.6 billion compared to the increase by \$ 5.74 billion in 1994-95. Thus since 1991 when the economic reform programme was initiated there has been a net addition of about \$ 18.2 billion to India's forex reserves. Of this, about \$ 8 billion have come from portfolio investments and \$ 5.8 billion as new NRI deposits showing that almost 70 percent of India's external reserves comprise volatility inflows. If these funds are withdrawn for some reason the Reserve Bank of India will come under pressure to sell dollars and buy rupees. This will exert a downward pressure on the rupee, drive more investors out and fuel a vicious cycle. In addition, the drain of liquidity from the market as the Reserve Bank buys up rupees with push domestic interest rates up and drag down industrial growth.

In the first six months of fiscal 1995-96 the forex reserves suffered an erosion of \$ 1.8 billion. According to the Reserve Bank of India, at the end of September 1995 the forex reserves had declined to \$ 19.02 billion from \$ 20.80 billion at the end of 1994-95. There was a slide in the external value of the rupee especially in relation to the dollar. For over two years the exchange value was Rs. 31.37 per US dollar. With the depreciation of the rupee caused by the excess demand for dollars the rupee sunk so low as Rs. 35.5 per dollar. The Reserve Bank, in the beginning stood ready to buy the incoming dollars to prevent the appreciation of the rupee. But when the rupee began to slide the Reserve Bank gave up the policy of market intervention and allowed the rupee to find its own level in the currency market. But when the slide became extreme the Reserve Bank returned to its earlier policy of market intervention. The decision of the Reserve Bank to sell dollars was due to the realisation that any further slide in the rupee beyond Rs. 35.50 can jeopardise macroeconomic stability. The Reserve Bank, in order to check the decline n the rupee has to augment the supply of dollars in order to meet the excess demand for them arising out of import payment, debt servicing and speculative transactions. It is obvious that the forex reserves are in for depletion. While in 1994-95 the Reserve Bank of India purchased $ 11.5 billion it is now under pressure to sell dollars.

During the current financial year the forex reserves declined by $ 1.8 billion. This was caused by two factors: (a) increase in the net outflow of funds on account of debt repayments and (b) the increase in the trade deficit inspite of higher imports because of the spurt in imports during this period. Since last year the net aid inflow has been negative after accounting for repayments of principal and interest. During the current financial year India had to pay back Rs. 2,359 crore for the period April-August 1995 against Rs. 1,777 crore for the corresponding period in 1994-95. The deficit in the trade balance is estimated to be Rs. 1,976 crore upto August this year (1995-96) against Rs. 798 crore for the same period of 1994-95. Though exports increased by an impressive 28 percent there is a jump of about 42 percent in non-petroleum imports of which capital goods formed an important part and a 17 percent rise in the imports of petroleum in sum, the draw down of forex reserves has been necessitated by both the increase in imports of capital good and petroleum products.

The trade gap and the depletion of forex reserves have made it necessary to keep a close watch on the movement of forex reserves. The drop in the dollar value of the rupee in the second week of October 1995 for the second time in six weeks has led to the demand from several quarters that Reserve Bank of India should intervene in the currency market to prop up the rupee value. This would mean that the Reserve Bank must use some of its dollar holdings to prop up the rupee in the same as it did earlier in the last week of October when it pumped $ 40-50 million to prevent a sharp rise in the exchange value of the dollar or a decline in the exchange value of the rupee. The question is: how long can the Reserve Bank go on using up its dollar reserves to defend the rupee. Going by the hawala rupee-dollar exchange rate, if the rupee continues to hold strong, the slide in the rupee appears to be temporary. But it is not possible to tell for sure. The Reserve Bank must decide just how far it will support the rupee and at what stage in the future it might even be necessary to tighten up imports to censure the future exchange value of the rupee. But given the fact that 45 percent of imports are inputs for exports, to tighten up these imports is to strangulate the rate of industrial growth and to impede the rate of export growth. This cannot be a solution. If the imports of consumer goods are tightened up their restraining influences on the rate of inflation will not be there. The import of petroleum cannot also be tightened considering the fact that domestic supply of oil is insufficient to meet the requirements. This means that not much can be expected from import tightening. If the Reserve Bank continues its policy of supporting the rupee by supplying dollars, there is the twin danger of the forex reserves falling to uncomfortably low levels and of the currency market losing faith in the stability of the external value of the rupee.

The Minister of State for Finance said in Calcutta on October 28, that the discomfiture of the rupee is due to a strong speculative lobby against it. Speculation can be curbed and the rupee would be back to its earlier position. He held out the assurance that the rupee crisis would be a short-term crisis. How short he did not elaborate. Speculation can be curbed in the context of stability of the exchange rate. In the absence of Reserve Bank intervention the rupee would float and this engenders speculation against the rupee. During 1993-95 there was a massive inflow of dollars which, in the absence of Reserve Bank intervention would have led to an appreciation of the rupee. Quite apart from its adverse consequences on the trade balance it would have triggered speculation. The speculators would have purchased rupees hoping it to appreciate further and this would have led to a further appreciation of the rupee. But the Reserve Bank intervened in the currency market and purchased dollar and thus stabilised the rupee dollar rate at Rs. 31.37 per dollar. When the rupee began to slide in the early part of 1995-96 consequent on the heavy demand for dollars to meet debt obligations, the rupee began to depreciate and it depreciated by 9 percent. The rupee dollar rate fell to Rs. 36 per dollar. As the depreciation continued unabated there was speculation against the rupee and those in possession of rupee balances began to sell rupees for dollars and this led to a further depreciation of the rupee. The Reserve Bank of India had then to intervene in the currency market but the intervention was half-hearted and was therefore ineffective in checking the slide in the rupee. The rupee is yet to recover and return to its old parity with the dollar. It is not known when the rupee-dollar rate would get stabilised. In the absence of a stable rupee, there would be speculation against it. The stability can be ensured if the Reserve Bank of India gives the assurance to the market participants that beyond a certain point either way the external value of the rupee would be protected. Thus, a limit to appreciation and limit to depreciation can be announced and if the rupee appreciates above this limit the Reserve Bank can stem the appreciation by actively intervening in the currency market to sell rupees in exchange for the inflowing dollars. Conversely, if the rupee depreciates below this point the Reserve Bank can stem the depreciation by actively intervening in the currency market to sell dollars in exchange for rupees. This will prevent the slide of the rupee. Thus, a band can be announced indicating the limits for appreciation and depreciation of the rupee. The bank has to be a narrow one. Within the band the rupee-dollar rate can fluctuate but the band being narrow the fluctuation will be narrow too. This combines the advantages of fixed exchange rate and of floating exchange rate. The Reserve Bank of India has left the market in a state of uncertainty about the external value of the rupee. The forces of speculation against the rupee causing its depreciation are very strong considering the fact that 70 percent of India's external reserves comprise volatile inflows. If, in the absence of intervention these funds are withdrawn the

Reserve Bank will be forced to sell dollars and buy rupees. This will cause a further downward pressure on the rupee and drive more investors out. In this situation it behoves the Reserve Bank of India to announce its policy initiative in order to stabilise the external value of the rupee. The present depreciation of the rupee is devaluation through the backdoor. This has increased the value of imports while its effect on exports is uncertain. This is also responsible for the widening trade gap. Announcing a narrow band within which the rupee can float and beyond which the Reserve Bank of India has to intervene is the need of the hour.

If the rupee is allowed to find its own level in the currency market it will create problems on many fronts. Imports become costlier, the burden of debt servicing will go up, foreign institutional investors will become cautious and even exporters are unlikely to be benefited though they may gain in future consignments. Although currencies commonly tend to fluctuate in foreign countries they can prove harmful in India more so when there are not many hedging instruments available.

The Reserve Bank of India believes that the current pressure on the rupee would not last long and at the end the rupee would stabilise. But the Reserve Bank intervention, being half-hearted, has not been able to break the market expectations that the rupee would weaken against the dollar further in the days to come. There is a general feeling that a sharp rupee depreciation would force foreign buyers to offer lower prices, thereby partly neutralising the benefits of depreciation. The sharp fall in the rupee rate might move counter productive even to exporters if the import content of their exports is very high. It is necessary not to all the rupee to cross the psychological barrier of Rs. 35 as it would have a major impact on the country's imports adding to inflationary spiral. Thus a limit has to be announced below which the rupee will not fall-the out limit of the band.

The current pressure on the rupee may continue for some more time, for how long, it is difficult to say. It had touched an all time low and hovered around Rs. 35.80 to the dollar before massive Reserve Bank intervention brought it back to Rs. 35.50. But the question is how far will the Reserve Bank have to go before it is able to peg the rate at Rs. 35. Chances are that it will soon touch Rs. 36 if the continued strong demand for dollar is any indication. This is considered to be a more realistic assessment especially since the six-month premia has of late been ruling a stiff Rs. 2.50. Less than a fortnight ago in the middle of October it crossed the Rs. 35 limit forcing the Reserve Bank to get into the resene act. What surprised many is why the Reserve Bank decided to start prop-up exercise in direct contrast with the earlier stand of leaving it to market forces to determine the exchange value of the rupee. This has caused confusion. Last year when the dollar was under pressure it had gone all out to prop it up—the explanation being that a weak rupee would give Indian exporters a shot in the arm. Again when the rupee began to fall last month it made known its firm determination not to intervene. These actions sent the market confused signals as to what the aim of the Reserve Bank is a stable currency in the long run or immediate but temporary gains through short-term fluctuations. Though earlier the Reserve Bank had prevented the rupee from gaining against the dollar to protect the competitiveness of Indian exports, inflationary trends in the country eroded the effect to a greater extent. This was compounded by the virtual drying up of portfolio investment by FIIs. The situation has changed now. The total inflow of external capital through the foreign direct investment route during January August 1995 stood at $ 1.34 billion averaging $ 166 million per month. Similarly the inflow of external capital through the FIIs route during January September 1995 stood at $ 926 million with a monthly average of $ 103 million. Again, the elimination of under invoicing of exports and over invoicing of imports which have led to an outflow of capital rom India, especially to the USA will add considerably to the dollar balances. Even given the volatility of 70 percent of forex reserves nothing definite can be said. If the rupee slides below the outer limit of the band the Reserve Bank of India can intervene to check any further slide. These developments on the forex front must alert the Finance Minister and the Reserve Bank Governor to make their intentions clear and to avoid the prevailing confusion in the currency market.

75

India's Export Performance Emulating the Korean Model is Needed

The balance of payments situation is causing concern despite the rise in foreign exchange reserves to Rs. 19,000 crore. The trends in foreign trade in April-June 1992 are in sharp contrast with those in the corresponding period of 1991-92. The deficit has risen from $ 733.91 million to $ 1,563.67 million despite the two-stage devaluation in 1991 and the partial convertibility of the rupee in March 1992. It can also be argued that the rise in the deficit is because of devaluation and the partial convertibility of the rupee. It is true that in theory devaluation is expected to remedy the deficit by reducing imports and stimulating exports. But this depends on the conditions (1) that the sum of the elasticities of demand for imports and the foreign elasticity of demand for exports should be greater than unity. (This is the famous Marshall Lerner condition) (2) the budget deficit should be constant and (3) the wage rates should remain constant following devaluation. There are no reliable estimates of elasticities of demand for imports and exports. However, a guess can be hazardous that the sum of the two elasticities is not greater than unity. The demand for imports is relatively inelastic considering the fact that the goods in great demand are those not available in India raw materials, intermediate goods and capital goods. These goods are necessary in order to meet the input requirements of exports and for this reason the rise in their prices following devaluation does not have the expected effects on their imports. Again, Indian exports do not have a ready market abroad. Indian exports have to compete with the exports of goods of other countries in world markets. Success in competition depends on both price and quality competitiveness of Indian exports. On both these goods Indian exports leave a lot to be desired. For this reason devaluation did not have the expected effect on exports.

Under the conditionality prescriptions of the IMF the fiscal deficit was brought down from 8.5 percent of GDP to 6.5 percent. But under the impact of rising oil prices and the prices of other imports the domestic price level rose. The supply of money led to rise to accommodate higher prices. Again, the wage rates did not remain constant. They were raised in the industries in the public and private sectors. This generated both cost-push and demand-pull inflations which became entwined and difficult to disentangle. Demand-pull inflation caused a rise in imports and a fall in the exportable volume; cost-push inflation reduced the competitiveness of Indian exports abroad. That despite devaluation the payments deficit becomes bigger is supportive of the "J-Curve Hypotehsis" which predicts a worsening of the payments deficit before it improves. Thus, the widening of the deficit may be attributed in part to the operation of the J-Curve Effect.

Partial convertibility of the rupee and its role to play is widening the deficit. Under this dispensation the exporters had to sell 40 percent of their export receipts to the Reserve Bank of India at the official exchange rate and the balance of 60 percent they had to sell to importers of goods at the market rate of exchange. Expectedly, the market rate of exchange was higher by Rs. 5 per dollar than the official rate i.e., Rs. 30 versus Rs. 25 per dollar. Those who wanted to import goods had to buy foreign exchange at the market rate and this naturally raised the rupee price of imports. This was a sort of hidden devaluation of the rupee. This raised the prices of imports and to the extent that they were used as inputs for exports, the prices of exports rose and this reduced the competitiveness of India's exports. Except in certain areas the quality competitiveness of Indian exports is no match to those of Japan or South Korea. These factors militated against the rise in exports to match the rise in imports. Furthermore, the policy of import liberalisation adopted under the new Export- Import policy announced on March 1, 1992 led to a surge of imports. The widening of the trade deficit can thus be accounted for. It can be said that the widening of the trade deficit is because of devaluation and the partial convertibility of the rupee rather than in mute of them.

The large imports in May and June can be ascribed to an increase in the quantum of crude and petroleum products. If there is a reduction in the quantum of these imports during the remaining three quarters of 1992-93, there will be some relief to the balance of payments. But it is felt that there will have to be an increase in the imports of crude and petroleum in the whole of 1992-93 because of a decline in indigenous production of crude and an increase in the demand for petroleum products, particularly diesel, kerosene and LPG. Even if the exports keep up their present tempo, the trade deficit is unlikely to be less than $ 5.0 billion or, in rupee terms around Rs. 15,000 crore at the market rate or at Rs. 13,000 crore at the official rate. With a pick up in domestic production of steel, petrochemicals and some other items, it may be possible to reduce imports of items in short supply to some extent. There may also be scope for reducing the import of edible oils or preventing a rise in food grains purchases in Foreign markets as the latest developments on the agricultural front are heartening.

Since crude, fertilisers and select petrochemicals, copper, lead, zinc and newsprint have to be imported, the trade deficit can be reduced only if there is a faster growth in exports. But the drastic devaluation of the rupee has resulted in the Foreign Customers getting Indian goods much cheaper in foreign exchange terms. The exporters have to be content with the realisation of a large value in rupees. This may provide the required incentives only to particular industries. But the target growth in exports by 13 percent in foreign exchange terms cannot take place without a well-thought-out Action Plan for exports. The adjustment to the new situation can be achieved in 2-3 years and a fairly large trade deficit is inevitable though it has to be ensured that there is no increase in foreign exchange expenditure on avoidable imports.

In the matter of designing an Action Plan for exports South Korea offers valuable lessons. Korea's export success has been the envy of most of the developing countries. Korea decided to embark on an export drive due to a severe balance of payments crisis in 1962 when its exports were only $ 52 million. By 1964 exports had crossed the $ 100 million mark; they reached $ 500 million in 1968, $ 1 billion in 1970, $ 10 billion in 1977, $ 20 billion in 1981 and were over $ 64 billion in 1990. With exports growing at almost 25 percent per annum in constant prices, the Korean economy has been growing at the phenomenal rate of 9 percent per year. Korea thus is poised to enter the ranks of the developed world.

Like India Korea had a colonial past; it was under the Japanese dominance. Korea learnt a lot from the Japanese export success. At the outset rather than opening up its border to free-trade, Korea continued a protectionist regime for the domestic market and, at the same time, established a free trade regime for exports along with a package of incentives. The establishment of a free trade regime for exports relied upon the following key strategies:

1. Allowing the currency to depreciate to its equilibrium rate and thereafter undertaking repeated devaluations of offset the impact of domestic inflation which was higher than world inflation.
2. Providing unrestricted and tariff free access to imported intermediate inputs for export production.
3. Granting automatic access to bank credit for working capital for all exports. Export credit was provided at concessional rates of interest to give a boost to the export drive as an added incentive.

The provision of duty-free inputs to exporters was a major challenge to export administration. In order to meet this challenge detailed input-output coefficients were worked out in consultation with the exporters product-wise. The input coefficients indicated the value of a particular input needed per unit of output. Based on this, the duty-free input was made available at world prices. This enabled the exporting firms to purchase the required inputs and to use them in the most economical way to increase the output of goods for the export market. The device was the most innovative one. In order to get the duty-free inputs, the Koreans used the domestic letter of credit (L/C). Once a Korean exporters got an export contract of L/C from a foreign buyer he could open a domestic line of credit with one of his suppliers through his bank. Based on this letter of credit, his domestic supplier was automatically entitled to the same export incentives of duty-free import of intermediates based on the relevant input-output coefficients along with instant working capital on preferential interest rates. The scheme of export incentives could cover as large a chain of manufacturers as necessary for the final finished product for export.

The Koreans also used a package of additional incentives in order to reorient firms towards exports. Tariff exemptions of input of capital goods were frequently granted. Priority in obtaining medium and long-term institutional finance was provided. As the banks were in the public sector this created no problems. Significant concessions in income tax and/or corporation tax were provided to exporters. Reduced rates of electricity tariff and freight rates were introduced to exporters. When entry into foreign markets proved difficult for exporters such exporters were given a liberal wastage allowance in the input-out co-efficient so that the exporters could offload some of their goods in the protected domestic market where they could make higher profits.

These were some of the initial incentives. After the export drive became successful some of these incentives were withdrawn. The duty-free imports were replaced by a duty drawback scheme where duties were first paid and reimbursements were claimed later. These incentives were important in the early years of export drive and in drawing even the smallest firms into the export network.

Export targets were fixed by every industry and they were all aggregated sector-wise through sectoral export associations and then for the whole economy. The incentives that were provided could be identified when once the targets were fixed. As the targets were fixed by the firms themselves the targets were not overambitious but were realistic and could be easily achieved.

Normal bureaucratic delays and hurdles in the way of smooth execution of export plans were minimised. The package of incentives and their operations were subject to intense and concurrent evaluation and was reviewed jointly by the government and the exporters and they were regularly find-tuned sector-wise to get enhanced results in terms of export performance. At the same time, those exporters who reached or overreached the export targets were awarded prizes which were greatly valued by them and which spurred them into greater activity. The President took personal interest in the export drive and left no stone unturned in making it a great success.

Korea's success in its export efforts is not due to free trade but due to the creation of a free trade regime for exports combined with a package of ingeniously designed incentives and an aggressive export policy implemented by an efficient and committed export policy implemented by an efficient and committed export bureaucracy. This was facilitated by the government's determination to achieve success on the export front and the political will for it.

The Export-Import policy of India announced on March 1, 1992 aims at achieving an export growth of 13 percent. But the success on the export front depends on several factors. The input-output coefficients for every export product has not been worked out in India and probably it has not occurred to the concerned authorities or to private research establishments that the working out of such input-output coefficients is very important. These coefficients result in greater output for a given input or a smaller input for a given output. This is conducive to economy in production and the achievement of cost competitiveness of goods for the export market. It is therefore necessary to workout the input-output coefficients for every export product. It is true that under bank nationalisation the export sector is given loans at concessional interest rates. But the tedious bureaucratic process of making the exporting firms run up to the banks several times to get the loans has acted as a disincentive to exporting firms. Industry-wise associations are not there to serve as instruments in focusing the attention of the government on such details. There does not seem to be any constructive partnership between the Government and the exporters in evolving institutional mechanisms for fostering of this partnership. This has to be fostered. Special income tax/corporation tax incentives should be offered to exporting firms in addition to higher rates of depreciation allowances.

It is also necessary for India to open export promotion offices in all major countries and to hold periodic exhibitions to highlight the quality, efficiency and grandeur of its exports. Export targets must be fixed by the industries themselves in which case it becomes their responsibility to make efforts to reach the targets. Those who reach targets must be awarded prizes and those who overreach them must be awarded prestigious honours. At present foreign direct investment is used to cover the balance of payments deficit. In future it should be attracted to export industries it must be export oriented. In these and other respects India will do well to emulate the example of Korea whose export performance is a model for all developing countries.

Despite periodic announcement of export promotion measures, India has not been able to make a breakthrough in exports. By and large, export growth rate is lower than the import growth rate. It is this situation that has led to periodic foreign exchange crisis compelling India to resort to external financing which has led to a burgeoning external debt making the detractors of government policy point to the danger of a debt trap. An export strategy of the type adumbrated above will increase India's foreign exchange earnings more than enough to pay for imports, enable India to repay external debt and to achieve external solvency so that India may achieve sustained growth untrammeled by the balance of payments barrier. It behoves the Government of India to restructure its export strategy with this end in view.

There cannot be much relief on the import front. With the liberalised import policy imports will surge forth. The World Bank has stated that India has miles to go before it can be said to have done enough "in reducing tariffs and in reducing quantitative restrictions" on imports. Inspite of liberalisation India has set up a protected and distorted trade policy regime. It cannot be denied that import and the exchange rate policies need further liberalisation. But it is just a question of speed.

The real question is whether India can benefit from liberalisation. The answer to this is generally affirmative though some obvious qualifications would apply to import liberalisation. The answer is generally affirmative because India would benefit from the liberalisation of economic regime. The simple truth is that its industrial structure is inefficient and the root of the inefficiency is in excessive protection and regulation. As India's experience during the past one year proves, liberalising the economy both within and without can go a long way in improving economic efficiency. This is why the World Bank calls the reform process as being very important for the survival of India in a global economy. This is also why the process should be pushed through expeditiously. In this situation the trade deficit has to be bridged not from the side of imports but from the side of exports. Hence the need for a well-designed export strategy of the Korean variety.

76

Freezing Dearness Allowance is Imperative

It is common knowledge that the Biju Patnaik Committee on austerity recommended inter alia, the freezing of Dearness Allowances in order to counter the on-going inflationary trend in the country. The subject came before the National Development Council at its meeting on Saturday 18th September 1993 when it deferred decision on DA freeze though the inflationary pressure warrants it. It agreed on the need for determined efforts by the Central and State Governments to cut down non-plan expenditure and raise additional resources for the plan but favoured less drastic measures for achieving this. Shri Pranab Mukherjee stated after the meeting that the austerity measures recommended by the Biju Patnaik Committee would be given effect at the time of finalisation of annual plans to the extent possible. It appreciated the view of political parties and trade unions that instead of such harsh measures there should be more rigorous efforts to control inflation which would automatically nullify the necessity for the payment of DA. The Centre and the State would work out further details on the austerity measures as and when the situation warrants. Atleast three States had already initiated action on austerity by putting the additional DA in provident fund accounts or other types of savings instruments. The NDC was in agreement with the recommendation of the austerity committee that users of services and facilities such as electricity, irrigation, water and transport should be made to pay for the cost.

The trade unions are opposed to freezing of DA obviously on the ground that this would make the workers tighten their belts and suffer deprivation. The trade unions argue that if the inflation is brought under control, there would be no need for DA payment. They seem to forget that DA payment and wage escalation are a cause of inflation. They generate (wage push) cost push and demand-pull inflations which get entwined and become difficult to disentangle. There is thus a vicious circle of wages and prices chasing each other endlessly. Higher prices generate demands for higher wages and higher wages in turn generate inflationary pressures. The austerity measure is based on the argument that if the DA is freezed for the present, the inflation of demand into the economic system gets reduced and this helps to control inflation. The Left parties and the trade unions argue that the need of the hour is the control of inflation engineered by other sources and if this is done, there would be no need for additional DA payment.

What are the various methods of inflation control? One of them is the reduction of the fiscal deficit as a proportion of GDP. Under the IMF dispensation, the fiscal deficit ought to be 4.7 percent of GDP in 1993-94 but because of burgeoning expenditure this target of fiscal deficit is unlikely to be realised. It is expected that the fiscal deficit would be the same as that in 1992-93 i.e., 5.7 percent of GDP. This means that unless the Government expenditure is reduced, the fiscal deficit will not be reduced and unless fiscal deficit is reduced inflation emanating from this source cannot be brought under control.

Can the fiscal deficit be brought under control? The Reserve Bank of India, in its annual report for 1992-93 released in Bombay on 9.9.1993 has stated that the wide-ranging reforms initiated in 1991 have begun to yield results with a deceleration of inflation. However, it has expressed caution at increasing gross fiscal deficit. According to the report, the revenue deficit of the Government as a percentage of gross fiscal deficit remains high. Reduction of the fiscal deficit and Government borrowing will be necessary to bring down interest payments as well as monetisation of the debt (Reserve Bank Credit to the Government). But the first quarter of the current fiscal year has witnessed a sharp rise in the budgetary deficit and also a large increase in the net Reserve Bank credit to the Government. The Reserve Bank has estimated the budget deficit for 1992-93 at Rs. 12,757 crore which was more than double the budget estimates at Rs. 5,389 crore and substantially higher than the revised estimates of Rs. 7,202 crore. The Bank expects the gross fiscal deficit for the year at 5.7 percent of GDP. The growth of primary liquidity in the economy recently is unprecedented and unless the gross fiscal deficit is drastically reduced in the next few months, the continuing excess liquidity would fuel inflationary pressures which could destabilise the economic reforms.

The borrowing by the Government has been continuously rising adding to the interest burden which in turn helps to increase the fiscal deficit. The Reserve Bank feels that with the proposed reduction in SLR for banks to 25 percent by 1996, the captive market for Government securities will shrink sharply over the next few years and the Government would need to move fully to a market determined rate of interest on borrowing. But the move will succeed only if Government borrowing is restricted. If the Government borrowing is excessive, as at present, under a market-determined interest rate system the rate of interest would move up to such high levels that the entire programme of reform would become counter-productive. There would thus emerge a vicious circle of rising interest rates and growing fiscal imbalances. It is, therefore, imperative that the borrowing requirements are kept within reasonable limits. It is thus obvious that not much relief can be expected from the fiscal side as the fiscal deficit is unlikely to be reduced.

India is faced with recessionary trends. The need of the hour is to counter recession. The Reserve Bank of India felt that recession can be countered by reducing the lending rate which has the effect of stimulating investment. But the degree of stimulation of investment depends on the interest elasticity of demand for investible funds. Even assuming that this demand is interest-elastic it may generate inflation in addition to countering recession. This danger cannot be ruled out completely. Furthermore a reduction of the deposit rate will reduce the real rate of interest and will reduce the magnitude of deposits given the empirically established truth that the volume of deposits varies directly with the real rate of interest. The savings of the households may be used to finance consumption or they may be used to purchase real estate or gold occasioning a rise in their prices. To the extent that consumption demand rises following a reduction in the deposit rate, it becomes a source of inflation.

In the manner the reduction of interest rate could fuel inflationary fires. The remedy for this is a rise in interest rate. But in a recessionary situation what is necessary is a reduction in the interest rate despite its inflationary consequences. Furthermore monetary growth which has fallen from 18 percent to 11 percent is excessive fuelling inflation in the economy. This warrants a reduction in the rate of monetary growth. But the authorities fear that reduction the rate of monetary growth would worsen the recession. Though a high rate of monetary growth is necessary to ward off recession, its inflationary consequences cannot be ignored. It is obvious from the foregoing that reduction of the rate of inflation, desirable as it is, cannot be brought about by reducing the fiscal deficit or by raising the interest rate or by reducing the rate of monetary growth.

At present various farm inputs are subsidised and these subsidies have the effect of widening the fiscal deficit. These are: electricity, irrigation, water and transport. These subsidies have the effect of holding down their prices of farm output. If as the NDC desires the users of these services and facilities should be made to pay for the cost of these services, the input costs rise necessitating a rise in the prices of output proportionately. This is also inflationary though the abolition of subsidies causes a reduction of the fiscal deficit and through it a reduction in the rate of inflation. Thus, while the NDC suggests that the users of these services should pay the cost and suffer in consequence, it does not want the working class to make a sacrifice in terms of the deferment of the DA payments. This is discriminatory.

Higher wages and DA payments are necessary when the prices are rising and these payments in turn exacerbate the price rise. Inflation emanating from the fiscal and monetary influences cannot be brought down. The alternative is a freezing of DA and additional wages. But the Government which has a soft corner for the trade unions is unwilling to bring this about. Instead it opts for a policy of wage escalation.

The proposed strike by the Central Government employees including railway men on October 12, 1993, has been averted following a settlement between the employees and the Government on Saturday, September 18. As per the settlement, this Government will immediately appoint the Fifth Pay Commission for revision of pay scales. This will advance pay revision by three to four years. All central employees including railwaymen in class III and class IV will be paid Rs. 100 per month as interim relief. Other demands agreed upon in the settlement are : those retiring will be benefited by a 20 percent merger of Dearness Allowance with pay for determining gratuity. The ceiling limit for payment of productivity linked bonus has been raised from Rs. 3,500 to Rs. 4,500 crore of railways and from Rs. 2,500 to Rs. 3,500 in other cases. Those class III railway employees who are not covered by the ceiling of Rs. 4,500 will be paid an ex-gratia. These unrestrained wage increases will fuel the fires of inflation.

It is obvious from this that the Government is keen on accommodating the insensate demands of the employees. The monetary system which is used to accommodate higher wage and DA payments is itself a source of inflation. In the good old days of the gold standard where the supply of money would depend on the supply of gold there would be no money to meet the higher wage demands unless the stock of gold increased. This helped to hold down the rate of inflation. Labourers who knew that the supply of money was inexpansible would not press their demands for higher wages for they knew that this would be an exercise in futility. Monetary system was on the gold standard and not on what Professor J.R. Hicks calls the "Labour Standard". But, at present, in India the monetary system can be said to be on the Labour Standard. Monetary expansion is permitted to meet the fiscal deficit which is due partly to the wage and DA escalation. It is necessary to restore some degree of inflexibility to the monetary system so that it will not be overly accommodative to frequent wage demands by means of unrestrained money creation to lend to the Government. This argument strengthens the case for making the Reserve Bank of India an independent institution subject to parliamentary control.

77

Case for Retaining Food and Fertiliser Subsidies

India is unfortunately in a tight corner. The US Government has issued a proclamation to do away with the duty-free entry of Indian pharmaceuticals to the US market. The US is keen on enforcing the acceptance of the Dunkel Draft which the Government of India is not prepared to do; the US Government wants India to sign the Nuclear Non-Proliferation Treaty while India wants to keep the option open. The US-controlled IMF wants India to abolish the food and fertiliser subsidies in order to make India fully market-friendly; the further release of the stand-by credit is conditional on India agreeing to abide by the US dictates.

The IMF announced a stand-by credit of $ 2.2 billion to be disbursed over an 18-month period in quarterly installments. The first two trenches of loan were released last year. The release amounted to $ 382 million. The third tranche of $ 650 million due at the end of March 1992 is expected to be released soon.

The Government of India signed an agreement with the IMF in the matter of fulfilling the conditionalities prescribed by it. The IMF deputed its review team to India to assess the progress of the structural adjustment reform measures. The team found several slippages in the agreement with the World Bank. But under the circumstances confronting India the Bank took a lenient view though it warned that "the release of the second tranche planned for April-May 1992 would be contingent on satisfactory overall progress in programme implementation and fulfillment of specific conditions. The lenient attitude of the Bank is probably due to the fact that the amount of the Bank's structural adjustment loan is only $ 500 million of which $ 300 million was released on signing the agreement when compared with the World Bank which is lenient, the IMF is fussy about the fulfillment of the conditions laid down by it.

Under the agreement the IMF was to conduct three reviews of the fulfillment of the programme. The first review was completed in March 1992; the second review will be held in September 1992 and the final review in March 1993.

India has fulfilled the performance criteria for domestic and financial policies for 1991-92. The Union Budget for 1992-93 is aimed at fulfilling the indicative targets for 1992-93.

The IMF is not happy over India's performance. According to it the quality of implementation of the programme leaves a lot to be desired. The IMF finds serious shortfalls in key macroeconomic objectives laid down in the agreement. The IMF has taken particular objection to the maintenance of food and fertiliser subsidies which it wanted to be reduced. The budgetary provision for fertiliser subsidy was increased from Rs. 4,000 crore in 1991-92 (estimate) to Rs. 5,000 crore in 1992-93. But if no action is taken the burden of fertiliser subsidy would be about Rs. 7,000 crore. The food subsidy is marginally reduced form Rs. 2,600 crore (estimate) in 1991-92 to Rs. 2,500 crore in the 1992-93 budget. However, with the recent increase in the procurement price paid to wheat producers, food subsidy has substantially increased. The economic cost of wheat for the public procurement agencies would be Rs. 400 per quintal against the issue price of Rs. 289 per quintal from the Central pool.

The IMF has taken a tough stand in the matter of subsidies. The Government applied for a loan of $ 7.0 billion under the Extended Fund Facility (EFF). But the IMF imposes stronger conditionalities like the abolition of subsidies, privatisation of all financial institutions and closure of all loss-making public sector units. The negotiations with the IMF for this loan should have started in April 1992. In view of the stiff conditionality prescriptions the Government of India is hesitating to take this loan under the EFF. Consequently the negotiations have been deferred indefinitely.

That apart, the IMF is insisting on the drastic reduction of food and fertiliser subsidies and the reduction of defence expenditure. But the IMF is unlikely to press this point to far and the Government has not given any formal undertaking to reduce it. However, the

Government of India is reported to have given an undertaking to the IMF to drastically reduce the fertiliser and food subsidies after the Presidential election in July 1992. This undertaking was considered necessary in order to mollify the IMF which had expressed unhappiness over the slippage of the reform programme. In view of this undertaking, the IMF and the World Bank are unlikely to be restrained in releasing the next tranche of the loan.

On any reckoning, the fertiliser prices are bound to rise. The fertiliser prices were raised in August 1991. The fertiliser industry and the Government seem to be agreed on raising fertiliser prices by July 1992 or just around the sowing season for the Kharif crop. The report of the Parliamentary Committee on fertiliser subsidy which will be released in mid-June will serve as a reference point for the Government to raise fertiliser prices. It must be admitted that the subsidy element in the Union Budget for 1992-93 is inadequate. How to accommodate the rise in the prices of inputs is a problem—should it be accommodated by raising the subsidy or should it be accommodated by deregulating fertiliser prices. Any further increase in subsidy will increase the budget deficit and exacerbate inflation in the economy; at the same time the Government has to take due note of the political reactions to decontrol of fertiliser prices. Even a partial price decontrol last year was resisted by the powerful elements in the Congress Party; furthermore, the original proposal regarding the extent of subsidy cut was revised in order to mollify the farm lobby which raised a hue and cry throughout the country. At present, the Government is faced with a similar problem and it would not be a surprise if the strategy runs along similar lines. There appears to be no way but to revise the fertiliser prices upward moderately. The extent to which the fertiliser prices may be raised depends on several factors quite apart from the cost of production which has been rising; they are the fertiliser demand-supply gap, import of fertilisers and the quality of the monsoon.

The fertiliser subsidy provided in the 1992-93 budget is less than it was in the 1991-92 budget. In 1991-92 there was a provision of Rs. 4,250 crore for fertiliser subsidy. But at the end of the financial year the quantum of subsidy had increased by Rs. 1,400 crore which had to be carried forward to the current year. The subsidy in the current year is Rs. 5,000 crore, of this Rs. 3,500 crore is for domestic producers and the balance of Rs. 1,500 crore is for imports. If out of the subsidy for domestic producers of Rs. 3,500 crore, the arrears of Rs. 1,400 crore carried forward from the previous year are paid out what remains for subsidy payment to domestic producers is only Rs. 2,100 crore. As the subsidy is linked to the cost of production it is estimated to go up by Rs. 2,000 crore over and above the budget estimate because of the rise in the prices of coal and natural gas and railway freight. This will take the total subsidy bill to Rs. 7,000 crore this year. The Government is unlikely to cover the gap through raising fertiliser prices as the farmers are bound to view it as a farmer-unfriendly policy. The alternative is to increase the subsidy though it widens the budgetary gap with all its inflationary consequences.

It must be noted that deregulation of fertiliser prices causes a rise in fertiliser prices. If the demand for fertiliser is price-elastic the demand for it falls, the input of fertilisers in the farm falls and this causes a fall in farm productivity and production. If the demand for farm produces is constant, a fall in their supply causes an excess demand which causes a rise in their prices. This is inflationary. If, on the other hand, the demand for fertilisers is price-elastic the demand for fertilisers and the input of fertilisers in the farm will not fall and consequently the farm productivity and farm production will not fall. Thus there will be no rise in farm prices on this score. But as the input costs have risen in farm prices on this score. But as the input costs have risen the farmers have to raise the prices of their output in order to cover the cost of production. Decontrol of fertiliser prices also means de-control of farm prices. In this case the consequence of decontrol is inflationary.

If, however, the subsidy is paid in full the prices of farm products will not rise. But the payment of subsidies will increase the budget deficit. This will be inflationary whether the budget deficit is debt-financed or money-financed. Thus, the payment of fertiliser subsidy and the deregulation or fertiliser prices are fraught with inflationary consequences. But the inflation emanating from the payment of subsidy is preferable to inflation emanating from deregulation of fertiliser prices. The subsidy element can be reduced by improving the efficiency element in the fertiliser industry as this results in a fall in unit cost of production and hence in unit prices.

If the food subsidy is abolished food prices rise. In India it is the food prices that govern the general price index and hence the rate of inflation. In the years when the food prices rise the rate of inflation rises though there is no budget deficit; in the years when there is a fall in food prices the rate of inflation declines though there is a budget deficit. If food subsidy is abolished, food prices rise, cost-of-living rises and this engenders demand for higher wages. If they are granted they will generate cost-push and demand-pull inflation. These two types of inflation get entwined and become difficult to disentangle. Even here food subsidies cause a rise in the budget deficit which is inflationary; abolition of food subsidies causes a rise in food prices which are also inflationary. But the inflation emanating from the payment of food subsidies is preferable to inflation emanating from the rise in food prices due to the abolition of food subsidies. The choice is difficult but the choice is to be made.

The IMF wants India to be market-friendly. India is not yet a free market economy though it is moving fast in that direction. Even in the United States farm subsidies are paid; the countries of the European Community and, in particular, France have maintained farm subsidies. These countries are more market-friendly than India is at present. Even so, they have retained subsidies. In view of this, it passes one's comprehension why the Fund-Bank combine insists on abolishing subsidies on food and fertilisers in India. It is held in certain quarters that India has not presented the case for retaining subsidies cogently and coherently before the IMF and the World Bank and this has generated all these complications. It is difficult to imagine that the Fund-Bank combine is too hard-headed to ignore the economic logic in the case for retaining subsidies.

Before the Government taxes the decision to abolish or drastically reduce the fertiliser and food subsidies it must present a closely argued case before the Fund-Bank combine for their retention. To abolish them or to drastically reduce them would be to generate hyper-inflation in the country and to make the claim of reducing the inflation rate to 7 percent sounds hollow. Subsidies are necessary at present though at a later date their abolition can be considered.

78

Hiking Procurement Prices: Lack of an Integrated Perception

Recently, the Government of India hiked the procurement prices of wheat and rice. This has generated a controversy. One school of thought supports the action of the Government while the other school opposes it. But the issue has to be examined in the right perspective.

The upward adjustments of procurement prices are held to have enabled the Government of India to effect large purchases of food grains and to replenish the buffer stocks to comfortable levels. It is argued on the basis of empirical evidence that the Indian farmers are sensitive to price movements in rearranging the cropping pattern. When the food prices fall the farmers are found to switch over from food crops to non-food crops thus causing a shortage of food grains and a rise in their prices. When the food prices rise, they are found to be increasing the area under food crops thus causing a rise in food output and a fall in food prices. The hikes in the procurement prices of rice and wheat are held to reverse the process of a shift from food crops to non-food crops. Furthermore, the hikes in procurement prices are also held to compensate the farmers for the rise in input costs and wages of farm labourers. Food production recorded an all-time high of 180 million tonnes in 1992-93 and the open market prices for wheat were lower than the procurement price of Rs. 330 per quintal announced early in 1993 for ensuring of a good wheat crop; the purchases by the Food Corporation of India and other agencies are likely to exceed 13 million tonnes against only 7.75 million tonnes out of the wheat crop for the 1991-92 season. The hike in wheat procurement prices by Rs. 105 per quintal, including the bonus payment in two seasons in succession is said to have placed the Government in a strong position and it is now felt that the imports of 1.5 million tonnes of wheat in the latter part of 1992 have become redundant. As regards rice, the hike in the procurement prices for all varieties by Rs. 40 per quintal is justified on the ground that it has led to a procurement of rice of the order of 12 million tonnes for the 1992-93 marketing season compared to 10.44 million tonnes in 1991-92. The buffer stocks thus have risen to 25 million tonnes thus making it possible for the Government to export limited quantities of food articles and to earn foreign exchange. A target of 188 million tonnes of food grains seems to be achievable in 1993-94 because of copious rainfall in regions which account for the bulk of the output of Kariff Crops.

Against this background, the latest decision of the Government to hike the procurement prices of wheat and rice has been hailed as a device to intensify the purchases of rice out of the Kariff Crops. This is higher than the price recommended by the Commission on Agricultural Costs and Prices. While the rate for the common variety of paddy has been raised by Rs. 40/- per quintal, that for the fine variety has been hiked by Rs. 50/- per quintal and that for the superfine variety has been hiked by Rs. 60/- per quintal. The yield may be higher than in the last season and the open market prices may tend to fall because of large arrivals into the markets in Punjab, Haryana and Andhra Pradesh later in 1993. If the food production goes beyond the target of 188 million tonnes the procurement of food may exceed the 25 million target in which case it is possible to export 2-3 million tonnes of fine cereals and wheat products. Because of satisfactory monsoons for the sixth season in succession, there is the likelihood of a rise in GDP by over 5 percent causing a decline in the rate of inflation.

It is claimed by the official agencies that the new price support norms restore the earlier differential between the various varieties of rice. About 6 years ago, the differential between common, fine and superfine varieties was Rs. 10 (about 6 percent). The 10 rupee difference continued and, as a result, the differential was reduced to about 3 percent in recent years. The Commission on Agricultural Costs and Prices recommended a Rs. 10 difference (for the 1993 Kariff season) between the varieties. The Ministry of Agriculture was prepared to widen the spread by accepting the CACP recommendation only for the common variety of rice. The prices of fine and superfine varieties were raised by an extra Rs. 10 thus widening the differential to Rs. 20. As most of the surplus rice producing areas cultivate predominantly fine and superfine qualities this serves as a bonanza for the farmers in the politically important North West. It is thus held that the hikes in the procurement prices smack of political expediency.

The satisfactory performance of the procurement operations of wheat so far has been attributed to the handsome increase announced by the Government in January 1993. The rabi procurement price increase announced in January 1993 was hefty judged by any standard: Rs. 55 per quintal of wheat, Rs. 50 per quintal of barley, Rs. 100 per quintal of gram etc. The recent enhancement of the procurement prices of food grains makes a mockery of one aspect of reform fostering cost competitiveness. In January when the prices of food articles were hiked, the impact of decontrol of fertiliser prices was offered as a justification. But as the Government only recently pushed up the fertiliser subsidy to neutralise the incidence of decontrol, there is really no justification for the present hike. The Government justifies its action on the ground of meeting farmers expectations. If the Government tries to woo the farming community year after year in this fashion the farm sector will be rendered more and more uncompetitive particularly when the Uruguay Round of GATT negotiations will bind the international community to increasingly competitive farming. The Government has raised objections to certain aspects of the proposals pertaining to trade in intellectual property rights and the Indian farmer has been sought to be pacified by assurances on seeds. However, over a period the Government has to accept the GATT norms on farm subsidies even though India is never likely to become one among the World's major exporters. The Government is obviously not preparing the farmers of diverse crops for the future by this posture of perpetual appeasement.

Indian industrial sector is not yet advanced and it is the objective of policy to provide the necessary incentives for this sector to develop along competitive lines. But the policy of favoured treatment adopted in respect of the farm sector appears to be unfair to the manufacturing sector and the urban consumers. Over the 1980s the terms of trade have dramatically turned in favour of the farm sector and this trend becomes strongest in the coming years. The industrial sector is exposed to global competition and the turn of the terms of trade in favour of the farm sector will impose considerable strain on the industrial sector. Furthermore, the Government has accepted the principle of international parity in respect of managerial remuneration. This makes it obligatory for the industrial sector to pay more and more to the workforce. The progressive rise in the prices of inputs coming from the farm sector will aggravate the problems of manufacturers in the country. The Government which is sensitive to the expectations of the farm sector and is prepared to help this sector, cannot be indifferent to the manufacturing sector. The Government cannot allow the industrial sector to be fleeced by the farm sector.

The urban consumers are bound to be hard hit by the favourable treatment accorded to the farm sector. The urban consumers who experience a rise in the cost of living index will have to demand higher dearness allowances to compensate them for the rise in the price index. The Government will be under pressure to freeze DA and then to reduce it in the attempt to reduce the rate of inflation. As on July 10, 1993 the rate of inflation had fallen to 5.39 percent, the Government has to attempt DA freeze in order to hold down the rate of inflation. A couple of months ago the Union Labour Ministry pushed up and DA points to public sector employees without realising that this was inconsistent with the essence of reform. This policy has to be eschewed as the nation has to move to the area of global cost competitiveness. In this situation a policy of appeasement of the farm sector will hurt the urban consumer. The reform enthusiasts seem to be proceeding on the premise that equity considerations can wait until the essential goals of reform are met. There is considerable poverty in the non-farm sector and there are also several working people in the unorganised and informal sectors without any access to the cost neutralisation benefit of DA. This means that in the hot pursuit of the reform process, the Government cannot overlook the equity considerations.

Furthermore, with such massive increases in procurement prices of food grains, the Government may not be able to hold on to the existing issue price of food articles to the Public Distribution System (PDS). If the Government is keen on holding the price line, it should not allow the higher procurement prices of food articles to be passed on to consumers in the form of higher food prices. If it does the inflationary fires would be stoked. In order to avoid this contingency the Government has to increase the food subsidy which helps to add to the fiscal deficit and to raise the rate of inflation. The other possibility is the reduction of subsidy on fertiliser, water and electricity now being supplied to farmers. It would be meaningless if the farmers are given enhanced prices for their products on the one hand and to extend subsidised inputs on the other. There is thus need to provide a level playing ground for the farmers on the one side and the manufacturers on the other. The Government has recently appointed the A.S. Kohlon panel to determines the terms of trade between industry and agriculture. It should await its findings before attempting further hikes in procurement prices of food articles.

79

Liberalizing Farm Exports

The Narasimha Rao Government which assumed office in June 1991 took a bold decision to adopt a policy of liberalization of the economy with intent to expose it to the bracing winds of external influences. Accordingly, the New Industrial Policy was adopted in July 1991 and the new EXIM policy was adopted in April 1992 and the modified EXIM policy was adopted in April 1993. Beside this several other sectors of the economy were also liberalized. Many economists and public men have been demanding the application of the policy of liberalization to agriculture also especially in matters of agricultural exports. Now that the rupee exchange rate is unified, it is expected that it would help promote agricultural exports. That the policy of liberalization should be extended to agriculture is the demand of the farm lobby. It is also the desire of the world bank.

In compliance with these demands the Government has taken a decision to integrate Indian agriculture with the global system. This is the first important step. Its objective is to facilitate the entry of Indian farm exports to the world markets. The EXIM policy announced by the Government in April 1992 was modified in April 1993. It has made possible what was considered impossible for many years. This modified EXIM Policy is expected to promote farm exports.

The Government of India is found to be encouraging exports in the context of the grave balance of payments situation. This policy is necessary to abate the foreign exchange crisis and to enable us to import those items that are necessary. But the main question is: Are we in a position to export farm commodities in sufficient quantity. Coffee, tea and other commodities are India's traditional agricultural exports. India is not in a position to export rice and wheat in sufficient quantities. Many a time we are compelled to import these food articles. In respect of oil India was not in a comfortable position.

There was indeed scarcity of oil. India has produced sugar in sufficient quantity and is in a position to register an exportable surplus. When we examine the production, domestic consumption and exportable surplus of many farm commodities we cannot say with confidence that India has a noticeable exportable surplus.

Many argue that the export prospects of farm products are bright. It can be demonstrated that we can export many food items; furthermore, it can be demonstrated that if production and domestic consumption of these articles are carefully managed India can export them to be able to earn foreign exchange. India can produce in large quantities those food articles which enjoy comparative advantage, export them and earn foreign exchange which can be used to finance essential imports. Basmati rice is an example of this. Last year India's export of Basmati rice fetched foreign exchange worth Rs. 455 crore for India. This supplied the finance for essential imports. India can export high quality and expensive rice and with the foreign exchange so earned can imports coarse varieties of food which are cheap. The poor reduce their demand for food from the PDS as they are in a position to buy cheap imported food articles. To that extent the burden of food subsidy on the exchequer falls. Even in respect of wheat it is argued that an intelligent policy of export-import can be adopted. When India produced surplus wheat, it can be exported and foreign exchange earned. In the years of scarcity this foreign exchange can be used to import wheat and other food articles. The cost of storing wheat is very high. If surplus wheat is exported there will be a saving in this expenditure. If the restrictions on the movement of food grains are removed the prices will be determined in the market. But we have to ponder over the question of whether India can adjust itself to a policy of liberalization as applied to agriculture.

As a consequence of the several policy measures adopted by the Government to achieve self-sufficiency in oil seeds and also of good monsoons. India has a comfortable surplus of oil seed production. The price of oil seeds has also started to decline. When the farmers find that the production of oil seeds is not profitable they can switch over to other crops with no difficulty. But oil seeds cultivation is heavily dependent on rains. In the area of dry farming India has not achieved a green revolution. For this reason the land can be used to grow coarse grains. But this is not economically viable. For this reason the extension of green revolution to the rain fed areas also become imperative. Therefore India should concentrate on those commodities in respect of which it has a comparative advantage, export them, earn foreign exchange and use it to purchase essential goods in the world markets at competitive prices. This is the first step in the direction of globalizing agriculture.

The recently announced agricultural exports policy has to be examined from this point of view. Just as the industries producing goods for the export market are enabled to import their essential requirements free of duty, the farm sector also has been given this benefit. The export-oriented industries can sell 25% of their output in the domestic market. If they sell more than this in the domestic market they cannot get duty free imports. Even if agro industries sell 50% of their output in the domestic market they can import their essential requirements duty free. This is as it should be. In the initial stages India's agro industries cannot export more. Processed food is becoming more and more popular in India. As these industries are enabled to import packaging materials, machinery and technology the export of processed food gets a boost. In recent years the exports of farm products are on the increase. During the past for years they have doubled. It is hoped that the present export policy in respect of farm products will be of great help to the export effort and to the earning of foreign exchange.

Removal of restrictions on the inter-state movements of agricultural products is a necessary condition for the success of liberalization policy in respect of agriculture. In this connection the Parliamentary Committee on Agriculture called the Chooka Rao Committee has suggested making a constitutional provision for compulsory implementation of the removal of inter-state restrictions on farm commodities. In its tenth report presented to the Lok Sabha on March 29, 1993 the committee said:

"Past experience as well as the present conditions prevailing show that most of the states may not implement the policy of removal of inter state restrictions. Therefore, there is need for a constitutional provision to implement this in totality".

This step is necessary as agriculture is a concurrent subject. Thus, the real implementation would have to be done by the states themselves.

The committee refers to the "extra-ordinary alarming situation" faced by the farm sector "where the farm sector was fetching lower prices for its produce while having to procure non-agricultural goods at higher prices". The committee noted that "agriculture being a vast and disorganized sector, it is the well accepted responsibility of the Government to regulate, control and guide the behaviour of production, supply and availability of commodities at reasonable prices to consumer prices to consumers and industry as well as ensuring reasonable remunerative prices to farmers".

Highlighting the discriminatory Government policies for agriculture the committee says that while industrial commodities were allowed free movement within the country, severe restrictions have been placed on the transport of farm products between the states. Furthermore, while Industrial commodities were allowed to be exported freely and fetch international prices, there was a near total ban on the export of agricultural produce. These factors have suppressed the prices of agricultural produce in general. While the prices of industrial goods are allowed to be determined by the market the Government intervenes to modulate the prices of farm products. As a consequence, the terms of trade have turned against the farm sector. This has led to a sharp decline in the average income of the farm sector. These policies of the Government towards the agricultural sector have caused a decline in the share of agriculture in GDP to 30% while the percentage of population approximately 70% — dependent on agriculture had remained at the same level. Indian agriculture has got a raw deal compared to the status of agriculture in the industrialized countries like USA, Canada, Japan and Germany where the farm sector not only enjoyed the minimum support price but also got additional income support by way of subsidy to get parity with income in the industrialized sector. In the USA the farmers got $47 billion as Government subsidy and an additional benefit of $28 billion by way of consumers having to pay higher prices in 1990.

Globalizing agriculture entails several measures to go with it and to make it a success. The Government which is under advice to reduce farm subsidy should resist this pressure for without it agriculture is bound to languish. Export and import of food grains should be free and open. In the years of surplus unless the export is permitted the prices of food grains decline making farming an unremunerative occupation. If the surplus food is exported it earns foreign exchange which can be used to import food in years of scarcity caused by natural calamities. For this reason there should be a separate foreign exchange budget for food. This is necessary to avoid inflation due to a rise in food prices in the years of scarcity and to prevent a decline in food prices in the years of surplus food production. When the prices of industrial goods are determined by the market forces, the prices of farm products should also be determined by the same forces to prevent hardship to the farmers. In this connection the recommendation of the Chokka Rao Committee for the setting up a center for monitoring agricultural prices in the Ministry of Agriculture for a self-sensitizing mechanism to observe prices appears thoughtful and it needs to be set up.

The modified EXIM policy attempts to give a thrust to farm exports. This is likened to an annual plan evolved within the parameters of the five year plan. The Government proposes to boost the share of agriculture in exports from the present 15% to 25% in the coming years. Value added exports may be alright in the short run to earn foreign exchange but if the country is to sustain its exports, the exportable items would have to be those which are renewable and fully produced within the country. The agricultural and agro-based products fulfill this condition. In this context the Indian planners felt that the country should step up exports of farm products to bring about a quantum jump in foreign exchange earnings in the coming years. There are schemes to enhance exports of tobacco, cotton and potatoes. In view of vast potential multinational companies are likely to enter the export business. The entry of multinational companies will bring about technological upgradation.

It must be admitted that agricultural exports will not be without hiccups. Even so, there is enormous potential and if properly harnessed the country would earn an additional Rs. 8,000 crore of foreign exchange every year. Farm exports would also lead to gainful employment in villages and also rural development through income generation and would go a long way towards arresting the increasing trend of migration to urban areas.

In order to promote agricultural exports certain modifications of the EXIM Policy are necessary. The commerce Minister has liberalized imports for exporters of agricultural products and services through the EPCG scheme under which the import duty concessions for agricultural units have been reduced to 15%. But the agricultural exporters perceive it as a mere drop in the ocean and not likely to provide sufficient impetus to such exports. When the maximum duty for import of capital equipment is 35% and for agricultural machinery is even less at 25% the duty reduction to 15% would not motivate exporters to go through all the procedural hassles and bank guarantees just to get 10% relief. The duty should be reduced to not more than 5%. Such a reduction would be meaningful given the trend towards liberalization and the efforts towards integration of the domestic market with the global economy.

80

Revenue without Tears

Addressing the 33rd meeting of the customs and central excise advisory council in Delhi on Saturday 7-11-1992. The Finance Minister enunciated the principle of "revenue without tears" in the effort to revamp the tax structure, especially in the area of customs and central excise duties. He came down heavily on his predecessors who had "produced a monster" by creating a duty rate structure which defied all logic. It was the considerations of revenue that prevailed in the matter of duty rate determination and nothing else. The customs duty rates were between 100 and 300 percent at a time when the international norms were around zero to 15 percent. For this reason, he underlined the need for falling in, with the rest of the world without hurting domestic industry. The tax rates structure should aim at maximum revenue generation without harassment to tax payers and with the least detrimental effects on industrial growth. While raising the revenue for development is necessary, it must be raised in such a way that it does not hamper industrial growth or its international competitiveness.

The principle of "revenue without tears" has to be given theoretical underpinnings. The objectives of revising the tax structure to make it conform to international norms of zero to 15 percent are:

1. Reduction in the burden of taxation on the tax payers.
2. The reduction in the rate of inflation.
3. Maximizing revenue yield.
4. Promoting industrial growth.

At present, the burden of indirect taxation is excessive. The duty between 100 and 300 percent, when compared with the international norms of between zero and 15 percent. The burden on the Indian Tax payer is over 20 times that on the tax payers in other countries. This means that the Indian tax payers is groaning under the heavy burden of indirect taxes. To reduce the rate of duties below its present level in gradual stages is to reduce the burden of indirect taxation on the consumers. This is a relief which is long overdue. In the attempt to get maximum revenue the successive Finance Ministers went on raising the rates of customs and excise duty rates. The structure became heavily weighted in favour of indirect taxes accounting for about 85 percent of total tax revenue. Therefore, the case for reducing the tax burden on the tax payers is just and fair. This is what the Finance Minister intends to do, when he enunciates the principle of "revenue without tears".

The present rates of duties are inflationary. These duties normally are forward shifted on to the consumers in the form of higher prices of the goods taxed. In the classical economic logic indirect taxes are inflationary as they are added on to the final market prices of the goods. But we have to analyze the issue within the Keynesian macro-economic framework. In a fully employed economy a general indirect tax which causes a rise in prices will, through the monetary mechanism, bring about a fall in the price level. A rise in the price level caused by the imposition of a general indirect tax releases three forces which cause a fall in the prices to the old level on the assumption that the supply of money is held constant. They are the real balance effect, the interest rate effect and the money illusion effect. A rise in the price level with a constant stock of money causes a fall in real balances. To the extent that consumption is a function of real balances, a fall in real balances causes a fall in consumption demand. A rise in the price level with a constant stock of money causes a rise in the transactions demand for cash. As the supply of cash is held constant the new demand for transactions balances has to be met some how. It will be met by the transistors selling their bond holdings in the bond market. This causes an excess supply of bonds which causes a fall in bond prices and a rise in the rate of interest. To the extent that investment is interest elastic a rise in the rate of interest will reduce investment and to the extent that consumption demand also is elastic to interest rate there will be a fall in consumption demand also.

The money illusion effect causes a fall in consumption demand. If the consumer is under money illusion they spend a constant sum of money on consumption despite a rise in the price level. This reduces real consumption expenditure. Thus, the two components of aggregate demand viz., consumption and investment will fall causing a fall in the prices to the pre tax level. This on the assumption that the supply of money is held constant. If the supply of money is allowed to expand the three forces do not come into operation and therefore, the prices having risen do not fall. This will be inflationary. Therefore in order to enable the new taxes to create a backlash which will generate anti-inflationary forces the supply of money should be held constant. In India the supply of money is expanding at the rate of 20 percent per anum. This does not release the anti-inflationary forces and so the inflation rate rises. If the indirect tax rates are reduced the rate of inflation is also reduced. If, at the same time, the supply of money is also reduced there will be reduction in the rate of inflation on this count also. Therefore along with a reduction in the duty structure there should be a reduction in the rate of monetary expansion. Otherwise, a reduction in the duty rates causes a reduction in the final market prices of goods. Even if the supply of money is held constant a reduction in market prices generates a real balance effect which increase demand and is inflationary. Therefore, the reduction of duty rates and the reduction in the rate of monetary expansion should go hand in hand.

The revenue yield is a function of two variables: the rate of duty and the elasticity of demand for the taxed goods. If the objective of tax policy is to raise revenue the taxes are to be levied on goods the demand for which is inelastic. In this case a rise in the rates of duty which causes a rise in the final market price of the goods will not cause a fall in the demand for them and a fall in the yield of revenue. But if the duty rates are raised on the goods the demand for which is elastic, the demand for the goods and therefore the revenue yield will fall. The demand for some goods is elastic while the demand for others is inelastic. In the aggregate, the demand for goods can be said to be elastic. It is for this reason that the tax yield is not commensurate with the rates of duty. Though the tax yield is larger it is not without tears of the consumers.

If the duty rates are reduce to conform to the international norms the final market prices of goods fall. As the demand for them is elastic the demand for them rises. On the assumption that the demand for goods has an elasticity greater than unity the outlay on the goods after duty reduction will be larger than it was before the tax. Therefore, though the duty rate per unit of the commodity is less the aggregate revenue will be larger than before the duty reduction. This larger revenue yield will be without tears. Thus duty reduction in the context of greater than unity elasticity of demand for goods causes a rise in revenue yield.

Duty reduction promotes industrial growth also. When the duties are raised to levels prevailing in India at present the market prices of the goods rise. When the demand for these goods is elastic the demand for them falls. A fall in demand occasions recession in the industries producing them and compels them to retrench the labourers employed there. This retards the rate of industrial growth. A fall in demand for goods also results in lower tax yield. As there is need to provide for unemployment relief the non-plan expenditure of the Government rises thus widening the fiscal gap. If, on the other hand, the duty rates are reduced the final market prices of the goods fall. As the demand for these goods is assumed to be elastic the demand for them rises enabling the industries to expand their output by utilizing plant capacity to the full and also be expanding plant capacity. This promotes industrial growth. At the same time it also increase the revenue yield. The increase in revenue yield helps to reduce, if not to close, the fiscal gap. As the capacity of the industry has to be expanded the demand for labourers increases and this will have an employment generating effect.

Thus the reduction in the rates of customs and central excise duties to a level consistent with international norms will yield greater revenue "without tears", will reduce the size of the fiscal gap, will reduce the rate of inflation, will reduce the duty burden on the consumers and will, more than all, promote industrial growth, seen in this perspective the Finance Minister's principle of "revenue without tears" is eminently appropriate to India in the present circumstances. It is hoped that he will incorporate this principle in his budget for 1993-94 to be presented to the Parliament in February 1993.

81

Export Growth and External Solvency

In the year 1992-93 Indian economy has faced with two problems; rising trade deficits due to near stagnation in exports and recession in the manufacturing sector. It was therefore expected that the Union Budget for 1993-94 would provide solutions to these problems.

The Finance Minister claimed that with full convertibility of the rupee on trade account the export market would be more attractive. This implies that exports were not growing because the exporters were required to surrender 40 percent of the earnings at the official rate which was lower than the market rate and with full convertibility of the rupee this problem faced by the exporter would be removed. It is also claimed that the excise concessions of Rs. 1,249 crore and an additional attraction of Rs. 720 crore export duty concession would help India industries to be price competitive. These claims need to be examined in the right perspective.

The Government has projected that the policies contained in the Budget for 1993-94 would help double the rate of growth of industrial output from an estimated maximum of 4 percent in 1992-93 to around 8 percent in 1993-94. They also hope that the export growth rate is dollar terms would also pick up from an estimates $10 billion (showing a maximum growth rate of 6 percent) in 1992-93 to $ 22 billion in 1993-94, a growth rate of 16 percent. The Government feels that the Budget would be both growth oriented and non-inflationary due to the continuation of fiscal discipline.

It is contended here that the stimulating effects of the package of incentives offered for industry and exports (along with other economic policies) have been overstated. This due to the under estimation of the constraints to be encountered by the industrial and export sectors. The industries and the exporting units are likely to face several impediments in changing gears from a highly protected and regulated environment to more competitive marketing environment being created by the budget. They need more time to adjust to the new environment.

The Government has improved the investment climate for both domestic and foreign investment through the package of incentives contained in the budget. The plan expenditure on central sector projects has been increased by 32 percent. Allocations to key infrastructural investment have been significantly increased. The interest rate on bank advances to industry has been reduced from 18 percent to 17 percent ensuring an increase flow of investment to industry. Powerful incentives to industrial growth have been offered through substantial cuts in both customs duties and excise duties. The excise duties have been significantly cut on a wide variety of consumer goods of mass consumption.

The economic strategy behind these measures including cuts in customs duties is to induce the supply side responses by cutting the costs of imported capital goods and raw materials and other inputs and thereby the costs of industrial production. Coupled with the introduction of full convertibility on trade account, the cuts in import duties should make the foreign direct investment into export oriented industries more attractive. Most of the export duty concessions also help in reducing the cost of production. These factors should increase the demand for goods of the industries hit by the recession. The Government thus expects the budget to provide a big boost to industrial production and to exports.

This optimism understates the impediments which the industries are facing. The Government preferred cuts in customs duties and excise duties to cuts in direct taxes, especially corporate taxes and this has disappointed the corporate sector. The stock market is unlikely to be stimulated to any appreciable degree as it discounted the alleged powerful impact of customs and excise duty cuts on industrial output. The domestic capital goods industries feel diffident about competing with liberalized imports and the MNCs producing foreign branded goods in India. The continuing world recession and the protective walls erected by the industries in the west have eroded the confidence of industry in expanding its exports. The industry has also got fears about the cascading effects of the hike in procurement prices, the hike in freight rates and the expected rise in the prices of petroleum and petroleum products. The expected cost push inflation due to likely decline in the value of the rupees is a factor engendering of export pessimism.

The budget has offered several incentives to exporters in order to enhance the relative profitability of exports. The most important of them is the decision to make the rupee fully convertible on trade account. This has effectively withdrawn the tax on exporters which the dual exchange rate system had imposed. Exporters have already started realizing higher exports (by 6 percent on average) under full convertibility. The export proceeds held back for expected lowering of the value of the rupee have begun to flow back thus strengthening the rupee. Foreign exchange which formerly was flowing through the havala channel has begun to flow through legal channels. The free market rate is likely to further depreciate by 5-10 percent thus rendering the rupee more competitive and this will motivate the exporters to export more so it is claimed.

This claim has to be examined. In February 1993 the official exchange rate was about Rs. 26/- US $ and the market rate was Rs. 33-24/ US $. After the introduction of full convertibility the market rate was about Rs. 32/- US $. Even if the exporter sells foreign exchange at the market rate he is likely to get about 8-10 percent more rupees. It is only after a while when the rupees depreciates that the exporter incentive may rise.

These incentives are not new. The export drive started in the late 1970s and since then export subsidies were raised. EPZ were started, 100 percent EOU were started and so on. But no material gains on the export front were realized. In July 1991 the rupee was devalued by 22 percent. But exports declined by 5 percent in 1991-92 over that in 1990-91. Then under partial convertibility in March 1992 when the exporters were free to sell 60 percent of their earnings at the market rate of exchange the exports failed to rise. In April December 1992 exports grew only by 3.4 percent in dollar terms over than in the same period in 1991. In fact a comparison with exporters in 1990-91 shows a decline.

The Government of India advanced the alibi that the decline in exports is due to the disintegration of the erstwhile Soviet Union. But facts show otherwise. In September-December 1992 exports to the GCA declined from $ 1,500 million is September to $ 1,400 million in December 1992.

Under the full convertibility dispensation all exporters and foreign exchange earners including the Indian workers abroad will be allowed to convert all their earnings at the market rate of exchange. The Government expects that it will give a boost to exports and will encourage the flow of foreign exchange into official channels. The risks inherent in the abolition of the dual exchange rate system will become evident in the near future. Under full convertibility the value of the rupee will be determined by four factors: the growth of exports compared to the growth of imports, the value of the rupee in the havala (illegal) market, inflation rate and the quantum of foreign exchange reserves. It is the primacy given to exports that has prompted the Government to provide one more incentive to exporters in the form of a unified exchange rate. Even with this incentive it is difficult to see how exports can register a fourfold growth of 12-16 percent a year from 3-4 registered between April and December 1992. A low export growth will further widen the trade gap as import growth can be expected to surge consequent on the reduction of customs duties. A widening of the trade gap will tend to depreciate the rupee further of course; this can be controlled by larger inflow of remittances through the legal channels. Under the single exchange rate system there should be no incentive for Indians working abroad to make their remittances through havala channels. Without an appreciable increase in remittance there is little likelihood of widening trade gap being partly covered. This means that with an excess demand for dollars the value of the rupee will drop. This may be of some advantage to exporters. At the same time this will make imports more expensive and will push up the rate of inflation. This will make Indian exports more expensive abroad and check export growth. The likely impact on domestic inflation cannot be discounted. India's dependence on oil imports is increasing every year and all these imports will have to be financed at the market rate of exchange compared to 1992-93 when, under partial convertibility dispensation, they were purchased at the official rate. A depreciation of the rupee and a firming up of oil prices which is likely will give a self-sustaining upward momentum to inflation. In this situation, the value of the rupee can be held up by intervention on the part of the Reserve Bank of India. But its ability to do so depends on the quantum of foreign exchange reserves in its possession. This is where the Government plan to seek $ 2.5 - $ 3 billion a year of exceptional financing come in. The new loans from the Fund-Bank combine will provide the necessary cushion. But the exceptional financing facility was supposed to cover the trade deficit and not support the value of the rupee. If exports do not increase as expected the country has to countenance a reversal of the recent trends in the rate of inflation.

There is another channel through which inflation is pushed up under full convertibility. The Government will have to buy foreign exchange at the market rate. As the policy of subsidies is being abandoned, a rise in import cost will be passed on by the Government to the Indian buyers. As a result, prices will rise. In this event the incentive to sell in the international market will decline as selling in the domestic market is more profitable.

The customs relief of the order of Rs. 720 crore is unlikely to be of much help. Its effect on lowering the prices is low and so it may not be of much value in increasing the competitiveness of Indian exports. Even assuming that the prices of exports are reduced by the full extent of fall in customs duties its impact will not be more than 1 percent in 1993-94. As there is already a rise in the prices of coal, steel and transport quite apart from the rise in the procurement prices of paddy, wheat and sugar the reduction in the excise duties will be offset by the rise in the prices of these goods. In India because of the distances between production and consuming centres the transportation cost is an important segment of the total cost. Unless the production cost is low enough to compensate for the rise in the transportation cost it is difficult to sell goods at competitive prices.

Domestic inflation is a factor that hinders export growth. In India inflation is projected to be 6-7 percent for 1993-94. This will be higher than the inflation rate of 2-3 percent in the OECD countries. India's exports to theses countries are 65-70 percent of total exports. This means that India does not enjoy relative price advantage. Again, in these countries the real GDP growth for 1993 and 1994 will be hardly 2-3% lower than that in India. The demand for Indian exports in these countries cannot be buoyant. Thus both the price and income effects are not conducive to a growth of exports. This will cause a slow growth of foreign exchange reserves. But the demand for foreign exchange reserves will rise. In 1992-93 the imports are expected to grow at the rate of 14-15% and in 1993-94 they are likely to rise by 18-20 percent due to a lowering of import duties. As the imports exceed exports people will hold their foreign exchange for speculative purposes. All these factors will cause a fall in the value of the rupee which will boost the domestic inflation rate causing a decline in the rate of export growth. There is thus a vicious circle of low exports, wide trade gap, fall in the value of the rupee, rise in prices in the domestic market and low export growth.

Devaluation of the rupee in the days ahead is a reality and this is bound to engender speculation. As the rupee is allowed to float a new element of uncertainty has crept into the determination of the exchange rate. This is currency speculation. If the holders of foreign exchange feel that the rupee is going to depreciate faster than the rate of inflation, they will be induced to hold foreign exchange. Such a trend is inherently dangerous. In the first place, it may reduce the flow of funds through normal, legal channels. The more important danger is that expectations of a large number of individuals about foreign exchange trends become self-fulfilling prophecies. If this happens the value of the rupee will sink. The Government holds the view that the Reserve Bank of India will intervene in the foreign exchange market to stabilize the rupee. But the Reserve Bank's ability to undertake stabilization operations is limited especially when companies like the Indian Oil Corporation enter the market for large amounts of hard currency to finance oil imports. If the Reserve Bank draws down its reserves it will have to replenish them again by fresh borrowing from the international financial institutions. The Government can only do that much and nothing more as evidenced by the recent depreciation of pound sterling despite strong intervention by the Bank of England. The Government of India knows fully well that the rupee will depreciate. The tide can be stemmed but only for a short while. Before long, the higher rupee costs of imports, despite cuts in customs duties are bound to exert strong cost-push pressures on prices and to reduce the rate of growth of exports.

Even assuming that devaluation of the rupee will confer a price advantage on exports, the increase in domestic prices related to the international price level would erode this advantage. Furthermore, Indian exports will also suffer from comparative disadvantage on the non-price front also like quality, packaging and delivery dates. Indian exports do not meet international standards. The export sector is labouring under infrastructural bottlenecks like shortage of power and it is also trammeled by labour troubles. Despite massive deregulation of exchange and trade controls the exporters are faced with several problems in the implementation of liberalized policies and procedures. The exporters of services are heavily taxed on their foreign exchange earnings. Recessionary trends and the protective walls in the global markets and the slow recovery in the CIS are not providing supportive environment for an overall growth of Indian exports.

The riots in Bombay in January 1993 have done great violence to India's export efforts. This situation has worsened with the series of bomb blasts in Bombay in the middle of March. According to the statistics compiled by the Commerce Ministry, the average increase in the dollar value of exports from April to December 1992 was reasonably healthy 5.41% but the one for the first ten months including January 1993 fell to 2.2%. The decline in exports has deeply hurt the dollar earning capacity of the country. In the first 10 months of 1992 India imported goods worth \$18.52 billion and the average growth rate of imports stood at \$18.52 billion. A comparatively stable import regime and a share decline in exports created a trade deficit of \$3.6 billion for the period April 1992 to January 1993. By the ends of the financial year 1992-93 this might go upto \$ 4.5 billion. The sale of goods to the general currency area

(GCA) has escaped a severe blow and has recorded modest increase of 10.51% upto January 1993. Trade with the former Soviet Union countries fell by 65.65% and this is expected to be reversed consequent on the agreement on the exchange rate between the rupee and the rouble.

India might suffer more than temporary damage by its failure to keep up a brisk growth rate of exports defaulting on deliver deadlines leads to cancellation of export orders. This would call for regaining the market which is not always easy. A low growth rate will make nonsense of one of the basic thrusts of the Budget easing the foreign exchange crunch. At present the country has a foreign exchange reserve of the order of $ 6 billion but it needs all this amount to balance the trade account and another $ 9 billion to meet the debt servicing obligations. India can hope to meet only a part of this huge need by borrowing from the multilateral lending agencies and to meet the balance it will have to resort to commercial borrowing. If exports grow by 10% as projected it will put more strain on the debt service ratio. According to the Eighth plan calculations reasonable debt service levels require exports to grow between 13 and 14% annually. If this does not materialize debt piles up. Borrowing from the Fund-Bank duo and commercial borrowing will together create the unseemly spectacle of India perched precariously on the brink of the classic debt trap if not the final entry into the debt trap.

The impediments to export growth mentioned above are likely to dampen the prospects of attaining the projected growth rate in exports and industry which are clearly interdependent. Action is necessary to remove these impediments. The Government is yet to implement the scheme for promoting exports of 34 thrust products identified two years ago. Strategic planning and restructuring of competitively export oriented industries and value based agricultural products and of the thrust markets such as the EC and the Asia Pacific and of the thrust export units based on the selectivity principle are urgently required. Finally the Export-Import Policy, 1992-97 announced in April 1992 needs to be revised to take care of the post-budget concerns of the export community. The recommendations of the Dr. Sundaram Committee on export credit need to be promptly implemented. India's salvation lies not in providing indiscriminate incentives to exporters but in upgradation of technology and selling the goods in the nearby countries. The scope for promoting exports to industrialized countries having 2-3 percent real growth in GDP is very limited. India must find economies with substantially higher growth rates and sell them there. To be able to achieve trade balance a strict control over imports of inessential goods has to be applied. Liberalized import policy should not mean license to enter the debt trap.

Indian export growth received a setback in the wake of the Bombay riots. This set back to exports could not have come at a more crucial time, as India was in the process of adjusting itself to the changes in global trading scenario particularly with the creation of the Single European Community market from January 1, 1993. While many feel that due to GATT restrictions. European community had become a fortress, there are also reports circulating of the pressure of international financial institutions on the Government of India to further liberalize imports of consumer goods and curb the negative list of imports.

With the market orientation of the Eastern European economies, India is forced to accept trading in hard currencies. This has cut down access to a secure market. India has to make up for this to sustain the export tempo. This makes the task of achieving the export target of Rs. 58,000 crore during 1992-93 financial year more difficult which in turn would have a cascading effect on India's debt servicing. The total debt servicing burden in 1992-93 is officially estimated at Rs. 1,760.9 crore. In this context India's trade deficit at $ 3,096.88 million during April-November 1992 is quite alarming and this is bound to go up on account of the loss of exports. In rupee terms the trade deficit has reached a staggering Rs. 8,828.71 crore already.

The Pre-Budget Economic Survey had revealed a disturbing development in the country's balance of payments. The current account deficit at $ 7 billion would exceed the anticipated trade deficit of $ 6 billion in the current year (1992-93). This implies that invisible receipts are less than invisible payments. The mounting external debt servicing obligations constitute the principal item of invisible out go. These are expected to increase in the medium term. In this situation action on two fronts is called for apart from searching for external financing: (1) The Government must negotiate with nation's creditors to re-configure the external debt so that external debt obligations may be trimmed: (2) greater stress has to be laid on reducing the trade deficit.

A trade deficit can be reduced by increasing exports and reducing imports. A recent study by the Reserve Bank of India indicated that import compression is not easy. The study has found that imports are determined by the level of domestic output. The reason is that imports consist largely of raw materials and intermediate inputs besides of articles of final consumption. It is found that a number of imports are price-elastic quite apart from being income elastic. The study avers that tariffs and exchange rate can be used to control the consumption of such imports. In the liberalized trade regime where cuts in import duties are the rule raising tariff duties involves self-contradiction. Depreciation of the rupee is not helpful as it has got inflationary implications. Inflation retards export growth. Higher growth will push up imports. Certain kinds of imports can be reduced crude petroleum for example. This calls for an integrated energy policy that seeks to reduce the dependence of imported oil. This cannot be a substitute for the accelerated growth of exports required to reduce the trade gap.

There are two problems facing the exporters. They pertain to credit facilities and infrastructural support. On the credit front the Reserve Bank of India has advised all commercial banks to ensure that the credit requirements of the export sector are promptly met. The need to fully meet additional credit requirements of exporters for implementing export orders, even if the sanction of such additional credit exceeded the maximum permissible bank finance limits has been impressed on banks. On the other hand, the Government has asked the State Governments to set up a separate Ministry for dealing with export matters. The Commerce Ministry has implemented most of the recommendations of the working group relating to extreme focus products which are within the purview of the exim policy and require direct action by the Ministry. Most of the recommendations made for increasing the export of 34 selected products, known as extreme focus products, involve removal of procedural irritants, creation of better infrastructural and institutional frame work and general macroeconomic policy changes aimed at creating a more conducive export environment.

There is no alternative to rapid export growth. The necessity to service the massive external debt makes increasing exports a sine qua non while the strategy of globalization of the economy also relies on exports as the engine for economic growth. The host of concessions announced in the Budget for the export sector will have an effect. So should the formation and revival of various joint business councils recently. Another heartening sign is the recent meeting of officials from India and ASEAN for a sectional dialogue which is expected to promote trade with non-traditional area.

On April 1, 1993 the Commerce Minister announced a new EXIM Policy geared to achieve a quantum jump of $ 35 billion annual exports including $ 5 billion agricultural exports by the end of the Eighth Plan Period. As averred above the country's export performance has been none too happy this year as it achieved only 2.2% growth from April 1992 to January 1993. The country was expected to end 1992-93 with an overall 3.5-4% export growth against a negative growth in the previous year. To be able to tackle the difficult balance of payments problem the country would have to achieve about 13.6% in value terms and 15-16% in dollar terms. To be able to reach this target the new EXIM Policy has contemplated several measures. The thrust area in the modified EXIM Policy is to enhance agricultural and service sector exports through greater investments.

All along India has been exporting traditional items like tea, coffee and spices. Now the attempt would be to break new ground by exporting agricultural, horticultural and floricultural products and export of fruits and vegetables. For this purpose of 144 items that were removed from the Negative list of exports several items pertained to agricultural commodities like cereals, coconut and fish meals. Further 36 consumer items had been removed from the Negative list for free exports and bring stability to agricultural exports. This would enable the country to achieve $ 2 billion exports this year $ 2.3 billion exports next year. The scheme of setting up technological parks by the State Governments would be finalized soon.

The Dunkel Draft Tax (DDT) is unlikely to have adverse effects on India's exports. The DDT has stipulated that the subsidy component for agricultural commodities should not be more than 10 percent for agricultural imports. The subsidy component is within the Dunkel limit. But if more is considered necessary, it could be negotiated. However, at the present state of the balance of payments the 3% stipulation of agricultural imports could not be applied. It could be applied when the balance of payments position improves. One should welcome further liberalization of the EXIM Policy to boost exports, particularly in the agricultural sector through duty-free imports under export-oriented unites (EOUs) and export processing Zones (EPZs) schemes, increasing domestic sales limit, widening definition of capital goods and removing some farm inputs and raw materials from the negative list of imports. These concessions are timely in the context of the decline in the share of agro exports to total exports form 20% in 1991-92 to 16.5% in 1992-93. There is need for a long-term and consistent policy for agro exports both in terms of minimum export prices and quantity allocations and incentives for investments in infrastructure in the agricultural sector.

Given the above strategy, the Government is confident of reaching the export growth target of 13.6 percent in value terms and 15-16 percent in dollar terms i.e., a rise in the value of exports to $ 35 billion in the current year. We should keep our fingers crossed.

82

Multinational Corporations (MNCs) to be made Growth-promoting

The Government of India adopted the policy of liberalization with intent to open the Indian economy to foreign capital, foreign technology and foreign trade. The idea was to encourage the inflow of foreign capital and technology and to strengthen the competitiveness of Indian industries in world markets. However, the inflow of foreign capital has fallen far short of expectations. The sectors laboring under capital shortage and technology gap have not registered much progress. However, the multinational corporations which have entered the Indian market have been very active. In particular, they are active in the consumer goods sector. They are increasing their clout by absorbing the indigenous industries. It is argued that the entry of these MNCs will not damage the Indian economy, foreign exchange inflow will increase, the domestic industries will grow to their optimum size and will be able to reduce the cost of production and to sell their goods at competitive prices, exports will increase and will earn larger amount of foreign exchange etc. The British East India Company which entered India in the early part of the 17th century admittedly exploited the Indian economy, drained India of its wealth and exterminated the indigenous industries which could not compete with the machine made goods imported by India. But the activities of the MNCs are different. In making profits for themselves they enable the Indian industries also to make profits. Therefore, it is held by the Finance Minister that the mindset that was there in the days of the British East India Company is not valid under the present conditions.

Under the policy of liberalization initiated by the Government in July 1991 the licensing procedure was given up, the restrictions on the size of the industrial units and the size of investments were removed and the EXIM Policy liberalized trade, reduced tariff duties, offered incentives for the growth of exports, the restrictive provisions of the Foreign Exchange Regulation Act (FERA) were relaxed. As a result of all these policies the MNCs have been increasing their activities in India. Formerly, these MNCs could not own more than 40% of the capital in the industries. As they owned less than half the capital they could not have complete control over the industries. Now they can own 51% of the capital invested. As they own more than half the capital they are in a position to exercise full control over the industries. India is a big country with 870 million people offering vast and expanding markets, cheap labours and growing demand for the products of these industries. As wages are low the cost of production is lower than in other countries. For these reasons among others, the MNCs are greatly interested in India.

When China invited foreign capital, it exercised great caution to check the exploitative proclivities of the MNCs. It directed investment to those sectors which needed foreign capital and technology and which needed to register rapid growth; but India did not exercise any caution of this type. Foreign capital did not flow in appreciable magnitude to sectors where rapid growth was necessary and to sectors whose exports needed to be promoted. Already the indigenous industries which either independently or through foreign collaboration are manufacturing consumer goods like soaps, shaving cream and blades, chocolate, cool drinks, tooth paste, foot wear, vehicles etc. The MNCs are rushing to these sectors finding them to be highly profitable. About two dozen MNCs are not only increasing their capital investment to 51% but are also engaged in amalgamating the indigenous industries with them. These MNCs are those with their parent companies in the USA, Britain, Japan, Germany, Sweden, Canada, Austria, Italy, Switzerland, France, Holland etc. These companies have been holding shares in Kinetic Honda, Maruti Udyog, Ashok Leyland, Digital, Cadbury, Bata, Madura Coats, Nestle, Glaxo, Phillips, Brooke Bond, Lipton, Pepsi, Indian oxygen and others. Now, after the introduction of the policy of liberalization the investment of foreign capital will come to be more than 50%.

This means that these MNCs will acquire monopoly position in these industries.

When the investment of MNCs in Indian industry goes beyond 50% they will be in a position to apply sophisticated equipment. It is argued that the demand for Indian goods, because of their cost and quality competitiveness in foreign markets increases. It is also held that the view that the MNCs will exploit India is the product of a mindset inherited from the days of the British East India Company and that this view is untenable at present. What happens is the growth of mutual trust between Indian companies and MNCs. At the same time, it cannot be forgotten that these MNCs conquer the domestic market, amalgamate the weak and unviable indigenous companies and spread their tentacles throughout the country. In an atmosphere of liberalization the big company tries to acquire the small company. The small and weak company has to surrender to the strong company and become a part of it as otherwise it is bound to become extinct. The MNCs have been making efforts to conquer and monopolies the vast Indian market.

The Hindustan Lever Company has recently acquired the Talco Company which was 65 years old. The Hindustan Lever is a subsidiary of the Unilever Company which is a MNC. For the Tomco share holders for every 15 shares a share of the Hindustan Lever become available. Mody, Revel, OK, Hamam, 510-all these soaps become the products of the Hindusthan Lever. All the production stages of Tomco become the single multi-stage production company. It commands one-third of the total supply of soaps and detergents sold in the Indian market. The universal company brings Rs. 31.34 crore of foreign exchange. The other industries are in trepidation about its rapid growth. One wonders whether India which has set foot on the road to liberalization is going in the direction of monopoly capitalism set into the Indian economy by the MNCs.

The International economic relations are not new. On many dimensions the world economy before 1914 was more open and internationalized than it is today. A genuine globalized economy would have four basic features:

1. It would be determined primarily by international processes, domestic polices would be subsumed by open world market processes.
2. The main players would be MNCs utilizing branch plants and internal investment to overcome locational and Governmental obstacles but try to keep core capital, basic R&D and the crucial components of value added in their home base.
3. It would signal a final decline in the political influence and bargaining power of organized labour. Capital would become internationalized and labour would be predominantly localized. Capital rather than labour would migrate rejecting policies that imposed high labour costs and high corporate taxation. Labour would have to trade down its social expectations to that minimum of provision requisite for advanced manufacturing efficiency.
4. Economies and politics would pull apart. The global system would have no single hegemonic or guarantor state. The states that reject the dominant logic of economic efficiency for national political considerations would lose out and the states that challenge the MNCs by threatening crucial resources would be subject to devastating economic sanction enforced by private economic actors.

MNCs have come to stay in the Indian economy and it would neither be possible nor desirable to get rid of them. India should make the best use of their resources, services and technological capability. So far, these MNCs are allowed to invade the consumer goods sector. But in future they should be directed towards sectors which are growth promoting. This is what China did and this what India needs to do. India is labouring under a balance of payments crisis. The remedy for it is export promotion. For this reason, MNCs should be asked to direct their investment into areas which produce goods for the export market. India cannot export soaps, detergents, tooth pastes and shaving sets. There is a surfeit of these goods for the Indian market and they cannot be absorbed by the world market. Foreign capital and technology to be brought by the MNCs are necessary for India but they must be diverted to non-consumer goods areas especially areas which produce goods for the export market. Restrictions should also be placed on the transfer of profits which could be asked to be ploughed back to the industries. The MNC, should be made growth promoting and not exploitative.

83

How to Bridge the Trade Gap

Recent estimates of India's foreign trade are unprecedentedly encouraging. This is most satisfying indeed. For the past two decades our foreign trade scenario was not encouraging. Our imports exceeded exports generating an unbridgeable import gap. Till the beginning of the 1980s it was possible to put up with it somehow. Certain international developments coupled with domestic distortions generated imbalances in our trade account consequent on the unexpected hike in the prices of petroleum and petroleum products the import prices of these imports rose suddenly. Our exports failed to rise to match surging imports. As a consequence the value of excess imports which was Rs. 1,085 crore in 1978-79 rose to Rs. 2,725 crore in 1979-80. This was more than twice the gap in 1978-79. India's efforts to achieve balance on trade account did not yield expected results. How to pay for the excess of imports over export remained an insoluble problem. This upsets the stability of the external value of the Indian rupee. The international community was not prepared to buy the rupee at the value prescribed by the Government/Reserve Bank of India. Indian goods became uncompetitive in world markets. This led to a decline in India's exports.

Thanks to the loans extended by the international financial institutions and the NRI deposits in Indian banks enabled India to meet the payments for excess imports. This could not be continued for long. The foreign exchange reserves declined to uncomfortable levels. Whatever was left in the foreign exchange kitty was made use of to pay for imports. At the same time the loss of the Soviet market for India's exports was a serious blow to our external solvency. India's trade deficit became large than ever before and the external value of the rupee declined.

The liberalization programme introduced by the Government in July 1991 was considerable assistance to the economy in general and to India's trade in particular. This was like the emergency surgery conducted on a seriously ailing patient. Import restrictions, reduction in customs duties unshackling of the industrial sector, measures to encourage the fee flow of foreign direct investment, opportunity to the foreign investors to invest 50% of total investment in Indian industries, opening up of the industrial sector to international financial institutions for investment; and in addition devaluation of the rupee all these measures were employed to reduce the import gap. To some extent the devaluation of the rupee helped to boost exports. Though the rupee was devalued there was the possibility of the value of the rupee falling in the international financial market. The partial convertibility of the rupee also helped to bride the traded gap. The exporters had to remit 40% of their exchange earnings to the Reserve Bank of India at the prescribed rate and they could sell the balance of 40% to the buyers at the market determined rate. In March 1992 it became possible for the exchange value of the rupee to change in accordance with the disparity in supply demand relationships. The full convertibility of the rupee in 1993 on trade account did not change the exchange value of the rupee. In fact it is practically stable. As a result of all these measures India's exports have picked up considerably. Measures have been adopted to promote exports to the former Soviet republics. India has entered into trade agreements with each of these states. Even the direction of trade has perceptibly changed. In terms of dollar value India's exports in April-November 1993 have increased by 19.37%. Its value has raised from $ 115.94 crore to $ 138.39 crore. At the same time there is a reduction in imports by 2.17 percent. In dollar terms it has fallen from $ 146.91 crore to $ 143.72 crore. As a result India's trade deficit has fallen from $ 309.69 crore to $ 53.2 crore.

India's exports in respect of textiles, diamonds and jewellery and agro-based products have significantly increased. This is the consequence of the new foreign economic policy evolved in 1993. Till then attention was focused on reducing imports. At present attention is focused on stimulating exports-especially exports of agro-based product. This shift of emphasis in trade perspective appears to have yielded result. Even the export-oriented industries have begun to improve their performance. As a result of the devaluation of the rupee which made imports costlier, imports have declined. But the rise in the prices of capital goods and spare parts which are to be imported has contributed to industrial recession in the country.

As a result of all these developments on our trade front, it is estimated that the trade deficit in 1993-94 may not exceed Rs. 2,500 crore. In 1992-93 it was Rs. 9,687 crore. As the trade gap in dollar terms is like to be less than 100 crore, it was expected that our foreign payments position is not likely to be critical. Now it is expected to be of the order of $ 300 crore. There is an inflow of foreign capital because of the announcement that foreigners can invest 50 percent of the total investment in the industrial sector. The foreign investment firms have begun to evince interest in the share market which is becoming buoyant. They are also participating in the share capital being floated. Our industries capital use a part of this capital to purchase capital goods and spare parts form aboard. This will enable the industrial sector to stage a recovery from the on-going recession. India's foreign exchange reserves have touched to $ 10 billion ($ 1,000 crore) mark. There may not be any occasion to use these reserves. Political stability and the growth-oriented budget of 1994-95 may act as a stimulus to out sagging economy.

It must be conceded that the surge of imports has declined considerably leaving the onus of adjustment on exports. A senior economist with the Reserve Bank of India Mr. D. Anjaneyulu in his study on external debt. It is pointed out that the technique of using imports to share up domestic production has important limitations. Contrary to the view that a certain buoyancy in imports is necessary to keep domestic industry knowing the study has found that for every one percent increase in imports, domestic output increases by 0.20 percent at the maximum and at that level there is a 1.01 percent increase in external debt. It is, therefore, necessary that an optimum level of imports be worked out. It is pointed out that if imports were to increase by 20 percent, then if the debt burden were to be kept at the same level either exports must also increase by 20 percent or domestic productivity should increase by atleast 9 percent. This is indeed a herculean task.

What about exports? The exchange value of the rupee has been declining ever since the rupee was put on full float. There has been a large inflow of US dollars form abroad as remittances shot sharply. This has tended to push up the value of exports against hard currencies. The Reserve Bank of India has, by now purchased more than $ 4.0 billion in accordance with the official strategy to keep the value of the rupee at about Rs. 11 to the dollar so that can retain their price advantage in the world markets. The study shows that for every one percent downward adjustment of the rupee, the rupee value of external debt will rise by as much as 0.39 percent. This clearly negates a significant part of the immediate gains of exports. This makes the policy of downward adjustment of the external value of the rupee unattractive as a device to push up exports for while it may be profitable strategy in the short run as it will benefit the exports it will also increase the rupee value of the country's debt obligations thereby adding to the public debt burden at home.

The recent export boom clearly contributed to the improvement on the trade balance. Exports in April-July were 27 percent larger than in the corresponding four months of 1992-93; the growth of exports fell sharply to 12 percent in August-November 1993. The convertibility of the rupee, which boosted the earning per dollar worth of exports by about 12 percent, gave a fillip to exports in April-June 1993. But this buoyancy wore out quickly. This is seen in the drop in the export growth rate to less than a half in July-September 1993. The rise in domestic costs of production, as measured by the increase in the wholesale price index by 8 percent eroded two-thirds of the exporter's gain from convertibility. The reduced margin was too insufficient to cover the hike in the exporters' cost of imported inputs brought about by convertibility. This had the effect of depressing sales abroad.

In the Union Budget 1994-95 there is every possibility of a reduction in import duties. This will provide relief to the exporters in terms of imported input costs. Aggregate revenue from import duties and excise duties will level down since reduced customs tariffs will put domestic (non-exporting) industries to disarray. The fiscal deficit as a proportion of GDP cannot continue at the current high level in order to reinforce inflation to the detriment of exports. The present recession will keep imports down. If the export deceleration is not reversed the trade deficit will be larger even as the stagflation deepens. The euphoria engendered about the external trade account cannot hide the disequilibrium imposed on the economy by the structural adjustment programme.

In view of this devaluation has to be ruled out for,

1. It will not lead to any dramatic improvement of the trade balance because of the operation of the "J-Curve Effect".
2. It will increase the value of the dollar debt and enhance the external debt burden considerably.
3. It will give an upward thrust to the rate of inflation through raising the prices of imports especially the price of imported inputs.
4. It will turn the terms of trade against India.

For these reasons devaluation as a method of stimulating exports can be easily ruled out. Exports have to be stimulated by means of enhancing the quality and price competitiveness of exports. Cost competitiveness can be enhanced by increasing the productivity of factors of production. Quality competitiveness can be enhanced by increasing the sophistication of Indian goods so as to meet the refined tastes of the consumers in world markets. Furthermore, as many items of goods imported by India are dumped goods, there is imperative need to impose anti-dumping duties to remove the price advantage enjoyed by dumped goods. The customs duties on imports of inessential goods have to be enhanced for free trade should not degenerate into unfair trade.